Sāmavedic Chant

Sāmavedic Chant

WAYNE HOWARD

New Haven and London
Yale University Press
1977

Printed in the United States of America by The Alpine Press, South Braintree, Mass.

Published in Great Britain, Europe, Africa, and Asia (except Japan) by Yale University Press, Ltd., London. Distributed in Latin America by Kaiman & Polon, Inc., New York City; in Australia and New Zealand by Book & Film Services, Artarmon, N.S.W., Australia; and in Japan by Harper & Row, Publishers, Tokyo Office.

Library of Congress Cataloging in Publication Data

Howard, Wayne, 1942-
Sāmavedic chant.

Bibliography: p.
Includes index.
1. Vedas. Sāmaveda. 2. Chants (Hindu) 3. Music, Indic—History and criticism. I. Title.
ML3197.H7 783.2'09'45 76-49854
ISBN 0-300-01956-4

To My Parents
Charlie and Viola Howard

CONTENTS

PART II: THE JAIMINĪYA SCHOOL

PART III: TRANSCRIPTIONS

ILLUSTRATIONS

TABLES

PREFACE

The purpose of this study is to examine, from a musical point of view, all of the known styles of Sāmavedic chanting. The basic materials for the study--tape recordings and notes from interviews--were gathered in India during a fifteen-month field research tour made possible by a Fulbright-Hays Fellowship. For assisting me in obtaining this grant I am very grateful for letters of recommendation submitted by Dr. Ralph T. Daniel, Dr. Walter Kaufmann, Dr. Hans Tischler, Dr. Thomas L. Noblitt (all of Indiana University) and Dr. Colin P. Masica (University of Chicago).

The idea of a project on Sāmavedic Chant originated in a "Seminar in Oriental Art Music" chaired by my teacher Professor Kaufmann, who had written the only major article in English on the Sāmavedic notations ("Some Reflections on the Notations of Vedic Chant," Essays in Musicology: A Birthday Offering for Willi Apel, pp. 1-18). His enthusiasm and counsel at every stage of the sometimes arduous and often frustrating field experience were sources of great encouragement and inspiration. Not the least of his contributions was the impartation of his deep love of India and her peoples; this influence has had untold rewards for me both personally and professionally.

Of the many people who assisted me in India I must thank first of all Dr. Prem Lata Sharma (Banaras Hindu University). It was she who began the chain of recommendations which introduced me to the Vedic cults of both the North and the South. The valuable assistance which she gave was often at great personal sacrifice, for which I shall be permanently indebted. Of the many introductions which she initiated, two of the most fruitful were to Professor J. F. Staal (University of California, Berkeley) and Dr. Asko Parpola (University of Helsinki), both of whom were in India during part of my tour. Staal's splendid book Nambudiri Veda Recitation (The Hague, 1961) had already made a deep impression upon me, and it was kept constantly at hand during my travels. In addition to writing several recommendations and offering many welcome suggestions, he has since provided copies of two important tape recordings of Sāmaveda from Saurashtra and North Arcot. Parpola, the leading authority on Sāmavedic ritual, was in South India investigating the rare Jaiminīya school of chant. It was indeed a happy coincidence that he was in need of someone to retrace his visits to Jaiminīya centers and to take recordings from the singers whom he had interviewed. On one such trek, to the village Tentirupperai, I was instrumental in discovering a palm-leaf manuscript of Jaiminīya verses and chants. Parpola has since arranged for its purchase by the Birla Institute at Hyderabad. He has furnished copies of several of his books and articles and has sent notes on the hand and arm movements used by the Nambudiri Sāmavedins of Kerala State.

The Brahman community as a whole has shown such kindness, hospitality, and interest in my work that adequate appreciation is impossible in these few pages. The contributions of Dr. Prem Lata Sharma have already been mentioned. Dr. E. R. Sreekrishna Sharma (Sri Venkatesvara University) has shown me many considerations. He arranged for a three-month stay at Tirupati and furnished copies of several of his recordings--among them examples of Rāṇāyanīya Sāmaveda from Tinnevelly and Gujarat. Of great assistance in Varanasi were Dr. K. C. Gangarade, Sri Gajanan Sastri Musalgaonkar, and Miss Indrani Chakravarty (all of Banaras Hindu University). In Mysore I received great help from Prof. G. Marulasiddhaiah (University of Mysore), Prof. B. K. Sivaramaiah (University of Mysore), Sri H. N. Narasimhamurthy (Maharaja's Sanskrit College), and Prof. Vishnu Narasimha Bhatta (Commerce College, Kumta). Professor Bhatta personally accompanied me during field trips to villages and temples of North and South Kannara. The time and effort which he spent on my behalf can never be fully repaid. Five additional friends who also went to great lengths to assist me are Sri Lakshmiprasad Daduram Brahmbhatt (Nadiad), Thiru S. Nambi Rajan (Tentirupperai), Thiru R. Venkatesan (Srirangam), Thiru K. Desikan Acharya (Srirangam/Chidambaram), and Sri V. Sankaranarayanan (Panjal). I would especially like to thank Thiru P. Sethuraman (Pinnavasal), Dr. V. R. Lakshmikanta Sharma (Kumbhakonam), Thiru T. R. Subrahmaniam (Madras), and Dr. V. Raghavan (Madras).

I am extremely grateful to the large number of Sāmavedins who graciously consented to share some of their precious treasures with me. I should especially mention the following: Sri Agnishwatt Sastri Agnihotri, Sri Krishnamurthy Srautigal, Sri Gopal Ram Tripathi (Varanasi); Sri M. Itti Ravi Nambudiri, Sri T. Narayanan Nambudiri (Panjal); Sri K. N. Sahasranama Aiyar, Sri K. S. Srinivasa Aiyar, Sri T. K. Tiruvenkatanatha Sharma, Sri Venkatarama Sharma (Kotuntirappulli); Thiru Venkatacala Upadhyaya, Thiru Kesava Upadhyaya (Tentirupperai); Thiru U. V. Narayanan Upadhyaya (Neduvenkurici); Thiru Balasubrahmanya Srautigal (Kumbhakonam); Thiru K. Raman Aiyangar (Madras); Thiru T. Rajagopala Aiyangar, Thiru R. Narasimhan; Swami Srinivasa Mahadesikan, Thiru P. T. Govinda Aiyangar, Thiru P. K. Srinivasa Aiyangar (Srirangam); Thiru Yajnarama Dikshitar (Pinnavasal) ; Sri N. Lakshminarayana Srauti, Sri S. Satyanarayana (Mysore); Sri Subbaraya Paramesvaran Bhatta Agni (Hadinbal); Sri Subbaraya Ramachandra Bhatta (Arolli); Sri Visvesvara Bhatta (Karikan Temple); and Sri M. Narasimha Acharya (Matapadi).

A large number of musical examples, transcribed from the tape recordings, appear both in the body and at the end of the study. Great care has been taken to notate pitch and rhythm as accurately as possible. Wherever a single syllable of text is sung to more than one pitch, those notes with flags (values of an eighth note or smaller) are barred together (for example: ). If one or more notes without flags (values of a quarter note or higher) appear, a phrase marking connects all of the notes attached to the syllable (for example: ). For the sake of clarity, very few additional signs are used. A sharp (#) above a note indicates that the tone it represents is slightly sharp; a flat (♭) signifies the opposite. A glide from one pitch to another is represented by ascending or descending diagonal lines (either — or —). Natural vocal vibrato is indicated by a wavy line (∿). An apostrophe (’) appears wherever breath is taken. Metronomic indications and relative pitches are given for all examples.

The Sāmavedic chants of course do not fall within our well-tempered scale, but the tone material of the various specimens can be approximated by the pitches of white-key octaves. At first I was undecided whether to employ exact transcription by electronic means or to adhere to the conventional method. The latter course was chosen for several reasons: (1) exact indication of microtonal intervals is superfluous when the same chant is never performed exactly the same way twice--even by a single chanter; (2) the hymns are taught in the traditional Indian manner of imitating after the teacher--not by consciously having the students concentrate on specific microtonal intervals; (3) when these two points are taken into consideration, an approximate transcription is, in the end, more representative of a style as a whole than an isolated exact reproduction; (4) the type of analysis which I wished to perform would have been exceedingly difficult and perhaps impossible by transcribing through other than conventional means; and (5) this study is intended for both the specialist and non-specialist in world music, and by necessity it had to make use of symbols understandable to both.

The text, preceded by an Introduction, is divided into two parts. Part I treats the related notations but divergent oral traditions of the Kauthumas and Rāṇāyanīyas; Part II discusses the notation and styles of Jaiminīya chant. A catalogue of recordings and an extensive glossary are included at the end, after the transcriptions. Personal and place names are not always scientifically transliterated.

ABBREVIATIONS

Complete bibliographical information is given in the Bibliography. See also the abbreviations list, pp. 455-56, which (with the exception of the Sāmaveda entries) refers only to the Catalogue of Recordings and not to the study proper.

ĀrG See under SV

ĀrGP See under SV

ĀrS See under SV

ĀrṣB *Ārṣeyabrāhmaṇa*, ed. Burnell

CH Caland-Henry, *L'Agniṣṭoma*

DED Burrow-Emeneau, *A Dravidian Etymological Dictionary*

DŚS Drāhyāyaṇa Śrautasūtra

JĀrG See under SV

JGG See under SV

JRG See under SV

JS *Jaiminīya Saṃhitā*, ed. Caland

JŪG See under SV

L/DŚS Parpola, *The Śrautasūtras of Lāṭyāyana and Drāhyāyaṇa and Their Commentaries*

LŚS Lāṭyāyana Śrautasūtra

MH Fox Strangways, *The Music of Hindostan*

ML *Mātrālakṣaṇa*, ed. B. R. Sharma

NVL Simon, "Die Notationen der vedischen Liederbücher"

NVR Staal, *Nambudiri Veda Recitation*

NŚ — Nārada Śikṣā, ed. Śrī Pītāmbara Pīṭha Saṃskṛta Pariṣad

PB — Pañcaviṃśa Brāhmaṇa, ed. Caland

PuS — Puṣpasūtra, ed. Simon

PVC — Raghavan, "Present Position of Vedic Chanting and Its Future"

PvS — Pañcavidha Sūtra, ed. Simon

RG — See under SV

Spb — Kṛṣṇasvāmin Śrautin, Sāmaparibhāṣā

SSV — Faddegon, Studies on the Sāmaveda, Part I

SUB — Saṃhitopaniṣad Brāhmaṇa, ed. Burnell

SV — Sāmaveda Saṃhitā

SV 1.1 = Sāmaveda Saṃhitā (ed. Sātvalekar), pūrvārcika, first verse

ĀrG 1.1 = Āraṇyakagāna, first chant on the first source verse (ed. Nārāyaṇasvāmi)

ĀrGP = Āraṇyakagāna Pariśiṣṭam

ĀrS 1.1 = Āraṇyakasaṃhitā, first verse of the first khaṇḍa

GG 1.1 = Grāmageyagāna, first chant on the first verse of the pūrvārcika (ed. Nārāyaṇasvāmi)

JĀrG = Jaiminīya Āraṇyakagāna

JGG = Jaiminīya Grāmageyagāna

JRG = Jaiminīya Rahasyagāna

JŪG = Jaiminīya Ūhagāna

RG 1.1.1 = Rahasyagāna, first parva, first daśati, first sāman (ed. Dīkṣita)

ŪG 1.1.1 = Ūhagāna, first parva, first viṃśati, first sāman (ed. Dīkṣita)

SvB Sāmavidhāna Brāhmaṇa, ed. B. R. Sharma

ŪG See under SV

VC van der Hoogt, The Vedic Chant Studied in Its Textual and Melodic Form

INTRODUCTION

The Four Vedas and the Mode of Preservation

The sacred lore of the Aryans, who crossed the Hindu Kush mountains into Northwest India many hundreds of years before the birth of Christ, is brought together in four collections (saṃhitās) designated by the general term "Veda" ("knowledge": from the root vid, "to know, to understand"). These compilations, which form the basis of the Brahmanical systems of religious philosophy, are: (1) the Ṛgveda Saṃhitā, which contains verses (ṛks) for sacrificial utterance; (2) the Yajuḥ Saṃhitā (Yajurveda), which is in essence a collection of sacrificial verses and prose formulae (yajus) appearing in two forms--with and without interspersed explanatory matter; (3) the Sāmaveda Saṃhitā, which consists of verses--most of them occurring also in the Ṛgveda Saṃhitā--and notated melodies (sāmans) set to these verses; (4) the Atharvaveda Saṃhitā, which is a collection of magical formulae and spells (atharvan). Appended to each saṃhitā are one or more Brāhmaṇas (theological exegeses), Āraṇyakas (philosophical texts composed or studied in the forest), and Upaniṣads (sources of the mystical doctrines which underlie the Vedānta philosophy). As a body these works are believed to have been revealed to the ṛṣis, the inspired seers of Vedic antiquity, through a "hearing" ("śruti"). They are thus set apart from works requiring "remembrance" ("smṛti") on the part of human preceptors. Belonging to the smṛti tradition are the six vedāṅgas ("limbs of the Veda": śikṣā, chandas, vyākaraṇa, nirukta, jyotiṣa, kalpa), the śrauta- and gṛhya-sūtras, the dharmaśāstras, the itihāsas, the purāṇas, and the nītiśāstras.

Only male members of the Brāhmaṇ or priestly caste are eligible to recite the Vedas, though members of the first two of the lower three castes[1] may sponsor and hence observe a Vedic sacrifice. Every Brāhmaṇ belongs by birth to one Veda, one śākhā (school) of this Veda, one gotra (ancestral family),[2] and one sūtra (manual of aphoristic rules). The sūtras, written in a terse, telegraphic style, describe in detail the functions of a particular Veda in the sacrificial (śrauta) rituals or domestic (gṛhya) ceremonies.

It is a truly remarkable phenomenon that most--indeed, perhaps all--Vedic literature was for hundreds of years handed down orally and not committed to writing. Such an achievement is almost beyond the comprehension of the Westerner, who relies far less on powers of memorization than

---

[1]In order of rank (high to low), they are: Kṣatriya, Vaiśya, Śūdra.

[2]The forty-nine gotras enumerated by the Āśvalāyana Śrautasūtra are listed in Max Müller's A History of Ancient Sanskrit Literature, rev. ed. by S. N. Sastri (Varanasi: Chowkhamba, 1968), pp. 344-49.

on the written word: "the Western religions (Judaism, Christianity and Islam) are primarily book religions, and Western culture is a culture of books,"[1] writes J. F. Staal. But the Vedic sages at all times cast aside any impulse to reduce their holy canons to writing. It was in fact never necessary for them to resort to the pen because of their superbly developed abilities for retaining orally transmitted information. These abilities were cultivated to the utmost degree due doubtlessly to the "implicit faith of the ancient Indian in the unlimited--almost divine--power of Vāc or the 'spoken word.'"[2]

Some conception of the scrupulousness with which the Vedic texts are handed down can be gathered from V. Raghavan's description[3] of one priest's mastery of Yajurveda. He was able not only to recite the lengthy text in reverse order, but also to supply a particular letter when the chapter and number of the letter were given. Mental feats of this sort are still to be observed among the Vedic reciters and chanters, despite the general breakdown of orthodoxy. During the course of my researches in India I had the rare opportunity to hear and tape-record a large

---

[1] Nambudiri Veda Recitation (NVR), vol. 5 of Disputationes Rheno-Trajectinae, ed. Jan Gonda (The Hague: Mouton, 1961), p. 12.

[2] V. M. Apte, "The 'Spoken Word' in Sanskrit Literature," Bulletin of the Deccan College Postgraduate and Research Institute 4 (1942-43): 277.

[3] "Present Position of Vedic Chanting and its Future," (PVC) Bulletin of the Institute of Traditional Cultures 1 (1957): 48-69.

number of Vedic hymns. On several occasions I chose to check the memory of the reciting Vaidika (Vedic chanter) by turning at random to any page in a printed edition of his Veda, reading the first few words of a verse or chant, and requesting the reciter to continue from that point on his own. Hardly ever was there the slightest hesitation or memory lapse; my admiration and respect were increased by the knowledge that even today some priests have the ability to recite the voluminous texts according to several memorization formulae (vikṛtis), schemes which require both grammatical and accentual alterations of the original or continuous text. Even the smallest error is abhorred and believed sufficient to produce catastrophe. Our appreciation of India's religious heritage can only be enhanced when we realize that a work such as the Ṛgveda, comprising over 10,000 verses in 1,017 hymns, has been passed down orally for at least 3,000 years with hardly any alteration of the original text. This has been possible at least partly because the transmitters have not considered translation and interpretation among their duties:

> . . . translation or interpretation are not necessarily thought of, for the words, which are one with the meaning and themselves sacred, should be preserved for the world and for posterity. In this sense the srotriya who recited without understanding should not be compared with a clergyman preaching from the pulpit, but rather with a medieval monk copying and illuminating manuscripts, and to some extent with all those who are connected with book production in modern society. To the copyists we owe nearly all our knowledge of antiquity, to the reciters all our knowledge of the Vedas . . . .[1]

---

[1]NVR, p. 17.

It is small wonder that written manuscripts of the Vedic texts were never thought of as necessary or even desirable.[1] But it was inevitable that the verses, hymns, and formulae would some day appear in written form. Louis Renou[2] refers to an eleventh-century manuscript, which is the oldest written source known to have once existed. However, even it is modern compared to the age of the Vedas. The relative dates of manuscripts are not as important as might be imagined, for "the most ancient manuscripts have no greater value than the evidence of the men who until only the other day still carried in their memory more or less extensive parts of the Veda."[3] This argument is enlarged upon by Arnold Bake, who asks:

> Why is it necessary to suppose beforehand that the practice of a certain Brahmin in Kumbakonam [a Vedic center in the Tanjore District of Tamilnāṭu]--who has been taught by his father, who in his turn had been taught the tradition of singing sāmans by his father and so on for thirty generations, which takes us back about a thousand years a time when, certainly in S[outh] India, Sāmaveda was not extinct by any means--why is it necessary to presume that the tradition of such a man is not sound, until one has proved that it is false when compared with the text books he professes to follow?[4]

---

[1]However, some scholars maintain that Veda recitation stems from texts which were originally written down.

[2]Classical India, vol. 3: Vedic India, trans. by Philip Spratt (Delhi: Indological Book House, 1971), p. 2.

[3]Ibid.

[4]"The Practice of Sāmaveda," Proceedings and Transactions of the Seventh All-India Oriental Conference, Baroda (Baroda: Oriental Institute, 1935), p. 144.

The preceding statements are highly significant for passing judgment on the authority of present-day reciters and chanters and consequently the legitimacy of tape-recordings of their recitals. They show the absurdity of Barend Faddegon's contention (regarding Sāmavedic chanting) that "it is . . . out of the question that modern Hindus educated in their śruti-system could sing a sāman correctly in the historical sense of the word; indeed their production of sāmans shows an indefinite number of personal differences and is in flagrant contrast with the notations of the Sāmavedic manuscripts . . . ."[1] Three points must be raised in refutation of this statement. First of all, it is presumptious to assume that all, or even a significant percentage, of the Vaidikas are performers of Indian classical music and hence "educated in their śruti-system." Even if this were true, it has been shown[2] that some of the most highly esteemed musicians in India realize the śrutis (microtones) of a particular rāga in different ways. The reasons for these variations are, according to Walter Kaufmann, the apparent disregard by the performers of the theoretical prescriptions and the reliance solely upon tradition:

> Despite the numerous arguments and calculations brought forth by Indian and Western authors, Indian performing

---

[1] Studies on the Sāmaveda, Part I (SSV), vol. 57, no. 1 of Verhandelingen der koninklijke nederlandse Akademie van Wetenschappen, afd. Letterkunde (Amsterdam: North-Holland Publishing Co., 1951), p. 13.

[2] N. A. Jairazbhoy and A. W. Stone, "Intonation in Present-Day North Indian Classical Music," Bulletin of the School of Oriental and African Studies 26, 1 (1963): 119-32.

> musicians pay no attention to these matters and are guided solely by the *rasa*, the sentiment and mood of a *rāga*, in order to achieve the required intonations. They refuse to define microtonal alterations by means of mathematical speculations.[1]

Vedic singers can hardly be accused of relying on the *śruti* system while in fact the most respected classical musicians ignore it completely. Secondly, that stylistically a "number of personal differences" exist among the chanters must not imply that the oral testament of any singer is somehow impure or invalid. Different styles of chanting are admittedly encountered in different localities and sometimes even in the same locality. But a chanter's reliability should not be impugned because of the geographic area in which he resides--a region which, for instance, may not be associated with Vedic tradition and orthodoxy. Apte rightfully contends that "*because* the Sāmavedins are confined for the most part to certain provinces or localities *today* and probably for a long time in the past, it does not automatically follow that the tradition of Sāma singing, the preservation of which was and is the *sacred duty and trust* of a Sāmavedin, is to be judged unsound on the ground that the Sāma-singer or his ancestors migrated to and settled in another province where the Sāmavedins do not muster strong!"[2] Thirdly and finally, Faddegon was in no position to determine who was and was not conforming

---

[1] *The Rāgas of North India* (Bloomington: Indiana University Press, 1968), p. 9.

[2] "Sound-Records of Sāmagānas: A Prospect and Retrospect," *Bulletin of the Deccan College Research Institute* 4 (1942-43): 299.

to the notations of the manuscripts. It will be shown in other sections of this study that he and other scholars of Sāmaveda have based their understanding of the musical notations on misconceptions of their symbolic role.

The Sāmavedic Texts

The Sāmaveda occupies a unique position in music history, for it preserves probably the world's oldest notated melodies. It is to be cherished all the more as a record of the sacral monophony, rooted in the remote past, which is carried to this very day in the memories of this Veda's adherents.

The *sāman* texts are collected in the Sāmaveda Saṃhitā,[1] though this title may refer also to the complete Sāmaveda corpus, both verses and chants. The Saṃhitā is divided into two parts (*ārcika*s). The *pūrvārcika* ("first *ārcika*") contains verses arranged according to divinity (Agni, Indra, Soma) and meter.[2] Appended to it is the Āraṇyaka Saṃhitā or "Forest Text." The *uttarārcika* ("last *ārcika*") presents verses arranged, usually in groups of three, according to the requirements of the Vedic ritual. The first verse of each group may ordinarily be found also in the *pūrvārcika*. Finally, there are four large *gāna*s (songbooks), the principal Sāmavedic texts, containing notated melodies. Found in the Grāmageyagāna ("Village Songbook")

---

[1]Henceforth SV = Sāmaveda Saṃhitā, ĀrS = Āraṇyaka Saṃhitā, GG = Grāmageyagāna, ĀrG = Āraṇyakagāna, ŪG = Ūhagāna, RG = Rahasyagāna. The prefix J indicates the Jaiminīya *śākhā*.

[2]The most common Vedic meters are the *gāyatrī* (three octosyllabic verses), the *anuṣṭubh* (four octosyllabic verses in two hemistichs), the *triṣṭubh* (four verses of eleven syllables in two hemistichs), and the *jagatī* (four verses of twelve syllables in two hemistichs).

are chants to be learned and sung within the confines of the village (*grāma*). Its melodies are set to *pūrvārcika* texts used in the same sequence in which they originally appear. As is true of each of the *gānas*, a single verse may be set to one or several melodies. The Āraṇyakagāna ("Forest Songbook") comprises chants of a more mystical and esoteric nature which are to be sung apart from the centers of human habitation. Here verses both from the Āraṇyaka Saṃhitā (in this instance taken in order but not necessarily one after the other) and the *pūrvārcika* are set to melodies not found in the Grāmageyagāna. The Grāmageyagāna and Āraṇyakagāna taken together are sometimes referred to as the Pūrvagāna ("First Songbook") or Prakṛtigāna ("Principal Songbook"). The last two *gānas* (collectively, the Uttaragāna ["Last Songbook"]) contain chants arranged for sacrificial usage. Their texts are drawn from the *uttarārcika*, each verse-group of which is set to a particular melody. The Ūhagāna borrows some chants from the Grāmageyagāna, and the Rahasyagāna (Ūhyagāna) is derived in part from the Āraṇyakagāna. The relationships of the texts are illustrated in the diagram:

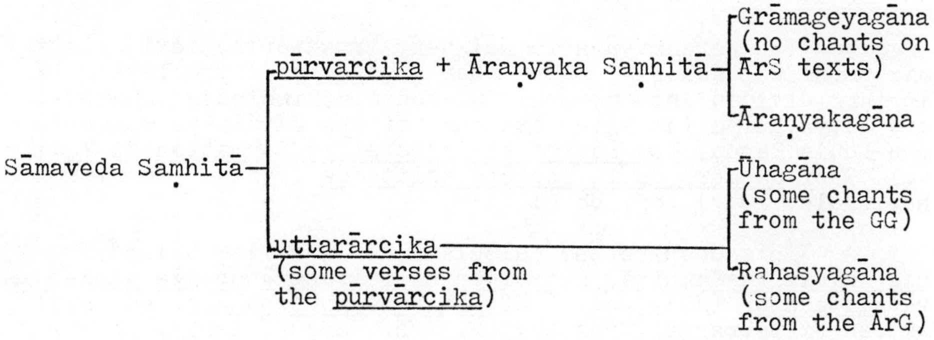

Śākhās (Schools) of the Sāmaveda

At the present time there are in India three schools of Sāmaveda: Kauthuma, Rāṇāyanīya, and Jaiminīya.[1] The Kauthumas and Rāṇāyanīyas share, to a great extent, the same texts: the ārcika portions are exactly alike, and there are only minor variants in the gānas--the chief among these is the employment in certain Rāṇāyanīya manuscripts of a syllable notation, in contradistinction to the numeral notation of the Kauthumas. The Jaiminīyas, on the other hand, share a distinctly different tradition, although the total number of chants does not markedly vary from the Kauthuma-Rāṇāyanīya count.[2] The principal differences consist of textual variants, some of which will be identified after first examining two features common to all sāmans regardless of śākhā.

First of all, every chant is divided into a number of sections (parvans), each of which is to be sung in a single breath. These units are marked in the manuscripts by vertical lines (daṇḍas), strokes which indicate the spots where pauses (virāmas) occur.

Secondly, the words of the source verses may undergo

---

[1]The Caranavyūha (a not very trustworthy text) lists six principal schools, among them Rāṇāyanīya. The latter is in turn divided into several sub-schools, including Kauthuma and Śāṭyāyanīya (an alternate name of the Jaiminīya school). See Louis Renou, Les écoles védiques et la formation du Veda, vol. 9 of Cahiers de la Société Asiatique (Paris: Imprimerie Nationale, 1947), pp. 88-91.

[2]This despite the calculations in Willem Caland, Die Jaiminīya-Saṃhitā, mit einer Einleitung über die Sāmavedaliteratur (JS), vol. 2 of Indische Forschungen, ed. by Alfred Hillebrandt (Breslau: M. & H. Marcus, 1907), p. 20. Caland, basing his figures on the Dhāraṇalakṣana, presumes the Jaiminīyas to possess 959 more chants than the other schools.

any one of a number of alterations. These changes are necessary so that text can be adapted more conveniently to melody--evidence which strongly suggests that the melodies were pre-existent. The six alterative devices as quoted by Staal[1] from Sātvalekar[2] are listed below. The illustrative examples (corrected by me) are taken from the opening *sāman* of the Kauthuma GG, based upon SV 1.1.

1. *vikāra*, "modification" (*agne* becomes *ognāyi*)
2. *viśleṣaṇa*, "dissolution" (*vītaye* becomes *voyitoyā 2̄ yi*)[3]
3. *vikarṣaṇa*, "suspension" (*ye* becomes *yā 2 3 yi*)
4. *abhyāsa*, "repetition" (*taye* becomes *toyā 2̄ yi* / *toyā 2̄ yi*)
5. *virāma*, "pause" (*gṛṇāno havyadātaye* becomes *gṛṇāno ha* / *vyadātoyā 2̄ yi*)
6. *stobha*, "insertion" (*au ho vā*)

Two additional devices are put forward by J. M. van der Hoogt[4] (the illustrations are my own):

7. *lopa*, "disappearance" (*pracodayāt* becomes *praco 1 2 1 2* / *hum ā 2̄* / *dāyo* / *ā 2 3 4 5*)

---

[1]NVR, p. 64.

[2]Dāmodar Sātvalekar, ed., *Sāmaveda [Saṃhitā]* (Pardi: Svādhyāyamaṇḍala, 1956), p. vi.

[3]The Kauthuma numeral notation will be discussed in detail in chap. 1.

[4]*The Vedic Chant Studied in Its Textual and Melodic Form* (VC) (Wageningen: H. Veenman & Sons' Press, 1929), p. 3.

8. āgama, "augmentation," the insertion of an extra letter or syllable within a radical word (vareṇyam becomes vareṇiyom)

Differences in Kauthuma, Rāṇāyanīya, and Jaiminīya readings of a single chant can be observed in GG 1.1 (= JGG 1.1). The three versions are presented below: the first is from a printed devanāgarī edition of the Kauthuma GG and ĀrG,[1] the second (with notational syllables italicized) is from Burnell Manuscript 89 (listed as 4291 in A. B. Keith's catalogue)[2] of the India Office Library (London), and the third is from a paper manuscript (copied from a palm-leaf original) belonging to the Vaidikas of Kōṭuntiṟappuḷḷi village (near Pālghāṭ [Pālakkāṭu] in Keraḷa).

1. o⁽⁴⁾ gnā i / ā⁽²ʳ⁾ yā⁽ʳ⁾ hī 3 vo⁽¹⁾ i to yā 2 i / to⁽¹⁾ yā 2 i /
gṛ⁽¹⁾ nā⁽ʳ⁾ no⁽²ʳ⁾ ha / vya dā to⁽¹⁾ yā 2 i / to⁽¹⁾ yā 2 i / nā⁽¹⁾ i
ho⁽²ʳ⁾ tā⁽¹⁾ sā 2 3 / tsā⁽¹⁾ 2⁽^⁾ yi / vā⁽³⁾ 2 3 4 au⁽⁵ʳ⁾ ho⁽ʳ⁾ vā /
hī⁽³⁾ 2 3 4 ṣī⁽⁵⁾ //[3]

2. o *ta* gnā i / ā⁽ᵒ⁾ *cho* yā⁽ᵒ⁾ hī *ṇa* vo i to yā *pre* i /

---

[1] R. Nārāyaṇasvāmi Dīkṣita, ed., Grāmageyagānam--Āraṇyageyagānam (Pārdi: Svādhyāyamaṇḍala, 1958), p. 1.

[2] Catalogue of the Sanskrit Manuscripts in the Library of the India Office (London: Secretary of State for India in Council, 1887-1935).

[3] The fourth syllable of the second parvan is given by Nārāyaṇasvāmi as "vī" instead of "vo." However, all of the Kauthumins whom I recorded use the latter reading.

o o
to kā yā pre i / gṛ kā ṇā no hā / vyā co dā to

o
yā pre i / to kā yā pre i / nā ghī i ho tā sā /

o o
[t]sā ve i bā au ho vā / hī ṭū ṣi //

ta ta sa thāc cā sa ṭā sa ṭā sa
3. o gnā i / ā yā hi vā i / tā yā i tā yā i /

cā sa ci ṭā sa ṭā sa ki
gṛ ṇā no ha vya dā / tā yā i tā yā i / nā i ho

ca ṭa ṭa khā si kha sa
tā / sā tsā i bā au ho vā / hī ṣi //

Apart from the obvious differences of notation (a subject of subsequent chapters), several structural and textual dissimilarities are apparent. Most notable among these is the disagreement of Kauthuma-Rāṇāyanīya and Jaiminīya parvan-division. For example, the former sing (omitting the notation):

/ ā yāhi voitoyāi / toyāi /

But the same passage is rendered by the Jaiminīyas as:

/ ā yāhi vāi / tāyai tāyāi /

The principal remaining differences are textual. The Sanskrit unaspirated lingual sonant, ḍ, is often replaced in Jaiminīya manuscripts by the Tamiḻ-Malayāḷam ḻ ("iḻā," for instance, instead of "iḍā"). Another variation is the pronunciation by the Jaiminīyas of the common Kauthuma-Rāṇāyanīya stobha "hāu" as "hābu." Vowels may be longer or shorter, or else they may be replaced by other vowels. The full nature and extent of the variants will not be known until the Jaiminīya gānas appear in print. Variations between Kauthuma and

Rāṇāyanīya texts are less significant and will be dealt with below, in Part I.

Sāmaveda in the Śrauta Ritual[1]

The Vedas are made manifest in one of two ways: (1) *svādhyāya*, recitation for its own sake, and (2) *prayoga*, recitation "for (sacrificial) use." When applied to the Sāmaveda these terms denote, respectively, the hymns as they appear in the *gānas* (the *rūpāntara* form) and the chants as performed at the elaborate *śrauta* ceremonies (the *svarūpa* form). Though this study treats primarily the *rūpāntara* forms of the chants, as they are found in the GG and ĀrG, some space must be devoted to the ritualistic or *svarūpa* chants of the ŪG and RG.

Sāmavedic chanting takes place specifically during rituals which feature libations of *soma*, an intoxicating juice obtained by pressing the stalks of the *soma* plant. These rites are solemnized either in the house of the *yajamāna* ("sacrificer": the one who sponsors the celebration and receives the benefit of its performance) or on a flat piece of ground close at hand. Here is constructed the *mahāvedi* ("great altar": see fig. 1 below),[2] where the most important functions take place (for instance, the receiving of the

---

[1] *Śrauta* ceremonies are sacrifices in which the chants and verses are heard in their secret, most potent forms, which have been established through divine revelation (*śruti*).

[2] See the entries "*yajamāna*" and "*mahāvedi*" in Louis Renou, *Vocabulaire du rituel védique* (Paris: Librairie C. Klincksieck, 1954), pp. 127, 124. See also id., *Vedic India*, p. 99.

Fig. 1. Mahāvedi (Kumbakoṇam, Tanjore District).

carts bearing the *soma* liquid). The *soma* sacrifices (*somayāgas*), which Asko Parpola rightly calls "the world's most complicated,"[1] are classified according to the number of days alotted for pressing: (1) *ekāha* ceremonies comprise only one pressing day, (2) *ahīna* rituals are made up of from two to twelve pressing days, and (3) *sattra* rites consist of pressings lasting twelve days or more.

The model for all *somayāgas* is the *jyotiṣṭoma*. Its length varies according to which of seven *soma saṃsthās* is being performed. Each of the seven forms is comprised of three services (morning, afternoon, evening); it is the length of the evening service which distinguishes one *saṃsthā* from another. As this third service increases in duration, so do the number of *stotras* ("lauds") sung by the Sāmavedic priests. The seven *saṃsthās*, along with the number of *stotras* belonging to each, are:

1. *agniṣṭoma*, 12
2. *atyagniṣṭoma*, 13
3. *ukthya*, 15
4. *ṣoḍaśin*, 16
5. *vājapeya*, 17
6. *atirātra*, 29
7. *aptoryāma*, 33

---

[1] *The Śrautasūtras of Lāṭyāyana and Drāhyāyaṇa and Their Commentaries: An English Translation and Study* (L/DSS), vol. 42, no. 2 of *Commentationes Humanarum Litterarum* (Helsinki: Societas Scientiarum Fennica, 1968-69), I:1, p. 5. Prescriptions for proper ritualistic observance are given in the Lāṭyāyana Śrauta Sūtra (LŚS), Drāhyāyaṇa Śrauta Sūtra (DŚS), and Jaiminīya Śrauta Sūtra (JŚS). They belong to the Kauthuma, Rāṇāyanīya, and Jaiminīya schools, respectively.

A stotra is not merely a single isolated chant; rather it is a chant complex in which several verses of text (drawn from the uttarārcika) are set to the same or different melodies. The verses of the uttarārcika are arranged usually in groups of two (pragāthas: two verses in mixed meters) or three (tṛcas: three verses in the same meter). In order to form the text of a stotra, the pragāthas are changed into tṛcas by a process of overlapping.[1] The stotra text comprises verses of one or more tṛcas; the verses (with modified texts)[2] are set to melodies, and the chants which result are called stotriyās. Some stotras are formed simply by going through the stotriyās once, without repetition; others require such repetition according to specific patterns (viṣṭutis), procedures which will be explained in more detail below.

Each stotriyā is divided into five sections (bhaktis), and each section is performed by specific members of a trio of Sāmavedic priests:

1. the prastāva, by the Prastotar
2. the udgītha, by the Udgātar
3. the pratihāra, by the Pratihartar
4. the upadrava, by the Udgātar
5. the nidhana, by Prastotar, Udgātar, and Pratihartar

---

[1]This change is described in Willem Caland and Victor Henry, L'Agniṣṭoma, description complète de la forme normale du sacrifice de soma dans le culte védique (CH), 2 vols. (Paris: Ernest Leroux, 1906-7), p. 307. See also NVR, pp. 71-72.

[2]Modified according to the devices listed above, pp. 11-12.

The principal *bhakti* of any chant is the *udgītha*, to which the *prastāva* serves as a short introduction. The *pratihāra* is essentially a response to the latter.[1] The *upadrava* is sometimes omitted, and the *nidhana* which follows it functions as a coda or cadence. The five *bhaktis* of a ritual chant are increased to seven by the addition of the *praṇava* (the mystic syllable *om*) and the *hiṃkāra* (the *stobha*-syllable *hum*). The *praṇava* occurs between *prastāva* and *udgītha* and is sung by the Udgātar. The *hiṃkāra*, inserted at the beginning of the *prastāva* and also between *udgītha* and *pratihāra*, is sung by various chanters.[2]

The ritualistic complexity and exactitude of the Vedic *soma* sacrifice are not even approximated by any other liturgy in the world--the involved prescriptions and chants of the Roman and related rites appear almost naive in comparison. Some of the intricacies associated with sacrificial Sāmavedic chanting can perhaps best be understood through a listing and description of the *stotras* of a particular sacrifice, the (Kauthuma-Rāṇāyanīya) *agniṣṭoma*.[3] It consists of twelve *stotras*; their names, the source verses (*yoni*) on which they are based (the arrangement in *tṛcas* and/or *pragāthas* is given in parentheses), and the required number (*stoma*) of *stotriyās*

---

[1]Renou, *Vocabulaire*, p. 109.

[2]Ibid., pp. 107, 175. See also Richard Simon, ed., *Das Pañcavidhasūtra* (PvS), vol. 5 of *Indische Forschungen*, ed. Alfred Hillebrandt (Breslau: M. & H. Marcus, 1913), pp. 2-3, nn. 4-5.

[3]From *agni-stoma*, the name given to the twelfth and final *stotra* (also known as the *yajñāyajñīyastotra*).

are as follows:

	stotra	ārcika source	stoma
1.	bahiṣpavamāna	SV 2.1-9 (3+3+3)	9
2.	first ājya	SV 2.10-12 (3)	15
3.	second ājya	SV 2.13-15 (3)	15
4.	third ājya	SV 2.16-18 (3)	15
5.	fourth ājya	SV 2.19-21 (3)	15
6.	mādhyandinapavamāna	SV 2.22-29 (3+2+3)	15
7.	first pṛṣṭha	SV 2.30-31 (2)	17
8.	second pṛṣṭha	SV 2.32-34 (3)	17
9.	third pṛṣṭha	SV 2.35-36 (2)	17
10.	fourth pṛṣṭha	SV 2.37-38 (2)	17
11.	ārbhavapavamāna	SV 2.39-52 (3+2+3+3+3)	17
12.	yajñāyajñīya (agniṣṭoma)	SV 2.53-54 (2)	21

The bahiṣpavamāna,[1] the first stotra shown in the foregoing list, is based upon 9 verses, which is the required number of stotriyās; therefore no repetitions are necessary. The stotra finds no setting in either ŪG or RG; as a result it is chanted on the Gāyatra-melody, which is nowhere notated

[1]See CH, pp. 177-180; LŚS 1.12.7-11 (= DŚS 3.4.22-25).

in the gānas.[1]

The four ājyastotras[2] are each based upon one tṛcā (3 verses), but the required number of stotriyās is 15. To meet this requirement the 3 verses (each set here also to the Gāyatra-melody) are repeated according to a particular pattern (viṣṭuti). The viṣṭuti prescribed for this particular stotra has the name pañcapañcinī ("five-fold"). As do all viṣṭutis, it consists of three rounds (paryāyas); each paryāya must be preceded by the hiṃkāra and must contain at least one setting of each of the 3 verses. If these are numbered 1-2-3, then the scheme of the viṣṭuti is: hum,1,1,1, 2,3; hum,1,2,2,2,3; hum,1,2,3,3,3.[3] As the stotra is chanted, the Prastotar marks the occurrence of each stotriyā by laying down a kuśā pin--a stick, about a span in length, made most often of udumbara wood. Thus a pattern of five sticks is formed for each paryāya of the viṣṭuti. According to the diagrams of Burnell and Parpola, the three paryāyas of the pañcapañcinī viṣṭuti are represented as follows:

---

[1] It is found, however, in Daivata Brāhmaṇa 3.24. See B. R. Sharma, ed., Devatādhyāya--Saṃhitopaniṣad--Vaṃśa--Brāhmaṇas (Tirupati: Kendriya Sanskrit Vidyapeetha, 1965), pp. 32-33. See also the entry "Gāyatra" in the Glossary below.

[2] See CH, pp. 236-38, 243-44, 247-48, 261-62; LŚS 2.5.18 (= DŚS 5.1.23-27), 2.6.4-12 (= 5.2.9-19).

[3] See Pañcaviṃśa Brāhmaṇa (PB) 2.4.1. The work is trans. in Willem Caland, ed., Pañcaviṃśa-Brāhmaṇa: The Brāhmaṇa of Twenty Five Chapters, work 255 of Bibliotheca Indica (Calcutta: Asiatic Society of Bengal, 1931).

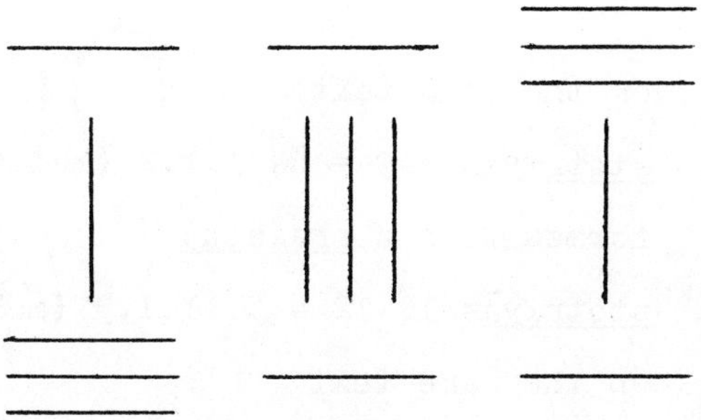

Burnell:	I	II	III
Parpola:	III	II	I

Burnell, who based his arrangement on oral information, specifies that the *viṣṭuti* is formed from left to right, with the bottom stick of each *paryāya* placed first.[1] Parpola believes the *śrautasūtras* to indicate that the *viṣṭuti* takes shape from right to left. Moreover, he writes that the order of placement for the individual *paryāya* is from top to bottom--except for the first three sticks (the top three of the rightmost diagram), where it is bottom to top (the three vertical sticks in the second *paryāya* are placed right to left).[2]

The *mādhyandinapavamānastotra*[3] requires 15 *stotriyās* from 8 verses:

1. *stotriyās* 1-3, on the text of the first *tṛca*,[4] are sung to the *Gāyatra*-melody
2. *stotriyās* 4-6 = ŪG 1.1.1 (melody: *āmahīyava*),

---

[1]A. C. Burnell, ed., *The Ārṣeyabrāhmaṇa (Being the Fourth Brāhmaṇa) of the Sāma Veda* (ĀrṣB)(Mangalore: Basel Mission Press, 1876), p. 105.

[2]L/DŚS, I:2, p. 214. [3]See CH, pp. 279-82.

[4]Refer to the *ārcika* listing above, p. 19.

on the same text

3. *stotriyās* 7-9 = ŪG 1.1.2 (melody: *raurava*), formed from a *prāgatha*

4. *stotriyās* 10-12 = ŪG 1.1.3 (melody: *yaudhājaya*), on the same text

5. *stotriyās* 13-15 = ŪG 1.1.4 (melody: *auśana*), on the concluding *tṛca*

The *pṛṣṭhastotras*[1] require 17 *stotriyās* each. These appear in the order of the *garbhinī viṣṭuti*, whose scheme is *hum*,1,1,1,2,3; *hum*,1,2,2,2,3; *hum*,1,2,2,2,3,3,3.[2] Each of the *pṛṣṭhastotras* is notated in the *gānas*; the corresponding *sāmans*, each sung to the pattern just cited, are:

1. RG 1.1.1 (melody: *rathaṃtara*), the first *pṛṣṭhastotra*, on a *pragātha*

2. ŪG 1.1.5 (melody: *vāmadevya*), the second *pṛṣṭhastotra*, on a *tṛca*

3. ŪG 1.1.6 (melody: *naudhasa*), the third *pṛṣṭhastotra*, on a *pragātha*

4. ŪG 1.1.7 (melody: *kāleya*), the fourth *pṛṣṭhastotra*, on a *pragātha*

The *ārbhavapavamānastotra*[3] comprises a total of 17 *stotriyās*, which are derived as follows:

1. *stotriyās* 1-3, on the text of the first *tṛca*, are sung to the *Gāyatra*-melody

---

[1]See CH, pp. 305-10, 314-15, 318-19, 323-25; LŚS 2.9.11--2.10.3 (= DŚS 6.1.15--6.2.3).

[2]PB 2.7.1. [3]See CH, pp. 337-43.

2. stotriyās 4-6 = ŪG 1.1.8 (melody: saṃhita), on the same text
3. stotriyā 7 = ŪG 1.1.9.1 (melody: sapha), on SV 2.42
4. stotriyā 8 = ŪG 1.1.10.1 (melody: pauṣkala), on SV 2.44
5. stotriyās 9-11 = ŪG 1.1.11 (melody: śyāvāśva), on a tṛca
6. stotriyās 12-14 = ŪG 1.1.12 (melody: āndhīgava), on the same text
7. stotriyās 15-17 = ŪG 1.1.13 (melody: kāva), on the concluding tṛca

A peculiar feature of this stotra is the omission of repeated portions of two sāmans (sapha and pauṣkala).

Finally, the yajñāyajñīyastotra (agniṣṭomastotra)[1] requires 21 stotriyās from a single pragātha. The stotra is constructed from ŪG 1.1.14 (melody: yajñāyajñīya) according to the saptasaptinī viṣṭuti, whose scheme is: hum,1,1,1,2,3; hum,1,2,2,2,3,3,3; hum,1,1,1,2,2,2,3,3,3.[2]

In addition to the formal and textual changes cited above, some further modifications are applied to certain chants. Notable among these is the replacement, in texts on the Gāyatra-melody, of udgītha- and upadrava-syllables by okāras (o-vowels). Singing a Gāyatra-melody with these sub-

[1]See CH, pp. 369-71; LŚS 2.10.15--2.10.20 (= DŚS 6.2.15--6.2.21).

[2]PB 2.15.1. A different pattern is given in CH, p. 369.

stitutions is referred to as "aniruktagāna" ("unexpressed chanting").[1] Another form of aniruktagāna is achieved in the udgītha section of the first pṛṣṭhastotra (on the rathaṃtara-melody, RG 1.1.1). Here each vowel is preceded by a bhakāra (the consonant bh), and also the original consonants are replaced by it.[2] Consequently the designation of the chant thus altered is "bhakāra rathaṃtara."[3]

There are occasions, especially during preliminary and auxiliary rites, when certain solo chants (parisāmans) are sung. For example, several of these are chanted by the Prastotar at the pravargya ceremony, an independent (apūrva) ritual preceding the soma sacrifice.[4] Also among the preliminaries (though it also occurs as well on the day of soma pressing) is the calling (āhvāna) of the subrahmaṇyā litany,[5] in which the god Indra is invited to be present at the sacrifice. A special Sāmaveda priest, the Subrahmaṇya, is solely

---

[1]See CH, p. 180; also see the Appendix below, specifically Tapes IIa(4), IXb(7A), XXVb(2, 22), XXVIIb(1-2). Alteration of the text apparently implies a corresponding change in melodic organization--a feature which I will discuss in a forthcoming article on "The Formation of Aniruktagāna in Sāmavedic Ritual Chants."

[2]See, however, the entry "bhakāra" in the Glossary below.

[3]See CH, p. 307. See also Parpola's lengthy note to LŚS 2.9.12-14a (= DŚS 6.1.16) in L/DŚS, I:2, pp. 242-44; and the Appendix below, Tapes Vb(10E), VIIIb(30), IXa(15), XXVb(3), and XXVIIIa(2).

[4]See LŚS 1.5.1--1.6.50 (= DŚS 2.1.1--2.2.53); also J. A. B. van Buitenen, The Pravargya: An Ancient Indian Iconic Ritual Described and Annotated (Poona, 1968).

[5]See LŚS 1.2.17--1.4.27 (= DŚS 1.2.23--1.4.31); L/DŚS, I:1, pp. 114-19; SSV, p. 23; NVR, p. 96; Tapes Ia(9), IVb(11), Vb(11), IXb(1), XXVb(18); "subrahmaṇya" in the Glossary below.

responsible for this task. Finally, solo chants are known to be sung in connection with the agnicayana,[1] a ceremony surrounding the construction of a large fire altar in the shape of an eagle with outstretched wings (see fig. 2 below). Though this ceremony proceeds simultaneously with soma rites, "an inner connection between the two is, however, not discernible; and it appears that the agnicayana, like the pravargya, has been brought only artificially in connection with the soma cult."[2] The solo chants are sung at various places around the completed altar as these parts of it are worshipped.[3]

---

[1]See Alfred Hillebrandt, Ritual-Litteratur: Vedische Opfer und Zauber, vol. 3, no. 2 of Grundriss der Indo-Arischen Philologie und Altertumskunde, ed. G. Bühler (Strassburg: Verlag von Karl J. Trübner, 1897), pp. 161-65.

[2]Ibid., p. 161. Translated by the author.

[3]See L/DṠS, I:1, pp. 120-25, where Parpola lists the sāmans as prescribed by numerous texts and, in a diagram of the altar, points out the specific spots where these chants are to be sung.

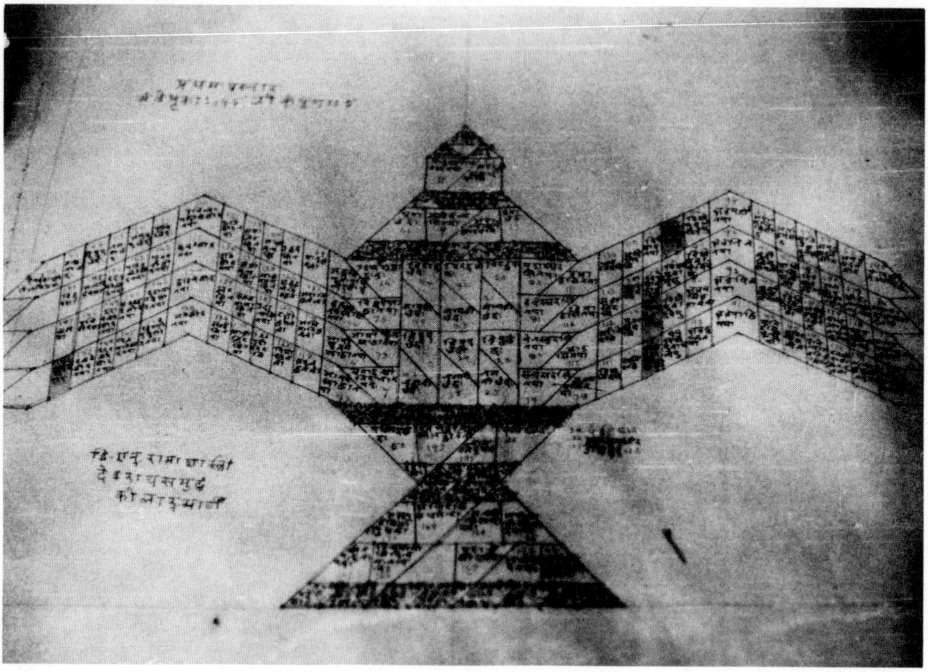

Fig. 2. Plan for a fire altar in the shape of an eagle (Kumbakonam, Tanjore District).

PART I

THE KAUTHUMA AND RĀṆĀYANĪYA SCHOOLS

CHAPTER 1

THE KAUTHUMA NUMERAL NOTATION

Notation of Svara

The seven svaras

The technical literature[1] names seven svaras ("sounds," "noises," "tones"): kruṣṭa, prathama, dvitīya, tṛtīya, caturtha, mandra, atisvārya (atisvāra, anusvāra, antya). The tṛtīya is alternately called madhyama ("middle"); mandra and atisvārya are sometimes called by their respective ordinals pañcama and ṣaṣṭha. In the gānas, svaras with ordinal names are designated by corresponding numerals: 1 = prathama, 2 = dvitīya, 3 = tṛtīya (madhyama), 4 = caturtha, 5 = pañcama (mandra), 6 = ṣaṣṭha (atisvārya).

Kruṣṭa

The kruṣṭa is indicated by either of two numerals: 1 or 11. Where it is specified by the former can be known only through oral tradition, for this numeral ordinarily designates the prathama.

The kruṣṭa is usually given first in lists of the

---

[1] Sāmavidhāna Brāhmaṇa (SvB) 1.1.8, Puṣpasūtra (PuS) 8.87, Nāradīya Śikṣā (NŚ) 1.1.12, et al.

seven svaras;[1] it is therefore the "highest" of the seven. The atisvārya is normally listed last; therefore it is thought to be the "lowest." Thus the numeral 1 is considered higher than the numeral 6, even though the latter is greater quantitatively.

It is said that the kruṣṭa occurs in only two sāmans;[2] however the Nārāyaṇasvāmi edition of the GG and ĀrG has it specifically notated in four chants. The parvans, all monosyllabic stobhas, in which it appears are:

1. / ū 2 / (with 1 above ū and ↑ above 2), in GG 284.2 (melody: ātra)[3]

2. / hai / (with 11 above), in GG 381.1 (melody: krośa)

3. / ū 2̄ / (with 11 above ū) and / ū 2̂ / (with 1 above ū), each occurring twice in ĀrG 141.1 (melody: kaśyapavrata anugāna [1])[4]

4. / ū / (with 11 above), occurring four times in ĀrG 144.1 (melody: kaśyapavrata anugāna [7])

The kruṣṭa possibly is found in other sāmans as well. The first example above makes use of the sign ↑̂, which indi-

---

[1]NŚ 1.1.12 has it in sixth place, before the atisvārya.

[2]PuS 9.26 reads: paṃcasv eva tu gāyaṃti bhūyiṣṭhāni svareṣu tu / sāmāni ṣaṭsu cānyāni saptasu dve tu kauthumāḥ // ("The Kauthumas sing most of their chants to five svaras, a few are sung to six, and two are sung to seven").

[3]See VC, p. 35.

[4]See ibid., pp. 36-37. The symbol 2̄ usually designates the preṅkha, a numerical succession involving prathama and dvitīya--not the kruṣṭa.

cates numerical disjunction. Here it takes the form of omission (atikrama) of the prathama in crossing from kruṣṭa to dvitīya. This symbol is notated fifty-eight times in the Nārāyaṇasvāmi edition,[1] and in all but six instances it is found above a 2 which is preceded by 1. The latter must designate kruṣṭa if atikrama is to take place, but whether this is always the intended pattern is open to question. Great care must be exercised in assigning specific functions to the notational signs. The editors of the printed editions are sometimes inconsistent and in error, and some symbols may denote more than one pattern: the circumflex, for example, accompanies four different types of number successions.

Theories on the Kauthuma scale

Students of Sāmaveda have, almost without exception, interpreted the term "svara" as "tone." Burnell was the first scholar to formulate, in the year 1876, a specific Sāmavedic gamut (of seven tones: F-E-D-C-B-A-G),[2] which he derived by checking one of the oral traditions[3] with a standard pitch pipe. He documented his finding by referring to a passage in the NŚ which equates the Sāmavedic svaras to the tones of

---

[1]The symbol is found in the following chants (multiple occurrences, excluding consecutively repeating parvans, are indicated in parentheses): GG 169.3, 245.4(4), 253.3(4), 284.2, 320.1, 340.1(3), 342.3, 417.1, 446.1, 465.1, 481.1(2), 545.1(3), 545.2(2), 554.2(2), 569.2(2), 570.3, ĀrG 8.1, 12.1, 30.1, 38.1, 44.1(3), 84.2(9), 91.5, 111.1, 112.1(2), 121.1(2), after 155.1:5; ĀrG pariśiṣṭa (ĀrGP): 2d mahānāmnī sāma (3), tavasyāvīya sāma (3).

[2]ĀrṣB, p. xlii.

[3]Probably that of the Kauthumas of South India; see below, pp. 102-13.

secular music:

> yaḥ sāmagānāṃ prathamaḥ sa venor madhyamaḥ svaraḥ /
>
> The *prathama-svara* of Sāmavedic Chant is the *madhyama-svara* of the flute;
>
> yo dvitīyaḥ sa gāndhāras tṛtīyas tv ṛṣabhaḥ smṛtaḥ // 1 //
>
> The *dvitīya* is considered the *gāndhāra*, the *tṛtīya* the *ṛṣabhaḥ*;
>
> caturthaḥ ṣaḍja ity āhuḥ pañcamo dhaivato bhavet /
>
> The *caturtha* is called *ṣaḍja*; the *pañcama* should be the *dhaivata*;
>
> ṣaṣṭho niṣādo vijñeyaḥ saptamaḥ pañcamaḥ smṛtaḥ // 2 //
>
> The *ṣaṣṭha* is heard as the *niṣāda*; the *saptama* is considered the *pañcama*.[1]

Burnell has overlooked the fact that the scale postulated by the NŚ has a *vakra* ("bent," "crooked") feature which places the *ṣaṣṭha* above the *pañcama*. Furthermore, a seventh (*saptama*) and lowest tone[2] is placed in correspondence with the *pañcama* of the secular scale. Since the NŚ gives here only the ordinal names of the *svaras*, it is possible that "*prathama*" refers here to "*kruṣṭa*" (which is actually the "first" *svara*), "*dvitīya*" to "*prathama*," "*tṛtīya*" to "*dvitīya*,"

---

[1]NŚ 1.5.1-2. Burnell (ĀrṣB, p. xlii) quotes only the first *śloka*, but he gives the entire passage in his ed. of the *Saṃhitopaniṣadbrāhmaṇa* (SUB) (Mangalore: Basel Mission Press, 1877), p. xix. If the secular scale of the NŚ is the same as the present *śuddha ṣaḍja-grāma* (approximately our major scale) on C, then *madhyama* = F, *gāndhāra* = E, *ṛṣabha* = D, *ṣaḍja* = C, *niṣāda* = B, *dhaivata* = A, and *pañcama* = G. However, the ancient *ṣaḍja-grāma* was comparable to the dorian mode.

[2]The numeral 7 ordinarily signifies the *abhigīta*, a numerical succession comprising *dvitīya* and *prathama*. See below, pp. 71-75.

and so on.[1] Clearly Burnell considered the topmost tone in the NŚ scale to be the prathama, not the kruṣṭa, and he set the prathama equivalent to the highest tone of the scale he had constructed by listening to actual Sāmavedic chanting. In his Introduction to the ĀrṣB he has given us transcriptions, in breves and semibreves, of the first two chants of the GG,[2] in which the atisvārya is not notated. Faddegon[3] noted this omission and questioned how the atisvārya could be set equal to the tone A--the pitch is relative, of course--when in fact the numeral 6 does not occur in the two chants from which he derived his scale pattern. The answer is fairly obvious. Burnell was not able to transcribe the chants as he listened to them; it was possible for him to take down only the seven pitches. He later attempted to reconcile this scale with the numeral notation of the gānas, and the result probably bears little resemblance to what he actually had heard. His transcriptions, therefore, are based not upon actual Sāmavedic chanting but strictly upon the gāna notation.

Later scholars constructed gamuts which generally differ from that of Burnell. Śeṣagiri Śāstrī, writing during the period 1901-5, recognized the transilient feature of

---

[1]See the table in A. H. Fox Strangways, The Music of Hindostan (MH) (Oxford: Clarendon Press, 1914), pp. 258-59. The reader should be aware that, in the pages following, the term "prathama" will denote the prathama-svara, not the kruṣṭa.

[2]ĀrṣB, pp. xlv-xlvi. The first chant is reprinted in modern notation in MH, p. 251, but with the omission of the 3d parvan.

[3]SSV, p. 47.

the NŚ scale and added that the second and sixth tones should be flattened; therefore his gamut reads F-E♭-D-C-A-B♭-G.[1] He observes that the sixth and seventh tones occur infrequently and that "the melody of the Sāmaveda is uniform and may be identified with the rāga . . . Ābhogi,"[2] which is a South Indian janya rāga containing five tones in both ascent and descent (hence: auḍava-auḍava) and belonging to the twenty-second meḷa (Kharaharapriya).

Fox Strangways, whose landmark work on Hindusthānī music--with a chapter devoted to Sāmaveda--appeared in 1914, believed the seven-tone sāman scale to have evolved from one of two tetrachords, E-D-C-B or F-E-D-C. The first, he writes, is identified by the Taittirīya Prātiśākhya as comprising the tones used by Yajurvedins of the Taittirīya school. The other has claim to authenticity from "the fact that the four ordinals (first to fourth) are assigned in every treatise to the notes F, E, D, C, and that . . . the Ṛgveda accents are appropriated [by the Taittirīya Prātiśākhya] to these notes."[3] The remaining three svaras, he thinks, were added successively only later and with the original four tones formed a scale similar to the old gāndhāra grāma, which, as Faddegon points out disbelievingly,[4] is built on the śruti system. Fox Strangways then acknowledges Śeṣagiri Śāstrī's interpretation

---

[1]M. Śeṣagiri Śāstrī and M. Raṅgācārya, A Descriptive Catalogue of the Sanskrit Manuscripts in the Government Oriental Manuscript Library, Madras, vol. 1: Vedic Literature (Madras: Government Press, 1901-5), pp. 76-78.

[2]Ibid., p. 78. [3]MH, p. 261. [4]SSV, p. 49.

of NŚ 1.5.1-2, adding that his transilient gamut must also be considered a possible form of the seven-tone scale.[1]

Finally, in 1951, Faddegon hypothesized that the original Sāmavedic scale was pentatonic and comprised one of two tone patterns--E-D-C-A-G or A-G-E-D-C--without a sixth tone: "The musicians of the Vedic times fixed the tones quintally, perhaps here and there correcting a third and sixth by auditive intuition."[2] Moreover, "in the classical period a fixed system of tuning was attained, with use of fifths, of melodious sixths and thirds; and this system penetrated even in the folksongs."[3] Thus, in his view, the pentatonic gamut was transformed only in the post-Vedic period to a scale based upon the _śruti_ system. He proceeds to connect certain types of _gāna_ melodization with the accents of the _ārcika_, partly justifying such a correlation on the PuS definition[4] of an _udūha_. This term refers to a _svara_ which is three positions higher than a lower _svara_. Accordingly, the _udūhas_ of _caturtha_, _mandra_, and _atisvārya_ are, respectively, _prathama_, _dvitīya_, and _tṛtīya_. Faddegon quite independently regarded them as "harmonic derivatives," for which the final three _svaras_ could be considered substitutes.[5] Among other alterations he believed to take place are:[6] (1) replacement of the _tṛtīya_ (_anudātta_)[7] by the _dvitīya_ or

---

[1] MH, pp. 263-64. [2] SSV, pp. 12-13. [3] Ibid., p. 13.

[4] See PuS 8.90. [5] SSV, p. 13. [6] Ibid., pp. 57-58.

[7] For an explanation of the Vedic accents, see the entry "_udātta_" in the Glossary below.

(less often) the *prathama*, and (2) continuation of the *prathama* (*udātta*) to the following syllable, where it replaces the *dvitīya* (*svarita*), provided that this syllable is not itself followed by an *udātta*. In this last procedure, first postulated by Hermann Oldenberg[1] and known as his rule of "acoustic metalepsis," a dependent *svarita* is replaced by an *udātta* if it is followed by a *pracaya* syllable or a pause concluding a phonetical unit.

The theories of Burnell, Śeṣagiri Śāstrī, Fox Strangways, and Faddegon raise serious questions regarding the Sāmavedic concept of tone and scale. Certainly the degree of authority in this matter of tracts such as the NŚ has not yet been determined. The age of the *śikṣās* was the subject of much dispute even among Sanskritists of the nineteenth century. The debate was succinctly summed up by Burnell:

> Profr. Haug considered that they are primitive; I have given reasons for believing that they belong to a school of grammar that preceded Pāṇini, though comparatively recent as regards their present form. Profr. Kielhorn, on the other hand, considers that they are modern. They often confound accentuation with the musical notes of the sāman chant, and have at least one sign of antiquity--that they are very naive in language.[2]

A word should be said of attempts by scholars such as Fox Strangways and Faddegon to link the notational numbers

---

[1] *Die Hymnen des Ṛgveda*, vol. 1: *Metrische und textgeschichtliche Prolegomena* (Berlin: 1888), p. 485.

[2] ĀrsB, pp. xx-xxi. Pāṇini was a great Sanskrit grammarian whose *Aṣṭādhyāyī* ("Eight Chapters") was probably written near the end of the 4th century B.C. For a description of the contents of the Nāradīya Śikṣā, see A. C. Burnell, *Catalogue of a Collection of Sanskrit Manuscripts*, pt. 1: *Vedic Manuscripts* (London: Trübner & Co., 1869), pp. 42-43.

to the accents of the source verses. Though such an analogy cannot be rejected outright, endeavors in this direction have not produced thoroughly convincing results. Faddegon, for instance, who has done perhaps the most research in this area, relied for his proof largely upon theories of tonal replacement and continuation--such as the acoustic metalepsis idea of Oldenberg. Although this theory was presented with some hesitation by Oldenberg himself, Faddegon went so far as to write that through it "we are witnesses of music's birth and we feel happy at India's rich literary inheritance which will in the course of time teach us music's spiritual development."[1] These are lofty but dangerous words, and greater credence could be placed in them if the evidence were more persuading. However, melody connected with accentuation is only one of four types of melodization which he has discovered in the gānas,[2] and there are numerous exceptions among the instances where such melody-accent correspondence is supposed to be found. He leaves unmentioned that representation by numerals is only one--and perhaps the most modern--of three Sāmavedic notational systems.[3] The other two make use of notational syllables which have not been connected in any way with ārcika accentuation.

None of the above named scholars spent adequate time tracking down and taking notes on the numerous oral traditions. This is a very serious deficiency which tends to negate the

[1] SSV, p. 24. [2] Ibid., p. 57.

[3] The notations cannot be said to predate the extant gāna MSS, none of which is older than a few centuries.

theories which they have proposed.[1] The present study, in which all of the known styles of sāman-singing are discussed, proves conclusively that the Sāmavedic concept of svara is much broader than believed by Burnell, Faddegon, and the rest. A central point which is made in forthcoming chapters is that the word "svara" implies a musical phrase or motive--not necessarily only a single isolated tone. The matter was stated to me simply and directly by Śrī M. Itti Ravi Nambūdiri (Pāññāl village, Trichur [Tṛśśivaperūr] District, Keraḷa), the principal living exponent of a style of singing which may represent Sāmavedic chant in its purest form:

> You must remember that the word "svara" we use is not the svara of the sapta-svaras [the seven tones of the secular scale]. We mean the movement or vibration of sound. [In describing this] we use the word "iḷakkam," which means "movement."[2]

In the remaining pages the term "svara" should be understood in this light.

Principles of Time Measurement

Mātrā

Temporal values are explained in a small treatise of fifty-six sūtras, the Mātrālakṣaṇa (known also as the Chandogapariśiṣṭa), a work of extreme importance to the

---

[1] Śeṣagiri Śāstrī admits that "the methods of singing the Sāmaveda are different in different countries [i.e., regions], and none of them agree[s] with the figures which are uniformly inserted over the vowels to indicate the notes with which they are to be sung." (Descriptive Catalogue, 1: 77)

[2] From a letter of May 20, 1973. "Iḷakkam" is a Malayāḷam word meaning "shaking, fluctuation, irresolution"; see T. Burrow and M. B. Emeneau, A Dravidian Etymological Dictionary (DED) (Oxford: Clarendon Press, 1961), no. 432.

Mātrālakṣaṇa (ML) cites the following example:

    2r 1 _   4r   r   r _5
    rāyāy ā 2 3 gne mahe tvā hāu (GG 93.2)

A long (dīrgha) syllable (that is, a syllable whose vowel is long)[1] contains two mātrās, and pluta and vṛddha syllables each contain three mātrās. A pluta syllable is formed by adding two mātrās to a hrasva syllable; a vṛddha syllable arises when one mātrā is added to a dīrgha syllable.[2] Long vowels are vṛddha ("augmented") if they do not have placed above them the repha (the semivowel r, written र) or the bindu (the sign °, found principally in South Indian manuscripts).[3] The ML establishes three additional time values:[4] adhyardha (1½ mātrā),[5] ardhatisra (2½ mātrās),[6] and ardha-atasra (3½ mātrās).[7]

ṛtti and kalā

The values described above are realized in any one of

---

[1]The long vowels are ā, ī, ū, ṝ, e, ai, o, and au ML 1.7-8).

[2]ML 1.4.

[3]When notated within instead of above the textual ne, the bindu denotes the nasalizations anusvāra or anusika; see NVL, p. 310.

[4]ML 1.5.

[5]Occurs in connection with certain numeral successions ed vinata, praṇata, utsvarita, and abhigīta. These are cussed individually below, pp. 69-75.

[6]Found in a special case of a particular number uence, the abhigīta. See below, pp. 71-75.

[7]This is the duration of the praṇava (the oṃkāra), h may be inserted into any chant as an additional bhakti. above, p. 18.

Sāmaveda scholar for its lucid and straightforward presentation of technical matters. Absolutely nothing is known about the authors of the text and commentary; we know only that the work is of comparatively recent origin.[1]

The temporal unit is the mātrā, which is equivaler to the length of a short (hrasva) syllable (that is, a sy lable whose vowel is short).[2] From the mātrā the other durational values are derived. Ardhamātrā and aṇumātrā refer, respectively, to one-half and one-quarter mātrā.[3] semivowel y is worth one-quarter mātrā when it occurs a end of a word before a vowel (when in saṃdhi [euphonic nation][4] a final i-vowel is changed to y before a diss vowel or dipthong); the vowel ṛ has this value when it at the beginning of a word.[5] As an instance of final

---

[1]B. R. Sharma, Pañcavidha-Sūtra and Mātrālak with Commentaries (Tirupati: Kendriya Sanskrit Vidy 1970), p. 18. This is a devanāgarī edition of both and commentary.

[2]The short vowels are a, i, u, and ṛ (Mātrā [ML] 1.3, 6).

[3]ML 1.2, 5.

[4]The Sanskrit sentence, verse, or quarter- a phonetical unity in which initial and final lett words are frequently combined euphonically. This (saṃdhi) may also occur between roots and stems a various endings.

[5]uttaro yakāro 'numātro . . . / ṛkārādir (ML 3.9). See Richard Simon, "Die Notationen de Liederbücher," (NVL) Wiener Zeitschrift für die Morgenlandes 27 (1913): 316, where r instead of for the second aphorism. This is obviously a mi the sūtra continues: repho 'rdhamātrā. One-ha the length of an r when it is combined with h, a sibilant in svarabhakti (a vowel sound separa from a following consonant).

(1 n na di se Wh Se

three vṛttis (tempi).[1] These are termed simply fast (druta), moderate (madhyama), and slow (vilambita). A mātrā is composed of 3, 4, or 5 kalās (temporal subdivisions), depending on which of the respective tempi is employed. Therefore the kalā has an absolute temporal value, while the mātrā varies in duration according to the vṛtti chosen by the chanter. The three tempi are related by the ML to colors and deities: druta to red and Vāyu, madhyama to blue-black and Bṛhaspati, vilambita to white and Sūrya.

Gati

The term "gati" refers to a prolongation of a vowel. Two types are explained by the ML:[2] lengthening of a guttural vowel (kaṇṭhya) by the addition of either a palatal vowel (tālavya) or a labial vowel (oṣṭhya). Both the ML commentator[3] and the hundreds of examples in the gānas indicate that the two cases in question are ā-i (or ā-yi) and ā-u. The elements (y)i and u of a gati are worth either one or one-half mātrā. The first element (ā) occurs either as a long (dīrgha) or augmented (vṛddha) vowel, but the two elements combined[4] must have the augmented value (three mātrās).

---

[1] ML 1.11-13.

[2] ML 1.15, 3.1-2. See also NVL, p. 315, and Richard Simon, Das Puṣpasūtra mit Einleitung und Übersetzung, vol. 23, no. 3 of Abhandlungen der philosophisch-philologischen Klasse der königlichen Bayerischen Akademie der Wissenschaften (Munich: n.p., 1908), p. 520.

[3] See his interpretation of ML 3.1.

[4] The phonetic result, of course, is a dipthong: either ai or au.

It appears that wherever the initial element (*ā*) is designated as long (2 *mātrās*), the final element (*[y]i* or *u*) is worth 1 *mātrā* to fulfil the requirement that the two elements combined should come to 3 *mātrās*.[1] But wherever the *ā*-element is not designated as long (that is, wherever it is augmented), the value of the final element must be subtracted from that of the vowel *ā* so that the total time of the two elements together comes to (and does not exceed) three *mātrās*. The *ā*-element is therefore reduced in value from 3 to 2½ (or, perhaps optionally, also to 2) *mātrās*.[2] The first *parvan* of GG 1.1 may illustrate this interpretation. It reads:

4
/ o-gnā-(y)i /

The *parvan* consists essentially of two syllables: first *o*, then *gnā*, to which the *gati* (*[y]i*) has been added. The first is an augmented syllable containing 3 *mātrās*; the second is an augmented *tālavya*, also of 3 *mātrās*. Therefore the *parvan* contains a total of 6 *mātrās* distributed in the following manner:

o	*gnā*		*(y)i*	
3	+ 2½	+	½	= 6
		or		
3	+ 2	+	1	= 6

[1]Such a case occurs especially in connection with *stobha*-syllables (e.g., *hā-[y]i* or *hā-u*).

[2]According to Simon (NVL, p. 315, n. 8), this explanation is confirmed by statements of the PuS.

Actually it makes little difference which of the two sets of figures is followed, for the end results--3 *mātrās* for the *tālavya* dipthong and 6 for the entire *parvan*--are the same in either case. The instances of *gati* which present the greatest difficulties are those in which numerals are placed between the two elements of the dipthong, as in *tsā 2 3 4 (y)i* (from GG 1.3). However, the ML is silent concerning cases such as this.

Primary and secondary numbers

The Kauthuma notational numerals appear both above and within the textual line. The two positions--and hence also the numerals themselves--are known respectively as primary (*prakṛti*) and secondary (*vikṛti*). If primary numbers alone were notated in the *gānas*, determining the precise number of *mātrās* in a *sāman* would be a fairly simple task. For example, the first four *parvans* of GG 133.1 contain primary numbers only, so *mātrā*-values can be assigned to the syllables of these *parvans* as follows:

```
Notation:  5r  r  r                4  5          2  1
Text:       ā ghā ye a-gnim in-dhā-tā-(y)i / stri-ṇan-ti
Mātrās:     2  2  2 1   1   1  3  2   1        1   1  1

          r            2r 1r         r    r
ba-r-hir ā-nu-ṣāk / ye-ṣām in-dro yu-vā-(y)i hā / u vā-(y)i/
 1 ½  1  2  1  3     2   2   1    2  1  2    1  3   3  2     1
```

The *parvan* totals are: 15 + 11½ + 14 + 6 = 46½ *mātrās* for the four combined.

Almost all chants contain secondary numbers, which occur either singly or in groups. They are viewed as being attached to the syllable (and consequently to the primary number associated with it) which immediately precedes. This combination of a primary number with one or more secondary numbers will be referred to henceforth as a sequence. In subsequent pages, sequences will occasionally be represented symbolically: thus, for example, 1_2 indicates a primary *prathama* followed by a secondary *dvitīya*, and 5_{656} symbolizes a primary *mandra* followed by three secondary figures (*atisvārya*, *mandra*, and again *atisvārya*).[1] The oral traditions, which are discussed below in detail, reveal that an individual numeral, though called consistently by the same name (*prathama*, *dvitīya*, and so on), does not represent a consistently identical musical tone or phrase. However, a particular sequence is usually sung the same way at all times.

Statements in the ML concerning the durations of sequences are often vague or, unfortunately, even non-existent, but the information which is given is extremely valuable for at least a partial understanding of the interrelationships of melody and *mātrā*. Eight sequence types are discussed in the ML; they are given the names *pratyutkrama*, *atikrama*, *karṣaṇa*, *svāra*, *vinata*, *praṇata*, *utsvarita*, and *abhigīta*. Each of these, along with several related types, are discussed below.

Pratyutkrama

A notational progression from a number to a higher number is termed *pratyutkrama*.[2] Eight different kinds of

---

[1]As a rule the same number is not notated twice in succession. Therefore a number, whether primary or secondary, holds true for subsequent syllables as well--until a different number is notated.

[2]See Simon, PuS, p. 521; NVL, pp. 313-14.

these progressions are listed by the ML,[1] and each is illustrated with one or more examples from the gānas. As these extracts show, the various types are found not only as sequences but also as patterns which occur between two primary or two secondary figures.

1. atisvārya to mandra (6 to 5). This case is found in the sequence named parisvāra or padānusvāra.[2]

padānusvāra

3 2 ^ 4 5
a) kayā 3 sthā S5 irā 6 5 6 n (GG 13.1)[3]

2. mandra to caturtha (5 to 4)

5r 5S
a) srāyanta iva sū 4 rāyam (GG 267.1)

5 r r 5
b) tarobhir vo vidā 4 d vāsum (GG 237.4)

5 r r 5
c) purojitī vo 4 ṃdhāsāḥ (GG 545.6)

3. caturtha to tṛtīya (4 to 3)

5r 4 2 ^
a) dūtā 3 ṃ vo 3 (GG 12.1)

5r 4 2 4 5r
b) devo 3 vo 3 draviṇodāḥ (GG 55.1)

5r 4 2 4r 5r
c) mā nā 3 ā 3 indrābhiyā disāḥ (GG 128.2)

4. tṛtīya to dvitīya (3 to 2)

---

[1] ML 1.18-26. See also Dīkṣita Rāmakṛṣṇa's commentary on PuS 9.160.

[2] See Simon, PuS, p. 521. The Hāvik Rāṇāyanīyas of Mysore and the "Old School" Kauthumas of Tamilnāṭu perform the padānusvāra in a manner which the term implies--with accompanying nasalization. See below, pp. 132-33; 135, n. 3.

[3] All examples from the Kauthuma gānas are from the Nārāyaṇasvāmi edition, unless otherwise noted.

  3   5
a) hī 2 3 4 ṣī (GG 1.1)[1]

5. *dvitīya* to *prathama* (2 to 1)

  2r
a) au ho 1 i (GG 5.2)

  2r 1
b) agne rāthā 2 3 m (GG 5.2)

6. *mandra* to *tṛtīya* (5 to 3)[2]

  4 3r 4 5r r 3r 2 3 5
a) sunota soma pā / āvnā o 2 3 4 vā (GG 285.2)

7. *mandra* to *dvitīya* (5 to 2)

  5
a) ṣibhā 2 / u (GG 559.2)[3]

  4 4 5
b) e 5 / abhi priyā 2̂ (GG 554.2)

8. *tṛtīya* to *prathama* (3 to 1)

  3 2
a) punā 3 1 (GG 511.16)

The ML has the following to say regarding *mātrā*-values of *pratyutkrama* numerals: "Wherever *mandra*, *tṛtīya*, or *dvitīya* proceed, without *karṣaṇa* [that is, without an intervening numeral], to the next higher numeral, they are

---

[1]The pattern $3_{234}5$ (or 3_{2345}) is that of the *nigada* (see Simon, PuS, p. 520), one of three kinds of *svāra*. See below, pp. 66-69.

[2]This and the following two cases are also examples of *atikrama* ("omission"). See below, pp. 48-50.

[3]The Nārāyanasvāmi edition reads: *ṣibhā 2 u* (with 4 above *bhā*). The example above is from the ML.

comprised of two mātrās."[1] This statement applies, therefore, to the second, fourth, and fifth cases. In addition to the above examples illustrating these cases, some further specimens are provided:[2]

1. the vairājanidhana,[3] a nidhana[4] equivalent to the following sequence, sung on the vowel ī:

   3 1 1 1 1
   ī 2 3 4 5 (found in many sāmans, including GG 72.1, 2; 317.1-5; 398.2; ĀrG 51.4; 54.1)[5]

2.
   3 2   3r 2
   ghnatā 3 4 vāmā 1 (GG 305.1)

3. the avanardana ("trill") of the Gāyatra-sāman:[6]

   [2] 1r r   2
   dhiyo yo naḥ praco 1 2 1 2 (on the Sāvitrī

   [2] 1 r r 2
   verse) or abhi devām iyā 1 2 1 2 (on SV 2.1, the first stotriyā of the bahiṣpavamānastotra)[7]

---

[1]ML 2.3: "yan mandradvitīyatṛtīyaiḥ svarair akṛṣṭam pratyutkrāmati anantarocce pratyaye tad dvimātrādiḥ." See NVL, pp. 313-14, n. 6, for an alternate reading, which, however, does not affect the translation. Concerning this passage Simon remarks, "So daß bei langer Silbe für den Ton, zu dem fortgeschritten wird, unter Umständen nicht mehr als 1 mātrā übrigbleiben würde" (Ibid.). The reasoning behind his statement will be explained below, in the discussion of karṣaṇa, pp. 53-54.

[2]ML 2.4-5.

[3]See the definition of svāra below, pp. 66-69.

[4]A nidhana is the final section (bhakti) of a sāman. See above, pp. 17-18.

[5]ĀrG 54.1 is named "mahāvairajyam."

[6]See PB 7.1.2.

[7]See above, pp. 19-20; see also the entry "Gāyatra" in the Glossary below.

Finally, specific durational values are prescribed for two particular cases. In

[5]r , 3r 2
pā / āvnā (GG 285.2) *mandra* and *tṛtīya* are each worth two *mātrās*. This is the expected value, for both numbers are written in the primary position and are accompanied by the *repha*. In

[4] 5 S 1 1 1 1
accha 2 u / vā 2 3 4 5 (GG 543.1) the *mandra* is worth one *mātrā*; the *dvitīya*'s duration is not mentioned.

Atikrama

Four types of *atikrama* ("omission") are listed,[1] all cases of a disjunct skip from a numeral to a lower numeral. In addition to these four patterns, the *Sāmaparibhāṣā*[2] (Spb) of Kṛṣṇasvāmin Śrautin records four instances of omission through ascending movement and provides one or more illustrations of each. The reason for the ML's silence regarding these four cases is not clear. However, three of the four had already been registered as examples of *pratyutkrama* (cases 6-8), so perhaps the author preferred not to repeat the obvious. The fourth and final case (5 to 1) occurs infrequently between primary and secondary numbers (only once, in ĀrG 103.1?), and the Spb example is the excerpt used by the ML to illustrate the fourth type of descending *atikrama* (1 to 5); the author again perhaps chose to avoid a needless repetition. *Atikrama*

---

[1]ML 1.27-31. See Dīkṣita Rāmakṛṣṇa's commentary on PuS 9.132.

[2]I have been unsuccessful in locating a copy of this rare *grantha* print. Its discussion of *atikrama* (p. 14) is cited in Simon, PuS, p. 516.

is discussed without reference to durational values. Like pratyutkrama it may be found between two primary or two secondary numbers, as well as between the numbers of a sequence. The eight cases (with examples) as established by the ML and the Spb are as follows:

1. Omission of 1 in crossing from 11 to 2 (kruṣṭa to dvitīya)

   a) ML: ū 2 / na â gā 2 3 4 hī (GG 284.2)[1]
   (marks above: 1 over ū, ↑ over 2, 3 over gā, 5 over hī)

   b) Spb: u 2 (GG 284.2)
   (marks above: 11 over u)

2. Omission of 2 in crossing from 1 to 3 (prathama to tṛtīya)

   a) ML, Spb: ā ro 3 hān (GG 92.1)[2]
   (marks above: 1r over ā, S over ro, ^ over 3, 2 over hān)

   b) Spb: nāke supārṇam upayāt patantām (GG 320.1)
   (marks above: lo o over nāke, 3 2 1 over patantām)

3. Omission of 4 in crossing from 3 to 5 (tṛtīya to mandra)

   a) ML, Spb: yajñā 5 ya (GG 35.4)
   (marks above: 4 3 over yajñā)

   b) Spb: o i trika (GG 457.1)
   (marks above: 2 over o, 3 5 over trika)

4. Omission of 2, 3, and 4 in crossing from 1 to 5 (prathama to mandra)

   a) ML, Spb: ī 5 hī hī hī hī hi (ĀrG 103.1)
   (marks above: 1 over ī, 1 over hī, 2r over hī, 3r over hī, 2 over hi)

---

[1] As noted above, p. 29, the numeral "1" here is the kruṣṭa, not the prathama.

[2] More precisely, the Spb reads: ā ro S 3 hān. (marks above: lo na over ā ro, 2 over hān) The "o" is the South Indian equivalent of "r," and the "na" symbolizes a sequence known as namana. See below, pp. 62-64.

5. Omission of 4 in crossing from 5 to 3 (*mandra* to *tṛtīya*)

    a) Spb: 5 3 2
             naram o i (GG 144.2)

6. Omission of 4 and 3 in crossing from 5 to 2 (*mandra* to *dvitīya*)

    a) Spb: 4   5
             abhi priyā 2 (GG 554.2)

    b) Spb: 5 o 2
             uccā tā 3 i (GG 467.13)

7. Omission of 2 in crossing from 3 to 1 (*tṛtīya* to *prathama*)

    a) Spb: 3o 1   5
             au ho 2 3 4 va (GG 139.1)

    b) Spb: 3o 2
             gayā 3 1 (GG 342.1)

8. Omission of 4, 3, and 2 in crossing from 5 to 1 (*mandra* to *prathama*)

    a) Spb: 1   1   2o 3o 2
             ī 5 hī hī hī hī hi (ĀrG 103.1).

Atikrama is often left undesignated, but it can be indicated by the circumflex (^) or the *avagraha* (S). The circumflex is always notated above the textual line, but the *avagraha* may appear either above or within the line. As many *avagrahas* may be notated as there are numbers which are omitted.[1]

Karṣaṇa

Five kinds of *karṣaṇa* (from the root *kṛṣ*: "to draw,"

---

[1]See Simon, PuS, p. 516.

"to pull") are illustrated;[1] all are attached to augmented vowels.

1. to the <u>dvitīya</u>: bo$\overset{1}{\text{dhā}}$ $\bar{2}$ (GG 15.1)[2]

2. to the <u>tṛtīya</u>: $\overset{1}{\text{ā}}$ 2 3 ind$\overset{2}{\text{rāḥ}}$ (GG 275.2)

3. to the <u>caturtha</u>: n$\overset{1}{\text{mā}}$ 2 3 4 bhā i (GG 87.1)[3]

4. to the <u>mandra</u>: $\overset{1}{\text{o}}$ 2 3 4 5 i (GG 3.1)

5. to the <u>mandra</u> from the <u>atisvārya</u>: t$\overset{5}{\text{van}}$ tvā 6 $\overset{5}{\text{me}}$ (GG 42.2).[4]

Long (<u>dīrgha</u>) <u>karṣaṇa</u> is differentiated from short (<u>hrasva</u>) <u>karṣaṇa</u>. In the former (<u>karṣaṇa</u> on a long vowel), <u>prathama</u> and <u>dvitīya</u> are worth two <u>mātrā</u>s each; the same holds true for <u>dvitīya</u> and <u>tṛtīya</u>. The excerpts quoted have, therefore, the following <u>mātrā</u> distributions:

1. $\overset{1}{\text{pra}}\overset{\underline{\text{r}}}{\text{prā}}\ \overset{\wedge}{\ }\ 2\ \overset{1}{\text{va}}\text{yam}$ (GG 35.1, 4)
   1 +2+2 +1+1

2. $\overset{1}{\text{bha}}\text{ra}\overset{\text{S}\underline{\text{r}}}{\text{tā}}\ 3$ (GG 98.2)[5]
   1+1+2+2

---

[1]ML 1.32.

[2]This is an example of <u>preṅkha</u>; see below, pp. 64-66.

[3]This is an example of <u>pratyavaroha</u> ("descent"); see Simon, PuS, p. 521.

[4]The example seems to conflict with the <u>sūtra</u>, which clearly has "<u>atisvārya</u>" in the ablative case.

[5]Here the <u>avagraha</u> probably is a symbol for the <u>namana</u>. See below, pp. 62-64.

```
      2  r r
3.  yat some 3  (GG 188.1)
     1  +2+2+2

    [2] r
4.  naryo 3  (GG 512.13).[1]
     1 +2+2
```

In short *karṣaṇa* (*karṣaṇa* on a short vowel) each of the two figures has the value of one *mātrā*.

```
     2
1.  suvita 3 m  (GG 316.2)
     1+1+1+1

     2
2.  turaya 3  (GG 337.1)
     1+1+1+1

     2 1    s r
3.  sahasradhāra 2 m vr  (GG 581.6)
     1+1 +1 +2+1+1 '+1'
```

Nowhere does the ML refer to augmented (*vṛddha*) *karṣaṇa*, and Simon takes this omission to mean that, in *karṣaṇa* (thus also perhaps in *pratyutkrama*, *atikrama*, and *svāra*, which are forms of *karṣaṇa*),[2] vowel length is determined according to the length of the corresponding syllable in the collection of verses (the *ārcika*), where vowels are either short or long: "Wie die Beispiele scheinbar erweisen, ist beim *karṣaṇa* 'kurz' oder 'lang' auf den Zustand der Silben im Ārcika zu beziehen."[3] But the very first example given by the ML to illustrate long *karṣaṇa* has the sequence on a long vowel which is short in the corresponding *ārcika* syllable.[4] Moreover,

---

[1]The *repha* is absent in the Nārāyaṇasvāmi edition.

[2]See above, pp. 44-50. *Svāra* is discussed below, pp. 66-69.

[3]NVL, p. 314, n. 3.

[4]See SV 1.35: *pra*, not *prā*.

Simon assigns the first two examples of short karṣaṇa to augmented syllables, but these syllables are short in the Nārāyaṇasvāmi edition.[1] Therefore the examples do not justify his argument.

A sentence from the ML may offer at least partial clarification: "visvaram akṣaram svare svare trimātraṃ bhavati pratyutkramātikramakarṣaṇasvāreṣu."[2] Simon, following the example of the Ṛktantravyākaraṇa,[3] reads "visvaram" as "unbetonten" ("unaccented"),[4] but the ML commentator gives the probable meaning of the passage: "A syllable connected with different svaras (kruṣṭa-svara, and so on) comprises three mātrās."[5] If this explanation is correct, "visvaram" would probably best be translated "discordant"--that is, "discord" resulting from the attachment of a sequence to a syllable. Vowel lengths are not mentioned, so the above rules relating to short and long karṣaṇa probably are nothing more than special cases of the general law that karṣaṇa syllables (mostly augmented) are worth 3 mātrās, 2 of which belong to the primary numeral and 1 to the first (and each subsequent) secondary numeral. Such an interpretation explains the ML's statement on pratyutkrama time value and clarifies Simon's comment that

---

[1]They are short also in the ārcika; see SV 1.316, 337.

[2]ML 1.16-17. [3]See Burnell's edition, p. 12.

[4]NVL, p. 313, n. 3.

[5]Commentary on ML 1.16: "nānā svaraiḥ saṃyuktam akṣaraṃ kruṣṭādiṣu svare[ṣu] trimātraṃ bhavati."

"under the circumstances [of a 2-*mātrā* primary number] not more than 1 *mātrā* would remain [for the secondary number]."[1] This holds true, as was mentioned earlier,[2] for the second, fourth, and fifth cases of *pratyutkrama*. The first case (6 to 5) could not have been included, for the *atisvārya* never occurs as a primary number. The third type (4 to 3) is found on short as well as on augmented syllables.[3] The sixth and seventh cases (5 to 3, 5 to 2) are found on all three types of syllables.[4] The eighth type (3 to 1) never occurs between a primary and a secondary number; it is discovered most often between secondary numbers.[5] When the above types (with the exception of type 8) are notated on short syllables, they fall under short *karṣaṇa*, where each numeral is worth 1 *mātrā*. But in regard to long *karṣaṇa* the ML refers only to *prathama*-*dvitīya* ($1r_2$) and *dvitīya*-*tṛtīya* ($2r_3$) combinations, so the presence of other patterns on long syllables leaves in doubt their proper time values. This problem can be solved by tabulating the kinds of sequences appearing on long (as well as on short) syllables in the Prakṛtigāna. For this purpose I have followed the reading of the Nārāyaṇa-svāmi edition, although errors and notational inconsistencies are found in this and every printed edition of the *gānas*.

---

[1]See above, p. 47, n. 1. [2]See above, pp. 46-47.

[3]See GG 428.1, 481.2.

[4]See GG 19.1, ĀrG 98.1 ($5r_3$); GG 168.2, 419.2 (5_3 on short vowels); GG 512.1 ($5sr_2$); GG 543.1, ĀrGP: *bhāruṇḍasya pāṭhāntaram* (5_2 on short vowels).

[5]See, for example, GG 17.2-3.

Due to the large number of sequences in the Prakṛtigāna (over 14,000) it was not possible to check each against the readings of available manuscripts. Such would be the task of the future editor of a critical edition--a publication which might give rise to a clearer understanding of some of the ML's less forthright sūtras. However, many of the results of the tabulations would not be affected by even a considerable number of errors; therefore, on the whole, they should be judged as fairly accurate. Not taken into account were numerous appearances of the abhigīta, a sequence whose symbol is the numeral 7 or the letter a notated in the primary position. The abhigīta occurs nearly always on short syllables which are not followed by notated secondary numerals.[1]

TABLE 1

DISTRIBUTION OF SEQUENCES ACCORDING TO GĀNA DIVISION AND VOWEL LENGTH

		Augmented	Long	Short	Total
GG	āgneyaṃ parva	1,472	24	16	1,512
	aindraṃ parva	5,818	95	142	6,055
	pāvamānaṃ parva	3,653	81	44	3,778
ĀrG	arka parva	684	18	55	757
	dvandva parva	739	0	11	750
	vrata parva	731	17	35	783
	śukriya parva	355	2	72	429
	pariśiṣṭam	174	3	7	184
	Total	13,626	240	382	14,248

---

[1]See the discussion below, pp. 71-75.

The figures in table 1 reveal the following overall percentage distributions: 95.6 percent (augmented), 1.7 percent (long), and 2.7 percent (short). Augmented syllables predominate heavily in each of the eight divisions; the number of long syllables exceeds the number of short syllables only in the āgneyam and pāvamānam sections of the GG.

Tables 2 and 3 below give the following data: (1) types of sequences occurring on long and short syllables, (2) references to the sāmans in which these sequences appear, and (3) total number of occurrences of each type. If a particular sequence is found more than once in the same chant, the number of times it appears is given in parentheses after the reference. Among the sequences on short vowels are instances of an intervening nasal between the vowel and the first secondary number: for example,

$$\overset{2}{\text{hum}}\ 3\ 4\ 3\ \text{(GG 203.1)}.$$

The nasal possibly causes the syllable to be augmented rather than short.[1] Each such appearance of the nasal is indicated by an asterisk before the reference; however, less than ½ of 1 percent of the sequences display this characteristic.

TABLE 2

SEQUENCES NOTATED ON LONG SYLLABLES

	GG and ArG Chants	Total
$1r_2$	GG 38.1, 39.1, 40.2, 44.3(2), 267.1, 295.1(2), 306.1, 308.1, 384.3(2), 386.1, 388.2(2), 388.3(4), 391.3(2),	35

[1]This is the practice, for instance, among the Nambūdiri Yajurvedins of Keraḷa.

TABLE 2--Continued

	GG and ĀrG Chants	Total
lr_2 (continued)	GG 419.1, 429.2, 510.1(2), 512.1, 512.3, 512.14, 513.1, 515.4, 529.1(2) ĀrG 114.2 ĀrGP: tavaśyāvīyaṃ sāma (2)	
lSr_2 or lrS_2	GG 73.1(2), 81.1, 87.1, 98.1, 98.2, 104.1, 124.1, 132.1, 171.1, 182.1, 188.1, 190.1(2), 206.1, 220.1, 226.1, 227.1, 235.2, 236.1, 237.1(2), 237.2(2), 239.3, 243.1, 244.1, 251.3, 253.1, 264.1, 275.1(2), 275.2, 279.2, 281.1, 289.2, 290.1(2), 312.1, 315.2, 317.3, 335.1, 335.2, 344.1(2), 352.1, 366.1, 378.2, 392.3, 399.1, 414.1, 417.2, 417.3, 422.1(3), 426.1, 429.1, 429.2, 430.1, 465.1, 469.4, 476.2, 480.2, 485.3(2), 491.1, 495.2, 505.1, 512.1, 512.2(3), 512.3, 512.4(3), 512.10(2), 512.14, 512.15(2), 513.1, 515.1, 515.5, 517.2, 518.6(2), 518.7(2), 539.1(2), 540.2(2), 545.3, 545.4, 549.2, 551.1, 563.1, 565.1(2), 565.2(2), 569.3, 576.2, 580.1, 580.4, 582.3(2), 582.4, 584.1, 584.2, 585.1 ĀrG 51.4(7), 51.5(6), 54.1(3), 147.1(13), after 155.1:5 ĀrGP: tavaśyāvīyaṃ sāma	144
$lr\hat{_2}$	GG 22.2, 35.1, 35.4, 568.5	4
$lvir_2$	GG 565.2	1
$lSr\hat{_2}$	GG 430.1, 551.1(2), 554.5, 565.1(2)	6
lr_{23}	GG 24.1, 429.1, 579.3 ĀrG 135.1	4
lr_{2345}	GG 236.3	1
lr_{2345}^{1111}	ĀrG 140.3	1
lSr_3	GG 98.2 ĀrG 51.5	2

TABLE 2--Continued

	GG and ĀrG Chants	Total
$2r_2$	GG 13.1, 289.1	2
$2r_3$	GG 100.1, 124.3, 188.1, 237.5(2), 237.6(2), 349.1, 390.3, 465.1(2), 465.2(4), 468.4, 468.5, 513.1, 534.1, 542.1, 547.5, 555.3(2), 566.3, 568.1 ĀrG 7.1, 157-59.1	27
$2\hat{r}_3$	GG 95.1	1
$2Sr_3$	GG 110.1, 119.3, 144.4, 344.3, 355.1, 566.2	6
$3r_3$	GG 427.3	1
$4r_2$	GG 22.1	1
$4r_5$	GG 79.1	1
$5Sr_2$	GG 512.1	1
$5r_3$	GG 19.1 ĀrG 98.1	2

TABLE 3

SEQUENCES NOTATED ON SHORT SYLLABLES

	GG and ĀrG Chants	Total
1_2	ĀrG 100.1(8), 114.2, 121.1(4)	13
$1S_2$	GG 337.2(4), 581.6 ĀrG 51.4(7), 51.5(8), 54.1(3), 114.2, after 155.1:6(2), 157-59.1, 160.1(4)	31
$1_{\bar{2}}$	GG 291.2 ĀrG *****1.3(5), 106.1	7

TABLE 3--Continued

	GG and ĀrG Chants	Total
1_{23}	GG 115.2, *584.1 ĀrG 89.1, 161-62.1	4
1^{1111}_{2345}	ĀrGP: **<u>tavaśyāvīyaṃ</u> <u>sāma</u> (2)	2
1_3	GG 433.1	1
2_1	GG 281.1, *371.3, *371.4 ĀrG 170-72.3, 170-72.4	5
2_2	ĀrG 114.2	1
2_3	GG 34.2, 70.2(2), 81.1, 90.1(3), 117.2, 133.2, 133.3, 142.2(2), 143.2(3), 144.4, 156.5(3), 160.3, 161.2, 165.1, 168.2(2), 172.1(2), 190.1, 193.1(2), 231.1, 233.1, 234.1, 235.2, *236.4, 237.3(2), 238.2(2), 246.1, 252.2(2), 253.1(2), 254.1(2), 256.1(3), 257.1(2), 258.2(4), 259.1(2), 264.2, 265.1, 271.3, 277.1, 283.1, 288.1, 291.1(2), 303.1(3), 313.2(4), 316.2, 332.2, 337.1, 337.2, 344.1, 344.3, 344.4, 349.1, 354.2(2), 355.1, 371.6, 376.1(2), 377.1(2), 378.1, 383.4, 384.1, 419.1, 423.1(2), 427.4(4), 430.2, 433.1, 433.2, 434.1, 434.2, 450.2, 454.1, 469.8, 469.9, 470.3, 475.3, *481.2, 491.1, 512.5, 512.6, 524.3, 534.1(2), 540.1, 542.1(2), 547.4(2), 547.5(2), 558.1 ĀrG 7.1, 13.1(2), 19.1(3), 33.1(4), 33.2(6), 35.1(2), 55.1(3), 63.1(3), 89.1(3), 90.1(3), 106.1(4), 106.2(2), 110.1(3), 137.1(2), 138.1(4), 137.1(3), 148.1(2), 153.1(3), 167-69.1(9), 167-69.2(9), 170-72.3(8), 170-72.4(8), 173-75.5(8), 173-75.6(8), after 175.6:2(6) ĀrGP: <u>udvayāmekaṃ</u> <u>sāma</u>	233
$2_{\hat{3}}$	GG 34.2, 70.2, 83.1, 90.1, 92.1(4), 515.1, 518.1(4), 524.3, 527.1(2), 542.1, 549.5, 555.3, 566.2, 566.3, 583.1 ĀrG 6.1(2), 7.1(2), 13.1, 33.2, 35.1(2), 63.1	31

TABLE 3--Continued

	GG and ĀrG Chants	Total
$2S_3$	GG **203.1(2), *236.4, *250.1, 419.2, *481.2, 509.2, *515.6	8
$2_{\hat{3}234}$	GG 580.2	1
2_{34}	ĀrG *after 155.1:2	1
2_{343}	GG *203.1, 328.2, 419.2	3
$2_{\hat{3}43}$	GG *515.6	1
2_4	GG 18.1	1
3_{23}	GG *343.7	1
3_{234}	GG 186.1, 233.2, 363.1, 371.7 ĀrG **52.1(2)	6
3^{1111}_{2345}	GG **251.3(2), *259.3, 317.1,[a] **325.2(2), ****328.2(4), *343.7, ***411.3(3)	14
3_3	GG *236.4	1
$3_{\hat{3}}$	ĀrG 6.1	1
$3S_3$	GG 504.1	1
3_4	GG *325.2(2)	2
4_3	GG 428.1	1
$4S_3$	GG *481.2	1

[a]This is probably a printing error, for the vairājanidhana occurs on the augmented ī-vowel.

TABLE 3--Continued

	GG and ĀrG Chants	Total
4_5	GG 433.1 ĀrG 141.1	2
5_2	GG 543.1	1
$5_{\hat{2}}$	ĀrGP: bhāruṇḍasya pāṭhāntaram (4)	4
$5S_3$	GG 168.2(2), *419.2	3
5_6	GG 579.4	1

Of the 240 sequences on long vowels, 224 (over 93 percent) involve prathama-dvitīya (1_2) or dvitīya-tṛtīya (2_3) patterns. None of the remaining sequences occurs more than four times in the entire Pūrvagāna, and many of these appear probably because of errors in the Nārāyaṇasvāmi edition. For example, it is extremely unlikely that the pattern 1_{2345} (or 1^{1111}_{2345}) belongs on anything but an augmented syllable. The sequences $2r_2$ and $3r_3$ are questionable, for as a rule the same number is not notated twice in succession. The pattern $4r_2$ is perhaps spurious, for it is not mentioned in any of the treatises as an example of either pratyutkrama or atikrama. The sequence 4_5 (utsvarita)[1] apparently has an absolute time value regardless of syllable length; therefore there is no reason for the presence of the repha. The pratyutkrama/atikrama type $5Sr_2$ is spurious, for the prathama occurs in place of the mandra in an Uttaragāna reading of the chant.[2]

---

[1]See below, pp. 70-71. [2]See ŪG 5.4.8.

The evidence given above suggests that only prathama-dvitīya and dvitīya-tṛtīya combinations are notated on long syllables; the pattern $1r_{23}$ also has claim to legitimacy, for, by the addition of a secondary number (3), it is but an extension of the former. Wherever the avagraha or the syllable vi (both notated in the primary position) appear in connection with the 1_2 arrangement, a sequence named "vinata"[1] is most certainly intended (there is some question about $1Sr_2^{\hat{}}$, where both avagraha and circumflex are present). Wherever the avagraha is absent and no other notational symbol is present (except, optionally, the circumflex), long karṣaṇa takes place. It occurs also in certain appearances of the 2_3 pattern, but here it is oftentimes impossible visually to distinguish long karṣaṇa from another sequence called praṇata.[2] This pattern has the circumflex only as an optional notational sign and often is not designated by a special symbol.

Namana

The sequence namana ("bending, sinking"; also called namata) is designated by the circumflex, the avagraha, or (in southern manuscripts) the syllable na.[3] These signs are placed in the primary position and are not preceded or followed on the same syllable by a primary number. Burnell writes that namana "consists of the first three notes (one, two, three),"[4] although he fails to state his source. That

---

[1]See below, pp. 69-70. [2]See below, p. 70.

[3]See NVL, pp. 310, 320, 322; see also Simon's theoretical transcription of ĀrG 25.1, ibid., pp. 318-19.

[4]ĀrṣB, p. xliii.

this sequence involves *prathama* and *tṛtīya* is known from certain manuscripts[1] which list selected *parvans* according to their initial notational numerals. Among the examples of *parvans* specified as beginning with *prathama* are a few in which the first notational sign is not the numeral 1 but the syllable *na*, a symbol used only for designating *namana*. Unquestionably, therefore, the primary numeral of the sequence is the *prathama*; the only other notated numeral is the *tṛtīya*, which appears always in the textual line. Six *parvans* which begin with *namana* are:[2]

na 2 2
1. au 3 ho 3 4 vā (GG 237.6)

na 2 2
2. o 3 hā 3 e 3 4 (GG 44.3)

na 2 3 5
3. svā 3 ho ā o 2 3 4 vā (GG 470.1)

na
4. au 3 ho 2 3 4 5 vā 6 5 6 (GG 128.2)

na 2
5. au 3 ho 3 1 i (GG 518.6)

na 2 2
6. au 3 ho 3 1 ye 3 (GG 469.5)

A further example was supplied to me by a Hāvik Rāṇāyanīyaka:

1r ^ 2
āro 3 hān (GG 92.1)

Both the ML and the Spb use this same example to illustrate *atikrama* of the *dvitīya*;[3] therefore *namana* is seen to be

---

[1]See the discussion of the Rāṇāyanīya syllable notation below, pp. 115-20.

[2]A. M. Rāmanātha Dīkṣita, ed., *Ūhagānam--Ūhyagānam*, Banāras Hindu University Vedic Research Series, no. 3 (Vārāṇasī: Banāras Hindu University Press, 1967), pp. 29-30.

[3]See above, p. 49.

nothing more than a special name given to the pattern 1_3. It is found almost entirely on augmented syllables[1] and therefore has a total value of three mātrās--two for the prathama, one for the tṛtīya.

Preṅkha

A sequence found frequently in the gānas is the preṅkha (from the root preṅkh: "to tremble, shake, vibrate, swing"), which has as notational signs either a horizontal line over the dvitīya ($\bar{2}$; the horizontal line sometimes appears over the syllable preceding the dvitīya) or (in South Indian manuscripts) the syllable pre. The primary number of preṅkha usually is the prathama, but occasionally a dvitīya appears in this position instead. The sole secondary number, which bears the notational symbol, is the dvitīya; the presence of this number also as the primary number may be nothing more than a printing or scribal error. Apparently preṅkha appears only on augmented syllables. No instances of this pattern on a long vowel are found in the Pūrvagāna; the sequence occurs only seven times on short syllables,[2] and five of these are questionable due to the interpolated nasal. According to Burnell, preṅkha "adds two mātrā to the preceding syllable [the syllable on which the sequence is found] and ends with the second svara."[3]

---

[1]It appears twice on long syllables (in GG 98.2 and ĀrG 51.5), only once on a short syllable (in GG 433.1). These occurrences, however, are perhaps due to printing errors.

[2]See type $1_{\bar{2}}$ in table 3 above, p. 58.

[3]ĀrṣB, p. xliii.

Furthermore, "where 'vinata' occurs in the Grāmageyagāna, preṅkha is put in the Ūha."[1] This latter statement has been shown by van der Hoogt[2] to be only partially correct. The four possibilities listed by him are:[3]

1. $\overset{S}{2}$ in the Pūrvagāna changing to $S\overset{S}{2}$ in the Uttaragāna (see RG 3.2.12-13 from ĀrG 51.4-5)

2. $\overset{S}{2}$ in both Pūrvagana and Uttaragāna (see RG 3.2.12-13 from ĀrG 51.4-5; RG 1.1.10 from ĀrG 54.1)

3. $\overset{S}{2}$ in the Pūrvagāna changing to $\bar{2}$ in the Uttaragāna (see UG 1.3.14 from GG 39.1; ŪG 4.3.2 from GG 87.1; ŪG 1.7.15 from GG 279.2; ŪG 1.7.16 from GG 290.1; ŪG 1.10.3 from GG 565.1)

4. $\bar{2}$ in both Pūrvagāna and Uttaragāna (see ŪG 6.2.6 from GG 7.1; ŪG 1.10.9 from GG 267.1; RG 1.1.5 from ĀrG 14.1).

The first and second cases are the same: some manuscripts characteristically place an avagraha before the first secondary numeral of a sequence,[4] and in such an instance the

---

[1]Ibid. [2]VC, pp. 44-46.

[3]His source is the edition of Satyavrata Sāmaśramī, Sāma-Veda-Saṃhitā, 5 vols, in Bibliotheca Indica (Calcutta: Asiatic Society of Bengal, 1874-78). Van der Hoogt fails to mention that a vinata in the Pūrvagāna may appear neither as vinata nor as preṅkha at the corresponding place in the same uttara-sāman. For example, a parvan from the acchidra-melody appears as / somo 2 . . . / (with "rSr" above "somo") in GG 512.1, as / prahinvā- . . . / (with "1" and "2r" above "prahinvā-") in ŪG 5.4.8 (the verse is different but the melody is the same).

[4]This is the general practice in the South.

symbol has little if any notational or musical significance. It is worth noting that the five examples illustrating the change from vinata to preṅkha (case 3 above) have the vinata on long vowels and the preṅkha on augmented vowels. Simon must have been referring to this particular case when he wrote that "in der Yoni [the Pūrvagāna] nur eine lange, im Uttaragāna nur eine vṛddhierte [augmented] Silbe karṣaṇa erfahren kann bzw. daß eine Silbe, die karṣaṇa erfahren hat, in der Yoni lang sein d. h. zwei mātrās enthalten, im Uttaragāna vṛddhiert werden d. h. drei mātrās enthalten muß."[1] From the example given by the ML to illustrate karṣaṇa to the dvitīya,[2] we may assume that preṅkha is simply a type of ordinary karṣaṇa lasting a total of three mātrās.[3]

Svāra

Three types of svāra ("sound, noise," or perhaps also "connected with the svarita accent;" known also as svārya and saṃprasāraṇa) are described:[4]

1. svāra beginning with the prathama (type $1_{2\overset{1}{3}\overset{1}{4}\overset{1}{5}}$) is worth nine mātrās, as in

```
 2        1   1 1 1
harī 3 śrī 2 3 4 5 ḥ  (GG 195.1)
```

---

[1] Simon, PuS, p. 518. It should be understood that, where sequences are involved, the presence of primary numbers on augmented, long, or short syllables does not necessarily imply that these numbers are worth, respectively, three, two, or one mātrā.

[2] See above, p. 51.

[3] The term "preṅkha," however, is never used by the ML.

[4] ML 2.1-2.

2. *svāra* beginning with the *dvitīya* (type 2^{111}_{345}) is worth six *mātrās*, as in

 3 2̄.1 1 1
rayā 3 4 5 im (GG 43.1)

3. *svāra* beginning with the *tṛtīya* (type 3^{111}_{2345}) is worth eight *mātrās*, as in

3   1 1 1
ī 2 3 4 5 (GG 67.2).[1]

In each of these cases, the final three numerals (*tṛtīya*, *caturtha*, *mandra*) are worth one *mātrā* apiece,[2] a characteristic indicated in the notation by placement of the numeral 1 above these figures.[3] The primary numbers may not exceed three *mātrās*, so the first secondary numbers of the first and third cases are worth three and two *mātrās* respectively.

Svāra is found frequently on final syllables in the *nidhana* sections of the chants. Here, according to the PuS, it is connected with the accents of corresponding *ārcika* or *stobha* syllables:[4] (1) to a dependent *svarita*[5] in the *ārcika* or *stobha* corresponds a *karṣaṇa* syllable in the Pūrvagāna and a *svāra* of the first type in the Uttaragāna, (2) to an *anudātta*[6] corresponds an *akarṣaṇa* syllable and a

---

[1]This type is known as *nigada*. See Simon, PuS, p. 520.

[2]ML 2.10.

[3]In the Nārāyanasvāmi edition, the numeral 1 is placed above all secondary numbers of this sequence.

[4]See PuS 9.30, with Dīksita Rāmakṛṣṇa's commentary. See also SSV, pp. 40-45, 61-65.

[5]The accents are explained under "*udātta*" in the Glossary.

[6]An *anudātta* "can . . . occur at the end of a pāda which does not close a phonetical unity." (SSV, p. 41, citing Macdonell, *Vedic Grammar*, p. 438, n. 2, and p. 449a)

svāra of the second type, (3) to a *pracaya* corresponds an *akarṣaṇa* syllable and a *svāra* of the second or third type, (4) to an *udātta* corresponds an *udātta* (*prathama*) and a *vṛdhesvara*, a type of *pratyutkrama* of the form 32_1.[1] By no means are these rules followed consistently. To give but one exception, SV 1.161 has a *svarita* on its final syllable:

1 2
". . . madam." Accordingly, this syllable should experience *karṣaṇa* in its Pūrvagāna melodization and have *svāra* of the first type (1_{2345}^{111}) at the corresponding place in the Uttaragāna. But the *ārṣabha*-melody based upon this verse has *svāra* type 3_{2345}^{111} in both *yoni* (GG 161.3) and *ūha* (ŪG 1.2.5), thus going against rule 1.[2]

Before concluding the discussion of *svāra*, mention should be made of a special case, the *padānusvāra*, which consists of the pattern 5_{656} on an augmented syllable.[3] Like the other types of *svāra* it occurs mainly on the final syllable of the final *parvan* of certain chants. According to Faddegon[4] the notational numerals of this final *parvan* are organized in one of three ways: / $12_3{}^4{}_5{}^5{}_{656}$ /, / $2_3{}^4{}_5{}^5{}_{656}$ /, or / $32_3{}^4{}_5{}^5{}_{656}$ /. The three forms "are connected with the versification and consequently with the distribution of the syllables over the parvans."[5] He continues,

---

[1]See Simon, PuS, p. 523; SSV, p. 45.

[2]For instances where the rules are observed, see SSV, pp. 41-44.

[3]See Simon, PuS, p. 521. [4]SSV, pp. 67-77.

[5]Ibid., p. 77.

The form[s] / $1\underline{2}_{3}{}^{4}{}_{5}{}^{5}{}_{656}$ / and / $32_{3}{}^{4}{}_{5}{}^{5}{}_{656}$ / are used in strophes with pādas of an even number of syllables. The form / $2_{3}{}^{4}{}_{5}{}^{5}{}_{656}$ / is found in triṣṭubhs.[1]

Vinata

A sequence involving prathama and dvitīya is the vinata ("bent, curved, sunk down, deepened"),[2] which has as symbols either the avagraha, notated in varying positions above the textual line, or (in South Indian manuscripts and prints) the syllable vi, notated above the syllable to which the sequence is attached. The duration of the prathama is 1½ mātrās on an augmented vowel, ½ mātrā on either a long or a short vowel; the dvitīya is worth ½ mātrā is all cases.[3] Among the examples of vinata in the ML are the following:

[2] 1 S 1S
1. yaṃ yaṃ ya 2 ṃ yām (GG 337.2)

1r Sr
2. ai hī 2 (ĀrG 147.1)

[2] 1 S 1 S 1
3. haṃ vaṃ va 2 m vaṃ va 2 ṃ vam (ĀrG, after 155.1:6)

1 S
4. uvi 2 (ĀrG 160.1).

The two chants of RG 3.2.12-13 (from ĀrG 51.4-5, but on a different text) consist almost entirely of bisyllabic parvans in which a prathama on the first syllable is followed by a vinata on the last.

[1]Ibid.

[2]See Simon, PuS, pp. 522-23; NVL, p. 315.

[3]ML 3.5; Spb, p. 15.

In the Uttaragāna preṅkha, vinata, or two primary numbers may appear in the spot where vinata occurs in the Pūrvagāna.[1]

Praṇata

The numbers 2 and 3 of praṇata ("bowed, inclined, bent")[2] bear the same mātrā-relationships as the respective numerals of vinata: the dvitīya is worth 1½ mātrās on an augmented vowel, ½ mātrā on either a long or a short vowel; the tṛtīya always has a value of ½ mātrā.[3] Occasionally the circumflex is used as a notational symbol, but praṇata ordinarily is left undesignated. The following examples are offered by the ML:

```
     2r  r       1
1.   ā yāhī 3 voitoyā 2̄ i  (GG 1.1)

    2  r ^    ,1
2.  tigmenā 3 so  (GG 22.1)

        [2] 1r r   2r r
3.  sy    apām oṣadhīnā 3 m  (ĀrG 157-59.1).
```

Utsvarita

The pattern 4_5, which occurs nearly always on augmented vowels,[4] is termed utsvarita.[5] The value of the caturtha is ½ mātrā, that of the mandra 1½ mātrās; these values hold true regardless of syllable length.[6]

---

[1]See above, p. 65. [2]See NVL, p. 315.

[3]ML 3.5.

[4]For the exceptions, which may be printing or scribal errors, see tables 2 and 3 above, pp. 58, 61.

[5]See NVL, pp. 315-16. [6]ML 3.6.

As the examples indicate, utsvarita is not designated by a special notational sign:

[5] 4r 4
1. manuṣye 5 bhir agniḥ (GG 79.1)

4 5r 4 4
2. ka ī vya 5 ktāḥ (GG 433.1).

Abhigīta

The single sequence lacking a notated secondary number is the abhigīta (literally, "addressed or praised in song"),[1] whose notational symbols are the number 7 (৭) or the vowel a. These signify a dvitīya of ½ mātrā followed by a prathama of 1½ mātrās.[2] The two examples given by the ML are:

[1]r 7 4
1. stomāṣm rudrā 2 3 yās (GG 15.2)

1 [7]r 1 1 1 1
2. pāinvo arkā 2 3 4 5 iḥ (GG 534.1).

The Nārāyaṇasvāmi edition omits the 7 of the second example, the reason for which becomes clear on examining the form of the entire chant. It consists of a four-fold musical repetition of only two parvans: the first contains stobha-syllables, and the second is comprised of one of four pādas of the text. The sāman concludes with a svāra on the stobha-syllable vā, the upāya.[3]

2r r ^ 2 2 r r r 1 7
hāu ho vā 3 hā i / pra te dhārā madhuma 3 tāir asṛgā

1 1 1 1 2r r ^ 2 r r r
2 3 4 5 n // hāu ho vā 3 hā i / vāraṃ yat pūto atī 3

---

[1]See Simon, PuS, p. 517; NVL, p. 316; ĀrṣB, p. xliv (here Burnell incorrectly calls it "abhigata").

[2]ML 3.7. [3]See Simon, PuS, p. 518.

1   1 1 1 1   2r r ^ 2   r
y āiṣi āvyā 2 3 4 5 m // hāu ho vā 3 hā i / pavamāna

r   1   1 1 1 1   2r r ^ 2
pavase 3 dhāma gonā 2 3 4 5 m // hāu ho vā 3 hā i /

r   1 r   1 1 1 1   2r r
janayant sūryam a 3 pāinvo arkā 2 3 4 5 iḥ / hāu ho

^ 2   2 1 1 1 1
vā 3 hāu // vā 2 3 4 5 // (GG 534.1)

It was considered necessary to indicate the *abhigīta* only once, in the second *parvan*, for the remaining textual *parvans* merely imitate this section tonally. Therefore the *abhigīta* is understood on the syllables *ṣi* (*parvan* 4), *ma* (*parvan* 6), and *vo* (*parvan* 8). It is possible that this and other sequences occur elsewhere in the *gānas* where they are not expressly indicated in the notation.[1]

The *abhigīta* is notated 281 times in the Nārāyaṇasvāmi edition: 255 times in the GG, only 26 times in the ĀrG, including its supplement. Table 4 gives the *sāmans* in which it appears. The number of occurrences (if more than one) in a single chant is given in parentheses after the reference.

TABLE 4

FREQUENCY AND DISTRIBUTION OF THE ABHIGĪTA

	GG and ĀrG Chants	Total
āgneyaṃ parva	GG 9.1, 11.1, 13.1(2), 15.2, 17.3, 18.2, 23.1, 29.1, 30.1, 31.1, 35.3(2), 37.1, 37.2, 38.1, 42.1, 43.1, 46.1, 48.1, 48.2, 54.1(2), 54.2(2), 55.1, 57.1, 64.1, 67.1, 68.1, 68.2, 74.1, 75.1, 77.2, 79.1, 81.2, 84.1, 88.1, 88.2, 94.1, 97.4, 101.1, 109.1, 110.1, 112.1	45

[1]See, for example, ĀrG, after 177.1:1.

TABLE 4--Continued

	GG and ĀrG Chants	Total
aindraṃ parva	GG 119.3, 121.1, 124.2, 124.3(2), 125.1, 130.1(6), 130.2(3), 133.2, 135.1, 140.1, 142.2(2), 148.1, 149.1(2), 151.1, 152.1, 154.1, 155.3, 158.2(2), 165.1, 166.2, 168.1, 171.1, 172.1(2), 184.1, 211.1, 221.1, 230.1, 233.1(2), 233.2, 234.2, 235.2(2), 235.3, 237.5, 237.6, 239.3(2), 241.1, 241.2, 243.1, 243.2, 252.2, 254.1, 254.2, 254.3, 256.1(3), 263.1, 264.2, 266.1, 268.1, 270.1, 272.3(2), 279.1, 279.2, 281.1, 282.2, 284.1(2), 285.2, 288.1, 289.1, 289.2, 291.2, 295.1, 296.1, 303.1(5), 305.1, 312.1, 319.1, 325.1(3), 327.1, 333.1(3), 344.3(2), 344.4, 351.1, 360.1, 372.1, 372.2, 374.1(2), 376.1, 382.2, 384.3, 388.1, 390.1, 392.2, 392.3, 401.1, 402.2, 403.1, 406.2, 408.1, 410.2, 424.1, 433.2, 435.1, 438.3, 440.1, 443.1, 446.1, 451.1, 454.1, 460.1, 461.1, 462.1(2), 463.3(2)	133
pāvamānaṃ parva	GG 467.10, 468.4, 468.9, 469.4, 469.8, 469.9, 472.5(2), 472.7, 473.2(2), 473.3, 475.5, 475.6, 477.1, 485.3, 486.1, 490.1, 491.2, 498.1, 502.1, 507.1, 512.5(2), 512.6(2), 515.2, 515.4, 517.2(2), 517.5(2), 517.7, 518.8, 519.1, 523.3(2), 523.5, 527.1, 534.1, 539.1, 540.2(3), 547.3, 547.4 (4), 547.5(2), 548.1(2), 549.1, 551.2(2), 551.3, 551.4, 557.5(2), 566.1, 566.2(2), 566.3(2), 566.5, 567.5, 569.3, 573.1(2), 580.5(2), 580.6(2), 581.1, 581.5, 584.4	77
arka parva	ĀrG 2.2, 13.2(2), 53.1(3), 56.1(2)	8
dvandva parva	ĀrG 65.2, 65.3	2

TABLE 4--Continued

	GG and ĀrG Chants	Total
vrata parva		0
śukriya parva	ĀrG 157-59.1(2), 161-62.1(4), 176-77.1(4), after 177.1:1(3)	13
ĀrG pariśiṣṭam	udvayāmekaṃ sāma (3)	3

As a rule abhigīta is preceded by the prathama and followed by the dvitīya,[1] though the latter may not necessarily be found on the syllable immediately following. The sequence is notated almost exclusively on short vowels, although in four cases--GG 151.1, 234.2, 296.1, and 547.4--it is found on augmented syllables. Two of these are used by the ML to illustrate abhigīta-kṛṣṭa:[2]

1. $\overset{7}{\text{to}}$ 2 $\text{dhv}\overset{3}{\bar{\text{a}}}$ 2 3 4 $\text{r}\overset{5}{\bar{\text{a}}}\text{i}$ (GG 151.1)

2. $\overset{7}{\text{to}}$ $\hat{2}$ kṣā 2 3 4 $\text{r}\overset{5}{\bar{\text{a}}}\text{n}$ (GG 547.4).

As the examples and the ML commentary prove, this term does not, as Simon conjectures,[3] refer to an abhigīta preceded by the kruṣṭa. Rather it denotes "lengthening" of the abhigīta syllable by the addition of a secondary numeral,[4] only two examples of which occur in the entire Pūrvagāna: the two cases cited above. The initial dvitīya has the value of ½ mātrā, as it does ordinarily, but the prathama is worth 2½

[1]For exceptions see GG 18.2, 149.1, 289.1, 312.1, 527.1, 549.1, ĀrG 65.2. Some or all of these may be mistakes or misprints.

[2]ML 3.8. See NVL, pp. 311, n. 2; 316.

[3]NVL, p. 316. [4]See SUB, p. ix, n. 1.

mātrās. Presumably the final dvitīya--the number notated in the textual line--bears 1 mātrā, as in karṣaṇa. Thus the syllable to in the examples above has a duration of ½ + 2½ + 1 = 4 mātrās.

CHAPTER 2

THE ORAL TRADITIONS

Kauthuma from North India

The general state of Sāmavedic chanting

The plight of Sāmaveda in North India can be ascertained from Raghavan's account[1] of his travels there as a member of the Sanskrit Commission. In the huge area comprising eleven states--Mahārāshtra, Gujarāt, Rājāsthān, Madhya Pradesh, Panjāb, Jammu and Kashmir, Uttar Pradesh, Assām, Bengāl, Bihār, and Orissa--indigenous Sāmavedic chanting can be found to a significant degree in only two states, Gujarāt and Uttar Pradesh. Of the two, Gujarāt is the major center, while in Uttar Pradesh the Sāmaveda is confined mainly to two localities: (1) near Lucknow,[2] and (2) in Banāras (Vārāṇasī), though here almost all Sāmavedins either belong to Gujarāti families or have had their Vedic training under Gujarāti preceptors. There is probably no

[1]PVC, pp. 50-52, 59-62.

[2]A trip I had planned to the village Baraura had to be cancelled due to flooding conditions. According to Staal there is resident near Lucknow a paṇḍit reputed to be the leading Kauthuma Sāmaga in the North. He has, I am informed, refused to be recorded even by another Brāhmaṇ.

single reason for the depressed state in the North of Vedic recitation in general and Sāmavedic chanting in particular. Certainly the region has been subjected more to foreign--and especially non-Hindu--influence and rule than has the South. This fact along with contemporary social, economic, and political trends prevalent almost everywhere--which often are anti-Brāhmaṇ and consequently anti-Vedic in nature--partly explains the deteriorated posture of Vedic chant in the area. Raghavan makes some further observations:

> Interest in Karmakāṇḍa [recitation during sacrificial rites] and the learning of Veda by rote had practically died out in most parts of the North. The Bhakti movements were no doubt responsible to some extent for throwing the Vedas and rituals into the background, and Brahmans there had forgotten even their _sākhās_ and _sūtras_; the surnames Chaubes and Chaturvedins, Tiwaris and Trivedins, Dubes and Dvivedins were still heard among Brahmans who were today in all walks of life, but they were no longer the repositories of the four, three, or two Vedas or even a single Veda.[1]

He goes on to offer an hypothesis to explain the style, unusual to him as a Southerner, of the northern chant:

> Owing to intonational differences, as also idiosyncracies of pronunciation, the effect of the recital on the ear differed very much [from that of South Indian Kauthumins]. It might be pointed [out] also that as these representatives of the rarer Śākhās lived amidst vast numbers of Śukla Yajurvedins, the latter's recital had always an unavoidable impact on the recitals of the less represented Śākhās, and the tempo, tone and style of even the Sāman was imperceptibly drawn towards those of the Śukla Yajurveda chanting.[2]

However, a difference in style from the Kauthuma chant of the South is not sufficient reason to judge the northern variety

---

[1]PVC, p. 50.

[2]Ibid., p. 61. See the entry "_Yajurveda_" in the Glossary below. The Śukla ("White") Yajurveda does not have prose interpolations in the _saṃhitā_. It appears in two recensions: Mādhyaṃdina and Kāṇva.

less pure. As will presently be shown, this northern chant does in fact move within a narrower range than does its southern counterpart and thus more closely approximates the range of the Mādhyaṃdina Śukla Yajurveda recitation of the North. Both stay largely within a minor third. But the styles are quite dissimilar, and it is no difficult task to perceive one as chant, the other as recitation. Furthermore it is much too simplistic to suggest that a Sāmavedin who has spent a good portion of his life committing to memory the huge body of hymns, with their numerous intonational rules and techniques, would in fact be able to forsake the results of years of discipline by imitating reciters of other Vedas. Such repudiations would intimate the presence of a multitude of Kauthuma styles in North India, when in fact the chant throughout Gujarāt and Uttar Pradesh appears to be remarkably uniform.

Mudrās

Kauthuma and Rāṇāyanīya chanting in both North and South is accompanied by various finger positions (mudrās) which correspond to the numbers notated in the gānas. As explained to me by a Gujarāti Sāmavedin living in Vārāṇasī, there are 13 positions of the right-hand fingers: 11 of these are employed when chanting sāmans, and 2 are used when reciting from the ārcika. These ārcika positions are associated with the symbols 2u and 3k. The former appears above the first of two successive udāttas followed by an anudātta,[1]

---

[1]See the entry "udātta" in the Glossary below.

as in the following example:

3 2u   3
iha nāsti (SV 1.345).

The latter marks an anudātta preceding an independent svarita, which is itself designated 2r, as in

3k   2r
ukthyam (SV 1.381).

The fingers of the left hand are used in three ways: (1) to indicate the occurrence of a long (dīrgha) syllable in the gānas, (2) to mark successive repetitions of words or stobhas, and (3) to show the accents udātta, anudātta, and svarita when reciting from the ārcika (that is, during saṃhitāpāṭha). Descriptions of the various positions, along with the corresponding numerals and signs in the gānas and the ārcika, are given in tables 5 (right-hand positions) and 6 (left-hand positions). Following this are presented fourteen photographs depicting most of the mudrās as demonstrated by Śrī Gopāl Rām Tripāṭhī (Kauṇḍinya gotra, Lāṭyāyana Śrautasūtra), a Gujarāti Kauthumin of Vārāṇasī.

TABLE 5

KAUTHUMA MUDRĀS (RIGHT HAND POSITIONS)

Symbol	Name or Explanation	Description of Finger Position
1	kruṣṭa or prathama	The thumb is held in a high position, apart from the other fingers (see fig. 3)
2	dvitīya	The thumb touches the middle joint of the forefinger (see fig. 4)
3	tṛtīya	The thumb touches the middle joint of the middle finger (see fig. 5)

TABLE 5--Continued

Symbol	Name or Explanation	Description of Finger Position
4	*caturtha*	The thumb touches the middle joint of the ring finger (see fig. 6)
5	*mandra*	The thumb touches the middle joint of the little finger (see fig. 7)
6	*atisvārya*	The thumb touches the lower joint (root) of the little finger (see fig. 8)
7	*abhigīta*	The thumb is flicked upwards from beneath the forefinger (see fig. 9)
$\bar{2}$	*preṅkha*	The thumb glides over the middle joints of the fingers, beginning with the forefinger and concluding with the little finger (see fig. 10)
none	*praṇata*	The thumb moves up the length of the forefinger, from base to tip (see fig. 11)
1 1 1 1 2 3 4 5	*svāra*	The thumb glides across the tips of the fingers, beginning with the forefinger and concluding with the little finger (see fig. 12)
$\hat{2}$ or 2^	*karṣaṇa*?	The thumb rubs the side of the forefinger as the hand forms a fist (see fig. 13)
2u	First of two successive *udāttas* followed by an *anudātta*. Found mostly in the *ārcika*, occasionally in the *gānas* (ĀrG 51.1)	The middle finger is bent forward onto the palm as the thumb touches the side of the forefinger (see fig. 14)

TABLE 5--Continued

Symbol	Name or Explanation	Description of Finger Position
3k	An <u>anudātta</u> preceding an independent <u>svarita</u>. Found in the <u>ārcika</u>.	The thumb moves down the length of the middle finger, from tip to base (see fig. 15)

TABLE 6

KAUTHUMA MUDRĀS (LEFT HAND POSITIONS)

Symbol	Name or Explanation	Description of Finger Position
1r	<u>dīrgha prathama</u>	The little finger is bent onto the palm
2r	<u>dīrgha dvitīya</u>	The ring finger is bent onto the palm
3r	<u>dīrgha tṛtīya</u>	The middle finger is bent onto the palm
4r	<u>dīrgha caturtha</u>	The fourth finger is bent onto the palm
5r	<u>dīrgha mandra</u>	The thumb is placed on the forefinger and the hand forms a fist. The hand is opened, then closed to again form a fist
(2) or <u>dviḥ</u>	Duple repetition of words or <u>stobhas</u>	For each statement of the word(s) or <u>stobha</u>(s), one finger is bent onto the palm, first the little finger and then the ring finger. The two fingers remain in the bent position until the conclusion of the second repetition.
(3) or <u>triḥ</u>	Triple repetition of words or <u>stobhas</u>.	Same as above, with the addition of the middle finger (see fig. 16)

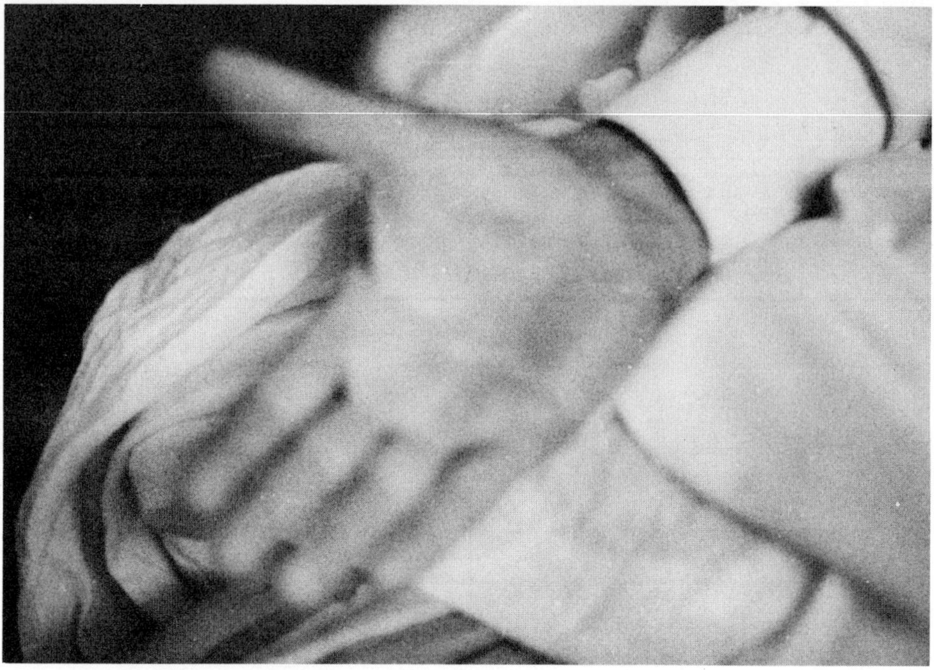

Fig. 3. *kruṣṭa* or *prathama* (1)

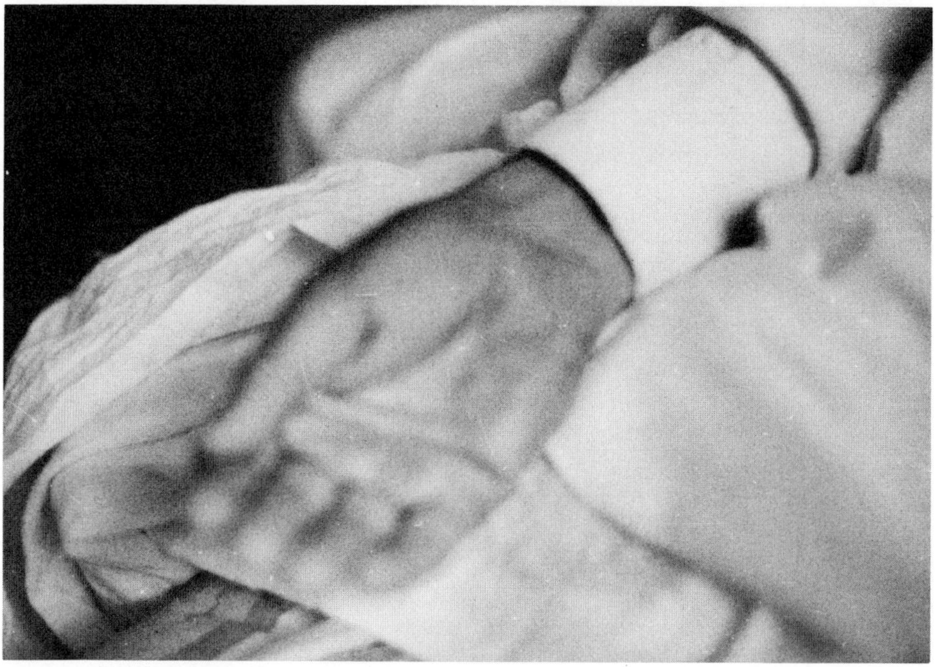

Fig. 4. *dvitīya* (2)

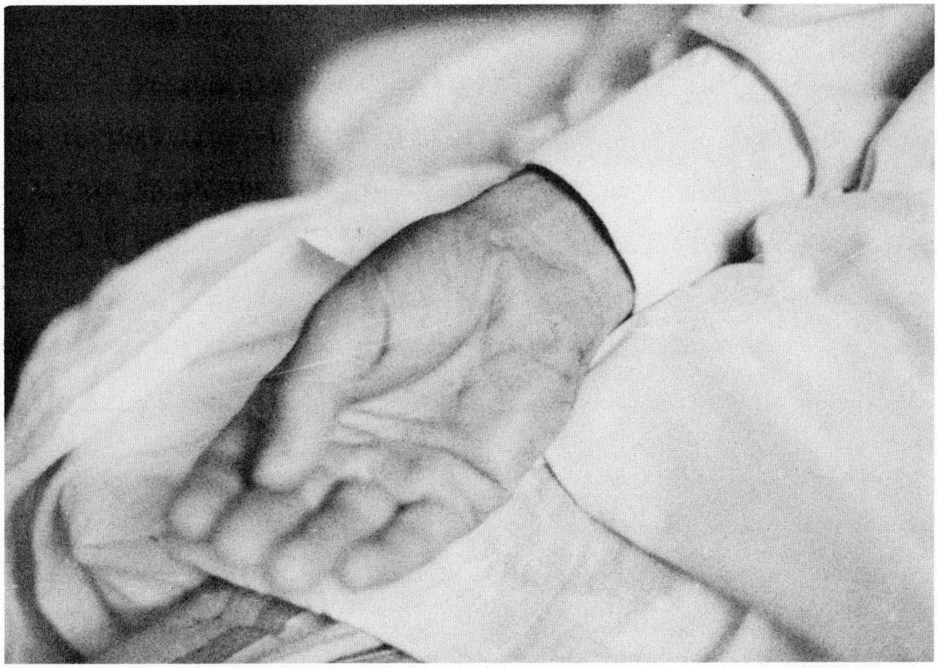

Fig. 5. <u>tṛtīya</u> (3)

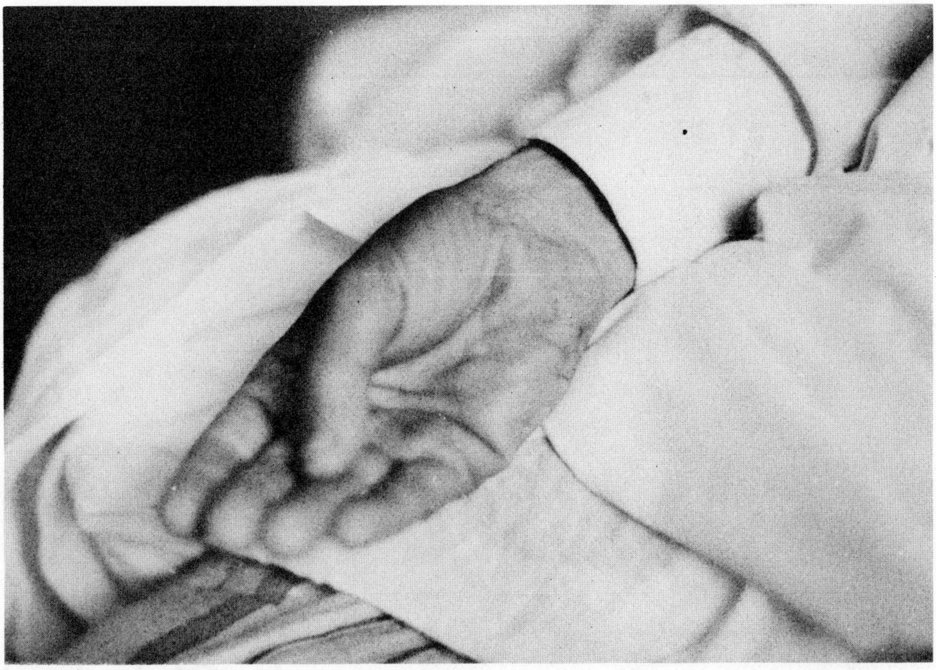

Fig. 6. <u>caturtha</u> (4)

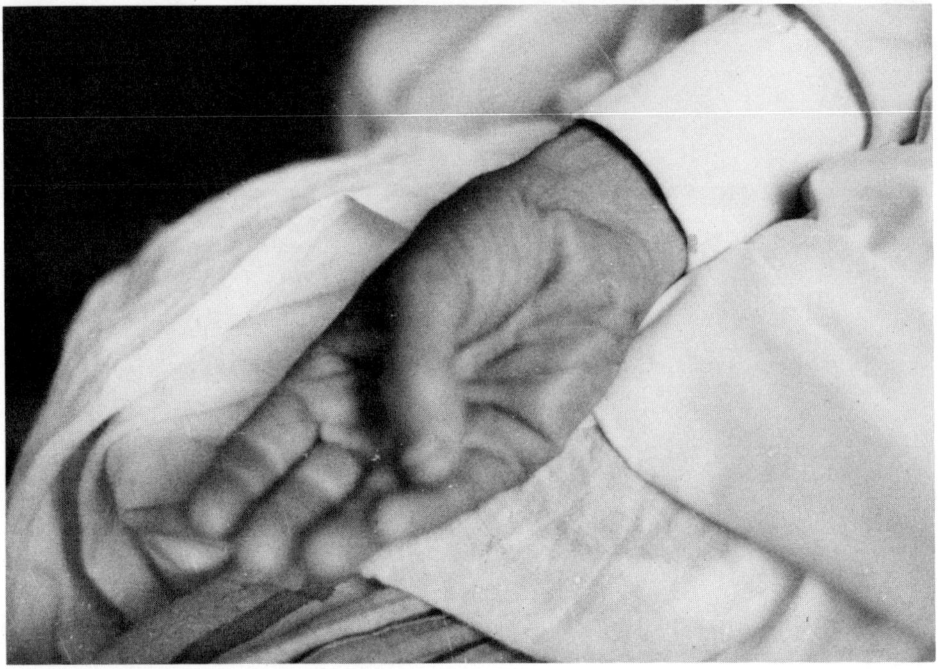

Fig. 7. <u>mandra</u> (5)

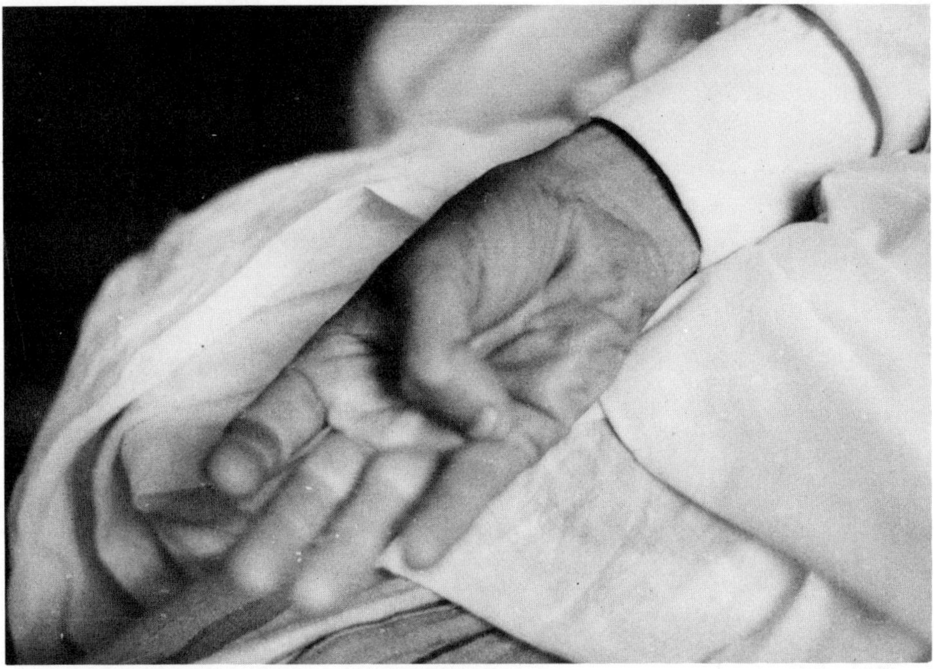

Fig. 8. <u>atisvārya</u> (6)

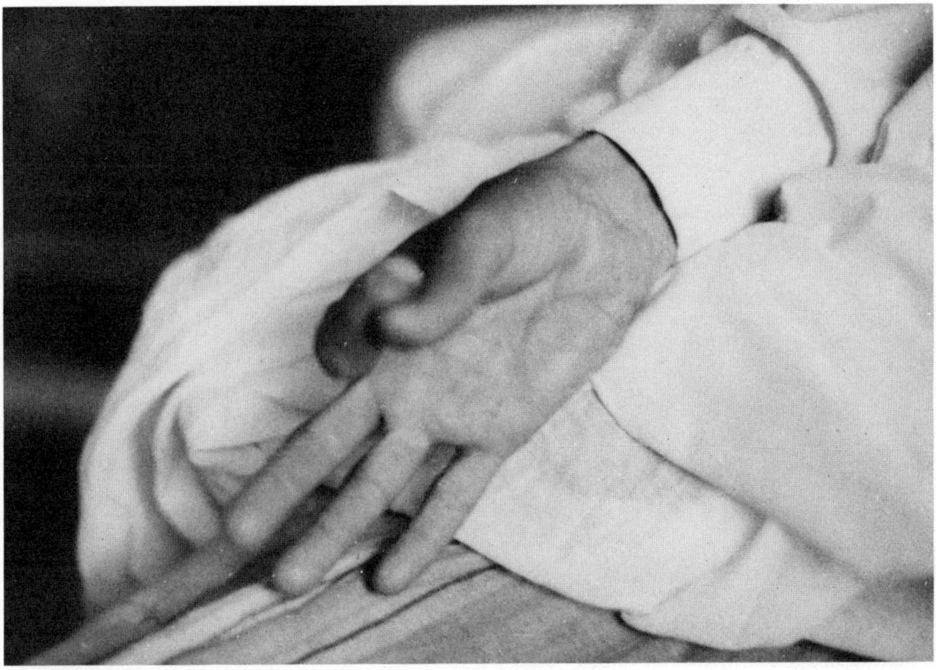

Fig. 9. abhigīta (7)

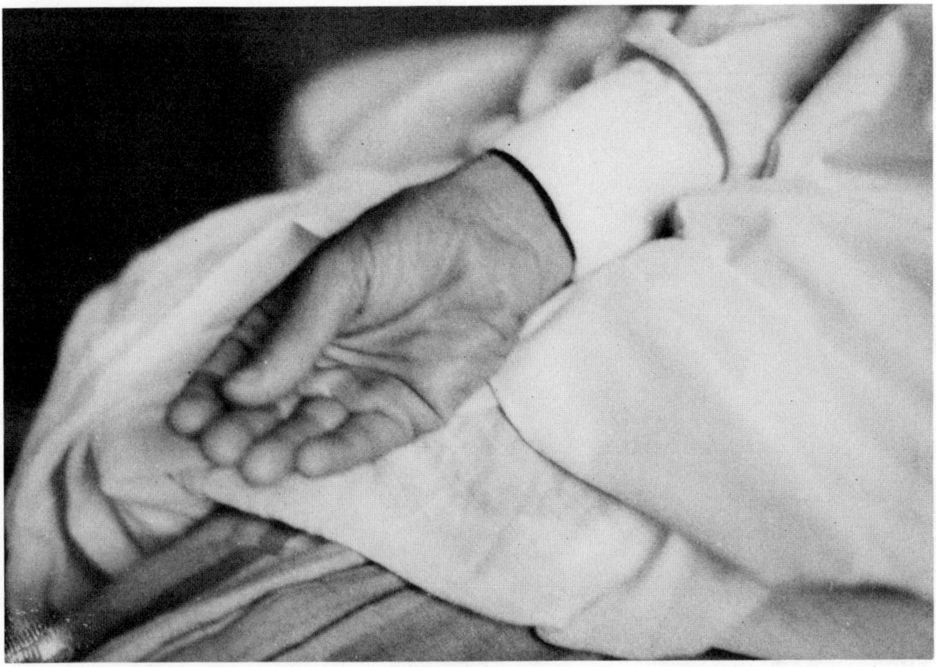

Fig. 10. preṅkha (2̄)

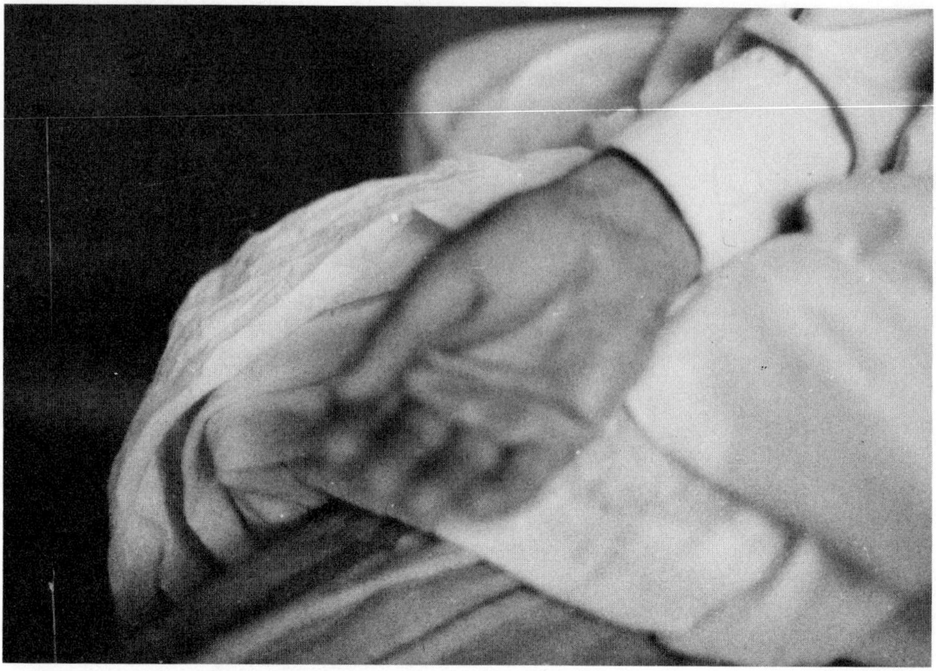

Fig. 11. praṇata (no symbol)

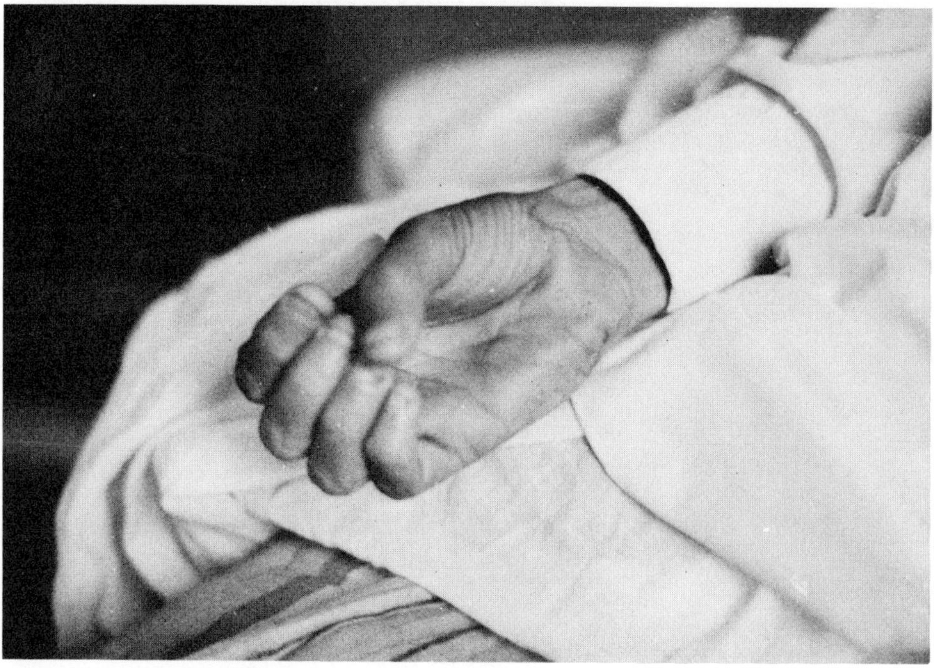

1111
Fig. 12. svāra (2345)

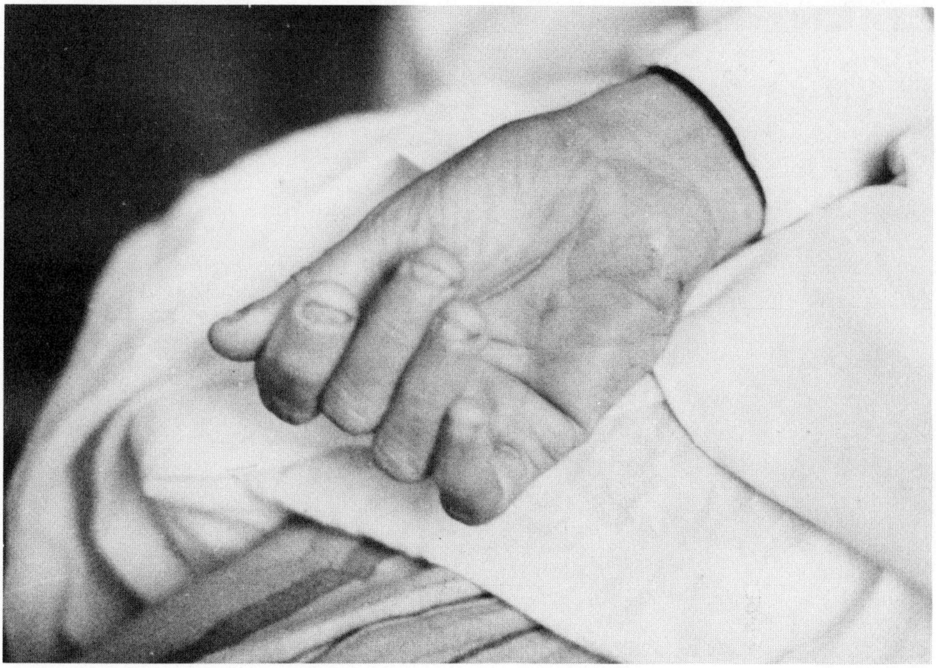

Fig. 13. *karṣaṇa*? ($\hat{2}$ or 2^)

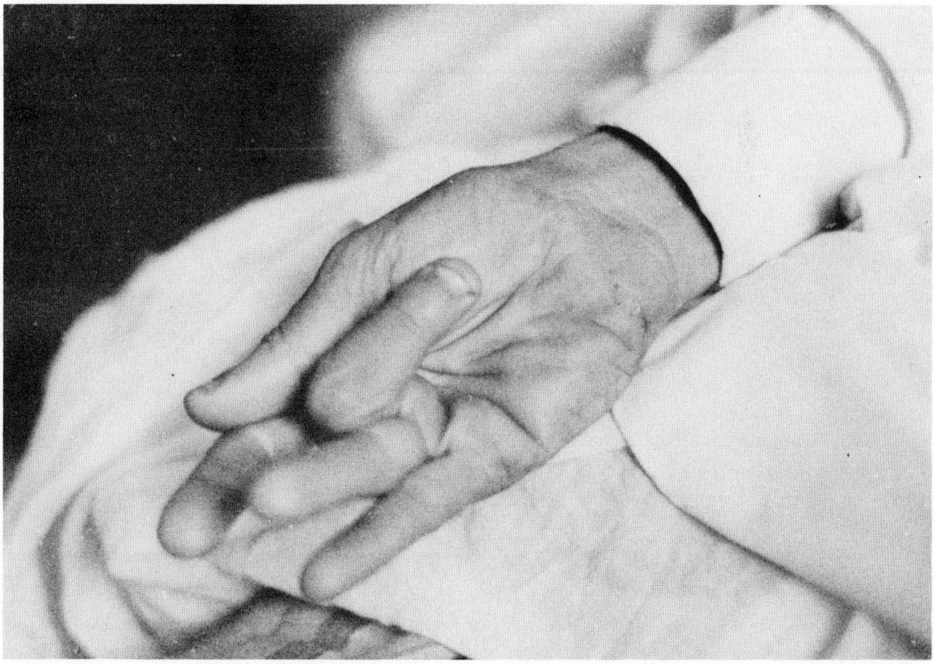

Fig. 14. First of two successive *udāttas* followed by an *anudātta* (2u).

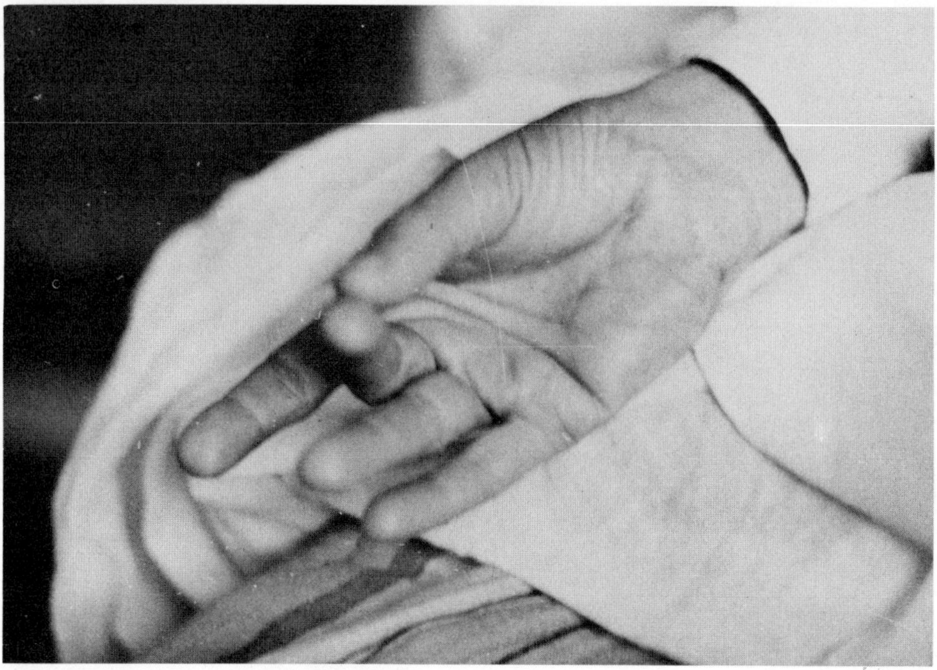

Fig. 15. _anudātta_ preceding independent _svarita_ (3k).

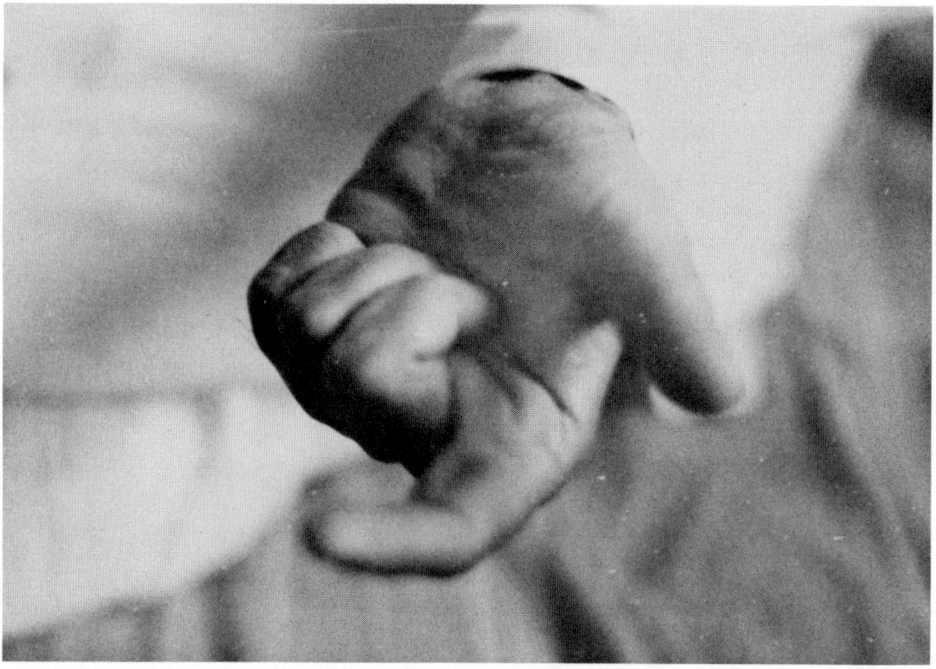

Fig. 16. Left hand indication of the third repetition of words or _stobhas_ [(3) or _triḥ_].

Some additional information on the mudrās is presented in the Introduction to a collection of Rudrapūjā chants edited by Ṛṣiśaṅkar Tripāṭhī Agnihotrī[1] of Vārāṇasī. Here the use of the first six finger positions as illustrated above is justified on the basis of the following passage from the NŚ:

aṅguṣṭhasyottame kruṣṭo hy aṅguṣṭhe prathamaḥ svaraḥ /

The kruṣṭa is [indicated] in the high position of the thumb; the thumb [designates] the prathama-svara;

pradeśinyāṃ tu gāndhāraḥ ṛṣabhas tad anantaram // 3 //

The gāndhāra is [indicated] on the forefinger, the ṛṣabha [on] the next [finger].

anāmikāyāṃ ṣaḍjas tu kaniṣṭhikāyāṃ ca dhaivataḥ /

The ṣaḍja is [indicated] on the ring finger, the dhaivata on the little finger;

tasyādhastāc ca yonyās [sic] tu niṣādaṃ tatra vinyaset // 4 //

And the lower part of the little finger should designate the niṣāda.[2]

Some North Indian Kauthumins employ separate indications for

---

[1] Sāmavedīyarudrajapavidhiḥ, comp. Yamunā Prasād Tripāṭhī (Varanasi: Chowkhamba, 1963), pp. 13-16. The editor, of Gujarāti ancestry, may be heard on the UNESCO album A Musical Anthology of the Orient: India I, ed. the International Music Council, directed by Alain Danielou (Kassel: Bärenreiter-Musicaphon, n. d.), BM 30 L 2006, Nos. 6-8, 14. The first three selections are from the gānas (ŪG 1.1.5, GG 91.1, ĀrG 51.1-3); the last is a mantra from the Vājasaneyi Saṃhitā (Mādhyaṃdina recension) recited according to various vikṛtis (repetition formulae).

[2] NŚ 1.7.3-4. As previously noted (p. 32 above, where NŚ 1.5.1-2 is quoted), the terms gāndhāra, ṛṣabha, etc. of secular music are related by the NŚ to the corresponding dvitīya, tṛtīya, etc. of the gānas.

kruṣṭa and prathama, and in this respect their practice is the same as that of Kauthumins and Rāṇāyanīyas in the South.[1] The first half-verse of the NŚ passage quoted above does not make a clear distinction between kruṣṭa- and prathama-mudrās, so it is not difficult to imagine how two interpretations could have arisen. The excerpt may have been kept deliberately vague so as to account for two practices in use at the time of its composition.

Riṣiśaṅkar Tripāṭhī refers to the symbols $\bar{2}$ and $\overset{1111}{2345}$ as designating vinata and utsvarita, respectively.[2] This is surprising, for the signs are thought to be connected only with preṅkha and svāra.[3] We have seen[4] that a sāman having vinata in the Pūrvagāna may have preṅkha at the same spot in the Uttaragāna, and it is possible that some Kauthumins came to verbalize this connection by assigning the same term to each sequence.[5] Such a correlation between svāra and utsvarita, however, is not discernible, although both bear a tenuous relationship with the svarita accent.

His remaining instructions may be summarized as follows:[6]

1. Wherever a notational numeral has no symbol

---

[1]See below, pp. 106-8.

[2]Sāmavedīyarudrajapavidhiḥ, p. 15.

[3]See above, pp. 64-69. [4]Above, p. 65.

[5]It should be remembered also that the term preṅkha is not mentioned in any of the Sāmavedic tracts and treatises.

[6]Sāmavedīyarudrajapavidhiḥ, p. 16.

placed above it, then the thumb touches the finger corresponding to that numeral, as in

$\overset{1}{\text{o}}$ 2 3 4 5 i (GG 3.1).

In this example the numeral 1 is not notated above the secondary numbers, so the hand movement associated with svāra is not performed. Rather the thumb touches the second, third, fourth, and fifth fingers in turn.

2. Wherever 2S or $\hat{2}$ appear, the gāndhāra-svara (dvitīya) and long articulation (dīrgha uccāraṇa) are intended.
3. Wherever the circumflex appears, long articulation is intended.
4. Wherever 3i is found, i is pronounced ai.

Particularities of musical style

The following discussion of the chant's musical characteristics is based upon recitals of five North Indian Kauthumins, who will henceforth be designated by capital letters (A, B, and D are single chanters; C represents two Brāhmaṇs who chant simultaneously):

A = Agnisvātt Śāstrī Agnihotrī (Vārāṇasī)

B = Revāśaṅkar Becarbhāī Trivedī (Paddhari, Gujarāt)[1]

---

[1]I am indebted to J. F. Staal for copies of two tapes of this Sāmavedin's chant. The former was recorded by the late Śrī T. K. Rājagopāla Aiyar (Madras) during or before 1957 (see PVC, p. 60). Staal's tape is a copy of this original, which has apparently been lost. The latter and more recent recording is, unfortunately, useless for analytical purposes, for the sāmans preserved here exhibit numerous stylistic and intonational peculiarities not found in the earlier recording. These irregularities are due no doubt to the chanter's advanced age.

C = Nārāyaṇ Śaṅkar and Hari Śaṅkar Trivedī (Vārāṇasī)

D = Gaṇapati Śaṅkar Kacarāśaṅkar (Ahmadābād)

The chant has a range of a perfect fourth, and within this interval four distinct tones are discernible. In relation to the lowest, the remaining three pitches are the upper major second, minor third, and perfect fourth.[1] The relative frequency of the four tones can be determined from table 7, where their distribution in three performances of GG 1.1 is shown.[2] Roman numerals designate the four tones in ascending order; Arabic numerals indicate the number of times the tones occur in particular durational spans. For example, in the transcription of A's recital[3] the lowest tone (I) appears once as a value between a quarter and a dotted quarter, eight times as values between an eighth and a double-dotted eighth, and twelve times as values between a sixty-fourth and a double-dotted sixteenth. The relative importance of a tone must be judged not only according to the total number of its appearances but also according to the number of occurrences as a note of long duration. The highest pitch (IV) occurs infrequently in each of the three performances. It is found no more than five times in any interpretation, and in almost all instances it occurs as a note of small durational value.

---

[1]The upper perfect fifth is heard occasionally in C's recital (twice in GG 1.1-3), but a lower tone was doubtlessly intended.

[2]See the transcriptions in Part III, pp. 251, 261, 263.

[3]See Part III, p. 251.

Furthermore, its appearances are not consistent with any particular notational numeral or sign in the <u>gānas</u>. The three lower tones are the principal pitches; consequently the chant moves mainly within the narrow range of a minor third. Of these remaining tones (I-II-III) the lowest is the least prominent in each interpretation, while the highest is the most important pitch in the recitals of A and C. In B's reading, the middle tone (II) is slightly more prominent than its upper neighbor. None of these tones, however, can be said to serve as a tonic or principal pitch.

TABLE 7

GG 1.1: TONAL DISTRIBUTIONS

	Reciter A				Reciter B				Reciters C			
	I	II	III	IV	I	II	III	IV	I	II	III	IV
♩ -- ♩.	1	4	10	0	6	8	3	0	1	3	1	0
♪ -- ♪..	8	6	9	0	7	9	11	0	8	12	17	1
𝅘𝅥𝅰 -- 𝅘𝅥𝅰..	12	27	32	2	17	25	28	3	14	36	47	4
Totals	21	37	51	2	30	42	42	3	23	51	65	5

There is no consistent adherence to temporal values as defined by the ML. For example, the fourth <u>parvan</u> of GG 1.2 should have (theoretically) the following <u>mātrā</u> apportionment:

```
notation:  1  r  r̲       2  1                   2
text:     ni ho-tā sa-tsi ba--r--hā-2 3-i ṣī
mātrās:    1 +2 +2 +1  +1 +1 +½  +4          +3
```

Performances of this extract by A and C reveal little agreement with the specified *mātrā* pattern:[1]

If the opening sixteenth note of these transcriptions (on the short syllable *ni*) is set equal to one *mātrā* (the theoretical length of a short syllable), then the relative durations of the syllables compare as follows to those put forth by the ML:

ML: $1 + 2 + 2 + 1 + 1 + 1 + \frac{1}{2} + 4 + 3 = 15\frac{1}{2}$

A: $1 + 3 + 1 + 5 + 3 + 1 + 16 + 4 = 34$

C: $1 + 4 + 1 + 8 + 5 + 1 + 16 + 2\frac{1}{2} = 38\frac{1}{2}$.

The interpretations of A and C are quite similar, but they both differ significantly from the ML model.

If one assumes that to each of the seven numerals notated in the songbooks corresponds a single, unique tone, then the North Indian chant with its four pitches cannot possibly conform to such a scheme. To the contrary, the fragment from GG 1.2 transcribed above demonstrates that in practice more than one tone may be associated with a notational numeral. The *prathama* is indicated in the *gānas* for the syllables *ni* *ho-tā*, but the oral tradition has a different pitch for each syllable.

---

[1]At the beginning of this and subsequent musical examples, the first note of the transcription is set equal to the actual sung pitch.

Sequences

A chanter is usually consistent in his realizations of a particular sequence, but there are sometimes discrepancies from one performer to the next. Moreover, *parvans* with the same succession of notational numerals and signs are generally performed in the same way by a particular chanter. An appreciation of this fact is crucial to an understanding of the chant's melodic organization, which, as will be shown below, cuts across boundaries of geography and *śākhā*.

The extracts below illustrate nineteen sequences as interpreted by northern Kauthumas. All of the various types of *pratyutkrama*, *atikrama*, *karṣaṇa*, and so on could not be given due to the limited number of recorded specimens.

1. *Pratyutkrama* (type 4_3)[1]

2. *Pratyutkrama* (type 2_1)

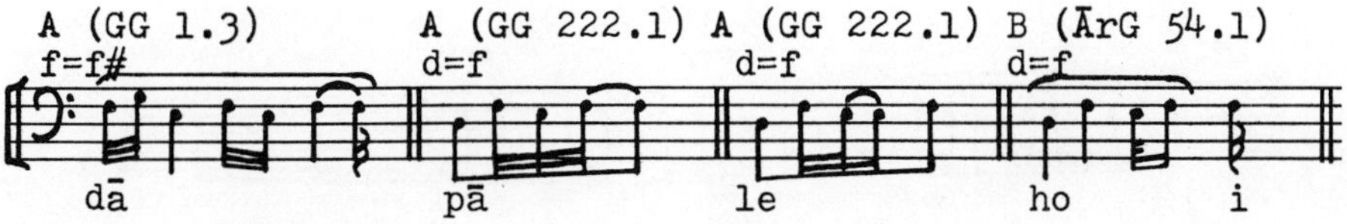

3. *Atikrama* (type 3_5)

---

[1] ♪= 120 for all examples.

4. Karṣaṇa (type $1^{\wedge}_{2}$)

5. Karṣaṇa (type 1_{23})

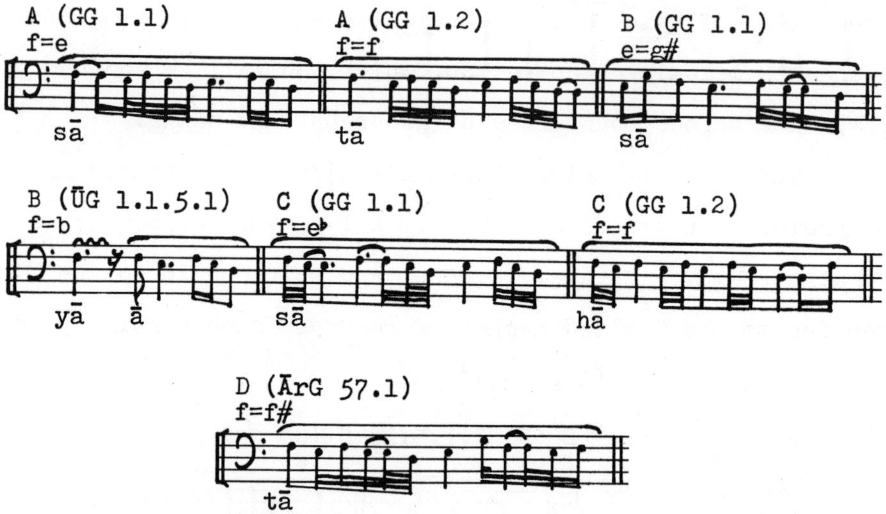

6. Karṣaṇa (type 1_{234})

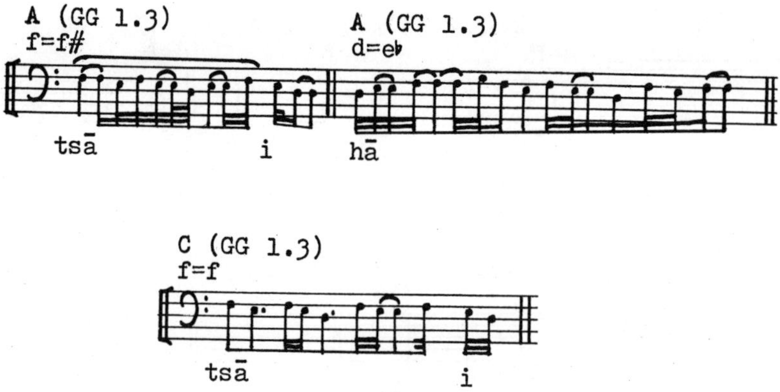

7. Karṣaṇa/Pratyutkrama (type 3_{234})

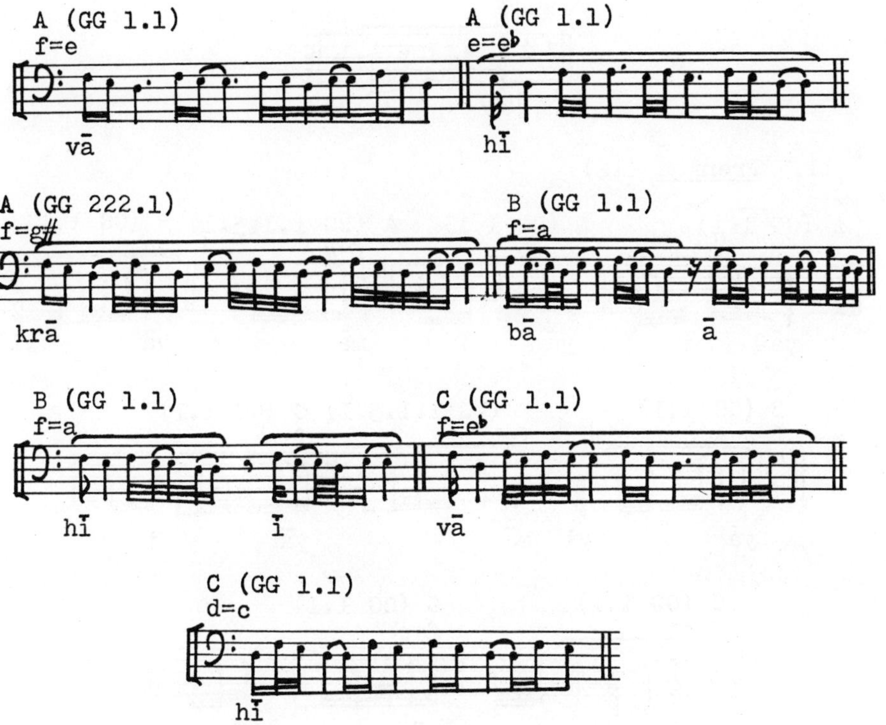

8. Karṣaṇa (type 3_4)

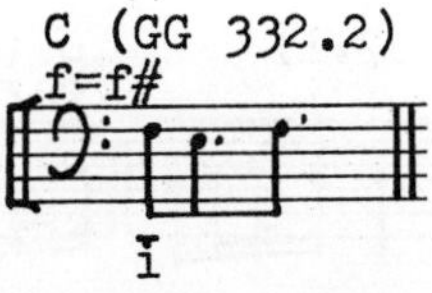

9. Karṣaṇa (type 5_6)

10. Namana (S_3)

11. Preṅkha ($1_{\bar{2}}$)

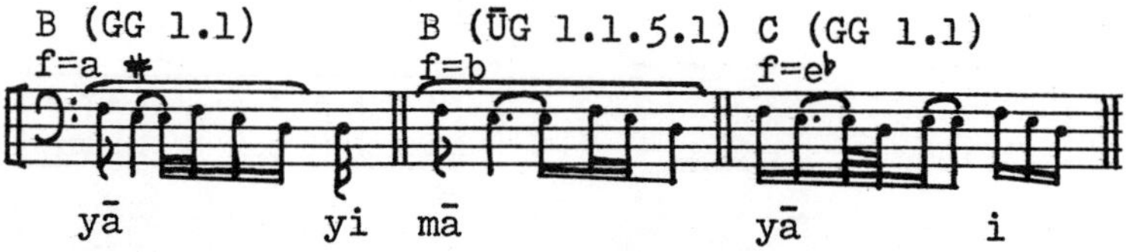

12. Svāra (type 1_{2345}^{111})

13. Svāra (type 2_{345}^{111})

D (ĀrG 57.1)
e=f

syā

14. Svāra (type 3^{111}_{2345})

A (GG 1.2) d=d — C (GG 1.2) f=f

sị̄ — sị̄

15. Padānusvāra (5_{656})

C (GG 332.2)
f=f#

mā

16. Vinata ($1S_2$)

B (ĀrG 54.1) f=b♭ — B (ĀrG 54.1) f=a

dri ḥ rvā

17. Praṇata (2_3 or $\hat{2}_3$)

A (GG 1.1) f=e — A (GG 1.2) f=f — A (GG 1.3) e=f — A (GG 1.3) e=f

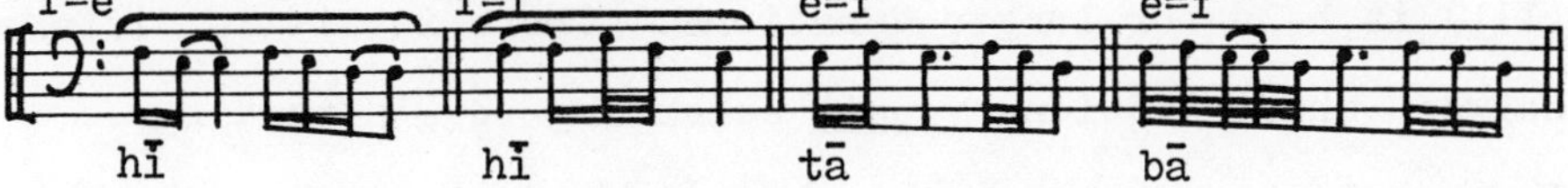

hī — hī — tā — bā

B (GG 1.1) f=a — B (ŪG 1.1.5.1) f=b — B (ŪG 1.1.5.1) f=b

hī — trā — au

B (ŪG 1.1.5.1) f=b | C (GG 1.1) f=e♭ | C (GG 1.2) f=f

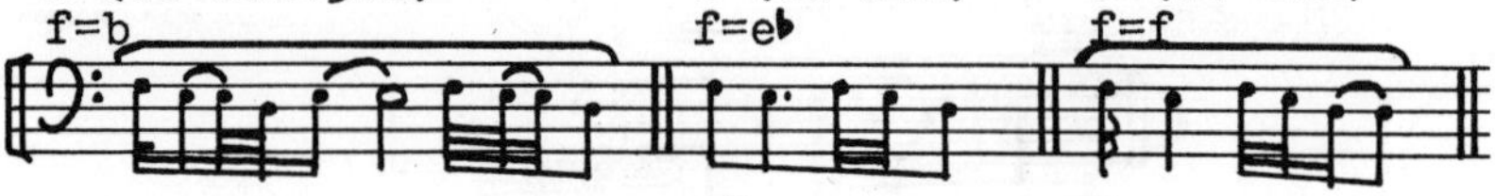

ho | hī | hī

C (GG 1.3) f=f | C (GG 1.3) f=f

tā | bā

18. Utsvarita (4_5)

A (GG 1.3) f=f# | C (GG 1.3) f=f

vā | vā

19. Abhigīta (7)

C (GG 333.1) f=g | C (GG 333.1) f=g | C (GG 333.1) f=g

ra | ra | ta

The above examples show that namana, preṅkha, and praṇata are performed almost exactly alike; karṣaṇa type 1_{23} is very similar to them, though here the beginning tone (III) is held for longer durations. There is little difference between short and long vinata according to B's readings. Three syllables bearing the abhigīta are chanted by C on a short single pitch (III). Discrepancies are noticeable among interpretations of the first and third types of svāra (1^{111}_{2345} and 3^{111}_{2345}), but three performers are in agreement on the second type (2^{111}_{345}). The four specimens of pratyutkrama type 2_1 generally agree, as do the two examples of utsvarita. There is lack of uniformity among the examples of pratyutkrama type 4_3, atikrama type 3_5, and karṣaṇa types 1_{234} and 3_{234}. Only one instance of padānusvāra was recorded; its durational value is approximately that of svāra type 1_{2345}^{111}, though the tonal patterns are different.

Early Kauthuma recordings

It is worthwhile to compare my recordings of the North Indian chant with those made some seventy years ago by Felix Exner, who had gone to India for meteorological studies. Such a comparison is made possible by transcriptions of Exner's records published in 1912 in a book by Erwin Felber and Bernhard Geiger.[1] Three northern Kauthumas were recorded by Exner: (1) Dharmavrata Chaṭṭopādhyāya, a student of the Sanskrit College in Calcutta, (2) Kṛṣṇavrata Chaṭṭopādhyāya, also a student of the Sanskrit College, and (3) Lakṣmīnārāyaṇa Śarmā, a Calcutta priest formerly of Paskara in Jodhpur. The recitals of the two students are suspect.[2] They each employ a range of a major sixth--an unusually wide interval for the North--and the general style of their chant, with its wide leaps, triadic figurations and occasional chromaticism, is unlike that of any Sāmavedin I have heard. However, Felber's

[1] Die indische Musik der vedischen und der klassischen Zeit, vol. 170, no. 7 of Sitzungsberichte der philosophisch-historischen Klasse der kaiserlichen Akademie der Wissenschaften (Vienna: Alfred Hölder, 1912), pp. 101-6.

[2] See Bake, "The Practice of Sāmaveda," p. 146.

transcriptions of four complete sāmans (GG 192.1-2, ĀrG 132.1, 133.1) as interpreted by the Jodhpur priest reveal his chant to be very similar to that of the Kauthumas whom I recorded: he strictly adheres to the ambitus of a perfect fourth, and the four tones he uses bear the same intervallic relationships as those of my 1971 informants. Moreover, his realizations of certain of the sequences generally echo the practices described above. This is sufficient proof that the Kauthuma style prevalent in the North can be traced back at least to the late nineteenth century. It undoubtedly hails from a much earlier age.

Tanjore Kauthuma

Geography and caste

Until fairly recent times, Western scholars interested in the practical aspects of Sāmaveda--that is, in the oral traditions--relied almost entirely upon the Kauthumas of southern Tamiḻnāṭu. These Sāmagas are present in large numbers in the Tanjore District, an area made fertile and luxuriant by the several branches of the Cauvery River which flow into the Bay of Bengal. It is one of three regions in all of India where authentic śrauta rituals are still performed and the only area where all seven soma saṃsthās are celebrated.[1] At least partly due to the dearth of Sāmavedic

[1]See J. F. Staal, "The Twelve Ritual Chants of the Nambudiri Agniṣṭoma," Pratidānam: Indian, Iranian and Indo-European Studies Presented to Franciscus Bernardus Jacobus Kuiper on His Sixtieth Birthday, ed. J. C. Heesterman, G. H. Schokker, and V. I. Subramoniam (The Hague: Mouton, 1968), p. 410.

chanting elsewhere, the Tanjore Kauthumas have migrated to various points in both the South and the North. In the South, outside Tanjore, they are represented in such urban areas as Tiruccirāppaḷḷi (Trichinopoly), Madras, and Mysore, as well as in the smaller temple towns. In the North they are resident mainly in the large cities, where they serve the needs of the often sizable South Indian communities; such an enclave is the Tamil̲ settlement around Hanumān Ghāṭ in Vārāṇasī.[1] Another center in the North is Darbhaṅga, sixty miles northeast of Patna (Pāṭaliputra) in Bihār, where Sāmavedic chanting in the southern style is subsidized by the mahārājā (or at least this was so up to the year 1957).[2]

Tanjore Kauthuma is perpetuated by _smārta_ Aiyar and _vaiṣṇava_ Aiyaṅgār Brāhmaṇs,[3] the two predominant Brāhmaṇ communities of Tamil̲nāṭu. Despite their numerous differences, the two castes show no apparent dissimilarity in the chanting of Sāmaveda. They study together in the _vedapāṭhaśālās_ (Vedic schools) and participate jointly in the rituals.

---

[1]Kṛṣṇamūrti Śrautigal, a Kauthumin who moved to Vārāṇasī permanently some twenty years ago from Maraiturai village (Vedaprī) in Tanjore District, can perform the incredible feat of reciting from memory the complete Sāmaveda corpus, including the Saṃhitā, the four songbooks, the eight Brāhmaṇas (Pañcaviṃśa, Ṣaḍviṃśa, Ārṣeya, Devatādhyāya, Saṃhitopaniṣad, Sāmavidhāna, Vaṃśa, Mantra), and the Chāndogyopaniṣad. For this achievement he has been honored by the Mahārājā of Banāras (in my possession is a photograph of the _śrautin_ seated on one of the royal elephants) with commendatory edicts and a pension. This is but one instance to show that competent Tanjore chanters are to be found as well outside the South.

[2]See PVC, p. 51.

[3]For a comparison of the two sects, see J. F. Staal, "Notes on some Brahmin Communities of South India," _Art and Letters: Journal of the Royal India Pakistan and Ceylon Society_ 32 (1958): 1-4.

Melodic components

The common gamut is made up of seven tones, which may be arranged and numbered as follows:

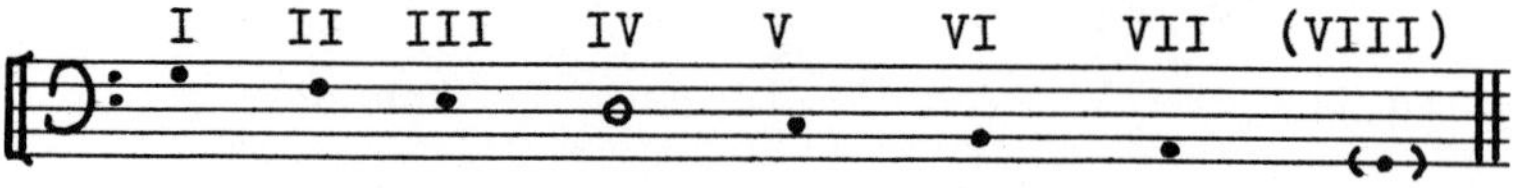

The Kauthuma Gamut: South India

Tone IV, the middle tone, clearly functions as a central or tonic pitch, although the singers do not necessarily consider it as such. However, it is the tone most often held for long durations and the one concluding most parvans. An eighth and lowest tone is heard occasionally, but its appearances are so rare that it cannot be considered an element of the scale. The gamut as it stands is thus quite similar to the hypodorian mode and the scale offered by Burnell in 1876.[1] It also comprises the tone material employed by Exner's South Indian chanters in 1904.[2]

The productions of some singers are characterized by much ornamentation and wavering--a sort of tremolo effect known as kampa. The degree of kampa and other forms of embellishment vary significantly from one performer to the next, as the following examples (extracted from the second parvan of GG 1.1) illustrate. The quoted fragment has preṅkha on the second syllable:

[1]
to yā 2̄ i

---

[1]See above, p. 31. He omits tone I but includes tone VIII.

[2]See Felber, "Die indische Musik," pp. 114-15.

The three Sāmagas are from Kumbakoṇam, Mysore, and Madras, respectively.

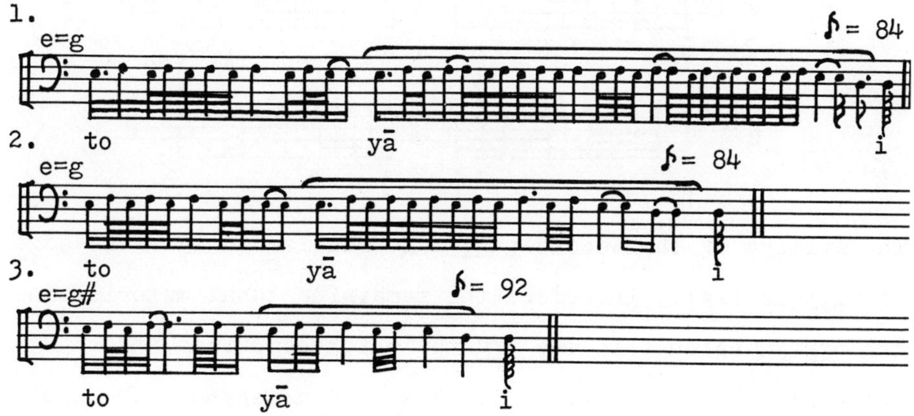

Despite these ornamental variations, the general contour of the melody is clearly perceived in each performance:

```
III-II-III-III-II-III-IV-IV
to        yā           i
```

Kruṣṭa

Like the North Indian chant, the Tanjore variety does not conform to the numeral notations of the *gāna*s; that is, the seven tones do not correspond to the seven *svara*s of the NŚ. That this is so as regards the *kruṣṭa* can be seen in the following examples from GG 284.2 (fourth and seventh *parvan*s), based upon recitals of Kṛṣṇamūrti Śrautigal (Vedaprī, Tanjore District; now residing in Vārāṇasī) and Śeṣādri Śāstrigal (Tiruvidaimarudūr, Tanjore District; now living in Madras). The two *parvan*s are notated respectively as:

$$/ \overset{1}{\bar{u}} /; / \overset{1}{\bar{u}} \overset{\uparrow}{2} /$$[1]

---

[1]See above, pp. 30-31.

The *dvitīya* of the second *parvan* is realized only as a short, final tone (IV). Therefore the remaining tonal material in the *parvan* belongs to the *kruṣṭa*, which comprises the pattern: III-II-III-(I)-III. There is a legend among the Kauthumas which says that the *kruṣṭa* is heard only by the gods and never by human ears. In this regard it is interesting that tone I is touched upon very briefly, but that nevertheless it is apparently an essential element of the *kruṣṭa*. Kṛṣṇamūrti Śrautigal informed me that he sings the *svara* "at a high pitch, only for a split second." Undoubtedly he was referring to this tone I. The impression should not be given, however, that this tone occurs only in connection with the *kruṣṭa*. For example, the pitch is heard twenty-one times in a performance by Bālasubrahmaṇya Śrautigal (Kumbakoṇam) of GG 1.1-3, although here too it is touched upon only briefly in each instance.

South Indian Kauthumas employ separate *mudrās* for *kruṣṭa* and *prathama*. The former is indicated by the hand--more or less in its relaxed, normal position--with thumb held somewhat apart from the remaining fingers. In specifying the *prathama* the thumb is moved closer to--but does not touch--

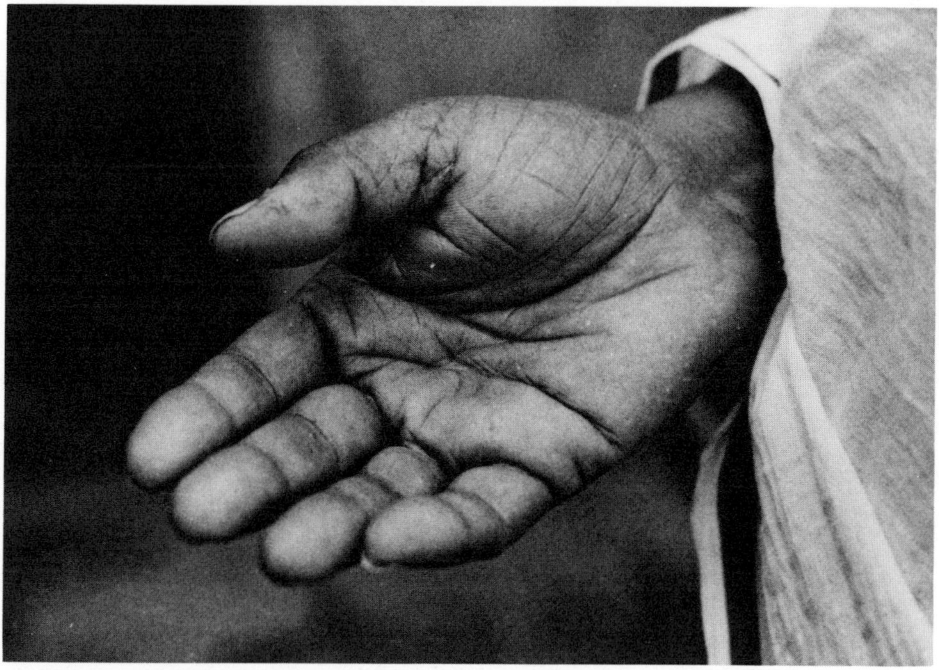

Fig. 17. <u>kruṣṭa</u> (South India)

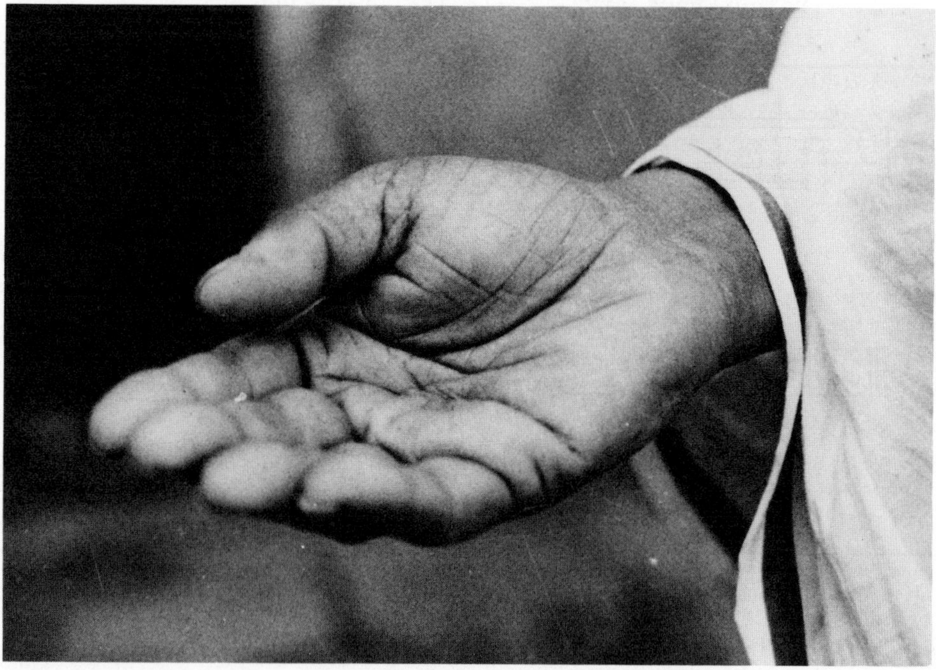

Fig. 18. <u>prathama</u> (South India)

the index finger. The two positions were illustrated for me by Kṛṣṇamūrti (see figs. 17-18). The five remaining postures, corresponding to numerals 2-6, are the same as those of the North Indians (see figs. 4-8).

Sequences

Tonal patterns (designated by Roman numerals) of sixteen of the most common sequences are given below. Each scheme is followed by one or more musical examples taken from performances of five masters of the Tanjore style:

A = Bālasubrahmaṇya Śrautigal (Kumbakoṇam)

B = Kṛṣṇamūrti Śrautigal (Vedaprī/Vārāṇasī)

C = K. Rāman Aiyaṅgār (Madras)[1]

D = S. Satyanārāyaṇa (Mysore)

E = N. Lakṣmīnārāyaṇa Śrautigal (Mysore)

1. Pratyutkrama (type 2_1): IV-III-II-III

---

[1]This Sāmaga gave the name of his śākhā as Gautama rather than Kauthuma, but there is no difference in style from the southern Kauthumas.

2. <u>Karṣaṇa</u> (type $1_{\hat{2}}$): III-II-III-IV

C (GG 1.1)
e=g#, 𝅘𝅥𝅯 = 92

D (GG 1.1)
a=c, 𝅘𝅥𝅯 = 84

E (GG 222.1)
e=b, 𝅘𝅥𝅯 = 84

E (GG 222.1)
e=b, 𝅘𝅥𝅯 = 84

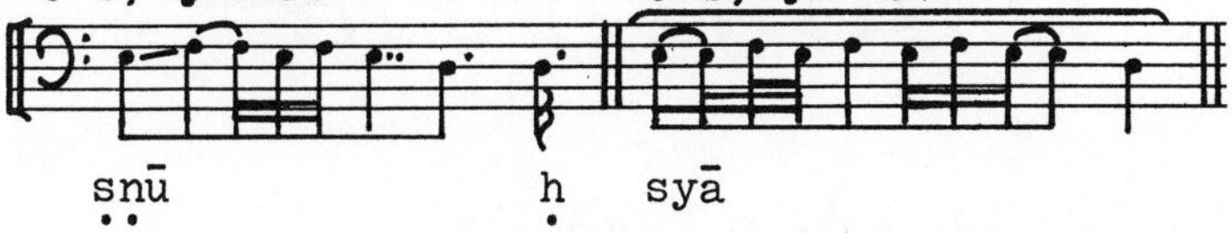

3. <u>Karṣaṇa</u> (type 1_{23}): III-II-III-IV

C (GG 1.1)
e=g#, 𝅘𝅥𝅯 = 92

C (GG 1.2)
f=a, 𝅘𝅥𝅯 = 92

D (GG 1.1)
e=g, 𝅘𝅥𝅯 = 84

D (GG 1.2)
e=f#, 𝅘𝅥𝅯 = 84

4. <u>Karṣaṇa</u> (type 1_{234}): III-II-III-IV

A (GG 1.3)
e=g#, 𝅘𝅥𝅯 = 84

D (GG 1.3)
a=b, 𝅘𝅥𝅯 = 84

5. Karṣaṇa/Pratyutkrama (type 3_{234}): (IV)-V-IV-V-(VI)

C (GG 1.1)
d=f#, ♪ = 92

D (GG 1.1)
c=e♭, ♪ = 84

vā vā

E (GG 222.1)
d=a, ♪ = 84

pā

6. Karṣaṇa (type 5_6): IV-V

A (GG 1.3)
a=c#, ♪ = 84

D (GG 1.3)
d=e, ♪ = 84

so̩ so̩

7. Namana (S_3): III-II-III-IV

B (GG 512.2)
e=g#, ♪ = 100

B (GG 512.2)
e=g#, ♪ = 100

au ī

8. Preṅkha ($1_{\bar{2}}$): III-II-III-IV

A (GG 1.1)
e=g, ♪ = 84

yā

B (Gāyatram)
e=f#, ♪ = 100

B (Gāyatram)
e=f#, ♪ = 100

hī ā

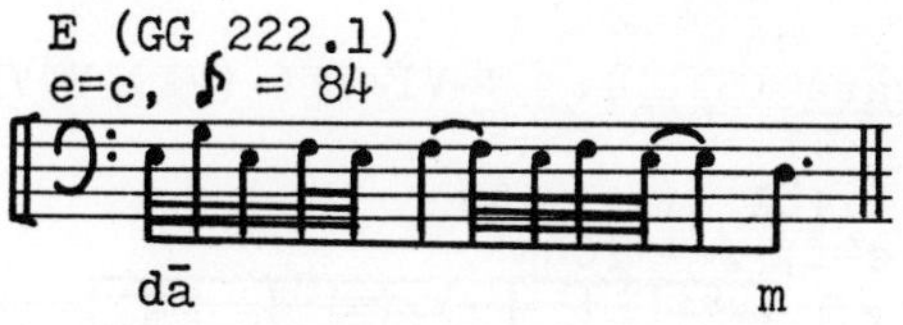

9. <u>Svāra</u> (type 1^{111}_{2345}): III-II-III-IV-V-(VI)-IV

10. <u>Svāra</u> (type 2^{111}_{345}): IV-V-VI-IV

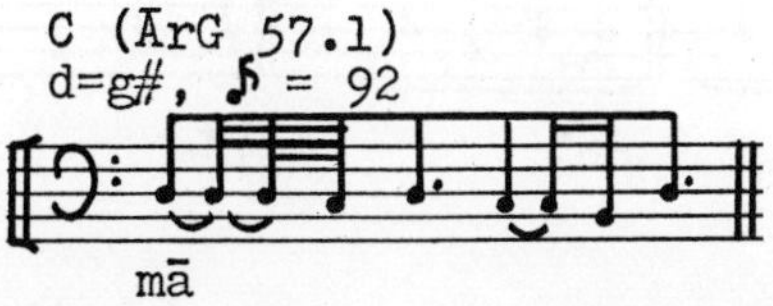

11. <u>Svāra</u> (type 3^{111}_{2345}): III-II-III-IV-V-IV

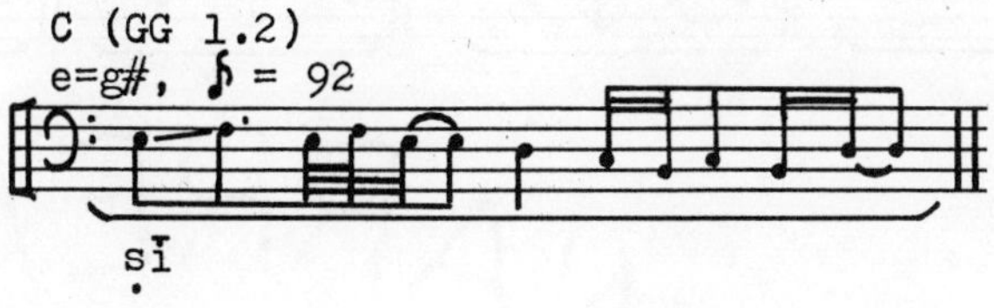

D (GG 1.2)
e=f#, ♪ = 84

12. Padānusvāra (5_{656}): V-VI-VII-(VI)-V-VI-IV

B (ŪG 1.1.13.1)
c=f, ♪ = 100

13. Vinata (type lrs_2): III-II-III-IV

B (GG 512.1)
e=g, ♪ = 100

B (GG 512.1)
e=g, ♪ = 100

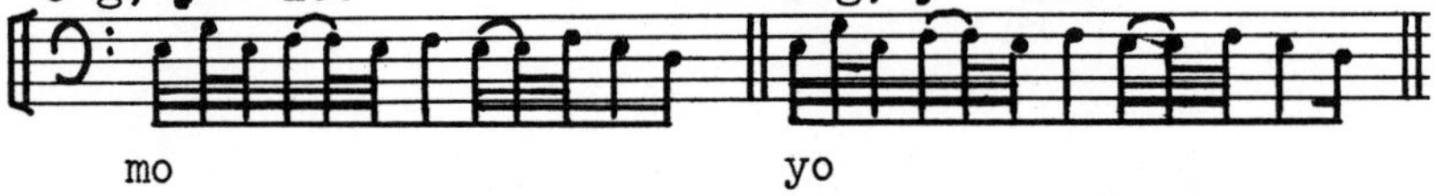

14. Praṇata (2_3 or $2\hat{_3}$): IV-(VI)-IV

A (GG 1.1)
d=f, ♪ = 84

A (GG 1.2)
d=f#, ♪ = 84

C (GG 1.1)
d=f#, ♪ = 92

C (GG 1.2)
d=f#, ♪ = 92

D (GG 1.1)
d=f, ♪ = 84

D (GG 1.2)
d=e, ♪ = 84

E (GG 222.1)
d=a, ♪ = 84

E (GG 222.1)
d=a, ♪ = 84

15. Utsvarita (4_5): VII-IV-V-VI-VII

16. Abhigīta (7): III-II

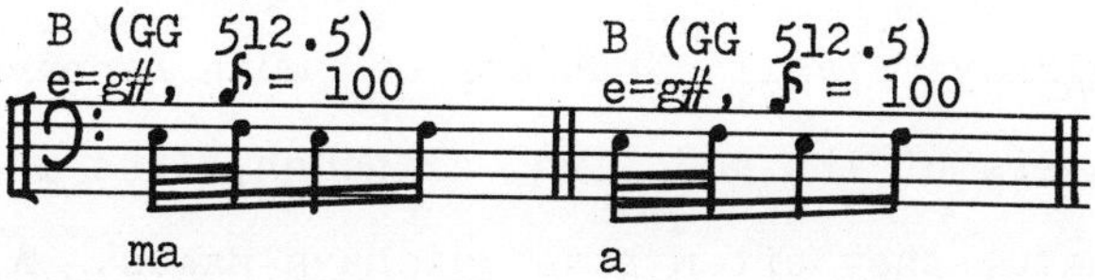

Six of the above (karṣaṇa types 1_2, 1_{23}, 1_{234}, namana, preṅkha, and vinata) are comprised of the same tone pattern: III-II-III-IV. Moreover, the time values allotted to each of the four tones are proportionately the same for each of the sequences, excluding namana. Tone I does not appear as a principal pitch in any of the examples, but we have seen that it is a necessary feature of atikrama from kruṣṭa to dvitīya. Hardly anywhere are the theoretical principles of the ML carried out in practice. With few exceptions, more tones are employed for a particular sequence than the notational numerals would indicate. This is but further evidence that the numbers signify tonal aggregates rather than single pitches.

Hāvik Rāṇāyanīya

Sāmaveda in North Kannara

Of the three extant Sāmavedic schools, the Rāṇāyanīyas and Jaiminīyas are dangerously approaching extinction. Until a few years ago the condition of the former was thought to be even more serious than it is in fact. Some reason for encouragement is the discovery of a small Rāṇāyanīya community near Honnāvār, in the North Kannara District of Mysore State. The Rāṇāyanīyas here are all of the Hāvik sect, a Brāhmaṇ sub-caste which has traditionally engaged not only in priestly but also in secular occupations--agriculture, for instance. In contrast to the *vaiṣṇava* Śivaḷḷi Brāhmaṇs of South Kannara,[1] the Hāviks are followers of the god Śiva, although, like the Aiyar Brāhmaṇs of Tamiḻnāṭu, they often have *vaiṣṇava* names. Apparently all Hāvik Sāmavedins are Rāṇāyanīyas.

Soma rituals were performed in North Kannara until about thirty-one years ago. An *agniṣṭoma* was celebrated at the village Salkod (two or three miles from Honnāvār) in 1946, but no *somayāgas* have taken place there since. A short distance to the north, in Gokarṇa, three *soma saṃsthās*--*agniṣṭoma*, *aptoryāma*, and *vājapeya* were last solemnized in 1951, according to best information), but the only ritual presently carried out is the *darśapūrṇamāsa*.[2] The probable

[1]Transcriptions of Sāmaveda from South Kannara are found below, pp. 452-54. The Sāmavedins here give Jaiminīya as their *śākhā*, but see NVR, p. 73.

[2]See J. F. Staal, "Some Vedic Survivals: Report on Research Done in India, Dec. 1970--March 1971, A.I.I.S. Grant" (Varanasi: 20 March 1971), p. 11. (Mimeographed.)

reason for this is that Gokarṇa has no Sāmavedins; hence the required trio (Prastotar, Udgātar, Pratihartar) had to be brought in from outside, especially from around Honnāvār. Nowadays, however, even this is impossible, for there remain among the Hāvik Brāhmans only two persons qualified to perform the difficult Sāmaveda parts. Thus an authentic performance in this area of a soma sacrifice is now a practical impossibility.

The Rāṇāyanīya syllable notation

That the śākhā of the Hāvik Sāmagas is Rāṇāyanīya is unquestionable, for they make use of a syllable notation peculiar solely to this school. The Rāṇāyanīya method of notating is readily comprehended. Around three hundred parvans have been extracted from various chants in the songbooks. Musically (and thus notationally) no two of the three hundred are exactly alike; but taken together they are said to constitute all of the melodic material used by the Rāṇāyanīyas in their 2,722 chants. Each of the motives or phrases is assigned a particular consonant-vowel symbol whose appearance in the songbooks signals the occurrence of the motive or phrase it designates. Every parvan of every chant in their repertoire has such a notational syllable, which in the manuscripts is found after the first textual syllable of the parvan.[1]

These "typical parvans" are systematized according to

[1]For the notation of GG 1.1, see above, pp. 12-13.

the consonants of the Sanskrit alphabet and their arrangement in five classes: guttural, palatal, lingual, dental, and labial. These are the five *varga*s (consonant categories); each is called by the first consonant of the group:

1. *ka*-*varga* (gutturals): k, kh, g, gh, ṅ
2. *ca*-*varga* (palatals): c, ch, j, jh, ñ
3. *ṭa*-*varga* (linguals): ṭ, ṭh, ḍ, ḍh, ṇ
4. *ta*-*varga* (dentals): t, th, d, dh, n
5. *pa*-*varga* (labials): p, ph, b, bh, m

The notational syllables are formed by assigning to each consonant ten vowels (*a*, *ā*, *i*, *ī*, *u*, *ū*, *e*, *ai*, *o*, *au*) and two grammatical signs (preceded by the short *a*-vowel), *anusvāra* (*aṃ*) and *visarga* (*aḥ*). Thus the five consonants of a *varga* may combine with the twelve vowels and signs to form sixty notational syllables. Those belonging to the *ka*-*varga* designate *parvan*s which begin with the numeral 1 (symbolizing *prathama* or *kruṣṭa*). Likewise the numbers 2, 3, 4, and 5 (*dvitīya*, *tṛtīya*, *caturtha*, and *mandra*) are the respective initial numerals of the *ca*-, *ṭa*-, *ta*-, and *pa*-*varga*s. Occasionally extra syllables must be added to a *varga* when the number of typical *parvan*s beginning with a certain number exceeds sixty. These extra syllables usually begin with sibilants, semivowels, or conjuncts.

Simon has based his catalogue[1] of syllable-types on four *grantha* manuscripts in the India Office and one *grantha*

---

[1] NVL, pp. 326-44.

print:[1] (1) Sāmalakṣaṇa (Svaraparibhāṣā), B. 133; (2) and (3) Chalākṣara (Rāvaṇabhaiṭ), B. 150 and B. 151 (incomplete); (4) Chalaprakriya, B. 496_8; and (5) Sāmaparibhāṣā of Kṛṣṇa-svāmin Śrautin, pages 17-33. The last-mentioned work is the only one giving the correspondence to the numeral notation. The sequence as given by Simon, who lists 297 syllables, is as follows:[2]

1. ka-varga: ka--kaḥ, kha--khaḥ, ga--gaḥ, gha--ghaḥ, ṅa--ṅaḥ, la--laḥ, va--vaḥ, tva--tvai
2. ca-varga: ca--caḥ, cha--chaḥ, ja--jhaḥ, ña--ñaḥ, śa--śaḥ, ṣa--ṣaḥ, sa--saḥ, ra--raḥ, ḷa--ḷī, śca--ścā, ścī--ścū
3. ṭa-varga: ṭa--ṭaḥ, ṭha--ṭhaḥ, ḍa--ḍau, ya--yū, yai--yaḥ
4. ta-varga: ta--taḥ, tha--thai, ha--hi
5. pa-varga: pa--paḥ, pha--phai

My recordings[3] of the melody-types as interpreted by two Hāvik Brāhmaṇs reveal a number of disagreements with Simon's edition:

1. The Hāvik singers include the syllables ści, śce, ścai, and ye, all absent in the manuscripts. They are associated by the chanters with the

---

[1]A devanāgarī edition of the typical parvans has appeared recently in Dīkṣita, Ūhagānam--Ūhyagānam, pp. 29-35.

[2]See also Walter Kaufmann, "Some Reflections on the Notations of Vedic Chant," in Essays in Musicology: A Birthday Offering for Willi Apel, ed. Hans Tischler (Bloomington: Indiana University School of Music, 1968), p. 5.

[3]See the transcriptions in Part III, pp. 289-362.

following <u>parvans</u>:

 2 1 r 2 lr ,2 r 1 2 1 r 2
<u>sci</u>: vrsabhas tvastā vrtrena sacīpatir annena

 1 2 1r 2 lr r
 gayah prthivyā srniko 'gninā visvam

 2r 1
 bhūtam a (ĀrG, after 127.1:1)[1]

 2 lr 4 5 4r 5 4 5 4
<u>sce</u>: ime tā 2 3 indra te vayam purustuto

 5
 va (GG 373.3)

 2 lr 1 2
<u>scai</u>: mahe tu na ai 2 hī 2 hī 3 yā (GG 509.1)

 3 2 3r 2
<u>ye</u>: stusā 3 4 i vām ā 3 (GG 178.1)

Therefore the Hāviks use 297 + 4 = 301 notational syllables.

2. They associate different texts with certain
 syllables:

 [2] 1 2 1r r 2 1r
<u>lā</u>: prthivy antariksam dyaurāpah kanikradāt

 2 1r r 2 1 r 2r r 1r
 sindhur āpo maruto mādayantām gharmo

 r
 jyotih (ĀrG, after 92.1:2)[2]

 [1] 2
<u>vī</u>: stā 2 3 mdr 3 4 (GG 243.2)

 7 2
<u>ña</u>: sya yo 2 3 hā 3 yi (GG 472.5)

 2
<u>sau</u>: o 3 2 3 4 5 vā 6 5 6 (GG 388.3)

[1]See VC, p. 112. This is the <u>parvan</u> of Simon's
syllable <u>lā</u>.

[2]See VC, p. 104.

4 2 1 1 1
thū: ho 3 vā 3 4 5 (ĀrG 98.1)

5 4 5
pī: agniṃ vaḥ (GG 21.3)

3. They refer to types tva--tvai as kva--kvai.

4. They place the syllables śca--ścai after saḥ and before ra.

Of the five parvan sources not given by Simon, four have now been identified: śā (GG 255.2), ṣī (GG 469.4), yau (GG 312.1), and hi (ĀrG 98.1). Moreover, the sources he gives for certain parvans should be changed to conform with Nārāyaṇasvāmi's edition of the GG and ĀrG: (1) kī: GG 236.4 to 236.5, (2) ṅe: GG 237[.1] to 237.1,2, (3) tva: GG 484.2 to 483.2, (4) ṣaṃ: GG 565.1,3 to 565.1,2, (5) ṭhai: GG 23.1 to 23.2, (6) phū: GG 22.1 to 22.3.

Three grantha gāna-manuscripts of the India Office make use of this notation: B. 141 (GG and ĀrG), B. 142 (GG and ĀrG), and B. 147 (ŪG, incomplete).[1] Apart from the syllables denoting the melody-types, other notational signs are employed sparingly, as Simon details:[2] (1) long syllables are designated by the bindu (°), placed above the line of text; (2) placed once within the textual line, the bindu denotes the isolated atisvārya; placed twice it designates the secondary number pattern 656 (parisvāra) of the

---

[1]There exist also Rāṇāyanīya manuscripts which use basically the same notation by numerals as South Indian Kauthuma manuscripts (see, for example, India Office manuscripts B. 138 [GG and ĀrG], B. 139 [ŪG], and B. 140 [RG]). For the differences, which are insignificant, see NVL, p. 322. The Hāvik Sāmavedins are familiar with both the numerical and the syllabic systems of notating.

[2]NVL, pp. 324-25.

padānusvāra; (3) additional notational syllables, appearing after the textual syllable to which they refer, symbolize certain ornaments: *a* = *abhigīta*, *an* = *anupadastubdha*,[1] *e* = *praṇata*, *na* = *namana*, *pre* = *preṅkha*, *vi* or *vin* = *vinata*, *ṇa* = *karṣaṇa* (type 2_3), *ṇaṇā* = *parisvāra*; (4) repeated syllables or *parvans* are designated *dviḥ* or *triḥ*. Some further symbols, not found in the manuscripts, are mentioned by the *Sāmalakṣaṇa*:[2] (1) *tra* = *tṛtīyadhāri*,[3] (2) *rtha* = *caturthadhāri*,[4] (3) *ma* = *kruṣṭa* to 2, (4) *mā* = 1 to 3, (5) *mi* = 3 to 5, (6) *mī* = 1 to 5, (7) *mu* = 5 to 1, (8) *mū* = 3 to 1, (9) *me* = 5 to 2, (10) *mai* = 5 to 3, (11) *va* = *atisvārya*, (12) *sthi* or *sthira* = *sthiramātrā*.[5]

Sāmavedic compositional technique

The Rāṇāyanīya notational system results from the technique used in constructing all Sāmavedic melodies, regardless of *śākhā*. Each chant consists of a certain number of standard phrases, part of a repertoire of melodic fragments constituting all of the musical material belonging to a certain style of singing. These phrases recur over and over again, in various patterns, to form the several thousand *sāmans*. This recurrence of melodic formulae is without doubt

---

[1]How this differs from *praṇata* is not clear.

[2]See NVL, p. 325.

[3]The pattern 434? See type *tha*, ibid., p. 342.

[4]The pattern 343? See type *ṭhai*, ibid., p. 340.

[5]Simon, who does not explain the term, refers to type *go*; see ibid., p. 328.

the raison d'être of the division into *parvans*, each of which corresponds to a specific musical phrase or motive. A melody-type is symbolized in the *gānas* by a particular syllable (in the case of the Rāṇāyanīyas), a certain sequence of numerals (in the case of the Kauthumas), or a specific sequence of syllables (in the case of the Jaiminīyas). In the latter two cases it is not the individual numeral or syllable which symbolizes always a specific melody-type; rather it is the arrangement of the numerals or syllables within a *parvan* which determines its musical content. One *sāman* is distinguished from another according to the choices of melody-types made by the "composers," who were perhaps the *ṛṣis* mentioned in the songbooks after the name of each chant. This technique of patchwork composition (centonization) is characteristic also of the ancient Hebrew chant and some of the oldest Gregorian chants, the Tracts. For example, Willi Apel has shown[1] that five Tracts of Holy Saturday, comprising in all sixteen verses and fifty-one phrases, are derived from only eight "standard phrases." If the latter are represented by letters (a--h), the Tracts by Roman numerals (I--V), and the verses by Arabic numerals (1--5), the musical content may be illustrated as follows:[2]

	1	2	3	4	5
I.	a c e (c e)	b c e	b h		

---

[1]*Gregorian Chant* (Bloomington: Indiana University Press, 1958), p. 316.

[2]Based upon the table in ibid. See also p. 319 for Apel's tabulation of the eighteen medieval Tracts in the eighth mode.

	1	2	3	4	5
II.	a d e	b c e	c e h		
III.	a d e	b c e	c e	b c e	e h
IV.	a c e	b c e f	b c e h		
V.	a d e f	b c g h			

The standard phrases a--h may be thought of as corresponding to *parvans* of Sāmavedic chant, but the Sāmavedic repertoire of basic motives and phrases is of course much larger. Several genres of oriental art music stem from a repository of melody types--the Indian *rāga*, the Arabian *maqām*, the Syrian *risqolo*, and so on.

A performance by a Hāvik Sāmaga of two *parvans* with identical notational syllables will illustrate some of the subtleties of Sāmavedic melodic structure. The *parvans* in question, taken from GG 1.1, are each designated in Rāṇāyanīya sources by the syllable *kā*; the Kauthuma numerical notation is *prathama* (1) followed by *dvitīya* (2). The first *parvan* has the *dvitīya* as a secondary number belonging to the sequence *preṅkha*, on the syllable *yā*. The number is in the primary position in the second *parvan*. The correspondence of the Kauthuma numeral notation to the Rāṇāyanīya syllable notation is given first; following this are musical transcriptions of interpretations by Subbarāya Rāmacandra Bhaṭṭa of Āroḷḷi village, North Kannara.

                                                  1
1. / to *kā* yā *pre* yi / = / to yā 2̄ yi /

                o   o   1 r 2r
2. / gṛ *kā* ṇā no ha / = / gṛ ṇā no ha /

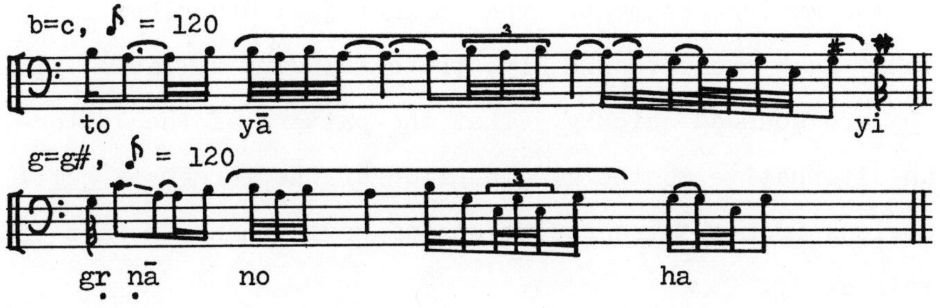

The two *parvans* contain three and four syllables respectively; therefore the short syllable *gṛ* is considered extra and is sung very quickly to a single pitch. It follows that syllable *to* of the first *parvan* corresponds to *ṇā* of the second--thus also *yā* to *no* and *yi* to *ha*. Syllable *ṇā* is sung somewhat differently from its counterpart, a variation due no doubt to the presence of the *bindu*. Likewise, the *preṅkha* syllable *yā* is seen to be more lengthened than the corresponding *no* of the second *parvan*. Clearly the former is divided into three parts according to the tonal scheme a-a-g. We have seen[1] that *preṅkha* consists of three *mātrās*, so the divisions are probably indications of this fact. The syllable *no*, on the other hand, is comprised of two parts (a-g), the number of *mātrās* due a long syllable. Therefore, though the two syllables are made up of the same tone material, one is more elongated (by one *mātrā*) than the other. I remember vividly a conversation with two Hāvik Sāmavedins, who cautioned that, although *parvans* of the same syllable-type are generally sung alike, certain "sub-combinations" (such as *preṅkha*, *namana*, *karṣaṇa*, and *abhigīta*) may slightly

[1]See above, p. 66.

alter the musical content. The variant just described is probably such a case. Finally, the concluding syllables *yi* and *ha* are sounded quickly. That the pattern of the latter is an alternative to the single pitch of the former (a *gati*) is obvious from the transcriptions of Hāvik chant in Part III of this study.

Tone material and sequences

Hāvik chanters sing their melodies to a six-tone gamut with an ambitus of a minor seventh. This is the range also of the Tanjore Kauthumins, though the intervallic relationships differ.

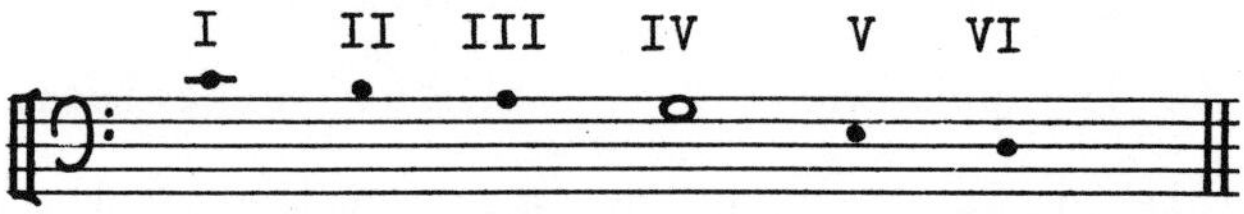

The Hāvik Gamut

Tone IV functions as a central pitch, and the second below it (the note F) is assiduously avoided. Tone II is hardly ever held for long durations; tone VI occurs occasionally, mainly in connection with the sequence *padānusvāra*. A glide from tone I to tone III is one of the most common features of the Hāvik style. Tones III, IV, and V are by far the principal pitches, as the sequence transcriptions below indicate. The latter are taken from recitals of three Hāvik chanters:

A = Subbarāya Rāmacandra Bhaṭṭa (Āroḷḷi)

B = Subbarāya Parameśvaran Bhaṭṭa Agni (Hadinbal)

C = Śiva Rāmacandra Bhaṭṭa (Āroḷḷi)

Principal tone patterns are indicated by Roman numerals corresponding to the pitches of the gamut.

1. <u>Pratyutkrama</u> (type 2_1): IV-III

A (GG 34.1--<u>ghi</u>)
g=e, ♪ = 120

A (GG 235.1--<u>ghu</u>)
g=f, ♪ = 120

2. <u>Pratyutkrama</u> (type 4_3): IV-V-III-IV

B (GG 282.2--<u>ha</u>)
g=g, ♪ = 100

B (GG 337.1,2--<u>hā</u>)
g=g, ♪ = 100

B (ĀrG 98.1--<u>hi</u>)
g=g, ♪ = 100

3. <u>Atikrama</u> (type 3_5): IV-V

B (GG 35.4--<u>the</u>)
e=e, ♪ = 100

4. <u>Atikrama</u> (type 1_5): III-IV

A (ĀrG 103.1--<u>gai</u>)
b=c, ♪ = 120

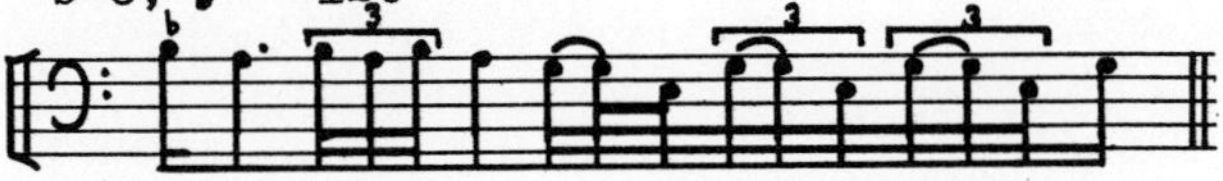

5. <u>Atikrama</u> (type 5_2): IV-V-III-IV

B (GG 554.2--<u>thai</u>)
g=g, ♪ = 100

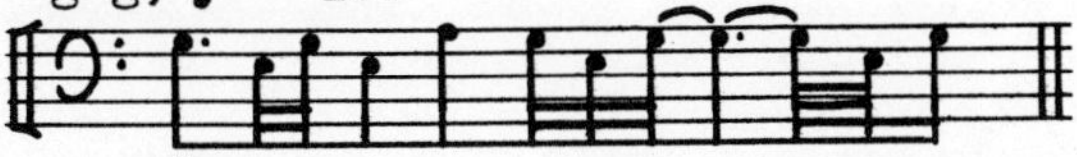

6. <u>Karṣaṇa</u> (type $1_2^{\wedge}$): III-IV

A (GG 1.1)
a=b♭, ♪ = 120

C (GG 222.1)
b=c#, ♪ = 120

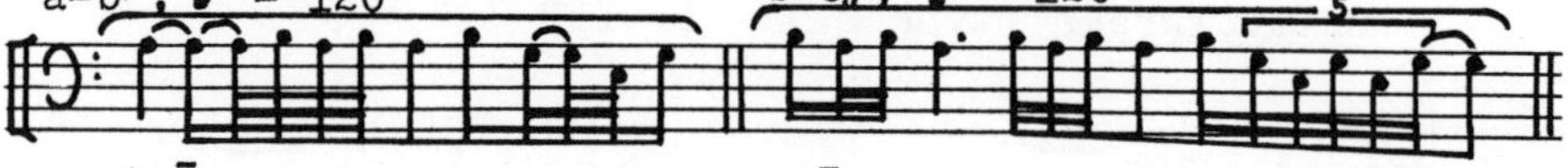

tsā syā

7. <u>Karṣaṇa</u> (type 1_{23}): III-(II)-IV

A (GG 1.2--<u>kah</u>)
b=b♭, ♪ = 120

A (GG 5.2--<u>kha</u>)
a=a, ♪ = 120

tā nā

A (GG 1.3--<u>vi</u>)
b=a, ♪ = 120

tsā

8. <u>Karṣaṇa</u> (type 1_{234}): III-(II)-IV-V

A (GG 236.5--<u>kī</u>)
b=b♭, ♪ = 120

A (GG 1.3--<u>kū</u>)
b=b, ♪ = 120

tā hā

B (GG 181.1--<u>chai</u>)
b=g#, ♪ = 100

trā

9. Karṣaṇa (type 2_{34}): V-VI-V

A (GG 44.3--kham) g=f, ♪ = 120 — A (GG 391.2--ghau) g=f, ♪ = 120

10. Karṣaṇa (type 2_{345}): IV-V

B (GG 5.2--cu) e=c, ♪ = 100 — B (GG 469.4--sī) g=f, ♪ = 100

11. Karṣaṇa/Pratyutkrama (type 3_{234}): V-IV-V

A (GG 1.1) g=g#, ♪ = 120 — B (GG 1.1--ṭū) e=f#, ♪ =100

C (GG 222.1) g=a, ♪ = 120

12. Karṣaṇa/Pratyutkrama (type 3_{2345}): V-IV

A (GG 128.2--gi) g=g, ♪ = 120 — A (GG 171.1--vai) g=e♭, ♪ = 120

13. <u>Karṣaṇa</u> (type 5_6): V

B (GG 21.2--<u>pā</u>) e=f#, 𝅘𝅥𝅯 = 100
B (GG 95.1--<u>ṭi</u>) e=eb, 𝅘𝅥𝅯 = 100̣
C (GG 222.1) e=f#, 𝅘𝅥𝅯 = 120

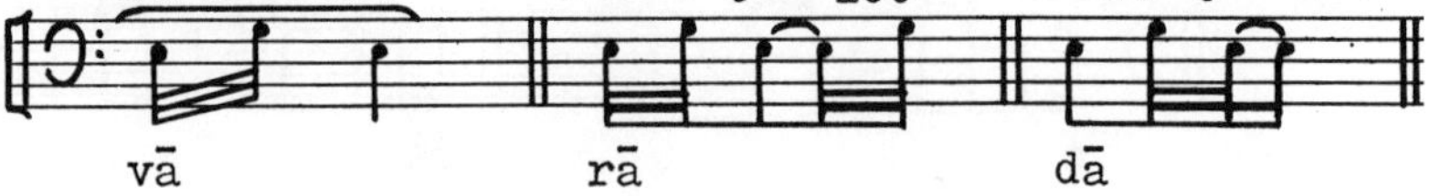

14. <u>Namana</u> (S_3): III-(II)-IV

A (GG 390.3--<u>khī</u>) a=a, 𝅘𝅥𝅯 = 120
A (GG 237.6--<u>khe</u>) a=a, 𝅘𝅥𝅯 = 120

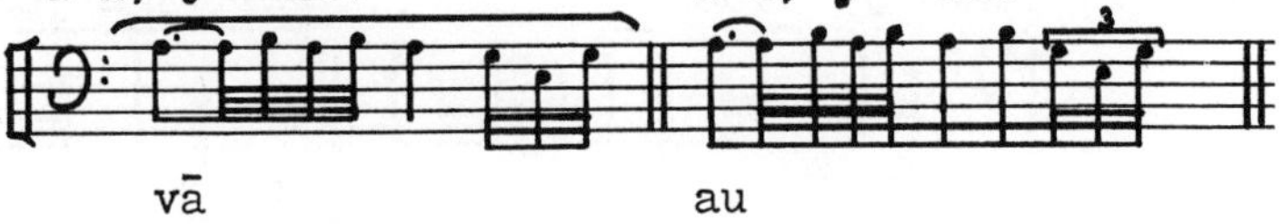

A (GG 323.3--<u>kho</u>) a=a, 𝅘𝅥𝅯 = 120
B (GG 166.2--<u>ñaḥ</u> c=a, 𝅘𝅥𝅯 = 100

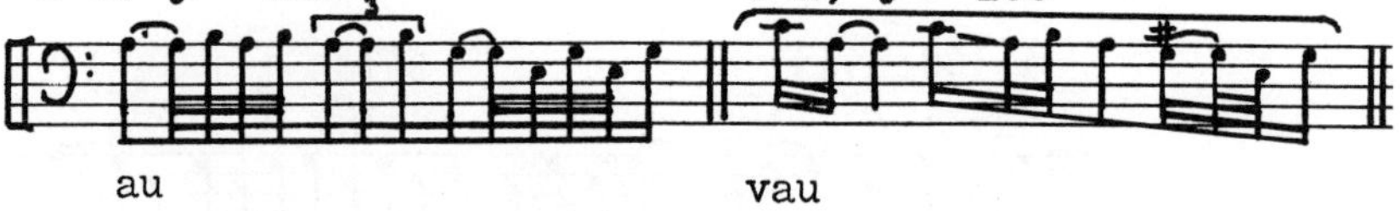

B (GG 312.1--<u>yau</u>) b=b, 𝅘𝅥𝅯 = 100

15. <u>Preṅkha</u> (1_3): III-IV

A (GG 1.1) b=c, 𝅘𝅥𝅯 = 120

A (GG 1.1) b=c, 𝅘𝅥𝅯 = 120

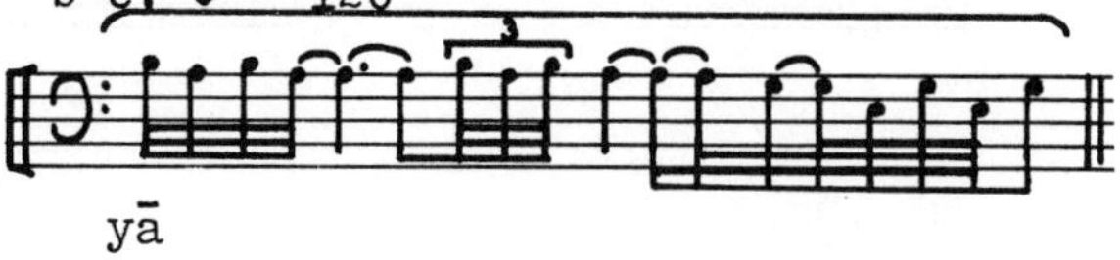

C (Gāyatram)
a=b, ♪ = 112

C (GG 222.1)
b=c#, ♪ = 120

16. <u>Svāra</u> (type 1^{111}_{2345}): III-(I)-IV-V-III-IV

A (ĀrG 57.1--<u>ṅau</u>)
a=g, ♪ = 100

B (ĀrG 63.1--<u>jha</u>)
b=g#, ♪ = 100

B (ĀrG 63.2--<u>sā</u>)
b=a, ♪ = 100

17. <u>Svāra</u> (type 2^{111}_{345}): V-IV-V-IV-III

A (ĀrG 57.1)
g=g#, ♪ = 120

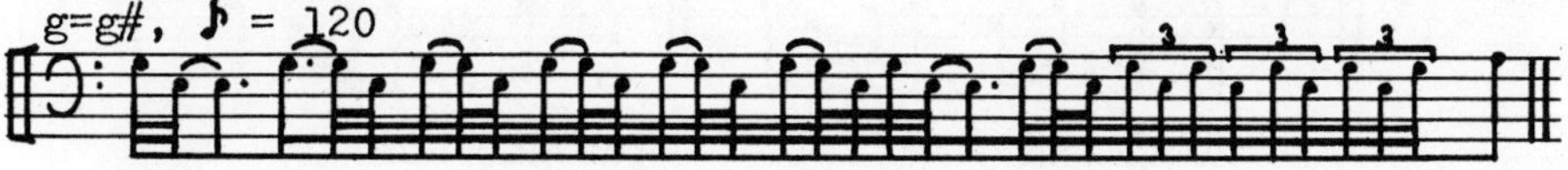

A (ĀrG 57.1)
g=g#, ♪ = 120

18. <u>Svāra</u> (type 3_{2345}^{111}): (III)-IV-V-IV-III

A (GG 1.2)
b=c#, ♪ = 120

A (ĀrG 156.7--<u>ṅū</u>)
a=g, ♪ = 120

B (GG 122.1--<u>jū</u>)
e=c#, ♪ = 100

19. <u>Padānusvāra</u> (5_{656}): VI-V-IV

A (GG 128.2--<u>gi</u>)
d=d, ♪ = 120

A (GG 171.1--<u>vai</u>)
d=b♭, ♪ = 120

B (GG 335.1,2--<u>cū</u>)
d=b♭, ♪ = 100

B (GG 21.2--<u>chī</u>)
e=c, ♪ = 100

B (GG 469.4--<u>ṣī</u>)
d=c, ♪ = 100

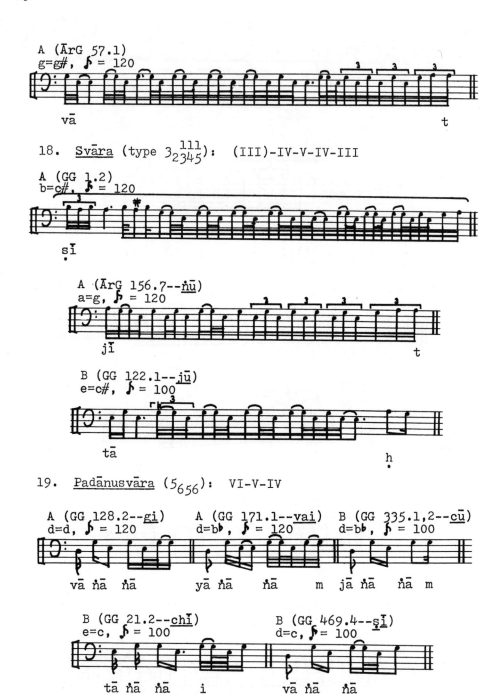

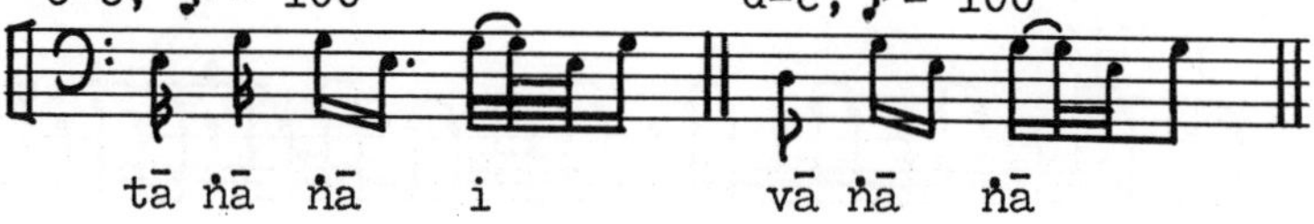

20. <u>Vinata</u> (type $1Sr_2$): I-III-IV

A (GG 237.1,2--<u>ṅe</u>) c=b♭, ♪ = 120 A (GG 540.2--<u>ṅaṃ</u>) c=b♭, ♪ = 120

ye dre

A (GG 584.2--<u>kvā</u>) c=a♭, ♪ = 120 B (GG 171.1--<u>jau</u>) c=a, ♪ = 100 B (GG 565.1--<u>jaṃ</u>) c=a, ♪ = 100

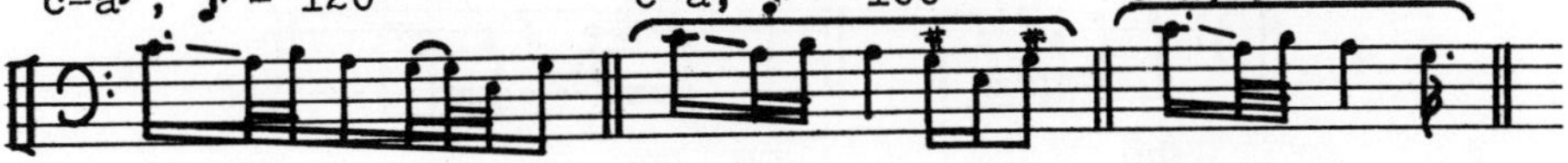

yā me dā

B (GG 565.2--<u>jhā</u>) d=b, ♪ = 100

yo

21. <u>Praṇata</u> (2_3 or $\hat{2}_3$): (III)-IV

A (GG 1.1) a=b♭, ♪ = 120 A (GG 1.2) e=f#, ♪ = 120

hī rhī

A (GG 1.3) a=b, ♪ = 120 C (GG 222.1) a=b, ♪ = 120

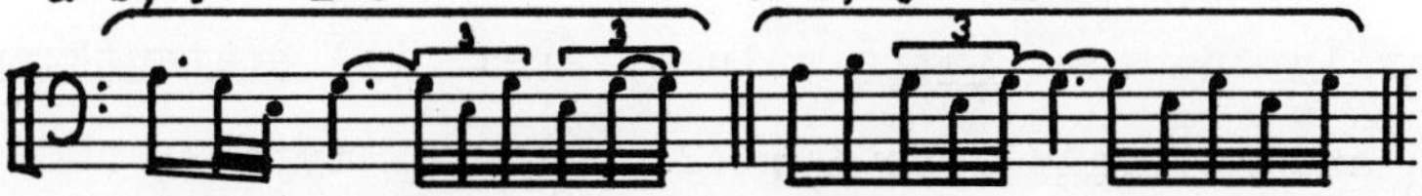

bā mā

C (GG 222.1) e=f#, ♪ = 120

e

22. *Utsvarita* (4_5): IV-V-VI

A (GG 1.3) g=a, ♪ = 120 — B (GG 335.1,2--*cū*) g=e♭, ♪ = 100

vā — vā

B (GG 4.3--*ti*) g=g, ♪ = 100 — B (GG 45.3--*phe*) g=b♭, ♪ = 100

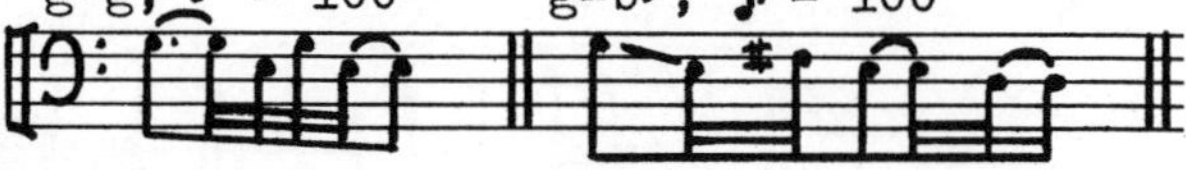

ho — me

23. *Abhigīta* (7): (I)-III-I-III

B (GG 130.1--*jhau*) c=a, ♪ = 100 — B (GG 124.2--*jhaṃ*) g=e, ♪ = 100

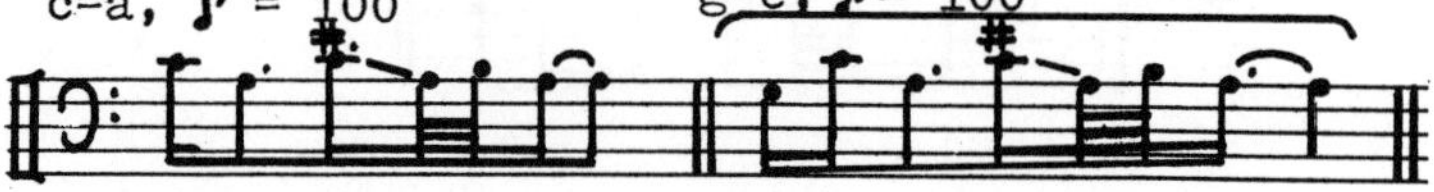

i — ra

B (GG 469.4--*ña*) g=e, ♪ = 100

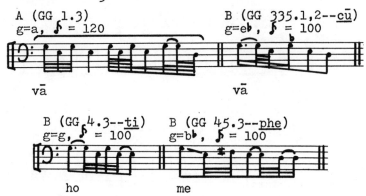

tsa

Sequences with identical tonal patterns, though not necessarily the same *mātrā* values, are: (1) *pratyutkrama* type 4_3 and *atikrama* type 5_2; (2) *atikrama* type 3_5 and *karṣaṇa* type 2_{345}; (3) *atikrama* type 1_5, *karṣaṇa* type $1_{\hat{2}}$, *preṅkha*, and *praṇata*; (4) *karṣaṇa* type 1_{23} and *namana*; (5) *karṣaṇa* type 2_{34} and *karṣaṇa*/*pratyutkrama* type 3_{234}. Each appearance of the *atisvārya* signals a nasalization, resembling the guttural nasal *ṅ*. In the case of *padānusvāra*, this nasal is sung to the vowel of the preceding syllable. Therefore [5] vā 6 5 6 (from GG 128.2) is sung as (omitting the notation) vā ṅā ṅā. In the case of karṣaṇa type 5_6, the nasal attaches likewise to the preceding vowel, but in this instance it is heard only once. Thus agniṃ⁵ vā 6 e⁵ (from GG 21.2) is sung agniṃ vāṅ e (or agniṃ vā ṅe). The Hāviks chant the hiṃkāra as him instead of hum, and to-i is sung as to-yi. Finally, they employ the same mudrās as the Tanjore Kauthumas.

The Composite Style of North Arcot

The "ka-ca-ṭa" notation

Our knowledge of the so-called old (prācīna) school of sāman-singing is based upon a single tape recording taken from Śrī Muḷḷantiram Rāmanātha Dīkṣitar (Muḷḷantiram village, North Arcot District, Tamilnāṭu) by Mr. T. K. Rājagopāla Aiyar (former Accountant General, Madras--now deceased). The original tape has since disappeared, but, fortunately for Sāmavedic research, a copy had been given to Staal,[1] who has graciously presented me with a duplicate. The North Arcot style is termed "old" because of the use there of a syllable notation which is believed to have been employed in the South long before the introduction, from the North, of notating by numerals. Thus the Tanjore Kauthumins, who follow strictly the numeral notation, are said to be exponents

[1]See NVR, p. 97.

of the "new school." The reason for the supplantation of the old syllable notation ("ka-ca-ṭa," as it is called) is detailed in a seminar address by the same Mr. Rājagopāla Aiyar; his important remarks will be quoted at some length:

> The defect of the Ka, Ca, Ṭa notation is that in the absence of guidance of a qualified teacher, the student following the written text is apt to pronounce the Ka, Ca, Ṭa letters as part of the song, with disastrous results to the rhythm and sense of the chants . . . . This defect was realised by the late Krishnaswami Śrauti of Tiruvaiyāru who therefore undertook a journey to Poona and copied out the whole of the Sāman texts available with the Chandogas of that city with the notation 1, 2, 3, came back to Tiruvaiyāru and printed them in Grantha characters. . . . [Then] he came to Kumbhakonam to obtain the approval of his late Holiness Śaṅkarācārya of Kāmakoṭi Pīṭham. . . . [But] it was decided that the Poona method cut up and dissected the musical phrases beyond all recognition and was therefore useless. However the printed book prevailed in the Southern districts, thanks to the inertia of the Pāṭhaśālā authorities, who found it much easier to buy the printed book than to make cadjan leaf copies of the authorised manuscripts in the old laborious way. Only the North Arcot and Kāñcīpuram Pāṭhaśālās seem to have resisted the invasion of the printed book and adhered to the genuine prācīna school.[1]

Raghavan, addressing the same seminar, noted that the Jaiminīyas also employ a syllable notation; he called for an investigation to determine "if in this older style of Muḷḷanṭiram . . . there was not really the survival of the Jaiminīya school of Samaveda."[2] However, Staal has shown[3] that this is not likely, for both text and parvan division of the Muḷḷanṭiram chant correspond to the Kauthuma-Rāṇāyaṇīya recension. But even of greater significance is that the "ka-ca-ṭa" notation is no different from the syllable notation of the Rāṇāyanīyas, a fact which has not heretofore

---

[1]PVC, p. 67. [2]Ibid., p. 56. [3]See NVR, p. 67.

been recognized. It is true that the syllables ka, ca, and ṭa are the initial three symbols in lists of the Jaiminīya svarabhedas;[1] but they also are names of the first three of the five vargas, according to which the Rāṇāyanīya notational syllables are classified.[2] In Jaiminīya manuscripts the syllables are written either above or below the line of text--or else they may be confined to "notational parvans"; but the Rāṇāyanīya symbols are mixed up with the syllables of the text, and thus it is explained how some of this non-textual material intruded into the recitals of some inexpert singers.

The stylistic dichotomy

Yet the most surprising feature of North Arcot Sāmaveda is the employment of two different styles in singing the chants of the Pūrvagāna (GG and ĀrG) and the Uttaragāna (ŪG and RG). The style of the former is the same as that of the Hāvik Rāṇāyanīyas, but the chants of the Uttaragāna are sung in the fashion of the Tanjore Kauthumins.[3] Such a mixture is perhaps the continuation of a very old trait. In the past the differences between the rūpāntara and svarūpa forms of Sāmaveda may have been greater than previously realized; such differences perhaps extended even to the use

---

[1]See below, pp. 148-49. [2]See above, pp. 116-17.

[3]See the transcriptions in Part III of GG 1.1 and the Gāyatram (which properly belongs to the Uttaragāna) as performed by Muḷḷaṇṭiram Rāmanātha Dīkṣitar. The peculiar way in which the Hāviks intone the atisvārya (see above, p. 133) is reflected also in North Arcot renderings of Pūrvagāna chants (see, for an example, NVR, p. 67).

of different scales and dissimilar styles of singing. It is probable that the Kauthumas and Rāṇāyanīyas in South India belong in fact to the same school--Rāṇāyanīya. They both name the Drāhyāyaṇa Śrautasūtra, a Rāṇāyanīya text, as their ritualistic authority, and there is uncertainty among some "Kauthumins" as to their true śākhā.[1] It is possible that true Kauthumins are to be found only in North India, where Kauthuma texts such as the Lāṭyāyana Śrautasūtra and Gobhila Gṛhyasūtra are followed exclusively. The problem should be investigated further in the villages where the South Indian prācīna style is said to survive: Aḍayappalam, Anakkāvūr, Perumāḷkoil, Panayūr, and Paranūr.[2]

Rāṇāyanīya from Gujarāt and Tirunelveli

Gurjarapāṭha

Brief mention must be made of two Rāṇāyanīya communities in Andhra Pradesh. I am very grateful to Dr. E. R. Sreekrishna Sarma (Tirupati) for sharing with me some of his recordings of these two styles of singing. Members of one of the communities (from the village Vijayanagaram) refer to their chant as "Gurjarapāṭha," that is, emanating from Gujarāt State in Northwest India. Raghavan was no doubt

---

[1]See, for example, NVR, p. 19, n. 38, where Staal quotes a Sāmavedin from North Arcot: "The name of my śākhā is not quite certain; it may be either Rāṇāyanīya or Kauthuma. For one thing, the name Kauthuma is quite new to me and my family." I recorded several South Indian Sāmagas who gave Gautama as their śākhā but whose recitals were no different from those of singers calling themselves Kauthumas. Gautama is a sub-school of the Rāṇāyanīya śākhā. See Renou, *Écoles védiques*, p. 89.

[2]PVC, p. 55.

referring to these Rāṇāyanīyas when he wrote of "the tradition here [in Andhra] among some Sāmavedins of Simhācala that their ancestors seven generations ago went to Surat, learnt, and brought back Sāma-gāna."[1] Musically, their productions utilize four tones with the intervallic relationships of the four pitches used by North Indian Kauthumins.[2] The major difference is that the lowest pitch is very seldom sounded (in the Kauthuma chant it is the highest tone that is least heard), so here too the range is mainly a minor third. The sequences as a rule differ tonally from those of the Kauthumas. If the four pitches are designated (I)-II-III-(IV) in descending order, then the sequences of the first three chants of the GG comprise the following tonal material:

1. Pratyutkrama (type 2_1):	III-II
2. Karṣaṇa (type $1_{\hat{2}}$):	II
3. Karṣaṇa (type 1_{23}):	II-III
4. Karṣaṇa (type 1_{234}):	II-III
5. Karṣaṇa/Pratyutkrama (type 3_{234}):	III-II
6. Karṣaṇa (type 5_6):	II-III
7. Preṅkha ($1_{\bar{2}}$):	II-III
8. Svāra (type 3_{2345}^{111}):	II-III-II
9. Praṇata (2_3 or $2_{\hat{3}}$):	III
10. Utsvarita (4_5):	(III)-II-III

Therefore the two middle tones are the only ones held for

---

[1] Ibid., p. 53. [2] See above, p. 92.

long durations in these particular chants; this Rāṇāyanīya style is seen to comprise the smallest compass of any method of singing discussed thus far.

The Tirunělveli style

A second Andhra Rāṇāyanīya community[1] consists of Brāhmaṇs with ancestral roots in the Tirunělveli District of Tamilnāṭu. Their scale is the gamut of the Tanjore Kauthumins (minus tone V), and the styles are also rather similar. But there are some traits which remind us as well of the Hāvik chant: (1) the disjunct scalar feature, (2) the frequent rapid alternation of the central tone with the lower minor third, and (3) the nasalization associated with the atisvārya (for example, in the final parvan of GG 1.3). A Rāṇāyanīya paṇḍit who has sung for the Deccan College Postgraduate and Research Institute, Lakṣmaṇa Śaṅkara Bhaṭṭa Drāviḍa, has attempted to explain the modus operandi of this style of chanting in an article entitled "The Mode of Singing Sāma Gāna."[2] But this is nothing more than a reiteration of the mistaken concept that the six numerals of the notation correspond to the svaras of secular music. His theory is made all the more implausible by the assertion that the numerals stand for different tones in different sāmans, a conjecture which is in no way substantiated by any of the oral traditions.

---

[1]The paṇḍits on Sreekrishna Sarma's recording are from the village Sītānagaram.

[2]The Poona Orientalist 4 (April-July, 1939): 1-21. The author's grandfather resided in Tirunělveli District. See also Apte, "Sound-Records of Sāmagāna," pp. 305-14.

PART II

THE JAIMINĪYA SCHOOL

CHAPTER 3

THE SYLLABLE NOTATION

The Consonant Symbols

As already stated,[1] the tradition of members of the third extant Sāmavedic school, Jaiminīya, is quite distinct from that of the Kauthumas and Rāṇāyanīyas. One of the most striking differences is the acquaintance of some Jaiminīyas with a syllable notation which on first examination appears to have little connection with either the numeral notation of the Kauthumas or the syllable notation of the Rāṇāyanīyas.

The principles of the Jaiminīya notation are set forth in the introduction to Sabhāpati's Dhāraṇalakṣaṇa, a work which has yet to be published or translated.[2] We know, however, that it lists thirty-three _svarabhedas_ ("_svara_ types") and describes the hand movements associated with each. A second listing, which excludes the hand move-

---

[1]See above, pp. 10-14.

[2]"Unfortunately the text is rather difficult, and my manuscripts of it incomplete," Parpola writes in a letter of 2/II/73.

ments, is found in the Sāmalakṣaṇa, a small treatise which merely records the *svarabhedas* in *grantha* and Tamiḻ.[1]

The system of Kŏṭuntiṟappuḷḷi

In the absence of a detailed study of the Dhāraṇa-lakṣaṇa, I have acquired from Śrī K. N. Sahasranāma Aiyar of Kŏṭuntiṟappuḷḷi village a list of the *svara* symbols and descriptions of the respective hand indications (*kai-lakṣaṇas*). He lists sixteen syllables representing single *svaras*, sixteen representing double or combined *svaras*. These are presented in table 8 in the order supplied to me; three additional symbols not connected with *svara* are explained at the end.

TABLE 8

JAIMINĪYA SVARABHEDAS AND KAI-LAKṢAṆAS

A. Single Svaras

	Grantha Symbol	Svara Name	Kai-Lakṣaṇa
1.	𑌕 (*ka*)	*avaroha*	The thumb touches the lower end of the ring finger.
2.	𑌖 (*kha*)	*anvaṅgulya*	The thumb touches in turn the middle portions of the middle finger, ring finger, and little finger.

[1]Both Dhāranalaksana and Sāmalaksana are preserved on paper in the Burnell collection of the India Office Library (Burnell manuscripts 497c-d [Keith 4326 and 4339]).

TABLE 8--*Continued*

Grantha Symbol		Svara Name	Kai-Lakṣaṇa
3.	ச (*ca*)	*udgama*	The thumb touches the middle portion of the ring finger and is then thrown upwards.
4.	ட (*ṭa*)	*yāna*	The hand is held sideways (thumb on top) and is then cast downwards towards the singer's right.
5.	ண (*ṇa*)	*ṇa-svara*	The thumb touches the lower end of the ring finger, then slowly moves upward until it reaches the tip.
6.	த (*ta*)	*āvarta*	The hand, with fingers stretched, is held so that the palm faces the floor. The fingers are then brought together, forming a fist. The fist is rotated so that the back of the hand now faces the floor. The fingers are again stretched outwards, and the hand is cast towards the floor.
7.	ഥ (*tha*)	*uttāna*	The hand, with fingers stretched, is held so that the back portion faces the floor. The fingers are then brought together forming a fist.

TABLE 8--Continued

Grantha Symbol	Svara Name	Kai-Lakṣaṇa
7. (continued)		The fist is rotated so that the back of the hand now faces upwards. The fingers are moved slowly in an upward direction (like an abhaya hasta) so that they resemble a serpent's hood.
8.  (pa)	kṣepaṇa	The fist is held sideways (thumb on top) and the fingers are thrown outwards.
9.  (pha)	pha-svara	The thumb touches the lower end of the ring finger and slowly moves upward until it reaches the tip. Then it moves back downward. (In ṇa-svara the thumb action is only in the upward direction.)
10.  (bha)	mardana	The hand, with fingers stretched, is held so that the palm faces upwards. It is moved in this position to the right. Then it is rotated so that the palm now faces the floor. The hand is moved to the left (to the original position) and then pushed (palm still facing downwards) towards the floor.

TABLE 8--Continued

Grantha Symbol		Svara Name	Kai-Lakṣaṇa
11. 	(ya)	marśana	The hand is held, palm upwards, with fingers slightly bent. Then the thumb slowly moves across the tips, beginning with the index finger.
12. 	(sa)	tarjanī-marśana	The hand is held, palm upwards, with bent index finger. The thumb touches the right side of this finger, near its tip, and then moves slowly to the left side. This action is similar to marśana, but here only the index finger is used.
13. 	(pla)	pla-svara	The thumb touches the lower end of the little finger, moves quickly up its length, over the tips of the remaining fingers, and down the length of the index finger.
14. 	(ṅa)	ṅa-svara	Same as for ṇa-svara but with quicker movement.
15. 	(tra)	tra-svara	The hand is held with palm facing the floor; then the ṇa-svara action occurs.
16. 	(kru)	kruṣṭa	The hand is held sideways (thumb on

TABLE 8--Continued

Grantha Symbol	Svara Name	Kai-Lakṣaṇa
16. (continued)		top). The fingers are drawn inwards, except for the index finger. This finger is moved upwards, then downwards.

B. Double or Combined Svaras

17.	 (ga)	avarohakṣepaṇa	(1 + 8)
18.	 (gha)	yānamarśana	(4 + 11)
19.	 (cha)	udgamottāna	(3 + 7)
20.	 (ja)	avarohamarśana	(1 + 11)
21.	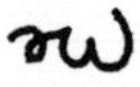 (jha)	āvartakṣepaṇa	(6 + 8)
22.	 (ṭha)	avarohottāna	(1 + 7)
23.	 (ḍa)	udgamakṣepaṇa	(3 + 8)
24.	 (ḍha)	āvartamarśana	(6 + 11)
25.	 (da)	udgamamarśana	(3 + 11)
26.	 (dha)	kṣepanamarśana	(8 + 11)
27.	 (la)	avarohayāna	(1 + 4)
28.	 (na)	yānānvaṅgulya	(4 + 2)
29.	 (va)	avarohāvarta	(1 + 6)

TABLE 8--*Continued*

	Grantha Symbol	Svara Name	Kai-Lakṣaṇa
30.	 (*ha*)	*udgamayāna*	(3 + 4)
31.	 (*ḷa*)	*udgamāvarta*	(3 + 6)
32.	 (*ba*)	*yānakṣepaṇa*	(4 + 8)
33.	 (*śa*)	Denotes absence of *svara* and occurs always *after* a *svara* symbol.	
34.	 (*ṣa*)	Denotes absence of *svara* and occurs always *before* a *svara* symbol.	
35.	 (*ra*)	Denotes, by combination with one of the vowels (a procedure explained below), the number of syllables in a notational *parvan*, in which it appears as the last symbol.	

Śrī Sahasranāma Aiyar[1] emphasizes that "there is some slight deviation in showing the kailakshana in [numbers] 3, 9, 13, [and] 14 as regards duration (timekeeping), but [this is] impossible to explain in writing or drawing."[2] Clearly motion pictures of the movements should be taken as the chants are being sung; this should be done not only at Kŏṭuntiṟappuḷḷi but also at other Jaiminīya centers in South India.

The order given by the Dhāraṇalakṣaṇa

The Kŏṭuntiṟappuḷḷi Vaidikas are in possession of a

---

[1]See above, p. 142. [2]Letter to me of 18/XI/71.

second listing which gives a different order and assigns to some syllables different names. Here the arrangement is primarily according to speech sounds: surd unaspirates, sonant unaspirates, sonant aspirates, surd aspirates--with the nasals, semivowels, ligatures, *ha*, *ḷa*, and *sa* at the end. A notable exception is the placement of *ya* (*marśana*) in sixth position, after *pa* (*kṣepaṇa*). *Svara* names in this second listing which differ from those of the first listing are given in parentheses after the symbol.

1.	*ka*	surd unaspirates
2.	*ca*	
3.	*ṭa*	
4.	*ta*	
5.	*pa*	
6.	*ya*	
7.	*ga*	sonant unaspirates
8.	*ja*	
9.	*ḍa*	
10.	*da*	
11.	*ba*	
12.	*gha*	sonant aspirates
13.	*jha*	
14.	*ḍha*	
15.	*dha*	
16.	*bha*	
17.	*kha*	surd aspirates
18.	*cha*	

19. ṭha
20. tha (kevalottāna)
21. pha (madhyamāṅgulya)
22. pla (anāmikāvaroha)
23. ṅa (kaniṣṭhikodgama)
24. ṇa (anāmikodgama)
25. [ña (kaniṣṭhāyās samudgatya-anvaṅguli-mardana)]
26. na
27. la
28. va
29. ha
30. ḷa
31. kru
32. sa
33. tra (kaniṣṭhikābhimarśa[na])

(Items 19–21 are bracketed together; items 22–33 are bracketed together and labelled "others".)

According to Parpola,[1] this last arrangement is evidently the traditional one, for it is used by both the Dhāraṇalakṣaṇa and the Sāmalakṣaṇa. He points out that these two works employ an additional syllable, ña (placed after ṇa), which is not found in either of the lists supplied to me. But in practice "it would indeed be strange if this akṣara was left unused when new ones had to be created from ligatures."[2]

---

[1] "The Literature and Study of the Jaiminīya Sāmaveda," Studia Orientalia 43, 6 (1973): 19.

[2] Ibid.

The Vowels, Anusvāra, and Visarga

Vowels and signs as number symbols

The consonants and ligatures combine with one of eleven vowels, *anusvāra*, or *visarga* (the latter two always follow the short *a*-vowel). The vowels are thought of in the order in which they occur in the Sanskrit alphabet; *anusvāra* and *visarga* are placed at the end.

1	2	3	4	5	6	7	8	9	10	11	12	13
a	ā	i	ī	u	ū	ṛ	e	ai	o	au	aṃ	aḥ

If, for instance, the consonant *k* were to combine with the short *i*-vowel (the third vowel in the series), then the *avaroha svara* would be intended for three syllables of text--the syllable on which the notational sign appears and the two preceding syllables. This same procedure is followed for all consonants and vowels. To give another example, the consonant *kh* together with the vowel *au* (eleventh in the series) signals the *anvaṅgulya svara* for eleven syllables of text--the syllable on which the sign is found and the ten preceding syllables.

Notational analysis of a Jaiminīya *sāman*

The procedures described above are perhaps best clarified by analyzing the *svara* patterns of a particular chant, the "Viṣṇu *sāman*," based upon JS 1.2.1.11.9. Text and notation are according to a Kŏṭuntiṟappuḷḷi paper manuscript of the JGG.[1]

---

[1]See below, pp. 155-62.

ti ṭā khi ṇa śa
Viṣṇoḥ sāma ca -- i dā me / vi ṣṇu rvi cā krā mā i / trā

ci kā ca yā ṭa ṭāc ya ṭa ta ṭa kha
i dhā ni d dhā i pā dāṃ sa mū ho ḍhā mā / syā pā au ho

śi ta tāc
vā / eṃ su le //

The analysis below takes each notational syllable in turn; the notation of the chant quoted above appears above the line of text.

1. The first notational symbol, ti, indicates the āvarta svara for text syllables i, dā, and me. Likewise:
2. ṭā = yāna for vi and ṣṇu.
3. khi = anvaṅgulya for vi, cā, and krā.
4. ṇa = ṇa-svara for mā.
5. śa = absence of svara for i.
6. ci = udgama for trā, i, and dhā.
7. kā = avaroha for ni and d.
8. ca = udgama for dhā.
9. yā = marśana for i and pā.
10. ṭa = yāna for dāṃ
11. ṭāc = yāna + udgama. Yāna is intended for sa and mū, and udgama is added at the end.
12. ya = marśana for ho.
13. ṭa = yāna for ḍhā.
14. ta = āvarta for mā.
15. ṭa = yāna for syā.
16. kha = anvaṅgulya for pā.
17. śi = absence of svara for au, ho, and vā.

18. ta = āvarta for eṃ.

19. tāc = āvarta + udgama. Āvarta is intended for su and le, and udgama is added at the end.

The above notation for compound svaras is apparently peculiar only to Kŏṭuntiṟappuḷḷi manuscripts. Elsewhere the short a-vowel is added to the second member: thus tā ca instead of tāc.

In most palm leaf manuscripts, notational consonants are sometimes combined with the semivowel y(a). According to the Vaidikas, the latter is merely a substitute for the long ā-vowel: thus tya is the same as tā.

CHAPTER 4

SURVIVALS IN SOUTH INDIA

Jaiminīya Sāmaveda exists only in a very few villages and towns in Tamiḻnāṭu and Keraḷa. From the available literary and epigraphical evidence,[1] we are led to assume that this school probably never existed outside the South. Within this region there are at present two main traditions: (1) that of the Tamiḻ-speaking Brāhmaṇs of Tamiḻnāṭu and Keraḷa and (2) that of the Malayāḷam-speaking Nambūdiri Brāhmaṇs of Keraḷa. The two "have stayed apart in their nucleus areas well over a thousand years," writes Parpola.[2] In his opinion the geographic core of the former "is the Cōla country (with the temples of Chidambaram, Thanjavur and Śrīrangam as the great centres), the communities in Tirunelveli . . . and in Pālghāt representing emigrations from this area."[3]

---

[1]Mahidāsa, commenting on the Caraṇavyūha, writes of Jaiminīyas existing in Karṇātaka. The school is mentioned also in two inscriptions: one from Tirunĕlveli (sixteenth century), the other from the Coḷa country (tenth century). See Renou, Écoles védiques, pp. 127-28.

[2]"Literature of the Jaiminīya Sāmaveda," p. 23.

[3]Ibid.

Tamil-Speaking Jaiminīya Communities

The three centers

Today the best Tamil chanters can be heard at: (1) Kōṭuntiṟappuḷḷi, near Pālghāt, (2) Śrīraṅgam, outside Tiruccirāppaḷḷi, and (3) Tĕntirupperai, near Āḻvārtirunāgari, in Tirunĕlveli District.[1] But everywhere the Jaiminīyas are in dire straits. Only two or three Vaidikas at each of the localities are able to chant substantial portions of the songbooks. Indeed I discovered that hardly anyone nowadays knows more than a few hymns from the JŪG and JRG. Only well-known sāmans like the āmahīyava (JŪG 1.1.1) and rathaṃtara (JRG 1.1.1) are still chanted, and these never according to the ritualistic applications of aniruktagāna or bhakāra-prayoga. By necessity, interest and effort are chiefly in the performance of domestic ceremonies (gṛhya rites), for which only the rūpāntara chants of the JGG and JĀrG are required. With the exception of Śrīraṅgam, where a Jaiminīya vedapāṭhaśālā has recently been established, the traditions are not being passed on to the younger generation; the chances are slim that the Kōṭuntiṟappuḷḷi and Tĕntirupperai styles will survive beyond twenty to thirty years from now--the latter may become ex-

[1]Jaiminīyas were also contacted at Vasiṣṭhapuram, near Tiṭṭaggudi (via Vṛttācalam) in the South Arcot District, and at Kiṭāmaṅgalam, a remote village near Tirupugalūr (Tirukaṇṇapuram, via Nannilam) in the Tanjore District. At the former, a single elderly Vaidika, Mutuveṅkaṭa Ācārya (eighty years old at the time of my visit), is the sole repository of Jaiminīya tradition; he is now too old to chant. At Kiṭāmaṅgalam, Satyamūrti Aiyaṅgār asked me to return at a future date for recordings; I was not able to honor his invitation due to the difficulties in reaching that village.

tinct even sooner.

Chanting in each of the three areas is confined to a very narrow range--the three principal tones are a central pitch, the major second above, and the minor second below. The lower minor third and perfect fourth are sounded occasionally but then only briefly. In some chants the upper minor third is prominent. Stylistically there is notable similarity, though the degree of ornamentation varies from one region and one performer to the next. These features can be observed in the following transcriptions of the first parvan of JGG 1.1 as sung by: (1) T. Rājagopāla Aiyaṅgār (Śrīraṅgam), (2) Tiruveṅkaṭanātha Śarmā (Kŏṭuntiṟappuḷḷi), and (3) Veṅkaṭācala Upādhyāya (Tĕntirupperai).

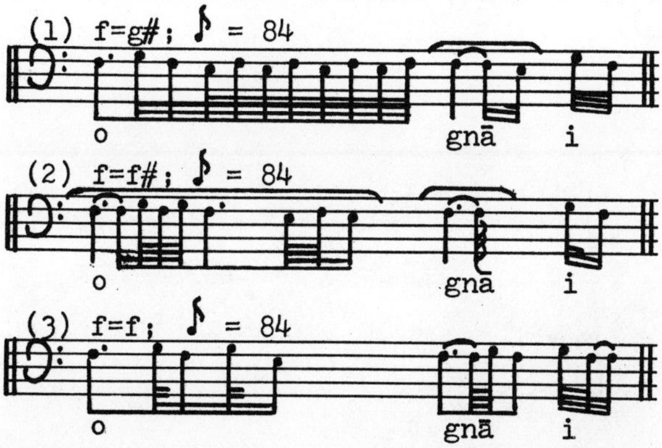

Kŏṭuntiṟappuḷḷi sāmans

The Kŏṭuntiṟappuḷḷi Sāmavedins are Aiyar Brāhmaṇs who speak Tamiḻ but write in the Malayāḷam script. They have kept a meticulous paper manuscript of the JGG--copied from a grantha palm leaf original--in which every textual

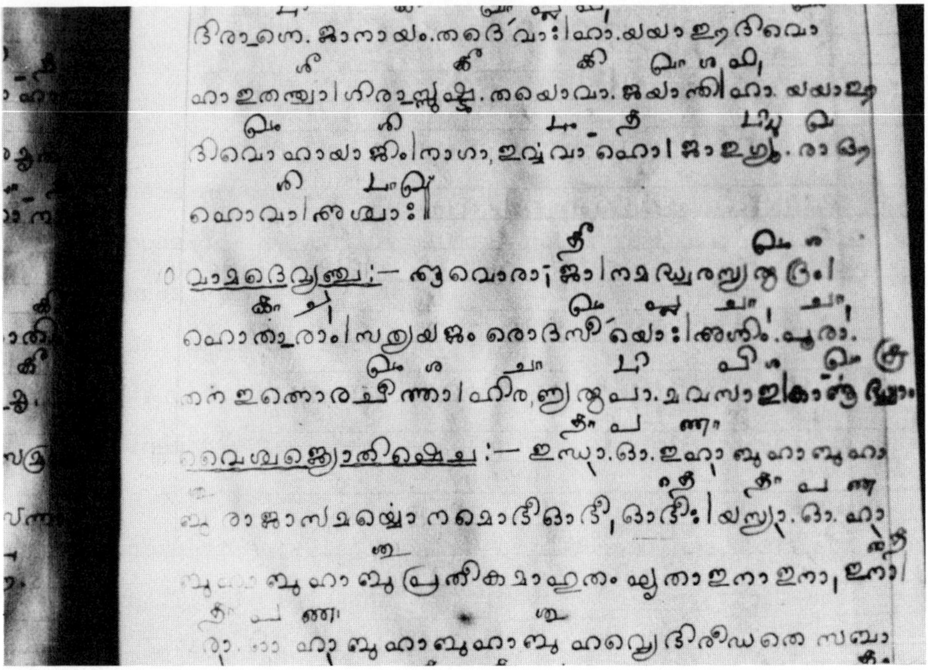

Fig. 19. Page from a Kŏṭuntiṟappuḷḷi paper manuscript of the JGG, showing JGG from JS 1.1.7.7 (vāmadevya).

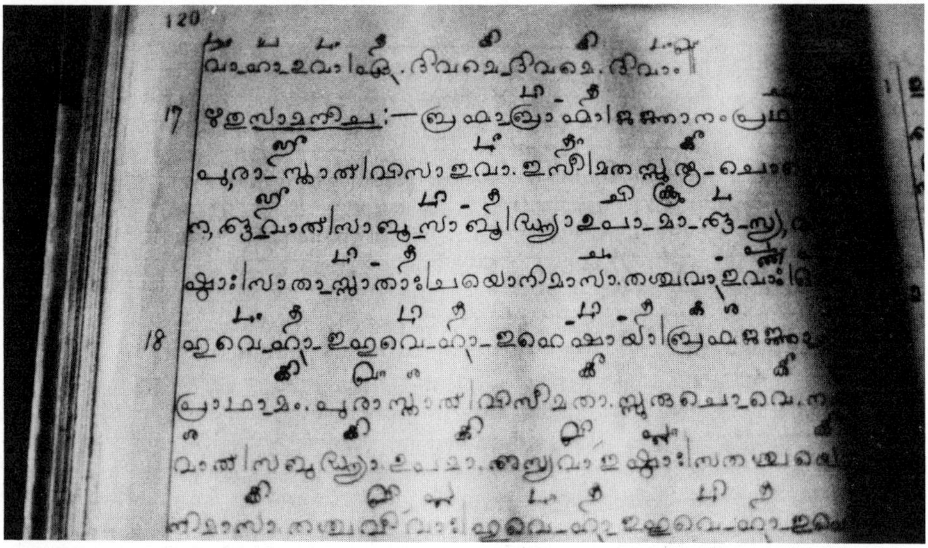

Fig. 20. Page from a Kŏṭuntiṟappuḷḷi paper manuscript of the JGG, showing JGG from JS 1.2.3.1.9 (ṛtu sāmanī).

syllable has been scrupulously accounted for in the notational designations. The text itself is written in Malayāḷam characters, and the notational syllables (in red *grantha* characters) are placed above the text (see figs. 19-20). Because few Jaiminīya *sāmans* have been published with the syllable notation, it will be worthwhile to include several specimens from this manuscript; some additional chants from other *gānas* were kindly copied for me by Śrī Sahasranāma Aiyar.[1] Each *sāman* is preceded by the name (abbreviated) of the *gāna* from which it is taken, the numerical designation of the source verse in the JS, and the *sāman* name.

(1) JGG from JS 1.1.1.1, *gautamasya parkaḥ*: see above, page 13, example 3.

(2) JGG from JS 1.1.1.1, *kaśyapasya barhiṣīyam*: a gna ā

tū sī tū ta śa
yā hi vī / ta yā i gṛ ṇā no ha vya dā tā yā i / ni

cā si tā tā tā khā si
ho tā sa tsī ba rhā i ṣī / ba rhā i ṣā au ho vā /

ca tākh
ba rhī ṣī //

(3) JGG from JS 1.1.1.1, *gautamasya caiva parkaḥ*: a gna

tū ti pūy pa śa
ā yā hi vā i ta yā i / gṛ ṇā no ha vya dā tā ye /

khi na ta tā pa plā sā
ni ho tā sat / sā i bā rhā i ṣo / hā i //

si
(4) JGG from JS 1.1.1.2, *sauparṇam ca*: tva ma gne ya

[1]See above, pp. 142, 147.

tū sa sī
jñā nā ntva ma gnā i / ya jñā nā mho tā vi sve sā

tu tā ka ṭi tā kāc kā ṭa kha
mhā i tāḥ / de vā i bhā i rmā / nu ṣe ja nā au ho

pla plā sa
bā / ho i lā //

(5) JGG from JS 1.1.1.3, vaiśvamanasam cāditya sāma vā:

tī sā tū ta cā
a gnim dū tām / vr ṇī ma hā i ho tā rā mvī sva ve da

sā ṭi ta kā ta ta cā ṭī
sam / a sya yā jñā o au ho vā / syā sū kra i mi lā

khaṇ pa plā
bhā / o i lā //

tī
(6) JGG from JS 1.1.7.7, vāmadevyam ca: ā vo rā jā /

khū sa kā ca
na ma dhva ra sya rū dram / ho tā ram / sa tya ya

khṛ pla cā cā khū
jam ro da sī yoḥ / a gnim pū rā ta na i tno ra cī

sa cā ṭi pi sa khā tra
ttā / hi ra ṇya rū pā ma va sā i / kā rṇū dhvām //

(7) JGG from JS 1.2.1.11.9, viṣṇos sāma ca: see above,
page 151.

tu sa
(8) JGG from JS 1.2.3.1.5, vātsapram: hā bu hā bu hā bu /

kī kī kī kā
o ho ho vā o ho ho vā o ho ho vā / ja gṛ hmā tā i

kī khā sī si si
dā kṣī ṇā min dra ha stam ndra ha stam ndra ha stam /

kā ki khā sī si
va sū ya vo vā sū pā tā i va sū nā mva sū nā mva sū

si kā ki khā sī si
nām / vi dmā hi tvā go pā tī msū ra go nā mra go nā

si ṣi ṭi kā kha
mra go nām / a sma bhyam cā i trā mvā rsā nam ra yin

si si si tu sa
dā ra yin dā ra yin dāḥ / hā bu hā bu hā bu / o ho ho

kī kī ṭiṭ kha si pha
vā o ho ho vā o ho ho vā au ho vā / ī //

ṭi
(9) JGG from JS 1.2.3.1.9, ṛtu sāmanī ca: bra hmā brā

ta cu ka bhī
hmā / ja jñā naṃ pra tha maṃ pu rā stā t / vi sā i

ṭī tā kī thā bhī ṭi
vā i sī / ma ta ssu rū co ve na ā vā t / sā bū sā

ta ci kru ṭa bhī ṭi
bū / dhnyā u pā mā ā sya vā i sṭhāḥ / sā tā ssā

ta cu pun pa plā
tāḥ / ca yo ni ma sā ta sca vā i vāḥ / o i lā //[1]

phā
(10) JGG from JS 1.3.10.3, sauktāni pañca (V.): sa khā

khī sa tu khā sa kā
ya yā u vo vā / ni ṣā i dā tā u vo vā / pu nā nā

kī tā ṭi khā sa
ya pra gā ya tā sā i sā u vo vā / na ya jñai ḥpa ri

tū ṭā khā sa tāc
bhū ṣā tā u vo vā / sri ye //

(11) JĀrG 1.1-2, vācovrate dve (on stobhas):

ki ta kā thā ṭā ta sa
I. hu ve vā cāṃ / vā caṃ vā caṃ hu ve vā k /

cā ṭi ṭā ta sa cā sa ṭā
sṛ ṇo tu sṛ ṇo tu vā gvā k / sa mai tu sa mai tu

ṭā ta sa ki ki ṭā kha si
vā gvā k / ra ma tā mra ma tā mra mā tā au ho vā /

tū
i hā i hā i hā //

II. hu vā i vā cāṃ / vā caṃ hu vā ī vā k / sṛ

---

[1] According to the Kōṭuntirappulli authorities, this sāman is the only chant of the JGG having the kruṣṭa svara.

```
cā sa , cā ka phapl ta sa        cā sa    cā ka
no tu sr no tū vā   gvā k  / sa mai tu sa mai tū

phapl ta sa          ti          khī        si
vā    gvā k  / ra ma tā mra ma tu vā  au ho vā /

            tu sa
mā i vā i mā ī  //
```

(12) JĀrG from JS 1.2.3.1.9, purusavratam nava (IX.):

```
                   ca       kā    pha  pha  pha
hā bu hā bu hā bu / bhā bham bham bham bham bham /

                  tu sa                si
(trih) / hā bu hā bu hā bu / bra hma ja jñā nam pra

             tū  ca sa            sī
tha mam pu rā stā t  / vi sī ma ta ssu ru co ve na

tū ca sa           si            tū    cā
a  vā t  / sa bu dhnyā u pa mā a sya vā i sthāh /

    su       tu  cā
sa ta sca yo ni ma sa ta sca vā i vāh / hā bu hā bu

tu sa     ca       kā    pha  pha  pha          sa
hā bu / bhā bham bham bham bham bham / (trih) / hā

             tū       kā              ku
bu hā bu hā u vā / bra hma de vā nām bhā ti pa ra

         ku sa      kā             ku
me vyo ma n  bra hma de vā nām bhā ti pa ra me vyo

ku sa      kā             ku          tī kha sa
ma n  bra hma de vā nām bhā ti pa ra me vyo mā  n  //
```

(13) from JS 4.3.8, prājāpatyam gāyatram: see below, page 514.

```
                                              tu
(14) JŪG from JS 3.24.9-10, vātsapram: hā bu hā bu hā
sa           kī         kī          kī  ka
bu / o ho ho vā o ho ho vā o ho ho vā / so ma pa vā

tī   kā kha        si        si        si    ca ka
te jā nī tā  ma tī nā mma tī nā mma tī nām / ja ni

        tī    kā kha            si          si
tā dā i vo jā nī tā  pr thi vyā hpr thi vyā hpr
```

si   ca ka ca   sā   ki kha   si
thi vyāḥ / ja ni tā gnā i rjja ni tā sū ri yā syā

si   si   ca ka   ṭi   kā kha
ri yā syā ri yā syā / ja ni te ndrā syā jā nī to ta

si   si   si   tu sa
vi ṣṇo sta vi ṣṇo sta vi ṣṇoḥ / hā bu hā bu hā bu /

kī   kī   ṭiṭ kha   si   kha
o ho ho vā o ho ho vā o ho ho vā au ho vā / ī //

tu sa   kī   kī
hā bu hā bu hā bu / o ho ho vā o ho ho vā o ho

kī   ṭu   kā kha   si
ho vā / bra hmā de vā nā ṃpā dā vī ka vī nā ṃka vī

si   si   ṭu   kā kha   si
nā ṃka vī nāṃ / ṛ ṣi rvi prā ṇā ṃmā hī ṣo mṛ gā ṇā

si   si   ka   ṭī   kā kha
mmṛ gā ṇā mmṛ gā ṇāṃ / sye no gṛ dhrā ṇā ṃsvā dhī tī

si   si   si   ka   tu
rva nā ṇā ṃva nā ṇā ṃva nā nāṃ / so ma pa vā i trā

kā kha   sī   sī   sī
ṃmā tī ye ti ra bha m sti re bha m sti re bha m /

tu sa   kī   kī   ṭiṭṭ
hā bu hā bu hā bu / o ho ho vā o ho ho vā o ho ho

kha   si   kha
vā au ho vā / ī //

(15) JRG from JS 3.4.1-2, <u>agneś ca rathaṃtaraṃ vasiṣṭhasya</u>

kūc   cā sa
<u>vā</u>: o bhi tvā śū ra no nū mo vā / ā du gdhā i va

ṣe   ṣe   tā   tā
dhe na va ī sā na ma sya ja ga taḥ su vā dṛ śāṃ /

thā   pā   sā   ṭāṭṭ   cā   sī
ī sā na mā in drā / tā sthu ṣā o vā hā u vā

ca sa
ā s //

cā sa   sū
ī so vā / nā min dra to sthu ṣo na tvā vaṃ an

kṛ ṭā tā ki pa śa
yo di vyo na pā rthi vāḥ / nā jā to nā jā / nā i

ṭiṭṭ cā kī ca śa
ṣyā tā o vā hā u vā ā s //

cā śa phū
nā jo vā / to na ja ni ṣya te a śvā yan to ma

kṛ ṭi tā kā pā śa
gha vaṅn in dra vā ji nāḥ / ga vyan ta stvā hā / vā

ṭāṭṭ cā kī ca śa
mā hā o vā hā u vā ā s //

(16) JRG from JS 3.15.7-9, bṛhatprājāpatyam bharadvājasya

sī tū ta
vā: au ho i tvā mi ddhi ha vā ma hā e / sā tau vā

kū kha ṇa pā ka thā ka
jā syā kā rā vāḥ / tū vā au ho vā / vṛ trā i ṣu vā

ṭṛ ki kha ṇa pī ka
in drā sā o tpā tīn nā rāḥ / tu vā ṃkā ṣṭhā au ho

thā ṭa pā śī tā ca śa
vā / sū va rvā tā o vā hā u vā hā s //

tu ta cā ka kha ṇa
au ho i tu vā me / kā ṣṭhā sū va rvā ṭāḥ / sa

pā ka thā ṭṛ ki
tvā au ho vā / na ścā i trā vā jrā hā o stā dhṛ

kha ṇa pī ka thā ṭa pā
ṣṇū yā / mā ha sta vā au ho vā / no a drā i vā ho

śa ti ca śa
vā hā u vā hā s //

tu ta cā ka khā ṇā pā
au ho i ma hā e / tā vā no a drā i vāḥ / gā mā

ka thā ṭṛ ki kha
au ho vā / śū vaṃ ra thā yā mā o dhin drā saṃ kā

ṇa ki pa ka thā ṭa pi
rāḥ / sa tra vā jā au ho vā / no jā i gū ṣā dhi

śī ti ca śa
ho vā hā u vā hā s //

Śrīraṅgam sāmans

Twenty-nine chants were recorded from Śrī T. Rājagopāla Aiyaṅgār, an expert interpreter of Śrīraṅgam (originally from the village Togūr, near Grand Amicut in the Tanjore District)[1] and head of the Jaiminīya pāṭhaśālā there. These sāmans were copied for me in grantha by Śrī Rājagopāla himself from his valuable grantha palm leaf manuscripts, which contain one of only two known sources of the Jaiminīya Uttaragāna (JŪG + JRG) with the syllable notation. These sāmans are reproduced below in transliteration. The consonant notational signs (k, c, ṭ, and so on) of this manuscript have been compared with the corresponding symbols (disregarding the vowels) in Jaiminīya manuscripts from the Burnell collection of the India Office Library (London): (1) B. 497 (Keith 4301, 4303), a grantha paper manuscript of the JGG and JĀrG copied from a palm leaf original from Tiruccirāppaḷḷi, (2) B. 61 (Keith 4300), a grantha palm leaf manuscript of the JGG, and (3) B. 62 (Keith 4302), a grantha palm leaf manuscript of the JĀrG. Where there is unanimous agreement among the manuscripts on a notational consonant, that symbol is preceded by an asterisk. The musical motives associated with these symbols are catalogued in the next section of this

---

[1]The Jaiminīyas of this area (Tanjore/Tiruccirāppalli) sometimes refer to themselves as Talavakāras, but these two names are merely different designations of one and the same śākhā. Burnell quotes a passage from the Dhāraṇalakṣaṇa which shows that Sabhāpati considered the two to be the same: see Burnell's The Jaiminīya Text of the Ārsheyabrāhmaṇa of the Sāmaveda (Mangalore: Basel Mission Press, 1878), p. vii. See also NVR, pp. 67-68.

study. The comparison of notational signs was greatly expedited by Caland's collation of B. 497 with B. 61 and B. 62. This notebook, Caland manuscript 7 of the University of Utrecht Library, gives the B. 61-62 variants in red; stobhas and notations are not collated for the JĀrG.

The sāmans which follow are preceded by designations of the gāna, source verse, and sāman name.[1] The final three chants belong to the Jaiminīya Uttaragāna; their notations are reproduced on the sole authority of the Śrīraṅgam manuscript, for additional readings are not available.

(1) JGG from JS 1.1.1.1, gautamasya parkaḥ:
*ta *ta *śa
o gnā i /

tha ca *ca *śa *ṭya ṭya *śa *cya
ā yā hī vā i / tā ya i tā yā i / gṛ ṇā

*śa *ci *ṭya ṭi śa *ka *ca
no ha vyā dā / tā yā i tā yā i / nā i ho tā /

*ṭa *ṭa *khya *śi *kha *śa
sat sā / i bā au ho vā / hī sī //

(2) JGG from JS 1.1.1.1, kaśyapasya barhiṣīyam:
a gna ā

*tū ṭū *ta *śa
yā hī vī / tā yā i gṛ ṇā no / ha vyā dā tā yā i /

*ci *ṭi *ta *ṭya *khya
nī ho tā sat sī ba rhā i sī / ba rhā i sā au

*śa ca *khya
ho vā / ba rhī ṣi //

[1]Chant names are those given by the Śrīraṅgam manuscript. For the names of all JGG and JĀrG chants, see Burnell, Jaiminīya Ārsheyabrāhmaṇa. Caland (JS, pp. 21-29) gives some variant readings for the JGG and lists the JĀrG sāmans with corresponding Kauthuma source verses and chants. See also B. R. Sharma, ed., Jaiminiyārṣeya-Jaiminīyopaniṣad-Brāhmaṇas (Tirupati: Kendriya Sanskrit Vidyapeetha, 1967).

(3) JGG from JS 1.1.1.1, gautamasya caiva parkaḥ:

*tū *ta *śa
a gna ā yā hī vā i tā yā i / gṛ ṇā no ha vya

yū *pa *śa *khi *ṇa *ṭa *tya *pa
dā tā ye / ni ho tā sāt / ṣā i bā / rhā i

pya pya
ṣo ha i //

(4) JGG from JS 1.1.2.7, agneś ca vāravantīyaṃ: a śvan

*tū *ta *śa *khi śa kya
na tvā bu ho ho hā i / vā rā vā ntam / va ndyā

pa *ṇa śa *pya *khu *ṇa
dhyo ṅā i / a gnā in na mā au ho vā i ho ṅā

*śa *khi *ṇa *ka *tha pa
i / u hu vā bhīḥ / sa mmrā ja ntā mā dhvā rā

*khu śa *pi pya *śa
au ho vā i ho hā i / u hu vā ṇā me hi yā hā

pya
ho i lā //

śu? *ṭi
(5) JGG from JS 1.1.4.1, śnuṣṭīgavaṃ: yā jñā yā jñā /

ṭī *ṭi *ṭī *śa
vo a gnā yā i / gā i rā gā i ṛā cā da kṣā śā i /

*ṭī *ca *ka ṭya *kha *ṇa
pra prā vā yā / mā mṛ ta ñjā tā ve dā saṃ /

ca ya ka ca ,ya *ṭa *khya *ṇa *pa śya
prā yā mmā i trā nnā saṃ ṣā i lā ā o i lā //

(6) JGG from JS 1.1.4.1, agneś ca yajñāyajñīyaṃ:

*ṇya *ṇya *pha *khya *ṇa *śa
ya jñā ya jñā vo a gna yā i / gā i rā gī

*ṭū *pya *śa ṭa ca *ka
rā cā dā kṣā sā i / pra pra vā ya ma mṛ ta ñjā

*pū *śa *śa *ta *ta
tā vā hi mmā i / dā sā / prā ya mmi trā nnā

```
*ka     ka      *kha
 śaṃ si ṣā bu /  bā  //
```

(7) JGG from JS 1.1.4.2, nārmmedhaṃ ca: pa hi no a gna

```
    *tya *ta   *ka                *pya *sa
e ka ya   e  /  pā hā u tā dvi tā i ya   yā / pā

*tya   *khya    *na                   *kū
 hā  i  gā    i ṛbhīḥ / tā i sṛ bhī ra  i   rjāṃ

  *ta           *khi *na   *pa          kya  tya
pā tā au ho au  ho   vā /  pā hī cā tā sṛ bhā au ho

   *khi *na   *pa            pya pya   sya
au  ho   vā /  vā sā ve hyā hā  ho   i lā  //
```

(8) JGG from JS 1.1.4.2, kārttaveśaṃ ca: pa hi no a gna

```
phi   kya  pa          pya  *ṅa *sa
e   ka yā / pā hyū ta dvī tī  ī yā  yā / pā hī gī

                     *khau?*na *sa     *cya *sa
rbhi sti sṛ bhī ū rjāṃ pā     tā  i  / pā hā    i

*kha        *sa          *ta     *ṭa *kha
 cā  tā hā o vā  / sṛ bhi rva  so /  ū   pā  //
```

(9) JGG from JS 1.2.2.1.1, indrasyārkau dvau: a bhi tvā

```
*ta           ti *ta   *tya *ta            ki   ca
 śū / rā no nu  mā o  nu    māḥ / ā du gdhā i vā dhā

    *kha      *ti *ta
 i nā  vā  o i nā  vāḥ / ā i śā na ma sya ja ga

cau?     *cya     kya    *ṭa *ṭa    ka   ka    ka ca
tā  / ssu  vā  rdṛ śā mo  dṛ  śāṃ / ā   ī śā na mi

             cya       *ṭa *ṭa *kha       *sa
ndrā ta sthū ṣaḥ / o  sthū   sā  au ho   vā / sthu

kya *ṭa [*kha]
ṣa  sthū  ṣaṃ //
```

(10) JGG from JS 1.2.2.1.1, indrasyārkau dvau: ā bhī tvā

```
            pya   ca               ku    *tā *ta
śū rā no nū māḥ / ā   du gdhā i vā dhā i  nā  vāḥ /
```

ca   kya   ku   ka   *ṭya *kha *ṇya
ā ī śa na ma sya ja ga tā ssu vā dṛ śāṃ /

ka , ṭī *ta   *cu   *ṭi *kha *na *pa
ī sā nā mī ndrā tā sthu ṣā i lā bā / o

sya
i lā //

(11) JGG from JS 1.2.3.5.1, *nānadaṃ tṛtīyaṃ*: pra tya smai

*phū *tya *pya ,   pya *ṅa *śa
pi pī ṣa tā i vā i svā nī vi du ṣe bhā rā /

*phū *khya   ,   *śū
a raṃ ga mā yā ja gma yo hā yā pā scā da dā /

*ka *pa *pya pya [*śā]
svā no / bā nā ro hā i //

(12) JGG from JS 1.2.4.10.5, *savituś ca sāma*: a bhi tyaṃ

*tau? *ta *śa
de vaṃ sa vi tā ra mau ho au ho vā / hā i /

*pya śa   *khi *na *ka *kya pa
o ṇa yoḥ / kā vi krā tuṃ / au ho au ho vā hā

*śa *khi *śa *khi *na   pi
i / a rccā mī sā tyā sāṃ vā rā / tnā dhā mā

*na pi *na śa *khi
bhī / prī ya mmā tīḥ / pra[1] / hā bu / ū rdhvā yā

na *khī *na *pi *na *pi
syā / ā mā tī bhyāḥ / ā di dyū tāt / sā vi mā

*na *khi *śa *kha *na khi
nī / pra / hī rā nyā pā nī rā mī mī tā sū krā

*na *śa *ta *ca ta *kha
tūḥ / pra / hā u vā / e kṛ pā svāḥ //

*tya *tha
(13) JGG from JS 1.3.1.1, *ājīkaṃ ca*: u ccā / te jā

ca ya *ṭya   kū
tā ma ndhā sā / di vi sat bhū myā da dā / u graṃ

---

[1]The syllable *pra* here denotes *pratistobha*: insertion of the *stobha* found at the end of the first *parvan* (*au ho au ho vā*).

ṡa *ta ṭa *kha *ṡa ṭa khi
ṡā rmmā / ṃā hā au ho vā / u pa śrā vāḥ //

*pi *ṇa
(14) JGG from JS 1.3.1.1, <u>ābhīkaṃ ca</u>: u ccā te jā /

pi *ṇa pi *ṇa *cya kya
tā ma ndhā ṡā / dī vā i sat bhū mī yā da dā u

pi *ṇa ṭi *kha *ṡa
graṃ ṡā ṛmmā / mā hā i śrā vā au ho vā /

*kha *ṡa
vā i //

(15) JGG from JS 1.3.1.1, <u>ṛṣabhaṃ ca pāvamanaḥ</u>: hā hā u

*tū *ta *ta *ṭi *kha *ṇa
ccā te jā / hā hā i ta mā ndhā ṡā / di vi sat

*yū *pa *ṡa *khi *ṇa ca ṭa
bhū mi yā dā de / u graṃ ṡā ṛmmā / oṃ oṃ ma

*khya pya [*ṡā]
ho bā śrā vo hā i //

pa pya
(16) JGG from JS 1.3.1.1, <u>ābhīkaṃ caiva</u>: u ccā te jā

*ṅa *ṡa *yū *pa [*ṡa]
ta mau ho ndhā sā / di vi sat bhū mi yā dā de /

*khi *ṇa *ṭa *khi pya *ṡya
u graṃ ṡā ṛmmā / ma hā u vā i śrā vo hā i //

*ṭi
(17) JGG from JS 1.3.1.1, <u>bābhrave dve</u>: u ccā te jā /

ṡa *ki *ki *ca
tā ma ndhā sā / o mo vā / pra / di vī sat bhū

kya *ya *ṭa *cya ya *ṭa
mī yā dā de / pra / u graṃ ṡā ṛmmā / pra /

*ṭa *ṭa *kha *ṡa *tya *ṭa [*kha]
mā hā au ho vā / śra vā ī //

*tī
(18) JGG from JS 1.3.1.1, <u>bābhrave dve</u>: u ccā te jā /

*ṭi *ta *ki *ṭi *ta *ṡa
tā ma ṅdhā sā / di vi sat bhū mi yā dā tā i /

*ṭya *ṭa *ṭi *ṭa *śa kya
ū gram hā / i sa ṛmmo hā i / ma hā ho i

*ṭa *ṭa *kha *śa *kha pya
śrā vā au ho vā / śvā bhiḥ //

(19) JGG from JS 1.3.1.1, <u>indrāṇyā sāma</u>: u ccā te jā ta

*tū *ṭya si *ki
mā / ndhā śa / o mo vā / pra / di vi sat bhū mī

kya *ya *ṭa *cya va? *ṭa
yā dā de / pra / u gram śa rmmā / pra / ma hā i

*ṭa *ṭa *kha *śa *khya *śa
śrā vā au ho vā / u ū pā //

(20) JGG from JS 1.3.1.1, <u>śaiśave dve</u>: u ccā te jā ta

*tr *ta tra *pi
ma ndhā sā / di vi sat bhū myā da dā u gram śa

*ṇa *khi *tra
ṛmmā / ma hā i śrā vāḥ //

(21) JGG from JS 1.3.1.1, <u>śaiśave dve</u>: u ccā te jā ta

*tr *ta *ṭr *tha
ma ndhā sā / di vi sat bhū mi yā dā dā / u gram

*ṭi *ta *ṭya *tha ṭa *ya
śā rmmā / ma hā ho vā au ho / pra / i śra

*ti *ṭa *ca *ka *ca *khya *tra *kha
vā / pra / i yā ho i yo vā / ū //

(22) JGG from JS 1.3.1.1, <u>prajāpater dohādohīye dve</u>:

*khya *tya *ṭya *khya *ṇa *pha *pya
u ccā au ho / te jā ta mā

*kha *sa *kr tha *ṭi
ndhā sā / di vi sat bhū myā da de ā u gram śā

*ta *cya *ka *ṭya *kha pya *sya
rmmā / mā hī srā vā au ho bā / ho i lā //

(23) JGG from JS 1.3.1.1, <u>prajāpater dohādohīye dve</u>:

*ti [*ti *ṭa *ta]
u ccā te jā ta ma ndha sā do hā i do hā e /

kṛ *ṭa *ta *ṭya *ṭa *ta
di vi sat bhū myā da dė do hā i do hā e /

*ṭi *ta *ṭi *kha *ṇa
pra / u graṃ śā rmmā / pra / mā hi śrā vā ḥ

pa *sya
o i lā //

*ṇya
(24) JGG from JS 1.3.1.1, *indrāṇyās sāma*: u ccā te

ṇya phya *khi *sya piʔ *ṇa *ṭa
jā ta mā ndhā sā / dī vā i sāt bhū myā da

*ṭya ṭa *ṭa *ṭa *ṭa *ṭi *ca *sa
dā / o vā o vā / u va u vā ho i / pra /

*ṭi *ta *cya ṭa ṭa *kha
u graṃ śā rmmā / pra / mā hī śrā vo yā / au

*sya *khi
ho vā / ya yu re //

*kha
(25) JGG from JS 1.3.1.1, *āmahīyavaṃ ca*: u ccā tā i

ṇa *ya *ṭa *ṭi
jā ī ta man dha sā / di vā i sāt bhū mi yā da

*ṭya *cya *ka *ca *ka *ṭa *ki *khya
dā i u graṃ śa rmā / mā hā i śra vā u vā

*ta *kha
stau ṣe //

(26) from JS 4.3.8, *prājāpatyaṃ gāyatraṃ*: ta tsa vi tu

*cū ci tya *ca
rva re ṇyoṃ / bha rgo de va sya dhī mā hā ī dhī

ṭa sa ca *cya ṭa *ka *ca ṭya ca ṭya ca
yo yo naḥ / prā cā hiṃ bhā o vā o vā o vā /

ca sa ka ca
hiṃ bhā o vā //

pya
(27) JŪG from JS 3.47.1, *devānām añjasāyi*: a dhva ryo

ṇa   bhā ṭa   kya pa ṇa   tha
a / o hā i ssu tāṃ / so maṃ pā vī / trā tū nā

ṭa   ca ṭa kha   sa   ṭi kha
yā / pu nā o ndrā au ho vā / ya pā ṭā ve //

                                             pha ta ta
(28) JRG, [bhargayaśasī]: u tso de vo hi ra ṇyā yā /

 kha sa   pa   sa   ta
u vo vā / ū tso de vo hī ra ṇya yā / hā u tso de

    ka ka pa   sa   ta   ka
vo hi ra ṇyā yā hā bu du hā na ū / dhā rdi vyaṃ /

       pa   sa ta ta kha
mā dhu prā yāṃ hā bu pra tnaṃ sa dhā om om o   /

  pya   pya sa
bā sā dā rhā i //

                                               ku sa
(29) JRG, vāsiṣṭhaḥ padastobhaḥ: hā ha hau vā u vo vā /

                   tū   ti ca sa
triḥ / e au ho au ho vā hā u vā / ī lā / hā ha hau

   kū sa   tū   ti   kya
vā u vo vā / triḥ / e au o au ho vā hā u vā / pa vā

     ki   khya   kū [sa]
sva vā ja sā ta ye   / hā ha hau vā u vo vā / triḥ /

             tū   ti ca sa
e au ho au ho vā hā u vā / ī lā / hā ha hau vā u

[kū sa]   tū   ta   ca sa
vo   vā / triḥ / e au ho au ho vā hā u vā / ī lā /

ka   kya sa   tū
hā ha hau vā u vo vā / triḥ / e au ho au ho vā hā u

ti   ṭa   tya ca   ka
vā / pa vi tre dhā ra yā su taḥ   / hā ha hau vā u

kya sa   tū   ti   ca sa
vo vā / triḥ / e au ho au ho vā hā u vā / ī lā /

          ku sa   tū
hā ha hau vā u vo vā / triḥ / e au ho au ho vā hā u

ti ca sa   ku sa
vā / ī lā / hā ha hau vā u vo vā / triḥ / e au ho au

tū ti kya cya ṭa , khi
ho vā hā u vā / i ndrā ya sso mā vi ṣṇa ve / hā ha

ku sa· tū ti
hau vā u vo vā / triḥ / e au ho au ho vā hā u vā /

ca sa ka ku sa
ī lā / hā ha hau vā u vo vā / triḥ / e au ho au

tū ti ca sa ka ku sa
ho vā hā u vā / ī lā / hā ha hau vā u vo vā /

tū ti kya ṭa
[triḥ] / e au ho au ho vā hā u vā / de ve bhyo ma

khu ka kya sa
dhu ma tta māḥ / hā ha hau vā u vo vā / triḥ / e

tū ti ca sa
au ho au ho vā hā u vā / ī lā //

Systematic catalogue of motives

The textual syllables covered by the starred notational signs have been extracted and placed in the following catalogue, where they are reproduced with the appropriate musical settings according to the recital of Rājagopāla Aiyaṅgār. The motives are systematized first according to syllable type (<u>avaroha</u>, <u>udgama</u>, <u>yāna</u>, and so on) and then according to the number of textual syllables specified by the notational vowel. Reference is made by numbers (1-29, in brackets) to the source chants given on pages 164-172.

(1) <u>Avaroha</u>: <u>k</u>

a. <u>ka</u> (<u>avaroha</u> on one textual syllable)

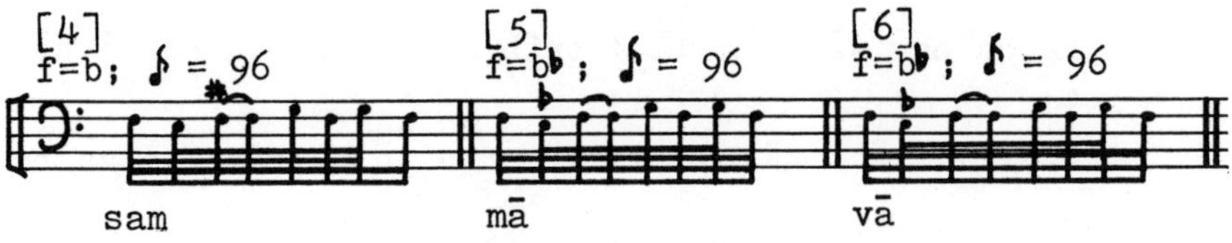

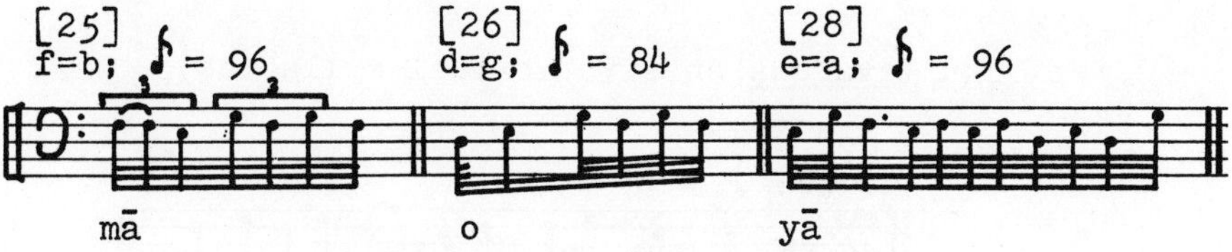

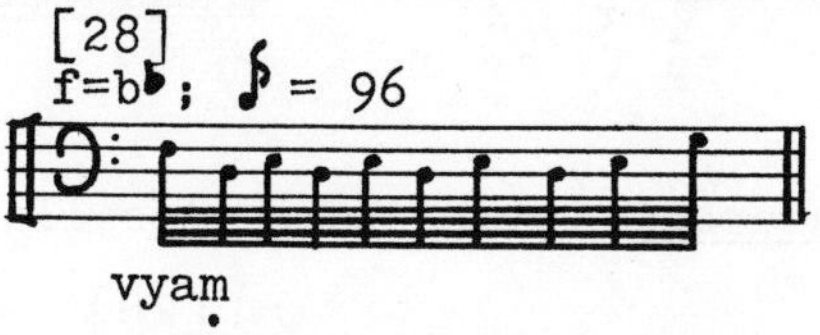

b. <u>kā</u> (<u>avaroha</u> on two textual syllables)

c. <u>ki</u> (<u>avaroha</u> on three textual syllables)

d. <u>kī</u> (<u>avaroha</u> on four textual syllables)

e. <u>ku</u> (<u>avaroha</u> on five textual syllables)

f. <u>kū</u> (<u>avaroha</u> on six textual syllables)

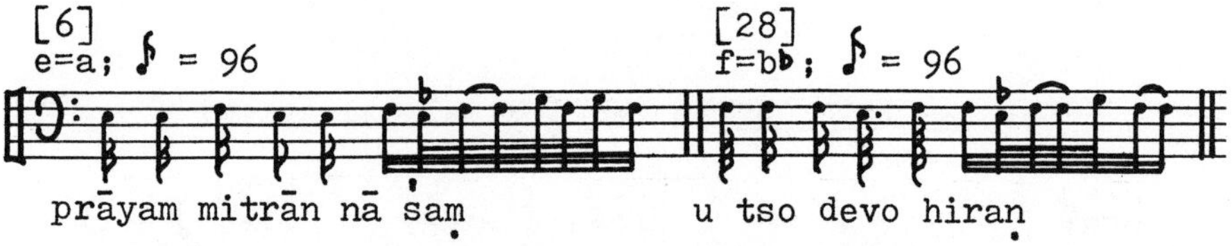

g. <u>kṛ</u> (<u>avaroha</u> on seven textual syllables)

(2) <u>Udgama</u>: <u>c</u>

a. <u>ca</u> (<u>udgama</u> on one textual syllable)

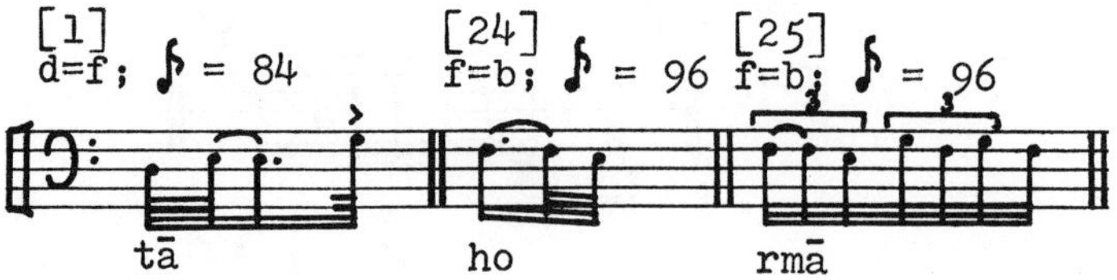

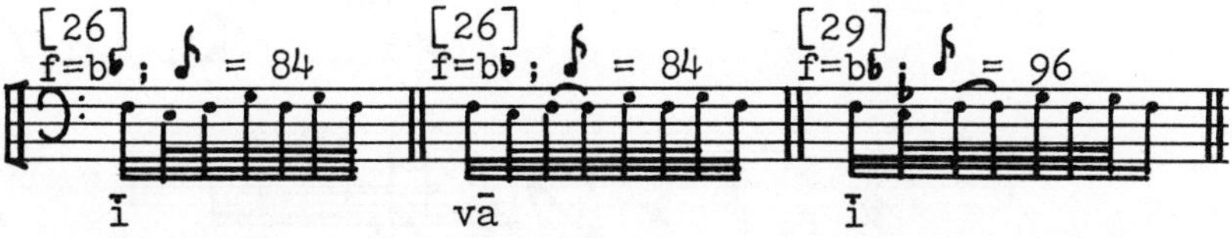

b. <u>cā</u> (<u>udgama</u> on two textual syllables)

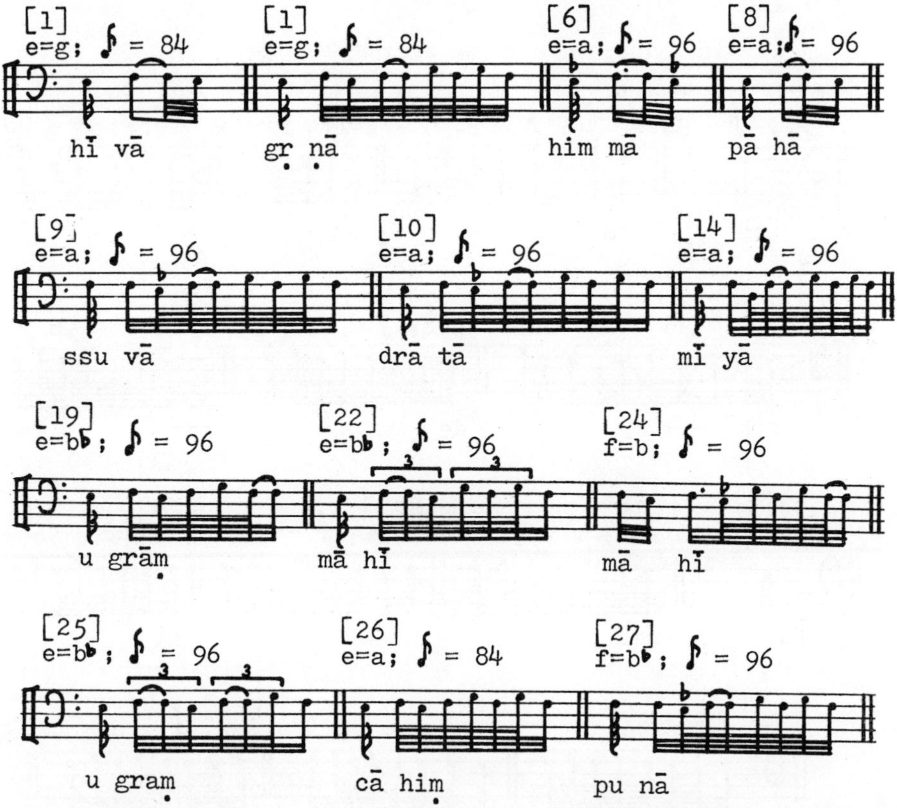

c. <u>ci</u> (<u>udgama</u> on three textual syllables)

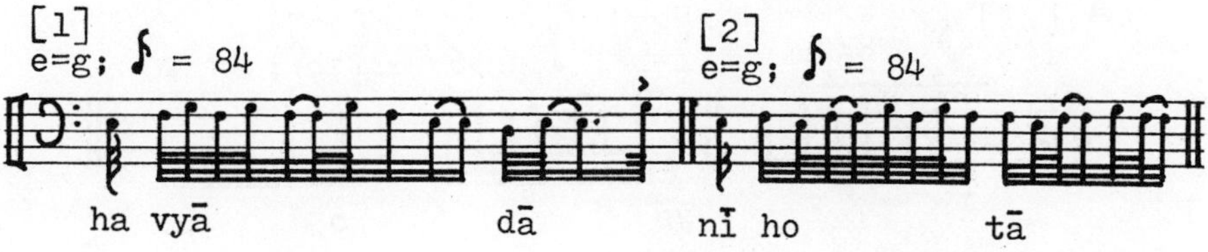

d. cū (udgama on six textual syllables)

(3) Yāna: ṭ

a. ṭa (yāna on one textual syllable)

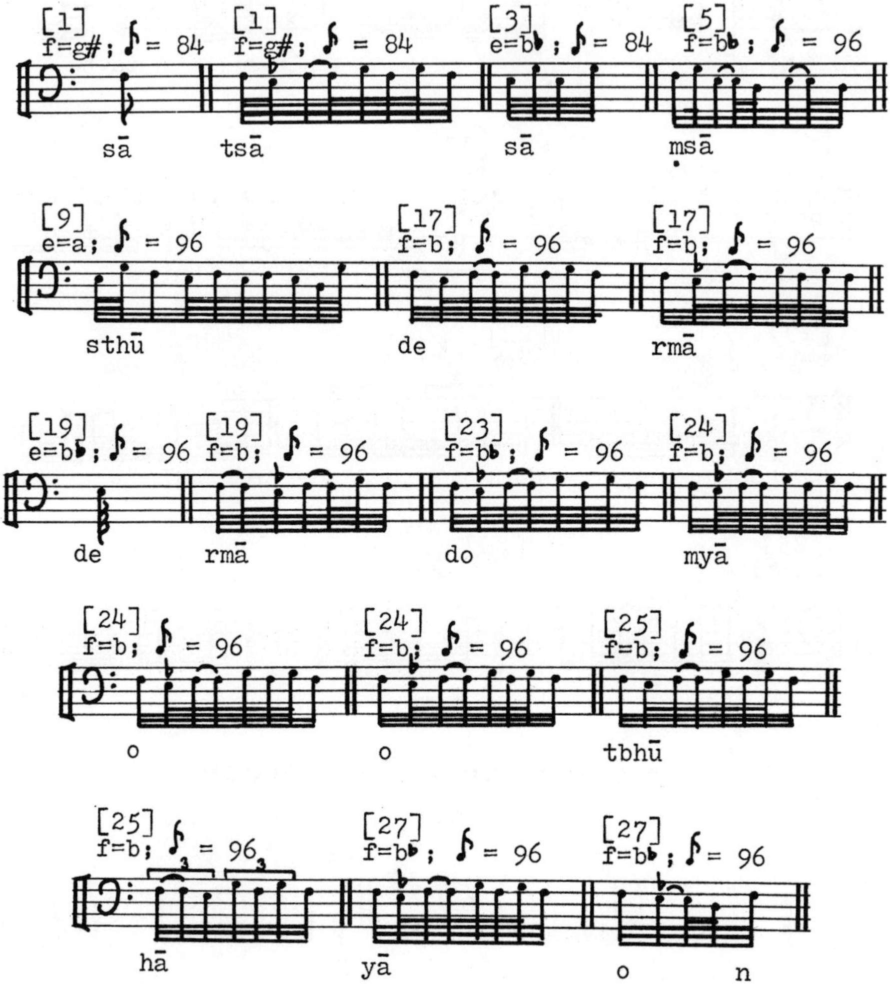

b. tā (yāna on two textual syllables)

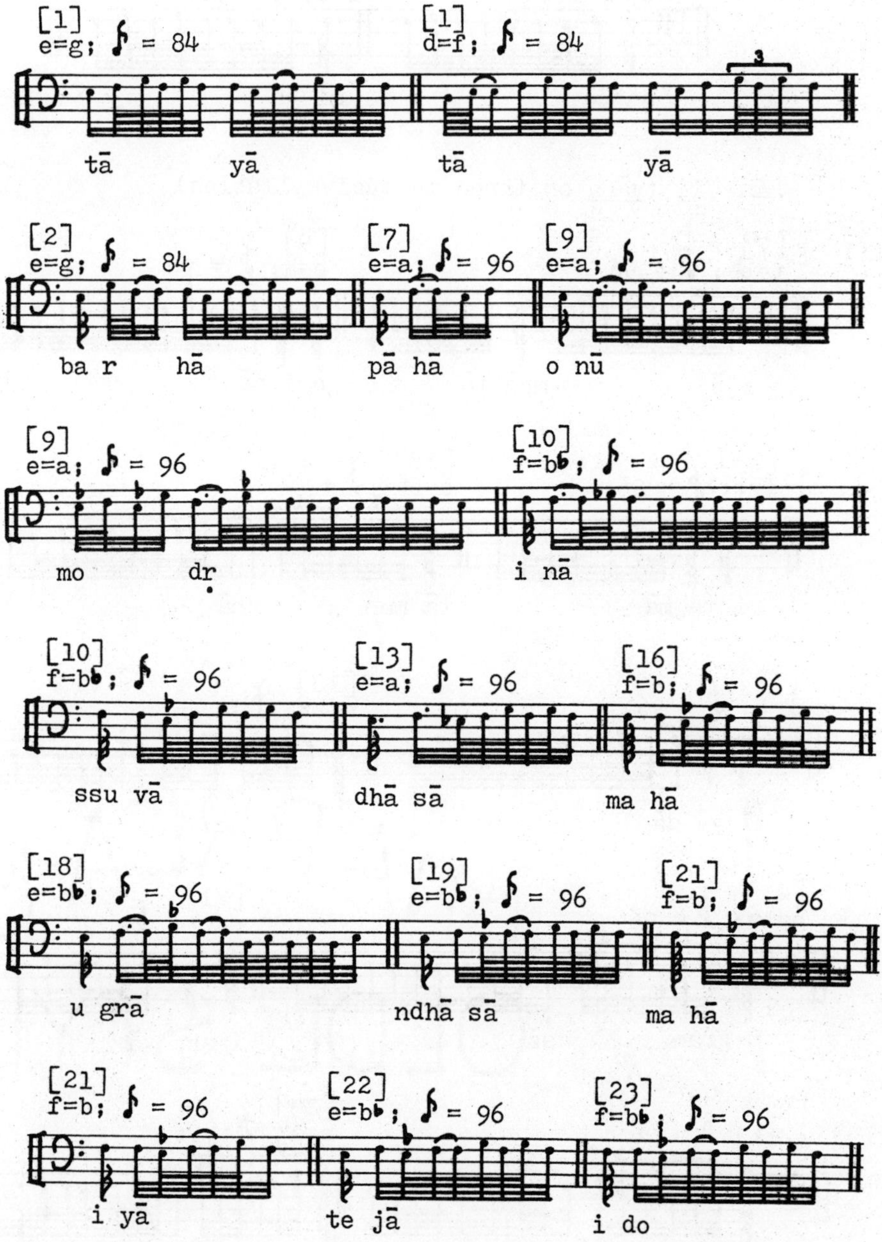

c. *ṭi* (*yāna* on three textual syllables)

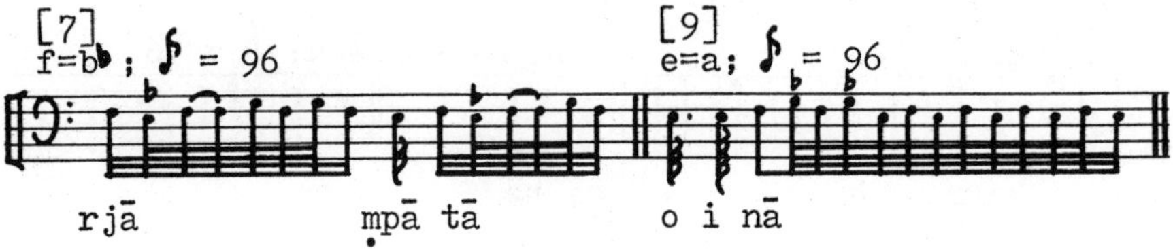

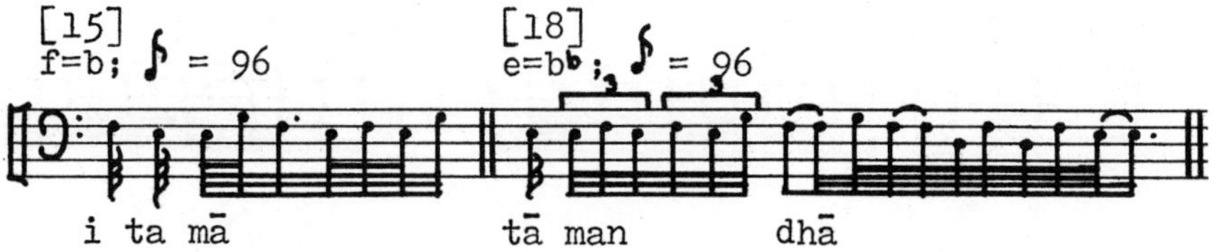

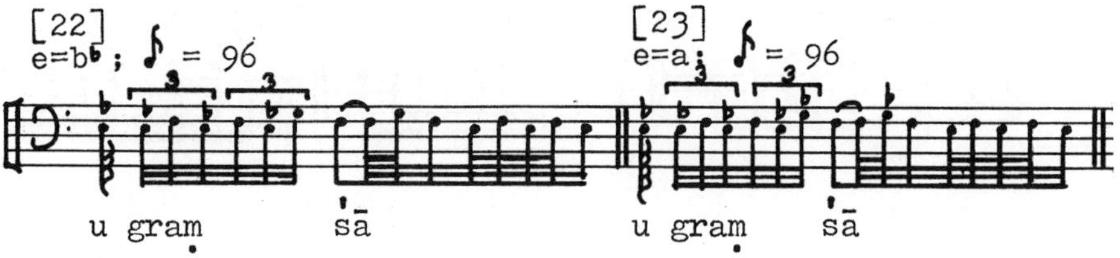

d. ṭī (yāna on four textual syllables)

e. ṭū (yāna on six textual syllables)

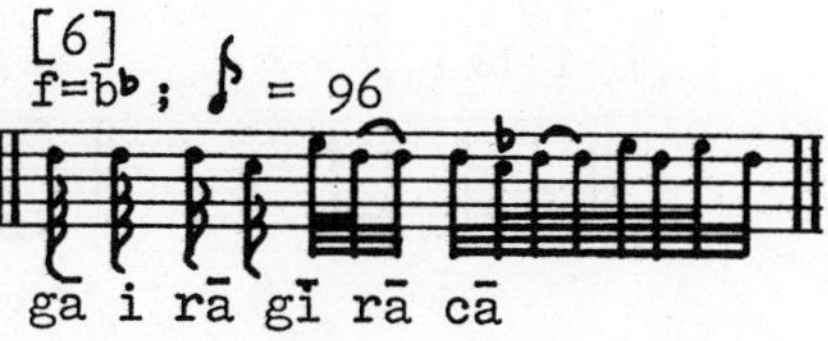

f. tr (yāna on seven textual syllables)

(4) Āvarta: t

a. ta (āvarta on one textual syllable)

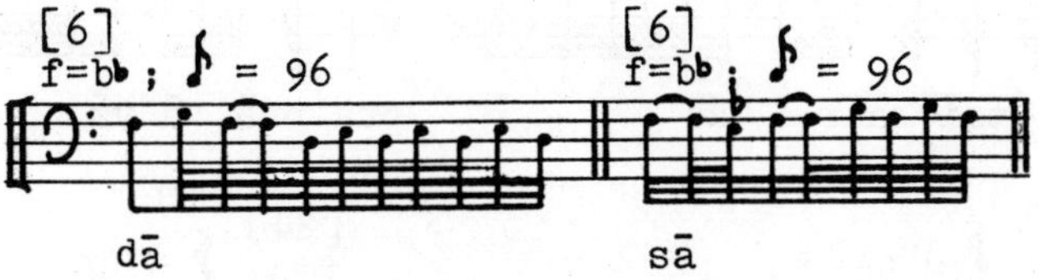

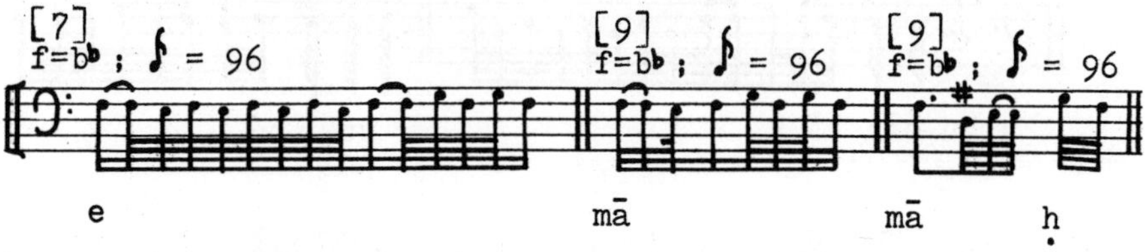

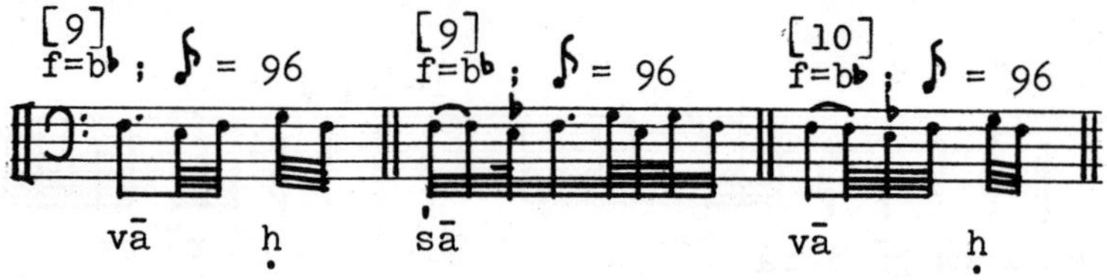

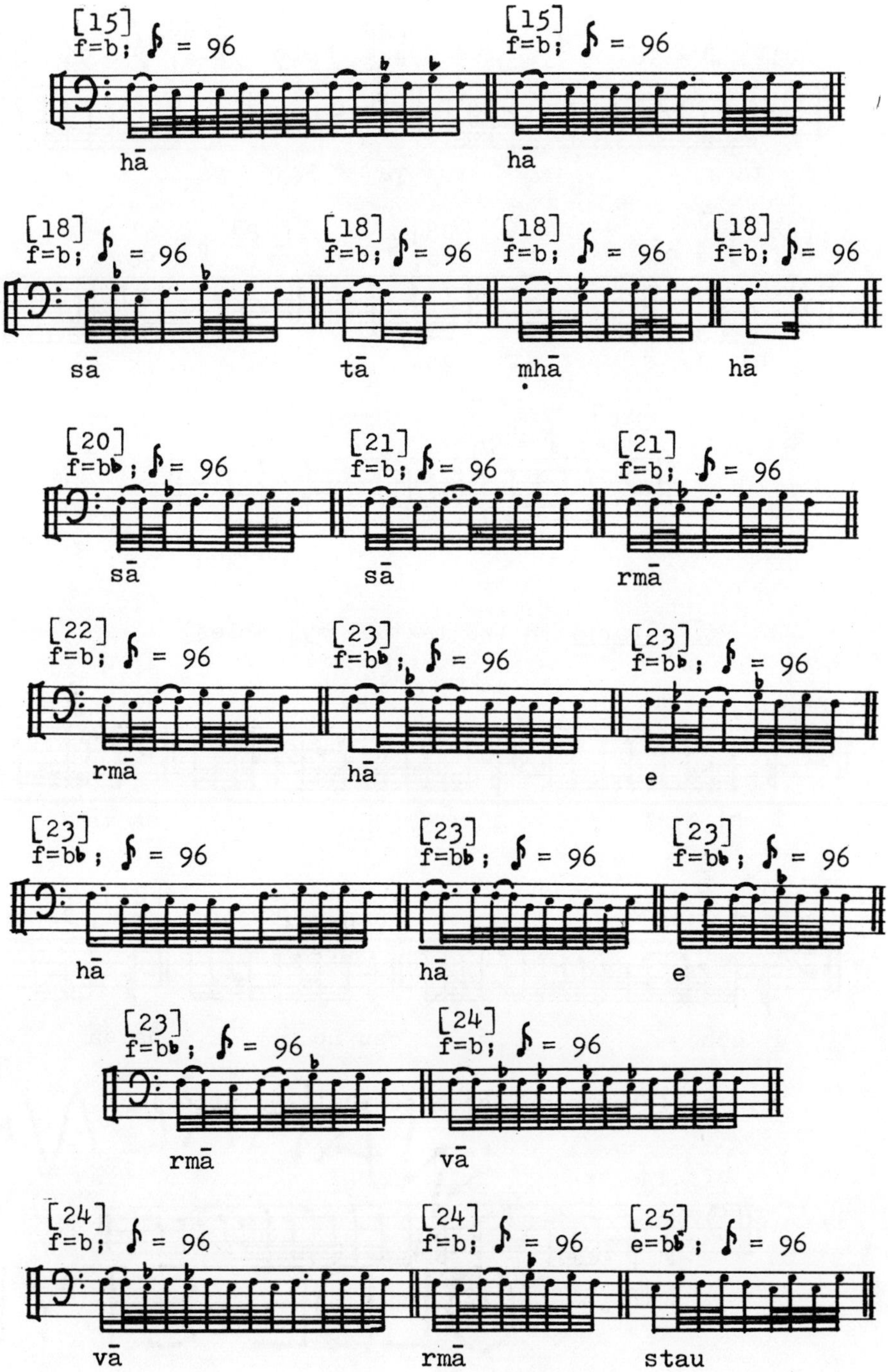
[15] f=b; ♪ = 96
hā
[15] f=b; ♪ = 96
hā
[18] f=b; ♪ = 96
sā
[18] f=b; ♪= 96
tā
[18] f=b; ♪ = 96
mhā
[18] f=b; ♪= 96
hā
[20] f=b♭; ♪= 96
sā
[21] f=b; ♪= 96
sā
[21] f=b; ♪ = 96
rmā
[22] f=b; ♪ = 96
rmā
[23] f=b♭; ♪ = 96
hā
[23] f=b♭; ♪ = 96
e
[23] f=b♭; ♪ = 96
hā
[23] f=b♭; ♪ = 96
hā
[23] f=b♭; ♪ = 96
e
[23] f=b♭; ♪ = 96
rmā
[24] f=b; ♪ = 96
vā
[24] f=b; ♪ = 96
vā
[24] f=b; ♪ = 96
rmā
[25] e=b♭; ♪ = 96
stau

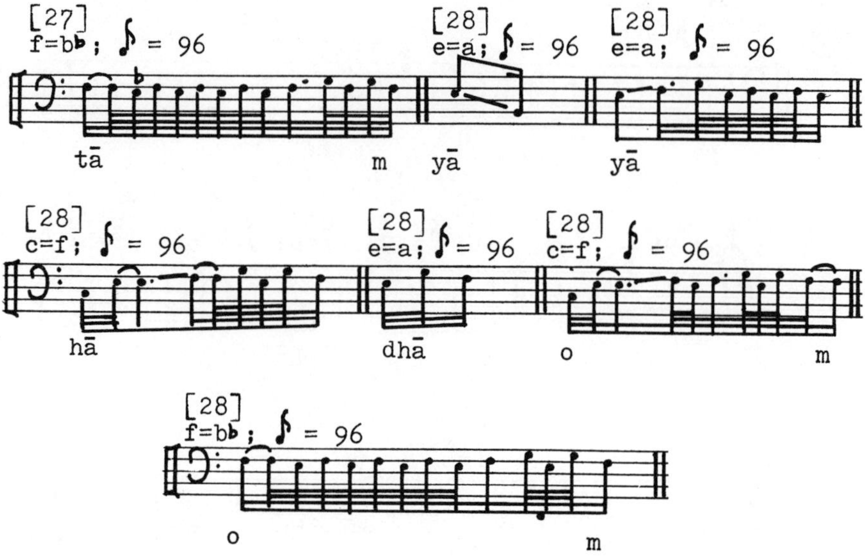

b. tā (āvarta on two textual syllables)

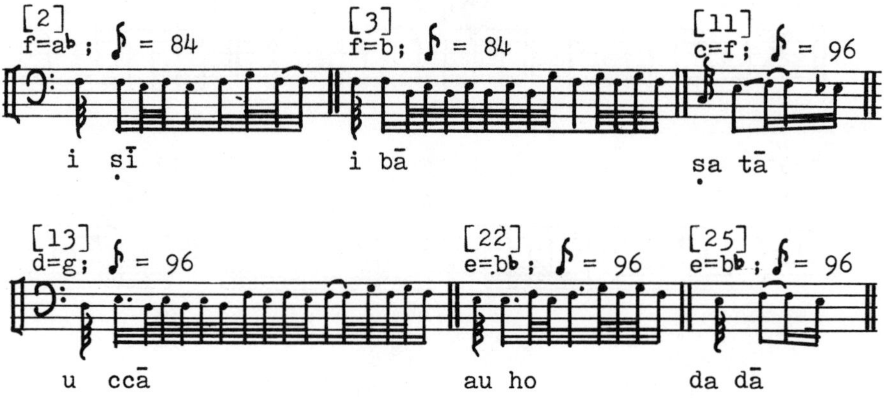

c. ti (āvarta on three textual syllables)

[29]
f=b♭; ♪ = 96

d. tī (āvarta on four textual syllables)

[9]
e=a; ♪ = 96

[17]
c=f♯; ♪ = 96

[18]
e=b♭; ♪ = 96

e. tū (āvarta on six textual syllables)

[2]
e=g; ♪ = 84

[3]
c=f♯; ♪ = 84

[4]
c=f♯; ♪ = 96

[15]

e=b♭; ♪ = 96
hā hā uccā te jā

[19]

e=b♭; ♪ = 96
uccā te jā ta mā

[23]

e=a; ♪ = 96
jātamandhasā do

f. <u>tṛ</u> (<u>āvarta</u> on seven textual syllables)

[20]

c=f; ♪ = 96
uccā te jātamandhā

[21]

e=b♭; ♪ = 96
uccā te jātamandhā

g. <u>te</u> (<u>āvarta</u> on eight textual syllables)

[7]

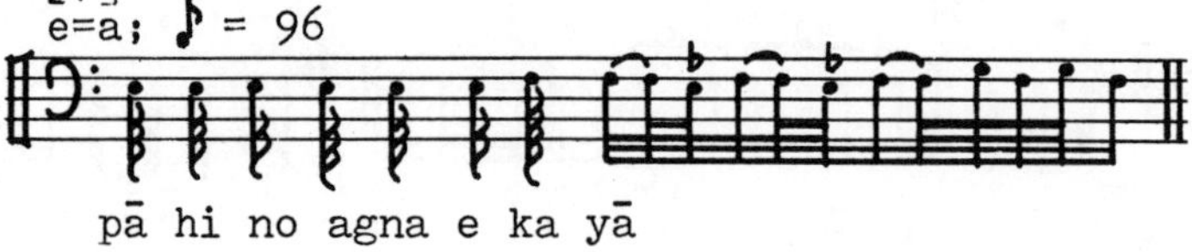
e=a; ♪ = 96
pā hi no agna e ka yā

h. tau (āvarta on eleven textual syllables)

(5) Kṣepaṇa: p

a. pa (kṣepaṇa on one textual syllable)

b. pā (kṣepaṇa on two textual syllables)

c. pi (kṣepaṇa on three textual syllables)

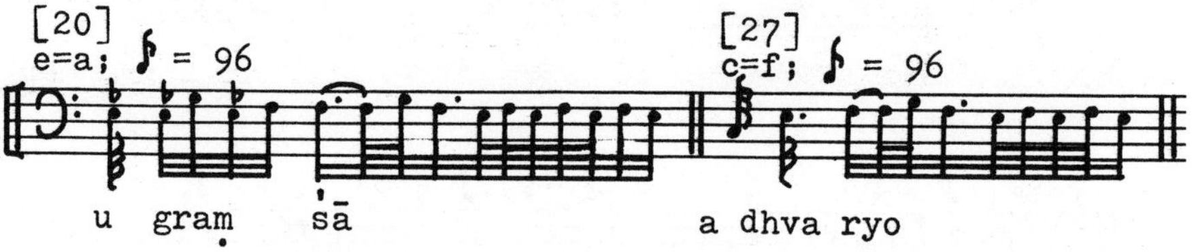

d. pu (kṣepaṇa on five textual syllables)

e. pr̥ (kṣepaṇa on seven textual syllables)

[7]
f=b♭; ♪ = 96

hā u tā dvi tā i yā

(6) Marśana: y

a. ya (marśana on one textual syllable)

[17] c=f♯; ♪ = 96 [19] f=b; ♪ = 96 [21] f=b; ♪ = 96

dā
dā
ho

b. yī (marśana on four textual syllables)

[25]
e=b♭; ♪ = 96

di vā i sā

c. yū (marśana on six textual syllables)

[15] e=b♭; ♪ = 96 [16] e=b♭; ♪ = 96

divi sat bhūmiyā
divi sat bhūmiyā

(7) Mardana: bh

a. bhī (mardana on four textual syllables)

[27]
e=a; ♪ = 96

o hā i ssu

(8) <u>Anvaṅgulya</u>: <u>kh</u>

a. <u>kha</u> (<u>anvaṅgulya</u> on one textual syllable)

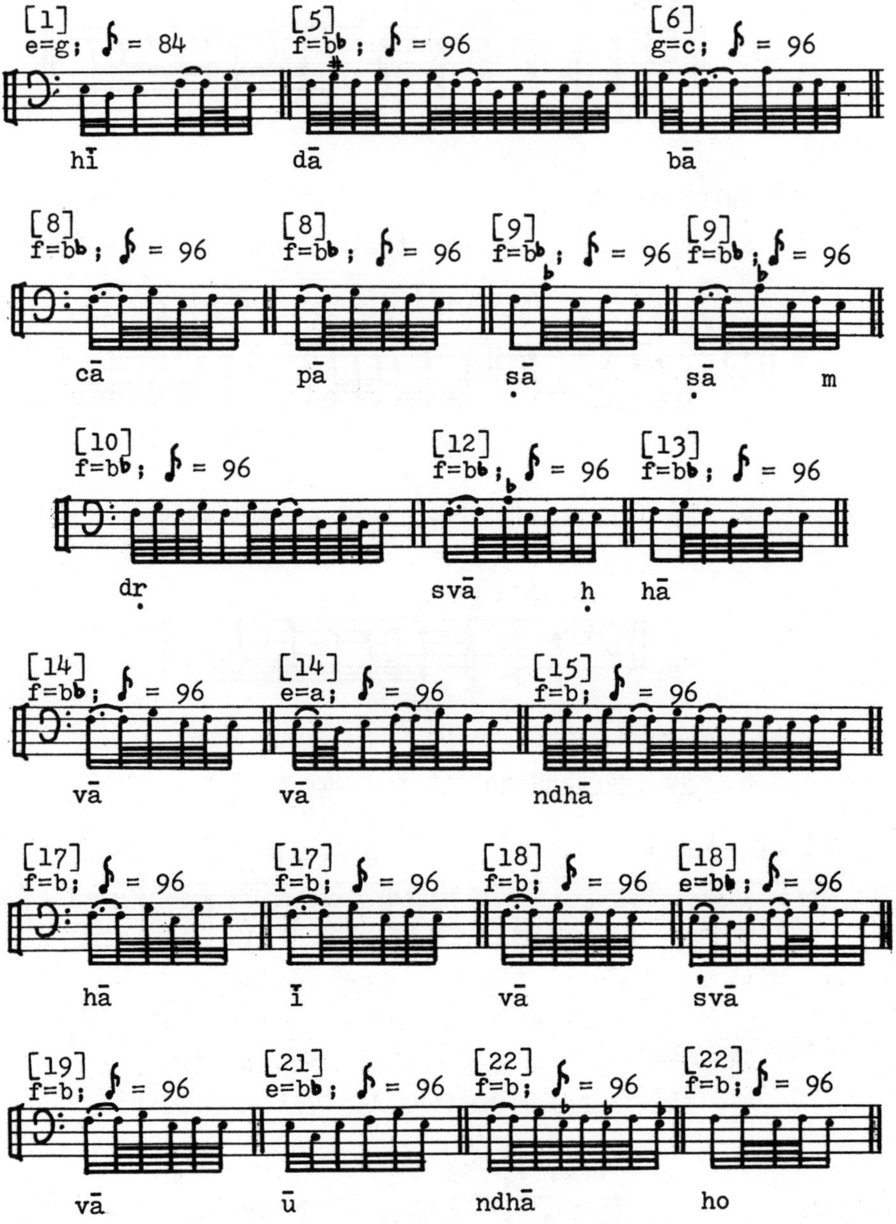

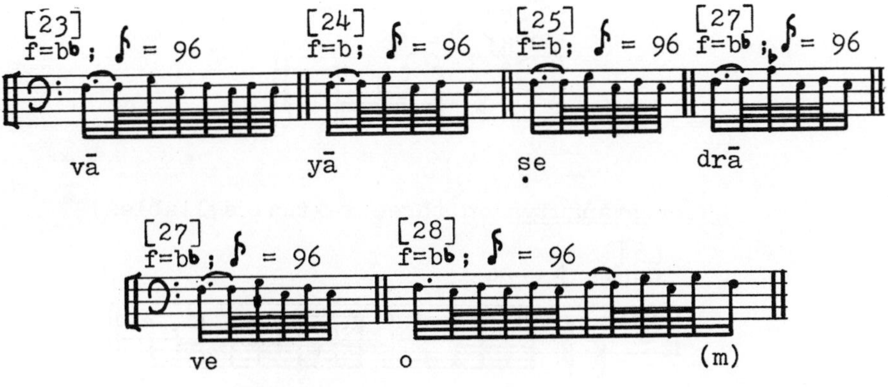

b. <u>khā</u> (<u>anvaṅgulya</u> on two textual syllables)

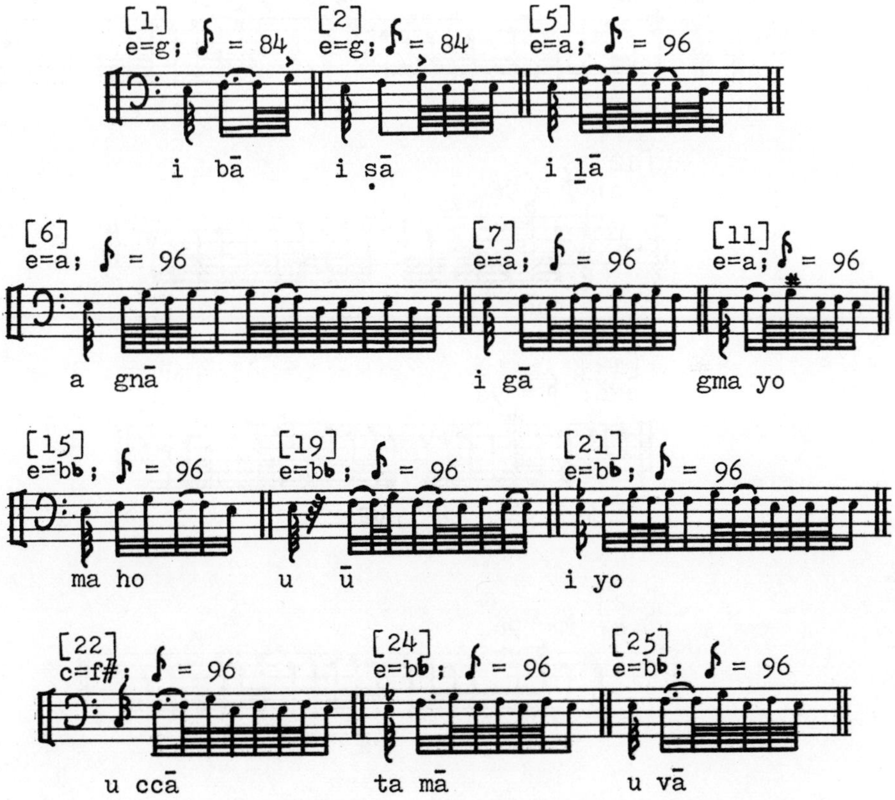

c. *khi* (*anvaṅgulya* on three textual syllables)

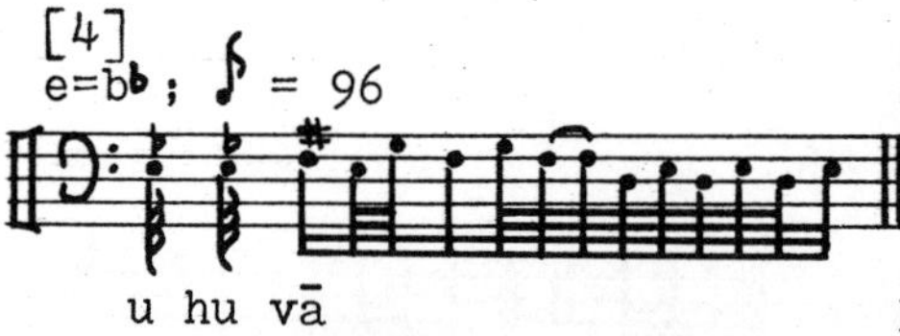

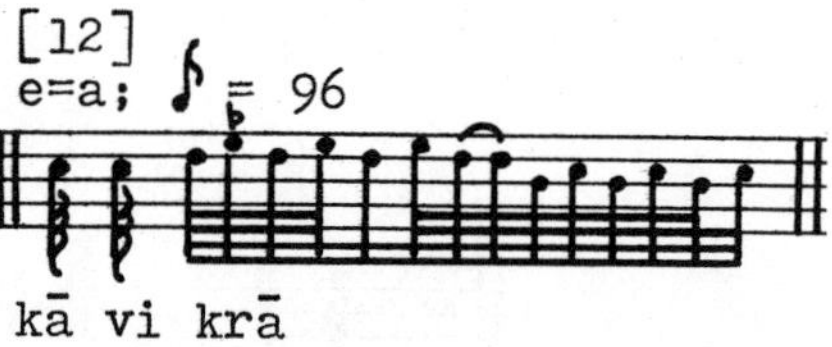

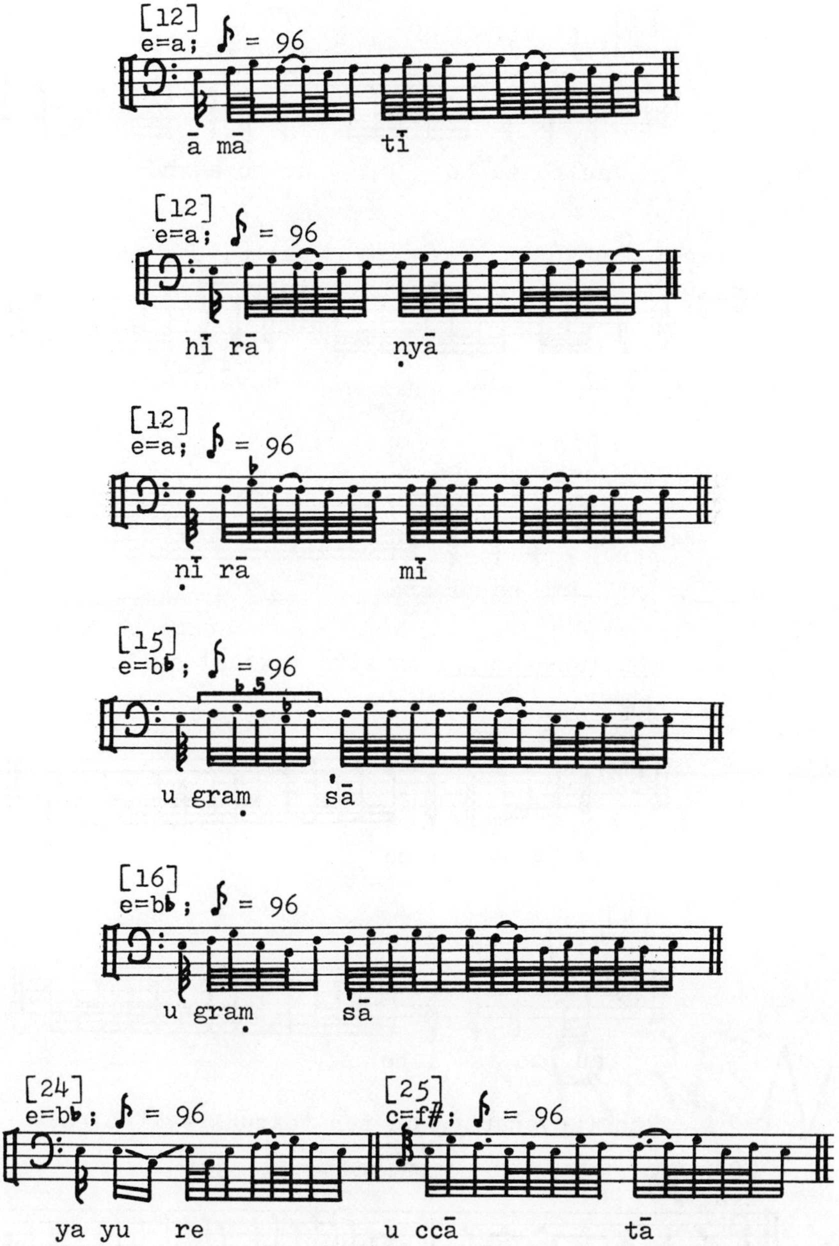
[12]
e=a; = 96
ā mā tī
[12]
e=a; = 96
hī rā ṇyā
[12]
e=a; = 96
ṇī rā mī
[15]
e=b♭; = 96
5
u graṃ sā
[16]
e=b♭; = 96
u graṃ sā
[24]
e=b♭; = 96
ya yu re
[25]
c=f#; = 96
u ccā tā

d. khī (anvaṅgulya on four textual syllables)

e. khu (anvaṅgulya on five textual syllables)

f. kho (anvaṅgulya on ten textual syllables)

(9) Kevalottāna: th

a. tha (kevalottāna on one textual syllable)

b. thā (kevalottāna on two textual syllables)

(10) Madhyamāṅgulya (Pha-Svara): ph

a. pha (madhyamāṅgulya on one textual syllable)

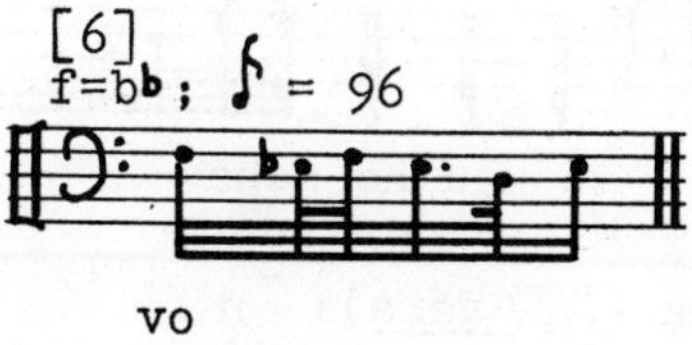

b. phu (madhyamāṅgulya on five textual syllables)

c. phū (madhyamāṅgulya on six textual syllables)

(11) Kaniṣṭhikodgama (Ṅa-Svara): ṅ

a. ṅa (kaniṣṭhikodgama on one textual syllable)

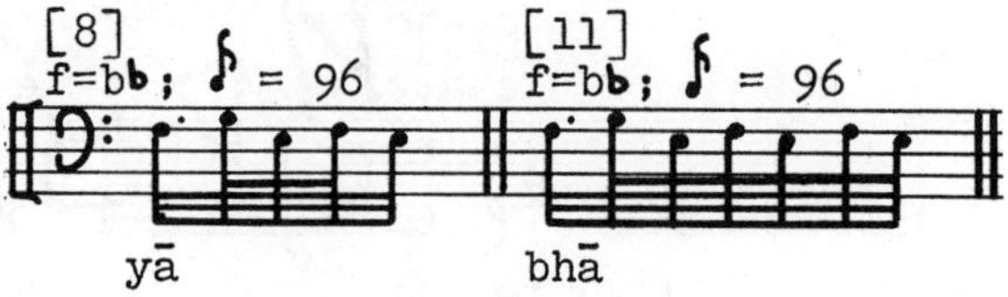

b. ṅī (kaniṣṭhikodgama on four textual syllables)

(12) Anāmikodgama (Ṇa-Svara): ṇ

a. ṇa (anāmikodgama on one textual syllable)

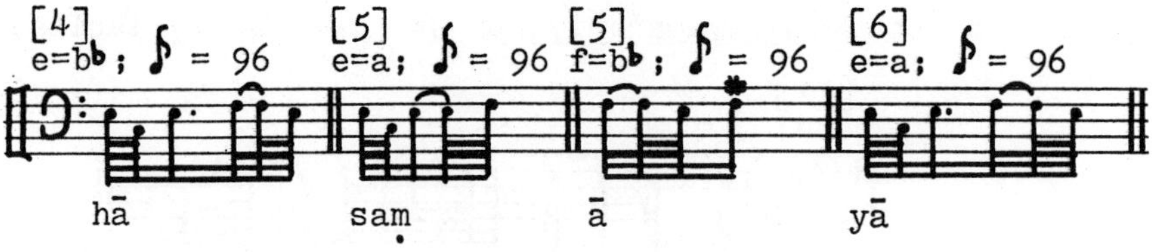

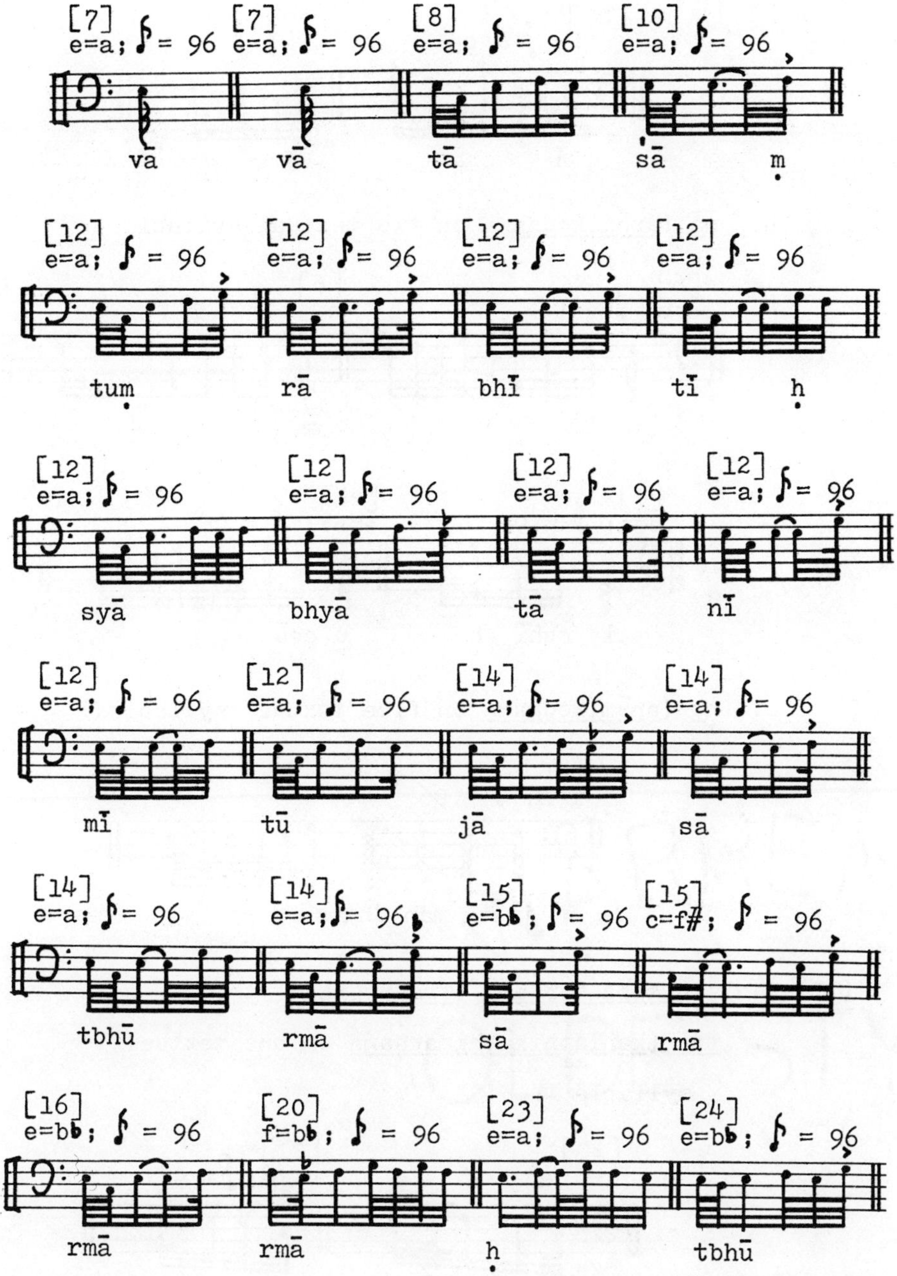
[7] e=a; = 96
[7] e=a; = 96
[8] e=a; = 96
[10] e=a; = 96
vā vā tā sā ṃ
[12] e=a; = 96
[12] e=a; = 96
[12] e=a; = 96
[12] e=a; = 96
tuṃ rā bhī tī ḥ
[12] e=a; = 96
[12] e=a; = 96
[12] e=a; = 96
[12] e=a; = 96
syā bhyā tā nī
[12] e=a; = 96
[12] e=a; = 96
[14] e=a; = 96
[14] e=a; = 96
mī tū jā sā
[14] e=a; = 96
[14] e=a; = 96
[15] e=b♭; = 96
[15] c=f#; = 96
tbhū rmā sā rmā
[16] e=b♭; = 96
[20] f=b♭; = 96
[23] e=a; = 96
[24] e=b♭; = 96
rmā rmā ḥ tbhū

b. ṇā (anāmikodgama on two textual syllables)

c. ṇu (anāmikodgama on five textual syllables)

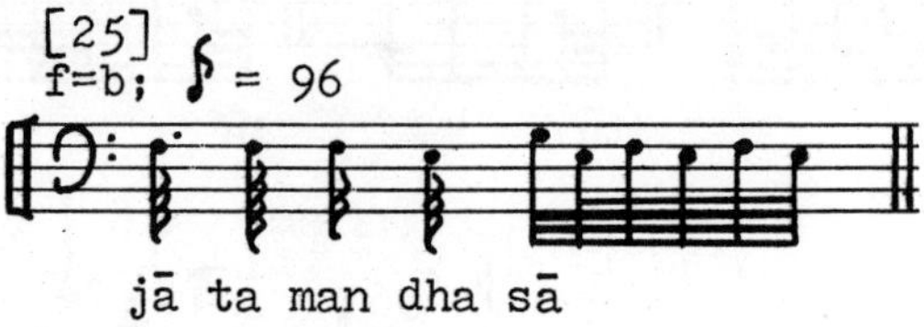

(13) Kaniṣṭhikābhimarśana (Tra-Svara): tr

a. tra (kaniṣṭhikābhimarśana on one textual syllable

From these examples it is clear how a svara is "adapted" to more than one syllable of text. The final syllable, on which the notational sign occurs, is set to a motive or melisma consisting usually of three or more tones. The preceding syllables are intoned rapidly in syllabic style (usually one tone per syllable, occasionally two); this is normally done on a single pitch, which more often than not is either the central tone or the minor second below. Thus it is explained why the notational symbols are found always on the last textual syllable of the svara. This final syllable bears the musical characteristic of the svara, and its importance is underscored by the presence of the notational sign. Some exceptions to this general rule are encountered occasionally. One notable departure is the notation syllable khi (anvaṅgulya on three textual syllables), where both final and penultimate textual syllables are often set to musical melismas.

The most important fact emerging from the catalogue is that a notational sign is not represented always by the same musical phrase; and if the examples are to be taken as any indication of sāman literature as a whole, the number of motives appears to be remarkably small. The most recurrent figure is:

Sometimes it appears in a more melismatic form as:

These two versions are associated in the twenty-nine Śrīraṅgam _sāmans_ (indicated by numbers) with the following notational syllables. Multiple occurrences in a single chant are given in parentheses.

(1) _Avaroha_

_ka_: 4, 5, 6, 7, 25 (2)

_kā_: 12, 22, 27

_ki_: 17, 25

_kī_: 18, 19

_ku_: 7

_kū_: 6, 28

_kṛ_: 22

(2) _Udgama_

_ca_: 25, 26 (2), 29

_cā_: 1, 9, 10, 14, 19, 22, 24, 25, 26, 27

_ci_: 2

_cū_: 26

(3) _Yāna_

_ṭa_: 1, 17 (2), 19, 23, 24 (3), 25 (2), 27

_ṭā_: 1 (2), 2, 10, 13, 16, 19, 21 (2), 22, 23, 24, 25

_ṭi_: 7, 21

_ṭī_: 2, 5, 24

_ṭū_: 5, 6, 29

(4) Āvarta

ta: 6, 7, 9 (2), 10, 13, 15 (2), 18 (2), 20, 21 (2), 22, 23 (4), 24 (3), 27, 28

tā: 2, 3, 13

ti: 29

tī: 9, 17, 18

tū: 2, 3, 4, 15, 19, 23

te: 7

(5) Kṣepaṇa

pa: 7 (2)

pā: 11

pu: 4

(6) Marśana

ya: 21

yī: 25

yū: 15, 16

(7) Mardana

bhī: 27

(8) Anvaṅgulya

kha: 28

khī: 9

(9) Kevalottāna

thā: 4, 13, 21

(10) Anāmikodgama

ṇa: 20

ṇā: 6, 24

Nambūdiri Jaiminīya

Another style of singing, radically different from anything previously shown, has to be mentioned. This style belongs to the tradition of Sāmavedins of the Nambūdiri sect, a Brāhmaṇ sub-caste resident in Keraḷa for so long that its origin cannot be traced elsewhere.[1] Partly because of their isolation from other Brāhmaṇ communities, the Nambūdiris are believed to preserve Vedic recitation and chant in their purest forms--a belief that has been shown to be well-based by the researches of Staal and others.

It is almost a certainty that Nambūdiri Sāmaveda will soon become extinct. Only a very few people--most of them quite old--are keeping the tradition alive, and they refuse to teach Sāmaveda to Nambūdiris who belong by birth to other Vedas. Fortunately--due to the initiatives of Sreekrishna Sarma, Staal, and Parpola--all Nambūdiri chants have now been recorded. This extremely important musical tradition has therefore been preserved for posterity.[2]

Motivic analysis of selected chants

Nambūdiri chanting is melismatic to such a degree

---

[1]The Nambūdiris as a class are discussed in Staal's "Notes," pp. 4-7, and in NVR, pp. 31-36. Nambūdiri Ṛg-, Yajur-, and Sāmaveda are dealt with in NVR. Nambūdiri agniṣṭoma chants are textually analyzed in his "Twelve Ritual Chants."

[2]The Nambūdiris celebrate two sacrifices, the agniṣṭoma and the atirātra agnicayana. The final performance of the latter--an event of considerable historical significance--was held in April, 1975.

that new terminology seems required. My transcription of a performance of JGG 1.1, for instance, shows at least 119 changes of pitch for the first two syllables of text.[1] The tones are grouped into motives consisting of from two to fifteen tones, although motives comprised of more than five or six pitches may be combinations of smaller motives. If such is the case, the motivic repertoire would appear to consist of not more than two dozen tonal patterns. These patterns are derived from an eight-tone gamut with an ambitus of a major sixth:

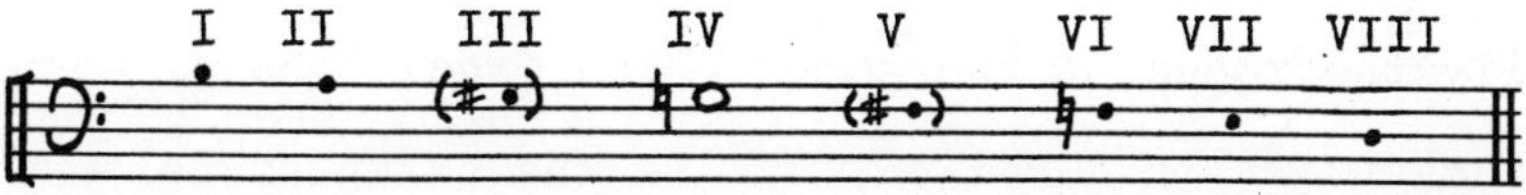

Tone I is heard infrequently, but its occasional appearance is clearly purposeful.[2] Tone III occurs in only one motive,[3] while tone V may result from natural vocal vibrato. The impression given is of continual ornamentation of a central pitch (IV). Most of the motives end on this tone, and it is the only pitch held for long durations. It, the upper major second (II) and some lower pitch (VI, VII, or VIII) are alternated in rapid succession to form most of the motives. This lower pitch varies, depending both on the performer and

---

[1]See Part III, p. 422.

[2]See, for example, Part III, p. 427: JGG 1.2, second parvan, on the syllable ha.

[3]See, for example, Part III, p. 422: JGG 1.1, second parvan, on the syllable yā.

on the amount of breath available.[1] In the chants of Śrī Itti Ravi Nambūdiri, sixty-seven years old at the time of my recordings, it is mainly the tone VII; in the performances of Śrī T. Nārāyaṇan Nambūdiri, a much younger singer, it is the tone VIII.

The motives, listed according to the number of pitches, will be referred to henceforth by numeral-letter symbols: 5b, for instance, indicates a particular motive with five pitches. One or more musical examples illustrate each motive, although all possibilities are not given for each designation. Roman numbers continue to be used to identify the tones of the gamut. The final tone of each motive may vary in duration, but in the examples below it is given always as a sixteenth note (𝅘𝅥𝅯 = approximately 116 for all examples). The pitches preceding the final tone are transcribed usually as thirty-second notes, occasionally (only in the transcriptions in Part III) as sixty-fourth notes.

A. Non-motivic tones (single pitches)

1a: IV

1b: II

---

[1]Technically, all <u>parvans</u> are to be sung in a single breath; however, the Nambūdiri chants are often extended to such a degree that strict adherence to this precept is made difficult or even impossible. Oftentimes the chanter is so short of breath at the conclusion of a <u>parvan</u> that he must strain in order to finish without breathing. Some <u>parvans</u> are extremely lengthy, so that performance in a single breath is out of the question. In such a case the singer chooses a spot in which to interrupt the melodic flow. The impressive stamina of Nambūdiri Sāmavedins is reminiscent of that required of <u>dhrupad</u> singers in North Indian classical music.

1c: VI

1d: VII

1e: VIII

1f: I

B. Two-member motives

2a: V, VI, VII, or VIII (that is, V-VIII) / IV

2b: IV-VIII / II

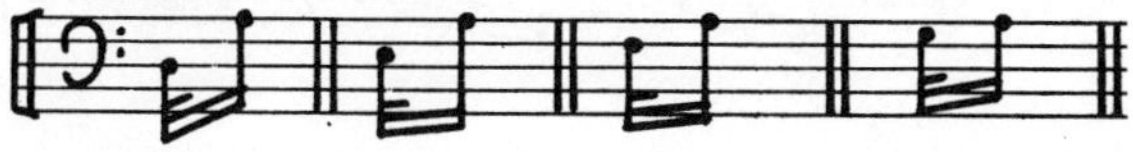

2c: VI-VIII / V-VI

2d: II / V-VIII

2e: II / IV

2f: V-VI / VI-VIII

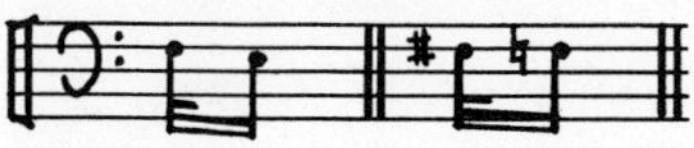

2g: II / III

2h: I / II

C. Three-member motives

3a: V-VIII / II, IV / V-VIII

3b: IV-VIII / II / IV

3c: II / VII-VIII / VI

3d: II / V-VIII / IV

3e: II / IV-VIII / II

D. Four-member motives

4a: V-VIII / II / IV-VIII / II

4b: V-VIII / II / V-VIII / IV

4c: II / V-VIII / II / IV

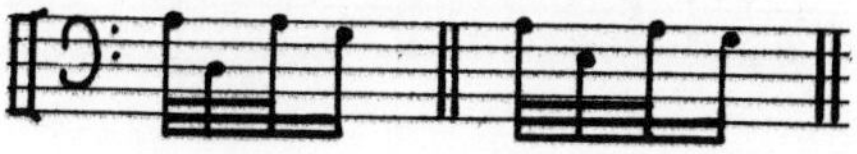

4d: II / V-VIII / II / V-VIII

4e: V-VIII / IV / V-VIII / IV

E. Five-member motives

5a: V-VIII / II / V-VIII / II / IV

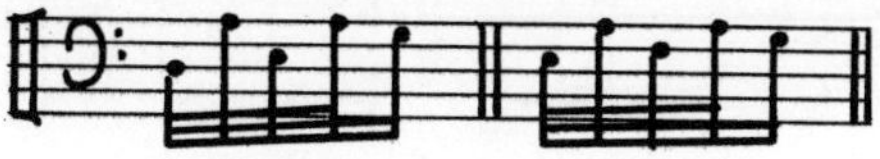

5b: II / V-VIII / II / IV-VIII / II

5c: II / V-VIII / II / V-VIII / IV

F. Six-member motives

6a: V-VIII / II / IV-VIII / II / IV-VIII / II

6b: II / V-VIII / II / IV-VIII / II / IV

6c: V-VIII / II / IV-VIII / II / V-VIII / IV

G. Seven-member motives

7a: V-VIII / II / V-VIII / II / V-VIII / II / IV

7b: II / V-VIII / II / IV-VIII / II / IV-VIII / II

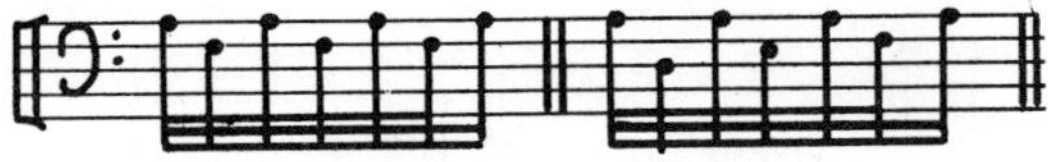

7c: II / V-VIII / II / IV-VIII / II / V-VIII / IV

H. Eight-member motives

8a: V-VIII / II / V-VIII / II / V-VIII / II / V-VIII / II

8b: II / V-VIII / II / V-VIII / II / V-VIII / II / IV

I. Nine-member motive

9a: II / V-VIII / II / V-VIII / II / V-VIII / II / V-VIII / II

J. Ten-member motives

10a: V-VIII / II / V-VIII / II / V-VIII / II / V-VIII / II / V-VIII / IV

10b: II / V-VIII / II, IV / V-VIII / II / V-VIII / II / V-VIII / II / IV

K. Twelve-member motive

12a: II / V-VIII / II / V-VIII / II / V-VIII / II / V-VIII / II / V-VIII / II / IV

L. Fifteen-member motive

15a: II / V-VIII / II / V-VIII / II / V-VIII / II / V-VIII / II / V-VIII / II / V-VIII / II / V-VIII / II

The above designations (2a, 2b, and so on) can be used symbolically to represent the various motivic constituents of entire *sāmans*. Below are presented ten such analyses, including: JGG 1.1-3, JGG 1.1-3 (abbreviated versions),[1] JĀrG 1.1-2, Jaiminīya Gāyatram, and JŪG from JS 3.6.9-11 (the sixteenth *stuti* [ritual chant] of the Nambūdiri *atirātra*).[2] Apart from the motivic designations, only a few additional symbols are used. A dash represents a continuation of the final tone of the preceding motive. An asterisk denotes where breath is taken. Wherever a motive is divided between two syllables of text, the tone (or tones) belonging to each syllable is indicated in parentheses. Two versions of the chants have been aligned where possible. I wish to thank Sreekrishna Sarma for supplementary copies of JGG 1.1-3 and JĀrG 1.1-2; his tapes were used for the first version of the former, the second version of the latter. The three *stotriyās* of the *ṣoḍaśi-sāman* are of course set to the same melody.

(1) JGG 1.1

1. Itti Ravi Nambūdiri with Nārāyaṇan Nambūdiri:
2. Itti Ravi Nambūdiri :
   Text :

[1] These shortened forms of the chants are, according to Itti Ravi, never employed during sacrificial performances. Whether they belong solely to the chants of the Pūrvagāna is a matter deserving investigation.

[2] See NVR, pp. 34, 80, 83.

```
2a    2a 2a 2a    4a 3b 3d 5b    2a 4c 2e 7b       3b 3d
2a 3a 2a 2a 5a 3d 3e 3b 3d 4c 3e 3b 3d 2e 4c 2e 3e 3b 3d
o

   3e 3b --    3e 3b 3d 5b   3b 3d    7b          3b 3d
4c 3e 3b -- 4c 3e 3b 3d 7b * 3b 3d 2e 4c 2e 2e 3e 3b 3d
         gnā                 ā

5b    3b -- * 2f 2a 2e 3d 4c    3d 3d 2g 3b    3e 3b 4c
4c 3e 3b -- * 2f 2a 2e 3d 4c 2e 3d 3d 2g 3b 2e 3e 3b 4c
         yi   ā     yā

      1b -- 2a(1) (2) 4c    3d -- 6b 3d * 2d 2a 2e 4c 5b
2e 2e    1b 2a(1) (2) 4c 2e 3d -- 6b 3d * 2f 2a 2e 4c 7b
         hi       vā          yi         tā

3b 3d 2e    3d -- 4c 3d 3b    6a 3b 2e    3e(1-2) (3)
3b 3d -- 2e 3d -- 6b 3d 3b 3b 5b 3b 2e 2e 3e(1-2) (3) 3b
      yā       yi       tā                       yā

2b 4a 3b 3d 2e 2e      4c 3e 3b    4c 5b 3b    * la 2a(1)
   5b 3b 3d       * -- 4c 5b 3b 3d 4c 3e 3b -- * 1d 2a(1)
                    ā                       yi   gṛ

(2) 4c    3d -- 2e 6a       3b 3d    5b 3b -- 2a 3d 1b le
(2) 4c 2e 3d -- 2e 3b 2e 3e 3b 3d 4c 3e 3b -- 2a 3d 2b --
ṇā           no                            hā          vya

       la 3e 5a lb   3b 4c    2e 3d * 2d 2a 2e 4c 3e 3b
2a(1) (2) 3e 5a    * 2e 4c 2e 2e 3d * 2f 2a 2e 4c 4c 4c
      dā             ā                tā

3d 2e 3d -- 4c    3d 3b 3b    3e 3b 2e 3e(1-2) (3) 3b 3e
3d 2e 3d -- 4c 2e 3d 3b 3b 2e 3e 3b 2e 3e(1-2) (3) 3b 3e
   yā    yi          tā                        yā

3b 3d      2e 4c 3e 3b 3d    5b 3b -- * 2d 2a    3e 5b
3b 3d * -- 4c 4c 3e 3b 3d 4c 3e 3b -- * 1b 2a 2e 4c 4c 3d
        ā                          yi   nā

3b 3d -- -- 1b 3b 1b 3b 3b       5c(1-4) (5)   3e 5a 3e
3b 3d -- 3d    4c 3e 3b 3b 2e 2e 4c(1-2) (3-4) 5b 5a 3e
      yi ho                            tā

3b 6b       3d * 2e 2a    5b 5a 3e 3b 4c    3d --  2a
3b 4c 2e 2e 3d * 2e 2a 4c 3e 5a 3e 3b 4c 2e 3d --  2a 4c
                 sā                            tsā

5b 3b    5b 3b 3d 3e 3b      -- 1b 2e    4c 3e 3b 3d 2e
3e 3b 4c 3e 3b 3d    4c * 2e -- 1b 2e 3d 4c 3e 3b 3d 2e
                          ā  yi    bā

4c 4c 3d 3d 2c 2a 2a 3a(1-2) * (3) 1a -- 2c 2a 2a 3b(1-2)
3d 4c 3d 3d 2c 2a 3b 3a(1-2) * (3) 1a -- 2c 2c 2a 3b(1-2)
                               au  ho vā
```

```
* (3)  2b 2b 2b 2a 5b 3b    5b 3b 3d    5b 3b 1d 1a 2b
* (3) 10a       4c 3e 3b 5a 3e 3b 3d 4c 3e 3b 3c 1a 8a
  hī                                          ṣi

2b 2b 3b
      3b //
```

(2) JGG 1.2

1. Itti Ravi Nambūdiri with Nārāyaṇan Nambūdiri:
2. Itti Ravi Nambūdiri :
Text :

```
1d 1a  -- -- 4c(1-3)       (4) 3e(1-2) (3) 3b   4c 3d
1d 1a  -- -- 3e      2a(1) (2) 3e(1-2) (3) 3b 3e 3b 3d
a  gna ā  yā               hi          vī

5b 3b 3d 7b       3b 3d 3e 3d * -- 1b -- 1a 2b -- 2h --
5b 3b 3d 4c 3e 3e 3b 3d 4c 4c * -- 1b -- 1a 2b -- 2h --
                                ta yā yi gṛ ṇā no ha vya

2b 2b    2a(1) (2) 4c    3d -- 2e 4a 3b 5b 3b 3d 3e 3b
2b 2b 2b 2a(1) (2) 4c 2e 3d 3b    4a 3b 5b 3b 3d 5b 3b
               dā           tā

-- 3e 3b 3d 5b   3b 3d    4c    3e 3b 3d 2e 2e 1b 3b -- *
-- 3e 3b 3d 5b * 2a 3d 2e 4c 2e 3e 3b 3d    4c 3e 3b -- *
yā                                                 yi

-- 2a(1) (2) 4c 3d -- 2e 3b 3e 3b 3d    5b 3b -- 2a    5b
2f       1a  4c 3d 3b    3b 3e 3b 3d 4c 3e 3d -- 2a 4c 3e
ni       ho     tā                              sa

3d 4c --    -- 2e  2e 4a 3b 5b 3b 3d 3e 3b -- 3e(1-2) (3)
3b 4c -- * 2e 2e  2e 6a 3b 5b 3b 3d 4c 4c -- 6b(1-2) (3-6)
      t    sī bar hā                      yi          ṣī

3b 5c 3d 5b   3b 3d 2e 7b    3b 3d    5b * 2e  2e 3b 3e
5b 3b 3d 5b * 3b 3d 2e 4c 3e 3b 3d 4c 4c * --  2e 6a
              ī                            bar hā

3b 5b 3b 3d    3e 3b -- 1b        --    1a 3d 5b 3b 3d 2e
3b 5b 3b 3d 4c 3e 3b -- 4c(1-2) (3-4)   3d 7b 3b 3d 2e
                     yi          ṣā

   4c 3d 3d   2c 2a 2a 2b 1d 1a 2e 2c 2c 2c      -- 5a 3e
3d 4c 3d 3d * 2e    2a 2b 1d 1a -- 2c 2c 2c 2b *
                          au ho vā                bar

3b 5b 3a(1-2) (3)        2a 4c 1b 3b
              1a  1b 2b 2b 2a 4c 3e 3b 3b 3e 2b 3b 3d 4c
              hī
```

```
5b 3b       3d 5b 3b 3d 8b 3d 3d 2a 2a 2a 3a
3e 3b 1c 1a    1b             2b 2b 2b 3b
         ṣi                                //
```

(3) JGG 1.3

```
    1.  Itti Ravi Nambūdiri with Nārāyaṇan Nambūdiri:
    2.  Itti Ravi Nambūdiri                          :
        Text                                         :
```

```
1d 1a -- -- 3e       1a  1b        --  4a 3b 3d    5b 3b
1d 1a -- -- 7c(1-6) (7) 6b(1-2) (3-6) 5b 3b 3d 4c 3e 3b
a  gna ā yā          hi             vā

3d    3d 7b    3b 3d    3e 3b -- -- 2a(1) (2) 3e 3b 3d
3d 2e 4c 3d 3e 3b 3d 4c 3e 3b -- -- 2a(1) (2) 5b 3b 3d
                              yi tā        yā

5b    3b 3d    4c 3e 3b 3d    5b 3b -- * le    1a  3e
7b * 2a 3d 2e 4c 5b 3b 3d 4c 3e 3b -- * 2a(1) (2)    2e
                                   yi   gṛ    ṇā

2a(1)    (2) 4c 3d 2e 2e  1b        --  4a 3b 3d 4c 3e 3b
3d(1-2) (3) 4c 3d -- --  6b(1-2) (3-6) 5b 3b 3d 4c 3e 3b
         no        ha vya           dā

3d 2e 2e 2e 3d 3e    5b 3b    5b 3b   2e 3d    5b 3b 6a
3d 2e 2e 2e 3d 3e 5a 3e 3b 4c 3e 3b * 2e 3d 4c 3e 3b 3b
                                       tā

      3b 3d    5b 3b 4c 1b 3b -- 4c    3d 3d 2c 2a 2a 3b
3d 3e 3b 3d 4c 3e 3b 4c 3e 3b -- 4c 2e 3d 3d 2c 2a 2a 3b
                              ye

   5b 3b * 1b 1a 2e 3b 3e 3b 3d 2e 4c 4c 3d 3d 2b
4c 3e 3b * 1b 1a 2e 3b 3e 3b 3d 2e 4c 4c 3d 3d 2b 2b 2b
           ni ho tā

3a       1a  2c 2a 2a       4a    5a 1b 3b 6b    3d
2c 2a(1) (2) 2c 2a 2a 2a 1b 2b 2b 5a 3e 3b 4c 2e 3d(1-2)
         sā

--  -- 2a 5b    3b 5b 3b 3d 5b 3b -- 3e(1-2) (3) 3b 1b 3b
(3) -- 2a 4c * 2e 5b 3b 3d 5b 3b -- 3e(1-2) (3) 3b 3e 3b
t  sā                            yi          ba

3d 4c          3d 3e 5c 3e 3b -- 3e 3b 5b 3b
3d 4c 2e 2e 3d 3e 5a 3e 3b -- 4c    3e 3b 6b(1-5) * (6)
                              r

2e 3d    5b 3b 3d    4c 4c 3d 3d 2b 2b 2b    3a 2a(1) (2)
2e 3d 4c 3e 3b 3d 3d 3d 4c 3d 3d 2b 2b 2b 2b 3a 2a(1) (2)
hā                                                    yi
```

-- 2c 2a   2b * la 2b 2b 2b   3b(1-2) (3) 2b
-- 2c 2a 2a 2b * la 2b 2b 2b 2b 2a(1)   (2) 2b
ṣo   hā   yi   //

(4) JGG 1.1 (abbreviated version)

Itti Ravi Nambūdiri: la 4e 3e 3b 4c -- 4d 4c -- *
Text   : o   gnā   yi

-- 1c 2a -- 3d 3d 3d 2e 3b -- -- 4c -- 5c * 1b 2a 5b 3b
ā   yā   hi vā   yi   tā

3d 1b la 4b -- 3d 3b 3b 8b(1-2) (3-8) 4c -- * 1d 3e 2a
   yā   yi   tā   yā   yi gṛ ṇā

-- 2e 3b 3d 4c -- 2c 2e 1b le la 5b 3b 3b 3d * 1b 2a 5b
no   hā   vya dā   tā

3b 3d -- 3d -- 3d -- 2e 3b 8b(1-2) (3-8) 4c -- * 1b 2a 5b
      yā   yi   tā   yā   yi   nā

3b 3d -- -- 3d 3b 3d(1-2) (3) 5b 3b 2e 3d * 2e 2a 8b --
      yi ho   tā   sā   t

-- 2c 4c -- 1b -- la 4e le la -- 4a * la 3e 2a 7b 3b 1d
sā   yi   bā   au ho vā   hī

la 4a 3b
ṣi   //

(5) JGG 1.2 (abbreviated version)

Itti Ravi Nambūdiri: 1d la   -- -- 3d(1-2) (3) 8b(1-2)
Text   : a gna ā yā   hi

(3-8) 4c * la 1b -- la -- 1b -- 2h -- 4b(1-3) (4) 2e 2e
 vī   ta yā yi gṛ ṇā   no ha vya   dā   tā

3b 4c -- 4c 4c -- * le la 1b 2a -- 2e 6c 4c -- 4b 4c --
      yā   yi   ni ho   tā   sa   t

-- -- 2e 3b 4c -- 8b(1-2) (3-8) 4c * -- 2e 3b 4c --
sī ba rhā   yi   ṣī   ba rhā   yi

4c(1-2) (3-4) 3d 6c 1d la -- 5b * la 2e(1) (2) 3e 3b
         ṣā   au ho vā   ba   r

4d(1-2) (3-4) la 4c 4c -- 2a 6a
         hī   ṣi   //

(6) JGG 1.3 (abbreviated version)

```
    Itti Ravi Nambūdiri: 1d la -- -- 3d(1-2) (3)
    Text               : a  gna ā  yā         hi

8b(1-2) (3-8) 4c -- -- 2a(1) (2) 4c 4c -- * 2a(1) (2)
         vā      yi tā        yā          yi    gṛ   ṇā

4c(1-2) (3-4) 1b 2a 2a -- 1b -- 5a 3d 4c 3d 6b 3d 5b 3b
         no         ha vya    dā

4c -- 3d 7b 3b -- 2e 2e 2a 3b 4c * 1b la 2e 3b 3d 6b 2e
   tā             ye                ni ho tā

3d 4a 2a 2a(1) (2) 2a 5b 3b 3b 3d -- -- 2a 4c 4c 3d 4c *
                sā                  t  sā

-- 1b -- 5a 3d 3d 7b 3b -- 4c 4c -- 3d 4c 3d 6b 2e 3d 4a
yi    bā                 r        hā

2a 2a(1) (2) -- 6a * -- la 2b 2b 2a(1) (2) 2b
         yi  ṣo      hā                yi      //
```

(7) JĀrG 1.1

```
    1.  Nārāyanan Nambūdiri: 2a(1) (2) 2b 2b 3b --
    2.  Itti Råvi Nambūdiri: la    --  2b 2b 3b --
        Text               : hu    ve           vā

3e(1-2) (3) 5a 3d 4c 3d 5b 3b 3d    4c -- * le la 2a 2a
3e(1-2) (3) 5a 3d 4c 3d 5b 3b 3d 3e 4c -- * le la 2a 2a
         cā                          m         vā cam̩

3b 4c    4d(1-3) (4) 2a -- 4c 4c 3d 2e -- 2e 4a 3b 4c 3d
4b 4c 3d 3c(1-2) (3) 2a -- 2b 2b 2a la -- 2e 2a    4c 3d
                  vā    cam̩            hu ve

4c -- 4c 3d 4c 3d 5b 3b 3d 4c -- * 2a(1) (2) 2a 2a 2a 3b
4c -- 4c 3d 4c 3d          4c -- * 2a(1) (2) 2a 2a    4b
   vā                         k    ṡṛ    ṇo

3e 3b 4d(1-3) (4) 2a -- 3d -- 4c 4c 3d -- 2e -- 2e 4a 3b
4c 3d 5b(1-4) (5) 2a -- 3d -- 4c 3b 3d -- 2e -- 2e 4a 3b
               tu    ṡṛ    ṇo            tu    vā

4c 3d 4c -- -- 4c 3d 4c 3d 5b 3b 3d 4c -- * 2a(1) (2) 2a
4c 3d 4c -- -- 4c 3d 4c 3d 5b 3b 3d 4c -- * 2a(1) (2) 2a
      g  vā                            k    sa        mai

2a 3b    2e 4d(1-3) (4) 2a 3b 3d -- 4c 4c 3d -- 2e --
2a 3b 4c 2e 4d(1-3) (4) 2a la 3d -- 4c 3b 3d --    --
                     tu    sa    mai           tu  vā
```

```
2e 4a 3b 4c 3d 4c -- -- 4c 3d 4c 3d 5b 3b 3d 4c -- * 2e
2e 4a 3b 4c 3d 4c -- -- 4c 3d 4c 3d 5b 3b 3d 4c -- * 2e
                  g  vā                          k    ra

2e(1) (2) 3d -- 4c 4c 3d -- 2e 2e(1) (2) 3d -- 4c 4c 3d
2e(1) (2) 3d -- 4c 3b 3d -- 2e 2e(1) (2) 3d -- 4c 3b 3d
      ma     tā          m  ra       ma     tā

-- -- 2e -- 2e 4a 3b 4c 3d 4c -- 4c 3d 8b 3d 2c 2c
-- --    -- 2e    3b 4c 3d 4c -- 4c 2e    3d 2c 2c 2a
ṃ  ra    mā                   tā

3a(1-2) (3) 1a 2e 2c 2c 2c 2b * 2f 1a -- -- 1b 2b 2b 2b
2b      1d  1a -- 2c 2a    2b * 2f 1a -- -- 1b 2b    2b
        au  ho vā               ī  hā ī  hā

1a 3e(1-2) (3) 5a 3d 4c 3d 5b 3b 3d    4c
1a 3e(1-2) (3) 5a 3d 4c 3d 5b 3b 3d 3e 3b
ī          hā                              //
```

(8) JĀrG 1.2

```
    1. Nārāyaṇan Nambūdiri:  2a --    5b 3b 3d -- 2e 4c
    2. Itti Rāvi Nambūdiri:  2a -- 2e 5b 3b 3d -- 2e 4c
       Text               :  hu vā                yi vā

7a(1-6)  (7)  3e 4a 3b 4c 3d -- * -- 2a 4c 8b(1-2) (4-8)
10a(1-9) (10) 5b    3b 3b 3d -- * -- 2a 4c 8b(1-2) (4-8)
         cā                  m    vā                caṃ

3d 3d 3d 2h 4a 3b       3e(1) (2-3) 3b(1-2) (3)    3d --
3d 3d 3d    4a 3b 4c 2e 3e(1) (2-3) 3b(1-2) (3) 4c 3d --
                               hu            vā        yi

2e 3d * 2a 2a 2a    4a 3b 3d 4c 3d 5b 3b 3d    4c -- *
4c 3d * 2a 2a 2a 2a 4a 3b 3d 4c 3d 5b 3b 3d 3e 3b -- *
        vā                                        k

2a -- 3d(1-2) (3) 3d(1-2) (3)    4c(1-3) (4)    4c 2d
1a -- 3d(1-2) (3) 3d(1-2) (3) 1b 4b(1)    (2-4) 4c 8b(1-2)
śṛ ṇo         tū          śṛ               ṇo

3e    3b(1-2) (3)   2b 3b -- 2a 2b 2a 4a 3b 3d 4c 3d 5b
(3-6)         (7-8) 2b 3b -- 2a 2a 2a 4a 3b 3d 4c 3d 5b
tu            vā          g  vā

3b 3d 4c -- * -- -- 3d(1-2) (3) 3d(1-2) (3) 4c(1-3) (4)
3b 3d 4c -- * -- -- 3d(1-2) (3) 3d(1-2) (3) 3d(1-2) (3)
         k    sa mai         tu          sā          mai

4c 5b(1-2) (3-5) 3b(1) (2-3) 2b 2b 3b 2a 2a 2a 4a 3b 3d
4c 5b(1-2) (3-5) 3b(1) (2-3) 2b 2b 5a 2a 2a 2a 4a 3b 3d
            tu          vā             gvā
```

```
4c 3d 5b 3b 3d 4c -- * -- 2d 4b 4a    3b 4c 3d       4c
4c 3d 5b 3b 3d 4c -- * -- 2d 3b 2b 2b 3b 4c 3d 1b 2b 3b
                  k    ra ma tā

-- -- 2a(1) (2) 2e -- 4c(1-2) (3-4) 3d 4c 3d 8b      3d
-- -- 2a(1) (2) 2e -- 4c(1-2) (3-4) 3d 4c 3d 4c 2e 2e 3d
ṃ  ra       ma     tu         vā

2e 2d 2e 3a(1-2) (3) 1a 3d 4c       2b * le la -- 5c(1-4)
2a 2a 2a 2b      1d  1a 2e 2a 2a 2a 2b * le la -- 3d(1-2)
                 au  ho vā               mā yi mā

(5) 3e(1-2) (3) 5a 3d 4c 3d 5b 3b 3d    4c --
(3) 3e(1-2) (3) 5a 3d 4c 3d 5b 3b 3d 3e 3b --
yi          mā                          yi //
```

(9) Jaiminīya Gāyatram

```
    Itti Ravi Nambūdiri:  1a 1b  -- --  2a(1) (2) 4c 3d
    Text               :  ta tsa vi tur  va    re

--  3e 5a 3e 3b 4c 2e 2e 3d -- * --  2h -- -- 2a(1) (2)
ṇyo                         ṃ     bhar go de va sya  dhī

3d -- 4c 3d -- 4c 3b 3d -- 2e(1) (2) 3d -- 5b 3b(1) (2-3)
   mā       hā          yi       dhī   yo            yo

3b 3d -- 2e 4a 3b 4c 3d 3e 3b * 2a   6a 2a 2e 4c 2e 2e
      nā                       ḥprā

1la(?) 3b 5b 3b 2e 2e 3d 4c 4c 4c 6a 2a(1) (2) 4c 2e 3d
                                           cā

--  4c 3d * --  4c 7c 3d 1d 1a 4c 6b 3e 3b 4c 2e 3d --
haṃ         bhā          o                         vā

2e 6a 3b 4c 2e 2e 3d
                     //
```

(10) JŪG from JS 3.6.9-11

```
    Itti Ravi Nambūdiri:  1a 2b 2b 2b 2a 6b 2e 9a 3b 5b
    Text               :  o

2b 3b 5b 3b 4c 2e 2e 3d 3e 5a 3e 3b 4c 2e 2e 3d -- 4c
                                                haṃ

6b 3e 3b 4c 2e 3d * -- --  2a 3b --  3e 3b --  3e 3b 3d
                    in drā       ju        sā
                    -- --  2a 3b --  3e 3b --     4c 3d
                    in drā       jā        thā
                    -- --  2a 3b --  3e 3b --     4c 3d
                    in drā       stu       rā
```

```
1.  6b 3d 3d 2b 2b 2b 2b 2a 3e 3b 3d 6b 3d 3d 2c 2a 2a   --
                                                          svā
2.  6b 2e 3d    2b 2b 2b 2a    4c 3d 6b 3d 3d 2c 2a 2a   --
                                                          ran
3.  6b 2e 3d 2b 2b 2b 2b 2a 3e 3b 3d 6b 3d 3d 2c 2a 2a * --
                                                          ṣā

1.  4b    * 1d 3d --  2a 2a 2a 4e -- * -- 2h
            prā   vā              ha    o yā
2.  5a    * 1d 3d --  2a 2a 2a 4e -- * -- 1f  1b  -- --
            nav   yan             na    o na  sva ma dho
3.  2c 2a   2b    la  2a 2a 2a 4e -- * -- 2h  --  -- --
            ṇmi   tro             na    o khā na  vṛ traṃ

1.  --  2a(1) (2)  3d -- 2e(1) (2) -- -- 2e     4a 3b 3b 3d --
    hi        śū      ra       ha  ri ha pā                 yi
2.  --  2a(1) (2)  3d --                          4c 3b 3d
    dri       vo      nā
3.  --  2a(1) (2)  3d 1b                 -- la 4a 3b 3b 3d --
    yya       tir     na                 bā                 yi

1.  2e 4a 3b 3d 6b 3d 3d 2c 2b   2b 2b 2a 3e 3b 3d      6b
    bā
2.  2e 4a 3b 3d 6b 3d 3d    2b * 2b 2b 2a    4c 3d      6b
    syā
3.  2e 4a 3b 3d 6b 3d 3d 2c 2b   2b 2b 2a    4c 1b * la 6b
    bhā

1.  3d 3d 2c 2c 2b 2b 3b 3d [unclear on tape]  * 1b 2a 3e
                                                 sū
2.  3d 3d 2c 2c 4a    3b 3d 4c 3d 5b 3b 3d 3e 3b * 1b 2a 3e
                                                 sū
3.  3d 3d 2c 2c 4a    3b 3d 4c 3d 5b 3b 3d    4c * 1b 2a 3e
                                                 dā

1.  3b 4c 3d -- 2e 4a 3b 3d 6b 3d 3d 2b 2b 2b 2b 2a    4c 3d
             tā
2.  3b 3b 3d -- 2e 4a 3b 3d 6b 3d 3d    2b 2b 2b 2a 3e 3b 3d
             tā
3.  3b 6c    -- 2e    3b 3d 6b 3d 3d    2b 2b 2b 2a    4c 3d
             vā

1.  6b 3d 3d 2c 2a 2a 4a 3b 3d 3d 5b 3b 3b 3d * 2e 4a 3b 4c
                                                syā
2.  6b 3d 3d 2c    2a 4a 3b 3d 3d 5b 3b 3b 3d * 2e 4a 3b 4c
                                                syā
3.  6b 3d 3d 2c    2a 4a 3b 3d 3d 5b 3b 3b 3d * 2e 4a 3b 4c
                                                lā

1.  3d 4c --    2a 2a 2a 4a 3b 3d 4c 3d 2e 4c 2e 2e 9a 3b 8b
          mā
2.  3d 4c 2a       2a 2a 4a 3b 3d 4c 3d 2e 4c 2e 2e 9a 3b 3e
          sū
3.  3d 4c --    2a 2a 2a 4a 3b 3d 4c 3d 2e 4c 2e 2e 7b 3b 8b
          ṃbhṛ
```

```
1.     2e 2e 7b    2a 3e * la 3d      6b 3d 3d 2b 2b 2b 2b

2.  5a 3e 2b 2b 2b 2a 3e   3b lb * la 6b 3d 3d 2b 2b 2b 2b

3.     3e       2a 3d 3e   3b lb * la 6b 3d 3d 2b 2b 2b 2a(1)

1.  la 5b 3b 3d 3e 3b --  2e 3d 4c lb * la 6b 3d 3d 3a 2a 2a
    tir               nā
2.  la 5b 3b 3d 3e 3b --     3d 4c 3d      6b 3d 3d 3a 2a 2a
    var               nā
3.  (2) 5b 3b 3d    4c -̇-     3d 4c lb * la 6b 3d 3d 3a 2a 2a
    gun               nā

1.  2a 2a 4b 2b 2b 2b 3b   -- 3e 3b 2e  3d 4c 3d      6b 2e
                           mā       dho
2.  2a    4b 2b 2b 4b lb * la    4c 2e  3d 4c 3d      6b 2e
                           ū        pā
3.  2a 2a 4b 2b 2b 2b 3b   --    4c 2e  4c 4c lb * la 6b 2e
                           sā       sā

1.  3d 2c 2c 2c 2b(1) (2) * --  2a 3e 3b 4c 3d    3b 4a 3b
                       h    cā                    kā
2.  3d 2c 2c 2a 2b     •  * --  2a 3e 3b 4a 2a    3b    4b
                            tvā                   mā
3.  3d 2c 2c 2c 2b        * --  2a 3e 3b 4c 3d -- -- 4a 3b
                            hā                 yi śā

1.  3d 6b 3d 3d 2b 2b 2b 2b 2a 4c 3d      6b 3d 3d 2c 2c

2.  3d 6b 3d 3d       2b 2b 2a 4c 3d      6b 3d 3d 2c 2c

3.  3d 6b 3d 3d 2b 2b 2b 2b 2a 4c lb * la 6b 3d 3d 2c 2c 2a

1.  4a 3b 3d 3d 5b 3b 3b 3d * --     3b 4c 3d      5a 2a
                              nā                      ścā
2.  4a 3b 3d 3d 5b 3b 3b 3d * --     3b 4c 3d      4c 2a
                              dā                      ssū
3.  4a 3b 3d 3d 6b 4c 3b 3d * 2e  4a 3b 4c lb * la 4c --  2a
                              trū                     nmā

1.  2a 2a 4a 3b 3d 4c 3d 2e 6b 2e 7b 3b 3e 5a 7b          2a

2.  2a 2a 4a 3b 3d 4c 3d 2e 5c 2e 7b 3b 3e 5a 2e 2e 5b    2a

3.  2a 2a 4a 3b 3d 4c 3d 2e 6b 2e 7b 3b 3e 5a 2e 2e 5b 2b 2a *

1.                7a 3d 3d 2c 2c    2b * la 2a 3e 3b 4c 3d
                                         o
2.  4c lb * -- la 6b 3d 3d 2a 2a 2a 2b * la 2a    4c 4c 3d
             ū                           o
3.  2e 3d          6b 3d 3d 2a 2a 2a 2b * la 2a 3e 3b 4c 3d
                                         o
```

```
1.  4c 3d 2e 2e 2e 3d 6b 4c    4c -- 3d 4c 3d        6b 3d 3d
                                  mo
2.  4c 3d 2e 2e 2e 3d 5b 3b    4c -- 3d 4c 3d        6b 3d 3d
                                  co
3.  4c 3d 4c    2e 3d 5b 3b 3e 3b -- 3d 4c 1b * 1a 6b 3d 3d
                                  so

1.  2b 2b 2b 3b * 1c_ la 2c 2a 3b 2c 2c 2c 2a 3b 1c la   2c
                  bbā dā                             yo
2.  2b 2b 2b 3b * 1c_ la 2c 2a 3b 2c 2c 2c 2a 3b 1c la   2c
                  bbā a                              sthu
3.     2b 2b 3b * 1c_ la 2c 2a 3b 2c 2c 2c 2a 3b 1c la   2c
                  bbā mā                             syo

1.  2c 2a 2b         * la 2b 2b 2b 2a(1) (2) 2b
                       hā                 yi    //
2.  2c 2a 2b(1) (2)  * la 2b 2b 2b 2a(1) (2) 2b
                 h     hā                 yi    //
3.  2c 2a 2b      •  * la    2b 2b 2a(1) (2) 2b
                       hā                 yi    //
```

The Nambūdiri tradition has been strictly oral, and therefore the Sāmagas are not acquainted with any system of notation. However, it may be useful to compare portions of some Nambūdiri chants which would have identical notational signs if the system of the Tamil̲ Jaiminīyas were employed. By comparing extracts from JGG 1.1-2 we obtain significant, though inconclusive, results. Following are patterns of four svarabhedas:

(1) Āvarta

```
             ┌──ādisvara──┐
        ta:  2a  3a 2a 2a 5a 3d 3e 3b 3d 4c 3e    3b 3d 2e 4c
             o
        ta:  la_             4c 3e 3b 3d 7b       3b 3d 2e 4c
             gnā
        ta:  la                 3e 3b 3d 5b    * 2a 3d 2e 4c
             yā

    2e       3e 3b 3d 4c 3e 3b (JGG 1.1)

    2e 2e 2e 3e 3b 3d 4c 3e 3b (JGG 1.1)

    2e       3e 3b 3d 4c 3e 3b (JGG 1.2)
```

(2) Yāna

ṭa: 2e 2a 4c 3e 5a 3e 3b 4c 2e 3d (JGG 1.1)
sā
ṭa: la 2a 4c 3e 3b 4c 3e 3b 3d 4c (JGG 1.1)
tsā

(3) Udgama

cā: 1b 2a(1) (2) 4c 2e 3d (JGG 1.1)
hi vā
cā: 1d 2a(1) (2) 4c 2e 3d (JGG 1.1)
gṛ ṇā

(4) Anvaṅgulya

khā: la 1b 2e 3d 4c 3e 3b 3d 2e 3d 4c 3d 3d
yi bā
khā: 4c(1-2) (3-4) 3d 7b 3b 3d 2e 3d 4c 3d 3d
yi ṣā

2c 2a 3b 3a(1-2) (JGG 1.1)

3d * 2e 2a 2a 2b (JGG 1.2)

Therefore the Nambūdiri chant appears to follow the syllable notation rather closely; in some respects it is more faithful to the individual notational signs than the chants of the Tamiḻ Jaiminīyas. There are some noteworthy discrepancies, however, and the problem demands further study. A svara is occasionally realized differently according to the vowel assigned the notational consonant. For example, ca is the pattern: 2e 5b 5a 3e 3b 4c 2e 2e 3d. But cā is 1d 2a 4c 2e 3d, and ci is la 2a 3d 2b 2a 3e 5a.[1] Possibly, as elsewhere in India, the sequence of notational symbols in the parvan (or vacana, as the Nambūdiris call it)--not the single sign--is the true notational unit.

[1]See JGG 1.1, parvans 6, 2, and 4, respectively.

Kai-kāṭṭuka and mudrā

The Nambūdiris employ hand movements (kai-kāṭṭuka: "hand showing")[1] which differ from those in use elsewhere. In September, 1971, I took still photographs of most of the positions as demonstrated by Itti Ravi Nambūdiri (see figs. 21-48 below). They were not explained to me at the time, but Parpola was able to take notes during his visit of March 14, 1971. He has very kindly forwarded to me that information, which has enabled me--after further correspondence with Itti Ravi--to present the sequence of hand movements for JGG 1.1-3.

The hand is held at three vertical levels: high (upari), middle (madhyam), or low (adhaḥ). A lower middle level, called pādam, is used occasionally. The hand may be moved to three horizontal positions: right (dakṣiṇa), middle, or left (vāma).

The hand may be held in four ways in each position:

(1) malartti (malarttuka):[2] "to place on the back, to lay open, to turn face upward." The palm of the hand faces the chanter (in the upari position).

(2) kamiḻtti (kamiḻttuka):[3] "to upset, to be turned upside down." The back of the hand faces the chanter (in the upari position).

(3) upariṣṭha-piṭikka: piṭi[4] = "to catch, seize, clutch, cling to."[5] Upariṣṭha (from Sanskrit) = "staying

---

[1]See DED 1683, 1209. [2]See DED 3880.

[3]See DED 1121. [4]See DED 3412.

[5]Parpola writes, "It seems that the word means 'holding (the hand in a certain position)' and is to be supplied also after malartti and kamiḻtti."

above." The hand is turned sideways so that the edge of the little finger faces the onlooker. In a letter of May 20, 1973, Itti Ravi has referred to this position as cĕriccu, which he defines as "the palm turned sideways to the left."

(4) maṭaki-piṭikka: maṭaki from maṭakku,[1] "to bend as the arms or knees, draw in, fold." The hand is held in a fist. This may be done in any of the preceding positions.

A procedure called kaṇakku (counting) is sometimes performed but only when the hand is motionless. The counts are made by bending forward each finger in its turn, beginning with the little finger.

In addition to these obligatory movements, which must be performed while chanting a sāman, there are certain optional mudrās which correspond to (long?) vowels, gati, anusvāra, visarga, and final ḷ, ṯ, and ṉ. There is also another movement, not photographed by me, which indicates vibrato. As described by Parpola, the thumb is placed upon the nail of the index finger; then the arm is moved horizontally back and forth. This movement is referred to as vilaṅṅattil,[2] "in transverse."

The movements for JGG 1.1-3 are given in table 9. In the first sāman the first two syllables of text (each designated by the āvarta in the manuscripts) have the same sequence of movements (excluding kaṇakku). However other

---

[1]See DED 3796. [2]See DED 4450.

syllables with the same notational sign do not have identical hand movements, even though the tonal patterns are sometimes the same. Thus it is impossible at this point to associate a particular motive or series of motives with any given symbol or hand movement.

TABLE 9

NAMBŪDIRI KAI-KĀṬṬUKA FOR JGG 1.1-3

A. JGG 1.1: <u>gautamasya</u> <u>parkaḥ</u>

Text Syllable	Kai-Kāṭṭuka
o	(1)-(3) kaṇakku (4) maṭaki-piṭikka, malartti, upari (5) maṭaki-piṭikka, malartti, madhyam (6) malartti, adhaḥ (7) malartti, upari (8) malartti, madhyam (9) malartti, adhaḥ (10) malartti, madhyam (11) kamiḻtti, upari (12) kamiḻtti, adhaḥ (13) cĕriccu, kamiḻtti, dakṣiṇa, upari (14) cĕriccu, kamiḻtti, madhyam (15) kamiḻtti, adhaḥ
gnā	(1) maṭaki-piṭikka, malartti, upari (2) maṭaki-piṭikka, malartti, madhyam (3) malar-tti, adhaḥ (4) malartti, upari (5) malartti, madhyam (6) malartti, adhaḥ (7) malartti, madhyam (8) kamiḻtti, upari (9) kamiḻtti, adhaḥ (10) cĕriccu, kamiḻtti, dakṣiṇa, upari (11) cĕriccu, kamiḻtti, madhyam (12) kamiḻ-tti, adhaḥ
yi	no <u>svara</u>

TABLE 9--Continued

Text Syllable	Kai-Kaṭṭuka
ā	(1) malartti, adhaḥ (2) malartti, madhyam (3) malartti, adhaḥ
yā	(1) malartti, upari (2) malartti, adhaḥ (3) malartti, upari (4) malartti, adhaḥ (5) malartti, upari (6) malartti, madhyam (7) malartti, upari
hi	(1) malartti, madhyam
vā	(1) malartti, adhaḥ
yi	(1) malartti, upari
tā	(1) malartti, vāma, madhyam (2) malartti, vāma, adhaḥ (3) malartti, vāma, madhyam (4) malartti, dakṣiṇa, madhyam (5) cĕriccu, madhyam (6) kamiḻtti, vāma, madhyam
yā	(1) cĕriccu, dakṣiṇa, adhaḥ
yi	(1) cĕriccu, vāma, upari (2) malartti, upari
tā	(1) malartti, adhaḥ (2) malartti, madhyam (3) kamiḻtti, upari
yā	(1) kamiḻtti, upari (2) kamiḻtti, madhyam (3) kamiḻtti, adhaḥ (4) cĕriccu, kamiḻtti, upari (5) cĕriccu, kamiḻtti, madhyam (6) kamiḻtti, adhaḥ
yi	(1) kamiḻtti, adhaḥ
gṛ	(1) kamiḻtti, adhaḥ
ṇā	(1) cĕriccu, kamiḻtti, upari
no	(1) cĕriccu, kamiḻtti, upari (2) cĕriccu, kamiḻtti, madhyam (3) cĕriccu, kamiḻtti,

TABLE 9--Continued

Text Syllable	Kai-Kāṭṭuka
	madhyam (4) cĕriccu, kamiḻtti, adhaḥ
hā	(1) malartti, adhaḥ (2) malartti, dakṣiṇa, madhyam (3) malartti, adhaḥ (4) malartti, upari
vya	(1) malartti, adhaḥ
dā	(1) malartti, madhyam (2) malartti, upari (3) malartti, madhyam (4) malartti, upari
tā	(1) malartti, vāma, madhyam (2) malartti, vāma, adhaḥ (3) malartti, vāma, madhyam (4) malartti, dakṣiṇa, madhyam (5) cĕriccu, madhyam (6) kamiḻtti, vāma, madhyam
yā	(1) cĕriccu, dakṣiṇa, adhaḥ
yi	(1) cĕriccu, vāma, upari (2) malartti, upari
tā	(1) malartti, adhaḥ (2) malartti, madhyam (3) kamiḻtti, upari
yā	(1) kamiḻtti, upari (2) kamiḻtti, madhyam (3) kamiḻtti, adhaḥ (4) cĕriccu, kamiḻtti, upari (5) cĕriccu, kamiḻtti, madhyam (6) kamiḻtti, adhaḥ
yi	(1) kamiḻtti, adhaḥ
nā	(1) kamiḻtti, dakṣiṇa, madhyam (2) kamiḻtti, dakṣiṇa, adhaḥ (3) kamiḻtti, adhaḥ (4) cĕriccu, vāma, adhaḥ (5) cĕriccu, vāma, upari (6) cĕriccu, madhyam (7) cĕriccu,

TABLE 9--Continued

Text Syllable	Kai-Kāṭṭuka
	dakṣiṇa, upari
yi	no svara
ho	(1) kamiḻtti, adhaḥ (2) kamiḻtti, madhyam (3) kamiḻtti, dakṣiṇa, upari
tā	(1) kamiḻtti, dakṣiṇa, upari (2) kamiḻtti, madhyam (3) kamiḻtti, adhaḥ
sā	(1) malartti, dakṣiṇa, adhaḥ (2) kamiḻtti, vāma, adhaḥ (3) malartti, dakṣiṇa, adhaḥ (4) cĕriccu, madhyam (5) cĕriccu, vāma, madhyam
tsā	(1) malartti, adhaḥ (2) kamiḻtti, upari (3) kamiḻtti, adhaḥ (4) kamiḻtti, madhyam (5) kamiḻtti, upari (6) kamiḻtti, adhaḥ (7) cĕriccu, dakṣiṇa, upari (8) cĕriccu, dakṣiṇa, madhyam
yi	(1) cĕriccu, dakṣiṇa, madhyam
bā	(1)-(2) cĕriccu, vāma, madhyam (3) cĕriccu dakṣiṇa, madhyam (4) cĕriccu, vāma, madhyam (5) cĕriccu, dakṣiṇa, madhyam (6) cĕriccu, vāma, madhyam (7) malartti, upari (8) malartti, adhaḥ (9) malartti, madhyam (10)-(13) kaṇakku
au	no svara
ho	no svara
vā	(1)-(4) kaṇakku

TABLE 9--<u>Continued</u>

Text Syllable	Kai-Kāṭṭuka
hī	(1) malartti, vāma, adhaḥ, kaṇakku (2) malartti, vāma, upari (3) malartti, dakṣiṇa, adhaḥ (4) malartti, adhaḥ (5) malartti, upari (6)-(7) malartti, adhaḥ (8) cĕriccu, malartti, dakṣiṇa, upari (9) kamiḻtti, adhaḥ
ṣi	(1) cĕriccu, kamiḻtti, dakṣiṇa, upari (2) kamiḻtti, dakṣiṇa, madhyam (3) kamiḻtti, madhyam (4) kamiḻtti, adhaḥ
	B. JGG 1.2: <u>kaśyapasya</u> <u>barhiṣīyam</u>
a	no <u>svara</u>
gna	no <u>svara</u>
ā	(1) maṭaki-piṭikka, kamiḻtti, adhaḥ
yā	(1) maṭaki-piṭikka, kamiḻtti, adhaḥ
hi	(1) maṭaki-piṭikka, malartti, upari
vī	(1) maṭaki-piṭikka, malartti, upari (2) maṭaki-piṭikka, malartti, madhyam (3) malartti, adhaḥ (4) malartti, upari (5) malartti, madhyam (6) malartti, adhaḥ (7) malartti, madhyam (8) cĕriccu, upari (9) kamiḻtti, adhaḥ (10) cĕriccu, kamiḻtti, dakṣiṇa, upari (11) cĕriccu, madhyam (12) kamiḻtti, adhaḥ

TABLE 9--Continued

Text Syllable	Kai-Kāṭṭuka
ta	no *svara*
yā	no *svara*
yi	no *svara*
gṛ	no *svara*
ṇā	no *svara*
no	(1) malartti, dakṣiṇa, madhyam
ha	(1) malartti, dakṣiṇa, upari
vya	(1)-(3) cĕriccu, vāma, madhyam
dā	(1) malartti, adhaḥ (2) cĕriccu, madhyam (3) kamiḻtti, upari
tā	(1) kamiḻtti, adhaḥ (2) kamiḻtti, madhyam (3) kamiḻtti, upari (4) kamiḻtti, adhaḥ (5) kamiḻtti, upari (6) kamiḻtti, adhaḥ (7) malartti, upari
yā	(1) malartti, upari (2) malartti, madhyam (3) malartti, adhaḥ (4) malartti, upari (5) malartti, madhyam (6) malartti, adhaḥ (7) malartti, madhyam (8) kamiḻtti, upari (9) kamiḻtti, adhaḥ (10) kamiḻtti, dakṣiṇa, upari (11) kamiḻtti, madhyam (12) kamiḻtti, adhaḥ
yi	(1) kamiḻtti, adhaḥ
ni	(1) malartti, upari
ho	(1) malartti, adhaḥ
tā	(1)-(3) malartti, madhyam (4) malartti, upari

TABLE 9--Continued

Text Syllable	Kai-Kāṭṭuka
sā	(1) cĕriccu, dakṣiṇa, madhyam (2) cĕriccu, vāma, madhyam (3) cĕriccu, dakṣiṇa, madhyam (4) cĕriccu, vāma, madhyam (5) malartti, upari
tsi	(1) malartti, adhaḥ
ba	(1) kamiḻtti, upari
rhā	(1) kamiḻtti, adhaḥ (2) kamiḻtti, madhyam (3) kamiḻtti, upari (4) kamiḻtti, adhaḥ (5) kamiḻtti, upari (6) kamiḻtti, madhyam (7) kamiḻtti, adhaḥ
yi	no *svara*
ṣī	(1) malartti, upari (2) malartti, madhyam (3) malartti, adhaḥ (4) malartti, upari (5) malartti, madhyam (6) malartti, adhaḥ (7) malartti, madhyam (8) kamiḻtti, upari (9) kamiḻtti, adhaḥ (10) kamiḻtti, dakṣiṇa, upari (11) kamiḻtti, madhyam (12) kamiḻtti, adhaḥ
ba	no *svara*
rhā	(1) kamiḻtti, adhaḥ (2) kamiḻtti, madhyam (3) kamiḻtti, upari (4) kamiḻtti, adhaḥ (5) kamiḻtti, upari (6) kamiḻtti, madhyam (7) kamiḻtti, adhaḥ
yi	no *svara*

TABLE 9--Continued

Text Syllable	Kai-Kāṭṭuka
ṣā	(1)-(2) cĕriccu, vāma, madhyam (3) cĕriccu, dakṣiṇa, madhyam (4) cĕriccu, vāma, madhyam (5) cĕriccu, dakṣiṇa, madhyam (6) cĕriccu, vāma, madhyam (7) malartti, upari (8) malartti, adhaḥ (9)-(12) kaṇakku
au	no svara
ho	no svara
vā	(1)-(4) kaṇakku
bā	(1) kamiḻtti, adhaḥ
r	(1) cĕriccu, vāma, madhyam (2) cĕriccu, dakṣiṇa, madhyam (3) cĕriccu, vāma, madhyam (4) malartti, vāma, upari
hī	(1) malartti, vāma, upari (2) malartti, adhaḥ (3) cĕriccu, dakṣiṇa, madhyam (4) cĕriccu, vāma, madhyam (5) cĕriccu, dakṣiṇa, madhyam
ṣī	(1)-(2) cĕriccu, vāma, madhyam (3) cĕriccu, dakṣiṇa, madhyam (4) cĕriccu, vāma, madhyam (5) cĕriccu, dakṣiṇa, madhyam (6) cĕriccu, vāma, madhyam (7) malartti, upari (8) malartti, adhaḥ (9) malartti, madhyam (10)-(13) kaṇakku

TABLE 9--Continued

C. JGG 1.3: <u>gautamasya</u> <u>caiva</u> <u>parkaḥ</u>

Text Syllable	Kai-Kāṭṭuka
a	no <u>svara</u>
gna	no <u>svara</u>
ā	(1) kamiḻtti, adhaḥ
yā	(1) kamiḻtti, madhyam
hi	(1) malartti, upari
vā	(1) malartti, upari (2) malartti, madhyam (3) malartti, adhaḥ (4) malartti, upari (5) malartti, madhyam (6) malartti, adhaḥ (7) malartti, madhyam (8) kamiḻtti, upari (9) kamiḻtti, adhaḥ (10) kamiḻtti, upari (11) kamiḻtti, madhyam (12) kamiḻtti, adhaḥ
yi	(1) kamiḻtti, adhaḥ
ta	no <u>svara</u>
yā	(1) malartti, upari (2) malartti, madhyam (3) malartti, adhaḥ (4) malartti, upari (5) malartti, madhyam (6) malartti, adhaḥ (7) malartti, madhyam (8) kamiḻtti, upari (9) kamiḻtti, adhaḥ (10) kamiḻtti, upari (11) kamiḻtti, madhyam (12) kamiḻtti, adhaḥ
yi	(1) kamiḻtti, adhaḥ
gṛ	no <u>svara</u>
ṇā	(1) cĕriccu, dakṣiṇa, madhyam
no	(1) cĕriccu, vāma, madhyam

TABLE 9--Continued

Text Syllable	Kai-Kāṭṭuka
ha	(1) cĕriccu, dakṣiṇa, madhyam (2) cĕriccu, vāma, madhyam
vya	(1) malartti, upari
dā	(1) malartti, dakṣiṇa, upari (2) malartti, dakṣiṇa, madhyam (3) malartti, dakṣiṇa, adhaḥ (4) cĕriccu, upari (5) kamil̲tti, vāma, madhyam (6) kamil̲tti, vāma, adhaḥ (7) cĕriccu, upari (8) malartti, adhaḥ (9) malartti, upari (10) malartti, adhaḥ (11) malartti, madhyam (12) malartti, upari
tā	(1)-(2) malartti, adhaḥ (3) malartti, upari (4) malartti, adhaḥ (5) kamil̲tti, upari (6) kamil̲tti, adhaḥ (7) kamil̲tti, adhaḥ (8)-(9) kamil̲tti, madhyam (10) kamil̲tti, dakṣiṇa, madhyam (11) kamil̲tti, upari
ye	(1) kamil̲tti, adhaḥ (2) kamil̲tti, dakṣiṇa, upari (3)-(4) kamil̲tti, madhyam (5) kamil̲tti, adhaḥ
ni	no <u>svara</u>
ho	(1) malartti, adhaḥ
tā	(1) malartti, upari (2) malartti, adhaḥ (3) kamil̲tti, upari (4) kamil̲tti, madhyam (5) cĕriccu, dakṣiṇa, adhaḥ (6) cĕriccu, vāma, madhyam (7) malartti, vāma upari

TABLE 9--Continued

Text Syllable	Kai-Kāṭṭuka
sā	(1)-(2) malartti, dakṣiṇa, adhaḥ (3) malartti, adhaḥ (4) malartti, vāma, adhaḥ (5) malartti, upari
tsā	(1) malartti, adhaḥ (2) kamiḻtti, upari (3) kamiḻtti, adhaḥ (4) kamiḻtti, madhyam (5) kamiḻtti, upari (6) kamiḻtti, adhaḥ (7) kamiḻtti, dakṣiṇa, upari (8) kamiḻtti, madhyam (9) kamiḻtti, adhaḥ
yi	no svara
bā	(1) malartti, dakṣiṇa, upari (2) malartti, dakṣiṇa, madhyam (3) malartti, dakṣiṇa, adhaḥ (4) cĕriccu, upari (5) cĕriccu, vāma, adhaḥ (6) cĕriccu, upari
r	(1) cĕriccu, upari (2) cĕriccu, dakṣiṇa, madhyam (3) cĕriccu, vāma, madhyam (4) cĕriccu, dakṣiṇa, madhyam
hā	(1)-(2) cĕriccu, vāma, madhyam (3) cĕriccu, dakṣiṇa, madhyam (4) cĕriccu, vāma, madhyam (5) cĕriccu, dakṣiṇa, madhyam (6) cĕriccu, vāma, madhyam (7) malartti, upari (8) malartti, adhaḥ (9) malartti, upari (10) malartti, madhyam (11) malartti, adhaḥ
yi	no svara
ṣo	(1) malartti, upari (2)-(4) kaṇakku, madhyam

TABLE 9--Continued

Text Syllable	Kai-Kāṭṭuka
hā	(1)-(4) kaṇakku, madhyam
yi	(1) malartti, madhyam

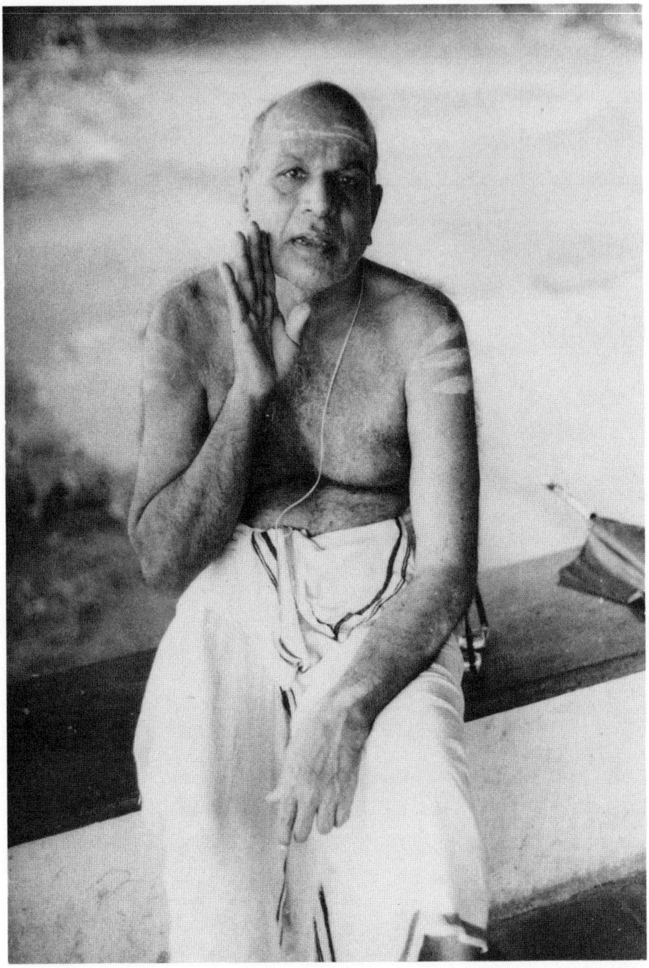

Fig. 21. kami<u>l</u>tti, upari

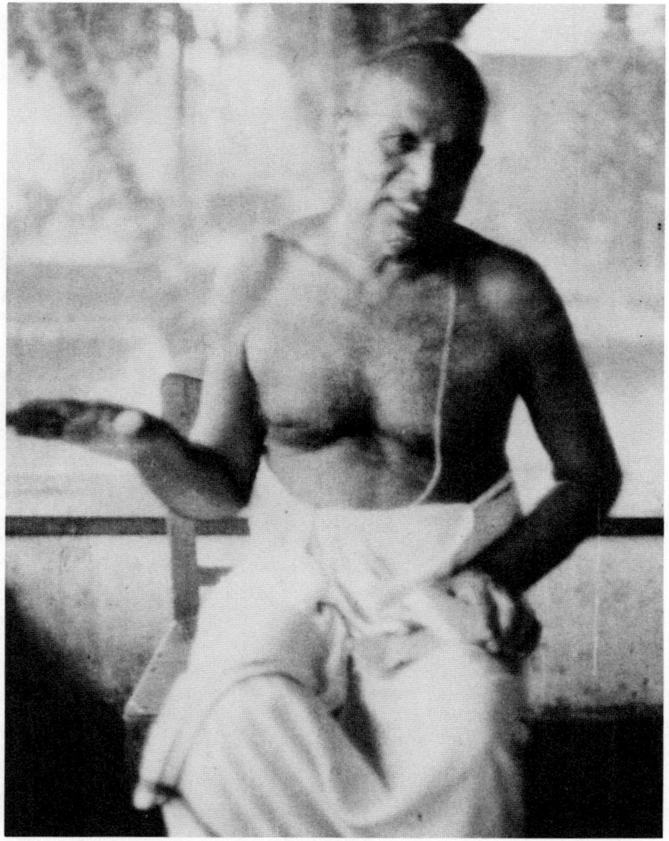

Fig. 22. kamil̲tti, dakṣiṇa, madhyam

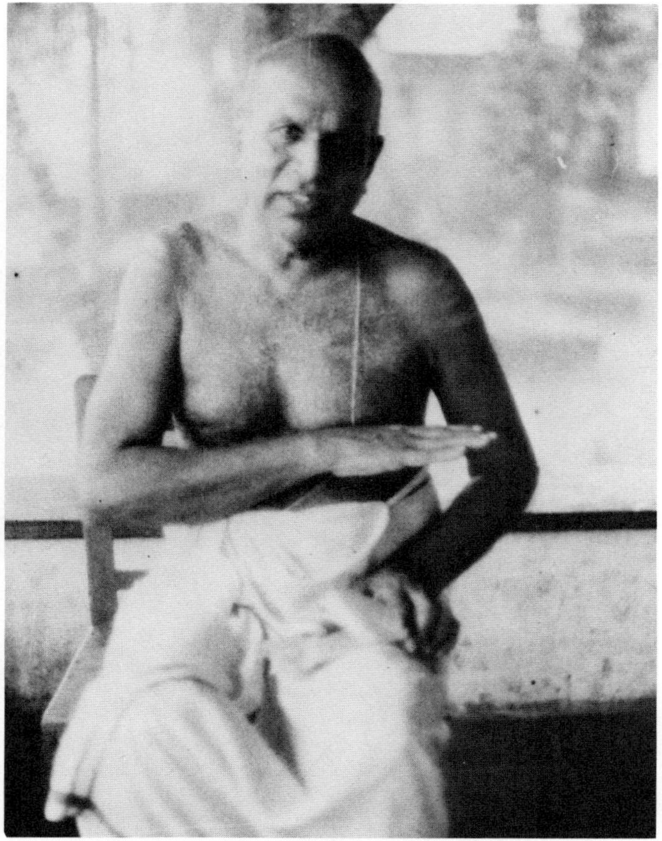

Fig. 23. kamil̲tti, vāma, madhyam

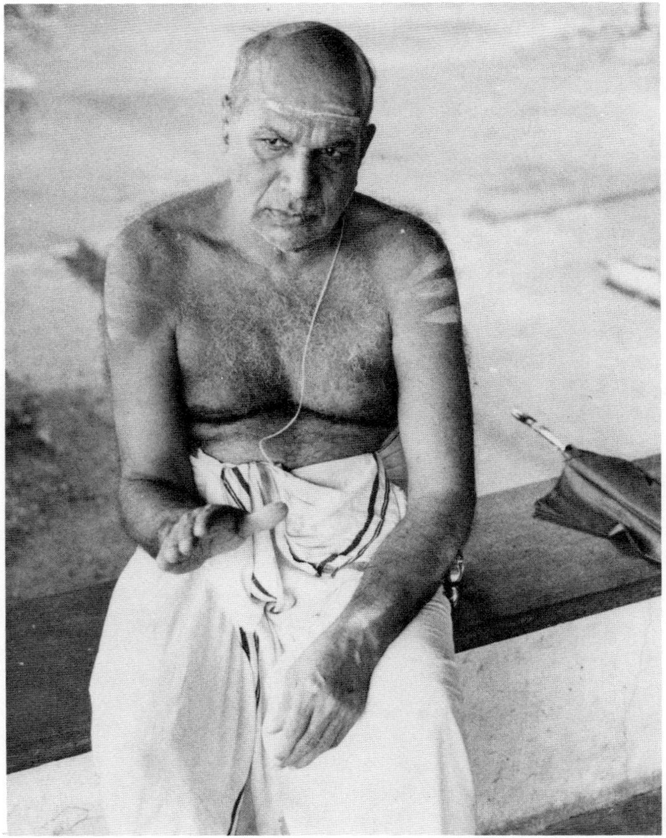

Fig. 24. kamiḻtti, madhyam

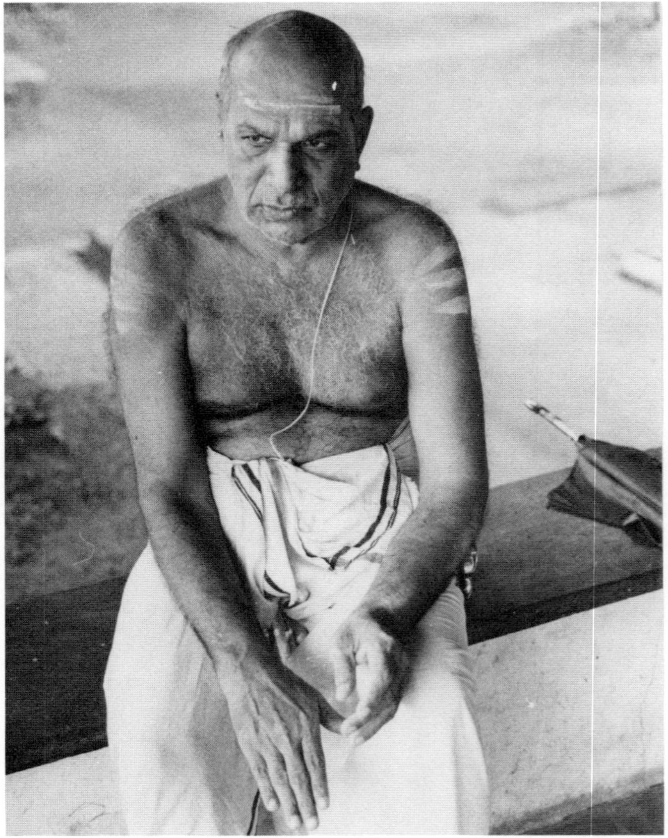

Fig. 25. kamiḻtti, adhaḥ

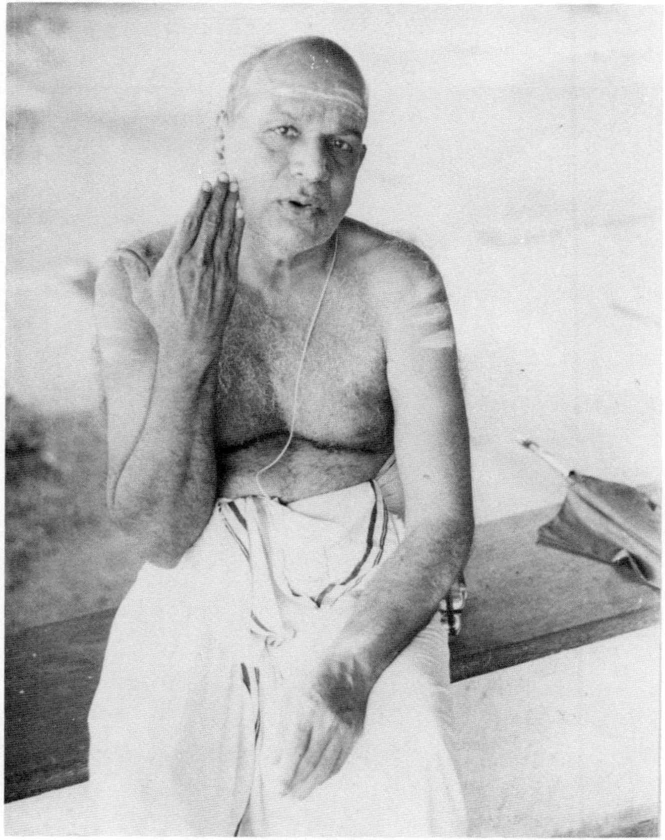

Fig. 26. <u>malartti</u>, <u>upari</u>

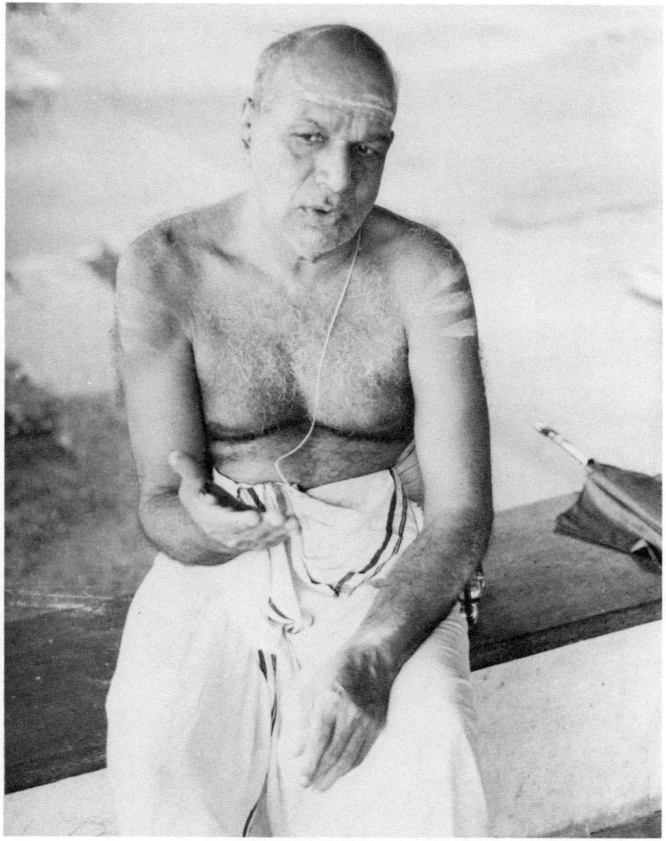

Fig. 27. <u>malartti</u>, <u>madhyam</u>

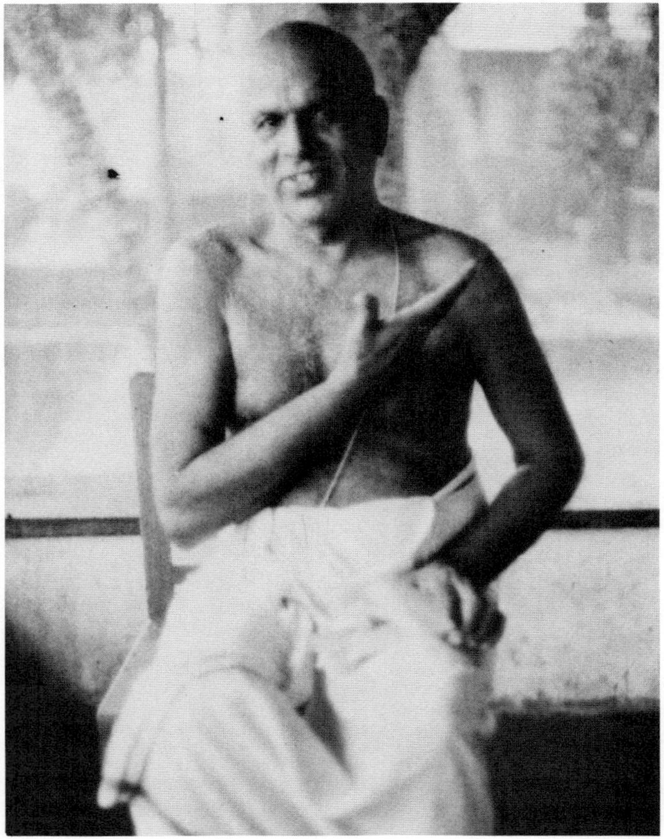

Fig. 28. malartti, vāma, upari

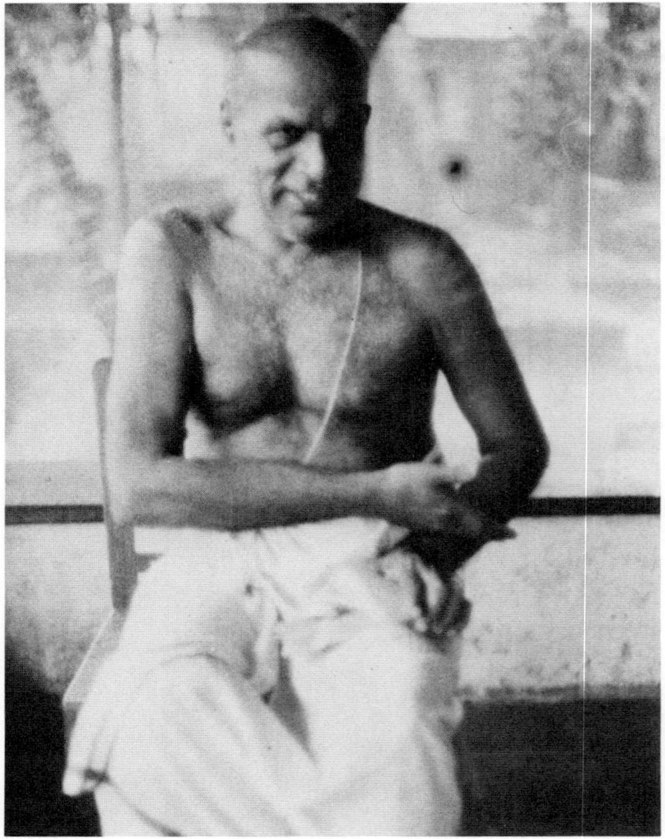

Fig. 29. malartti, vāma, madhyam

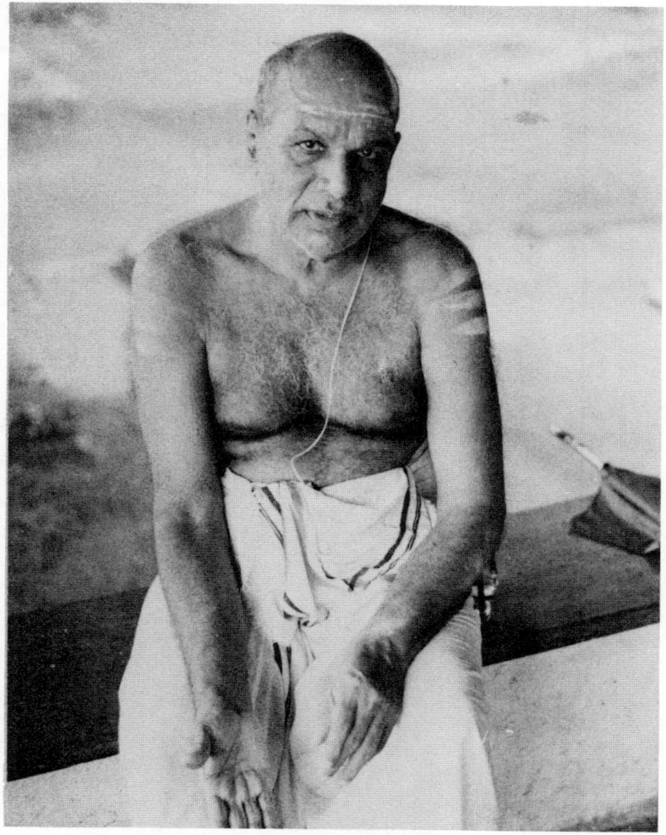

Fig. 30. malartti, adhaḥ

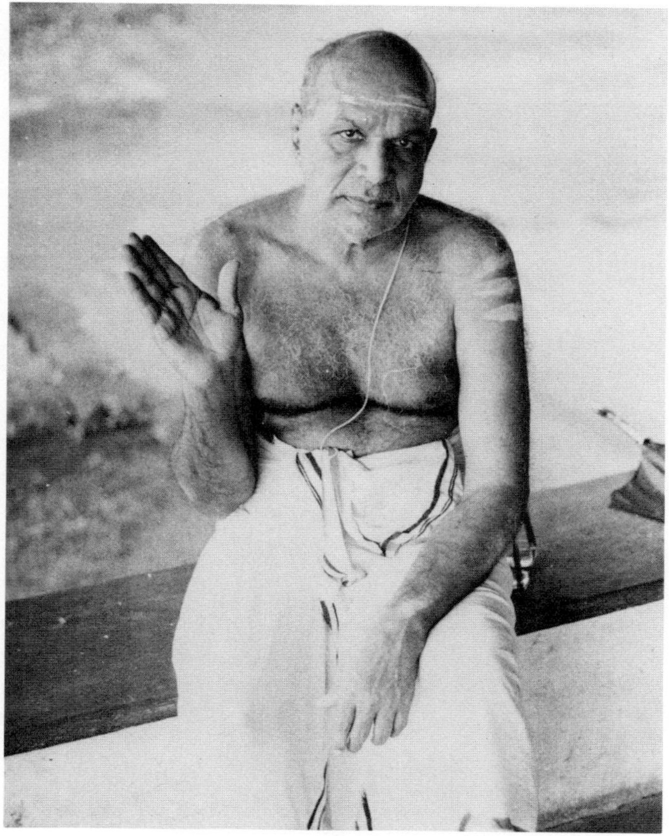

Fig. 31. cĕriccu, upari

Fig. 32. cĕriccu, dakṣiṇa, madhyam

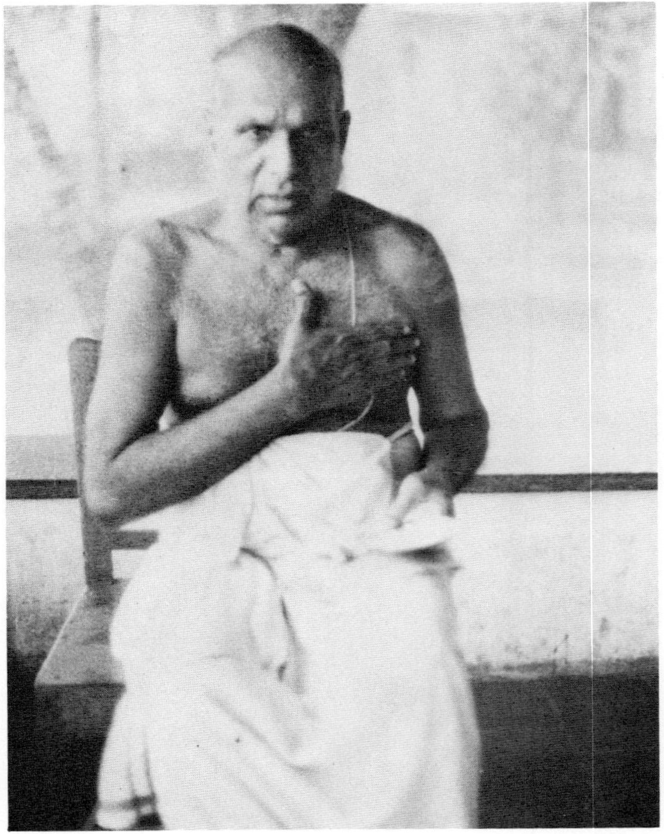

Fig. 33. cĕriccu, vāma, madhyam

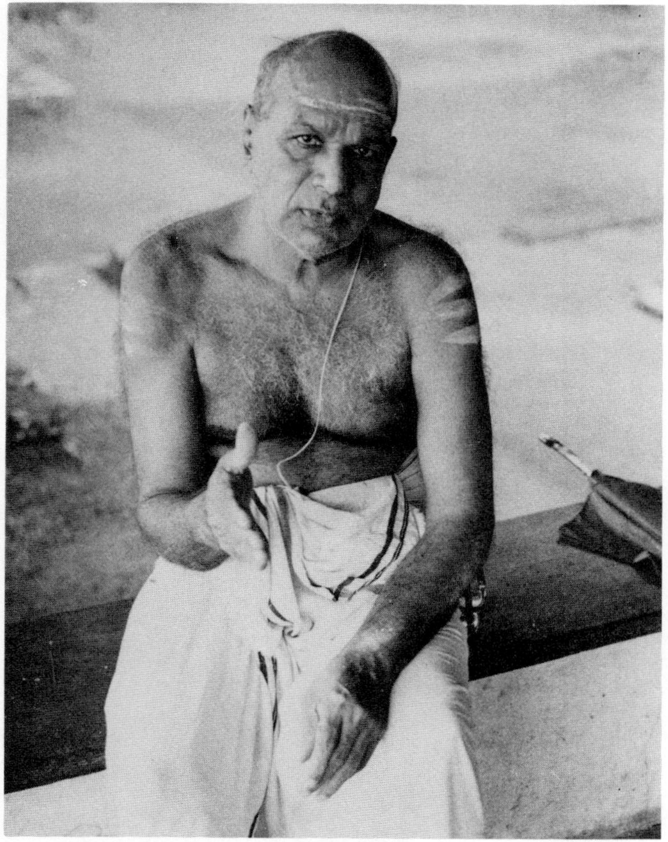

Fig. 34. <u>cĕriccu</u>, <u>madhyam</u>

Fig. 35. <u>cĕriccu</u>, <u>adhaḥ</u>

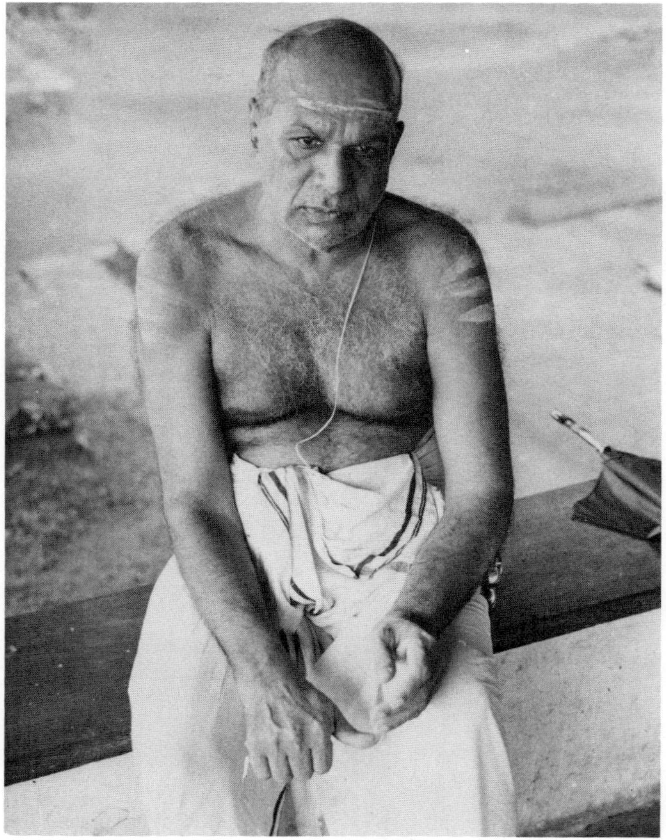

Fig. 36. maṭaki-piṭikka, kamiḻtti, adhaḥ

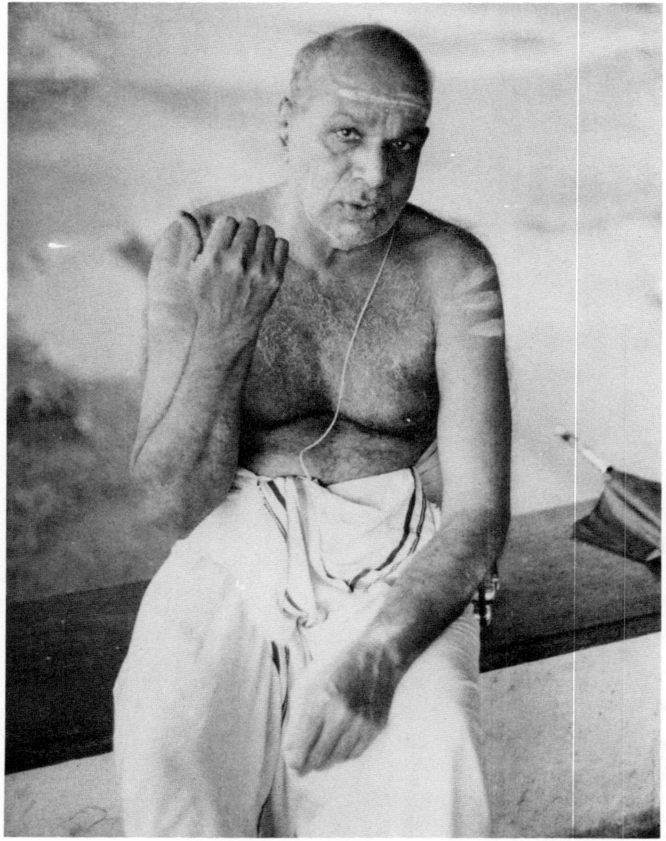

Fig. 37. maṭaki-piṭikka, malartti, upari

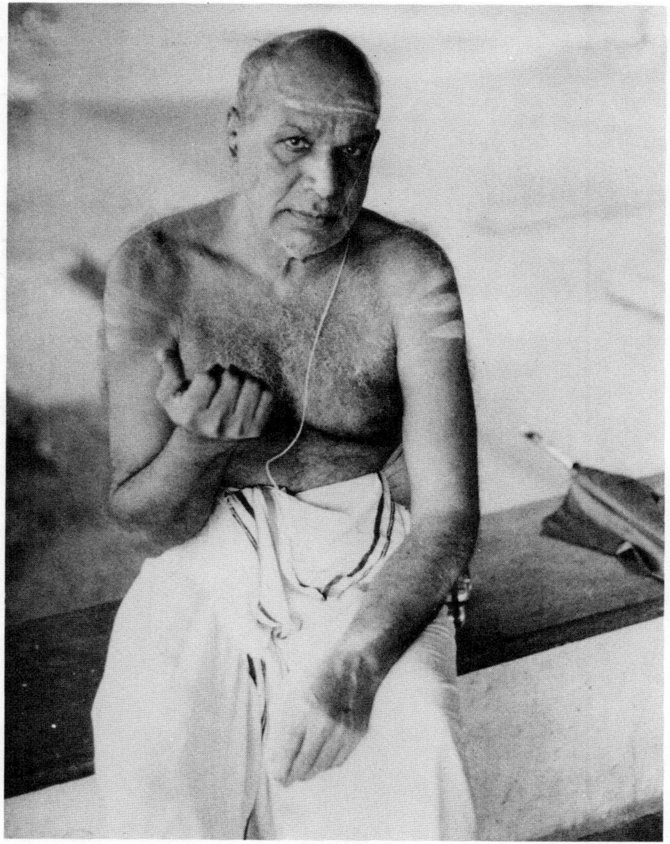

Fig. 38. _maṭaki-piṭikka_, _malartti_, _madhyam_

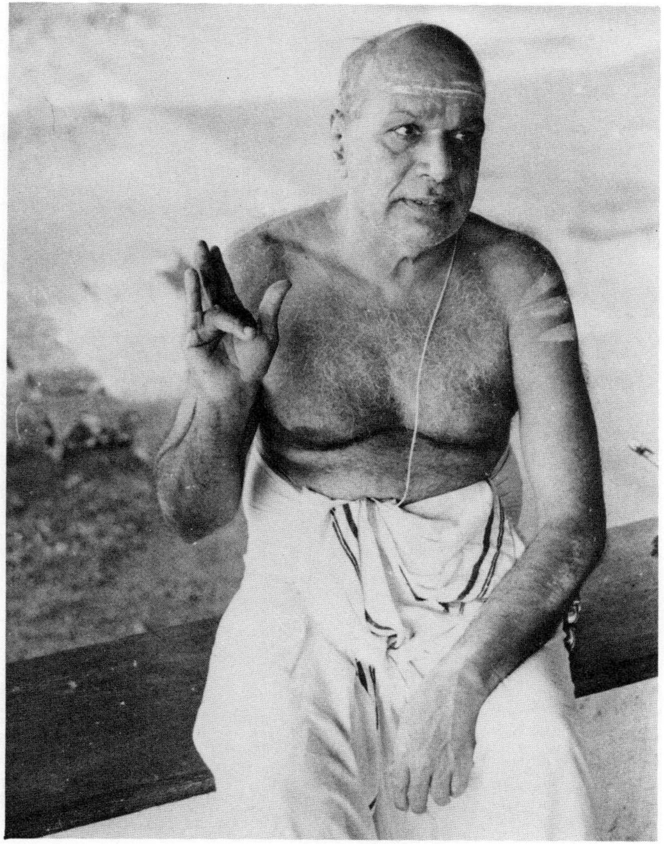

Fig. 39. _ā-kāra_

Fig. 40. _ī-kāra_

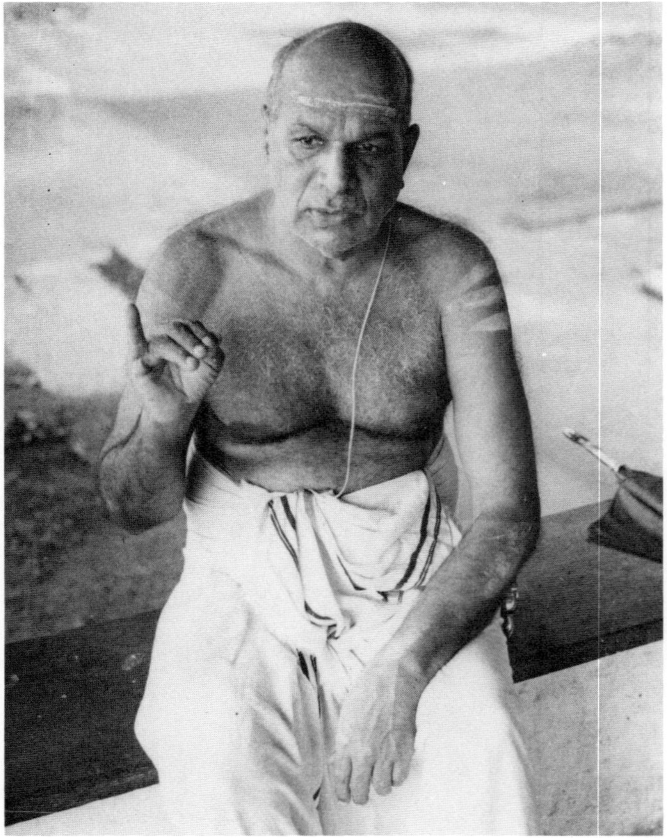

Fig. 41. _ū-kāra_

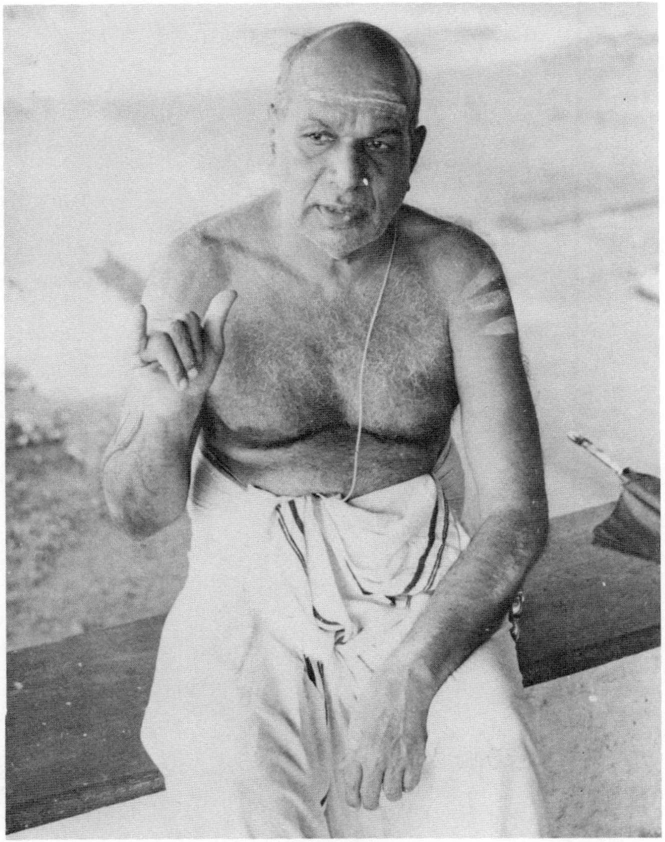

Fig. 42. e-kāra, ai-kāra

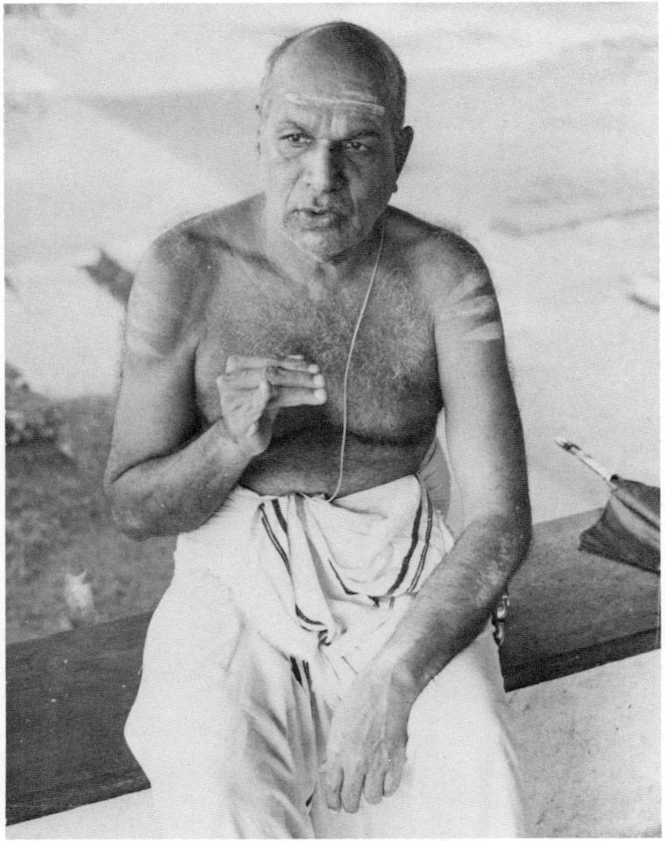

Fig. 43. o-kāra, au-kāra

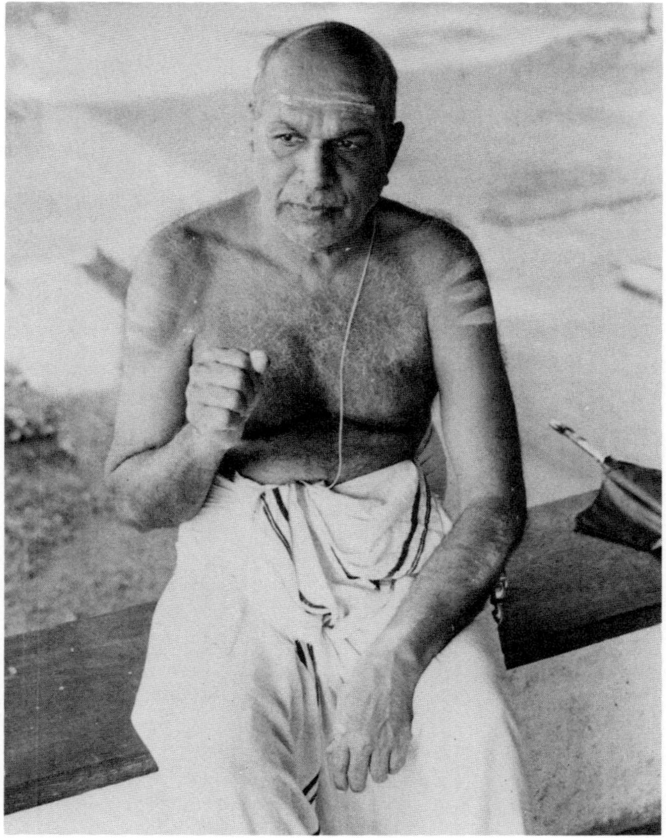

Fig. 44. <u>anusvāra</u>

Fig. 45. <u>visarga</u>

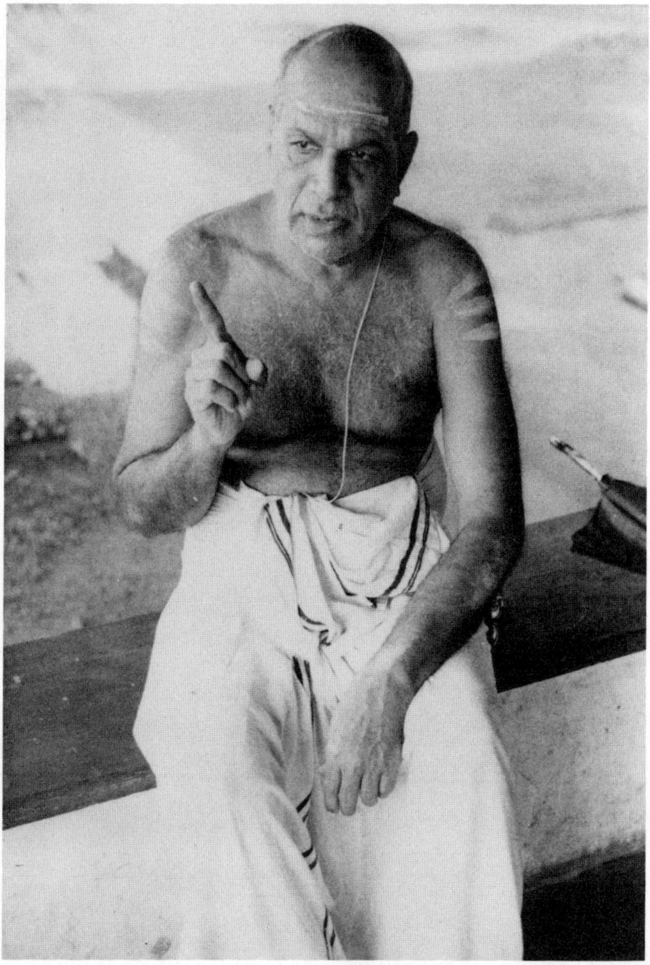

Fig. 46. dīrgha-visarga

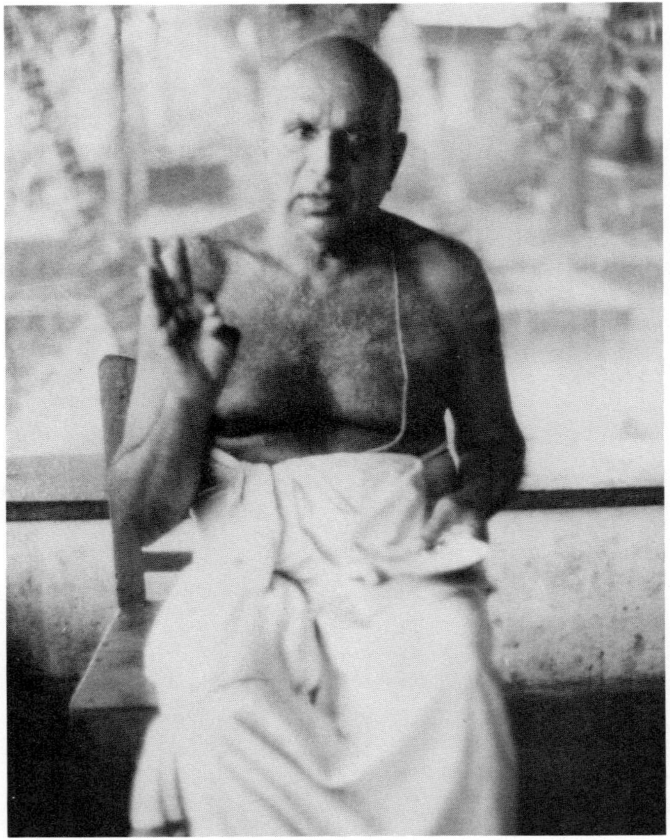

Fig. 47. il̤-kāra, ta-kāra

Fig. 48. na-kāra

PART III

TRANSCRIPTIONS

Tape Ia(8)
GG 1.1

♪ = 120

Agnishvatta Sastri Agnihotri
Kauthuma School
Varanasi

F=E

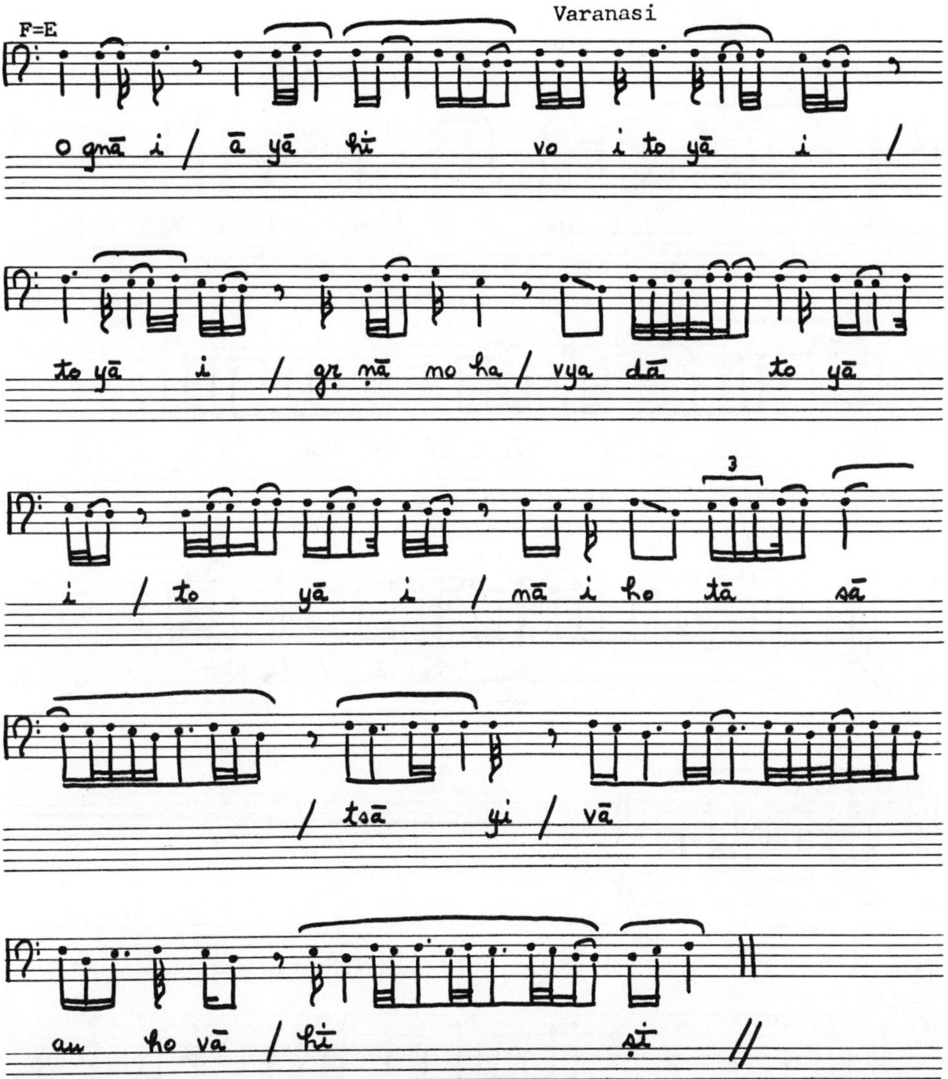

o gnā i / ā yā hi vo i to yā i /
to yā i / gṛ ṇā no ha / vya dā to yā
i / to yā i / mā i ho tā sā
/ tsā yi / vā
au ho vā / hi ṣi //

Tape Ia(8)
GG 1.2

♪ = 120

Agnishvatta Sastri Agnihotri

F=F

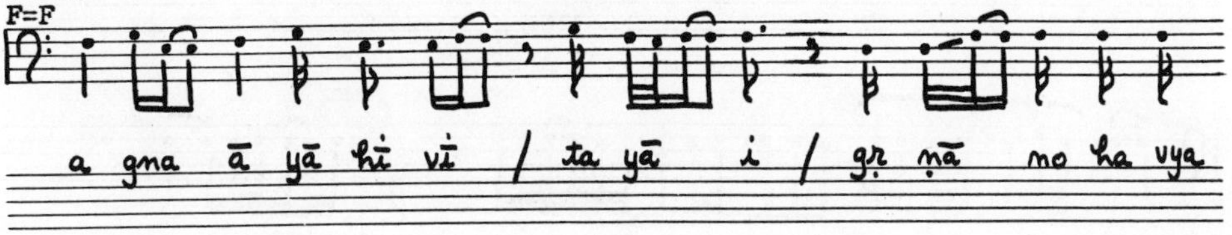

a gna ā yā hi vi / ta yā i / gṛ ṇā no ha vya

GG 1.2 (cont.) Agnishvatta Sastri Agnihotri

3
dā tā yā i / mi ho tā sa tsi ba
rhā i ṣī / ba rhā i
ṣā au ho vā / ba rhī
ṣī //

Tape Ia(8) Agnishvatta Sastri Agnihotri
GG 1.3
F=F#

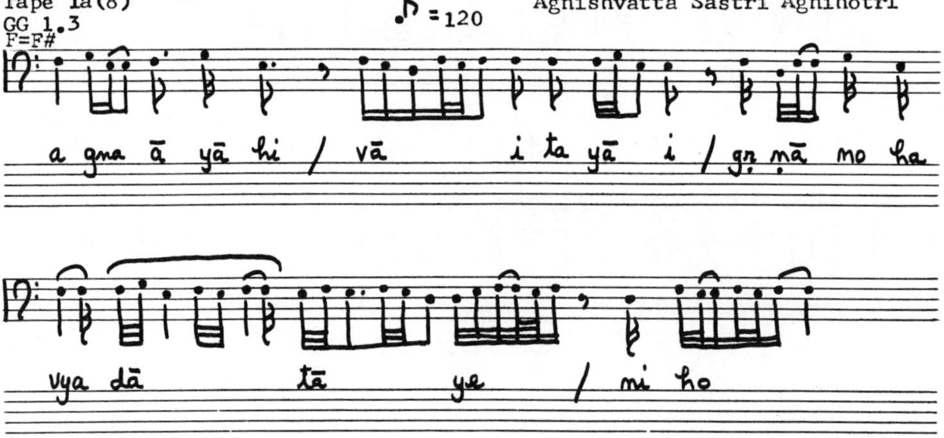
= 120
a gna ā yā hi / vā i ta yā i / gr ṇā mo ha
vya dā tā ye / mi ho

GG 1.3 (cont.) Agnishvatta Sastri Agnihotri

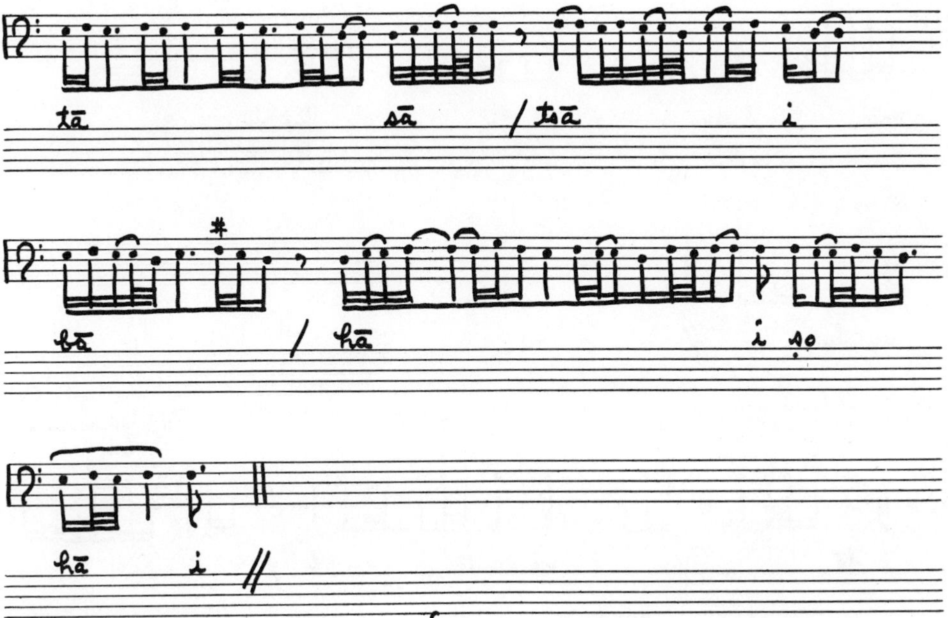
tā sā / tsā i
bā / hā i ṣo
hā i //

Tape VIIIb(32) ♪=120 Agnishvatta Sastri Agnihotri
GG 222.1
D=F

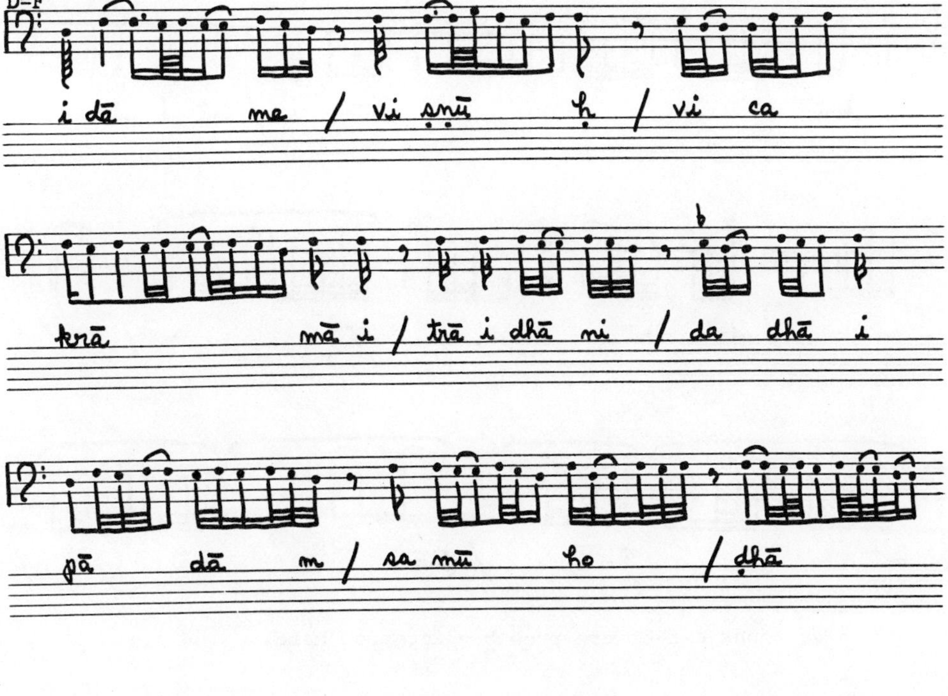
i dā me / vi ṣṇū ḥ / vi ca
krā mā i / trā i dhā ni / da dhā i
pā dā m / sa mū ho / ḍhā

Agnishvatta Sastri Agnihotri

GG 222.1 (cont.)

mā / syā pā au ho vā / e /
au le //

Tape VIIIb(33)
GG 222.1: sacrificial form ♪: 120 Agnishvatta Sastri Agnihotri
D=F

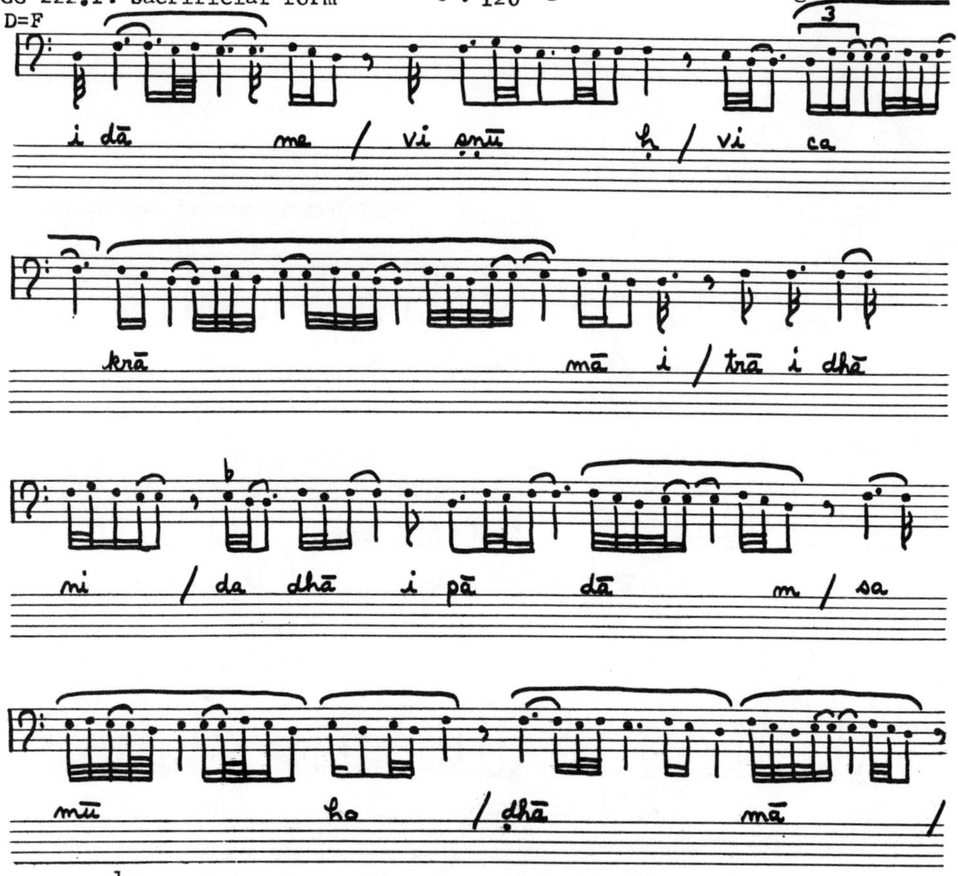
i dā me / vi ṣṇū ḥ / vi ca
krā mā i / trā i dhā
ni / da dhā i pā dā m / sa
mū ho / ḍhā mā /

[1]The tones e-f-e were probably intended here.

GG 222.1: sacrificial form (cont.) Agnishvatta Sastri Agnihotri

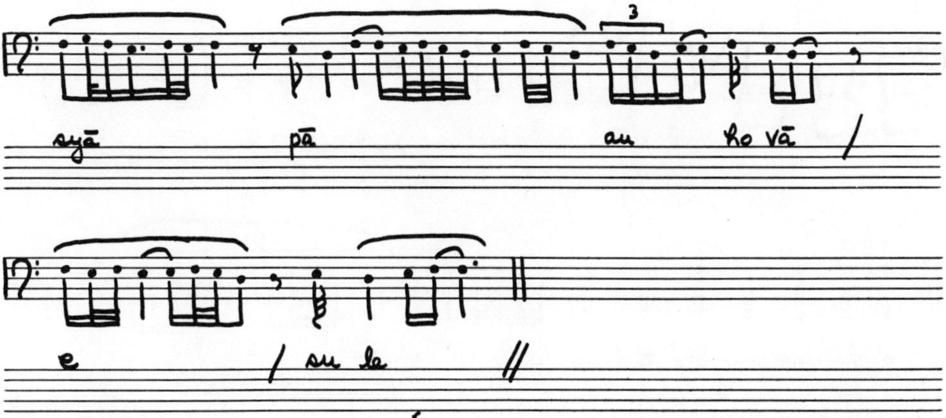

Tape Ib(1)
ArG 57.1
F=F

♪ = 120 Agnishvatta Sastri Agnihotri

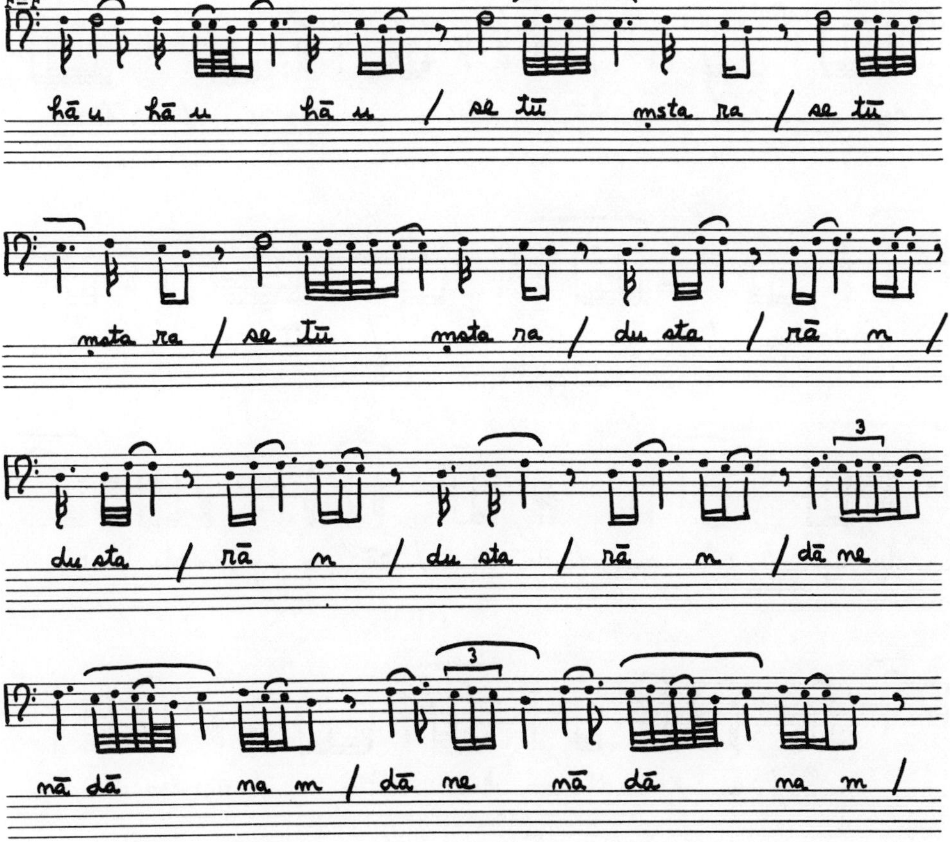

ĀrG 57.1 (cont.) Agnishvatta Sastri Agnihotri

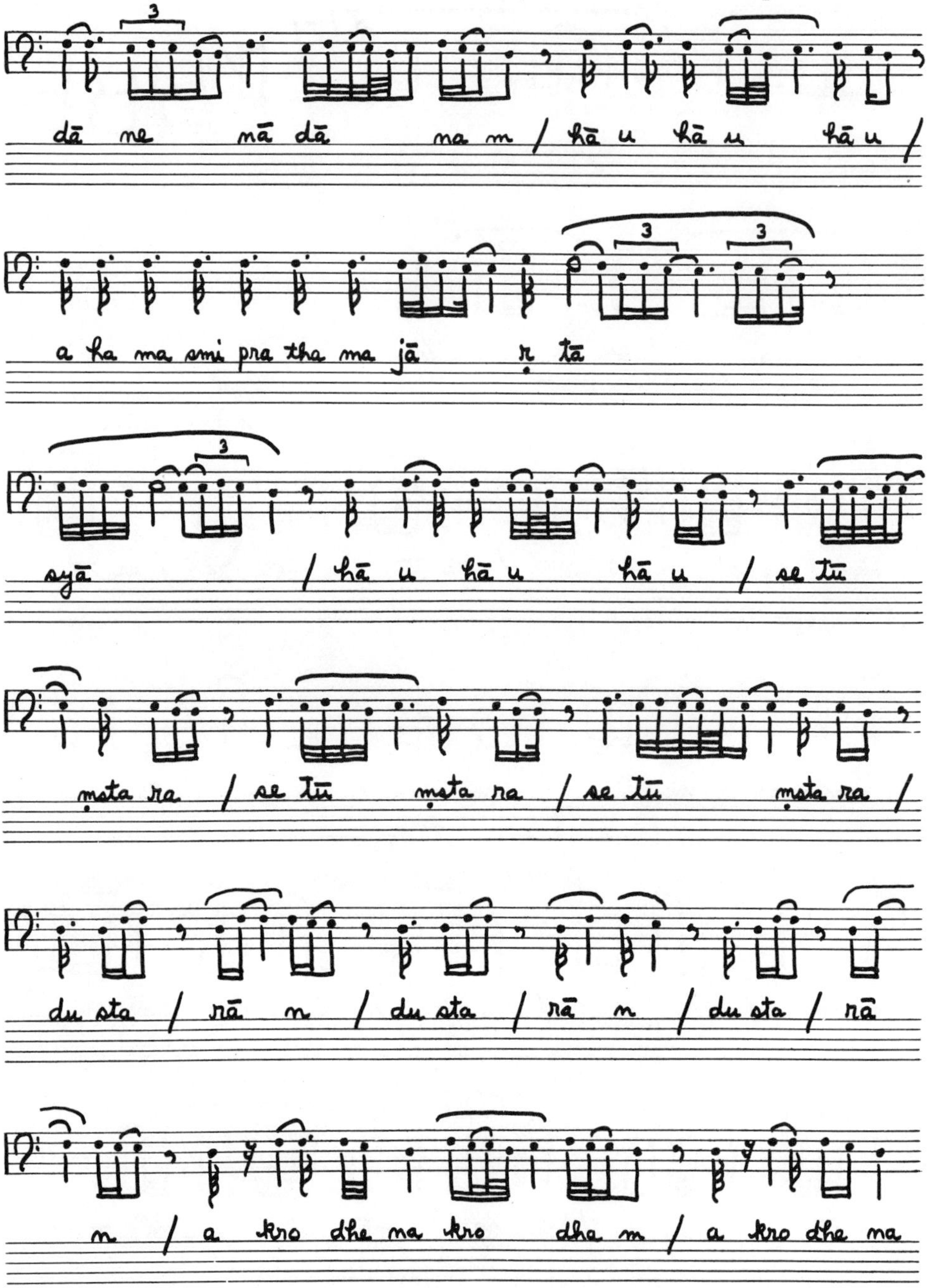

ĀrG 57.1 (cont.) Agnishvatta Sastri Agnihotri

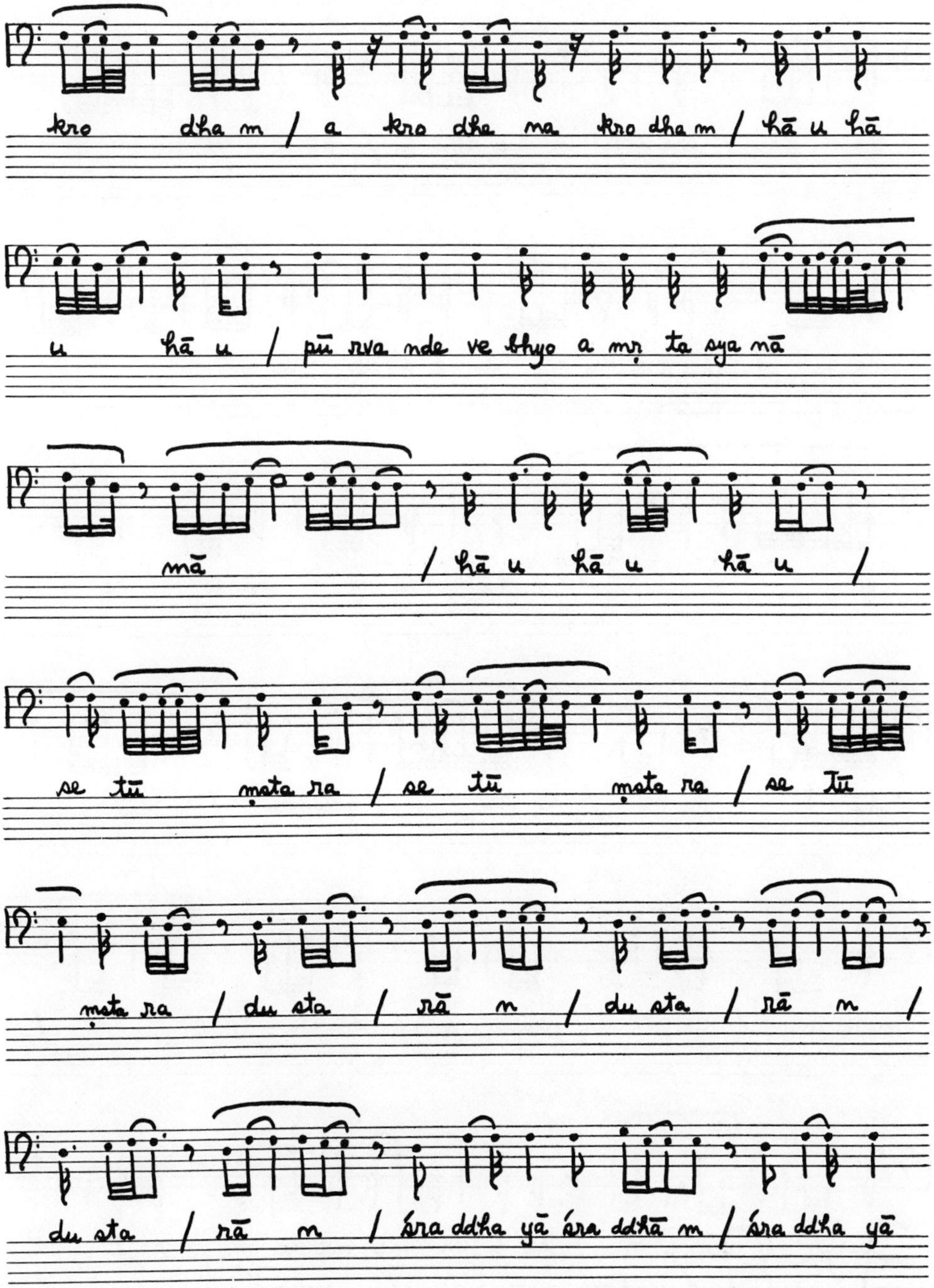

ĀrG 57.1 (cont.) Agnishvatta Sastri Agnihotri

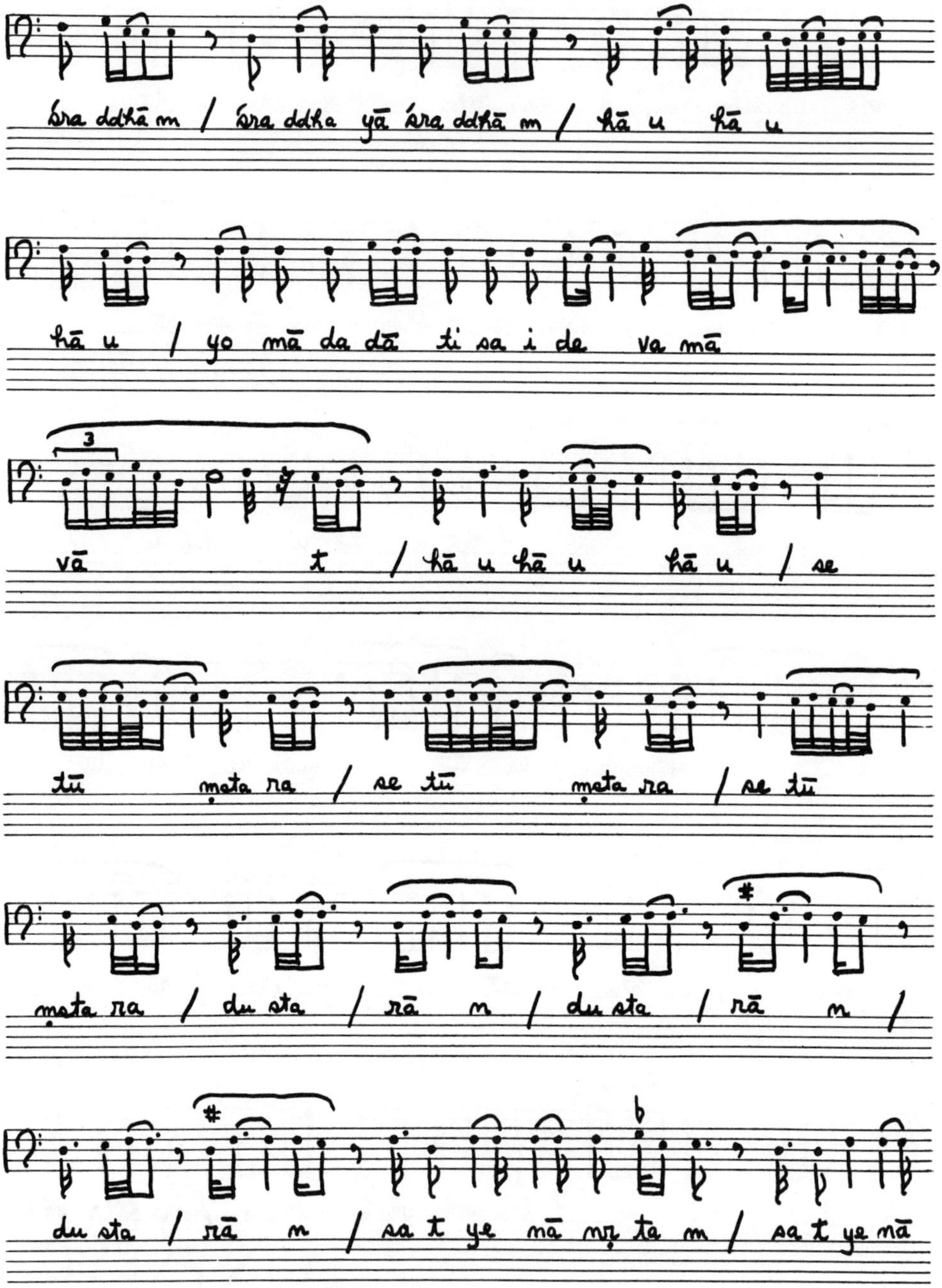

ĀrG 57.1 (cont.) Agnishvatta Sastri Agnihotri

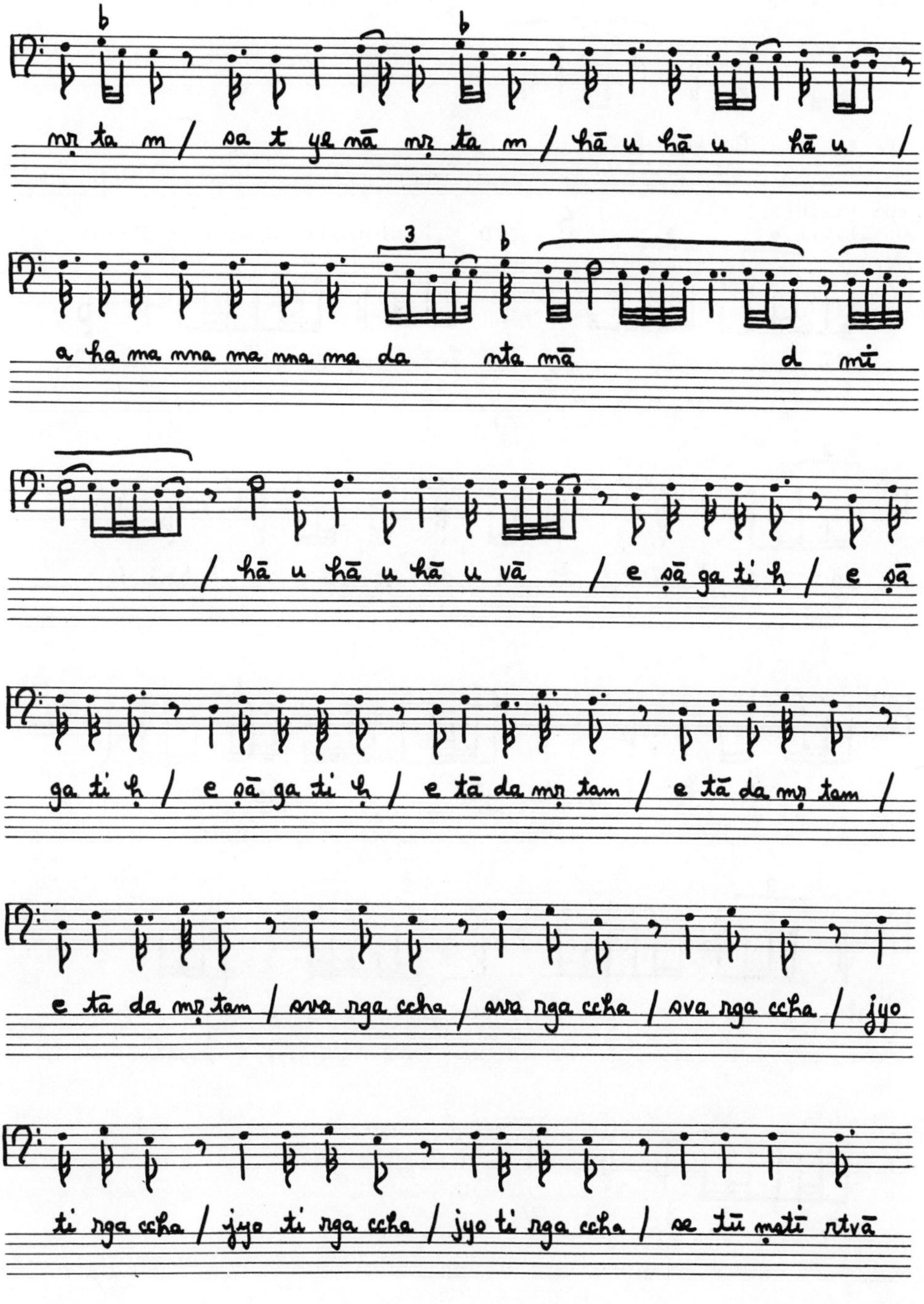
mṛ ta m / sa t ye mā mṛ ta m / hā u hā u hā u /
a ha ma mna ma mna ma da nta mā d mī
/ hā u hā u hā u vā / e ṣā ga ti ḥ / e ṣā
ga ti ḥ / e ṣā ga ti ḥ / e tā da mṛ tam / e tā da mṛ tam /
e tā da mṛ tam / sva rga ccha / sva rga ccha / sva rga ccha / jyo
ti rga ccha / jyo ti rga ccha / jyo ti rga ccha / se tū mṣtī rtvā

ĀrG 57.1 (cont.) Agnishvatta Sastri Agnihotri

Tape VIIIb(31)
ŪG 1.1.5.1
F=G

♪ = 120 Agnishvatta Sastri Agnihotri

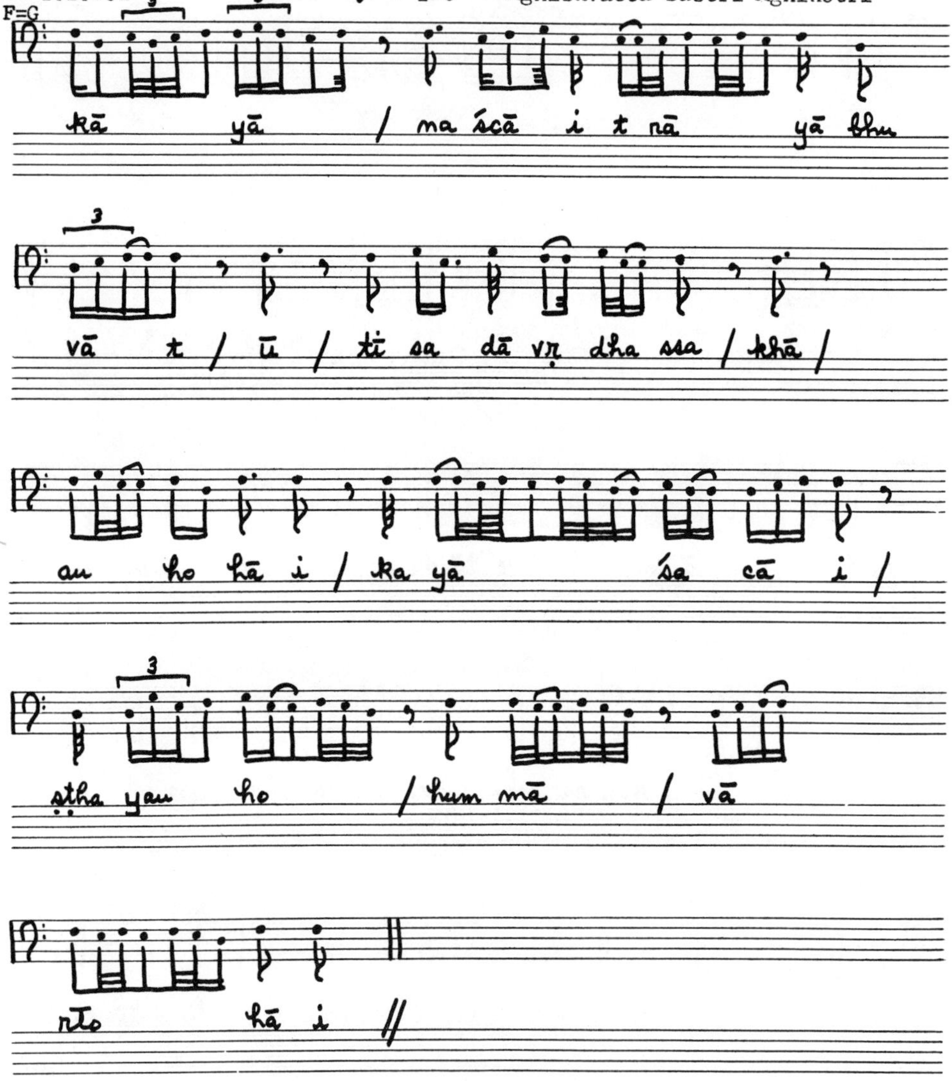

GG 1.1

F=A

♪=120

Revasankara Becarbhai Trivedi
Kauthuma School
Saurashtra

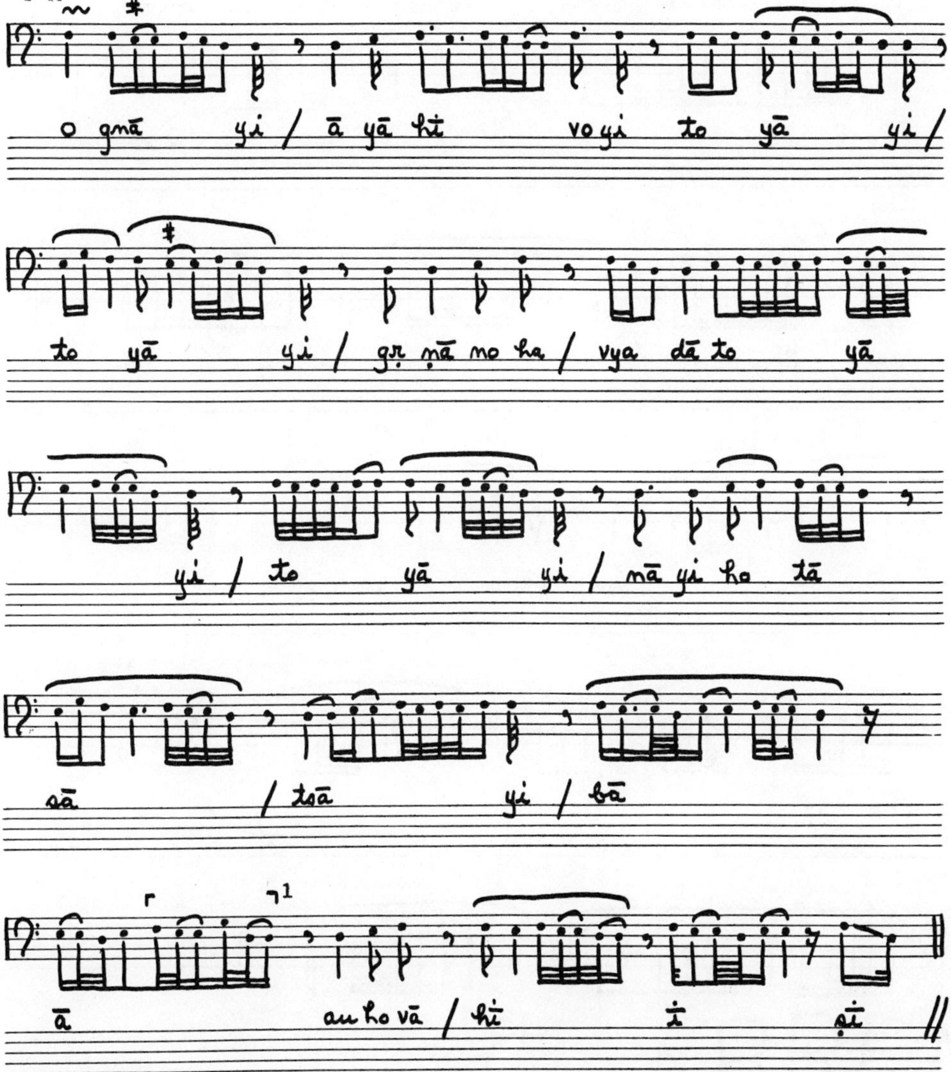

ŪG 1.1.5.1

F=B

♪= 120

Revasankar Becarbhai Trivedi

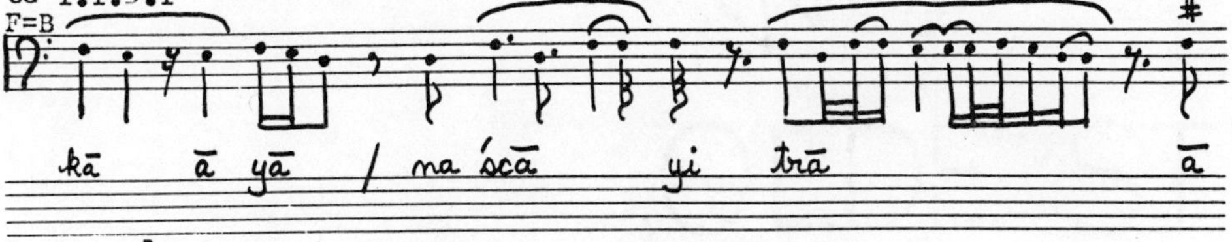

[1]Unclear on tape: approximate transcription.

ŪG 1.1.5.1 (cont.) Revasankar Becarbhai Trivedi

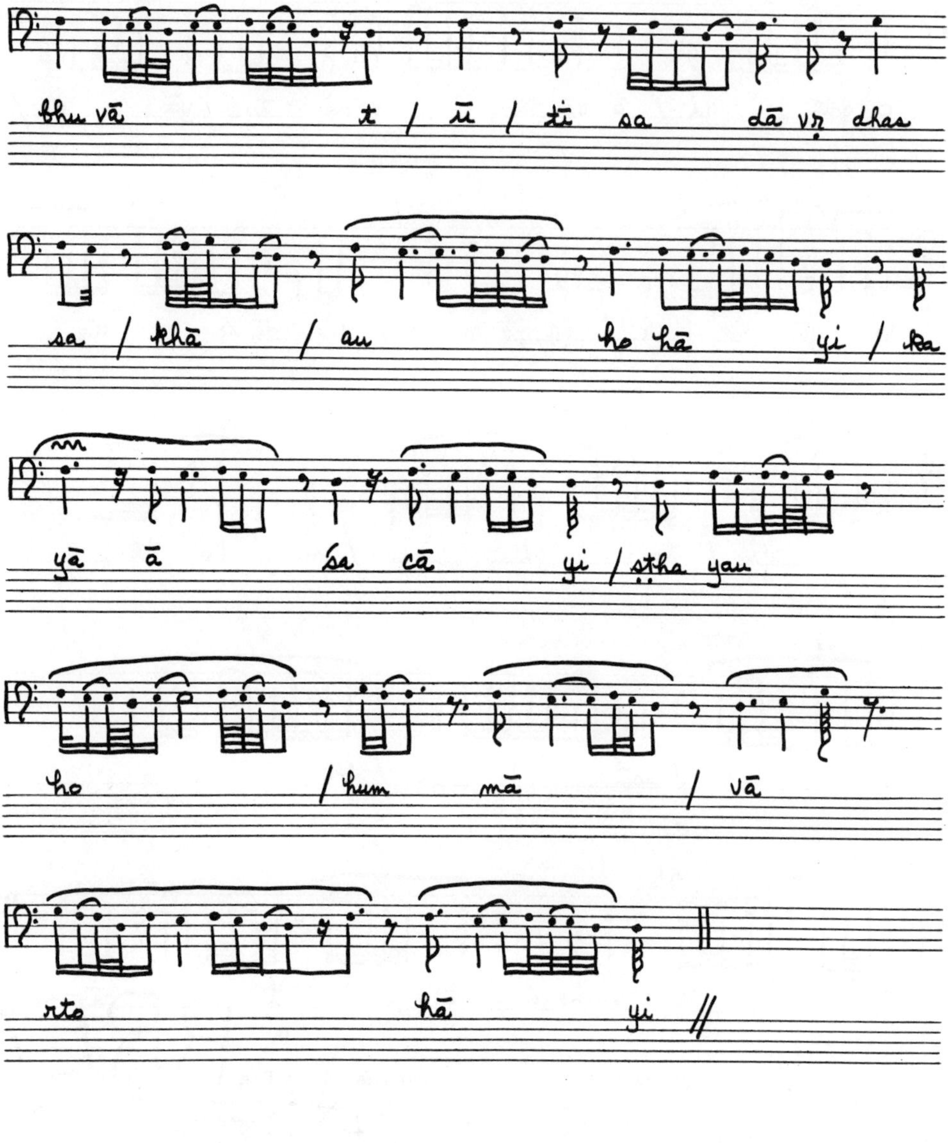

Tape IVb(1)
GG 1.1
A=G

♪ = 120

Narayan Sankar
Hari Sankar Trivedi
Kauthuma School
Varanasi

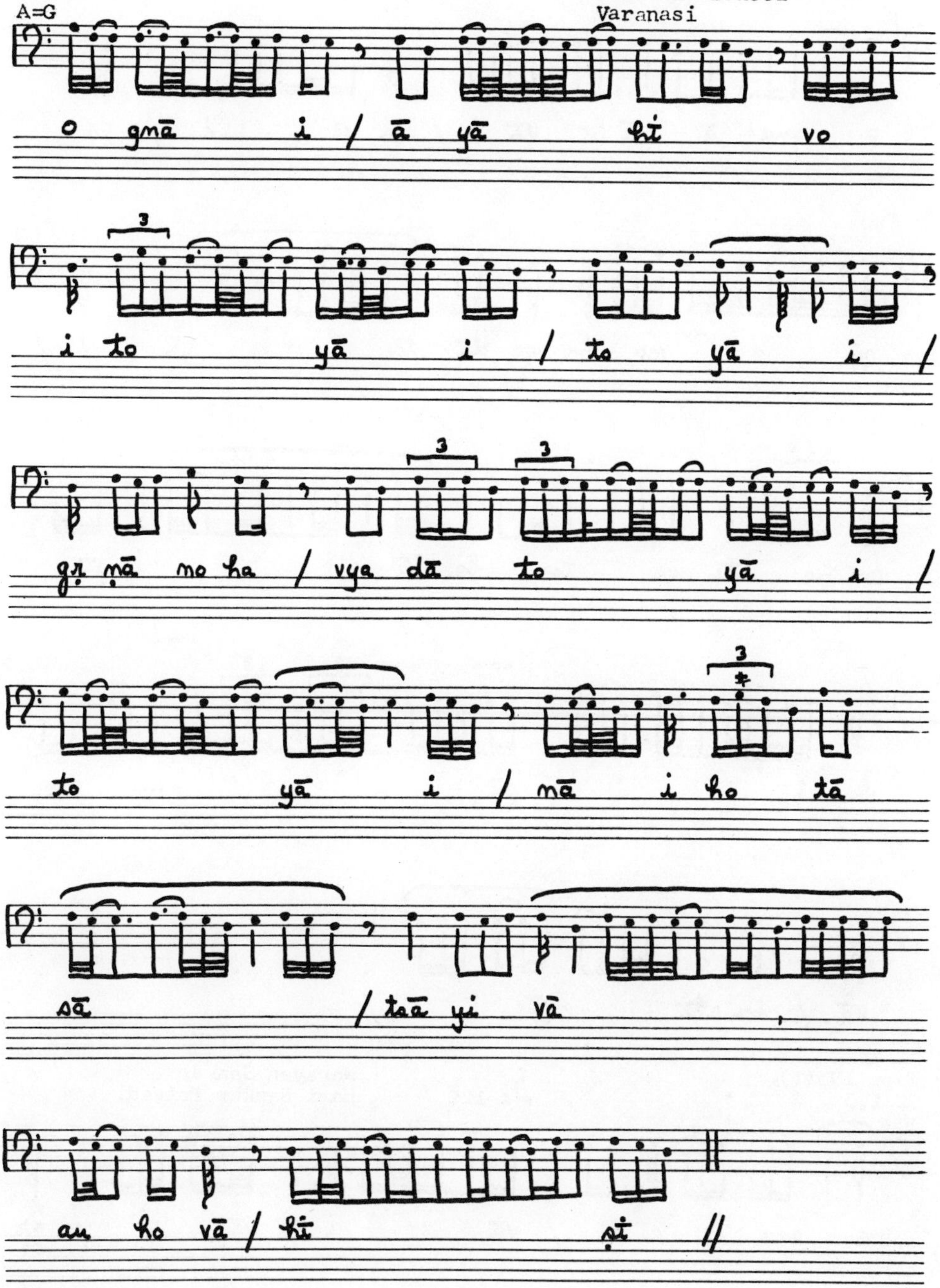
o gnā i / ā yā hī vo
i to yā i / to yā i /
gṛ ṇā no ha / vya dā to yā i /
to yā i / mā i ho tā
sā / taā yi vā ,
au ho vā / hī ṣī //

Tape IVb(1)
GG 1.2

♪ = 120

Narayan Sankar
Hari Sankar Trivedi

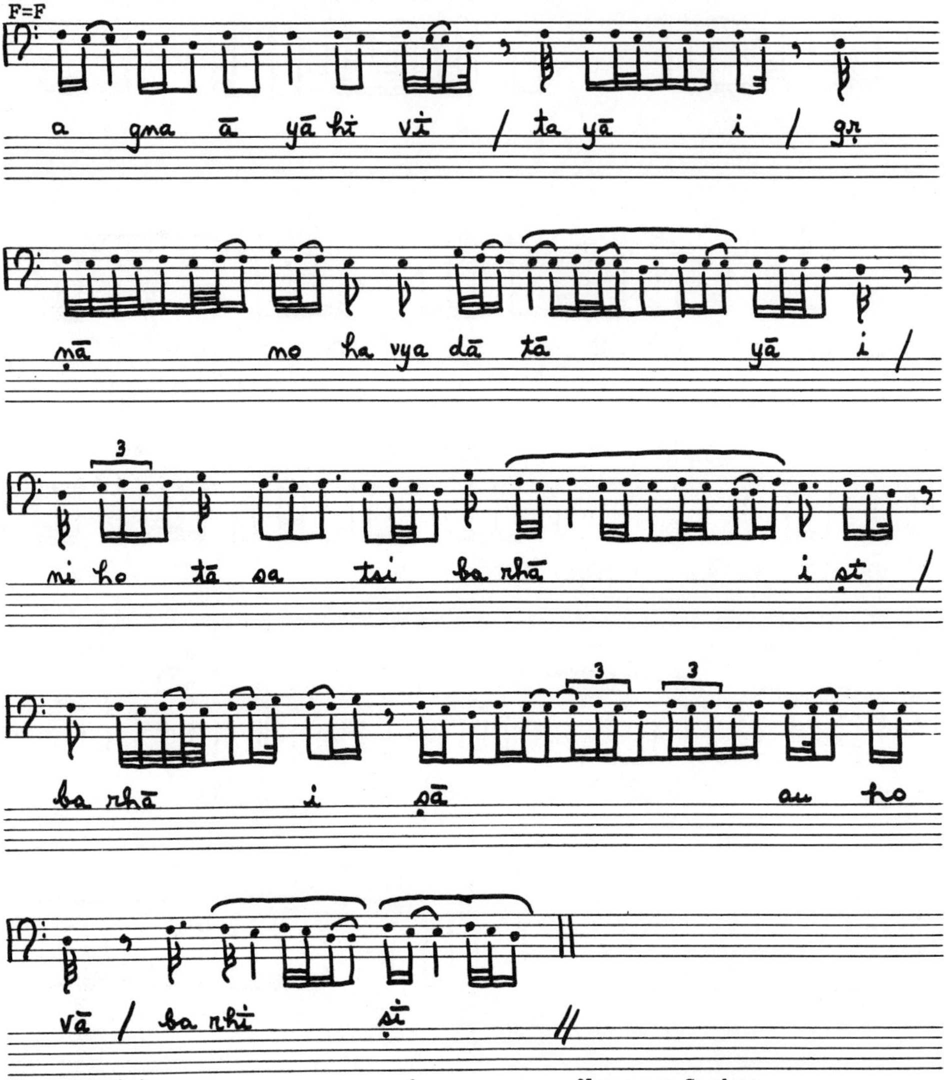
F=F
3
3 3
a gna ā yā hi vi / ta yā i / gr̥
n̥ā mo ha vya dā tā yā i /
ni ho tā sa tsi ba rhā i ṣt /
ba rhā i ṣā au ho
vā / ba rhi ṣi //

Tape IVb(1)
GG 1.3

♪ = 120

Narayan Sankar
Hari Sankar Trivedi

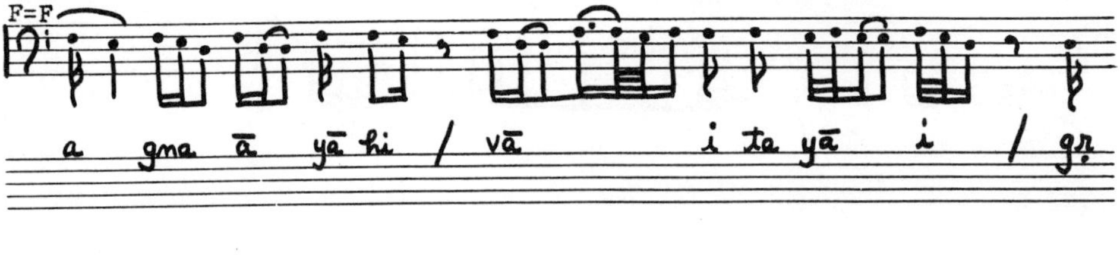
F=F
a gna ā yā hi / vā i ta yā i / gr̥

GG 1.3 (cont.)

Narayan Sankar
Hari Sankar Trivedi

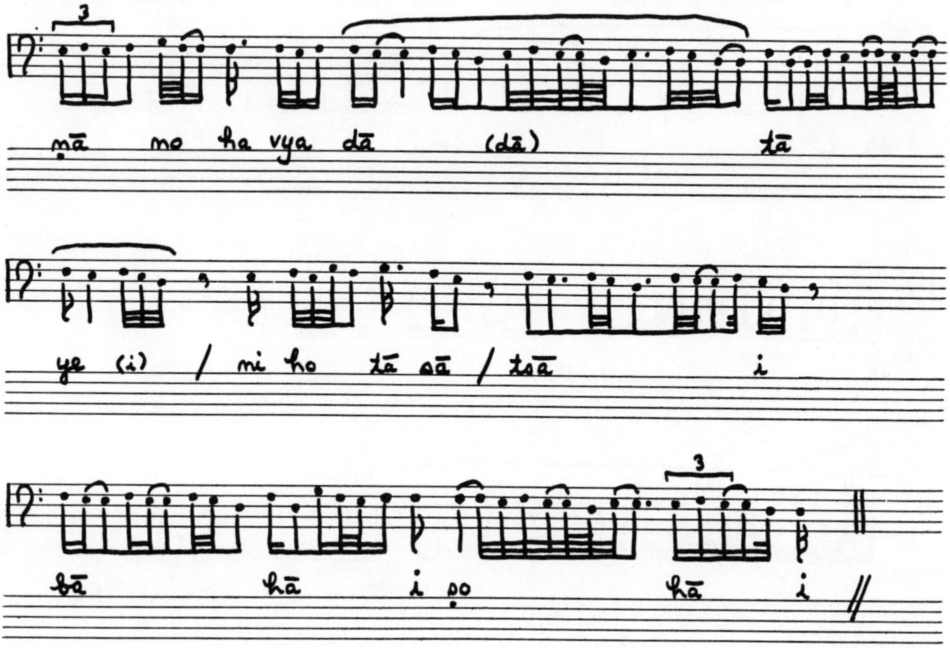
mā mo ha vya dā (dā) tā
ye (i) / mi ho tā sā / tsā i
bā hā i po hā i //

Tape Ia(3) ♪. = 120 Ganapati Sankar Kacarasankar
ĀrG 57.1 (opening stobha) Ahmedabad (Kauthuma School)

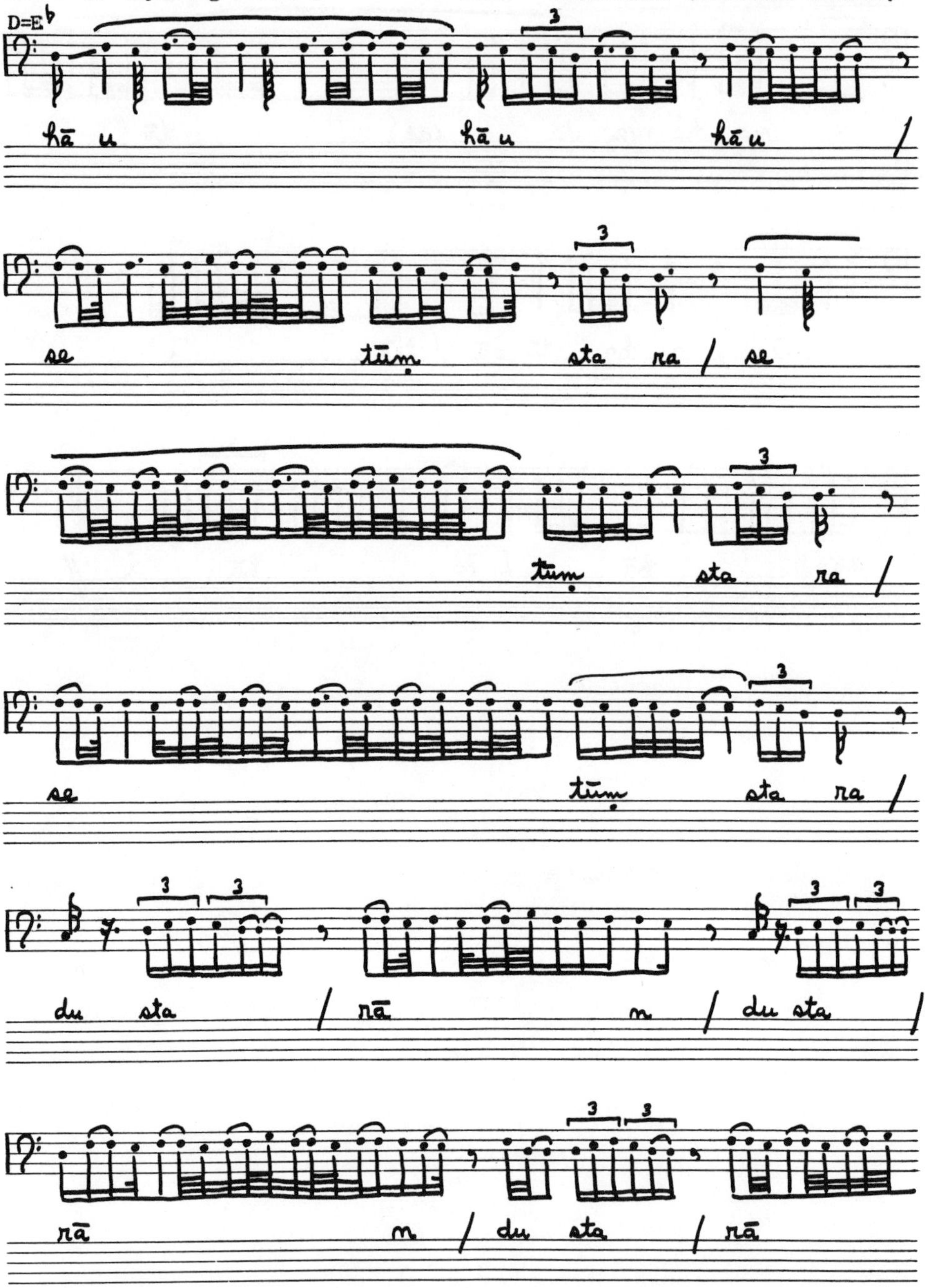

ĀrG 57.1 (opening stobha), cont. Ganapati Sankar Kacarasankar

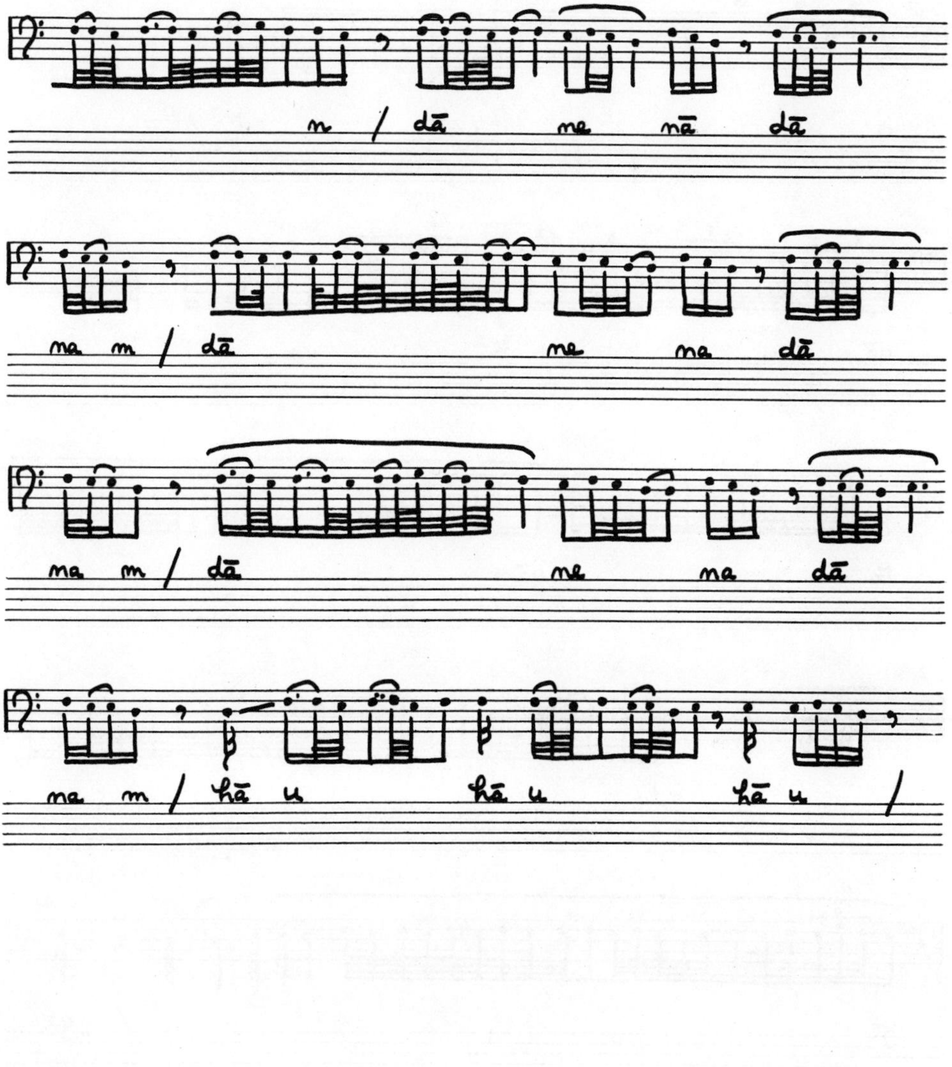

Tape Vb(10)B
GG 1.1

♪ = 84

Balasubrahmanya Srautigal
Kumbakonam, Tanjore District
Kauthuma School

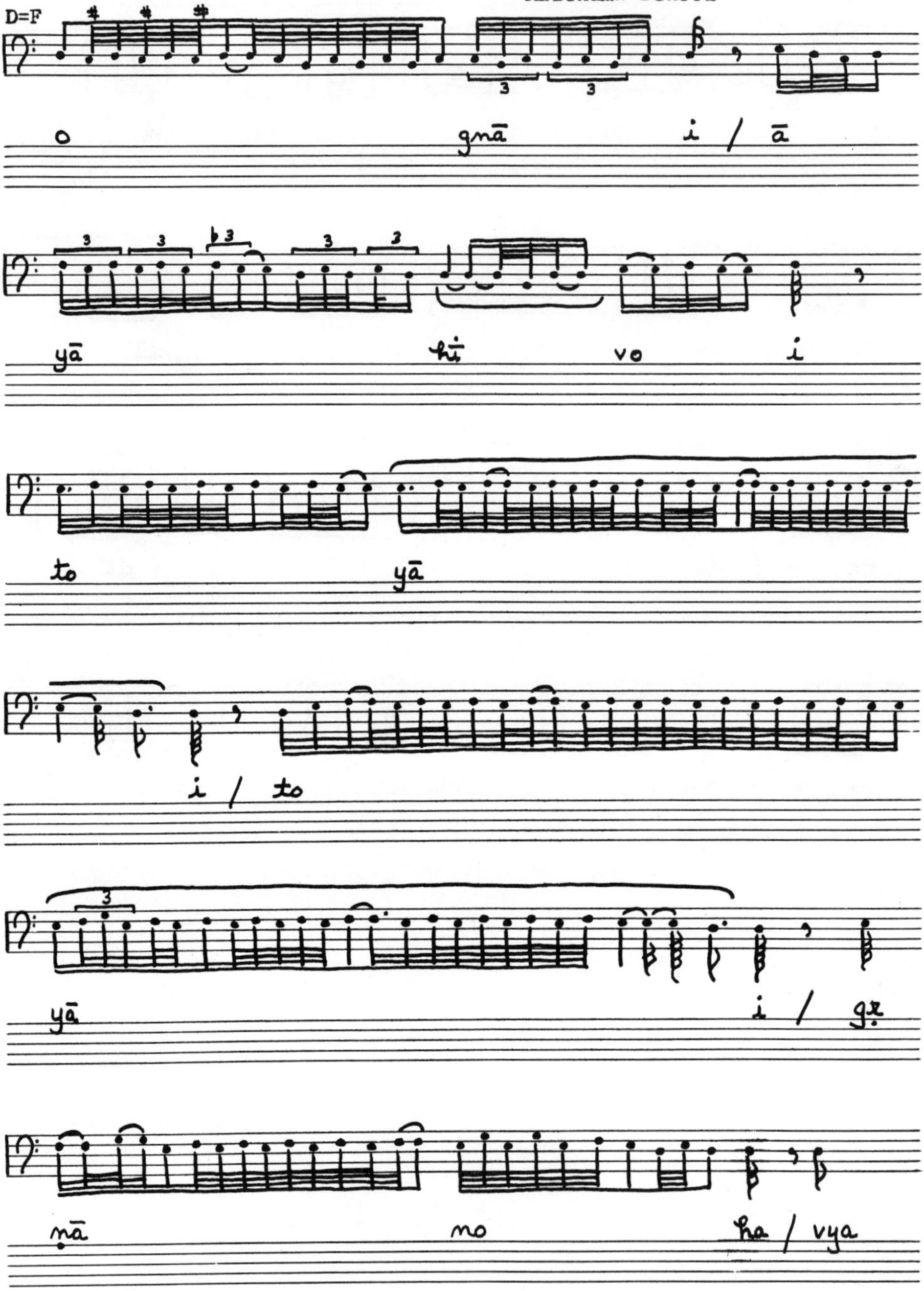
D=F
o gnā i / ā
yā hi vo i
to yā
i / to
yā i / gṛ
ṇā no ha / vya

GG 1.1 Balasubrahmanya Srautigal

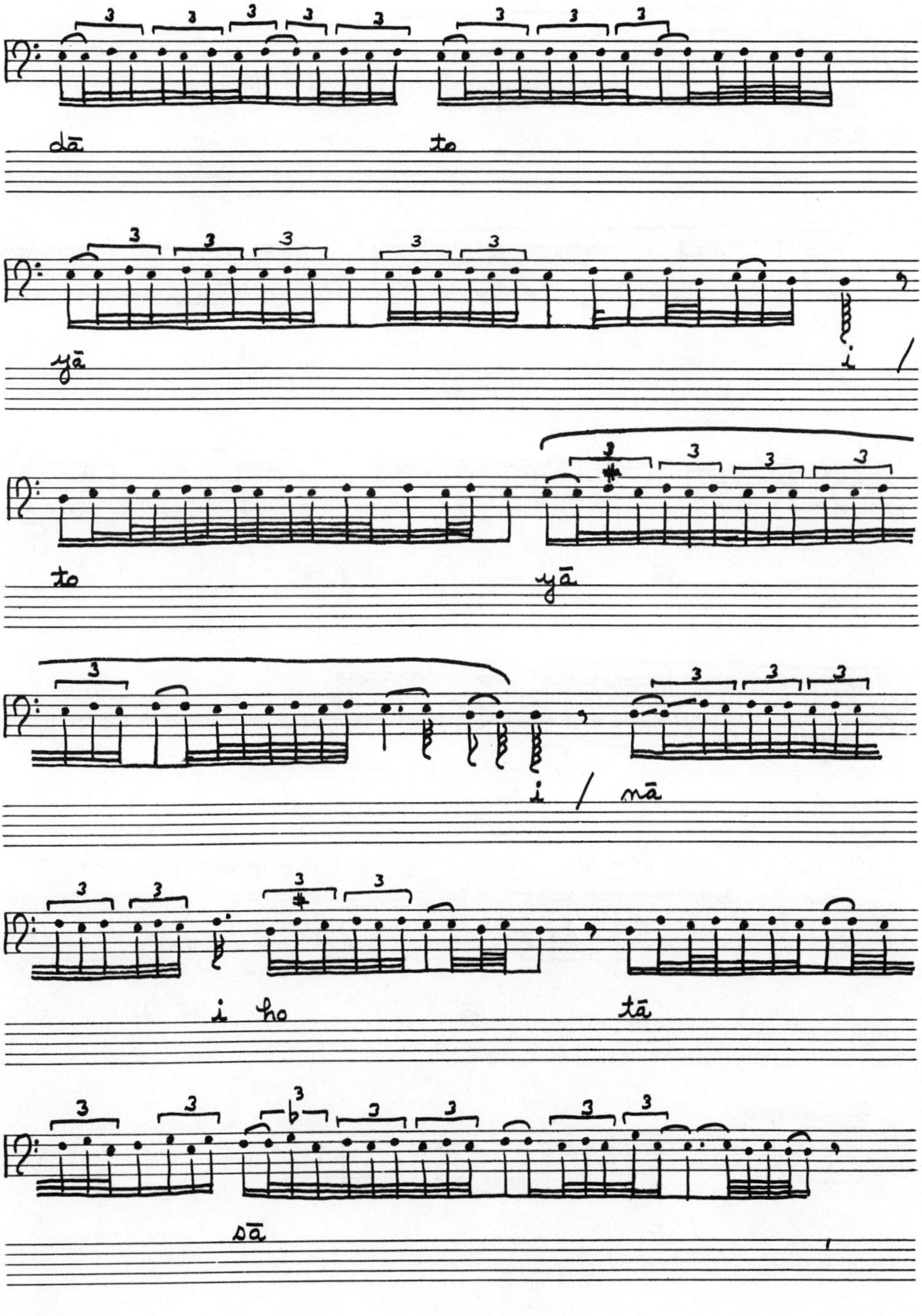
dā
to
yā
i
to
yā
i / nā
i ho
tā
sā

GG 1.1-2 Balasubrahmanya Srautigal

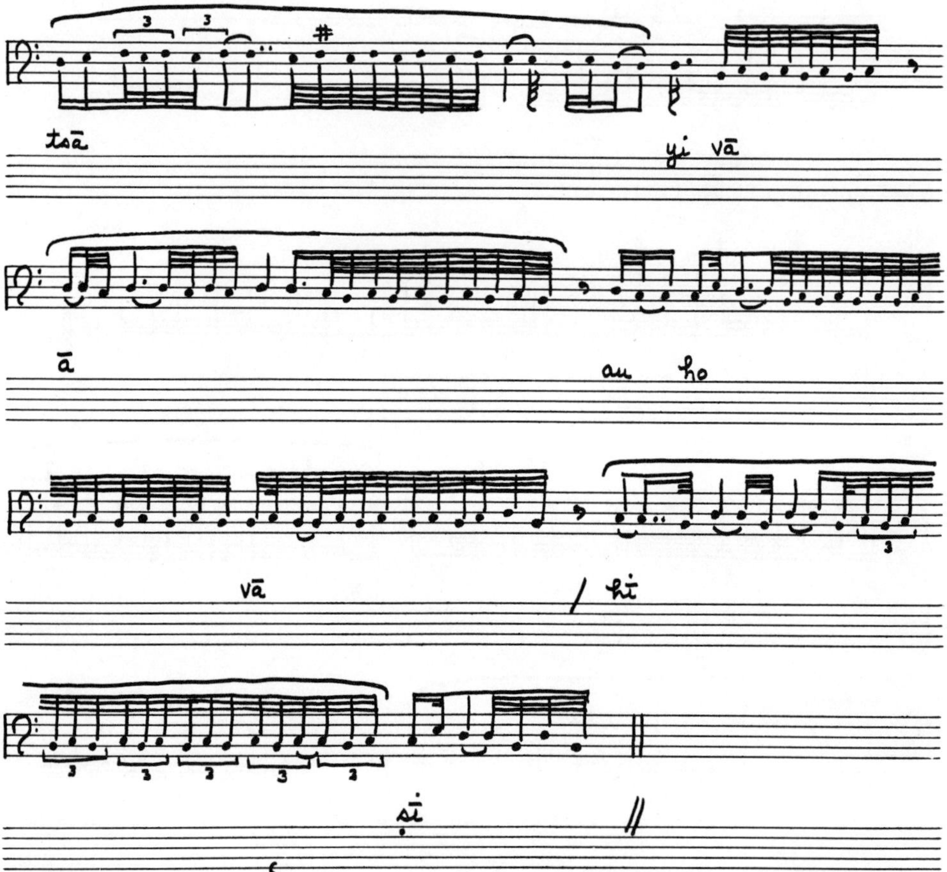
tsā
yi vā
ā
au ho
vā
/ hi
ṣi
//

GG 1.2 ♪ = 84 Balasubrahmanya Srautigal

C=E

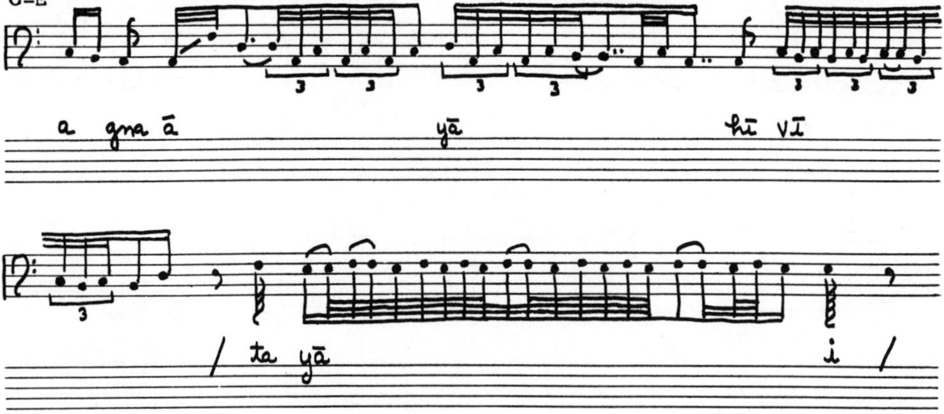
a gna ā
yā
hī vī
/ ta yā
i /

GG 1.2 Balasubrahmanya Srautigal

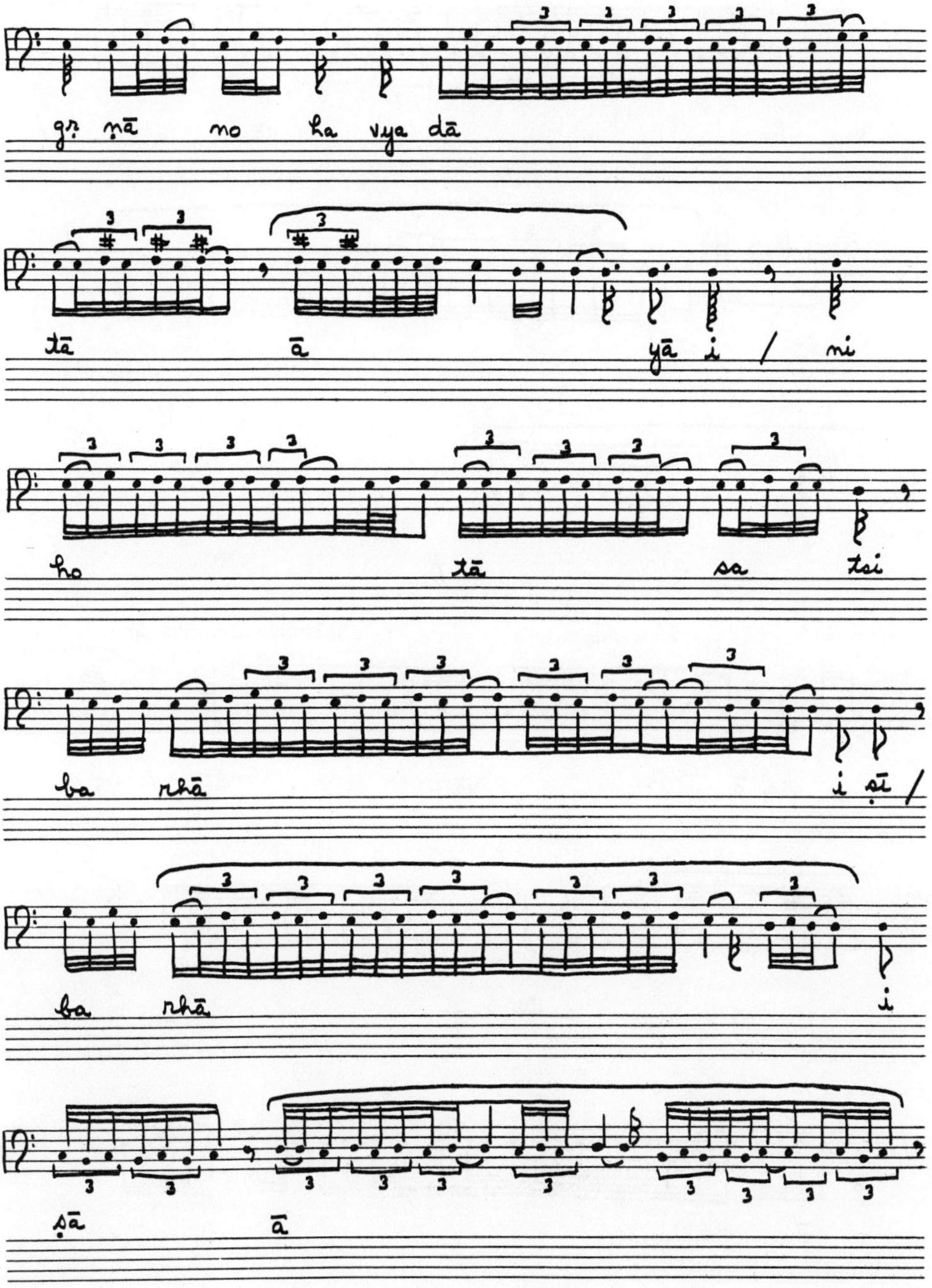
gṛ ṇā no ha vya dā
tā ā yā i / ni
ho tā sa tsi
ba rhā i ṣī /
ba rhā i
ṣā ā

GG 1.2-3 Balasubrahmanya Srautigal

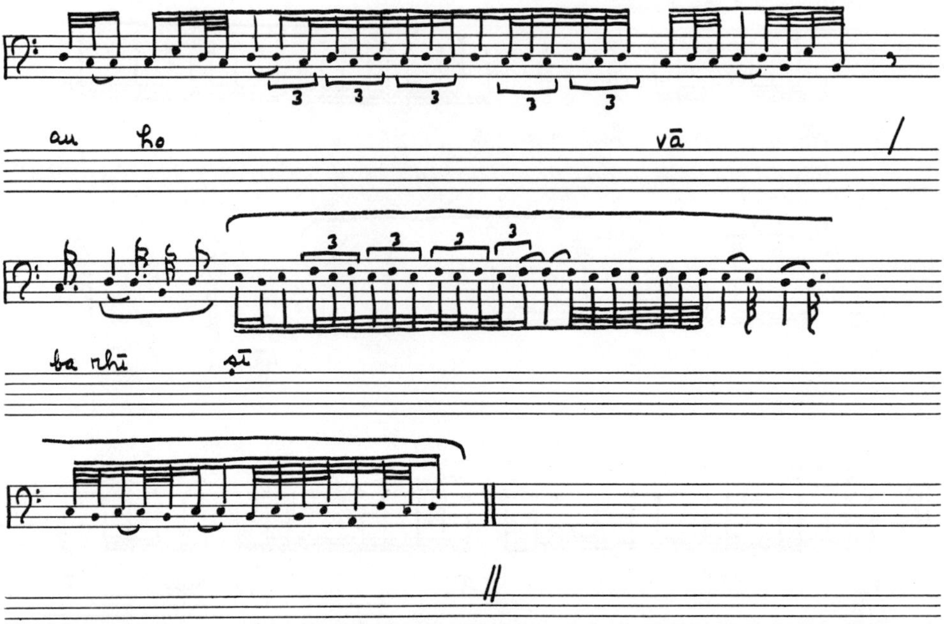
au ho vā /
ba rhī ṣī
//

GG 1.3 ♪ = 84 Balasubrahmanya Srautigal

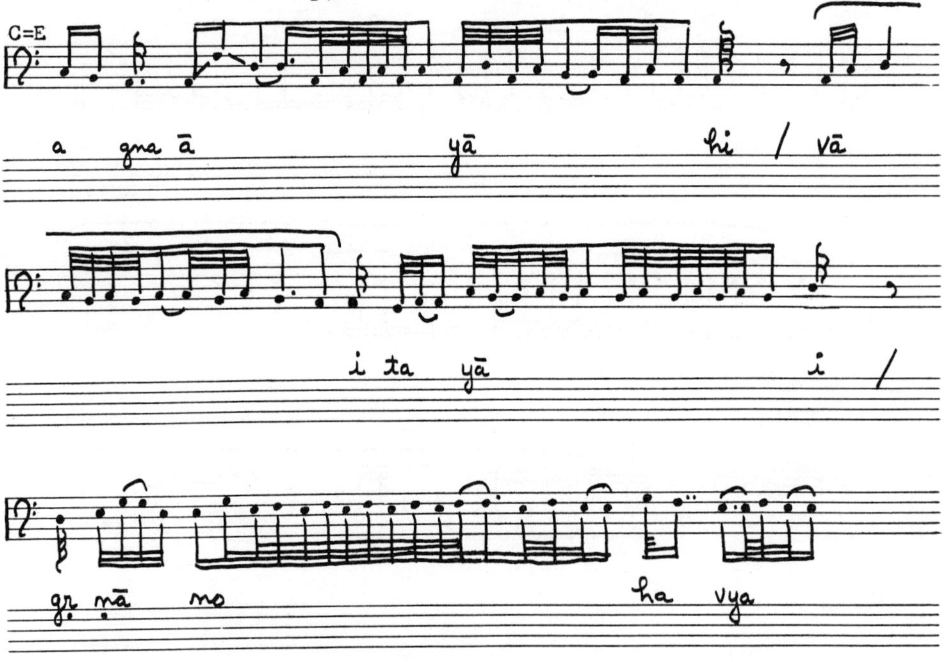
C=E
a gna ā yā hi / vā
i ta yā i /
gṛ ṇā no ha vya

GG 1.3 Balasubrahmanya Srautigal

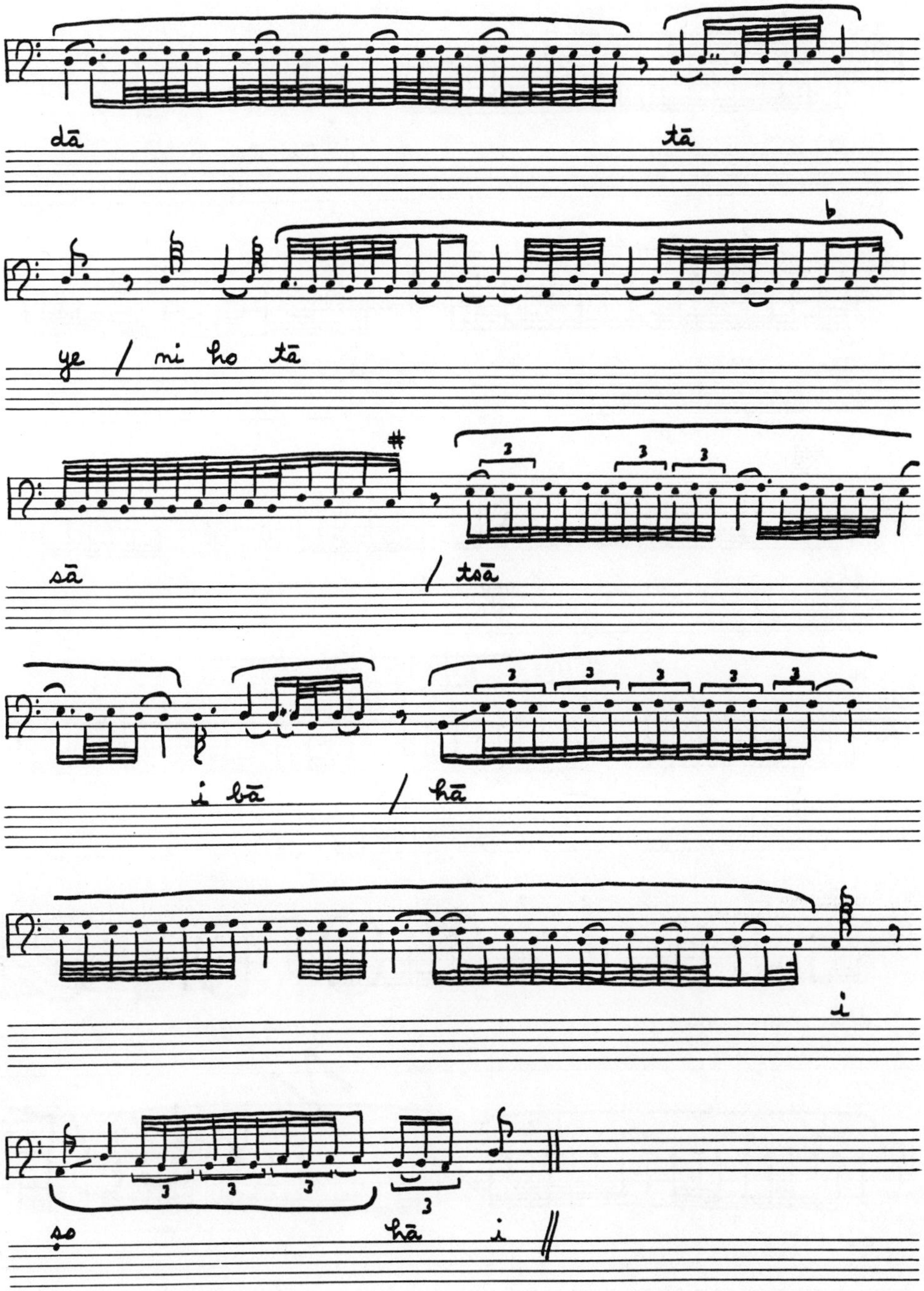
dā tā
ye / mi ho tā
sā / tsā
i bā / hā
i
so hā i //

Tape Vb(10)A
Kauthuma Gāyatram ♪ = 84 Balasubrahmanya Srautigal

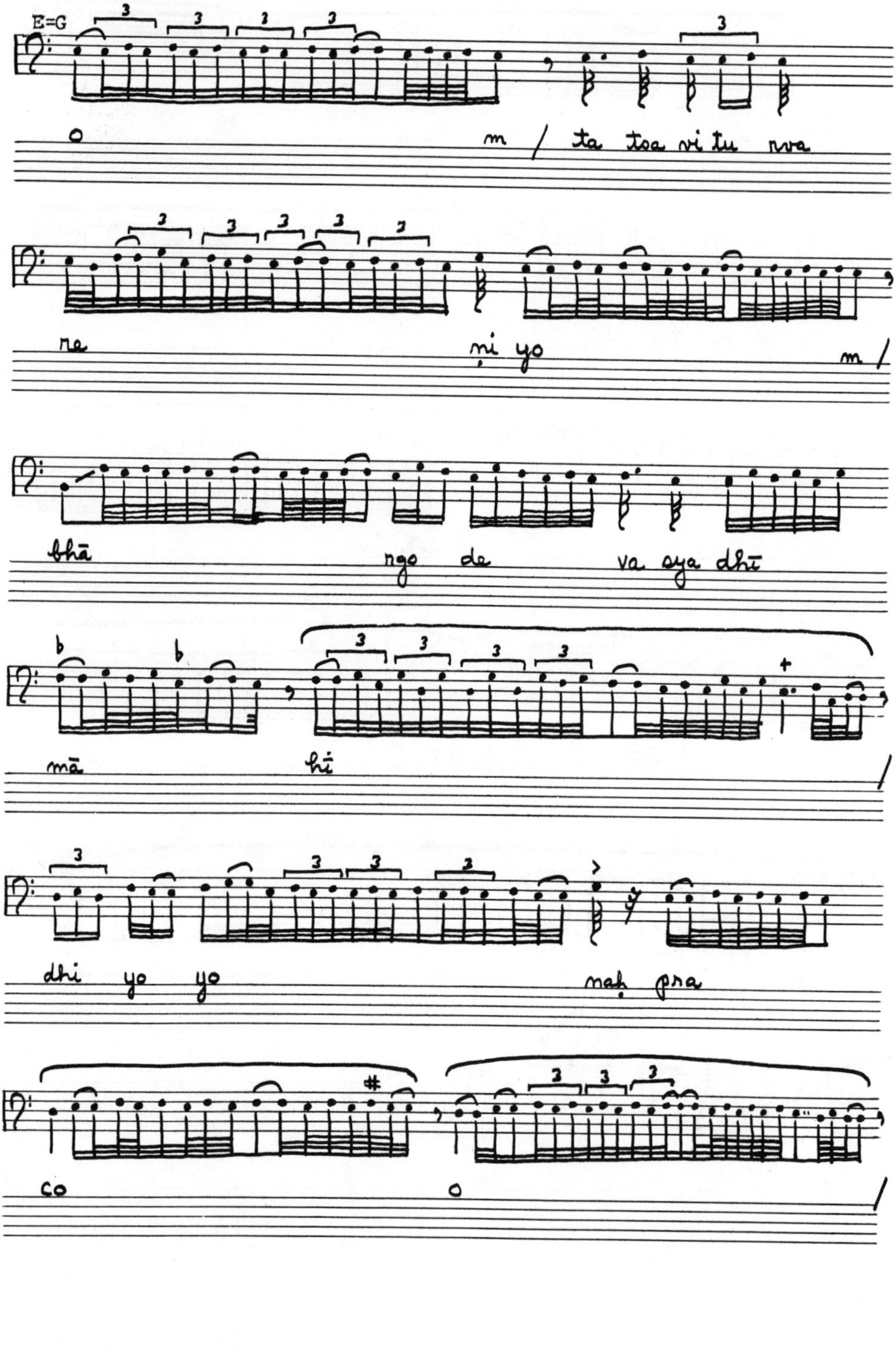

Kauthuma Gāyatram (cont.) Balasubrahmanya Srautigal

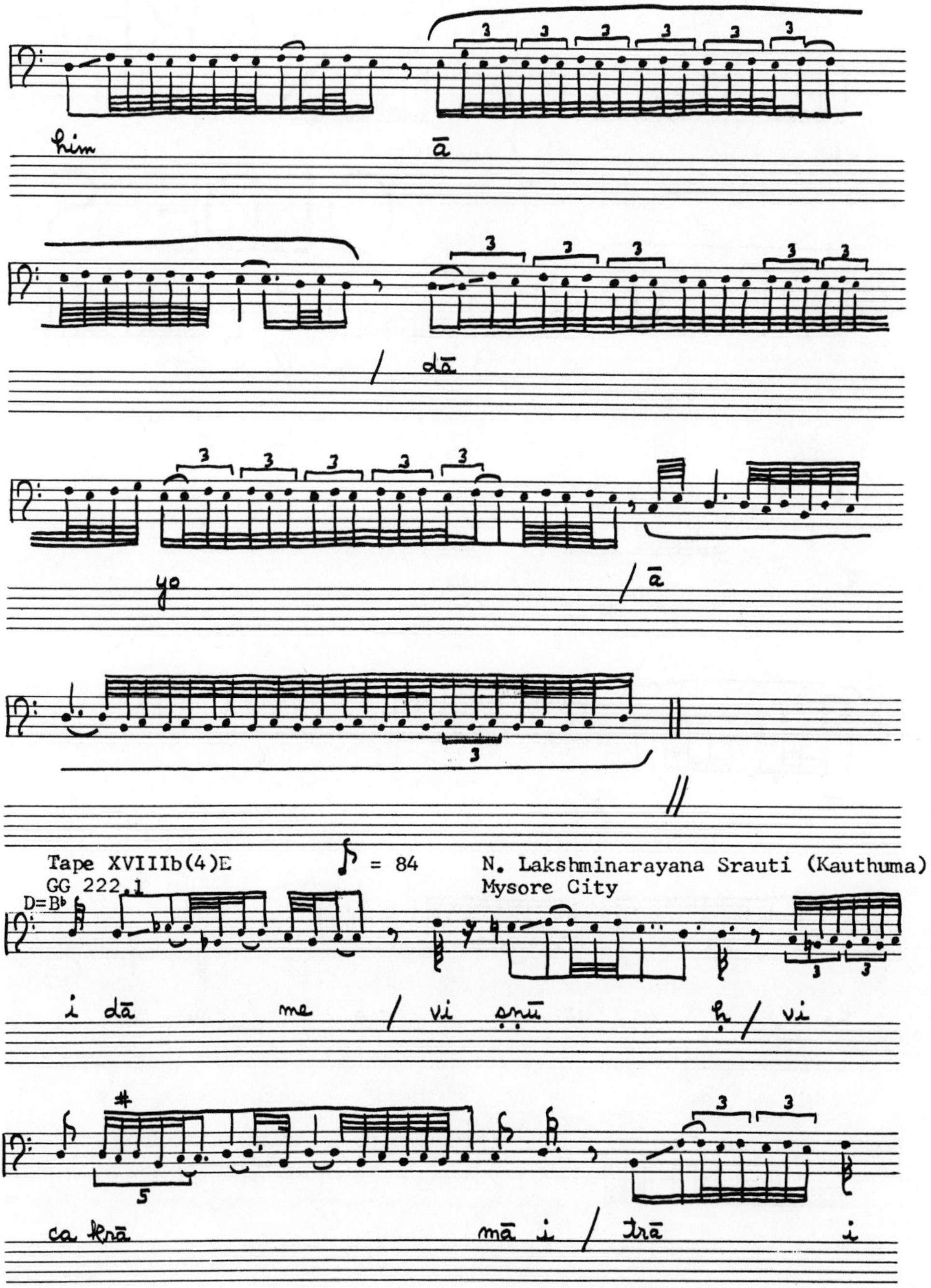
him
ā
dā
yo
ā
Tape XVIIIb(4)E
GG 222.1
= 84
N. Lakshminarayana Srauti (Kauthuma)
Mysore City
D=B♭
i dā me vi ṣṇū ḥ vi
ca krā mā i trā i

GG 222.1 (cont.) N. Lakshminarayana Srauti

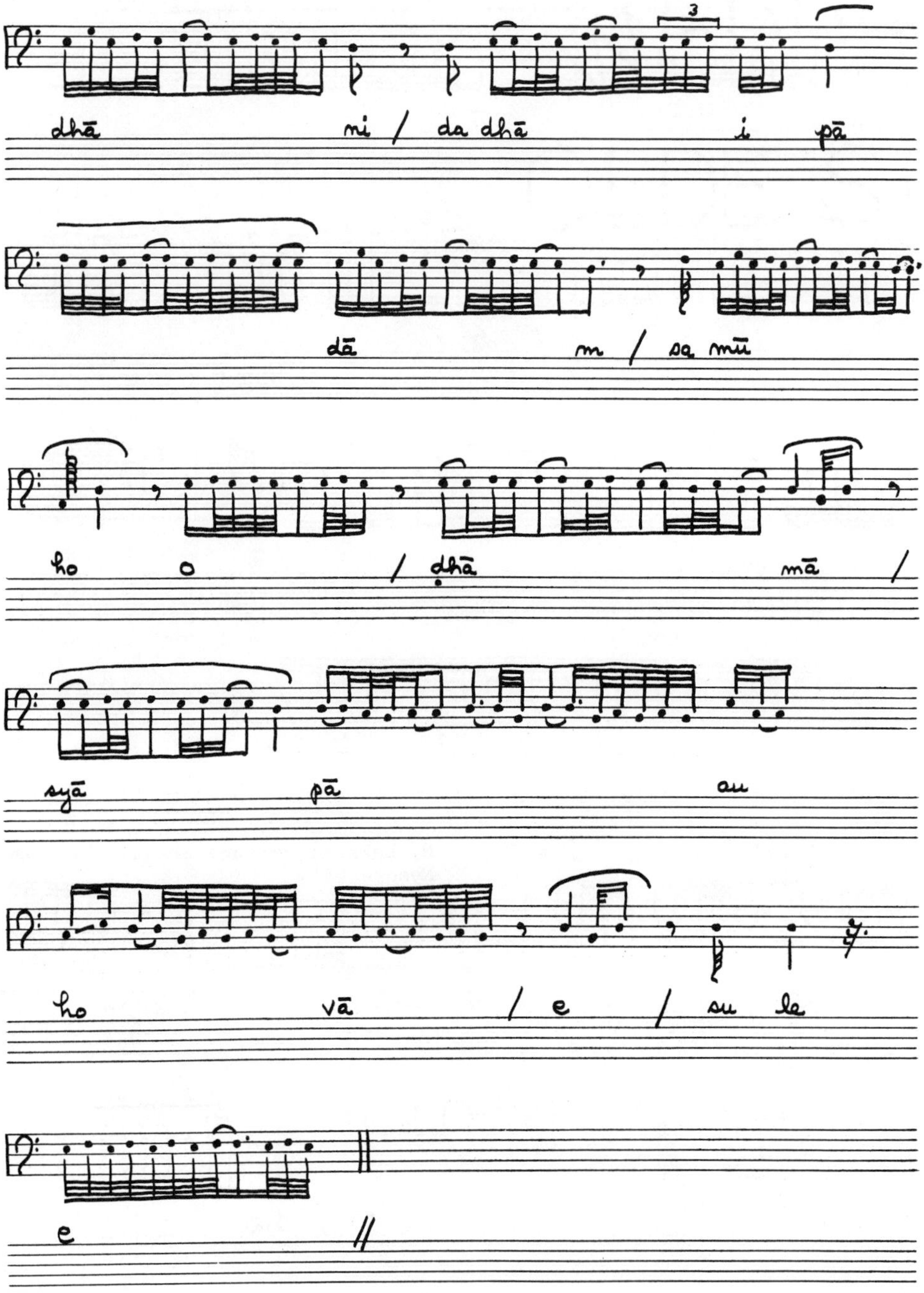
dhā ni / da dhā i pā
dā m / sa mū
ho o / dhā mā /
syā pā au
ho vā / e / su le
e //

♪ = 100

Tape IIa(4)
from the bahispavamānastotra
gāyatragāna

Krishnamurti Srauti (Kauthuma)
Varanasi, formerly of Maraiturai,
Tanjore District, Tamilnadu

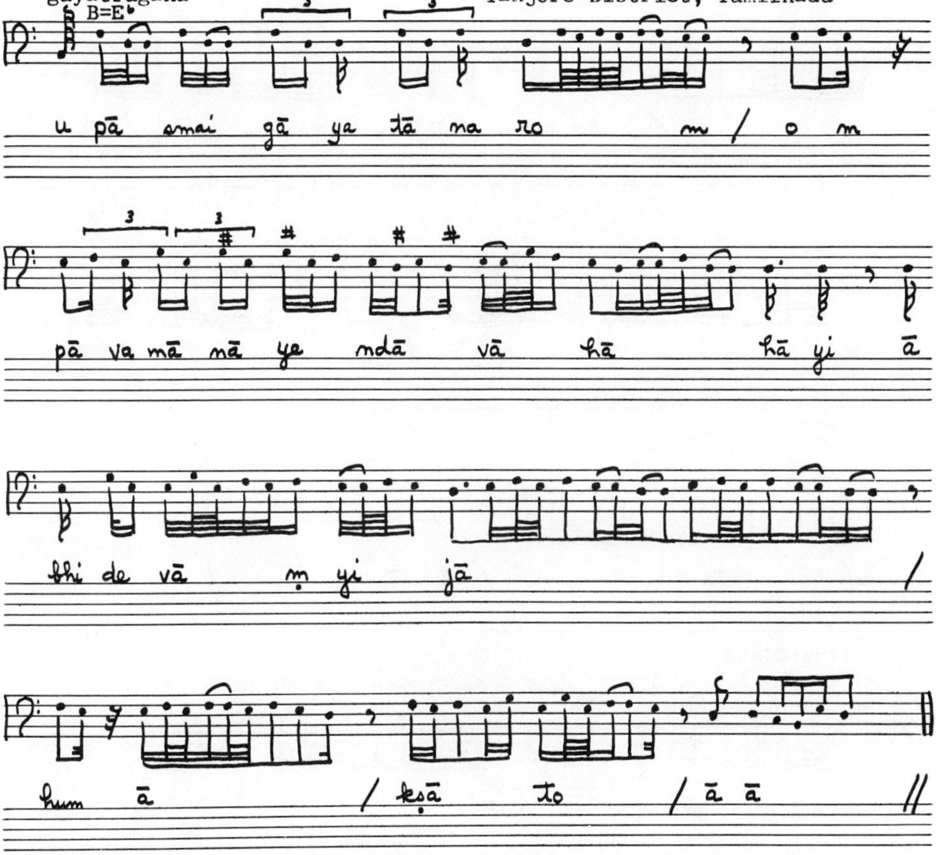

niruktagāna

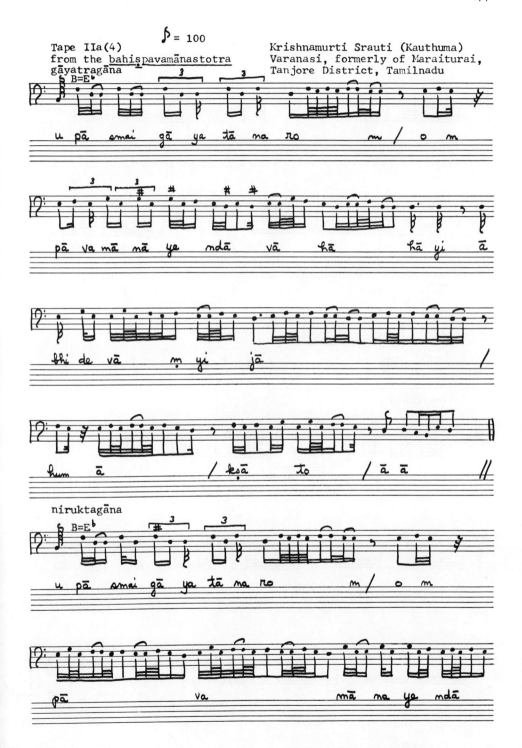

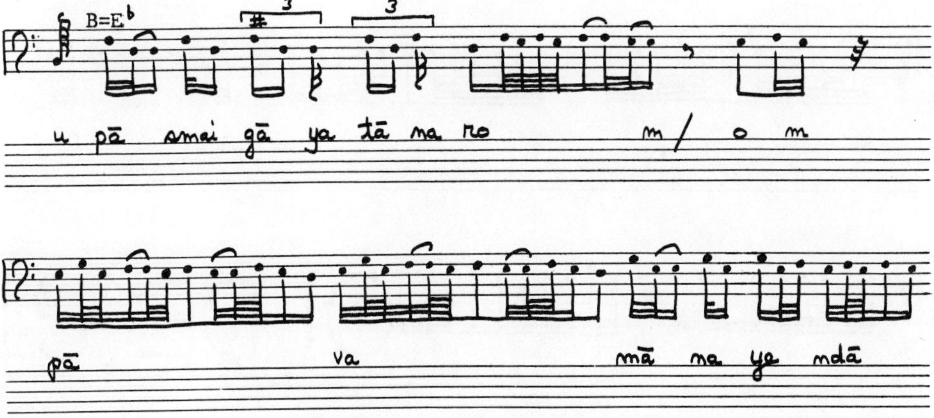

from the bahiṣpavamānastotra (cont.) Krishnamurti Srauti

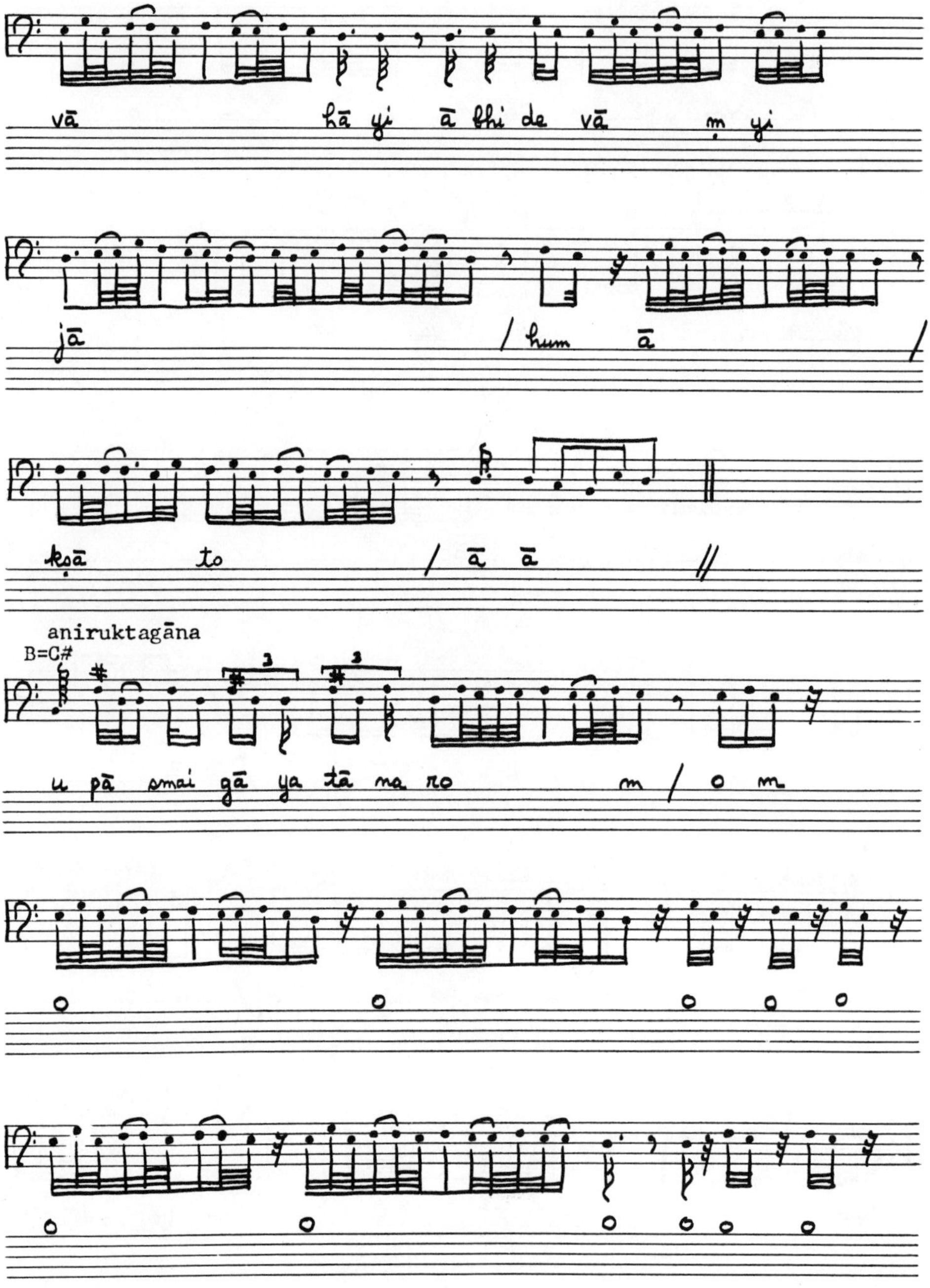

from the <u>bahiṣpavamānastotra</u> (cont.) Krishnamurti Srauti

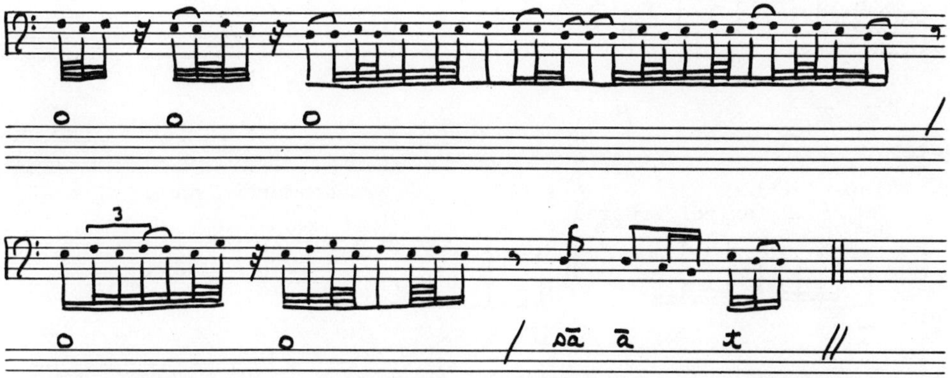

Kauthuma Gāyatram ♪ = 100 Krishnamurti Srauti
Tape IIa(5)
E=F#

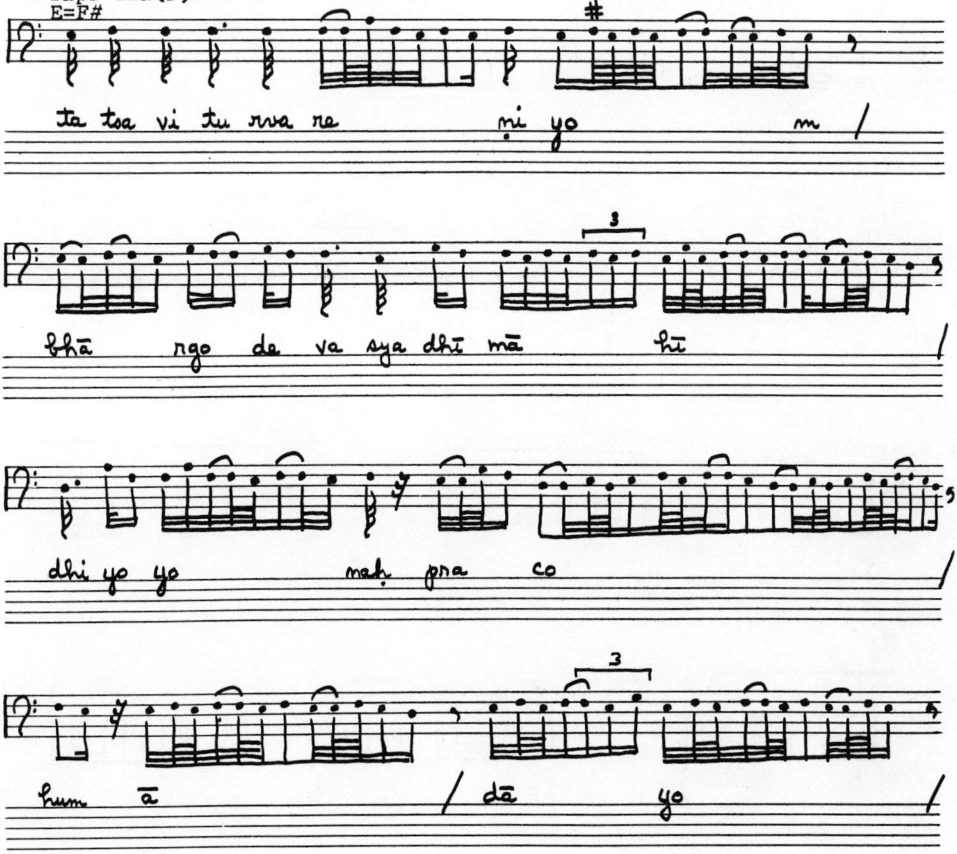

Kauthuma Gāyatram (cont.) Krishnamurti Srauti

ā ā //

Tape Ib(3) ♪ = 100 Krishnamurti Srauti
GG 284.2 (ex. of kruṣṭa)

E=G
ū
ū

Tape XXVIa(8) ♪ = 100 Seshadri Sastrigal (Kauthuma)
GG 284.2 (ex. of kruṣṭa) Tiruvidaimarudur, Tanjore Dist.

E=C
ū
ū

Tape IVa(9) ♪ = 92 K. Raman Aiyangar (Gautama)
GG 1.1 Madras

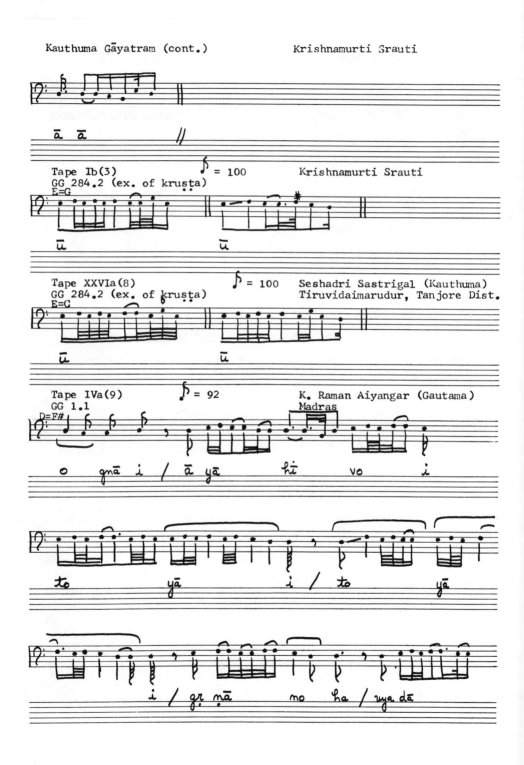

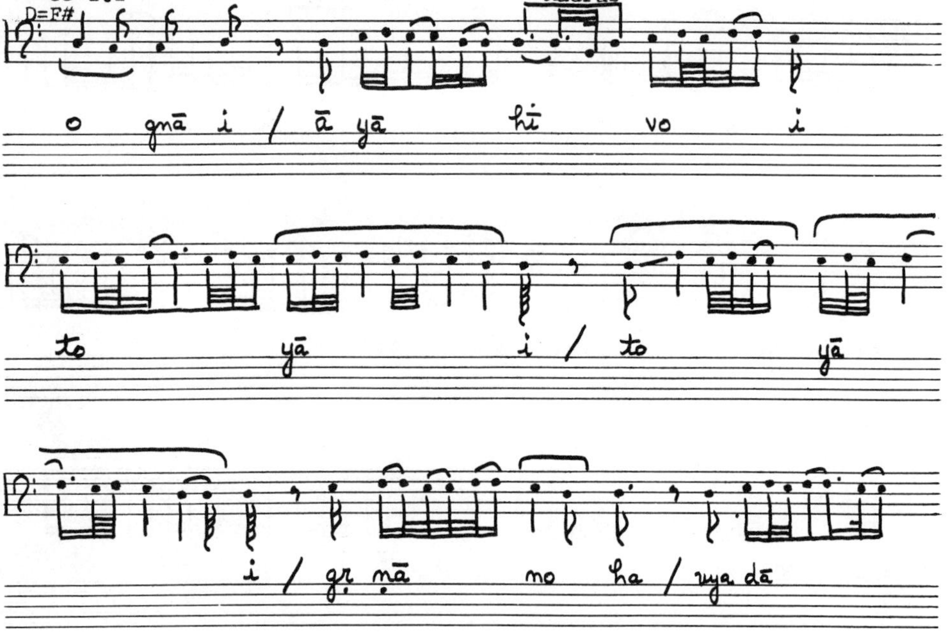
D=F#
o gnā i / ā yā hi vo i
to yā i / to yā
i / gṛ ṇā mo ha / vya dā

GG 1.1 (cont.) K. Raman Aiyangar

to yā i / to yā i /
mā i ho tā sā / tsā
i vā au ho vā /
hi ṣi

GG 1.2 ♪=92 K. Raman Aiyangar
Tape IVa(9)

C=E
a gna ā yā hi vī / ta yā i / gṛ
ṇā no ha vya dā tā yā i / ni ho tā sa

GG 1.2 (cont.) K. Raman Aiyangar

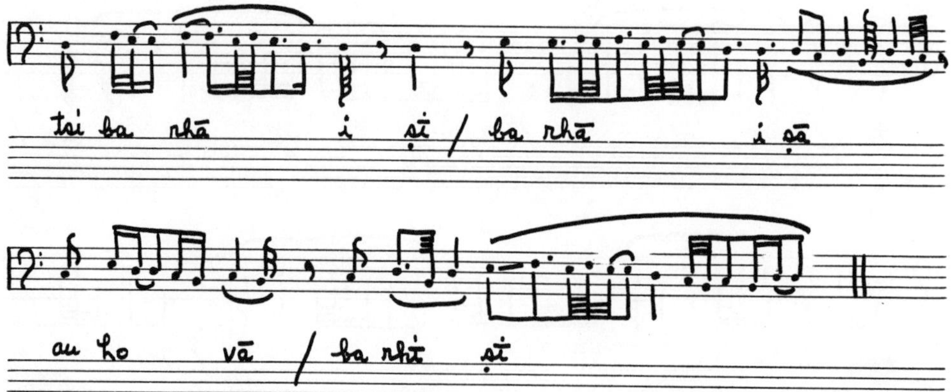
tsi ba rhā i ṣi / ba rhā i ṣā
au ho vā / ba rhi ṣi

Tape IVa(9) ♪ = 92 K. Raman Aiyangar
GG 1.3
C=E

a gna ā yā hi / vā i ta yā i /
gṛ ṇā mo ha vya dā tā ye / ni ho tā
sā / tsā i bā / hā
i ṣo hā i //

Tape XVIIIb(4)B
GG 1.1

♪ = 84

S. Satyanarayana (Kauthuma)
Mysore City

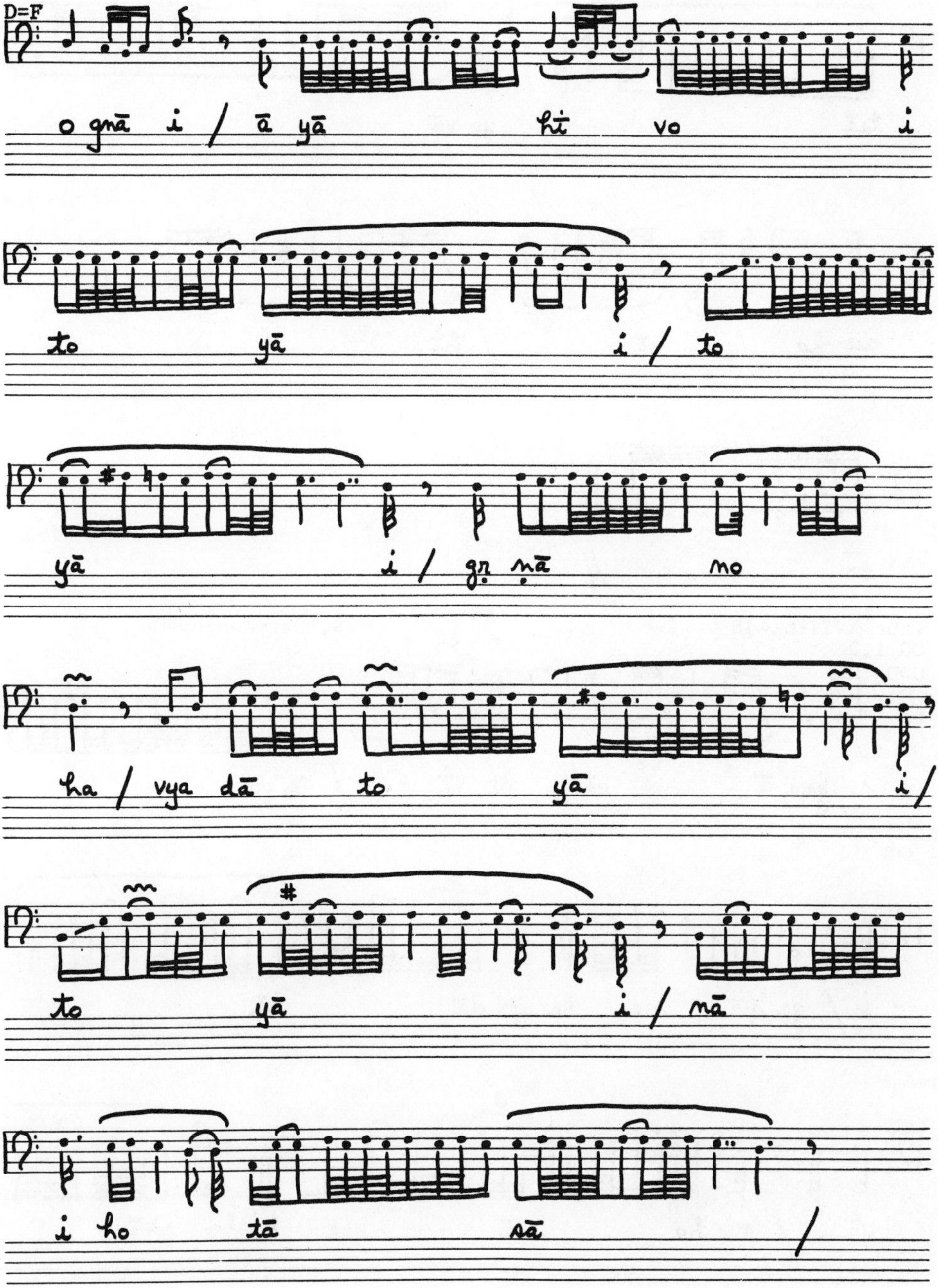
D=F
o gnā i / ā yā hi vo i
to yā i / to
yā i / gṛ ṇā mo
ha / vya dā to yā i /
to yā i / mā
i ho tā sā /

GG 1.1 (cont.) S. Satyanarayana

tsā yi vā
au ho vā / hi
si
//

Tape XVIIIb(4)B ♪ = 84 S. Satyanarayana
GG 1.2
C=D

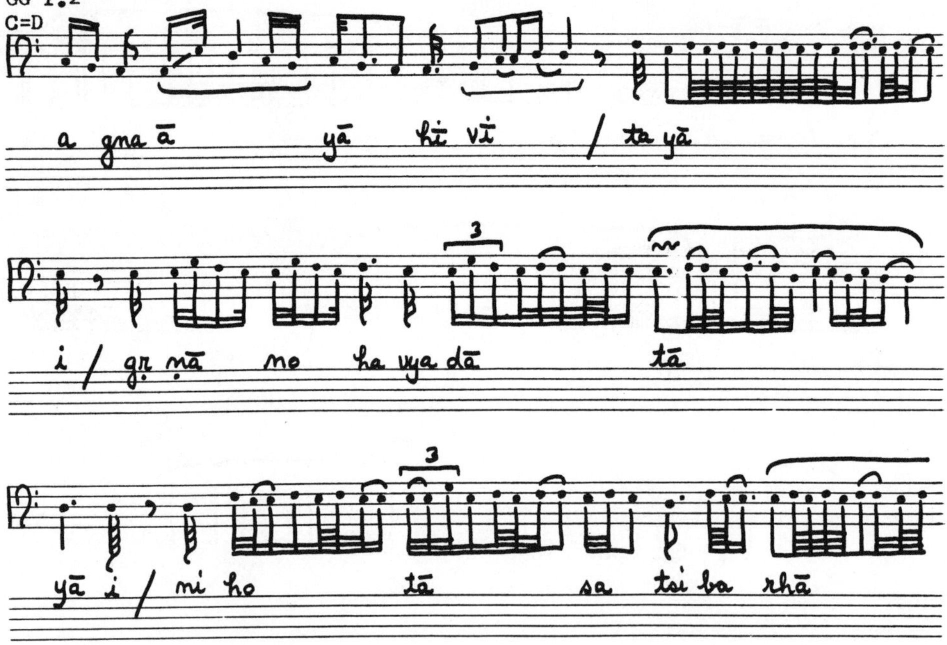
a gna ā yā hi vi / ta yā
i / gr̥ nā no ha vya dā tā
yā i / ni ho tā sa tsi ba rhā

GG 1.2 (cont.) S. Satyanarayana

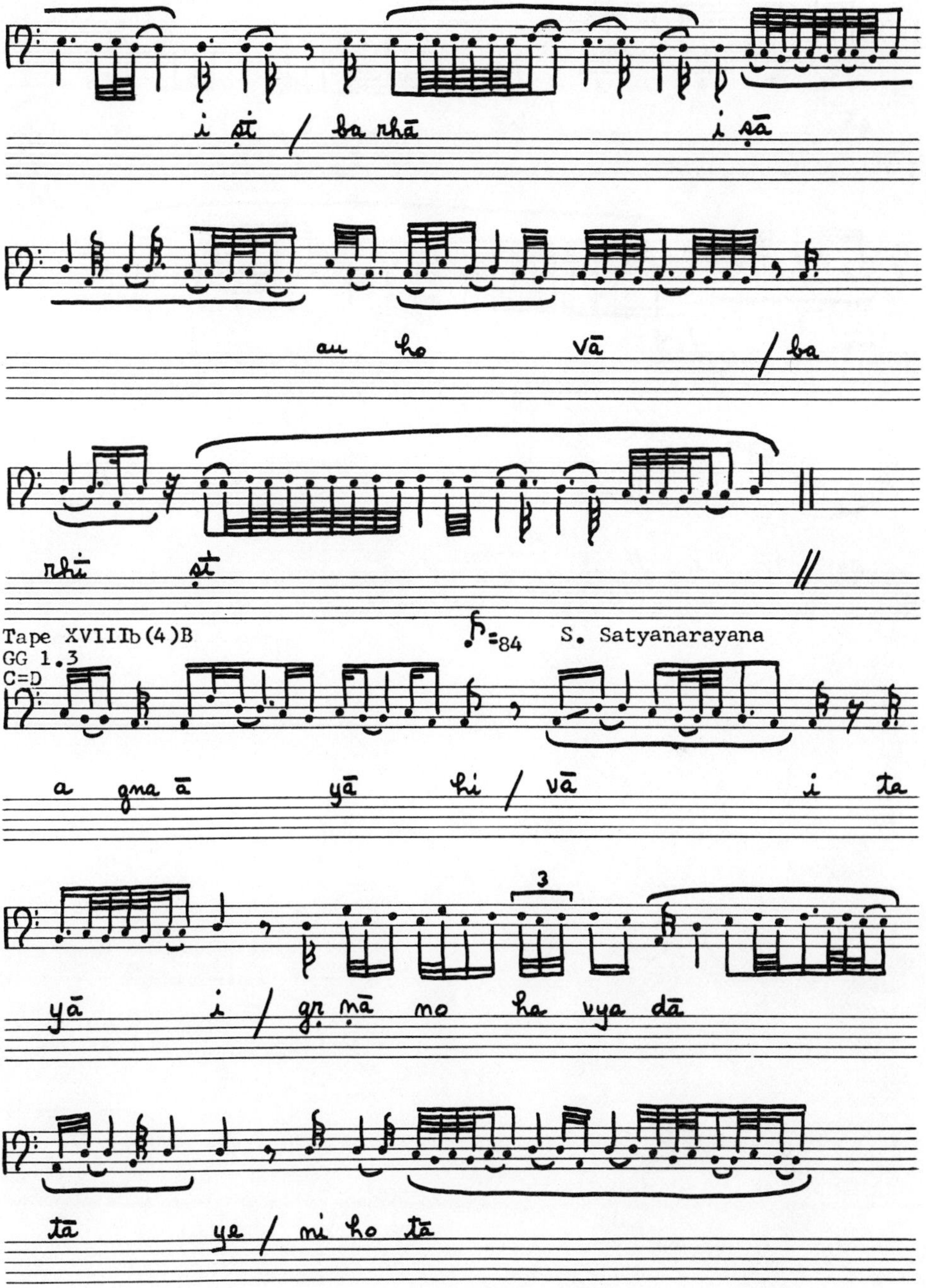

GG 1.3 (cont.) S. Satyanarayana

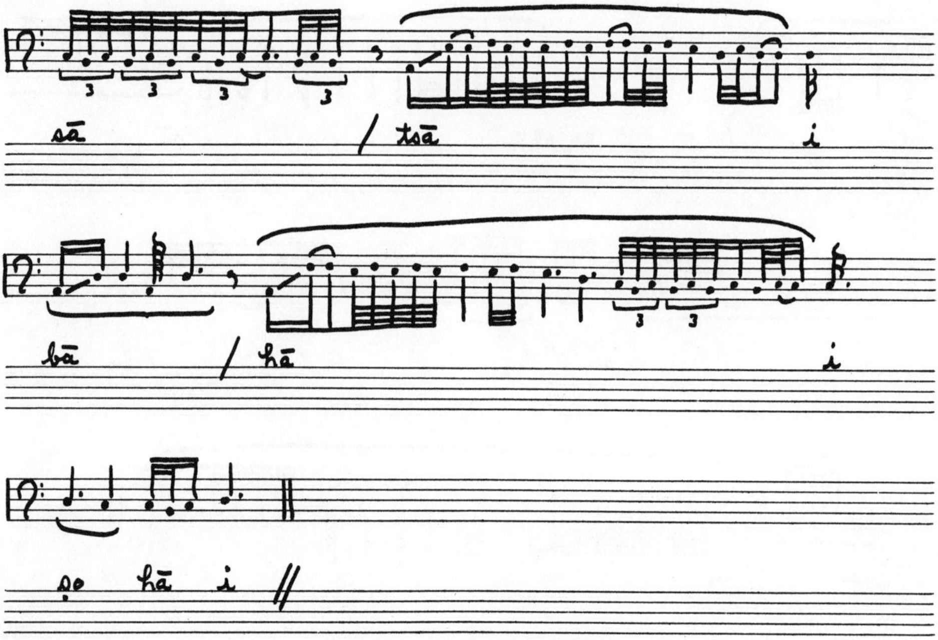
sā
tsā
i
bā
hā
i
hā
i

GG 1.1

♪ = 84

Mullantiram Ramanatha Dikshitar
Kauthuma School
Mullantiram, North Arcot District

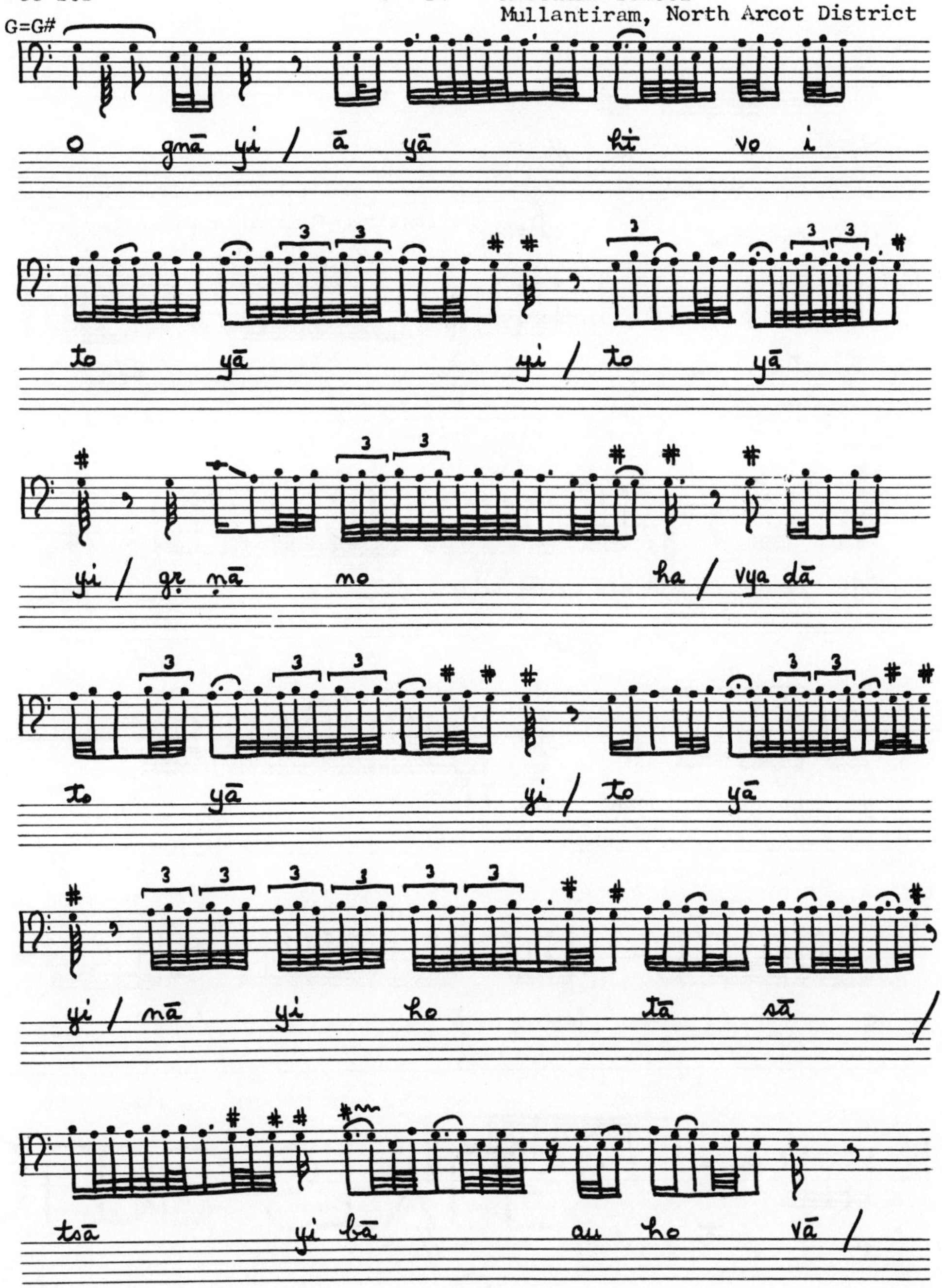
G=G#
o gnā yi / ā yā hi vo i
to yā yi / to yā
yi / gṛ ṇā mo ha / vya dā
to yā yi / to yā
yi / nā yi ho tā sā /
tsā yi bā au ho vā /

GG 1.1 (cont.) Mullantiram Ramanatha Dikshitar

Kauthuma Gāyatram ♪= 84 Mullantiram Ramanatha Dikshitar

D=B

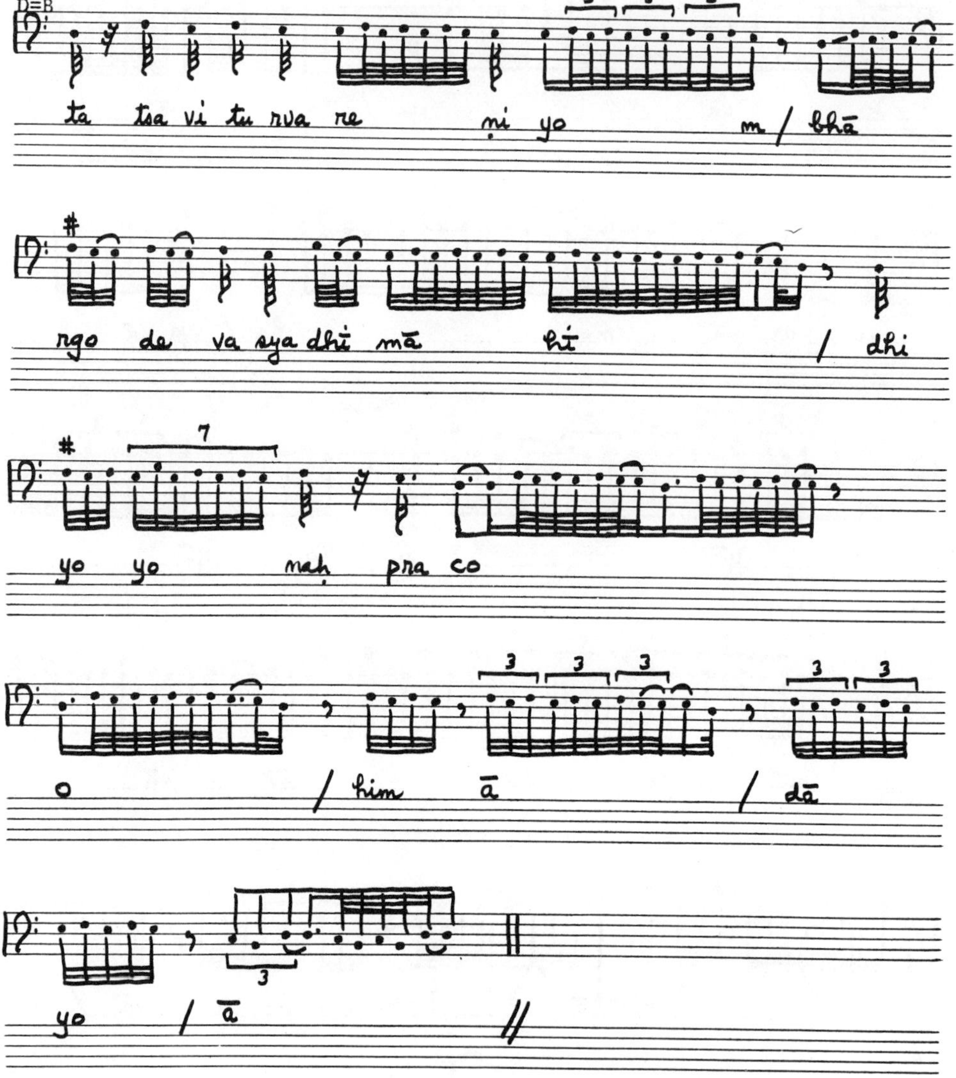

Tape XXVa(12)
The 301 typical parvans of the Hāvik Rāṇāyanīyas ♪ = 120 for ka-varga

ka-varga: Subbaraya Ramacandra Bhatta (Arolli village, Mysore)

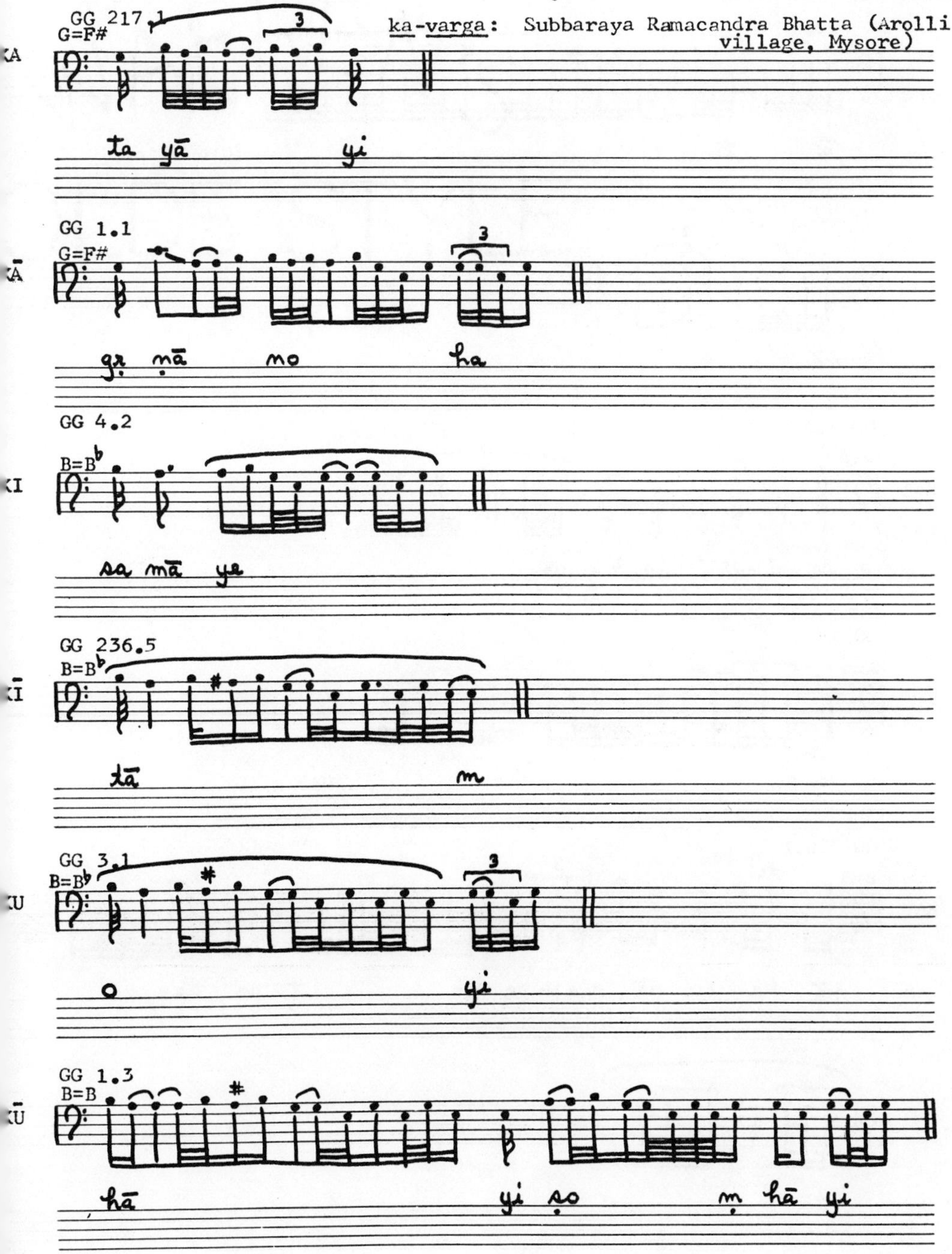

ka-varga (cont.) Subbaraya Ramacandra Bhatta

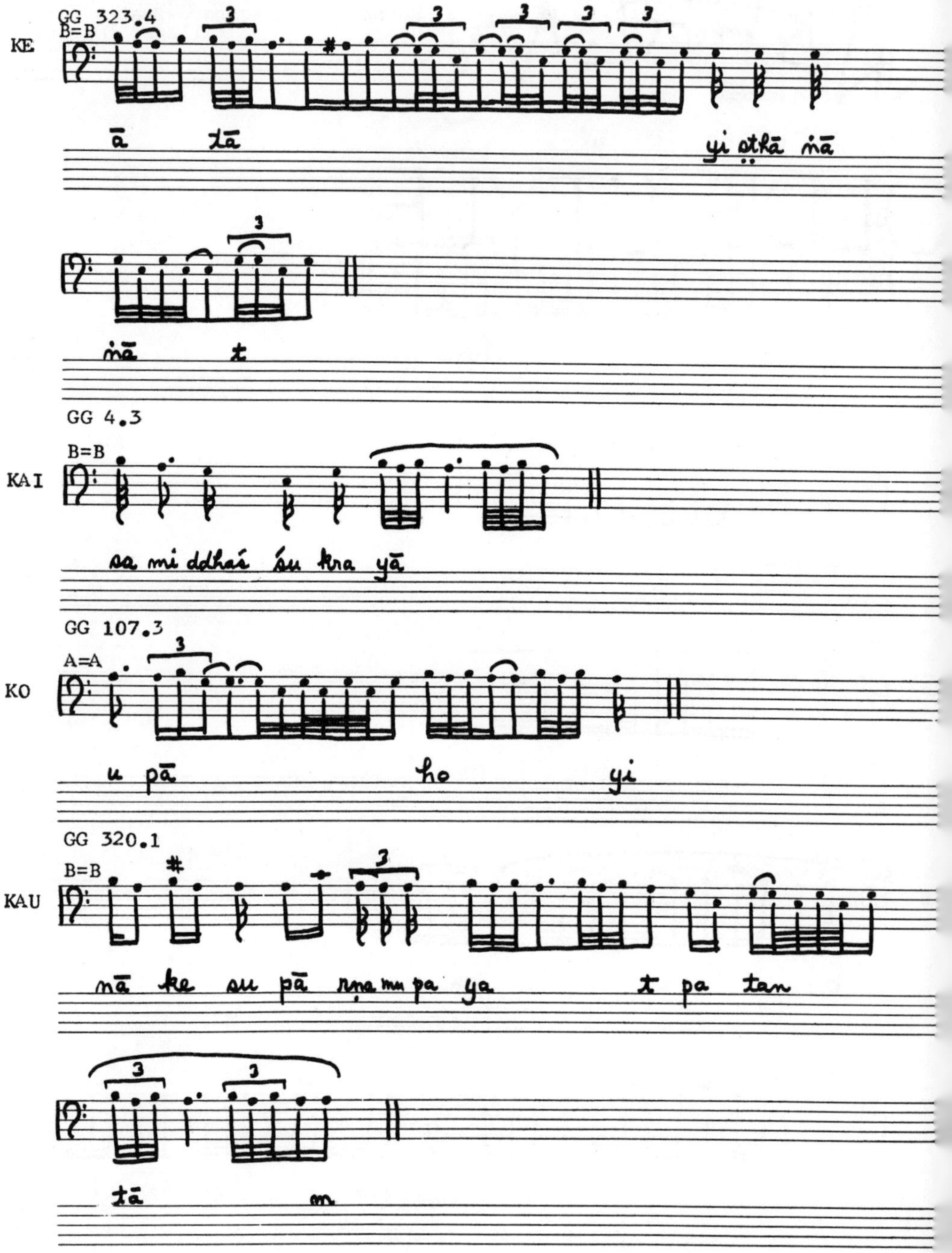

ka-varga (cont.) Subbaraya Ramacandra Bhatta

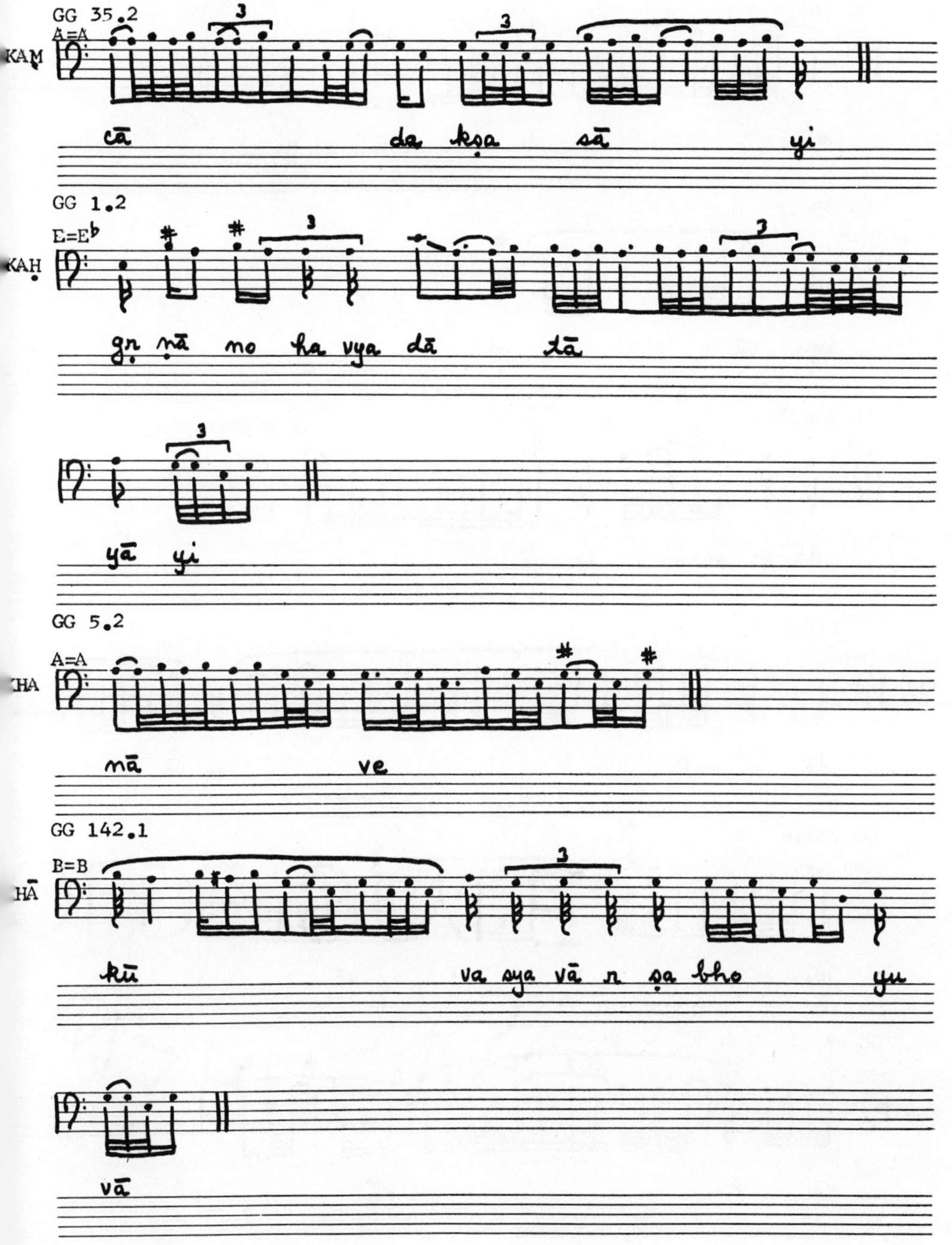

ka-varga (cont.) Subbaraya Ramacandra Bhatta

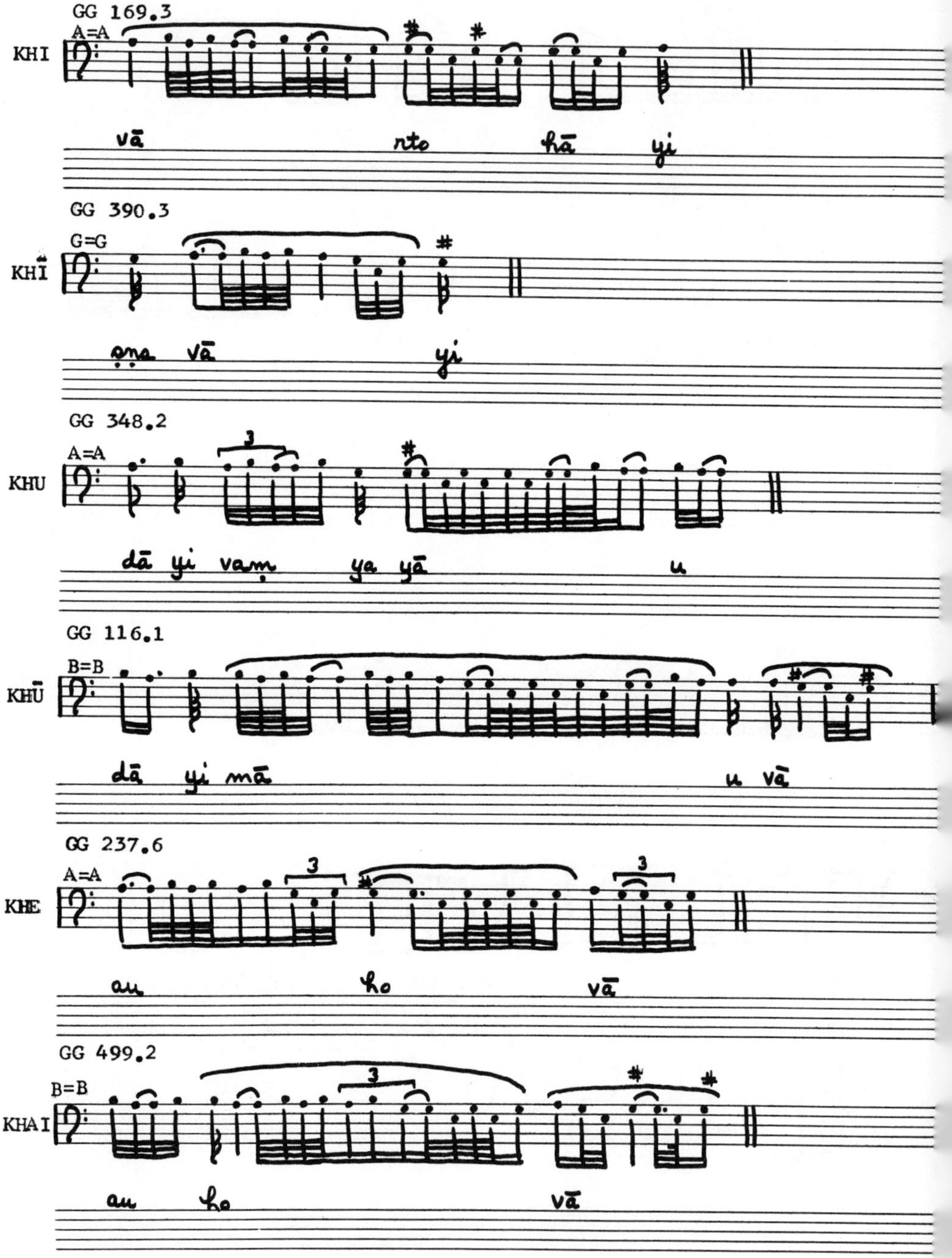

<u>ka</u>-<u>varga</u> (cont.) Subbaraya Ramacandra Bhatta

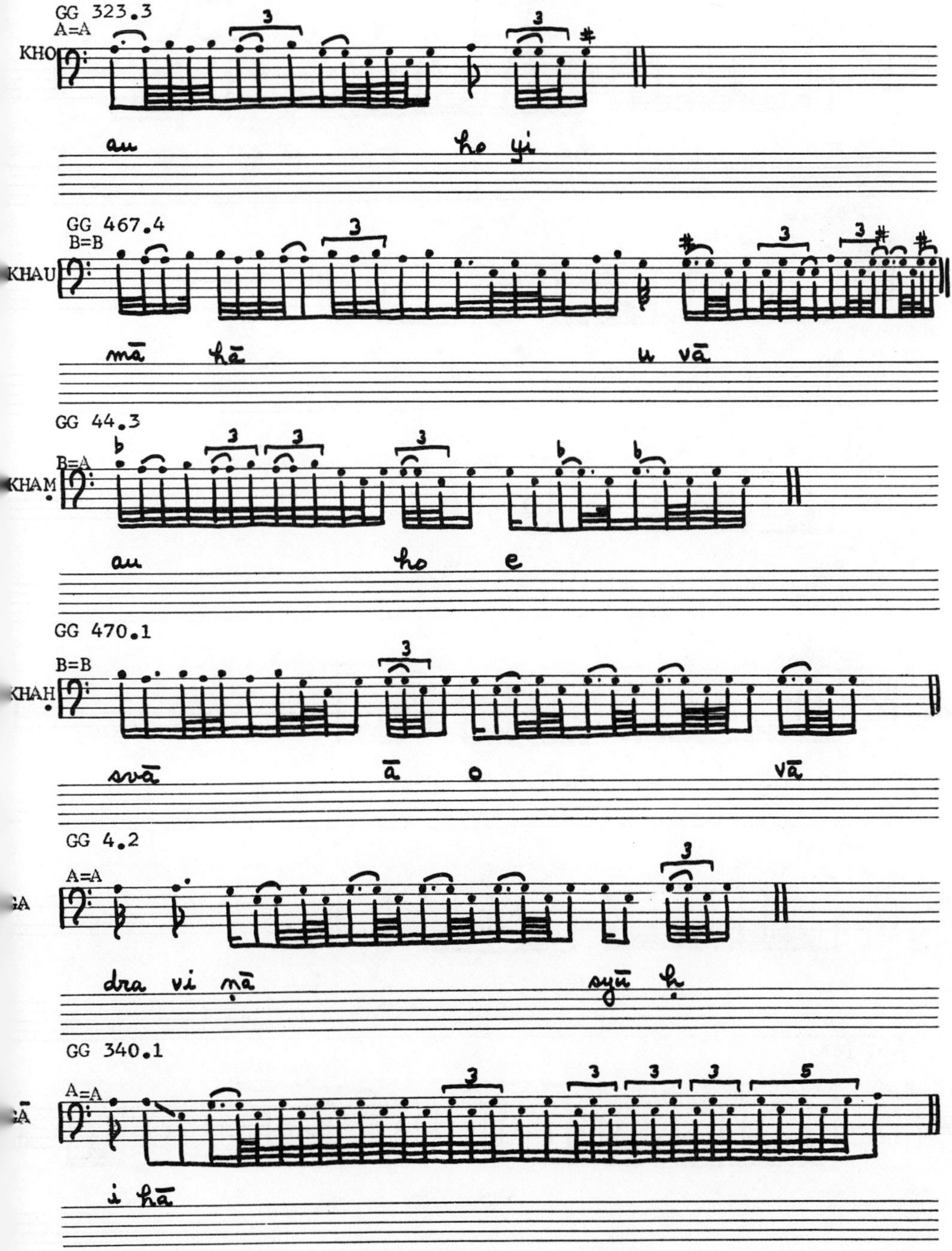

<u>ka</u>-<u>varga</u> (cont.) Subbaraya Ramacandra Bhatta

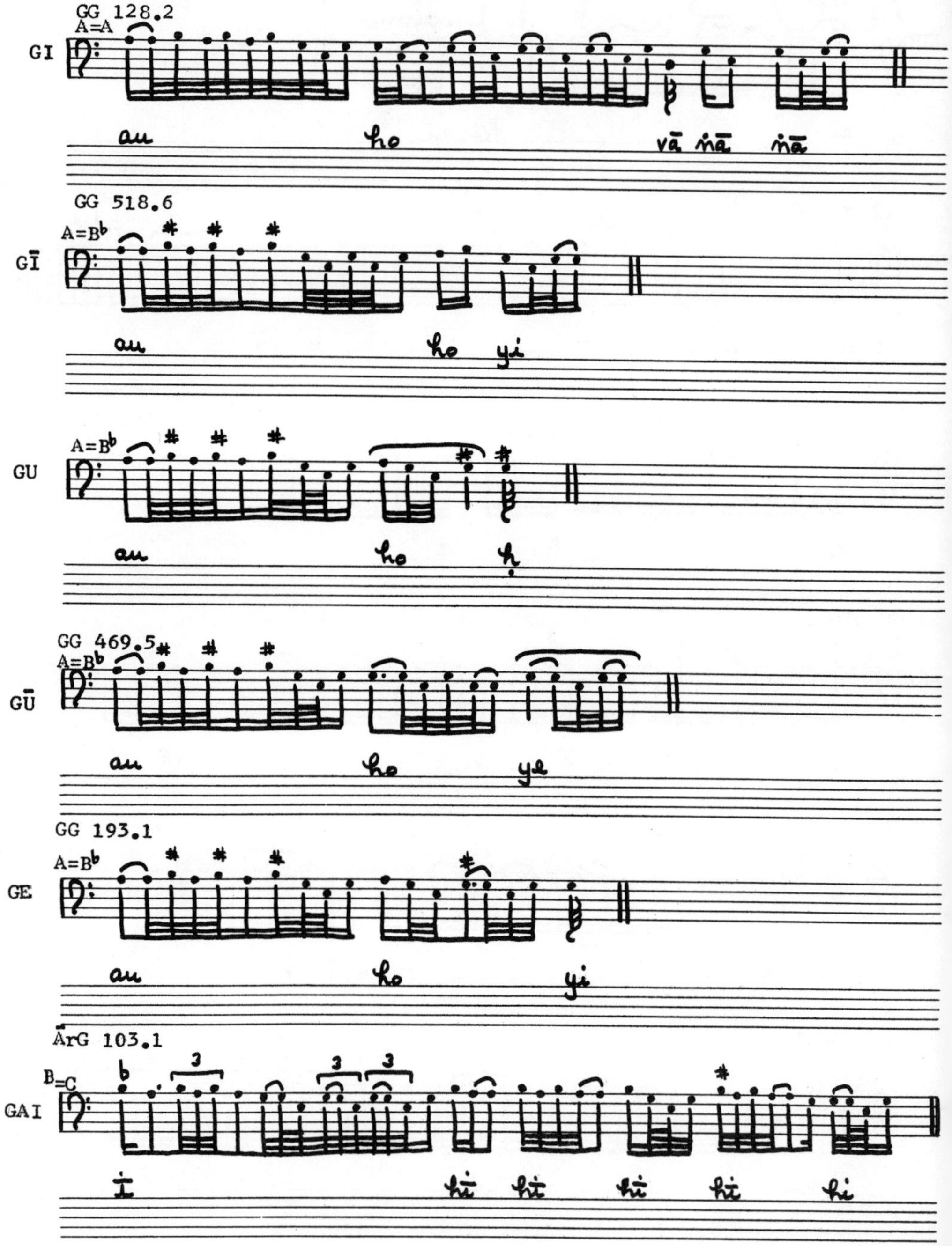

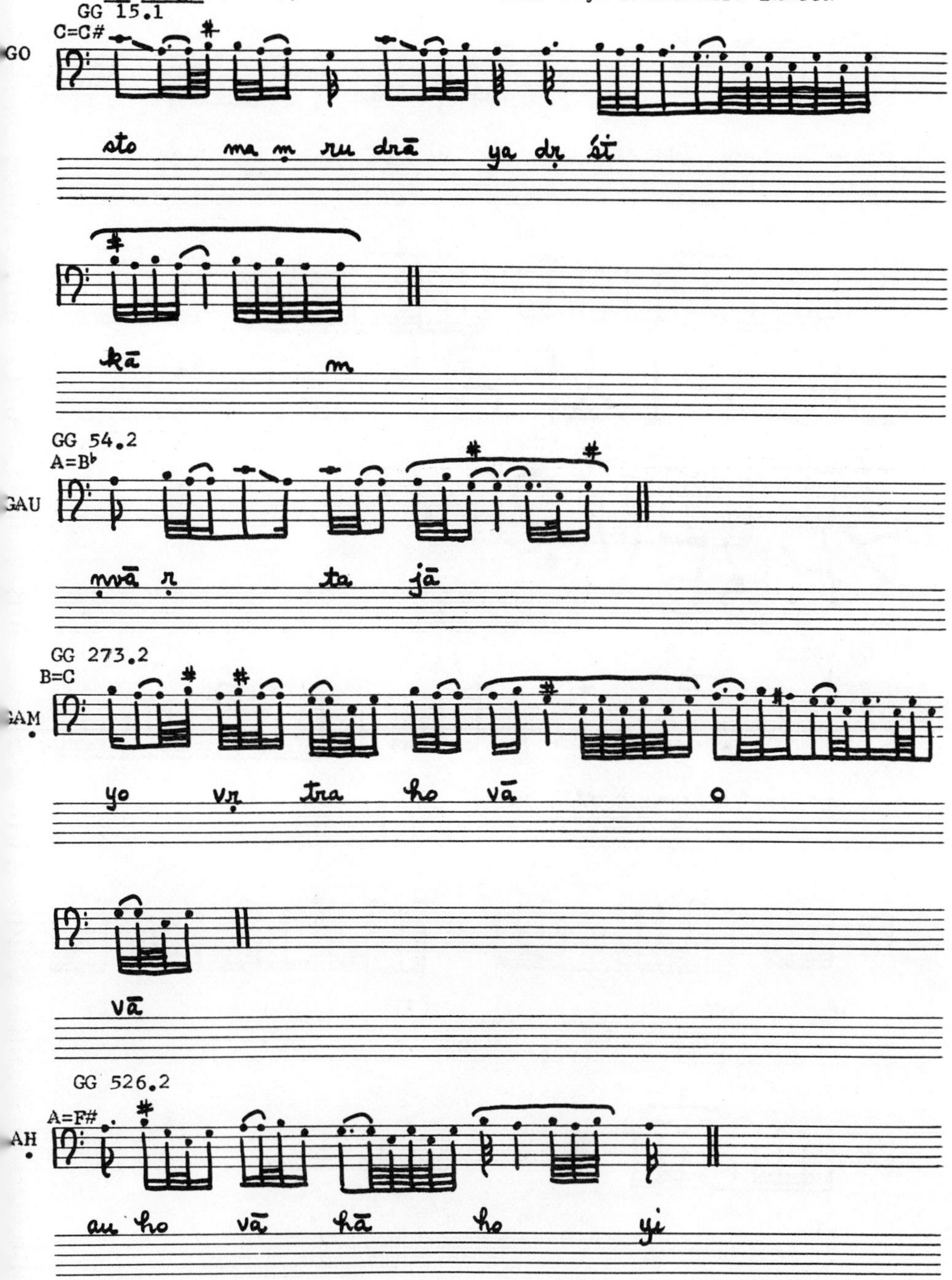
GG 15.1
C=C#
GO
sto ma m ru drā ya dṛ śt
kā m
GG 54.2
A=B♭
GAU
ṇvā ṛ ta jā
GG 273.2
B=C
AM
yo vṛ tra ho vā o
vā
GG 526.2
A=F#
AH
au ho vā hā ho yi

ka-varga (cont.)

GG 147.2

Subbaraya Ramacandra Bhatta

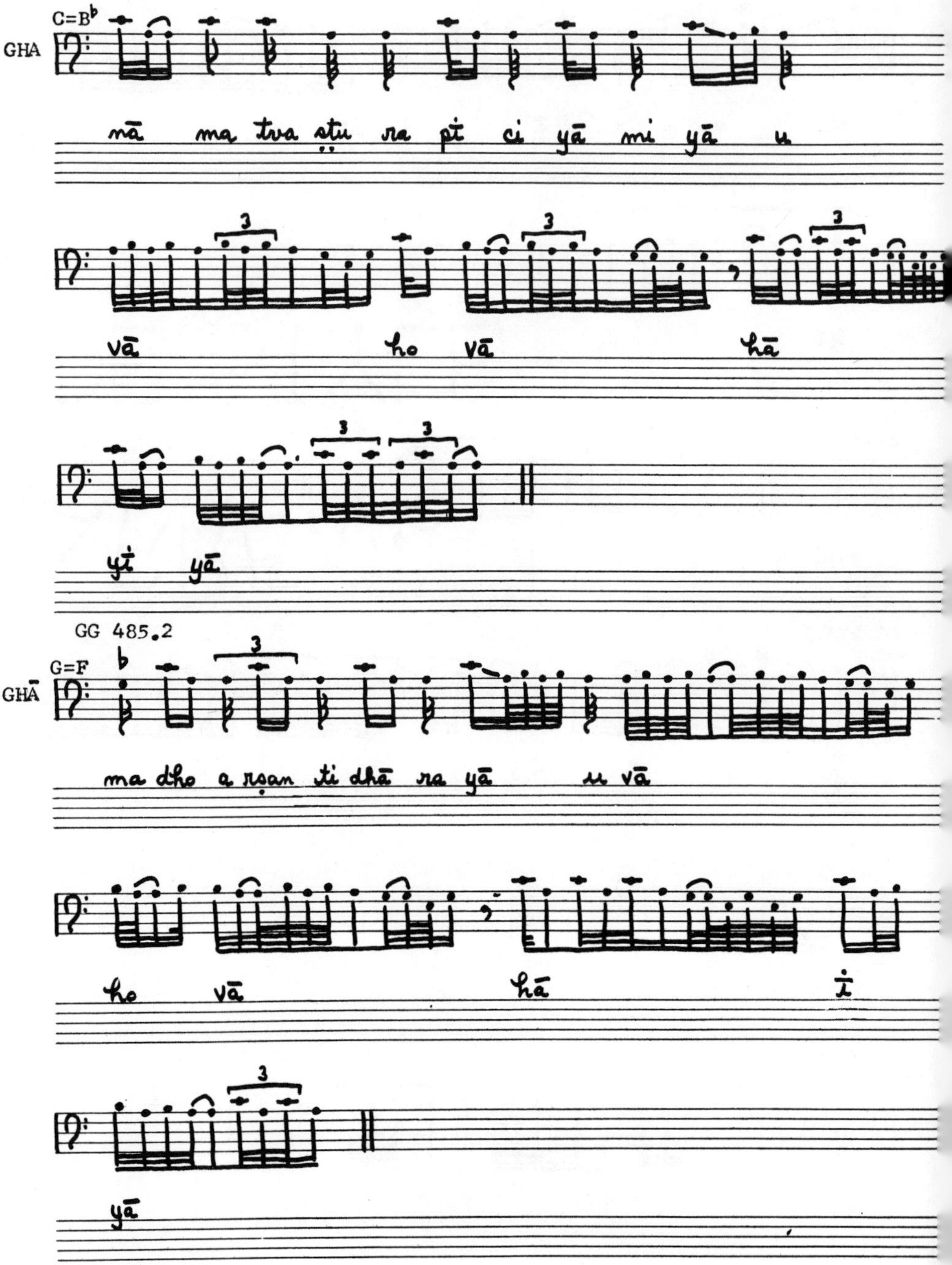

ka-varga (cont.) Subbaraya Ramacandra Bhatta

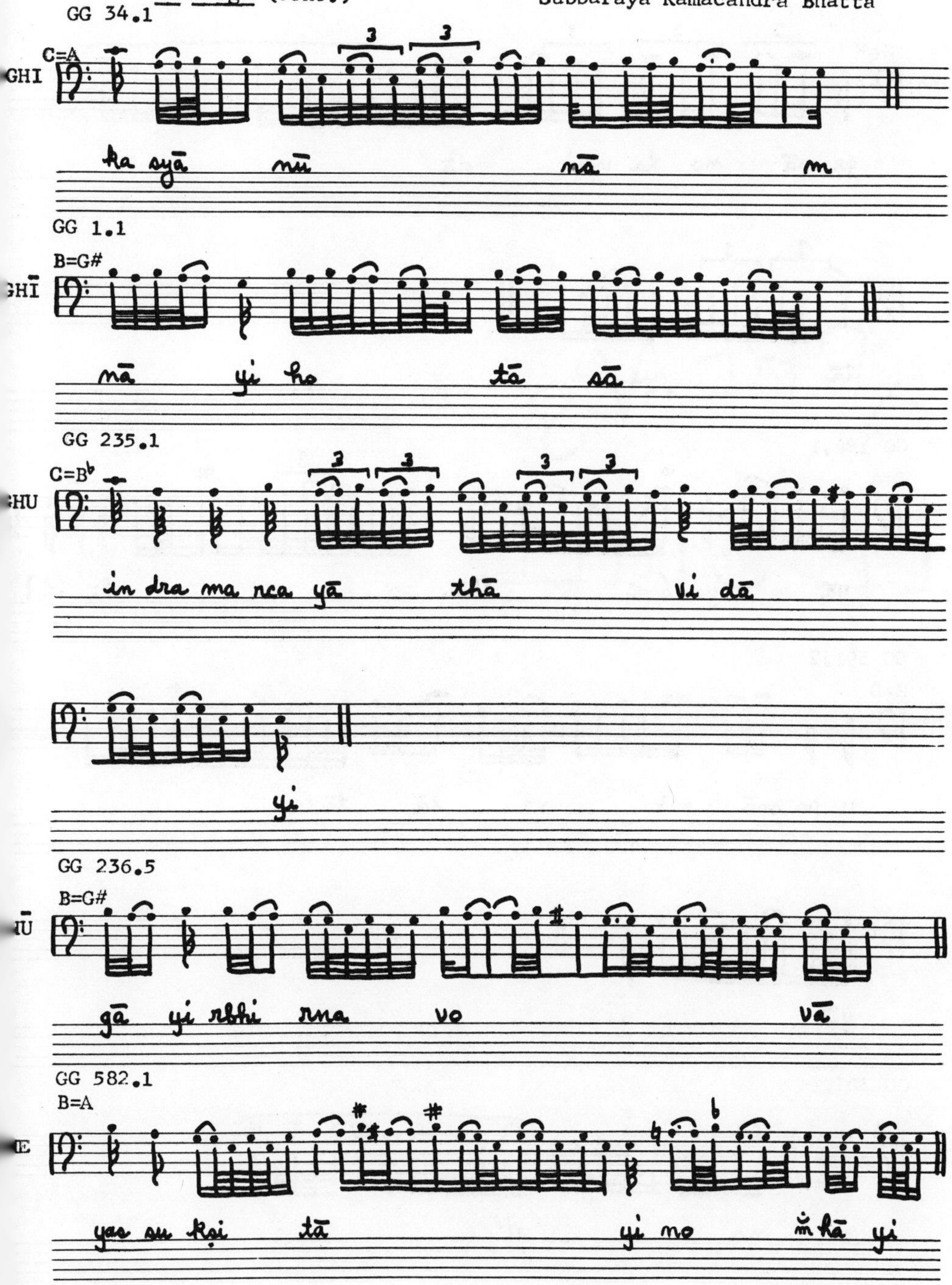

<u>ka-varga</u> (cont.) Subbaraya Ramacandra Bhatta

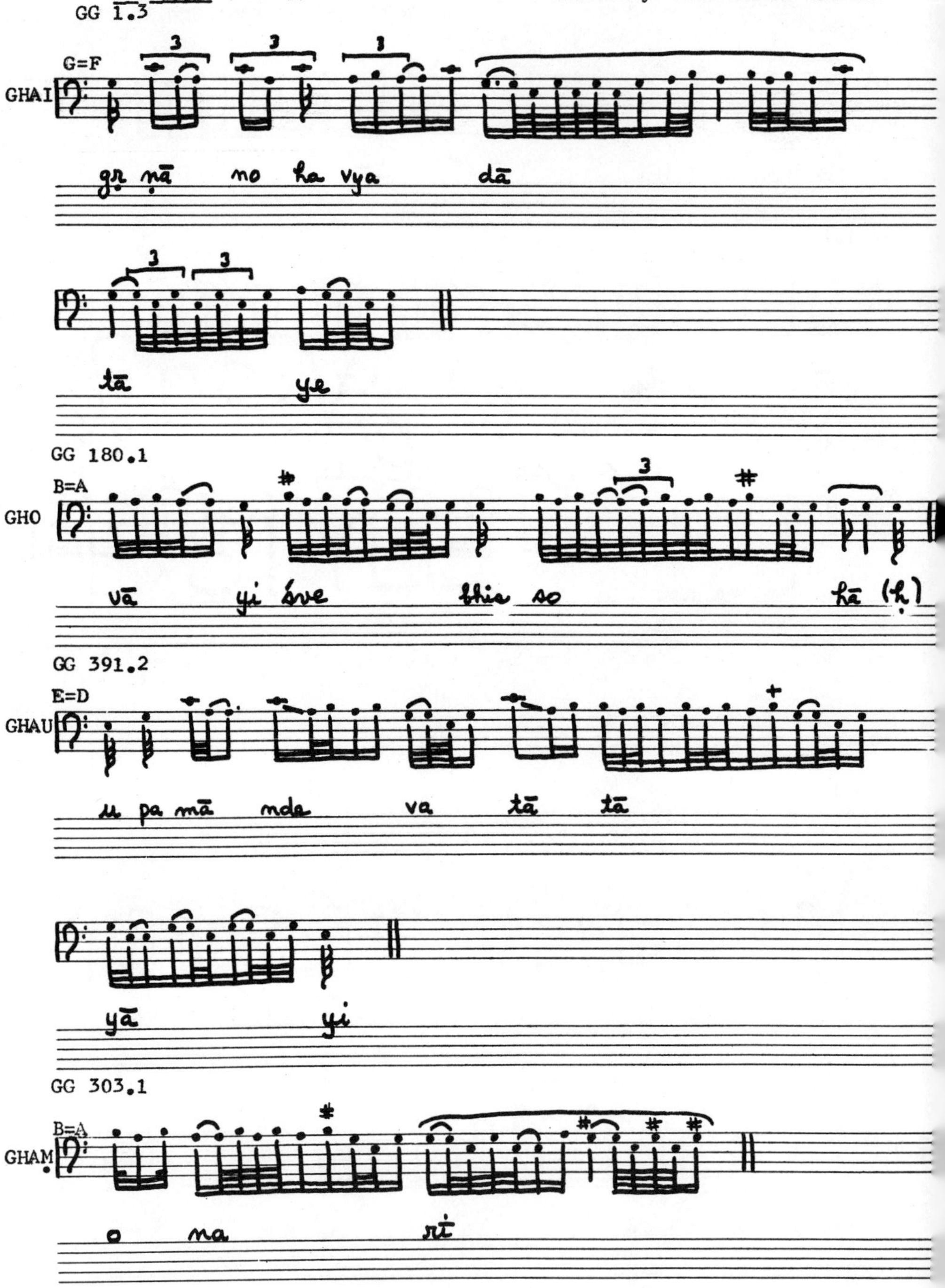

ka-varga (cont.)
GG 417.5

Subbaraya Ramacandra Bhatta

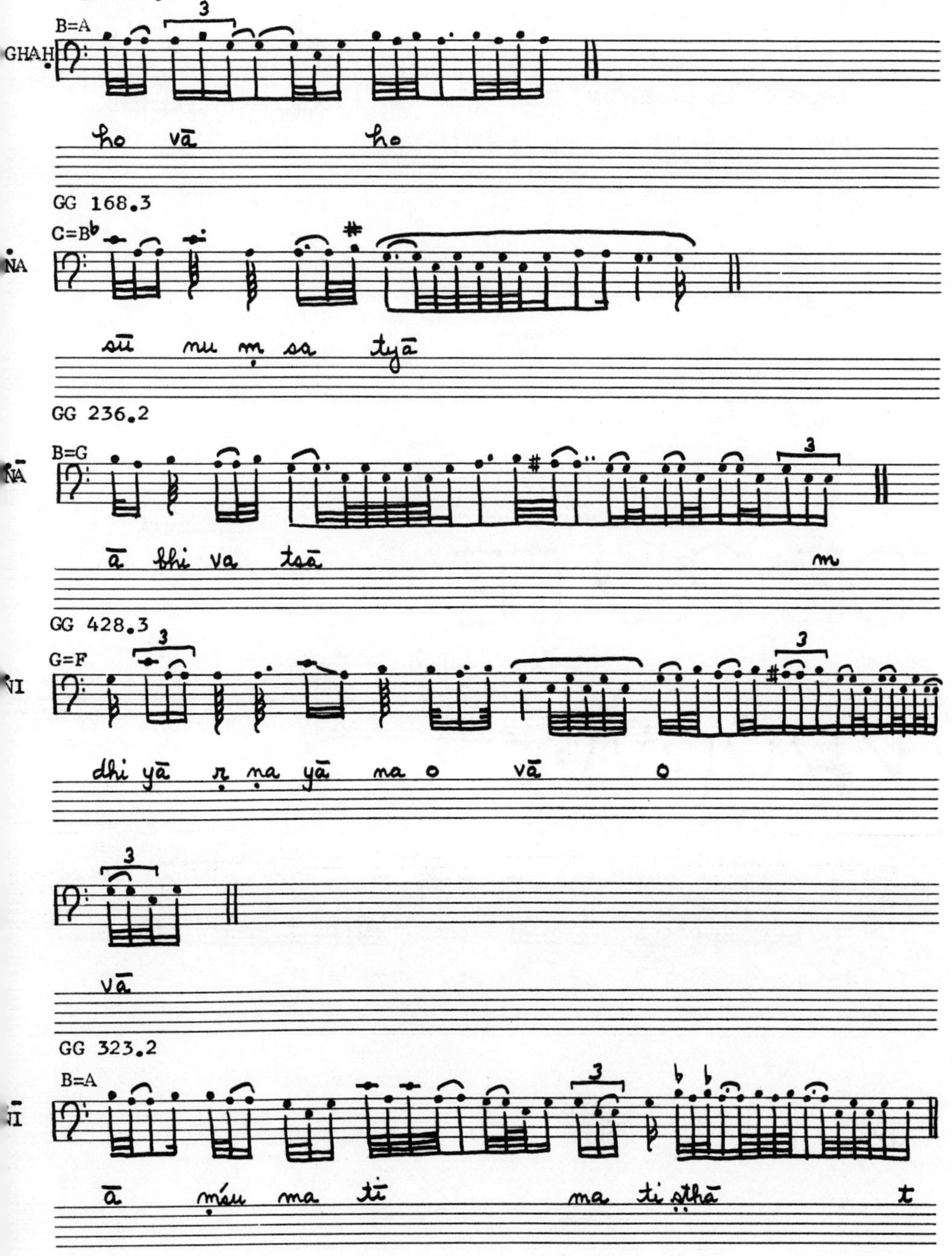

ka-varga (cont.) Subbaraya Ramacandra Bhatta

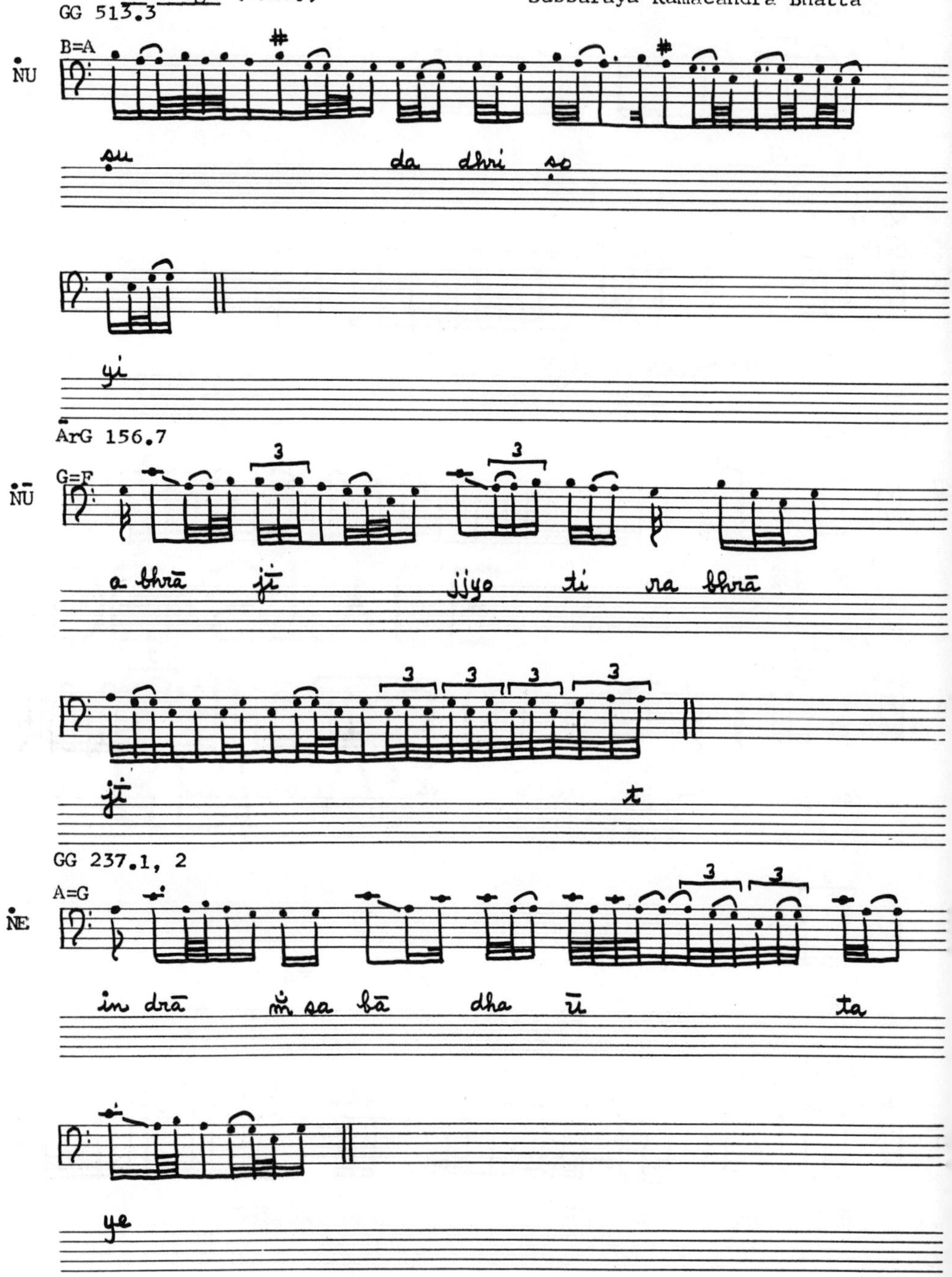

ka-varga (cont.) Subbaraya Ramacandra Bhatta

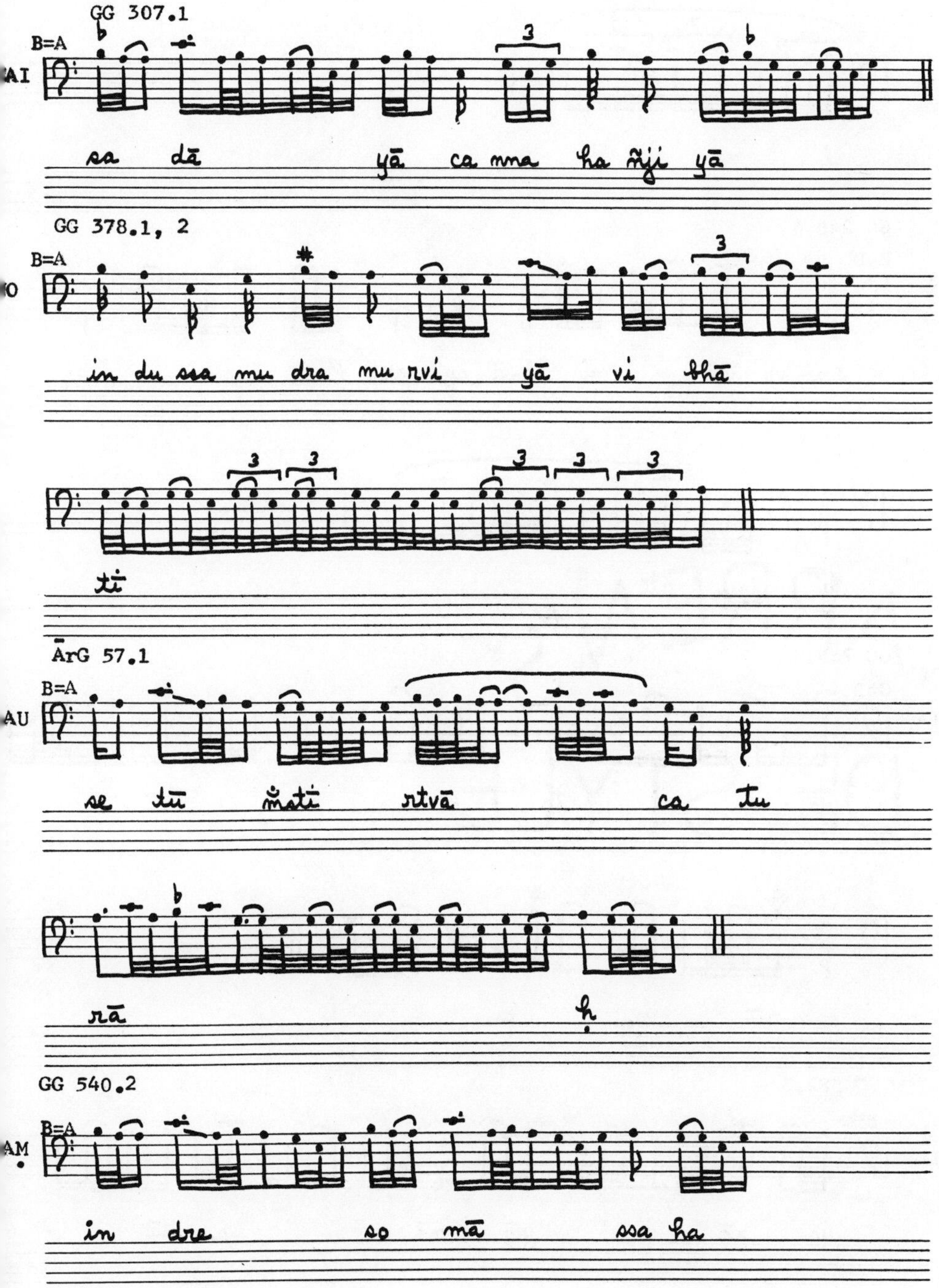

<u>ka</u>-<u>varga</u> (cont.) Subbaraya Ramacandra Bhatta

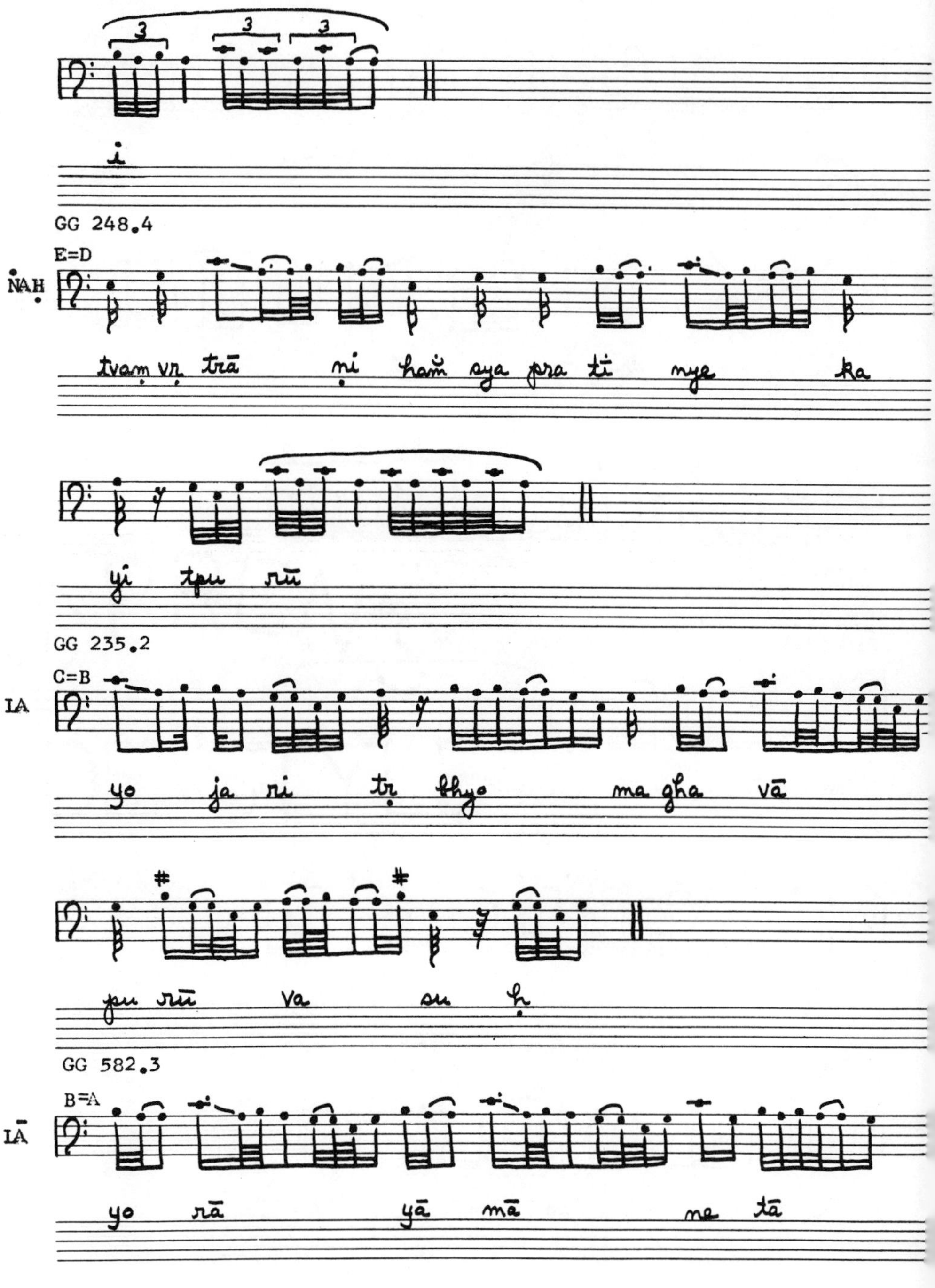

ĀrG 56.1

ĀrG, after 93.5

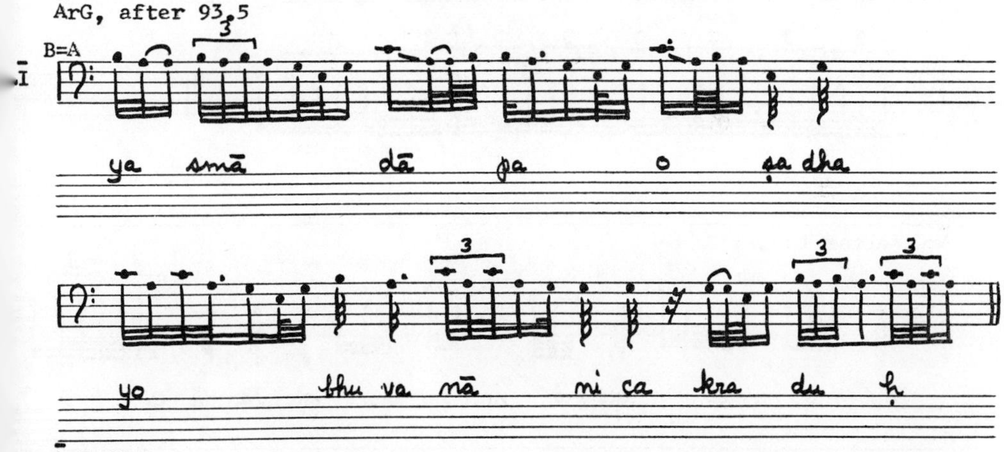

ĀrG 98.1

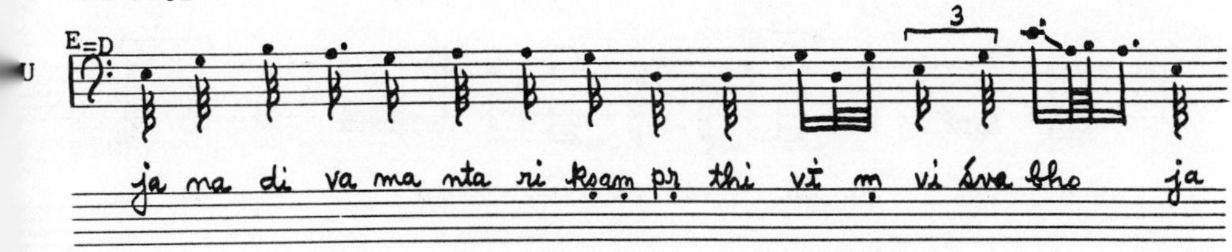

<u>ka-varga</u> (cont.) Subbaraya Ramacandra Bhatta

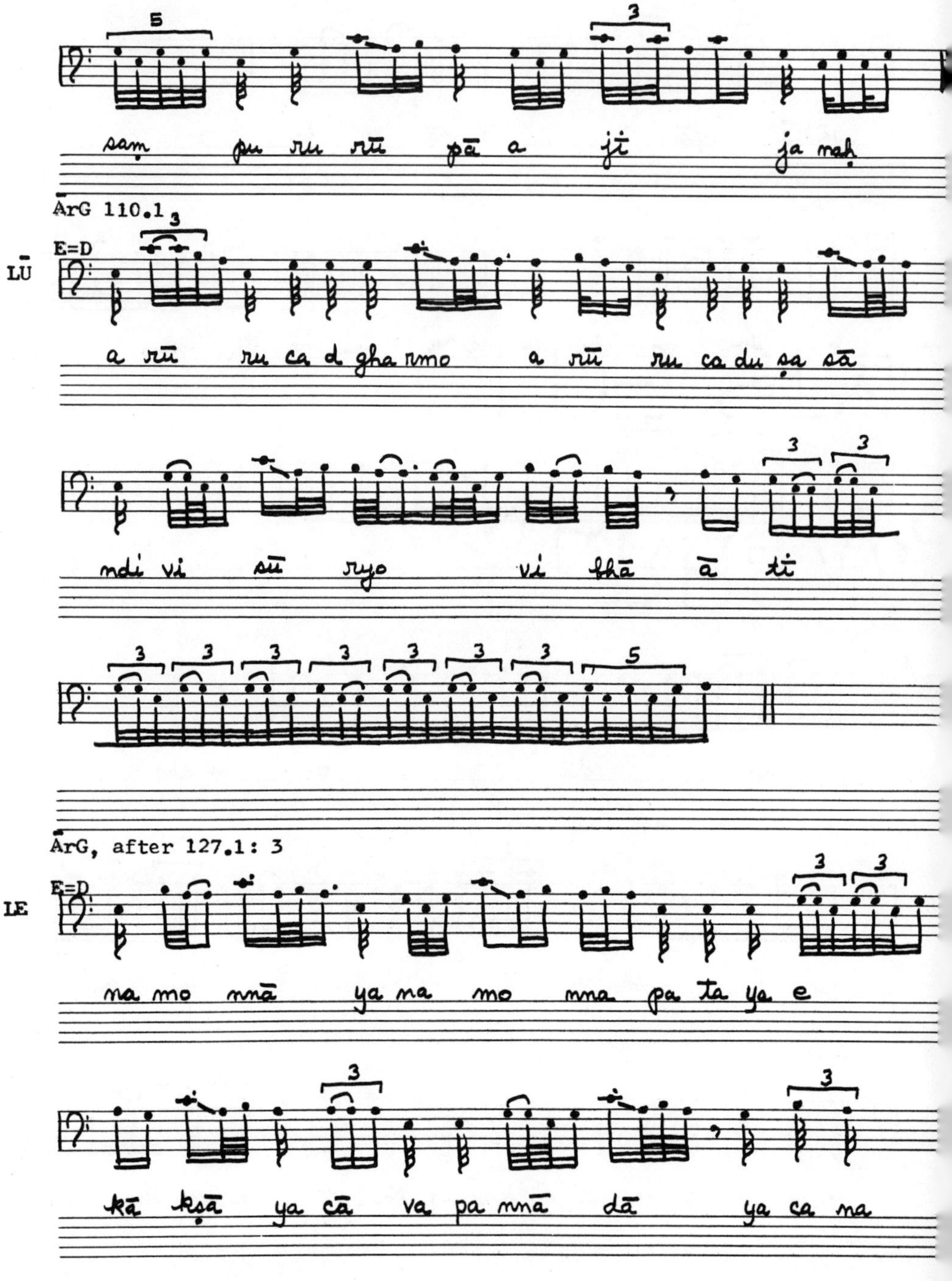

ka-varga (cont.) Subbaraya Ramacandra Bhatta

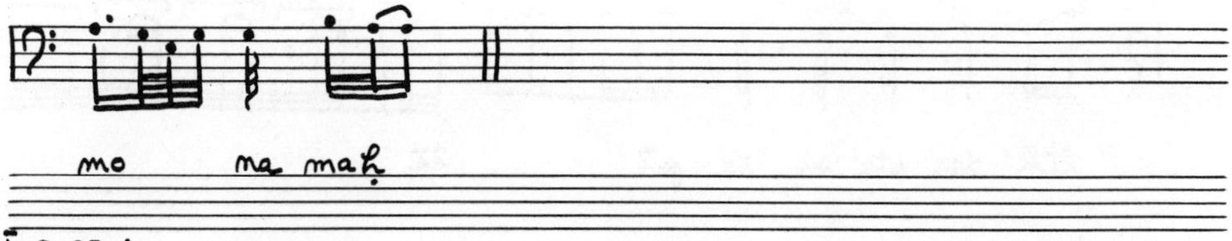

ĀrG 93.4

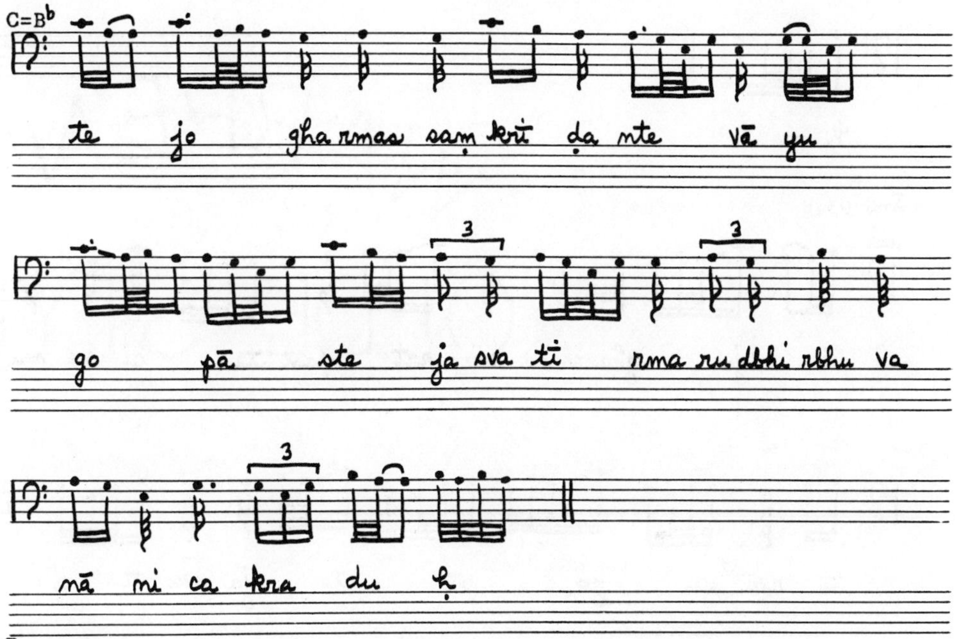

ĀrG 139.1

ka-varga (cont.) Subbaraya Ramacandra Bhatta

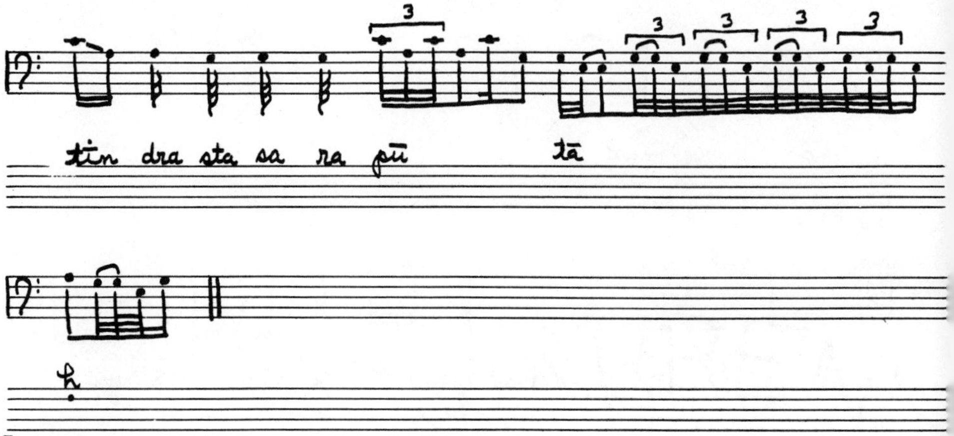

ĀrG 93.2

ĀrG, after 127.1: 1

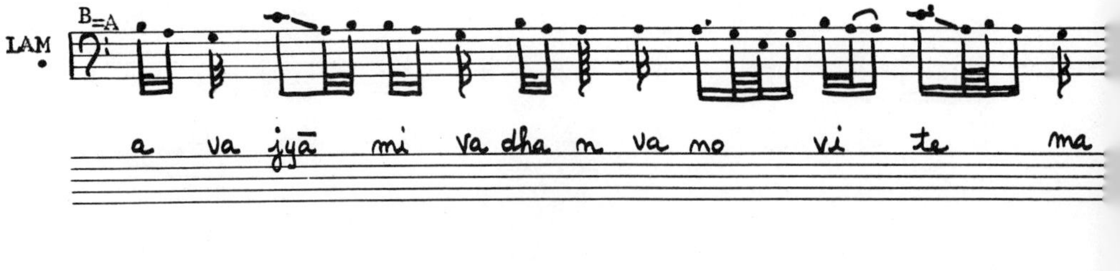

ka-varga (cont.) Subbaraya Ramacandra Bhatta

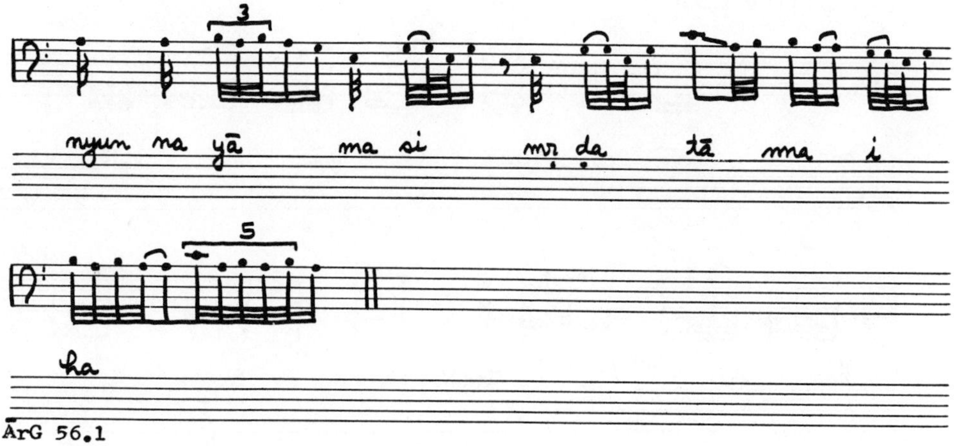

ĀrG 56.1

[1] Unclear on tape: approximate transcription.

ka-varga (cont.) Subbaraya Ramacandra Bhatta

ĀrG, after 175.6

ĀrG, after 127.1: 2

[1]Unclear on tape: approximate transcription.

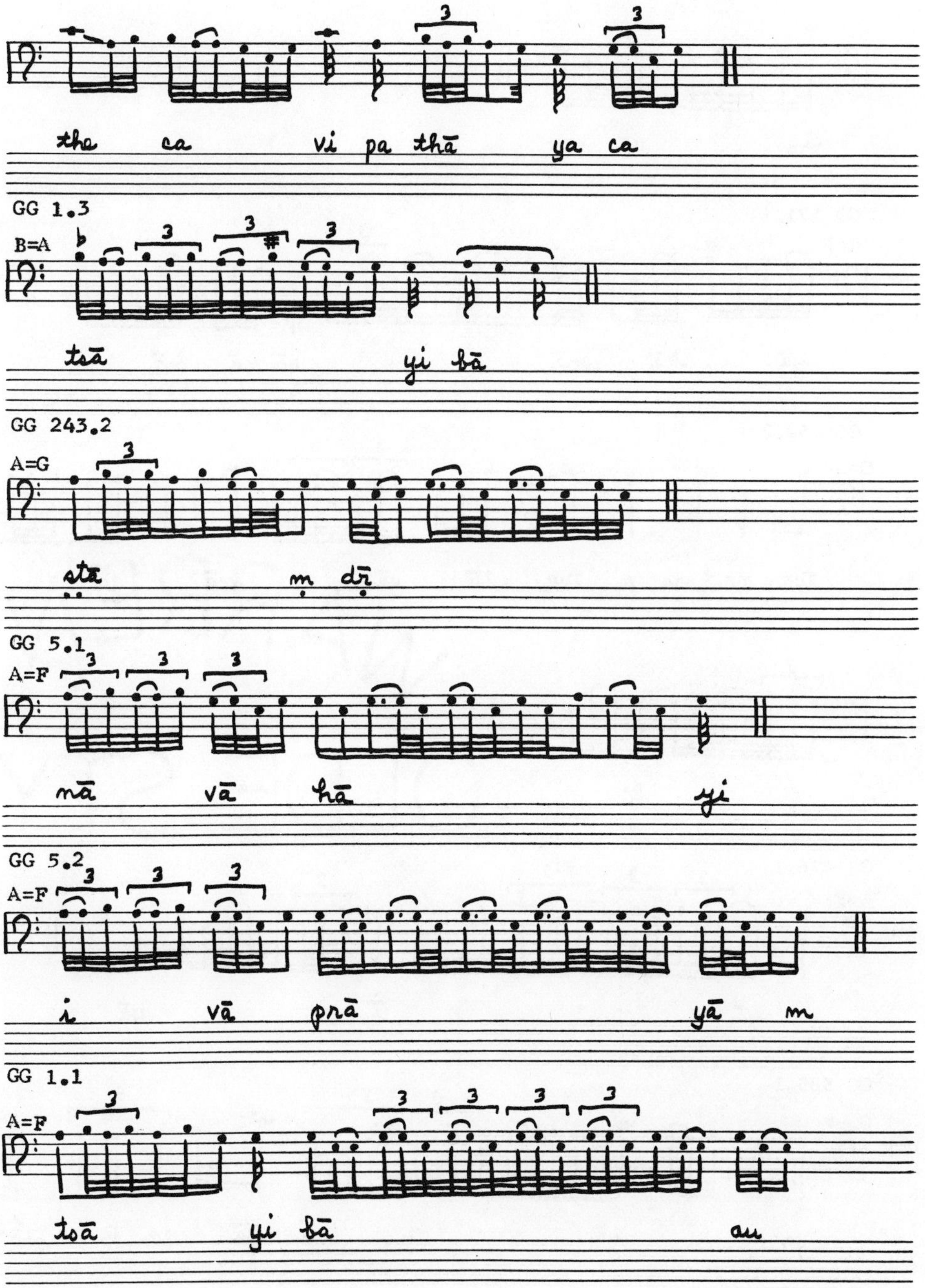
the ca vi pa thā ya ca
GG 1.3
B=A
VI
tsā yi bā
GG 243.2
A=G
VĪ
stā m dṛ
GG 5.1
A=F
U
nā vā hā yi
GG 5.2
A=F
Ū
i vā prā yā m
GG 1.1
A=F
E
tsā yi bā au

ka-varga (cont.) Subbaraya Ramacandra Bhatta

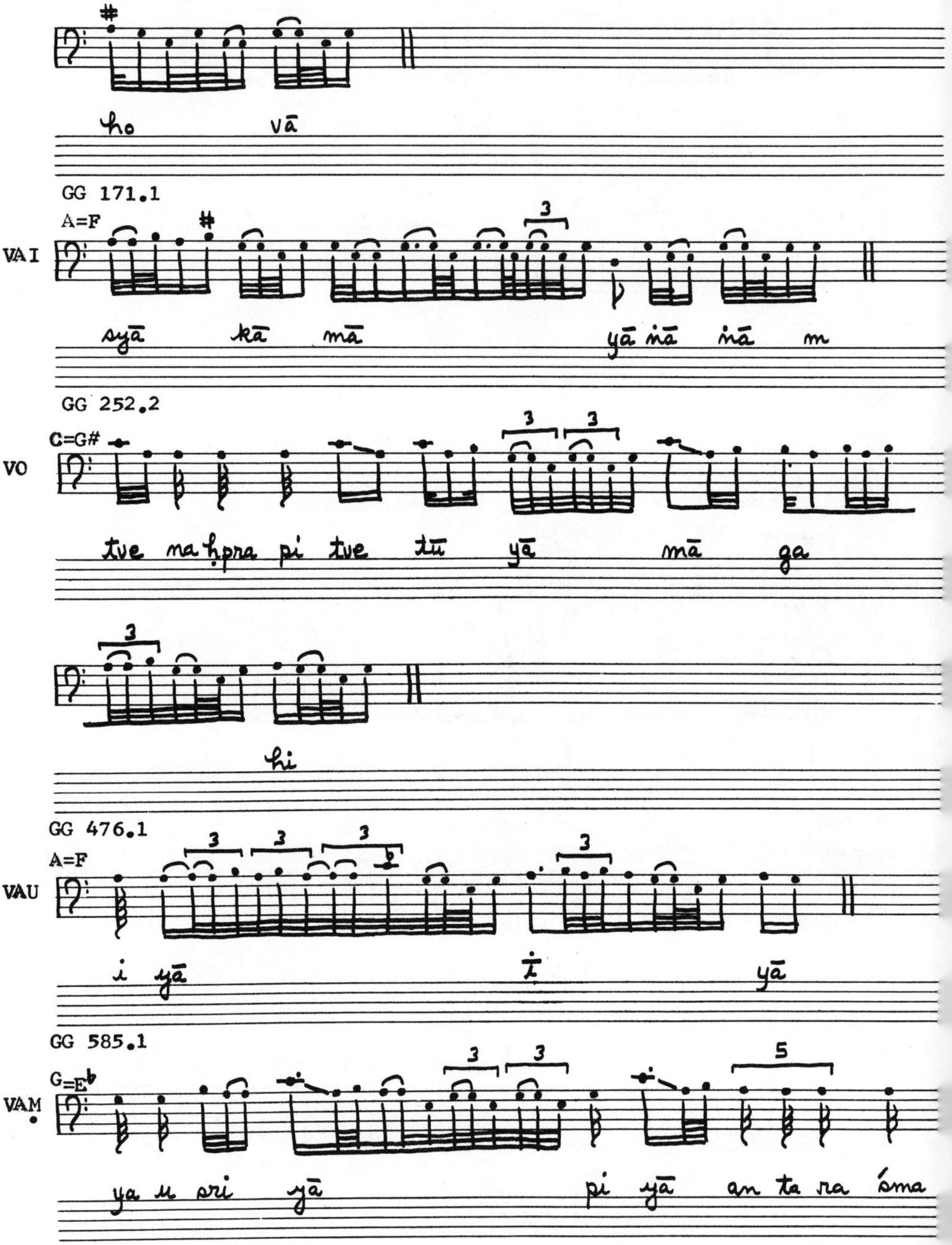

ka-varga (cont.) Subbaraya Ramacandra Bhatta

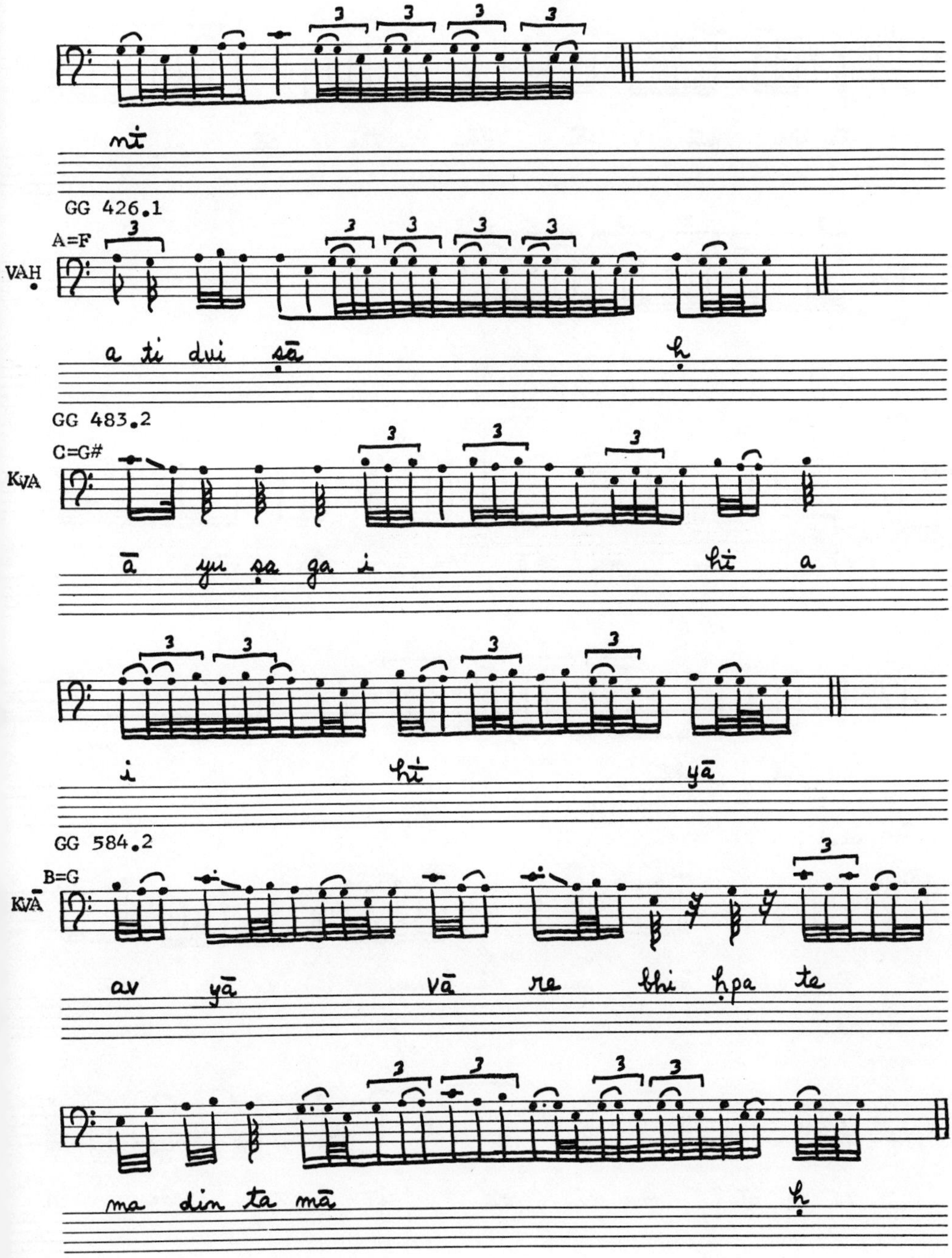

ka-varga (cont.) Subbaraya Ramacandra Bhatta

GG 148.1

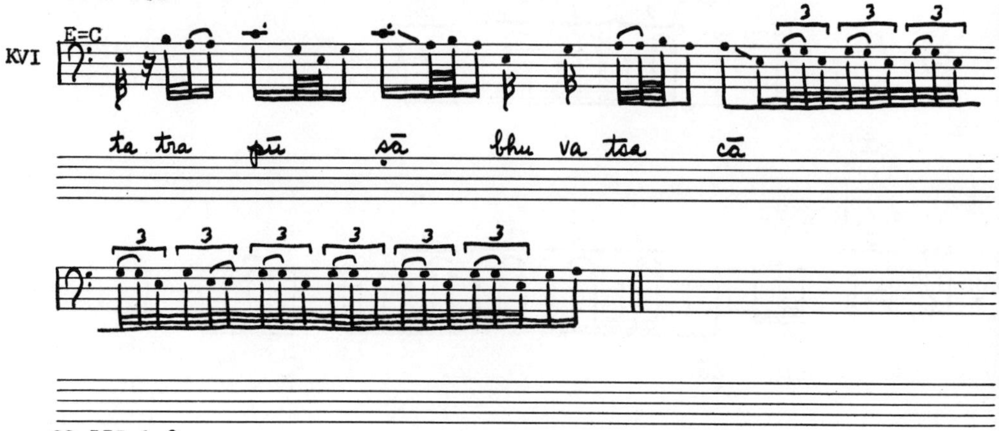

GG 335.1,2

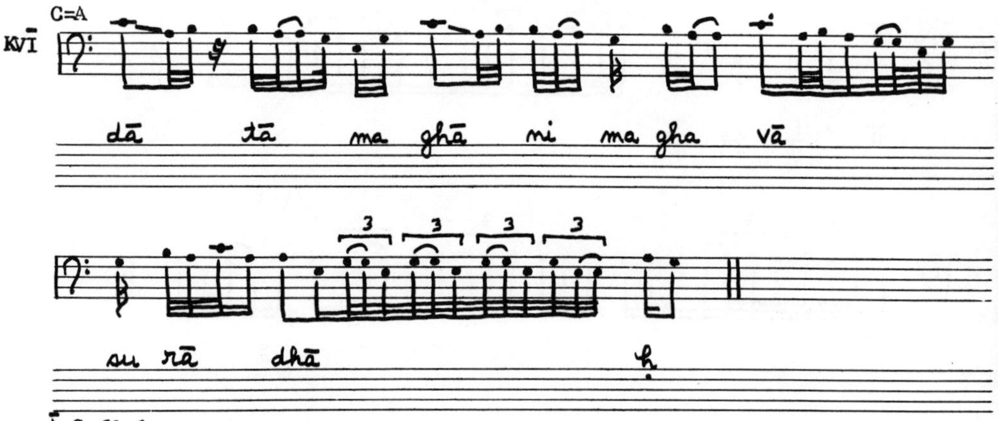

ĀrG 61.1

ka-varga (cont.) Subbaraya Ramacandra Bhatta

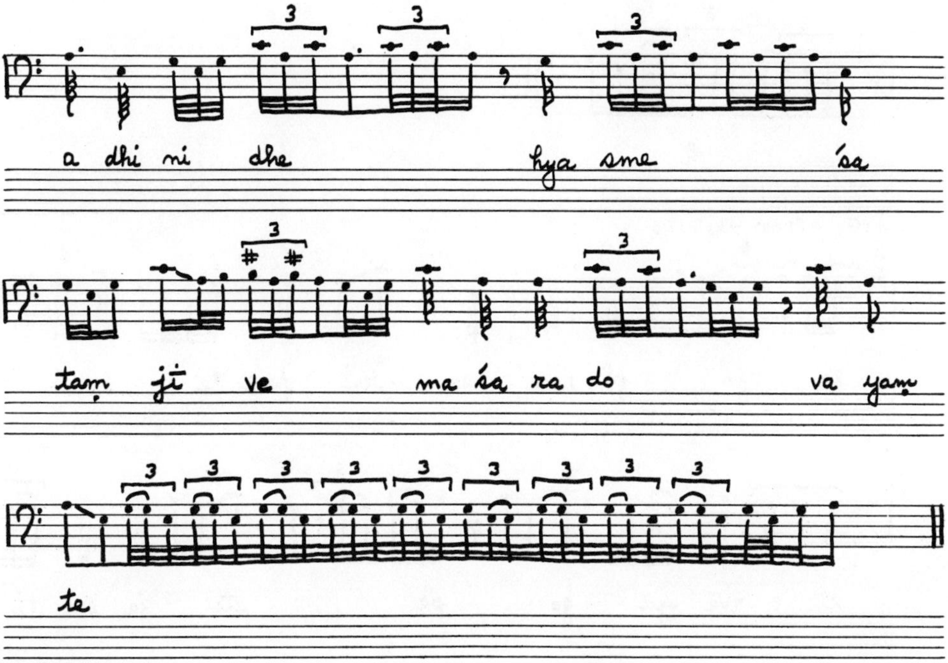
a dhi ni dhe hya sme śa
taṃ jī ve ma śa ra do va yaṃ
te

GG 463.1

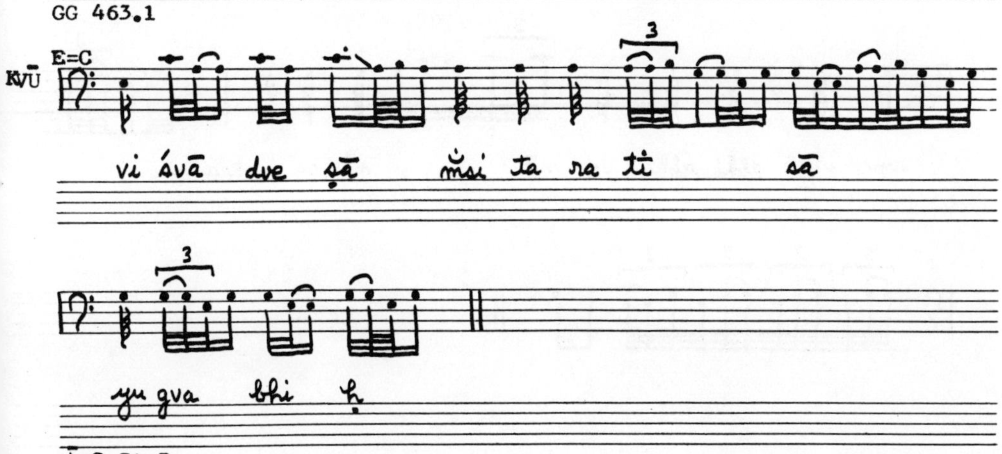
E=C
KVŪ
vi śvā dve ṣā ṃsi ta ra ti sā
yu gva bhi ḥ

ĀrG 51.5

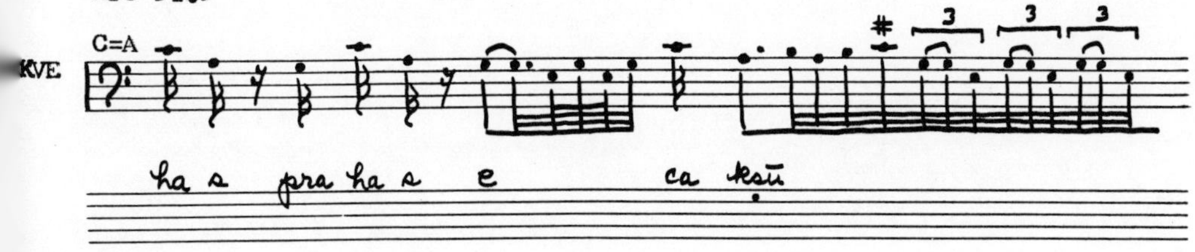
C=A
KVE
ha s pra ha s e ca kṣū

ka-varga (cont.) Subbaraya Ramacandra Bhatta

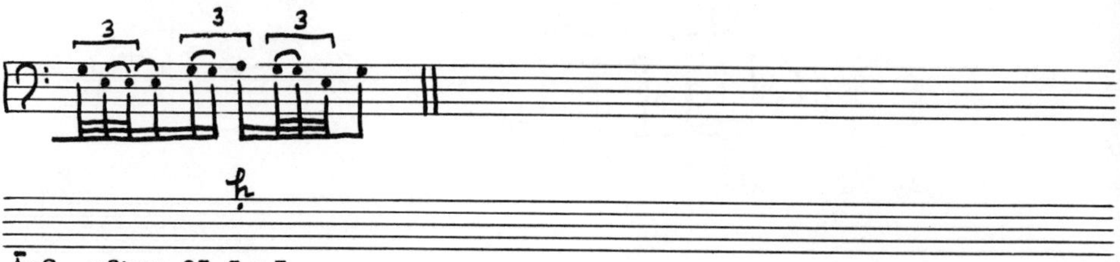

ĀrG, after 93.5: 3

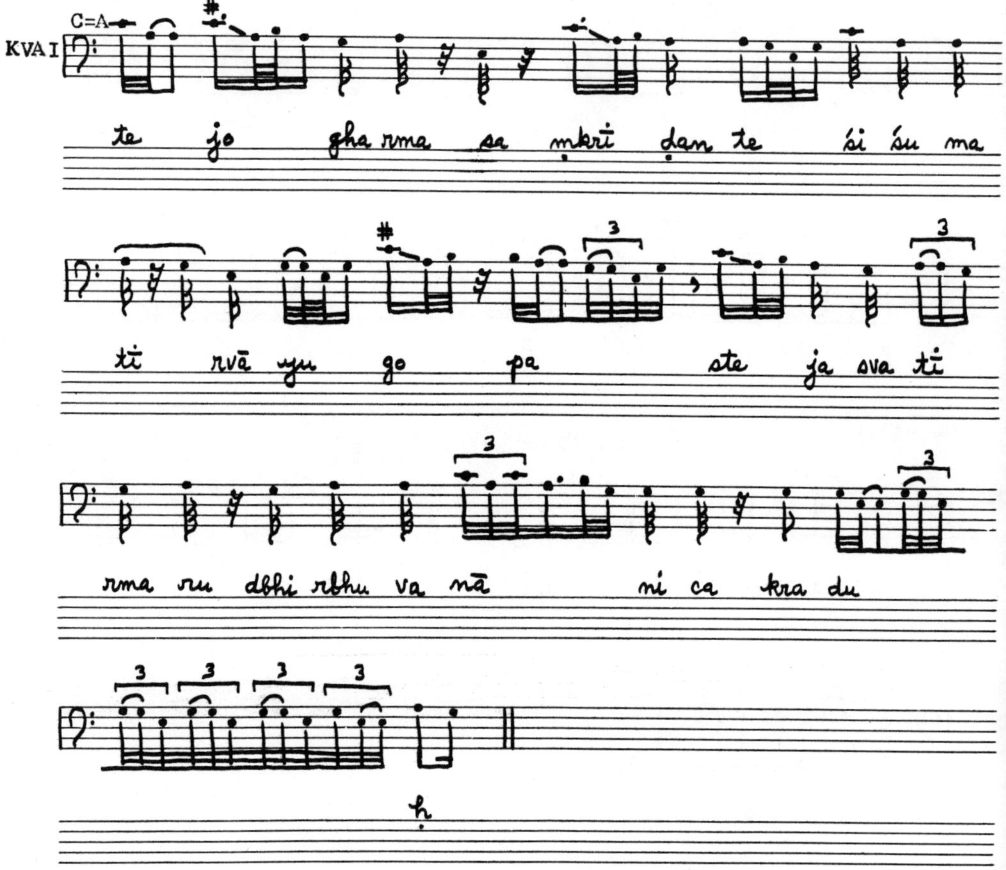
C=A
KVAI
te jo gha rma sa ṃkṛī ḍan te śi śu ma
tī rvā yu go pa ste ja sva tī
rma ru dbhi rbhu va nā ni ca kra du

ca-varga: Subbaraya Paramesvaran Bhatta

GG 8.2

♪ = 100 for ca, ṭa, ta, & pa vargas

G=E♭

CA

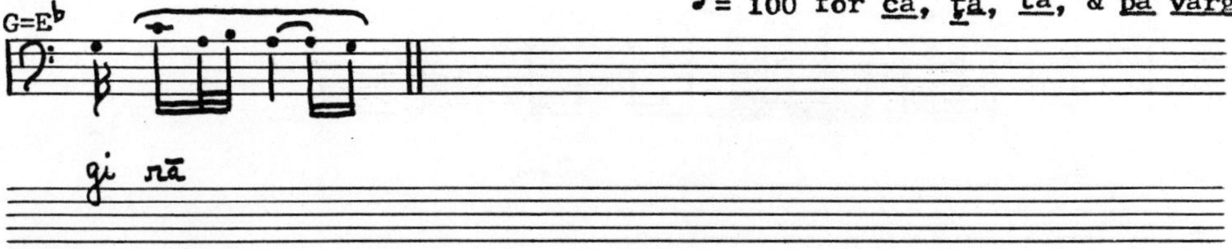

GG 5.2

E=C

CĀ

GG 170.2

G=E♭

CI

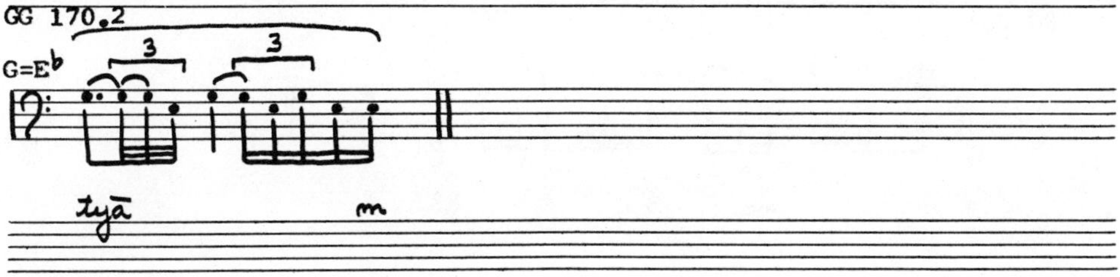

GG 2.1

G=E♭

CĪ

GG 5.2

E=C

CU

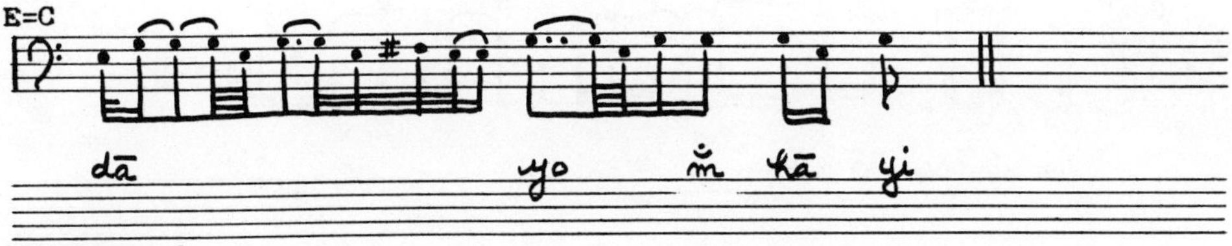

GG 335.1, 2

G=E♭

CŪ

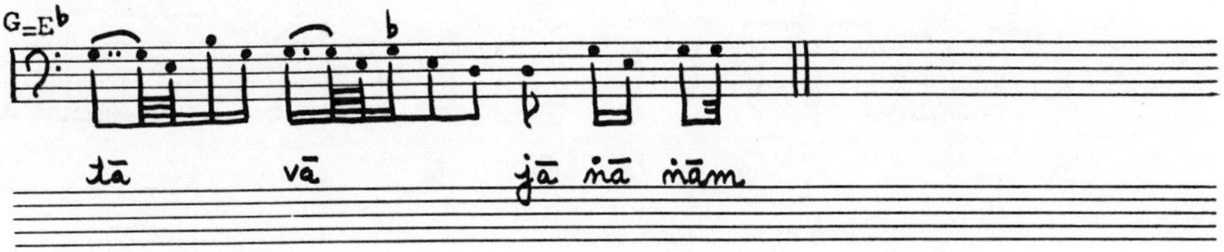

ca-varga (cont.) Subbaraya Paramesvaran Bhatta

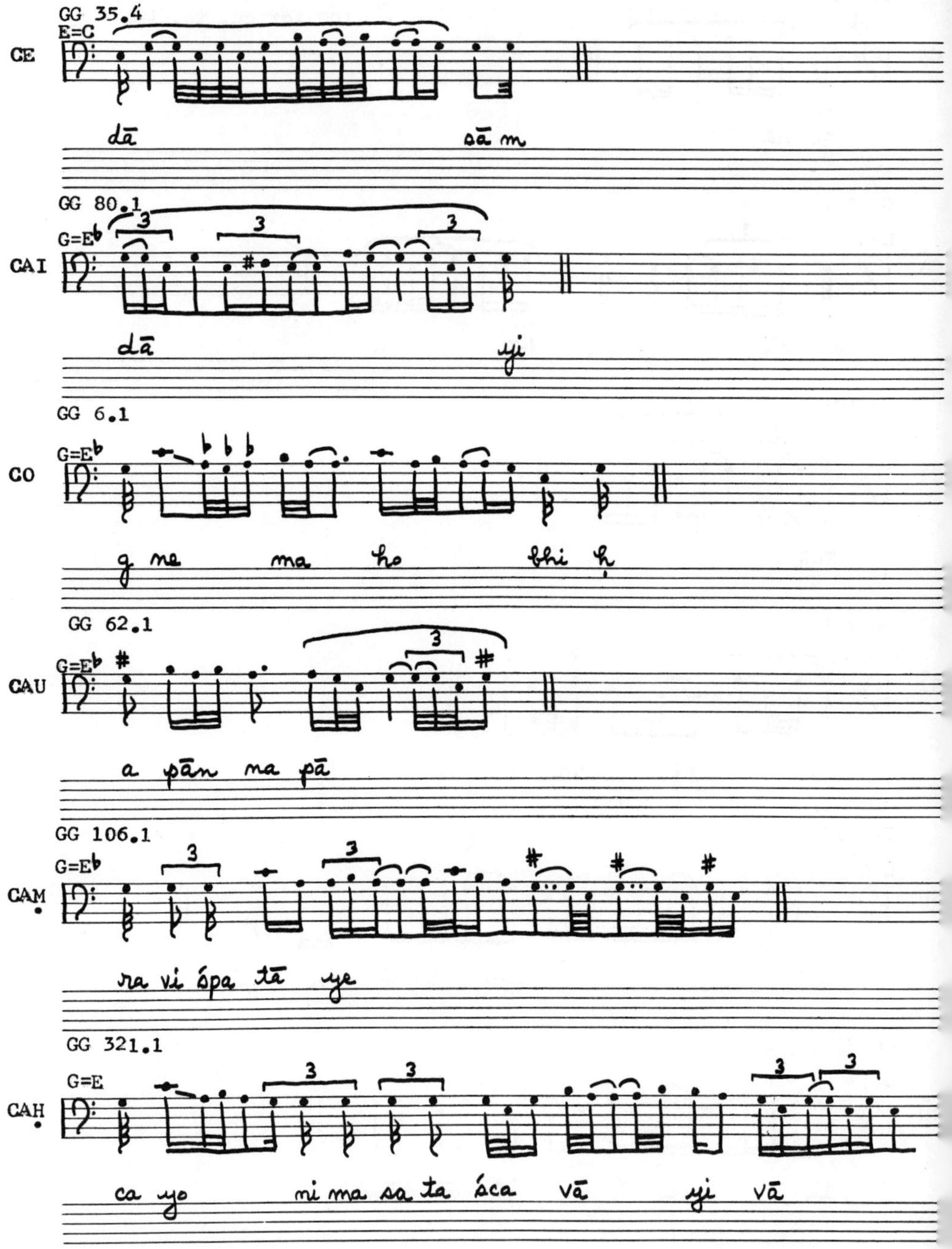

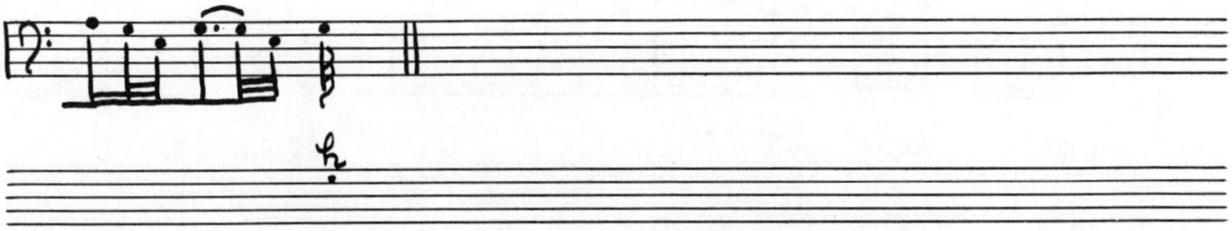

GG 16.1

GG 37.1

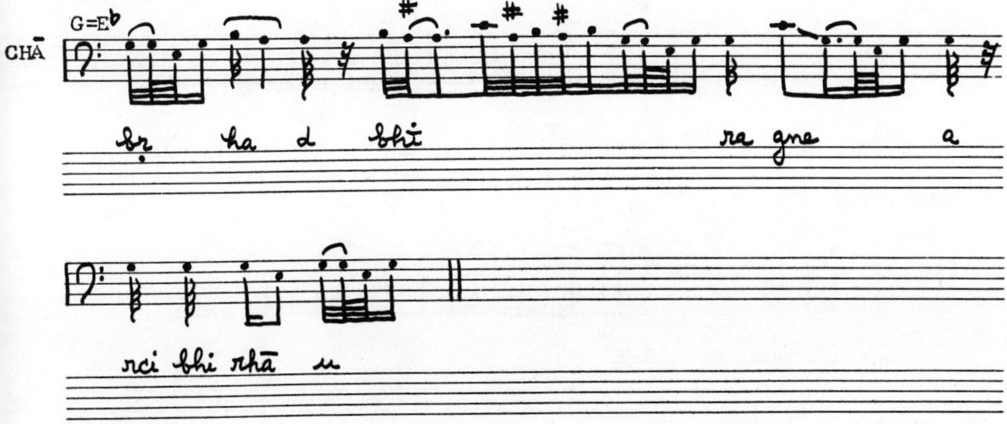

GG 248.3

<u>ca-varga</u> (cont.) Subbaraya Paramesvaran Bhatta

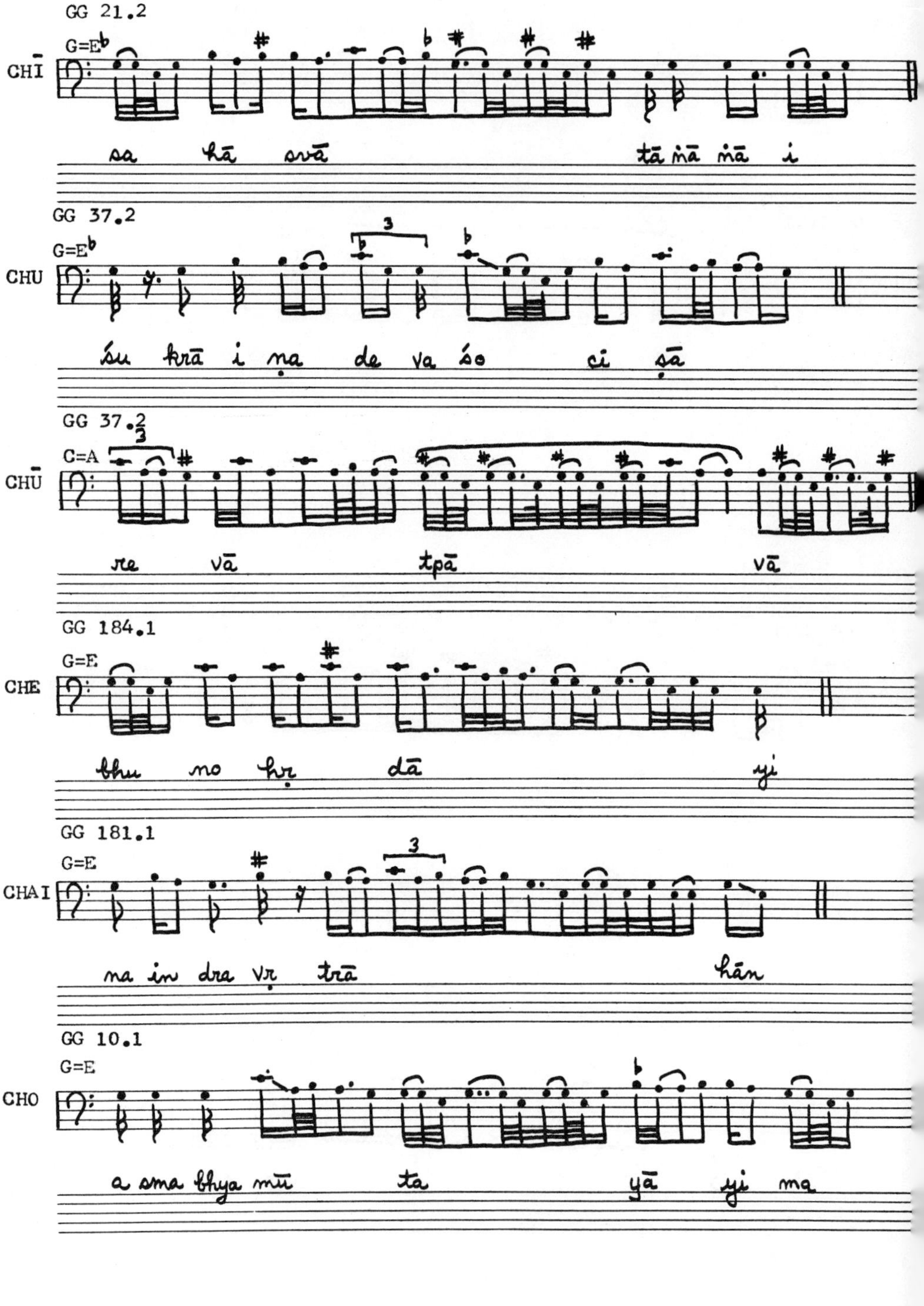

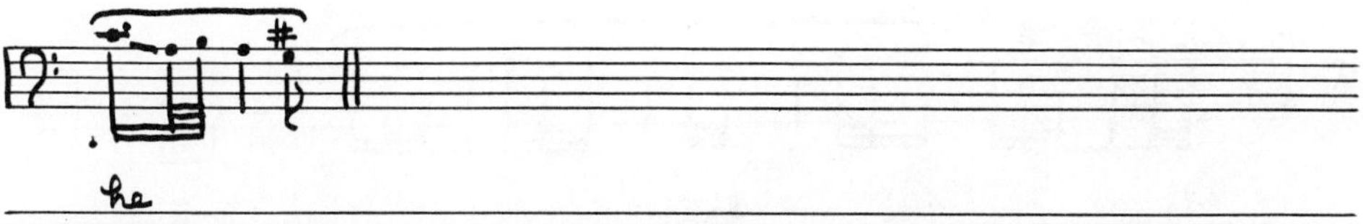

GG 34.2

GG 35.4

GG 64.2

GG 57.1

ca-varga (cont.) Subbaraya Paramesvaran Bhatta

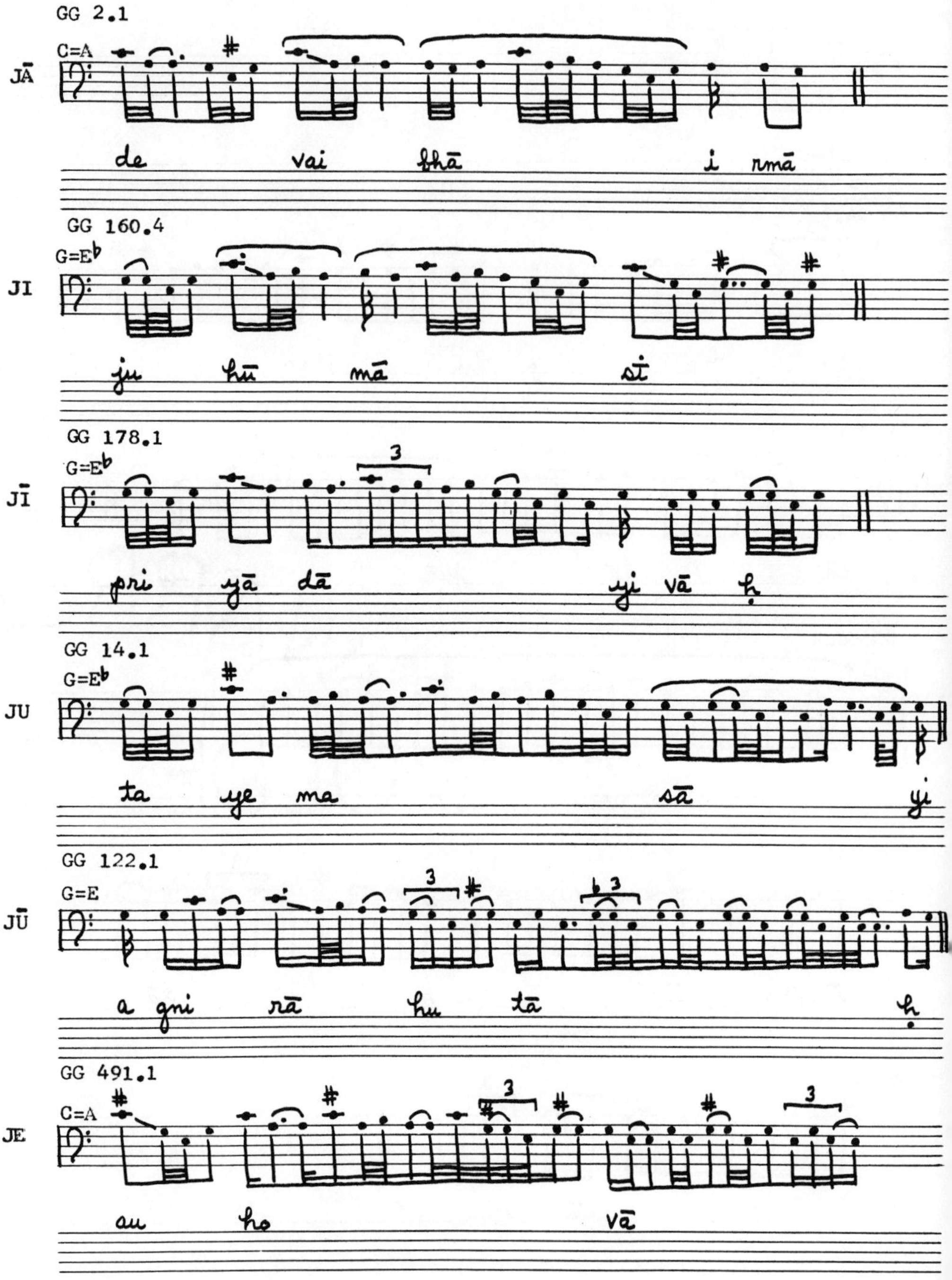

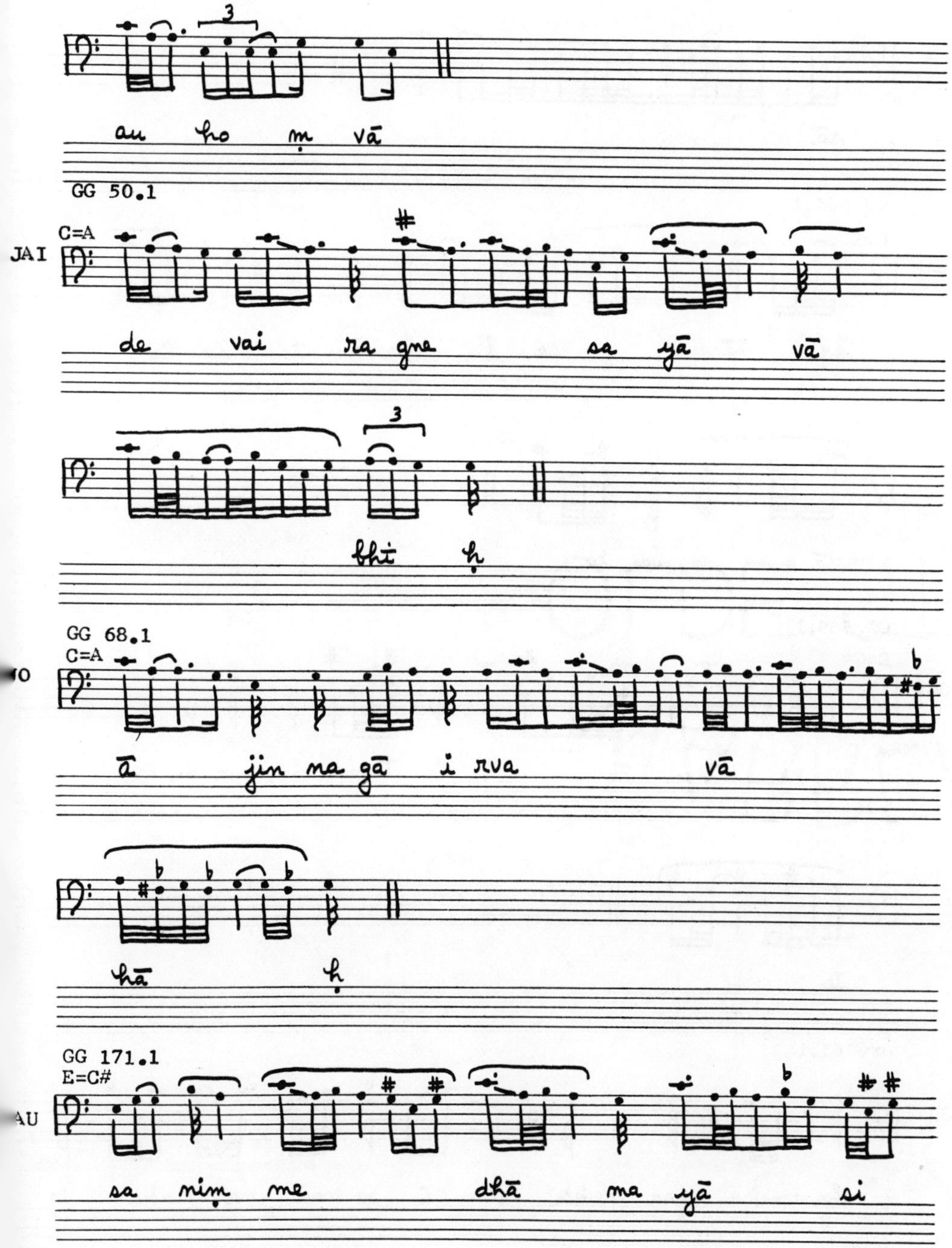
au ho ṃ vā
GG 50.1
C=A
JAI
de vai ra gne sa yā vā
bhi ḥ
GG 68.1
C=A
ā jin ma gā i rva vā
hā ḥ
GG 171.1
E=C#
AU
sa niṃ me dhā ma yā si

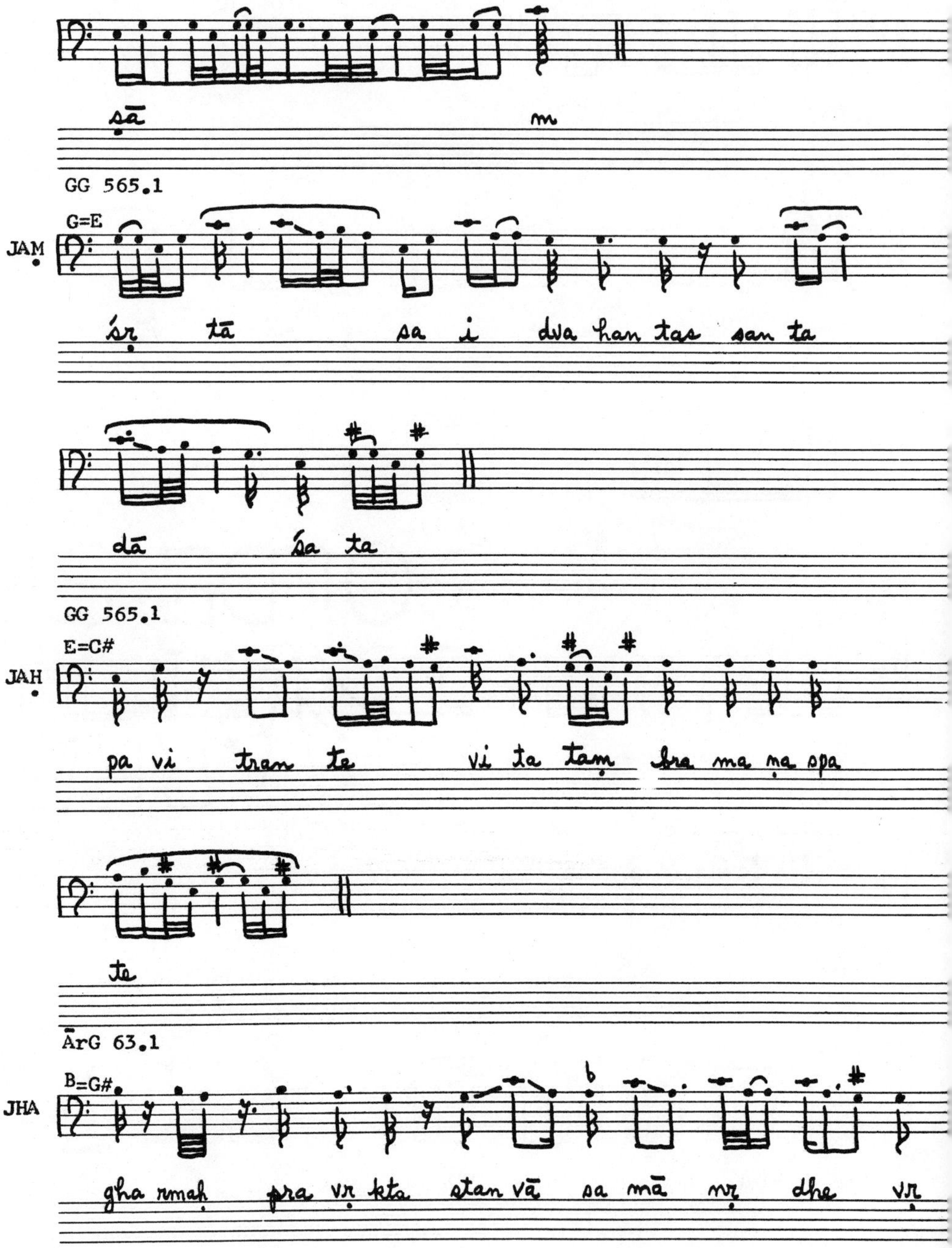

sā m
GG 565.1
G=E
JAṂ
śṛ tā sa i dva han tas san ta
dā śa ta
GG 565.1
E=C#
JAḤ
pa vi tran te vi ta taṃ bra ma ṇa spa
te
ĀrG 63.1
B=G#
JHA
gha rmaḥ pra vṛ kta stan vā sa mā nṛ dhe vṛ

GG 565.2

G=E

JHĀ
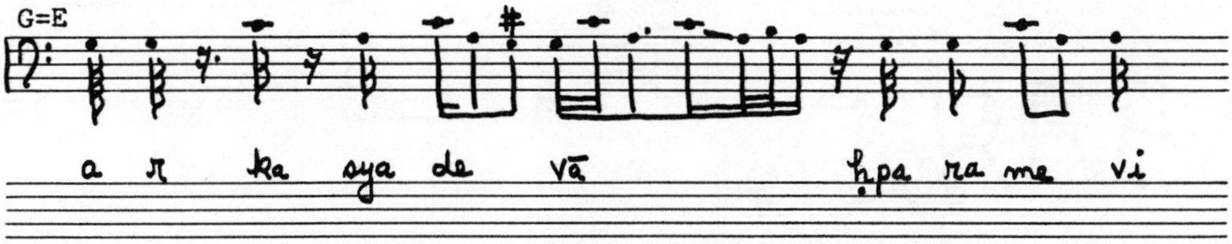

GG 247.1

D=B

HI

GG 104.1

G=E

HĪ

ca-varga (cont.) Subbaraya Paramesvaran Bhatta

GG 537.2

GG 18.1

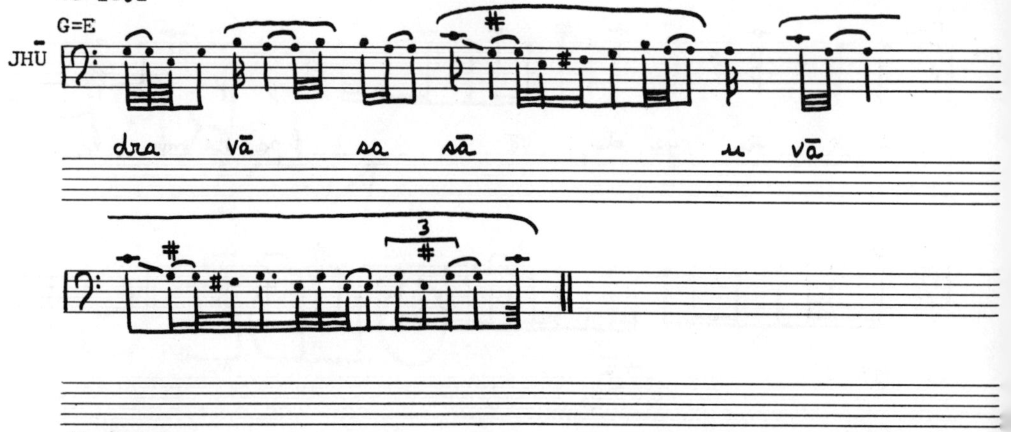

GG 422.1

GG 103.1

GG 346.2

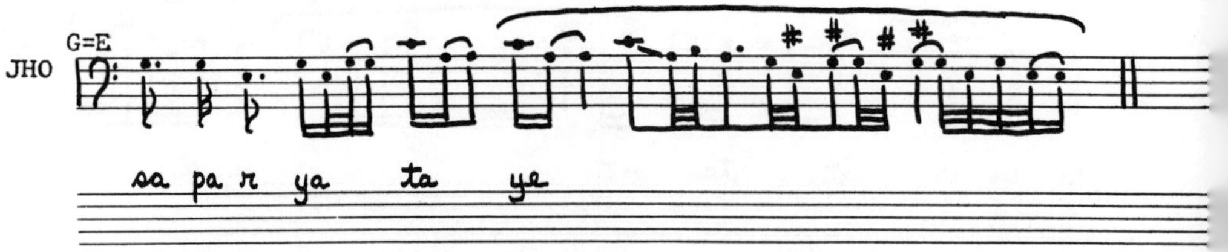

ca-varga (cont.) Subbaraya Paramesvaran Bhatta

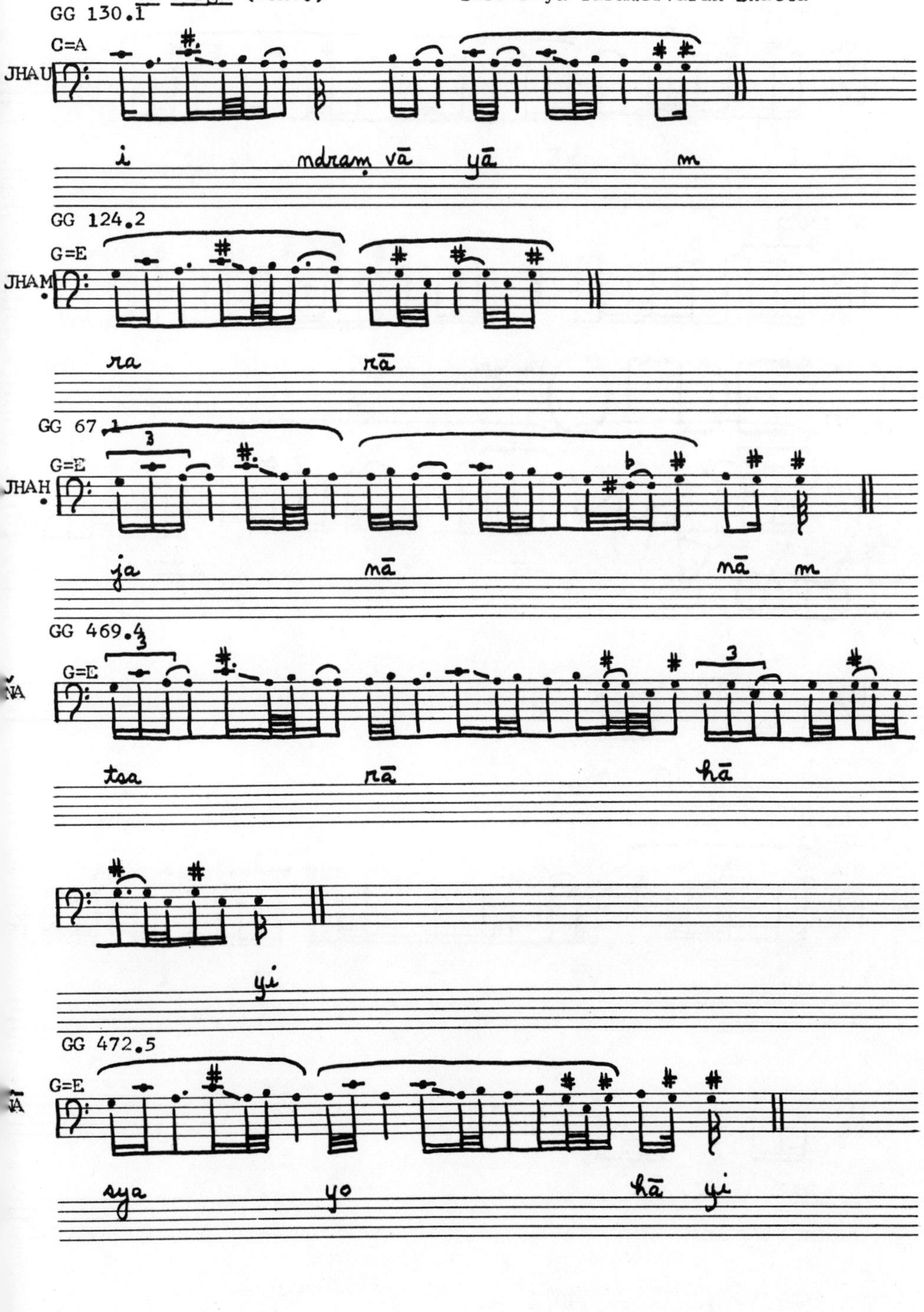

ca-varga (cont.) Subbaraya Paramesvaran Bhatta

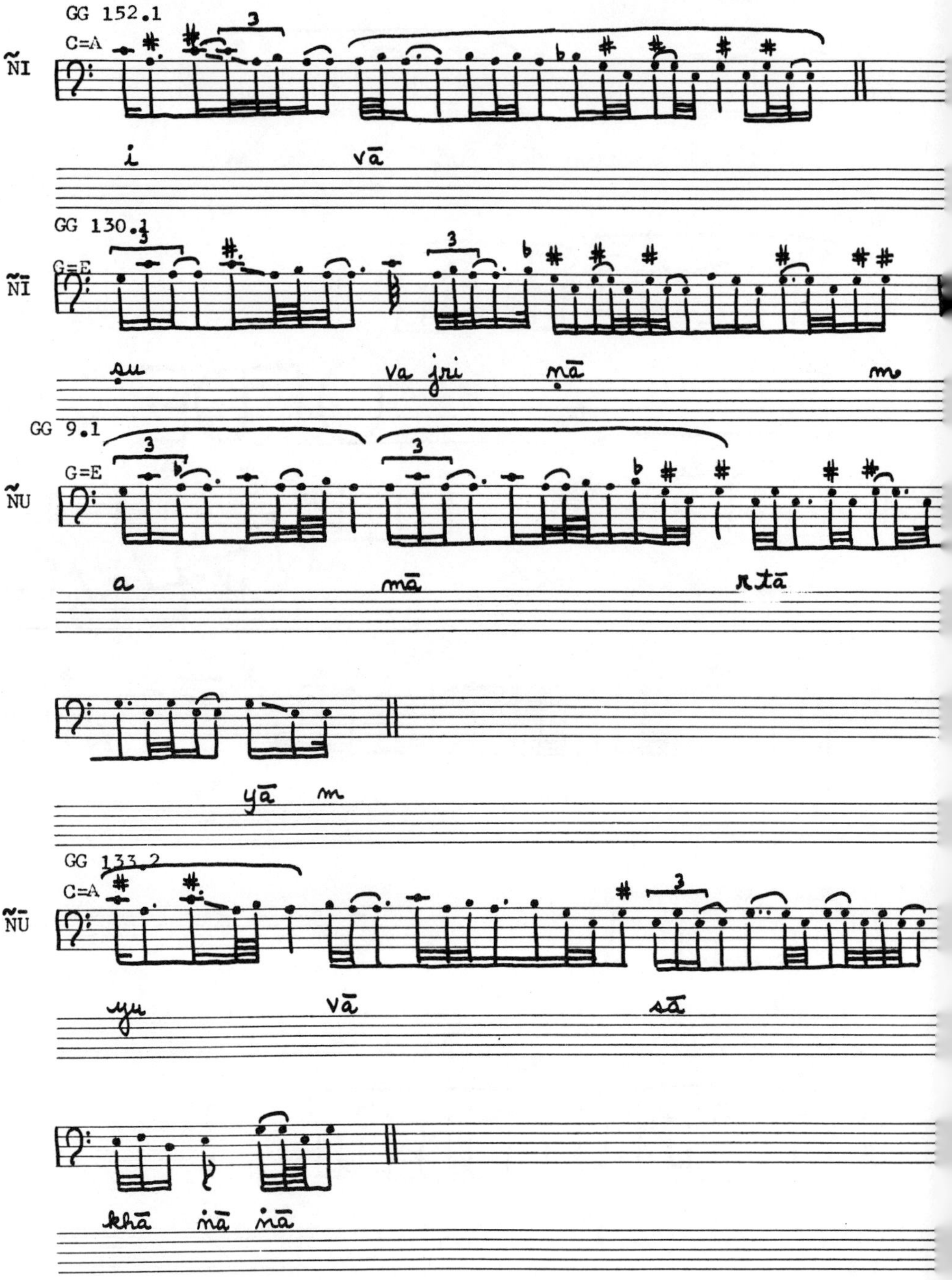

ca-varga (cont.) Subbaraya Paramesvaran Bhatta

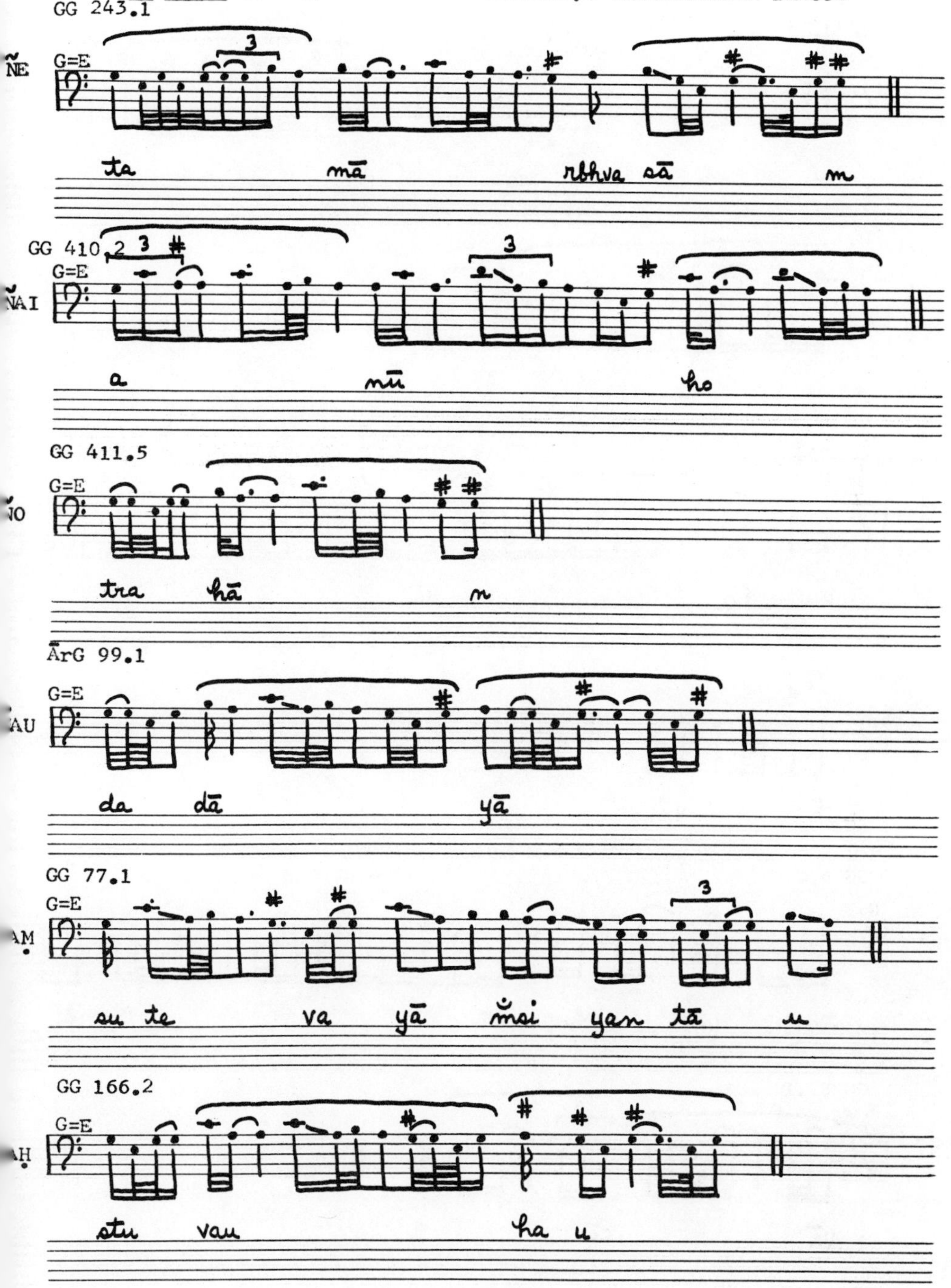

ca-varga (cont.) Subbaraya Paramesvaran Bhatta

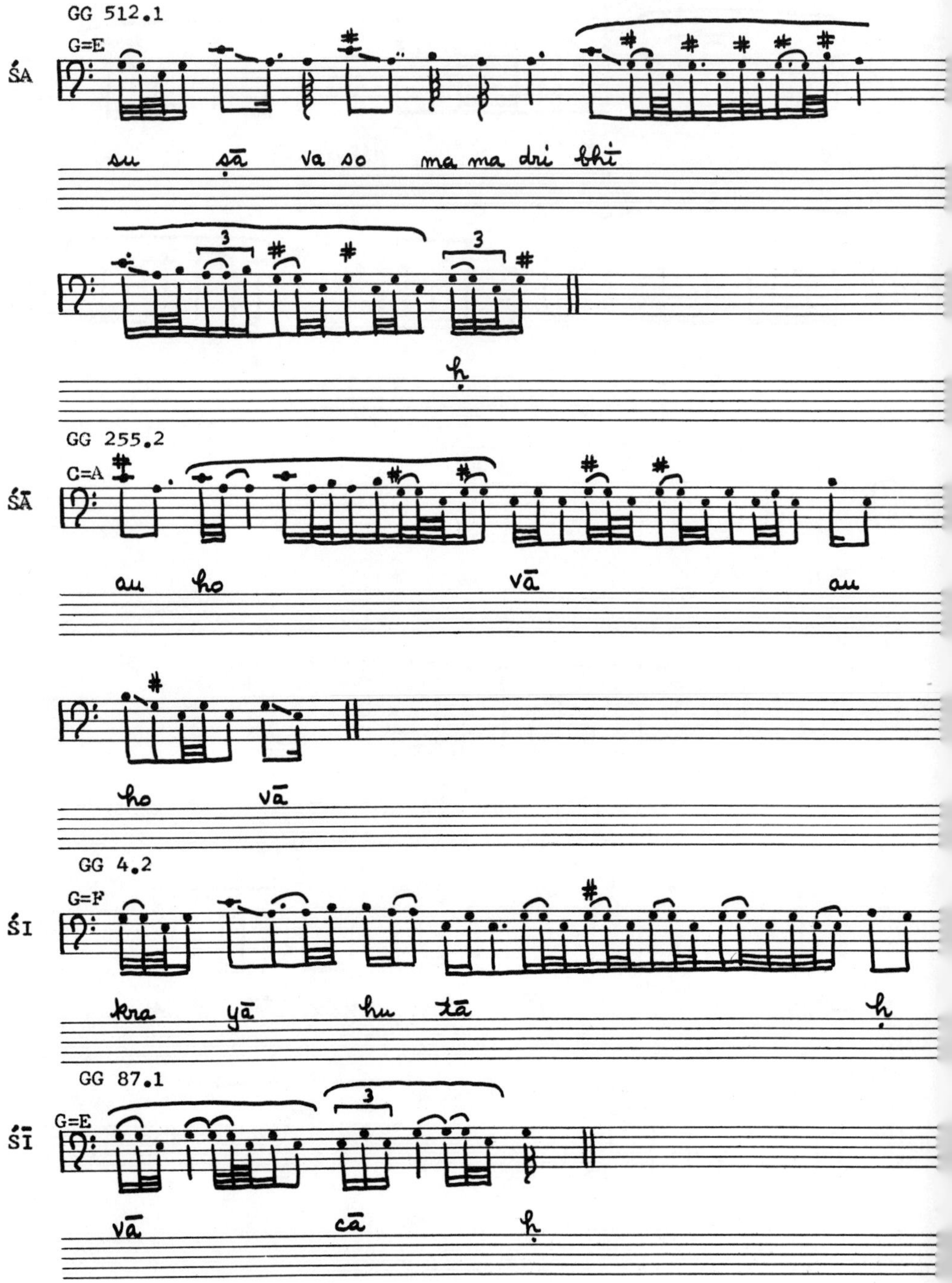

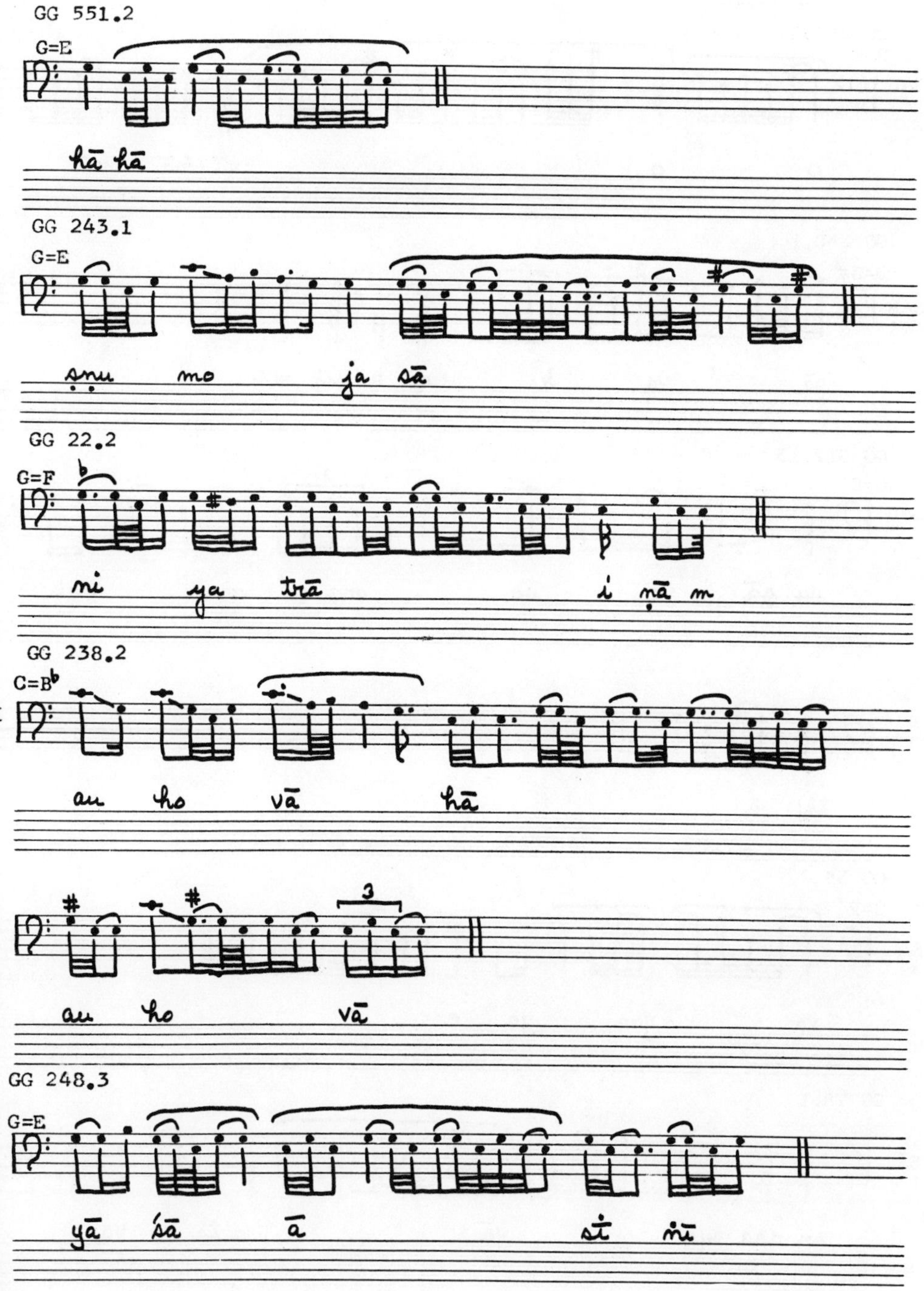
GG 551.2
G=E
hā hā
GG 243.1
G=E
ṣṇu mo ja sā
GG 22.2
G=F
ni ya trā i ṇā m
GG 238.2
C=B♭
au ho vā hā
3
au ho vā
GG 248.3
G=E
yā śā ā sī nī

ca-varga (cont.) Subbaraya Paramesvaran Bhatta

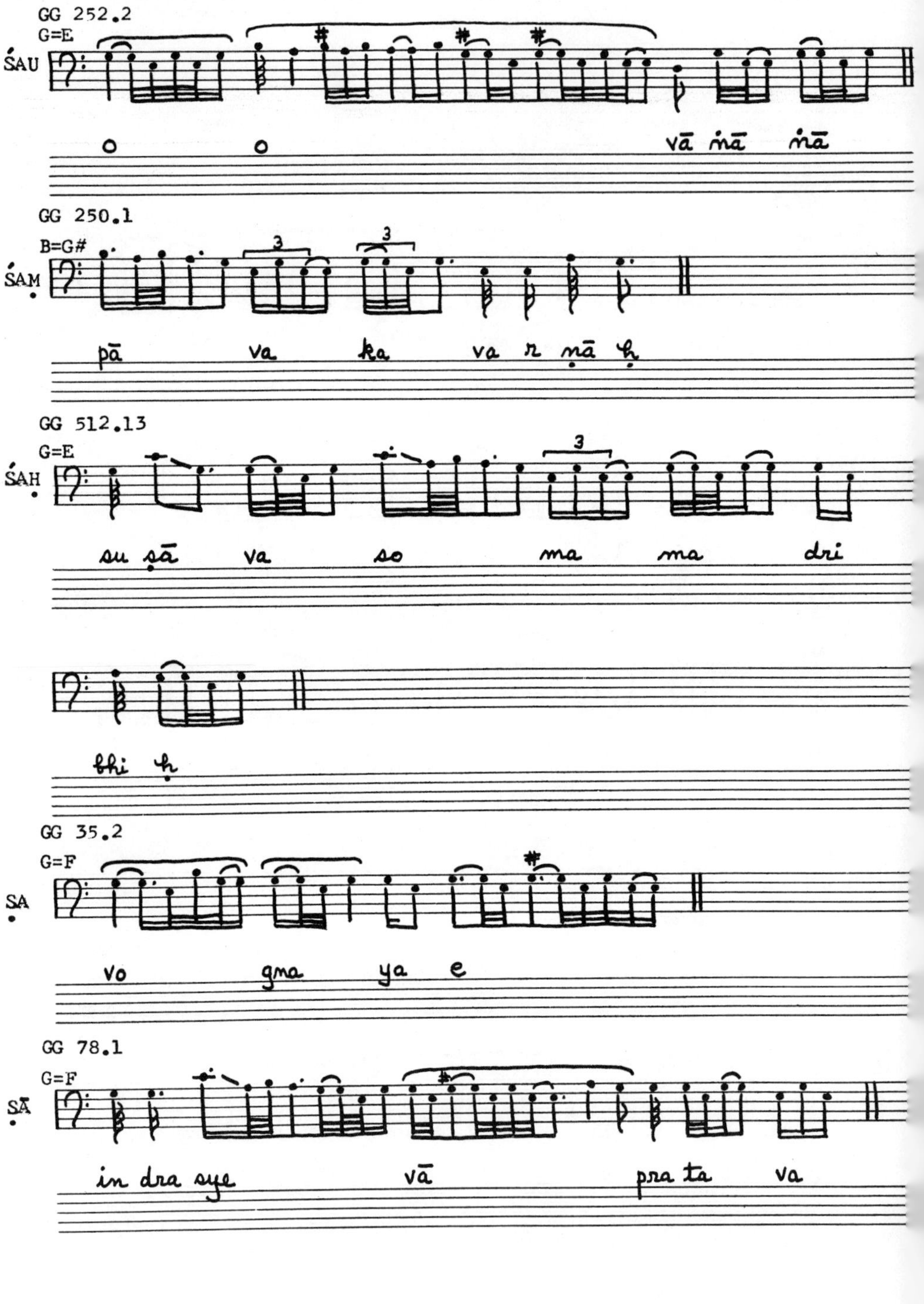

ca-varga (cont.) Subbaraya Paramesvaran Bhatta

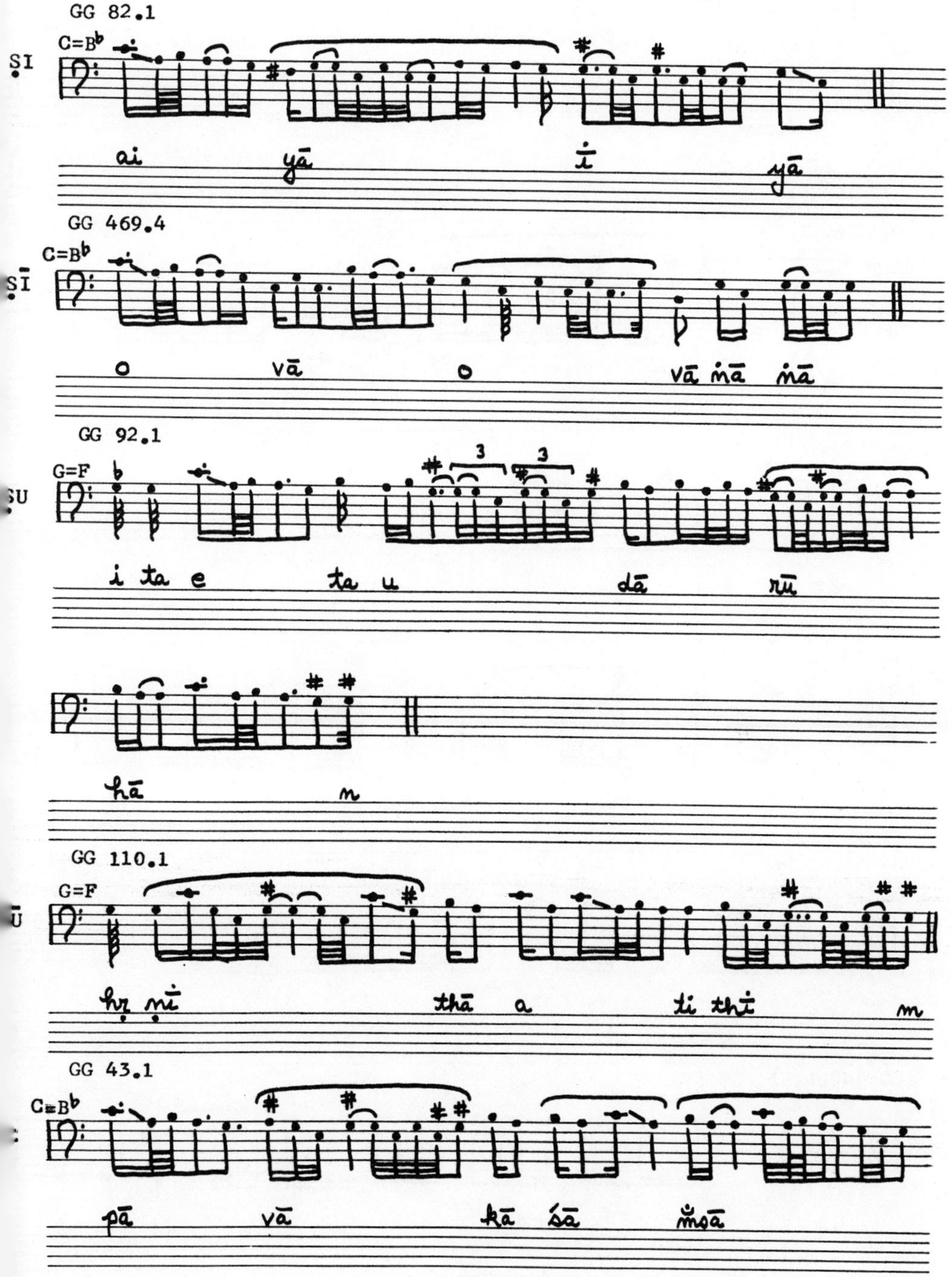

ca-varga (cont.) Subbaraya Paramesvaran Bhatta

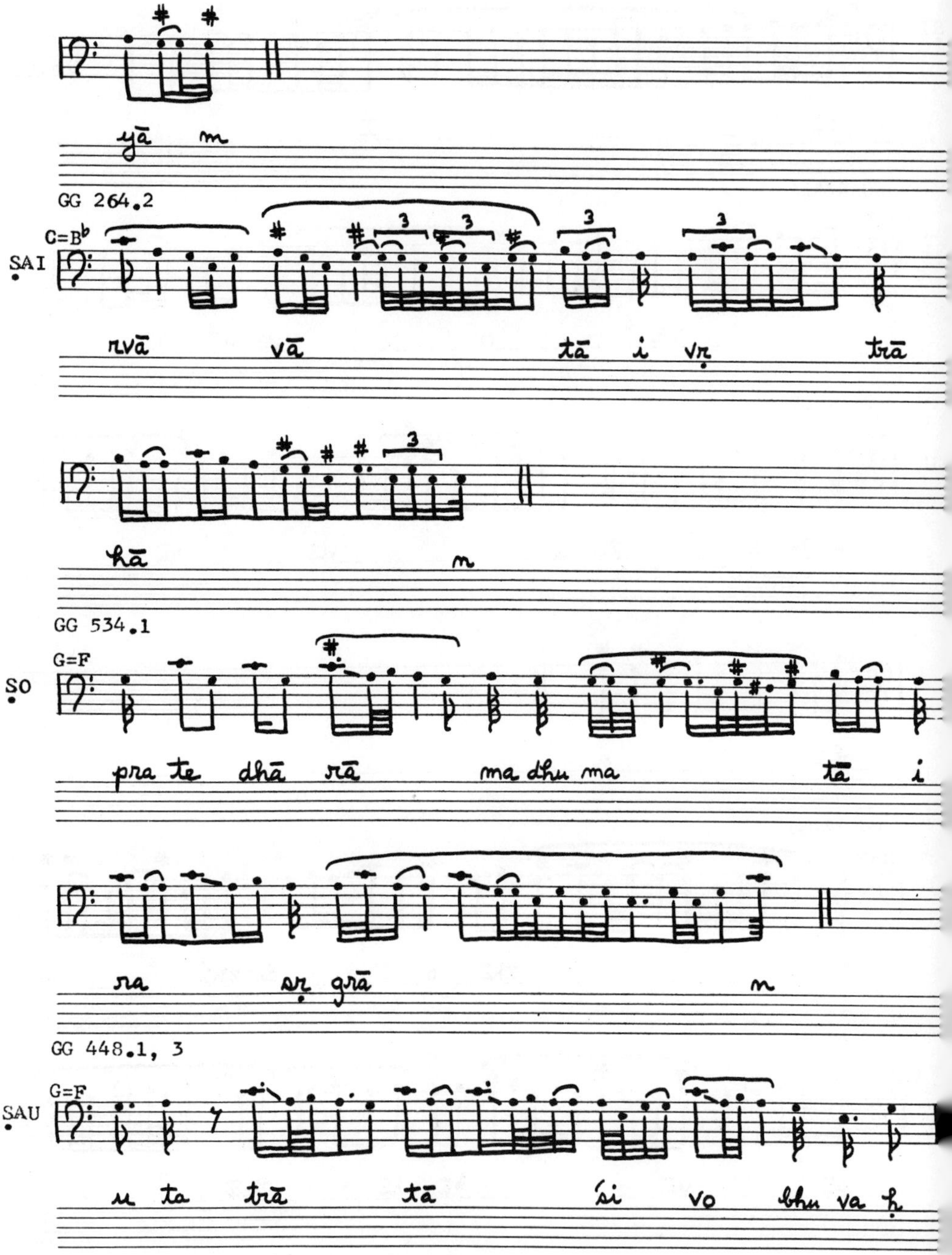
yā m
GG 264.2
C=B♭
SAI
rvā vā tā i vṛ trā
hā m
GG 534.1
G=F
SO
pra te dhā rā ma dhu ma tā i
ra sṛ grā m
GG 448.1, 3
G=F
SAU
u ta trā tā śi vo bhu va ḥ

GG 565.1, 2

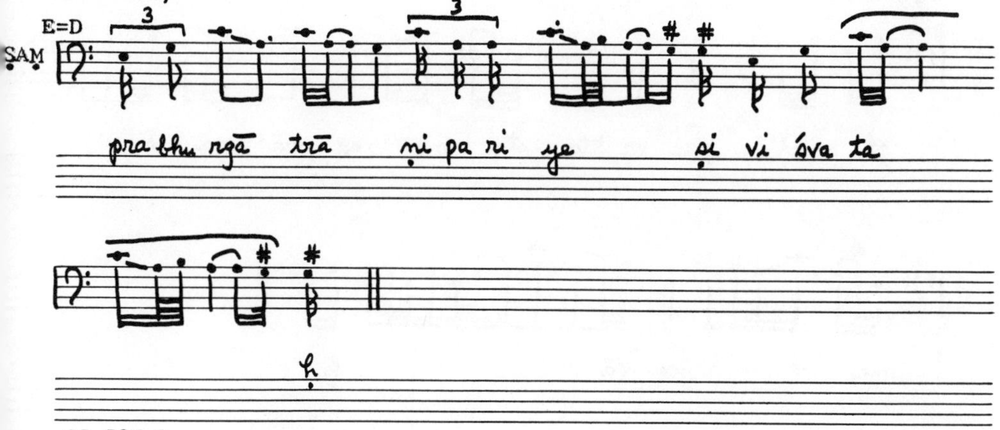

GG 326.1

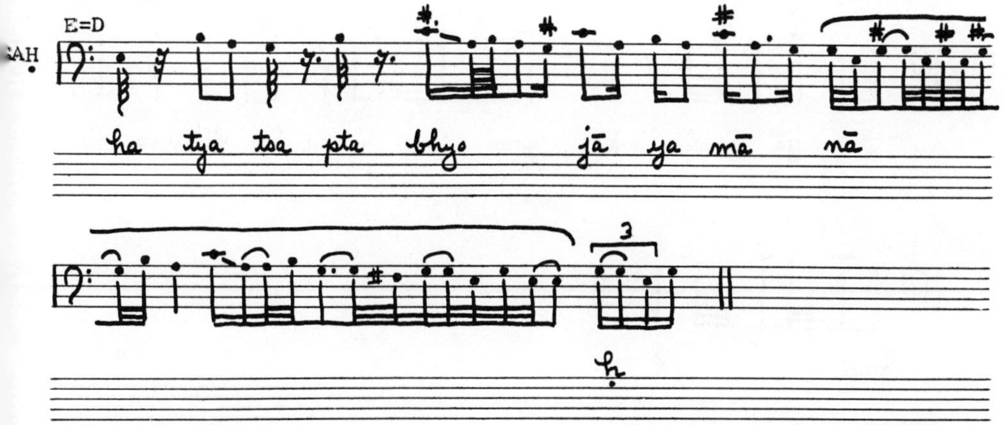

GG 554.5

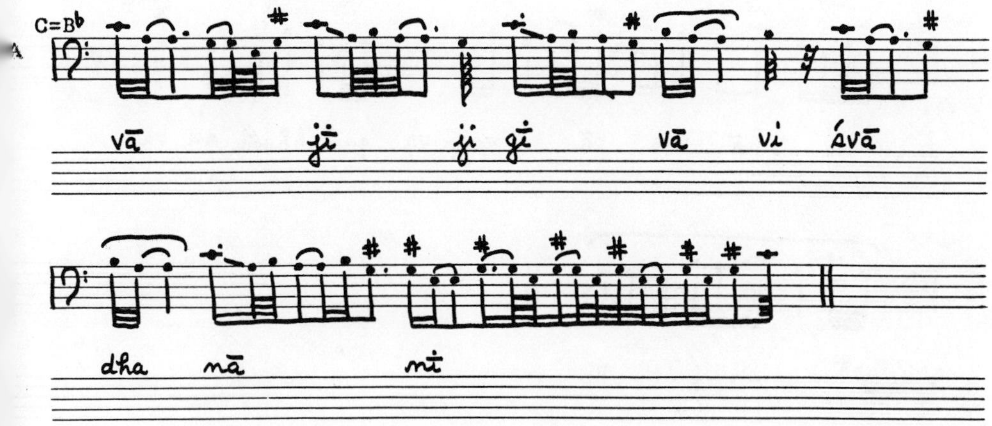

<u>ca</u>-<u>varga</u> (cont.) Subbaraya Paramesvaran Bhatta

ĀrG 63.2

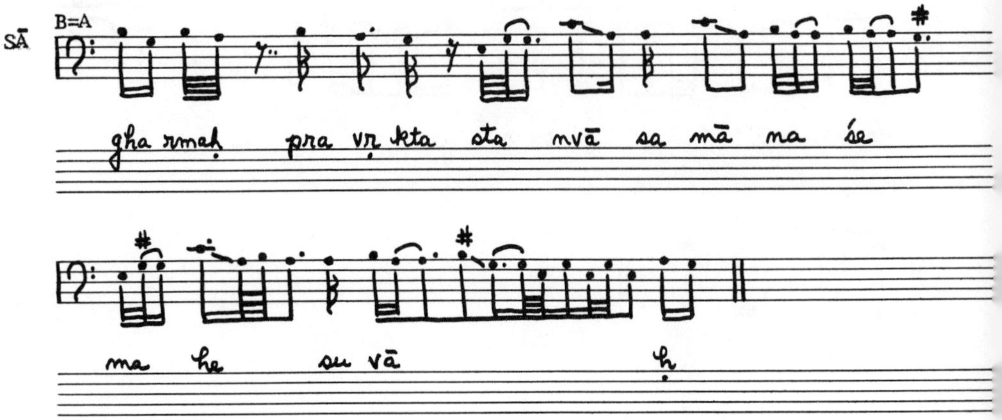

GG 323.4

GG 335.1, 2

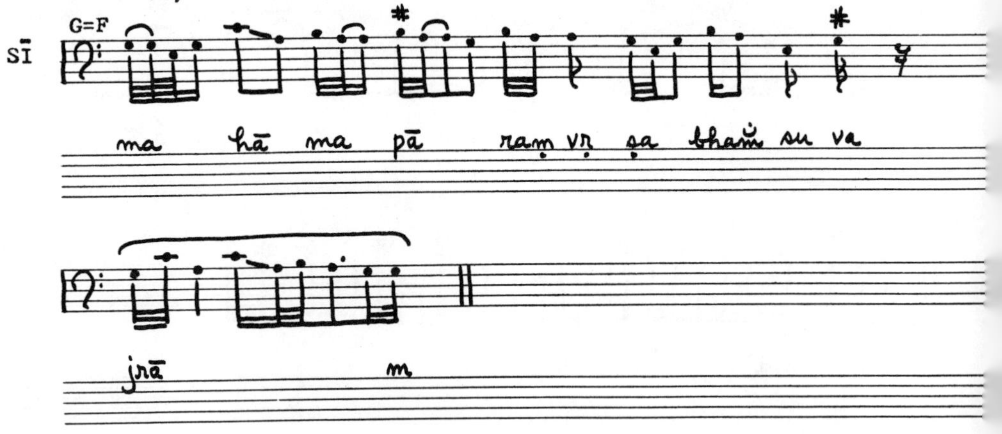

ca-varga (cont.) Subbaraya Paramesvaran Bhatta

ĀrG 115.1

SU
G=F
vṛ trañ ja gha nvā m̐ma pa ta dva vā ra
ya tta mā ḥ

ĀrG, after 127.1: 2

SŪ
E=D
3
ti da dhā ne bhya śca na maḥ pra vi dhya dbhya
śca pra vyā dhi bhya śca na maḥ tsa ra dbhya śca
tsā ri bhya śca na maḥ śrī

ĀrG, after 127.1: 1

SE
E=D
ma nyu nā vṛ tra hā sū rye ṇa sva rā

ca-varga (cont.) Subbaraya Paramesvaran Bhatta

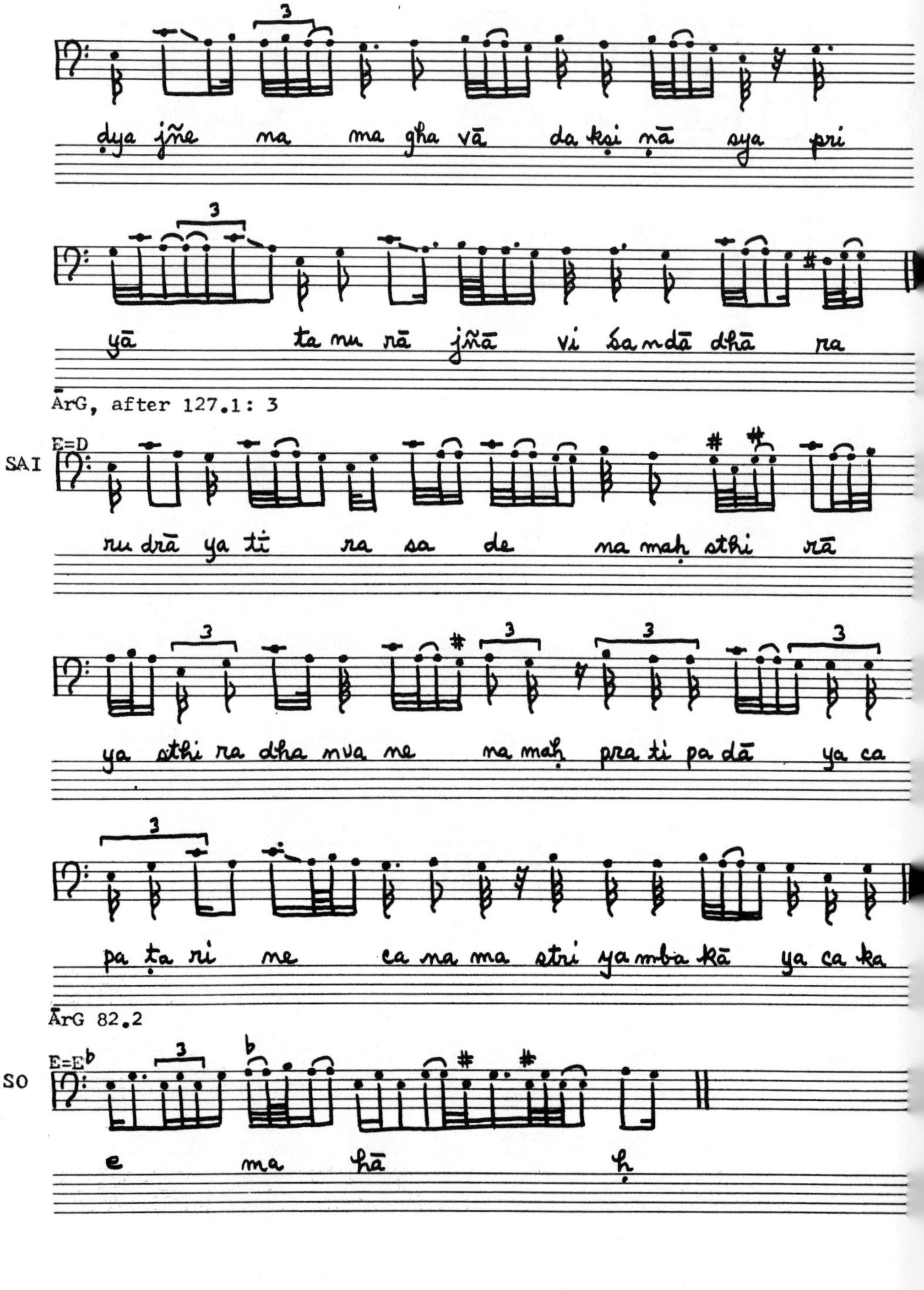
dya jñe ma ma gha vā da kṣi ṇā sya pri
yā ta nu rā jñā vi śa ndā dhā ra
ĀrG, after 127.1: 3
E=D
SAI
ru drā ya tī ra sa de na maḥ sthi rā
ya sthi ra dha nva ne na maḥ pra ti pa dā ya ca
pa ṭa ri me ca na ma stri ya mba kā ya ca ka
ĀrG 82.2
E=E♭
SO
e ma hā ḥ

ca-varga (cont.)   Subbaraya Paramesvaran Bhatta

GG 585.2

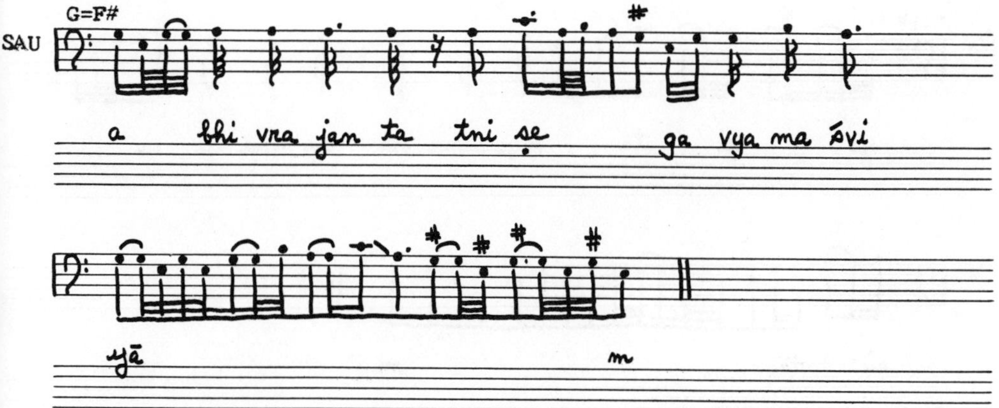
G=F#
SAU
a bhi vra jan ta tni ṣe ga vya ma śvi
yā m

GG 527.3 2

G=F#
SAM
ja ni te ndra sya ja ni to ta vi
ṣṇo ḥ

ĀrG 102.1

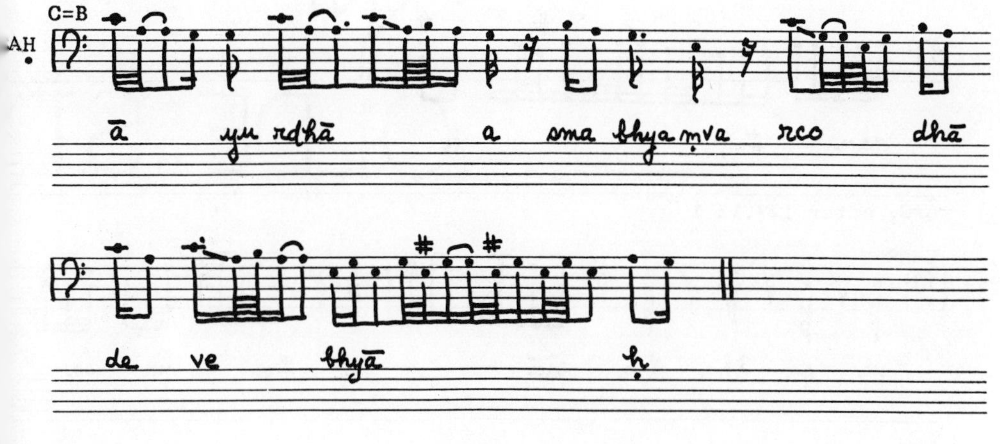
C=B
AH
ā yu rdhā a sma bhya ṃva rco dhā
de ve bhyā ḥ

ĀrG 55.1

ĀrG 93.5

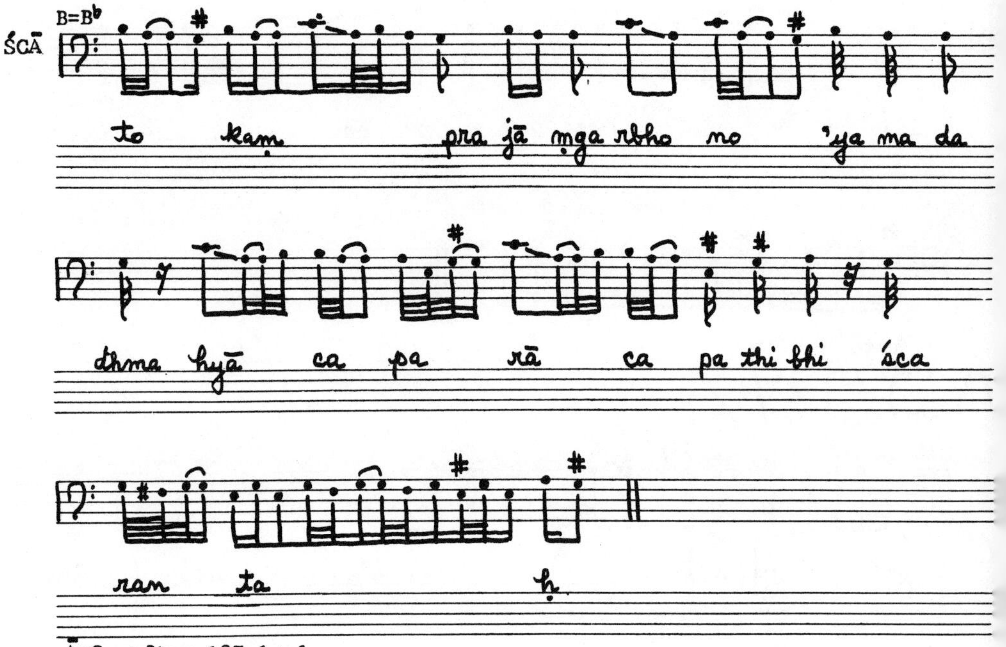

ĀrG, after 127.1: 1

ca-varga (cont.) Subbaraya Paramesvaran Bhatta

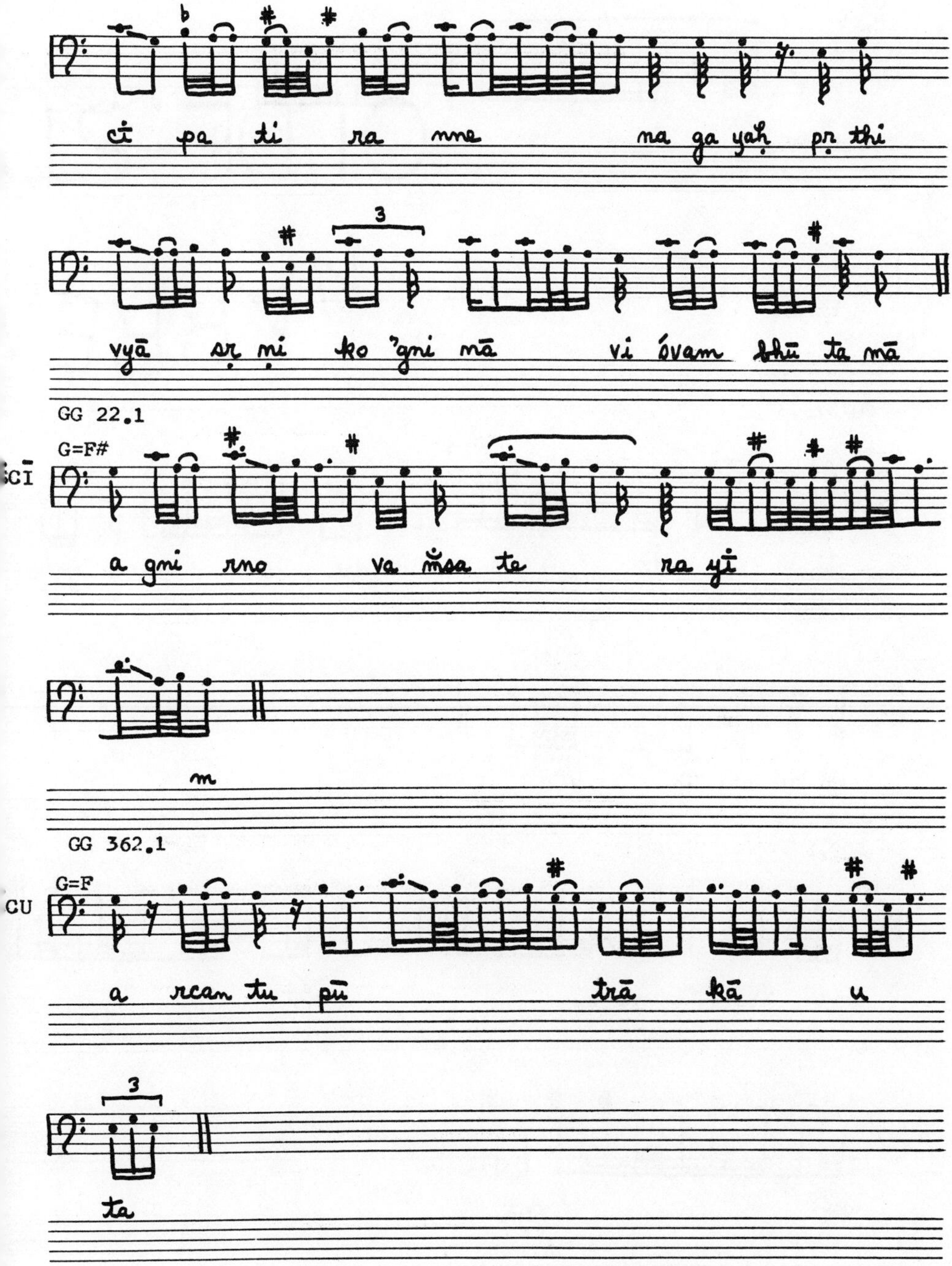

<u>ca</u>-<u>varga</u> (cont.) Subbaraya Paramesvaran Bhatta

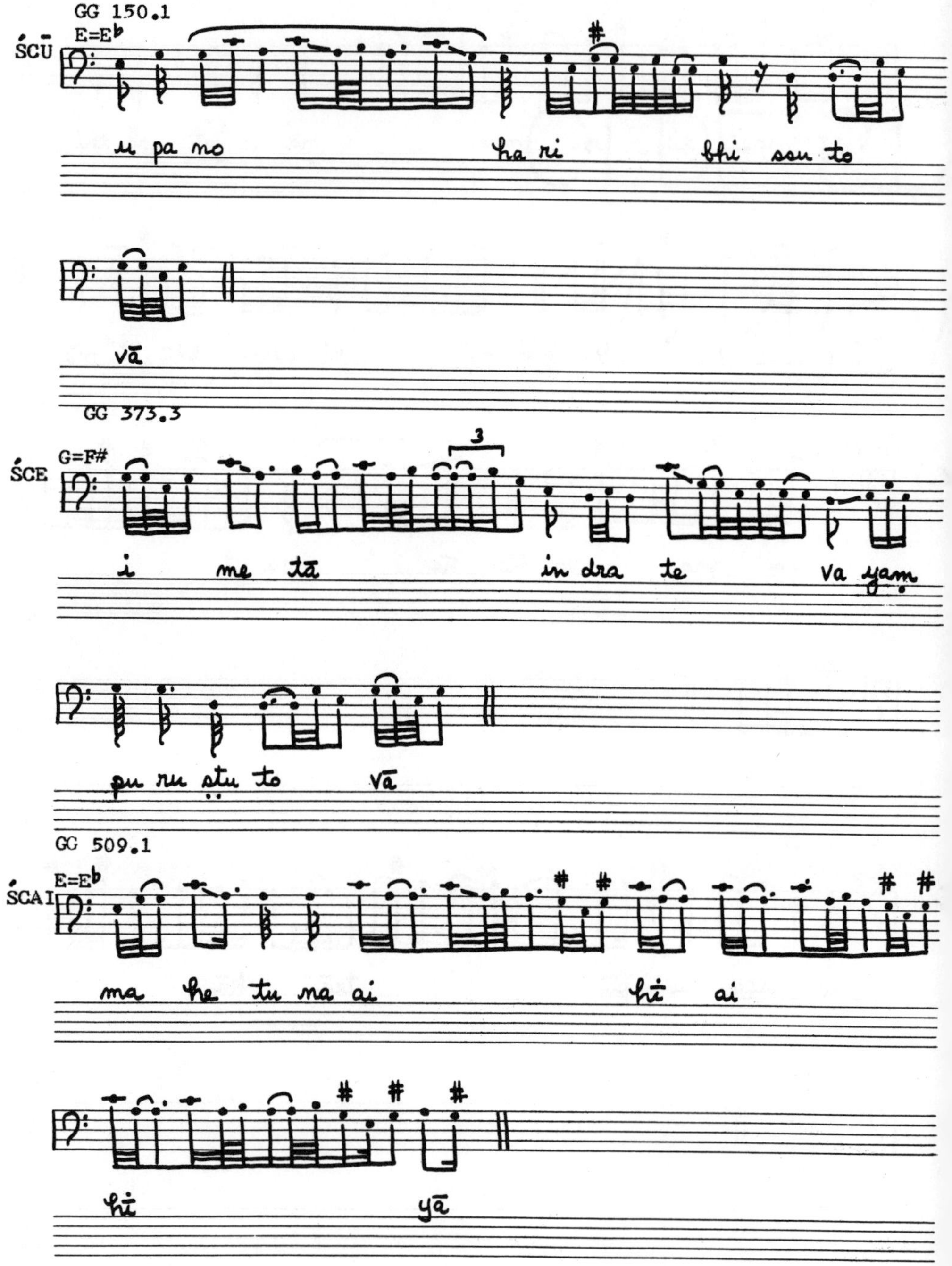
GG 150.1
E=E♭
ŚCŪ
u pa no ha ri bhi ssu to
vā
GG 373.3
G=F#
ŚCE
3
i me tā in dra te va yam
pu ru stu to vā
GG 509.1
E=E♭
ŚCAI
ma he tu na ai hī ai
hī yā

ca-varga (cont.)   Subbaraya Paramesvaran Bhatta

GG 67.2

RA

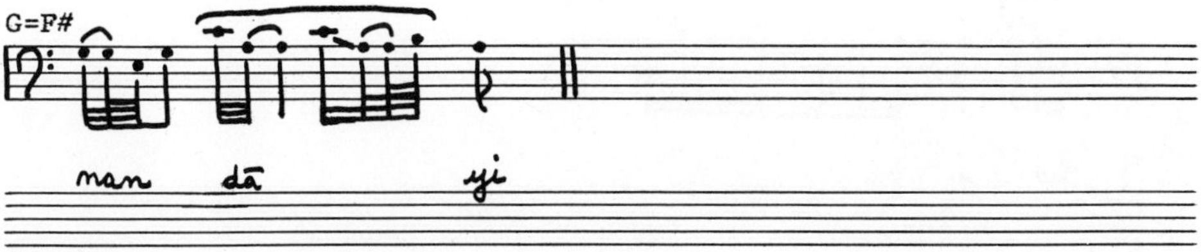

GG 65.1

RĀ

GG 35.2

RI

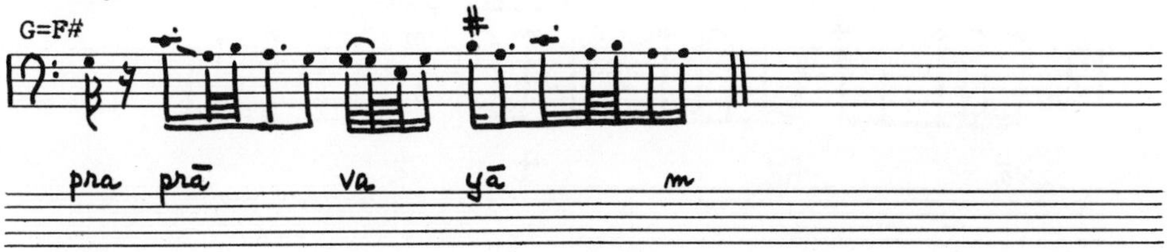

GG 53.2

RĪ

GG 457.1

RU

GG 8.2

RŪ

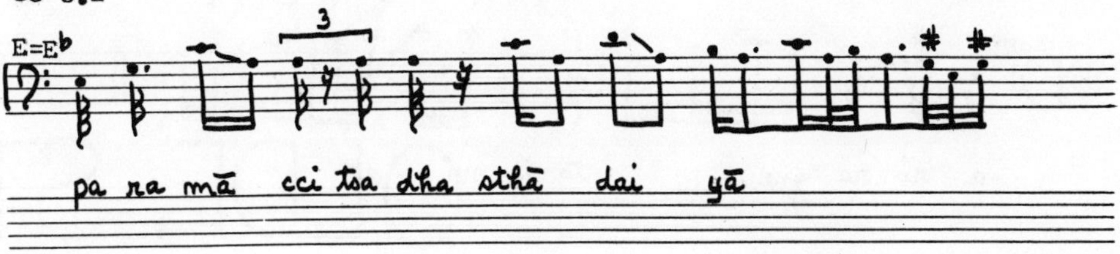

<u>ca</u>-<u>varga</u> (cont.) Subbaraya Paramesvaran Bhatta

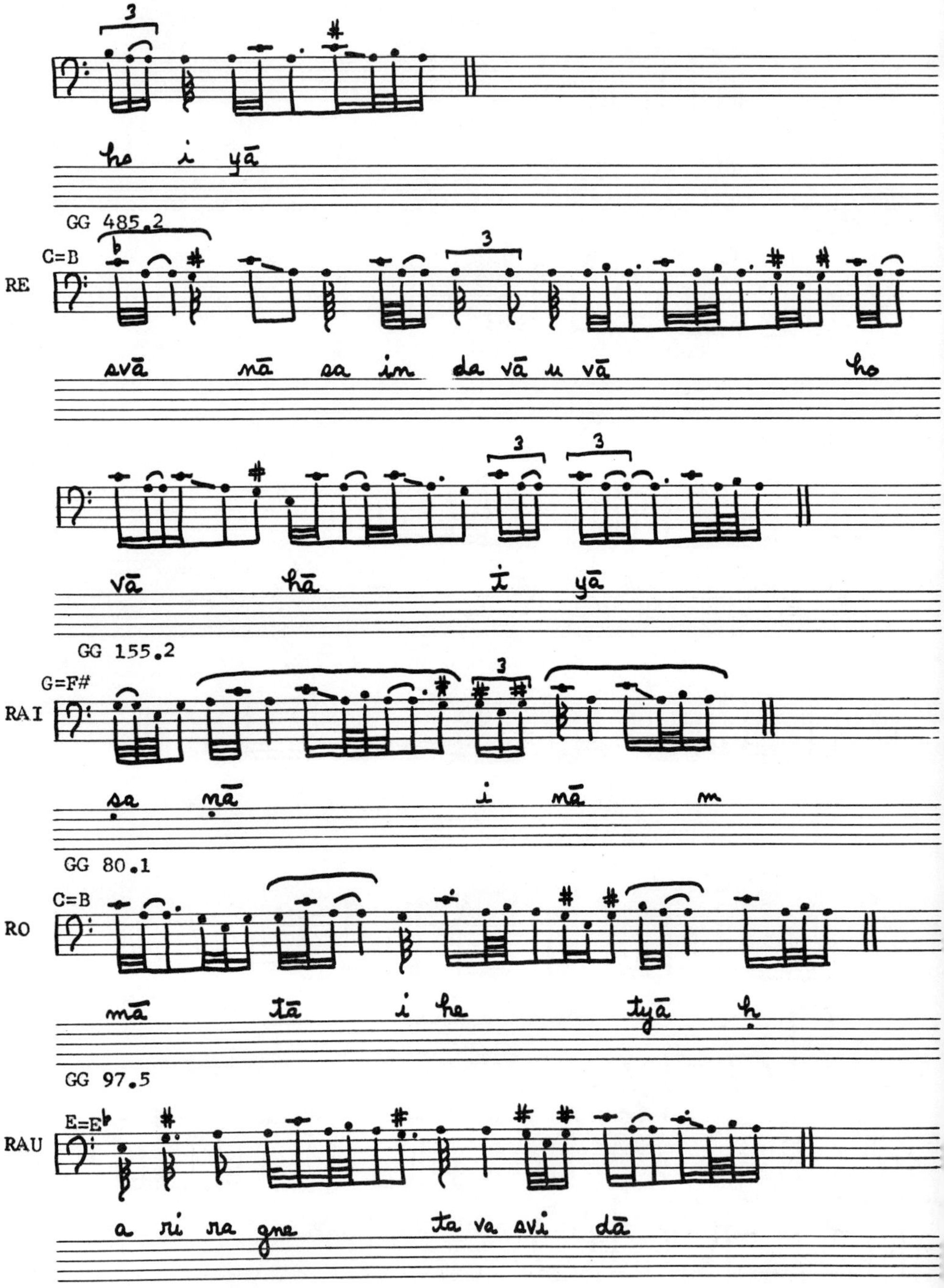

<u>ca</u>-<u>varga</u> (cont.) Subbaraya Paramesvaran Bhatta

GG 527.2

G=F#

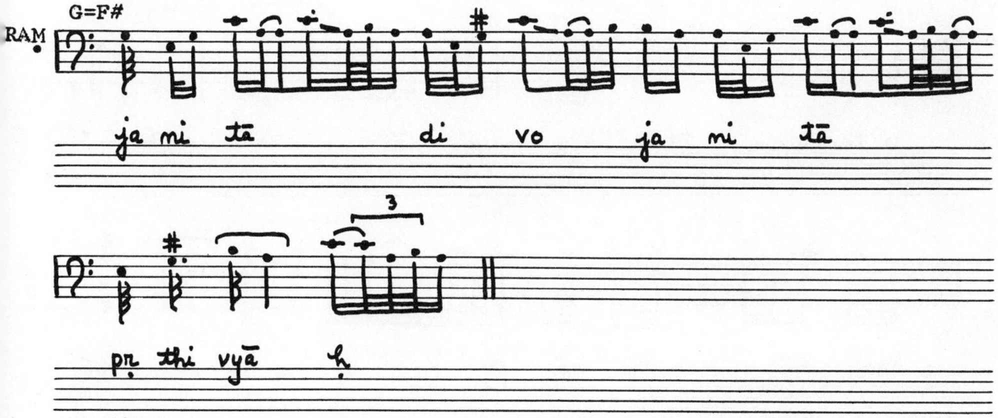

GG 541.3

G=F#

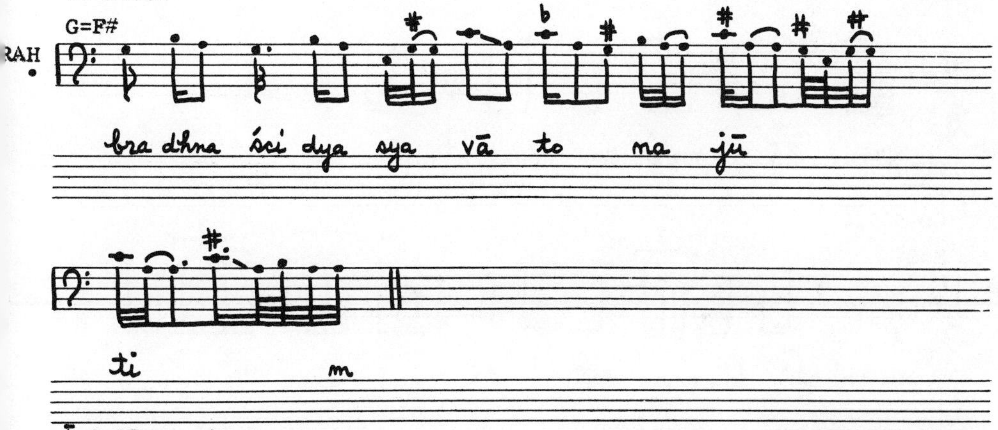

ĀrG 53.1, 147.1

G=F#

ca-varga (cont.) Subbaraya Paramesvaran Bhatta

ĀrG, after 92.1: 2

IĀ

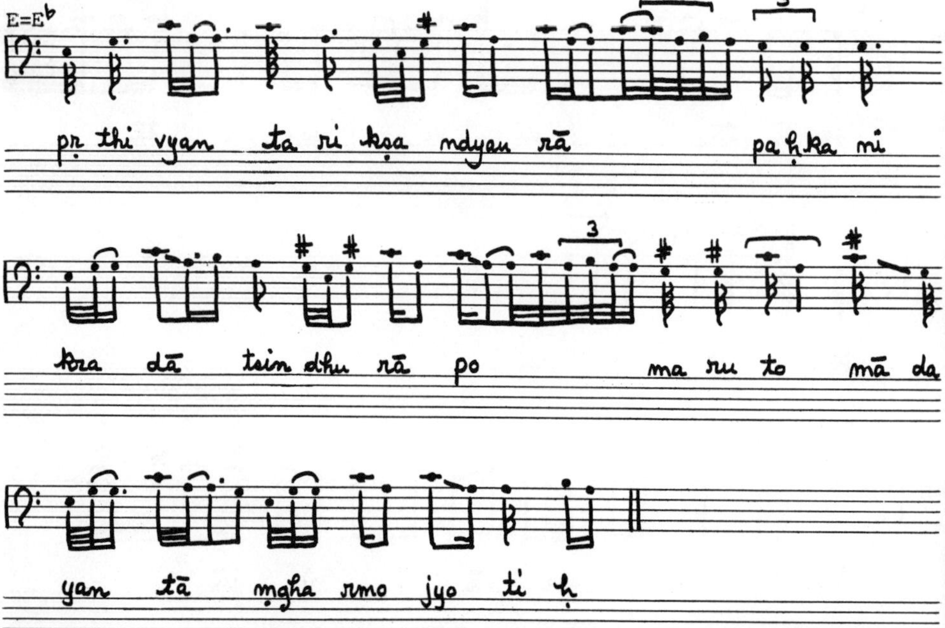
E=E♭
pṛ thi vyan ta ri kṣa ndyau rā pa ḥka ni
kra dā tsin dhu rā po ma ru to mā da
yan tā mgha rmo jyo ti ḥ

GG 545.4

LI

E=E♭
su vṛ ktí bhi rnṛ mā da naṃ bha re su
vā

ĀrG 115.1

LĪ

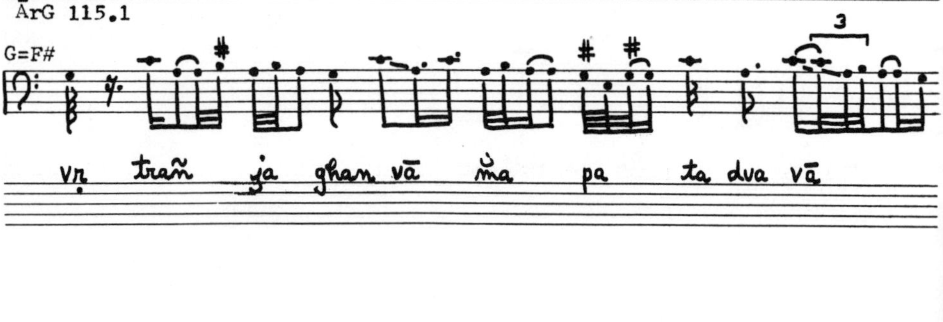
G=F#
vṛ trañ ja ghan vā m̐ma pa ta dva vā

<u>ca</u>-<u>varga</u> (cont.) Subbaraya Paramesvaran Bhatta

ṭa-varga: Subbaraya Paramesvaran Bhatta

GG 272.2

ṬA

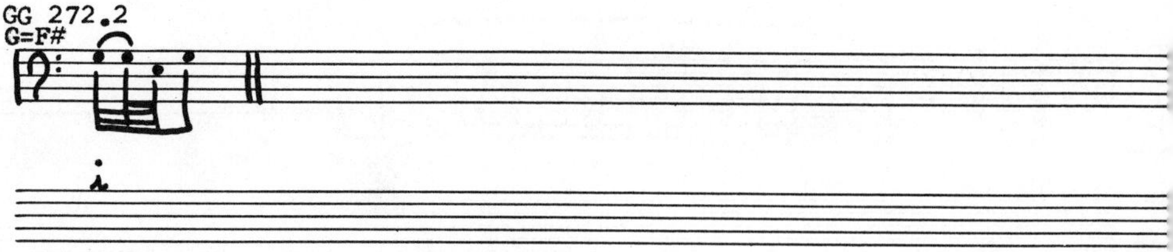

GG 95.1

ṬĀ

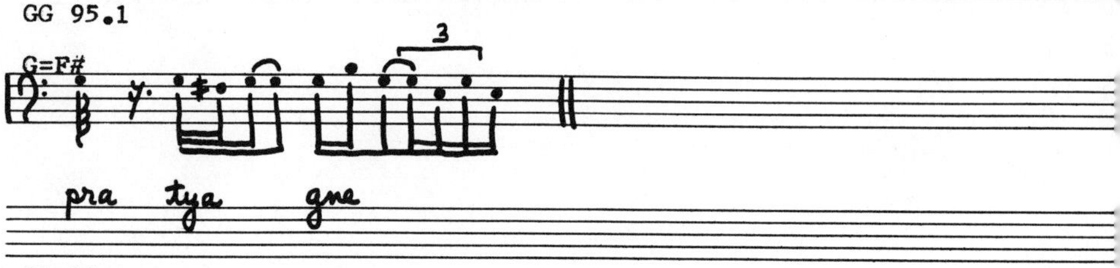

GG 95.1

ṬI

GG 168.3

ṬĪ

GG 99.1

ṬU

GG 1.1

ṬŪ

ṭa-varga (cont.) Subbaraya Paramesvaran Bhatta

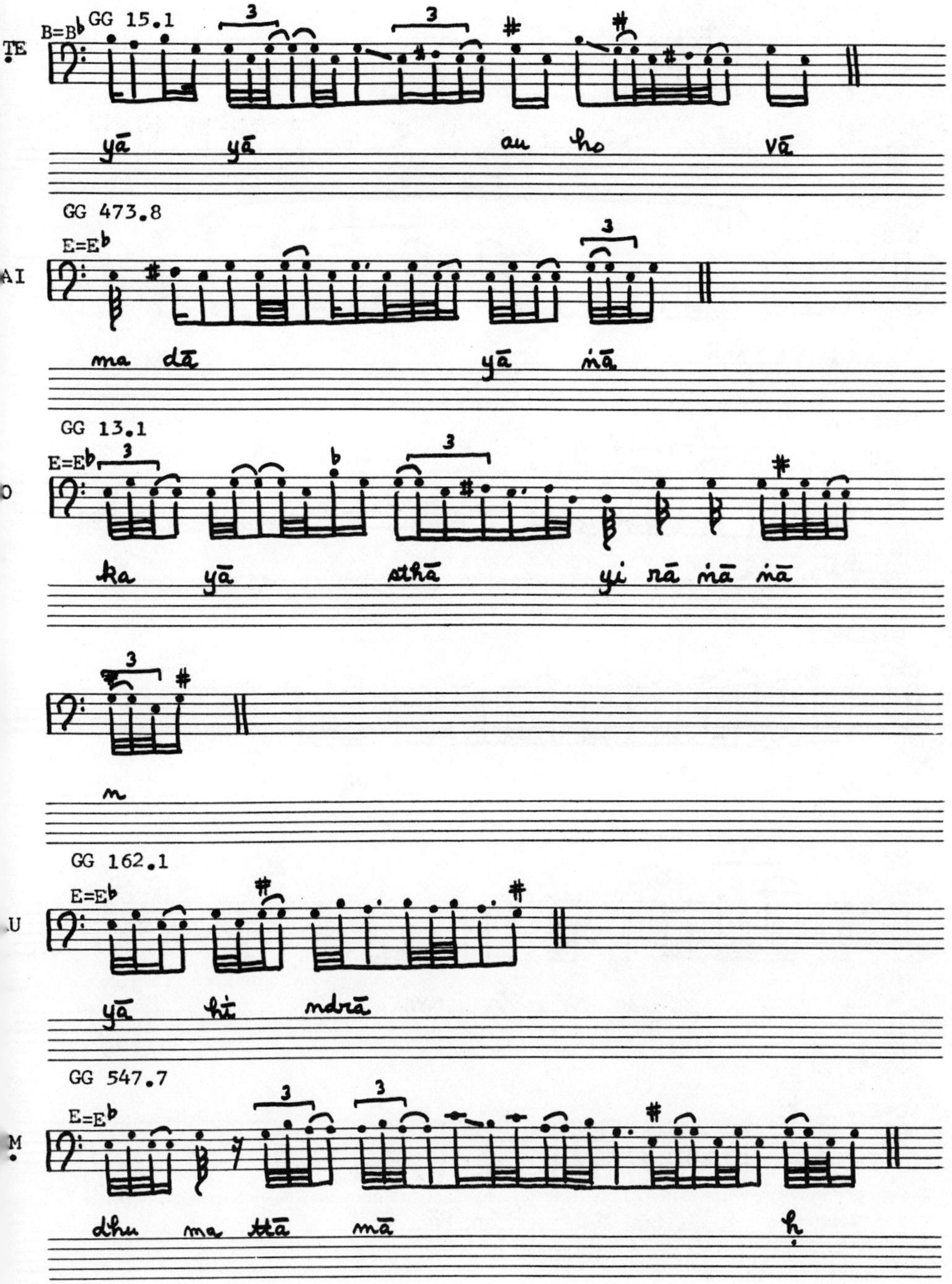

ta-varga (cont.) Subbaraya Paramesvaran Bhatta

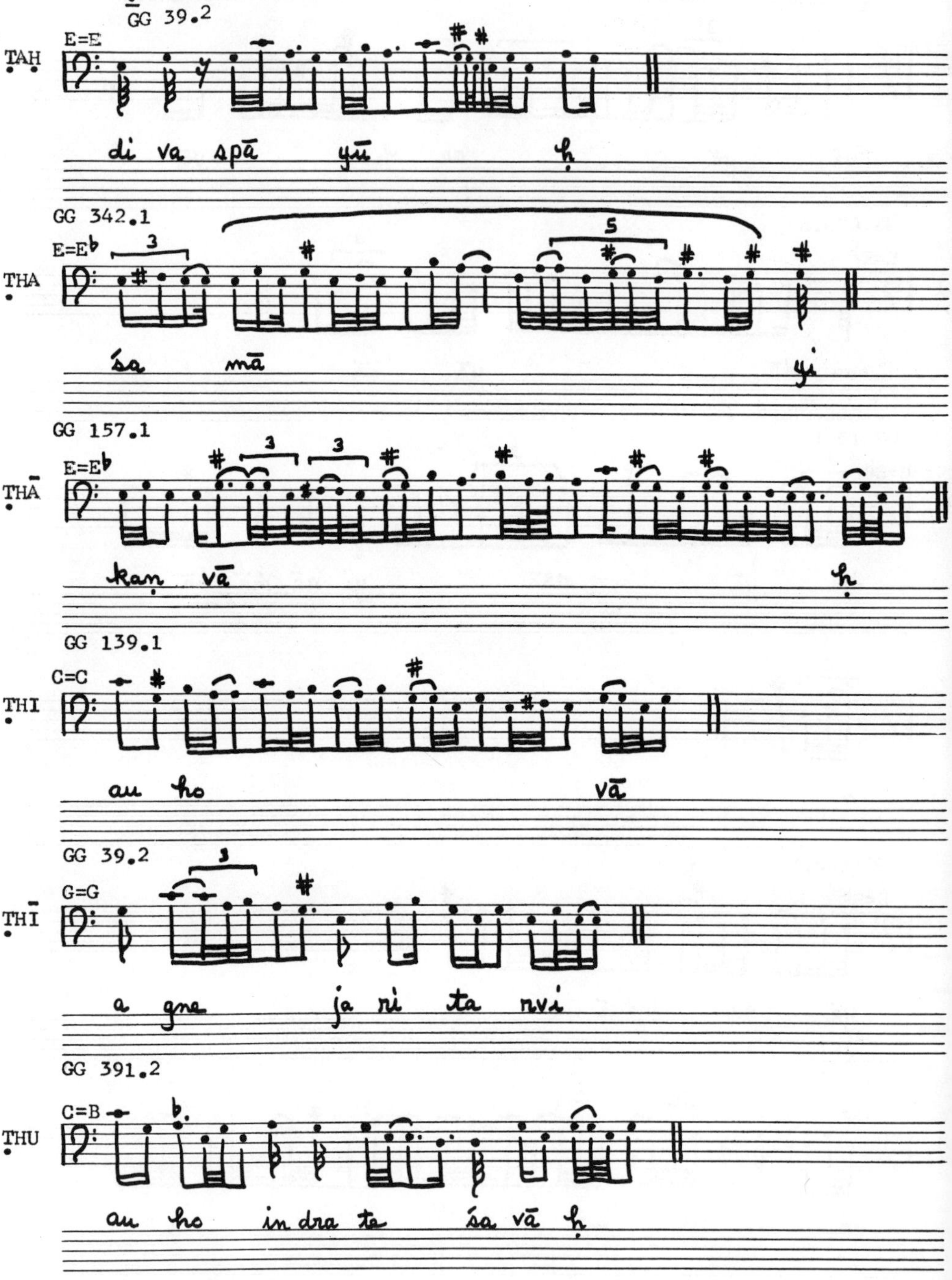

GG 43.1

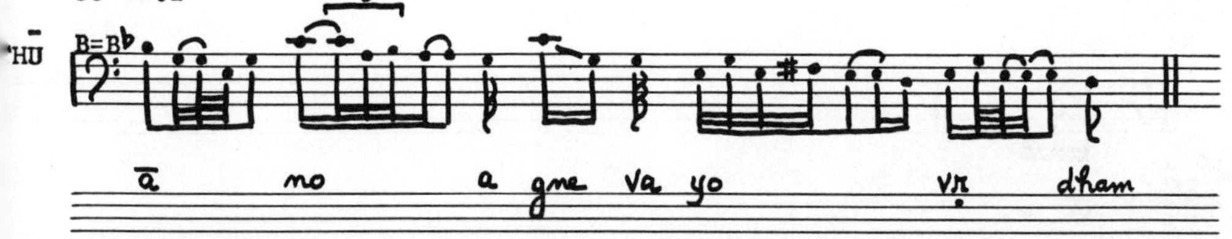

GG 323.3, 4

GG 23.2

GG 544.1

GG 192.1

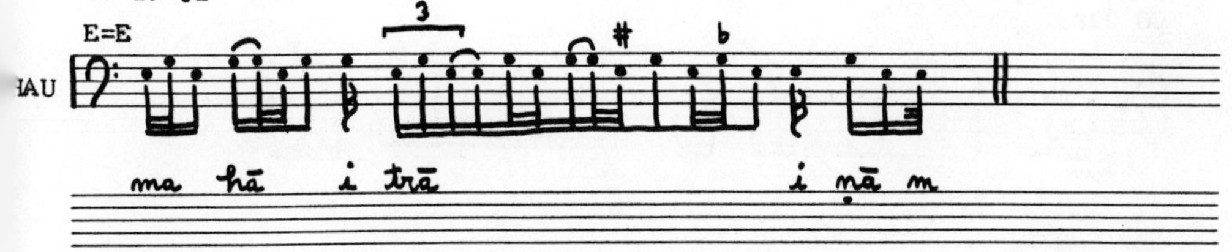

GG 385.1

ṭa-varga (cont.) Subbaraya Paramesvaran Bhatta

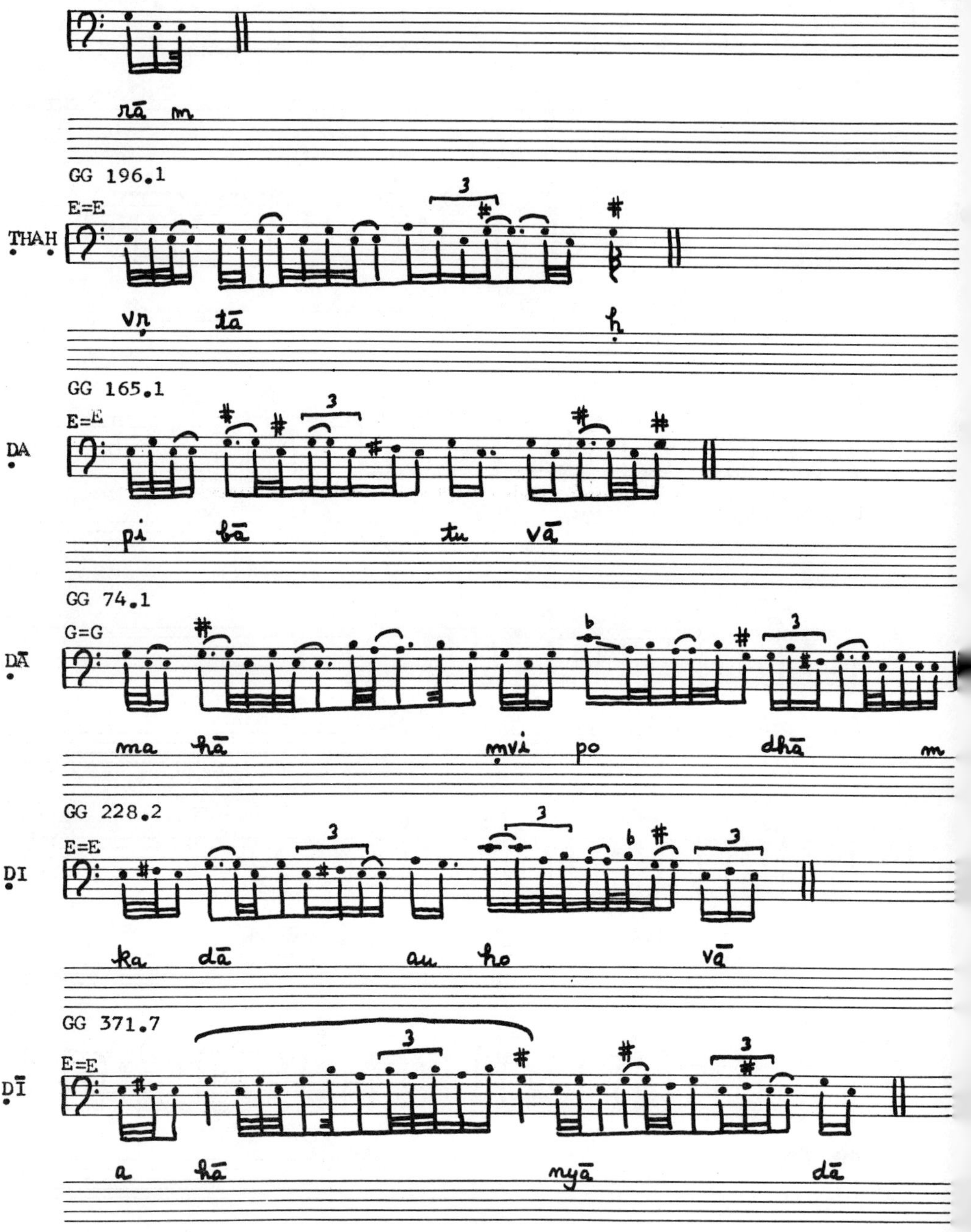

ṭa-varga (cont.)   Subbaraya Paramesvaran Bhatta

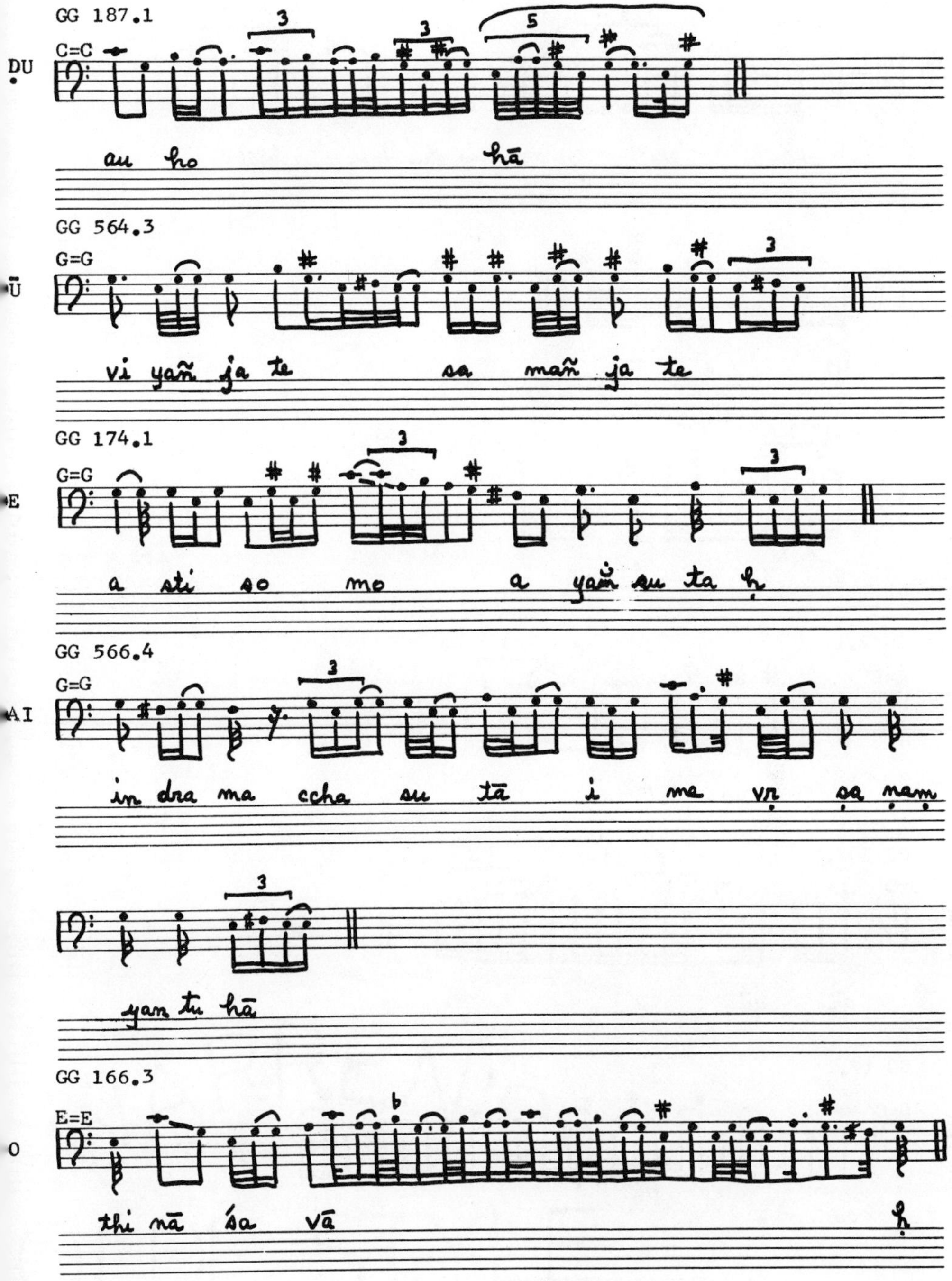

ṭa-varga (cont.) Subbaraya Paramesvaran Bhatta

GG 300.1

ḌAU

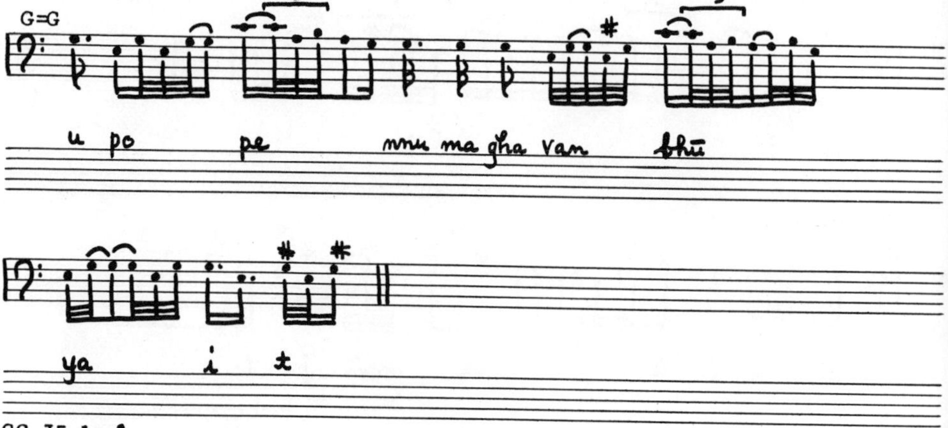

GG 35.1

YA

GG 2.1

YĀ

GG 342.1

YI

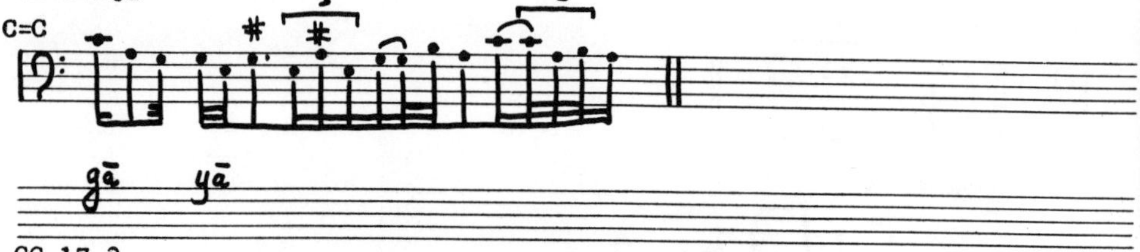

GG 17.2

YĪ

ṭa-varga (cont.) Subbaraya Paramesvaran Bhatta

GG 476. 1, 2

GG 235.1

GG 178.1

GG 305.1

GG 495.2

GG 312.1

ṭa-varga (cont.) Subbaraya Paramesvaran Bhatta

GG 236.2

YAṂ

GG 166.3

YAḤ

GG 1.1 ta-varga: Subbaraya Paramesvaran Bhatta

TA

GG 15.1

TĀ

GG 4.3

TI

GG 5.1

TĪ

ta-varga (cont.) Subbaraya Paramesvaran Bhatta

GG 1.3

GG 74.1

GG 1.2

GG 39.1

GG 10.1

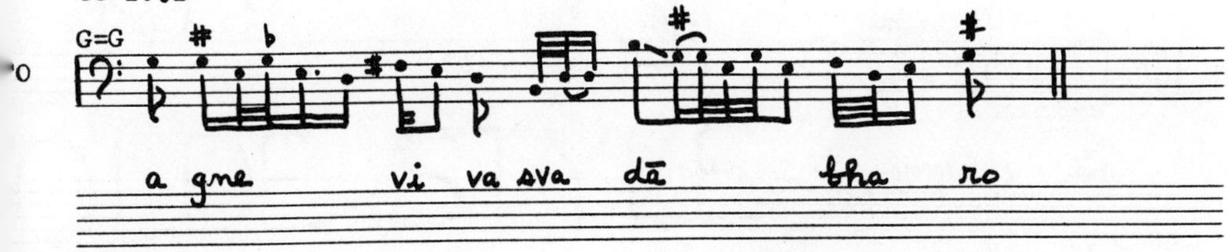

GG 64.2

ta-varga (cont.)   Subbaraya Paramesvaran Bhatta

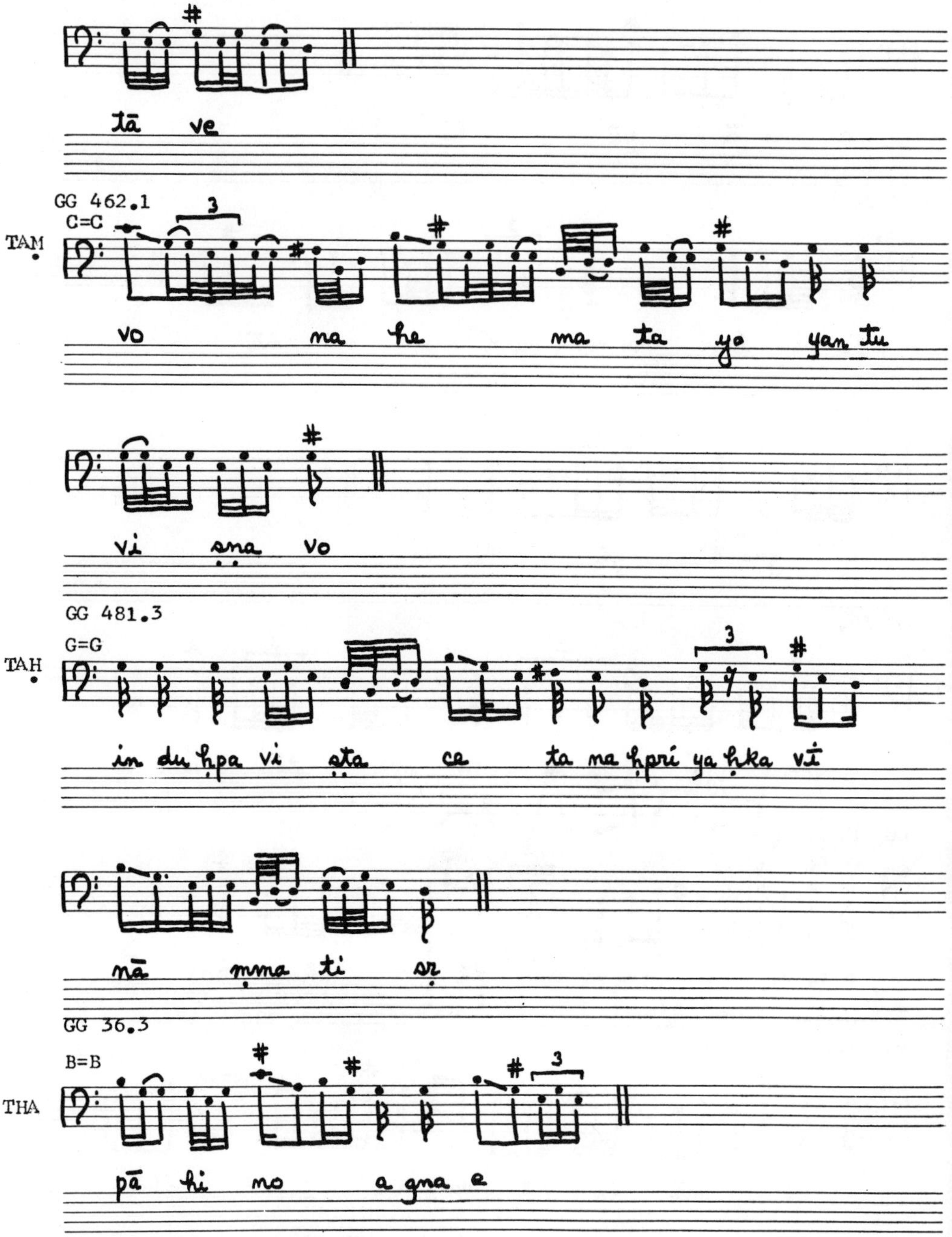

<u>ta</u>-<u>varga</u> (cont.) Subbaraya Paramesvaran Bhatta

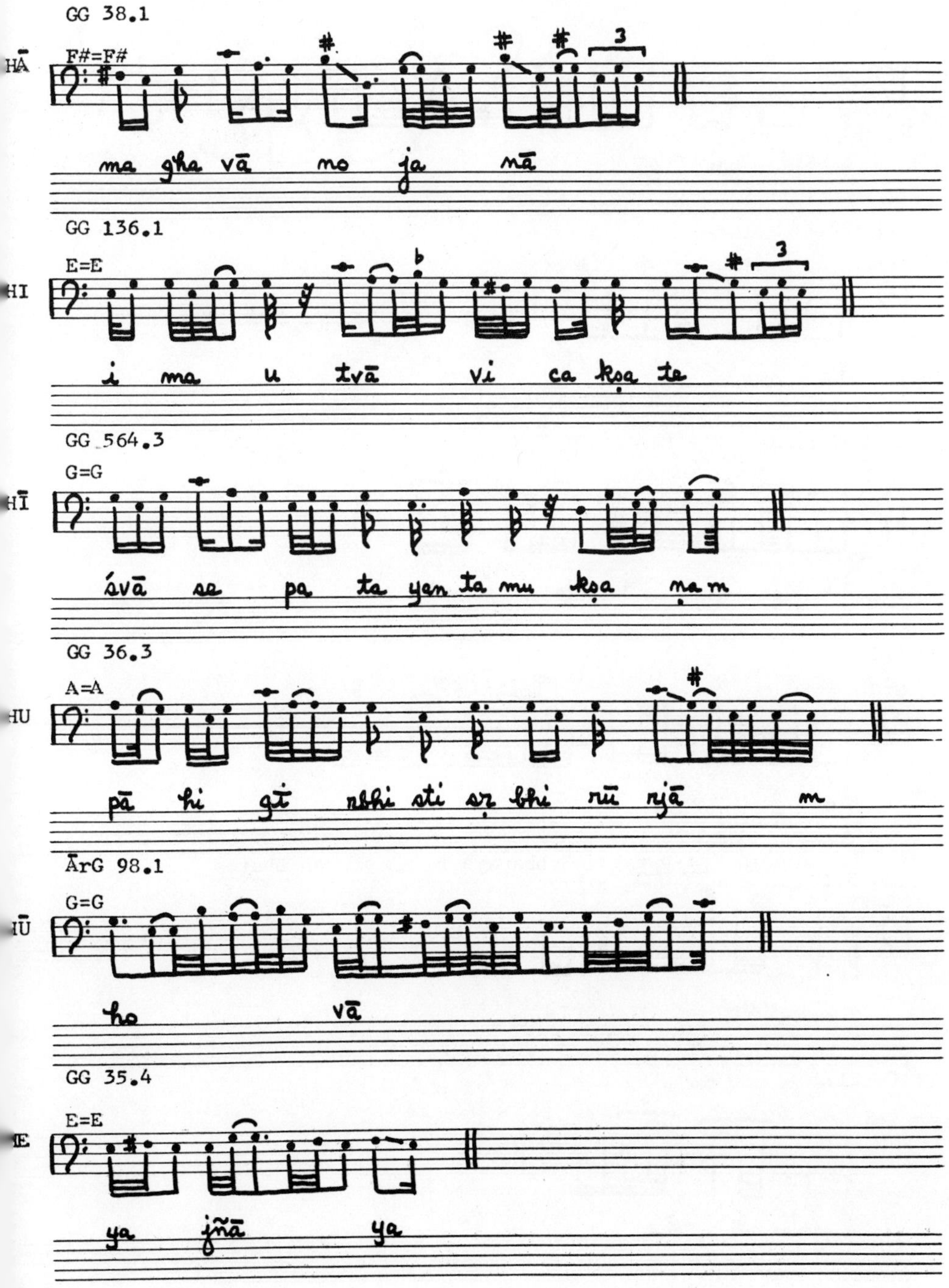

ta-varga (cont.) Subbaraya Paramesvaran Bhatta

GG 554.2

THAI

GG 282.2

HA

GG 337.1, 2

HĀ

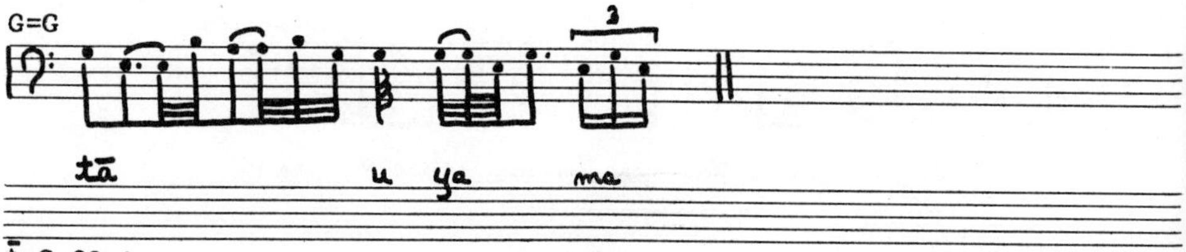

ĀrG 98.1

HI

pa-varga: Subbaraya Paramesvaran Bhatta

GG 3.1

PA

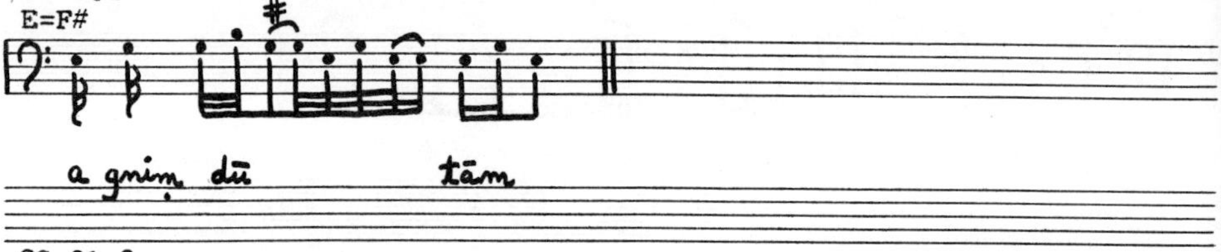

GG 21.2

PĀ

pa-varga (cont.) Subbaraya Paramesvaran Bhatta

GG 97.1

E=F#

[illegible]I

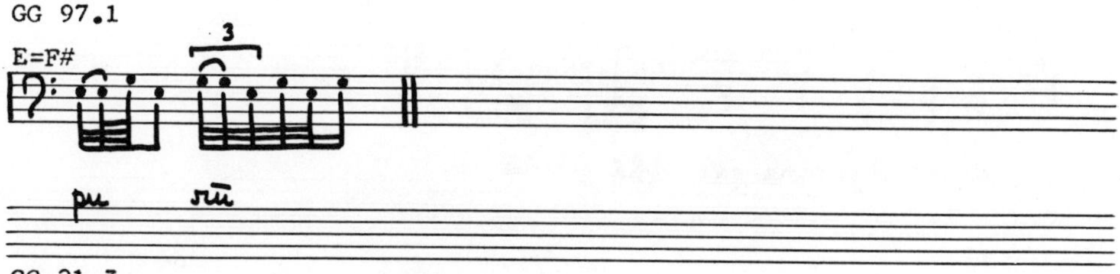

GG 21.3

D=E

[illegible]Ī

GG 144.2

E=F#

U

GG 144.2

B=C

Ū

GG 332.1,2

F#=G#

E

GG 15.2

E=F#

[illegible]I

pa-varga (cont.) Subbaraya Paramesvaran Bhatta

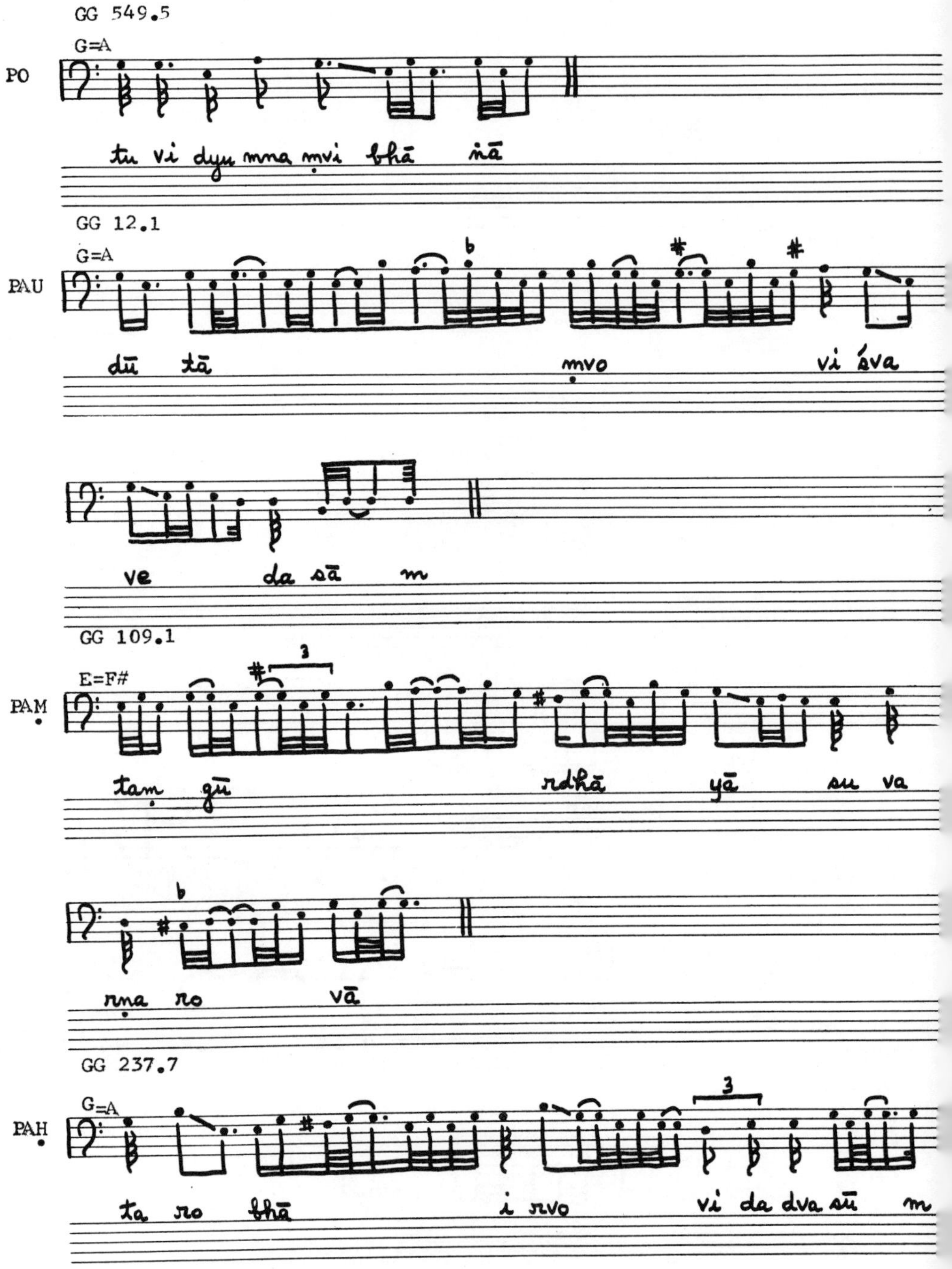

pa-varga (cont.)   Subbaraya Paramesvaran Bhatta

GG 107.1

E=G

PHA

GG 7.1

G=B♭

PHĀ

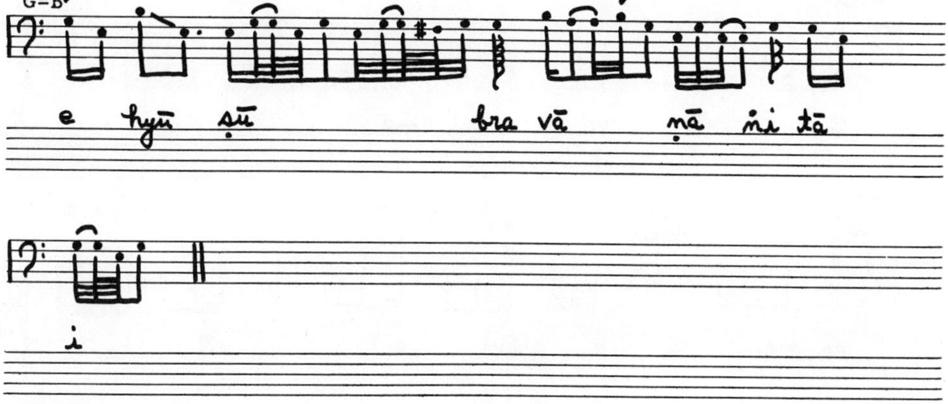

GG 93.1

E=G

HI

GG 19.1

D=F

HĪ

GG 75.1

D=F

HU

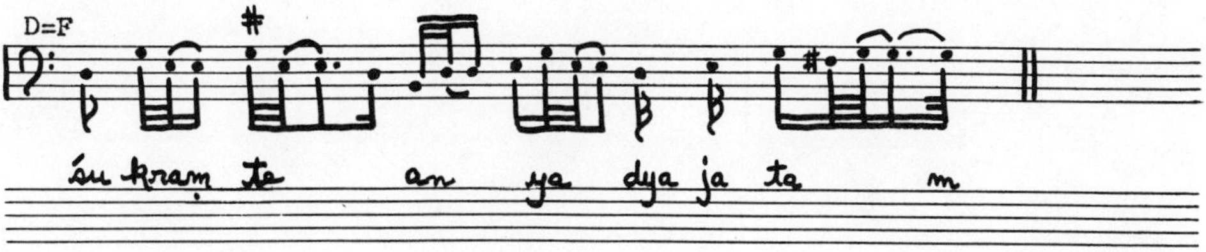

pa-varga (cont.) Subbaraya Paramesvaran Bhatta

GG 22.3

GG 45.3

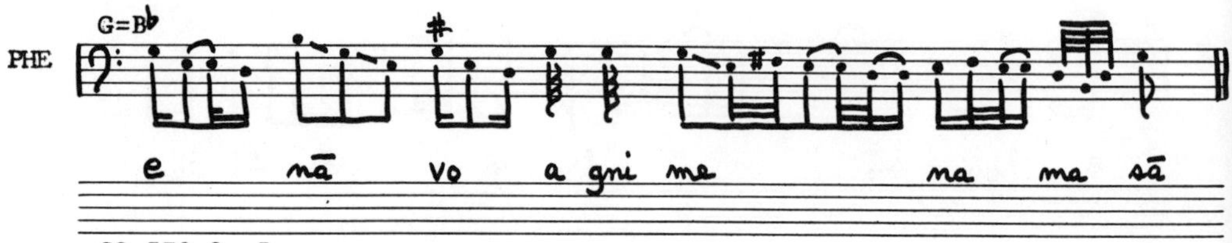

GG 372.2, 3

Tape XXVa(5) ♪= 120

Subbaraya Ramacandra Bhatta
Rāṇāyanīya school (Arolli village, Mysore)

GG 1.1

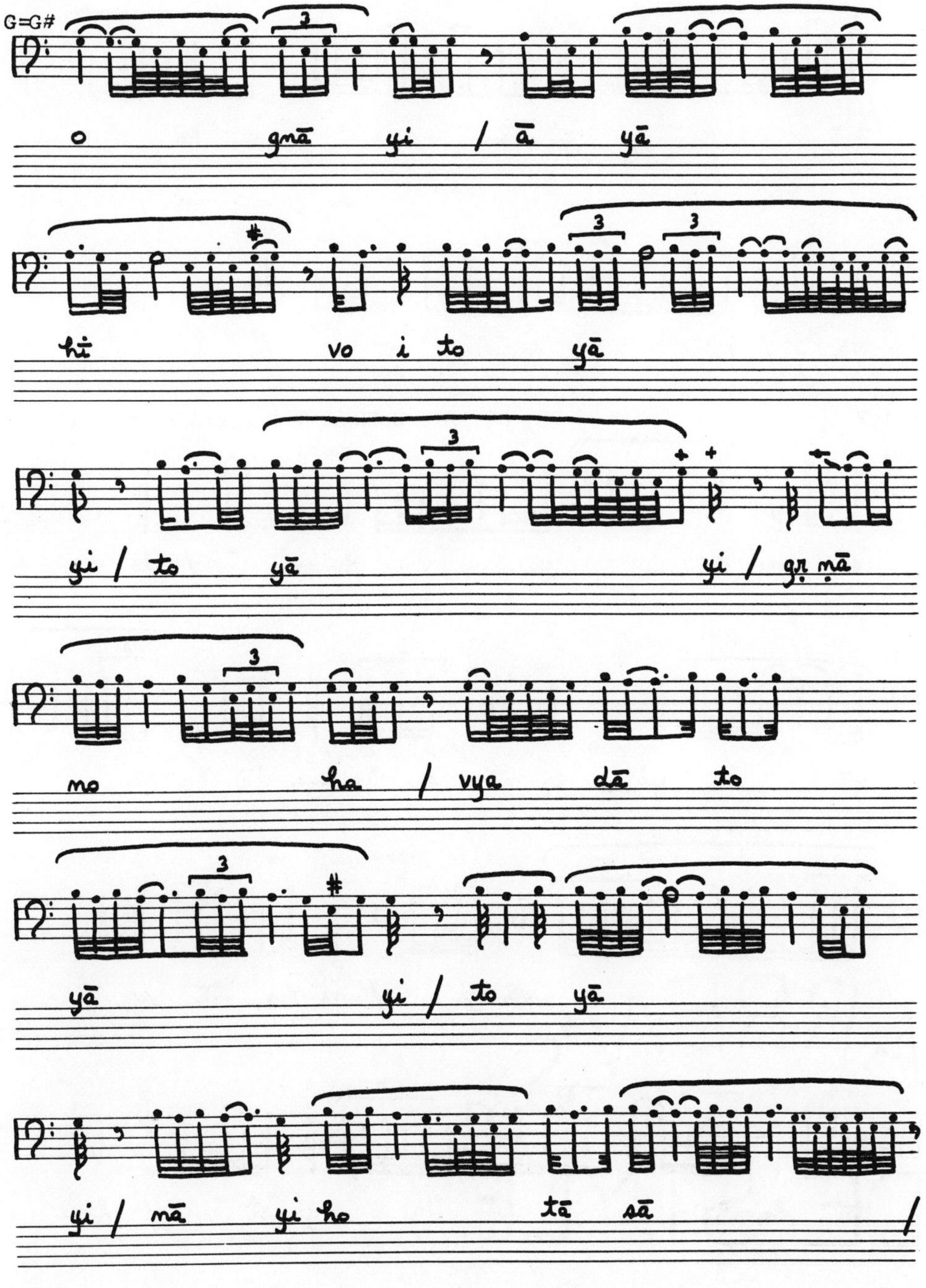
G=G#
3
o gnā yi / ā yā
hī vo i to yā
yi / to yā yi / gṛ ṃā
mo ha / vya dā to
yā yi / to yā
yi / mā yi ho tā sā /

GG 1.1 (cont.) Subbaraya Ramacandra Bhatta

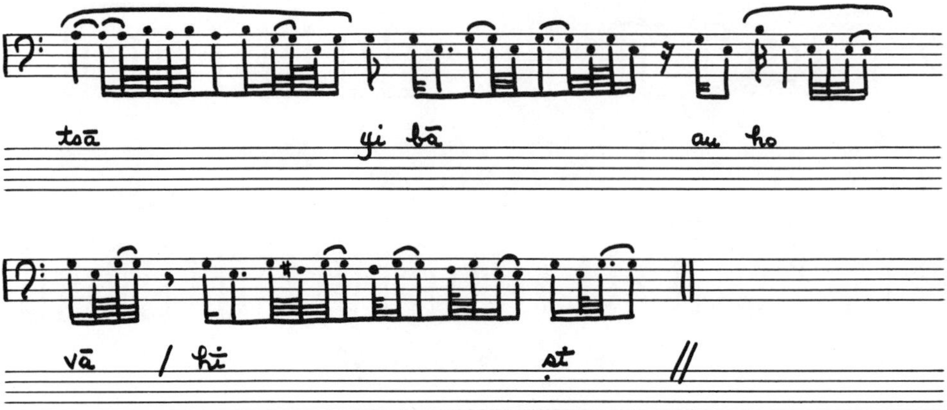
tsā yi bā au ho
vā / hi ṣṭ //

GG 1.2 ♪=120 Subbaraya Ramacandra Bhatta

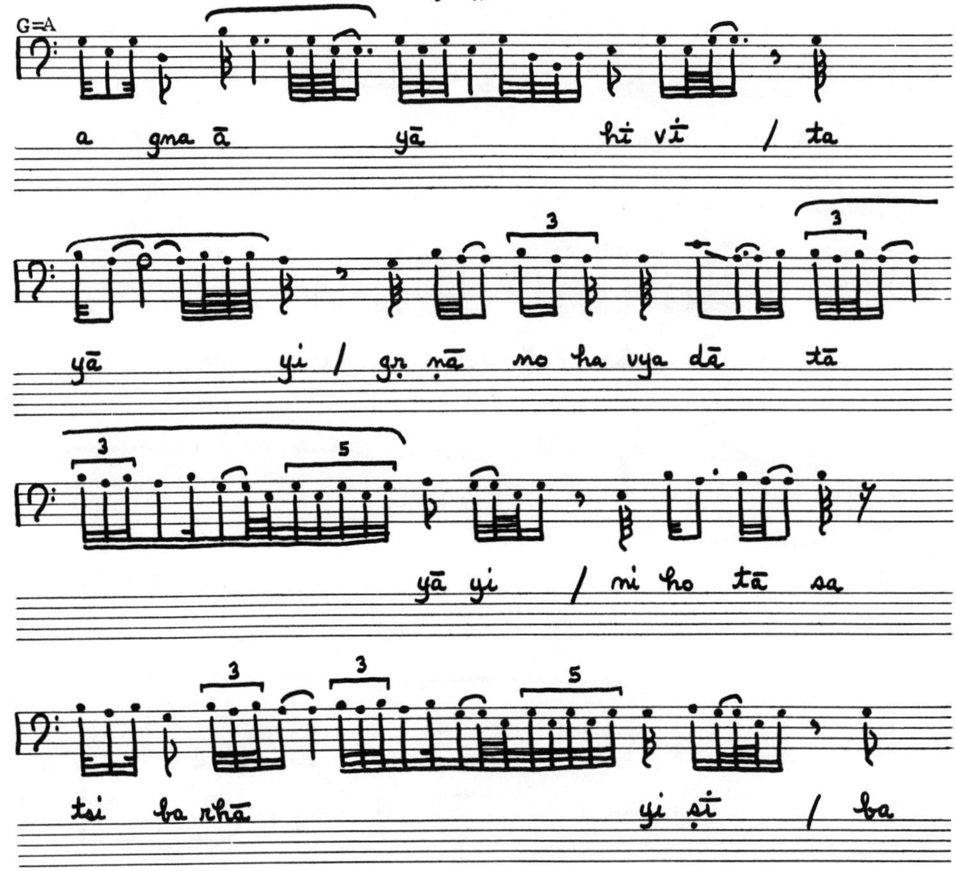
G=A
a gna ā yā hi vī / ta
yā yi / gṛ ṇā mo ha vya dā tā
yā yi / ni ho tā sa
tsi ba rhā yi ṣī / ba

GG 1.2 (cont.) Subbaraya Ramacandra Bhatta

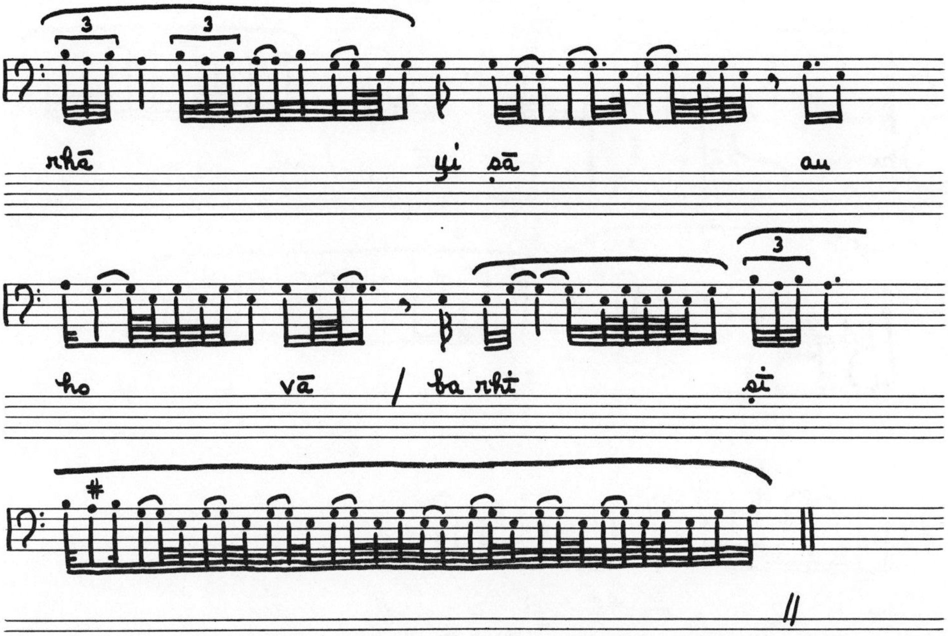
rhā yi ṣā au
ho vā / ba rhi ṣi
//

GG 1.3 ♪ = 120 Subbaraya Ramacandra Bhatta

G=A

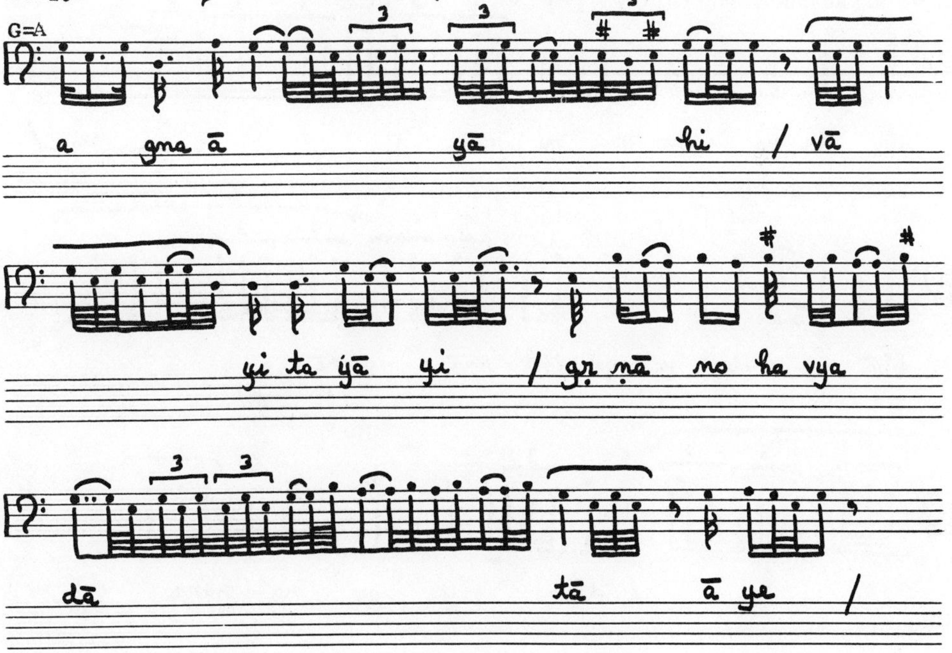
a gna ā yā hi / vā
yi ta yā yi / gṛ ṇā no ha vya
dā tā ā ye /

GG 1.3 (cont.) Subbaraya Ramacandra Bhatta

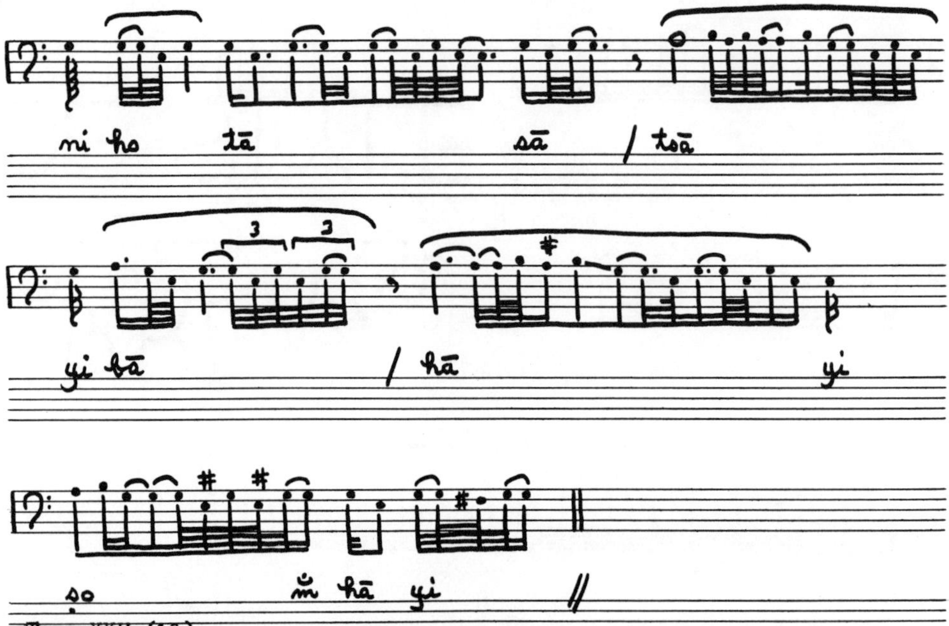
ni ho tā sā / tsā
yi bā / hā yi
so m̐ hā yi //

Tape XXVa(10)
Raṇāyanīya Gāyatram
Siva Ramacandra Bhatta (Arolli)
A=B

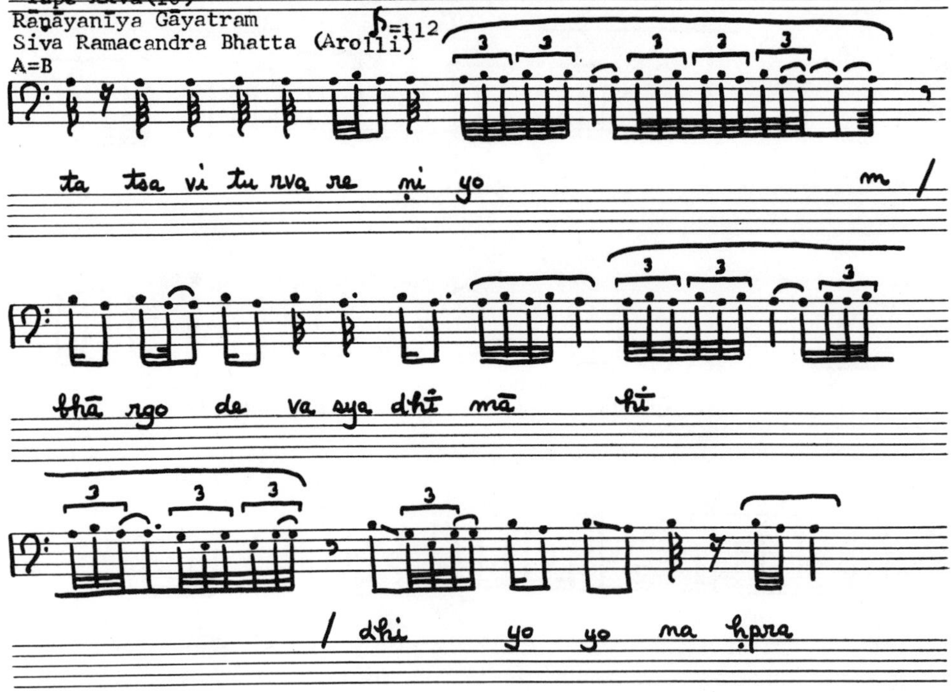
=112
ta tsa vi tu rva re ṇi yo m /
bhā rgo de va sya dhī mā hī
/ dhi yo yo na ḥpra

Rāṇāyanīya Gāyatram (cont.) Siva Ramacandra Bhatta

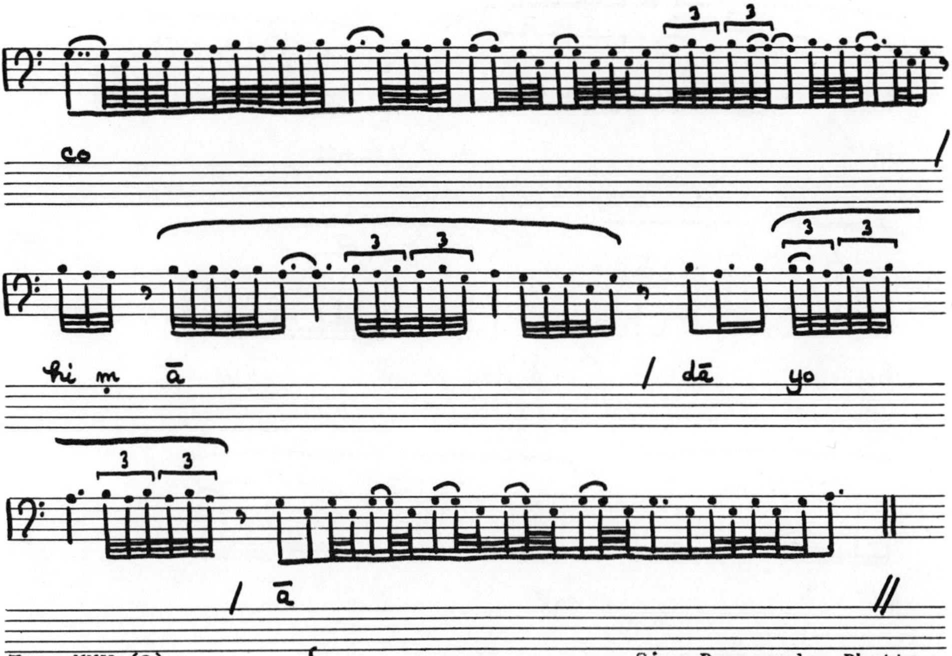

Tape XXVa(8)
GG 222.1
E=F#

♪=120

Siva Ramacandra Bhatta

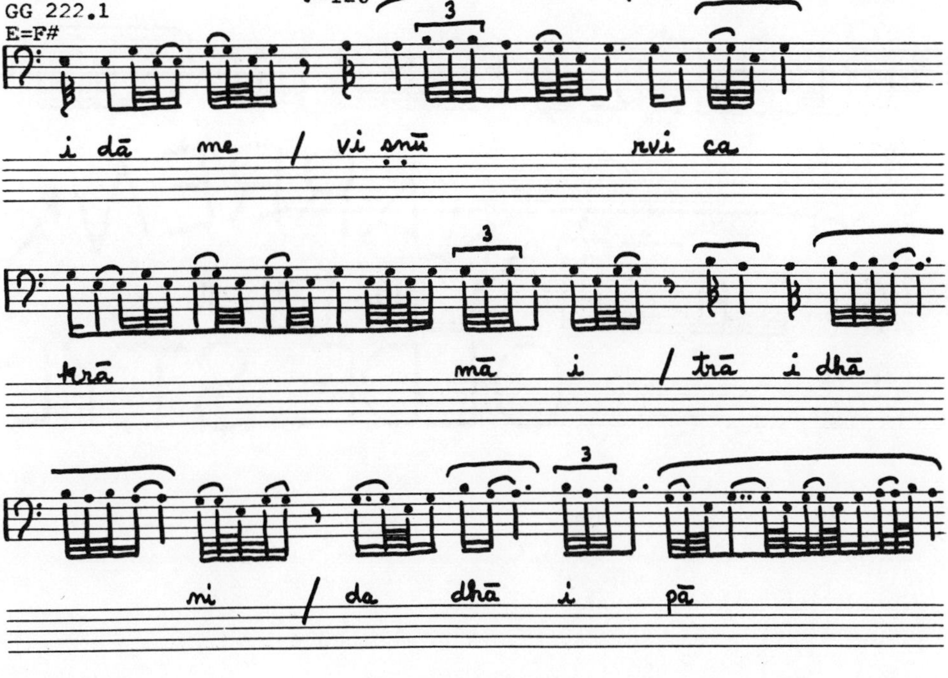

GG 222.1 (cont.) Siva Ramacandra Bhatta

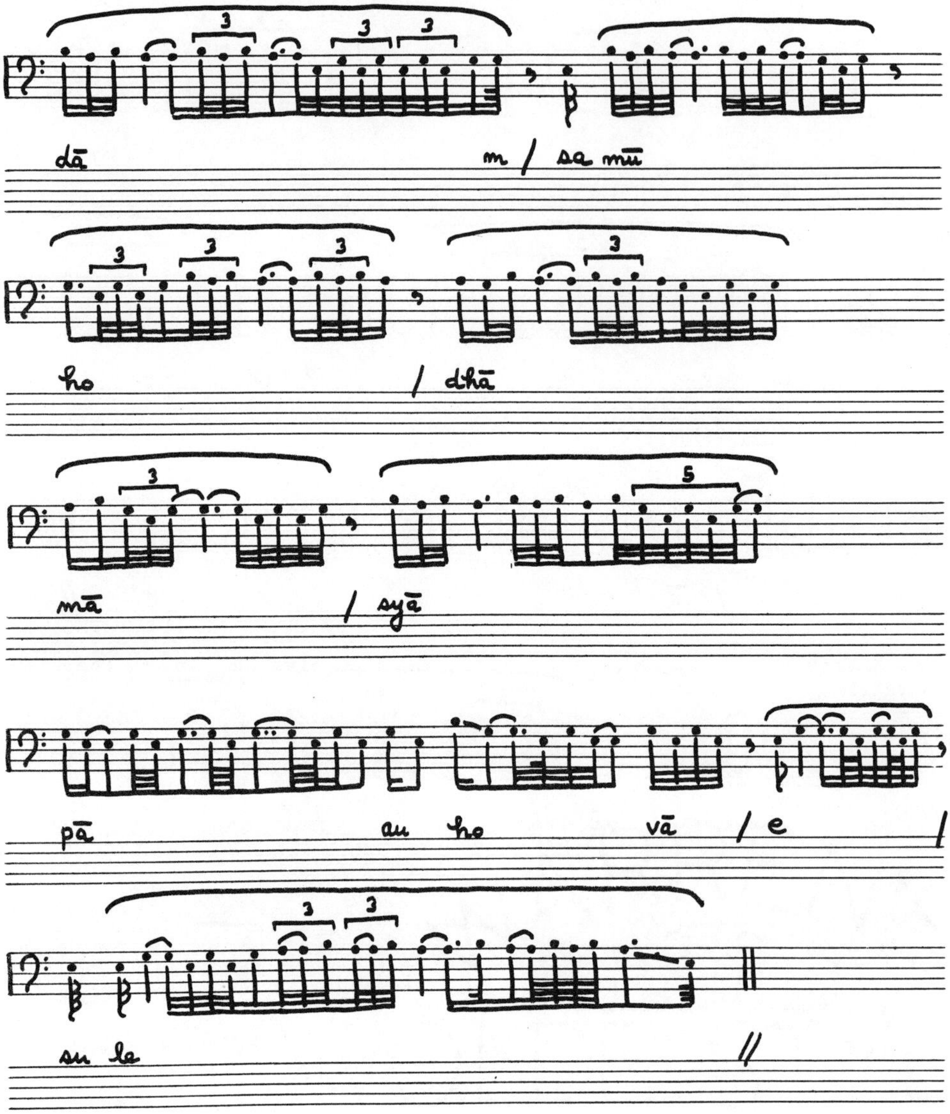
dā
m / sa mū
ho
/ dhā
mā
/ syā
pā
au ho
vā / e
/
su le
//

Rāṇāyanīya Gāyatram ♪ = 138

Vedulu Gopala Avadhani and
Srigovinda Sarma
(Vijayanagaram, Andhra Pradesh)
"Gurjarapāṭha"

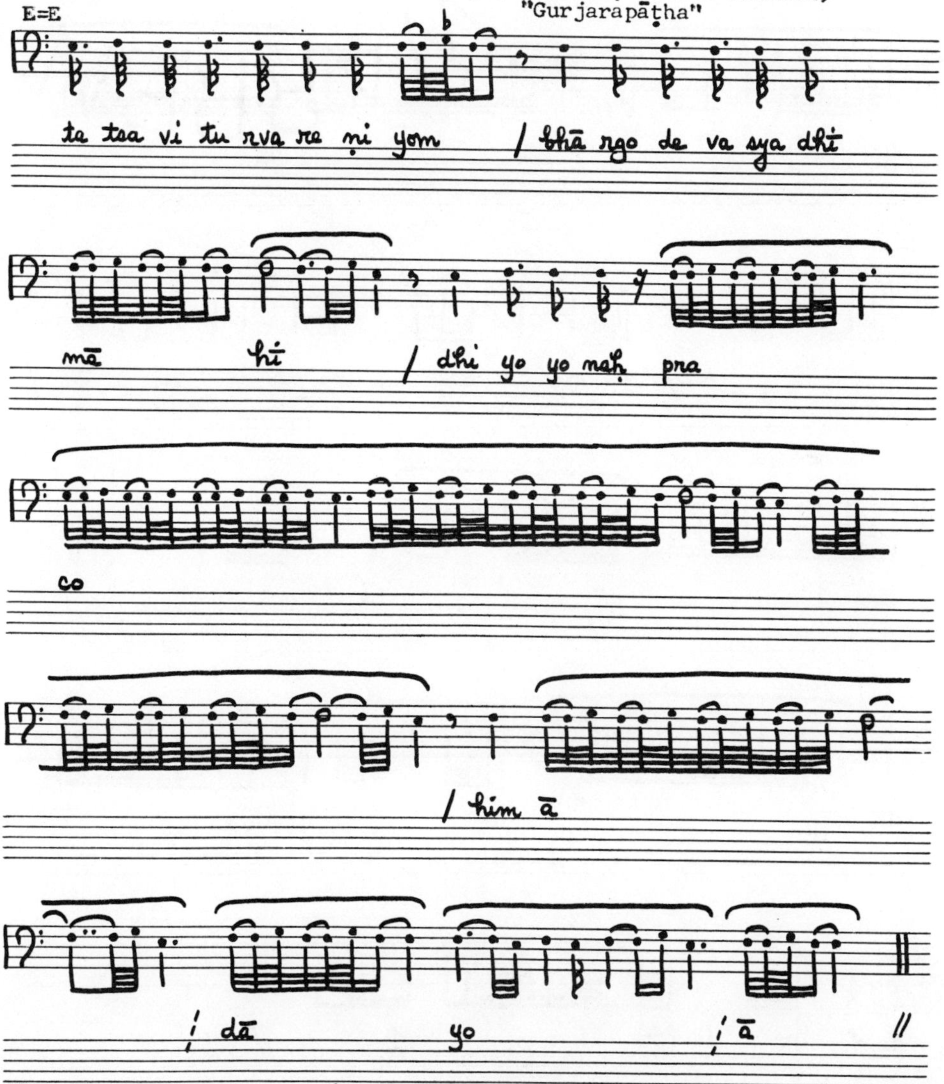
E=E
ta tsa vi tu rva re ṇi yom / bhā rgo de va sya dhī
mā hī / dhi yo yo naḥ pra
co
/ him ā
/ dā yo / ā //

GG 1.1 ♪ = 138

Vedulu Gopala Avadhani
Srigovinda Sarma

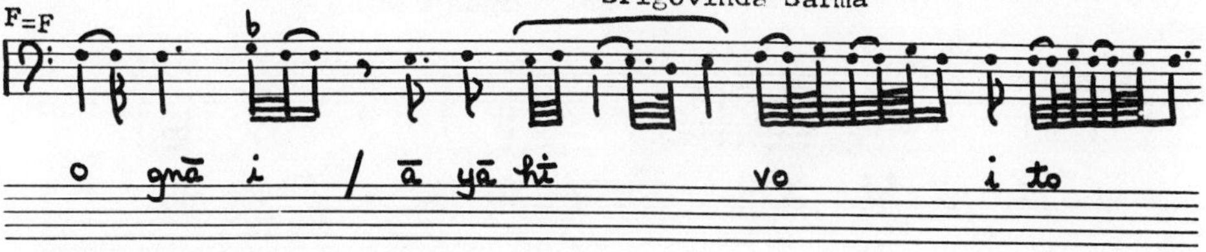
F=F
o gnā i / ā yā hī vo i to

GG 1.1 (cont.)

Vedulu Gopala Avadhani
Srigovinda Sarma

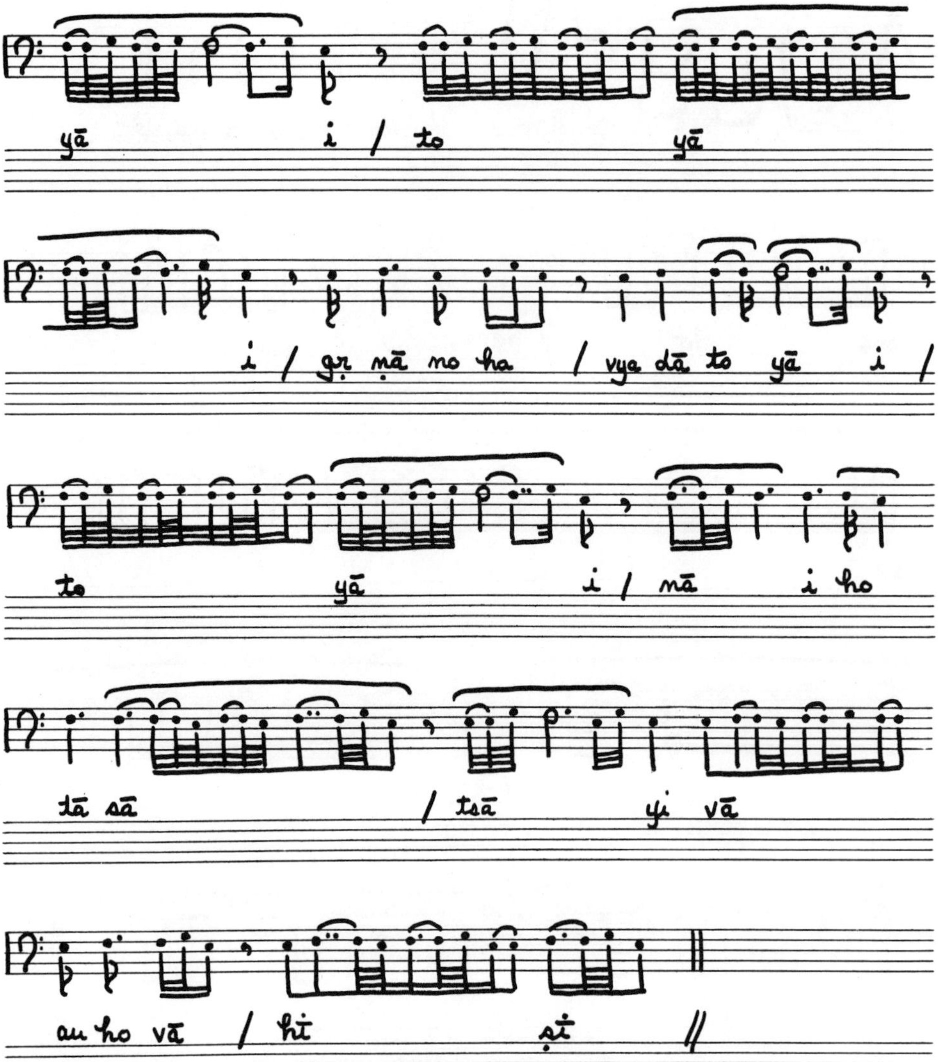
yā i / to yā
i / gṛ ṇā no ha / vya dā to yā i /
to yā i / nā i ho
tā sā / tsā yi vā
au ho vā / hi ṣi //

GG 1.2

♪= 138

Vedulu Gopala Avadhani
Srigovinda Sarma

F=F

a gna ā yā hi vi / ta yā i / gṛ ṇā

GG 1.2 (cont.)

Vedulu Gopala Avadhani
Srigovinda Sarma

no ha vya dā tā yā i / ni ho tā
sa tsi ba rhā i ṣī / ba rhā i ṣā
au ho vā / ba rhī ṣī

GG 1.3

♪ = 138

Vedulu Gopala Avadhani
Srigovinda Sarma

F=F

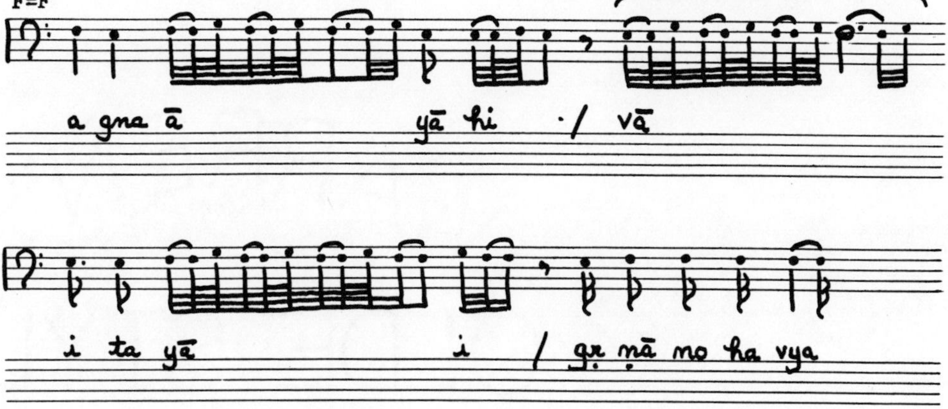
a gna ā yā hi · / vā
i ta yā i / gṛ ṇā no ha vya

GG 1.3 (cont.)

Vedulu Gopala Avadhani
Srigovinda Sarma

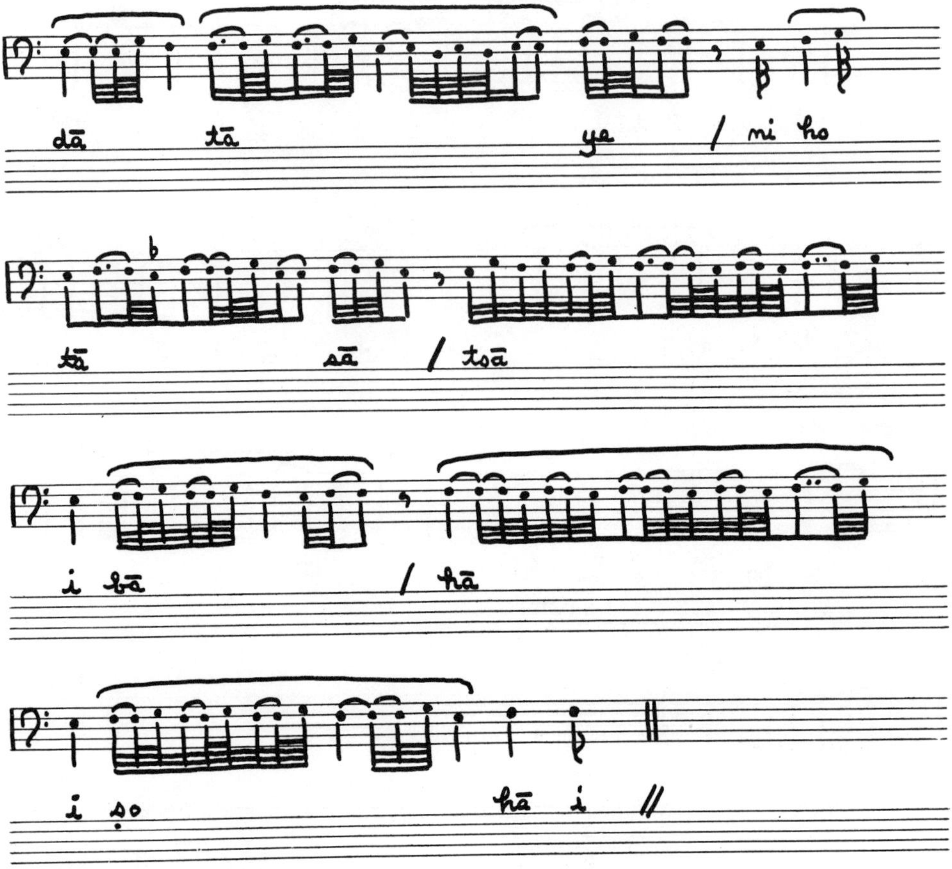
dā tā ye / ni ho
tā sā / tsā
i bā / hā
i ṣo hā i //

Rāṇāyanīya Gāyatram = 112 S. Ramagopala Sastri and S. Narayana Sastri (Sitanagaram, Andhra Pradesh)

"Rāṇāyanīya from Tirunēlveli"

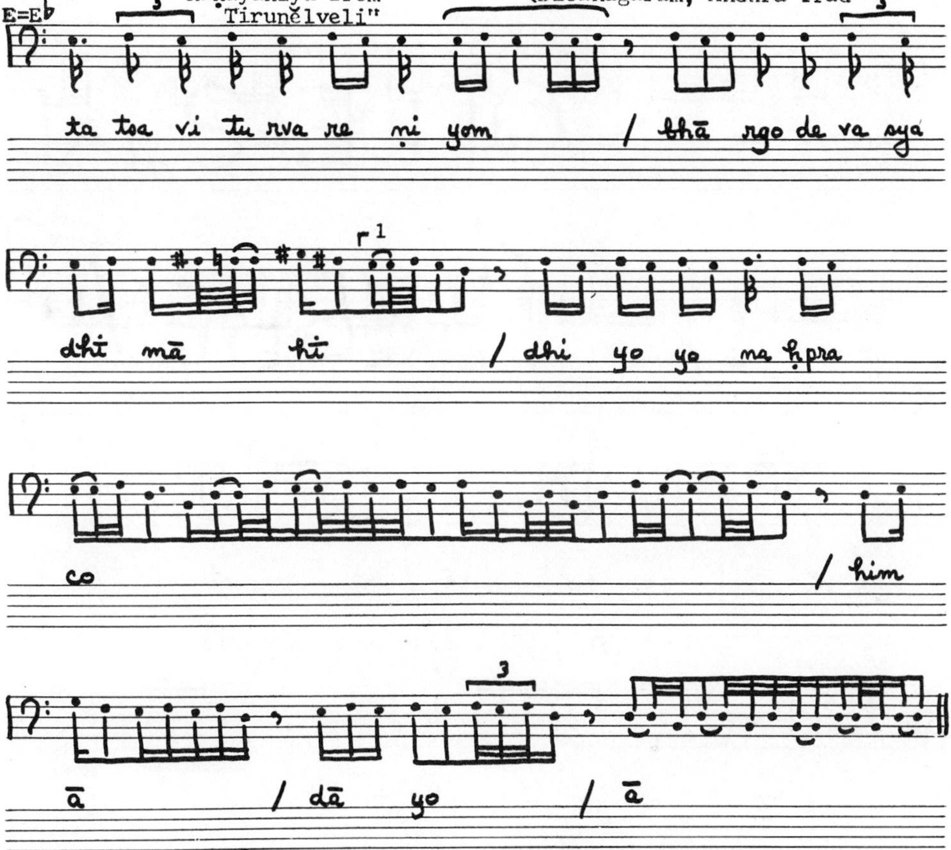
E=E♭
ta tsa vi tu rva re ṇi yom / bhā rgo de va sya
dhī mā hī / dhi yo yo na ḥpra
co / him
ā / dā yo / ā

GG 1.1 = 112 S. Ramagopala Sastri S. Narayana Sastri

o gnā i / ā yā hī vo i to
yā i / to yā i /

[1]Tonal center shifts here a half step higher.
[2]Unclear on tape: approximate transcription.

GG 1.1 (cont.)

S. Ramagopala Sastri
S. Narayana Sastri

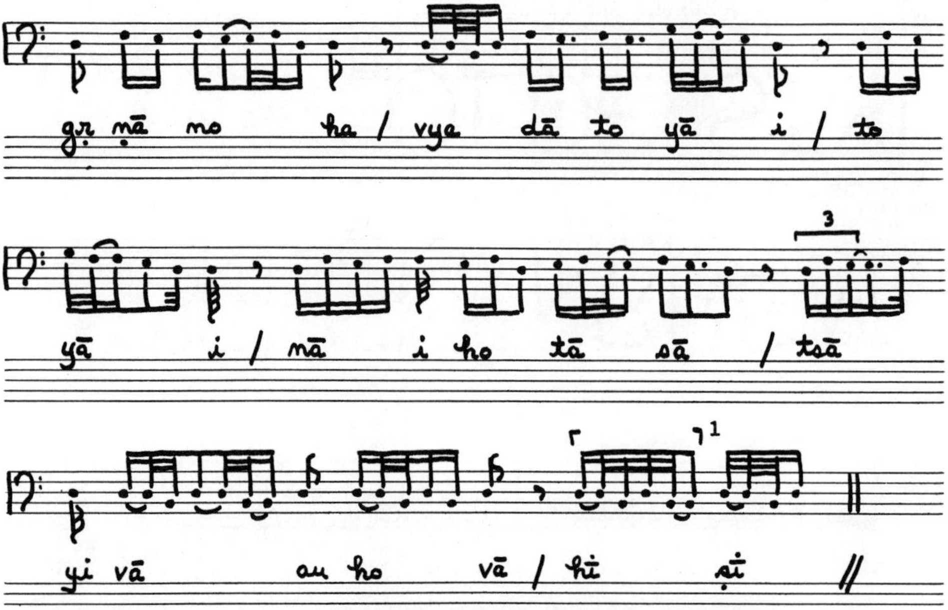
gṛ ṇā no ha / vya dā to yā i / to
yā i / nā i ho tā sā / tsā
3
1
yi vā au ho vā / hi ṣi //

GG 1.2

♪ = 112

S. Ramagopala Sastri
S. Narayana Sastri

D=D
3
a gna ā yā hi vi / ta yā i /
gṛ ṇā no ha vya dā tā yā i / ni ho tā
sa tsi ba rhā i ṣi / ba rhā i

[1]Approximate rhythmic transcription.

GG 1.2 (cont.)

S. Ramagopala Sastri
S. Narayana Sastri

ṣā au ho vā / ba ṛhi
ṣi //

GG 1.3 ♪ = 112

S. Ramagopala Sastri
S. Narayana Sastri

D=D

a gna ā yā hi / vā i ta yā i /
gṛ ṇā no ha vya dā tā ye /
ni ho tā sā / tsā i bā /
hā i som hā i //

[1]Approximate rhythmic transcription.

Tape IVb(3)
JGG 1.1

T. Rajagopala Aiyangar
Srirangam
Jaiminiya School

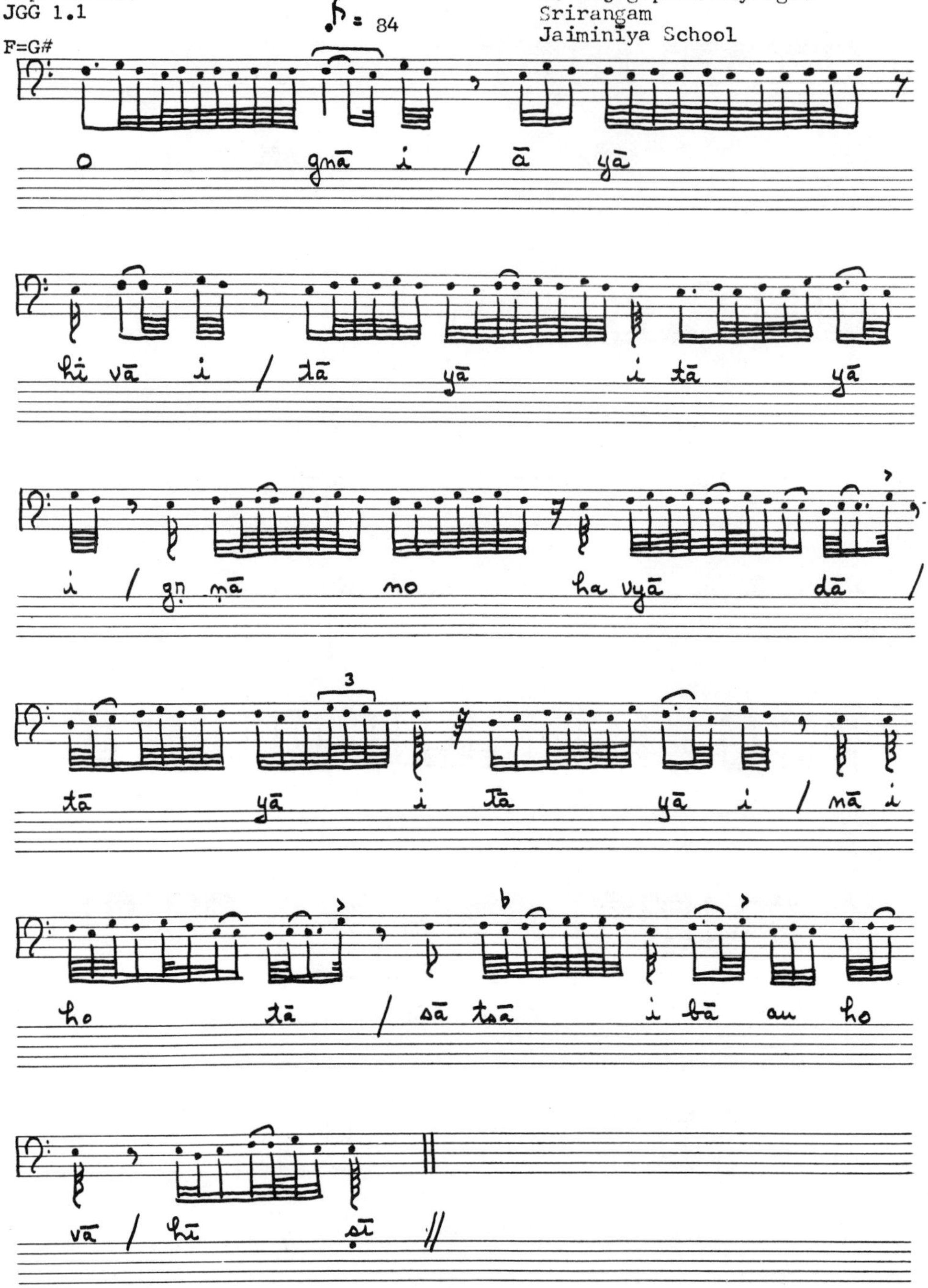
♪ = 84
F=G#
o gnā i / ā yā
hi vā i / tā yā i tā yā
i / gn ṇā no ha vyā dā /
3
tā yā i tā yā i / mā i
ho tā / sā tsā i bā au ho
vā / hi ṣī //

Tape IVb(3)
JGG 1.2

♪ = 84

T. Rajagopala Aiyangar

E=G

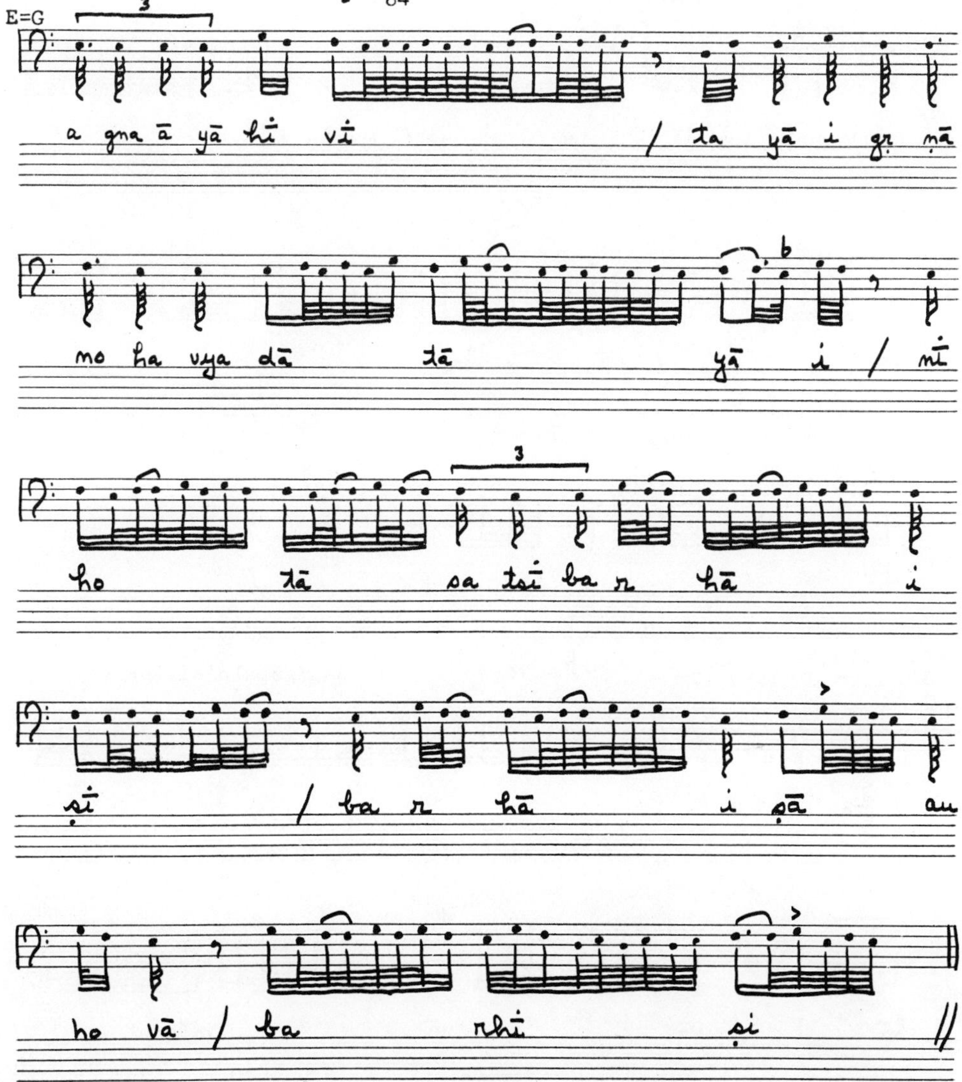
a gna ā yā hi vi / ta yā i gṛ ṇā
mo ha vya dā tā yā i / ni
ho tā sa tsi ba ṛ hā i
ṣi / ba ṛ hā i ṣā au
ho vā / ba rhi ṣi //

Tape IVb(3)
JGG 1.3

♪ = 84

T. Rajagopala Aiyangar

C=F#

a gna ā yā hi vā i tā yā i /

JGG 1.3 (cont.) T. Rajagopala Aiyangar

gṛ ṇā mo ha vya dā tā ye / ni ho tā
sā t / sā i bā / r
hā i ṣo hā i //

Tape IVb(4)
JGG from JS 1.1.2.7 ♪ = 96 T. Rajagopala Aiyangar

C=F♯

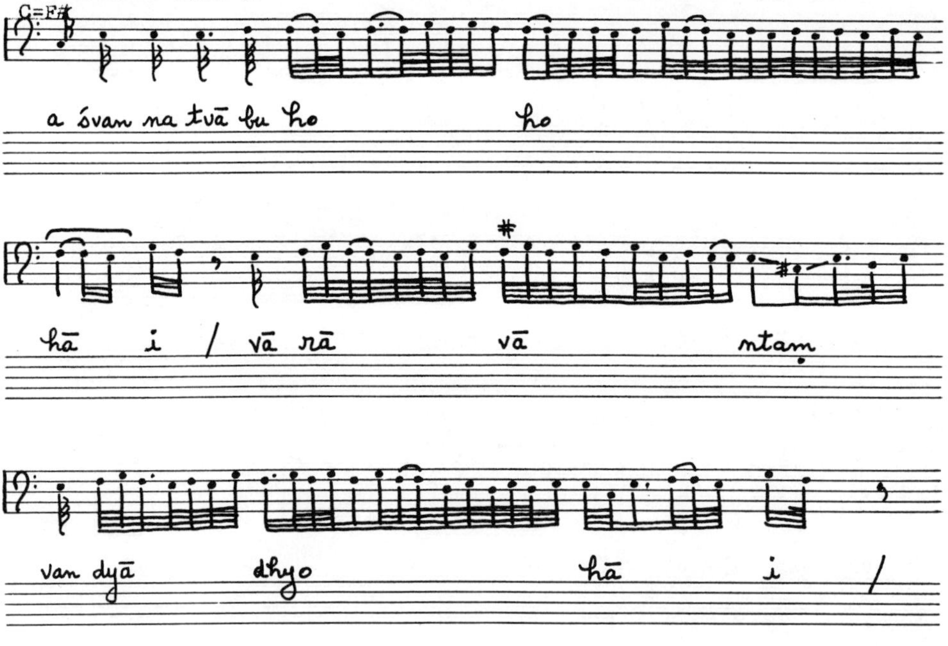
a śvan na tvā bu ho ho
hā i / vā rā vā ntaṃ
van dyā dhyo hā i /

JGG from JS 1.1.2.7 (cont.) T. Rajagopala Aiyangar

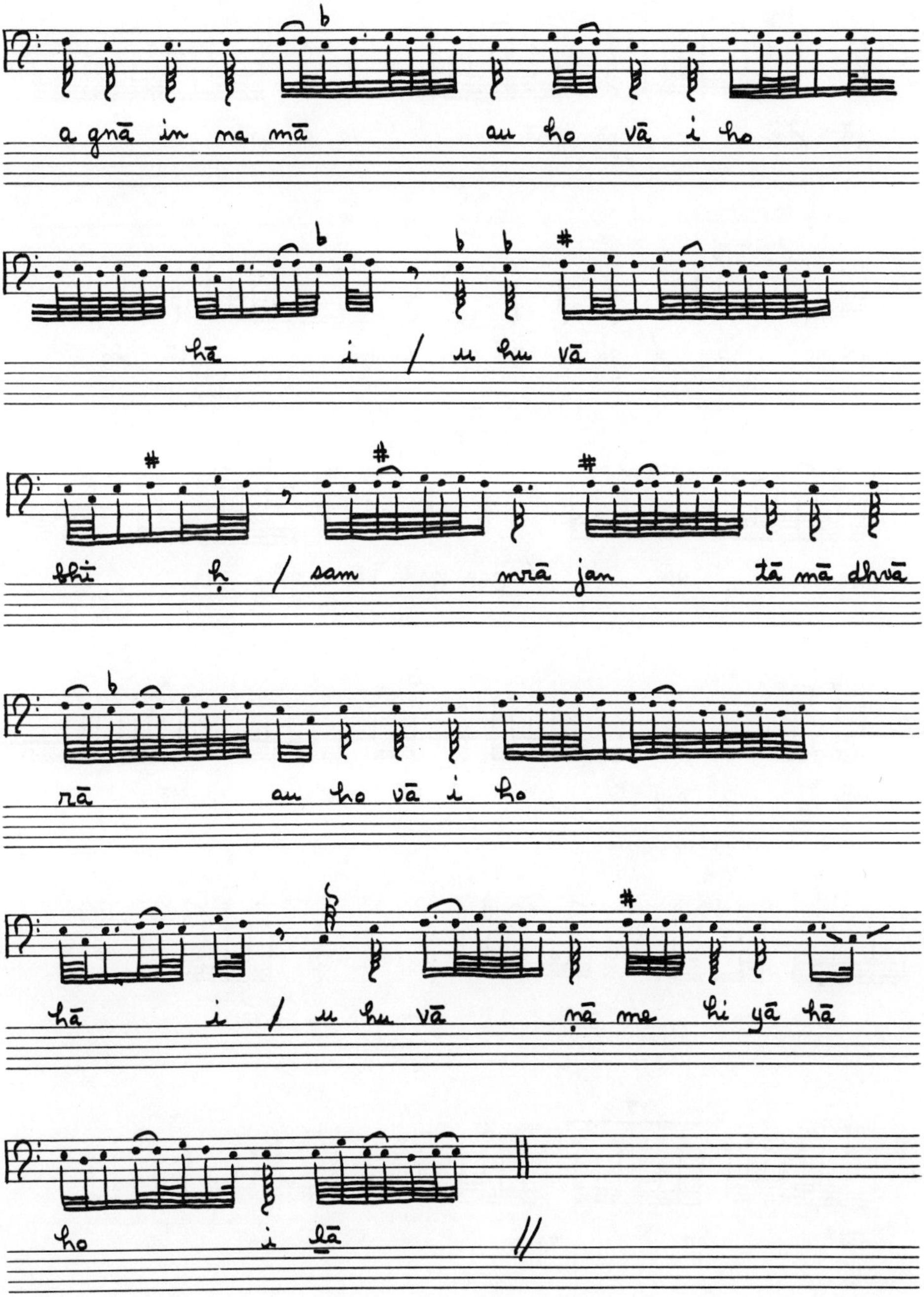

Tape IVb(5)
JGG from JS 1.1.4.1 ♪=96 T. Rajagopala Aiyangar

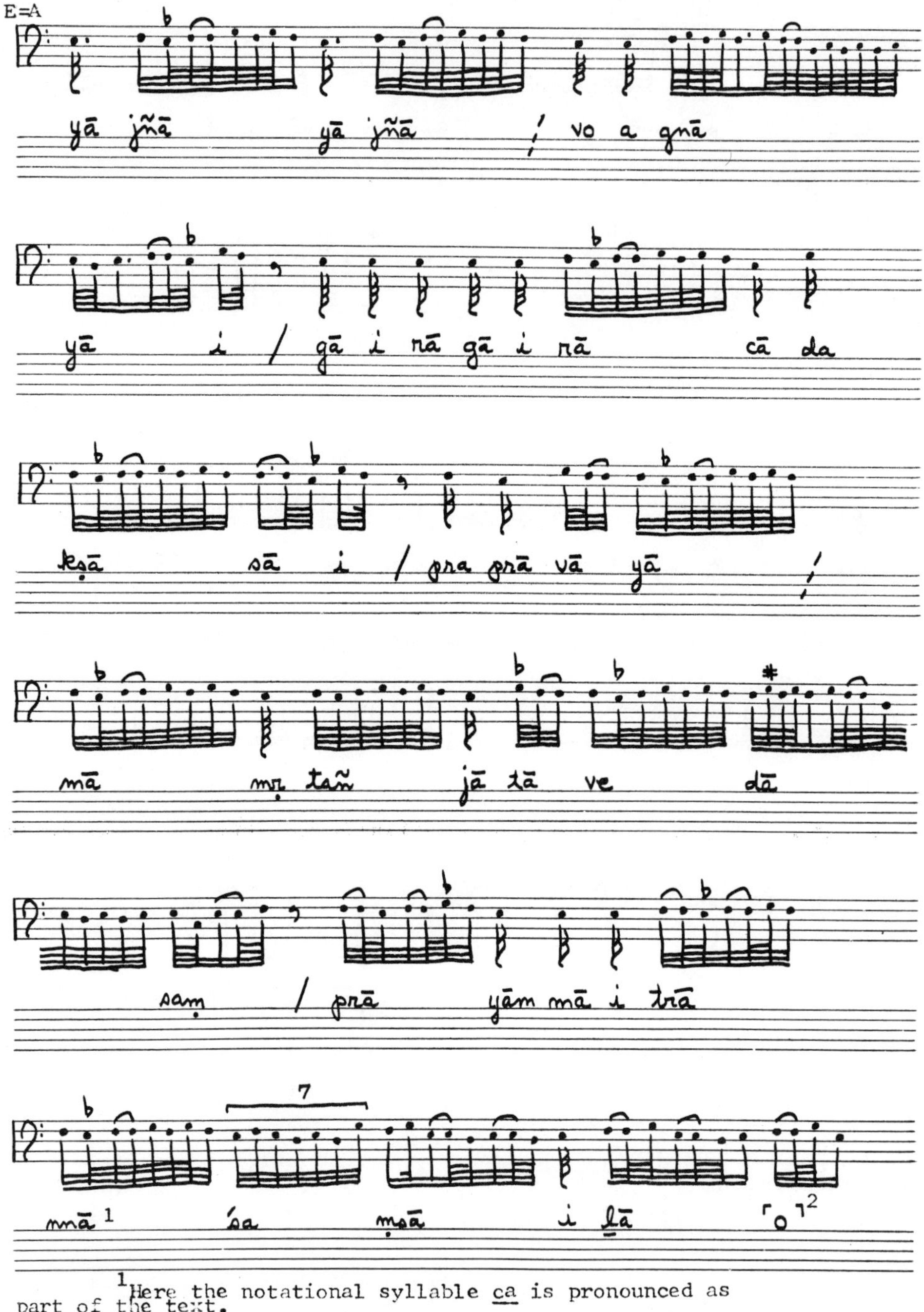
E=A
yā jñā yā jñā / vo a gnā
yā i / gā i rā gā i rā cā da
kṣā sā i / pra prā vā yā /
mā mṛ tañ jā tā ve dā
saṃ / prā yām mā i trā
mā 1 śa mṣā i lā ⌜o⌝ 2
7

[1] Here the notational syllable ca is pronounced as part of the text.

[2] Absent in the chanter's manuscript.

JGG from JS 1.1.4.1 (cont.) T. Rajagopala Aiyangar

Tape IVb(5)
JGG from JS 1.1.4.1 ♪=96 T. Rajagopala Aiyangar
E=A

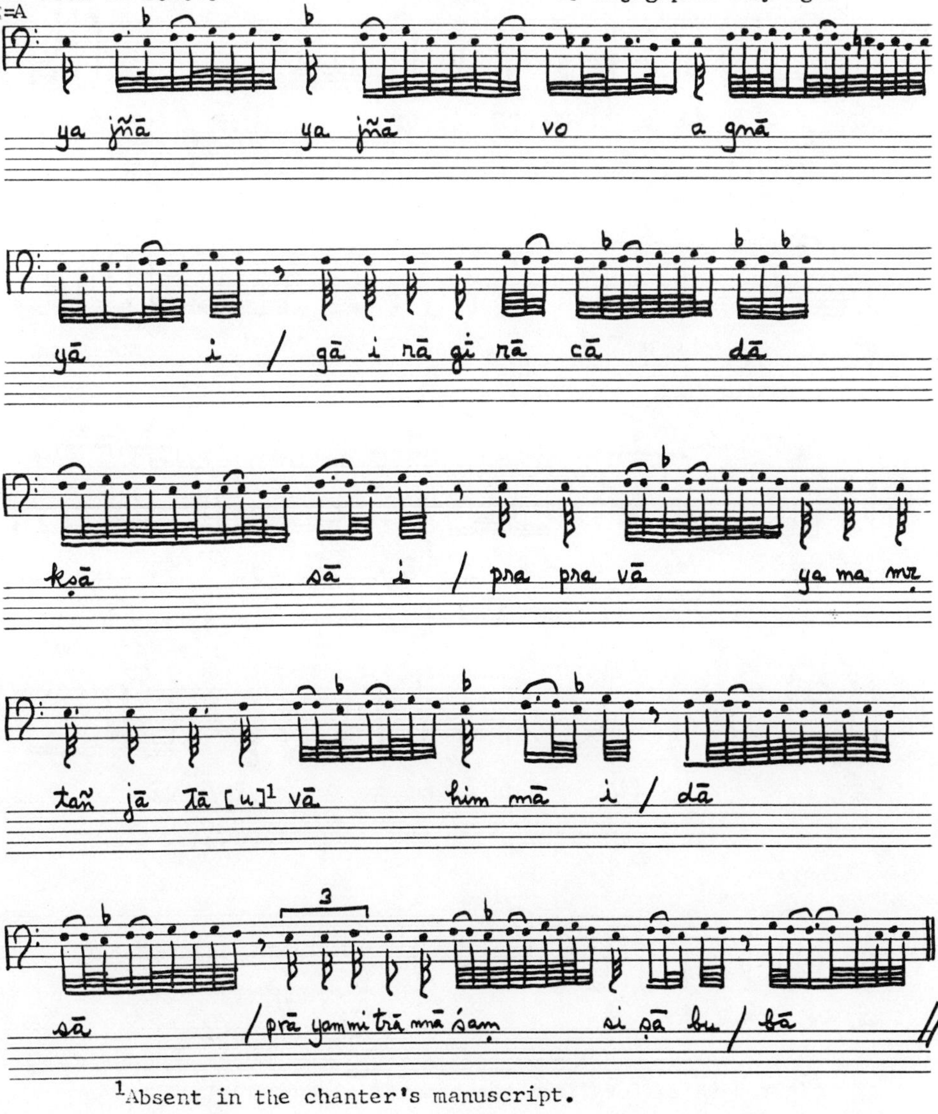

[1]Absent in the chanter's manuscript.

Tape IVb(6)
JGG from JS 1.1.4.2 ♪ = 96 T. Rajagopala Aiyangar

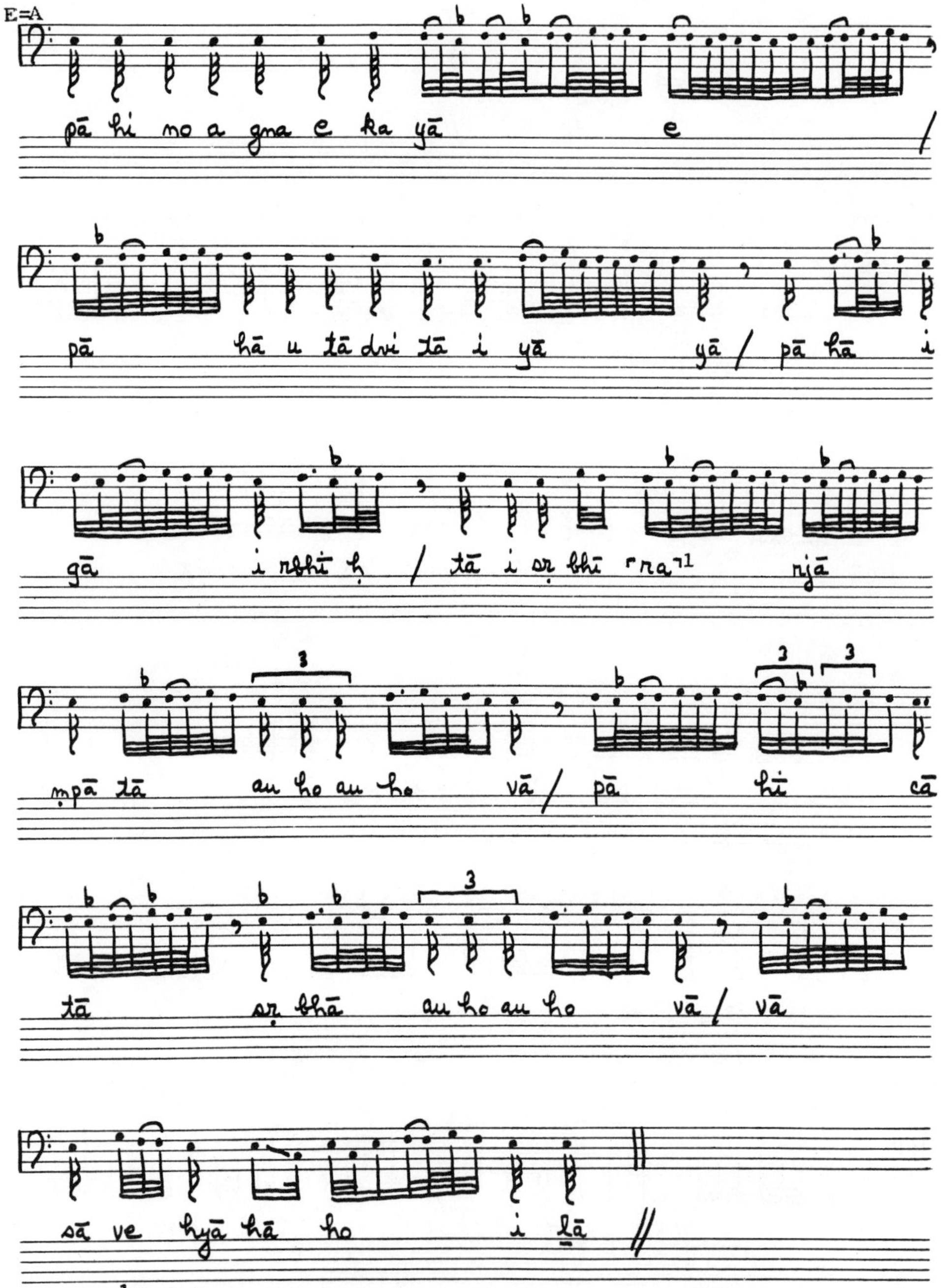

[1]Text here differs from the chanter's manuscript.

Tape IVb(6)
JGG from JS 1.1.4.2

♪ = 96

T. Rajagopala Aiyangar

E=A

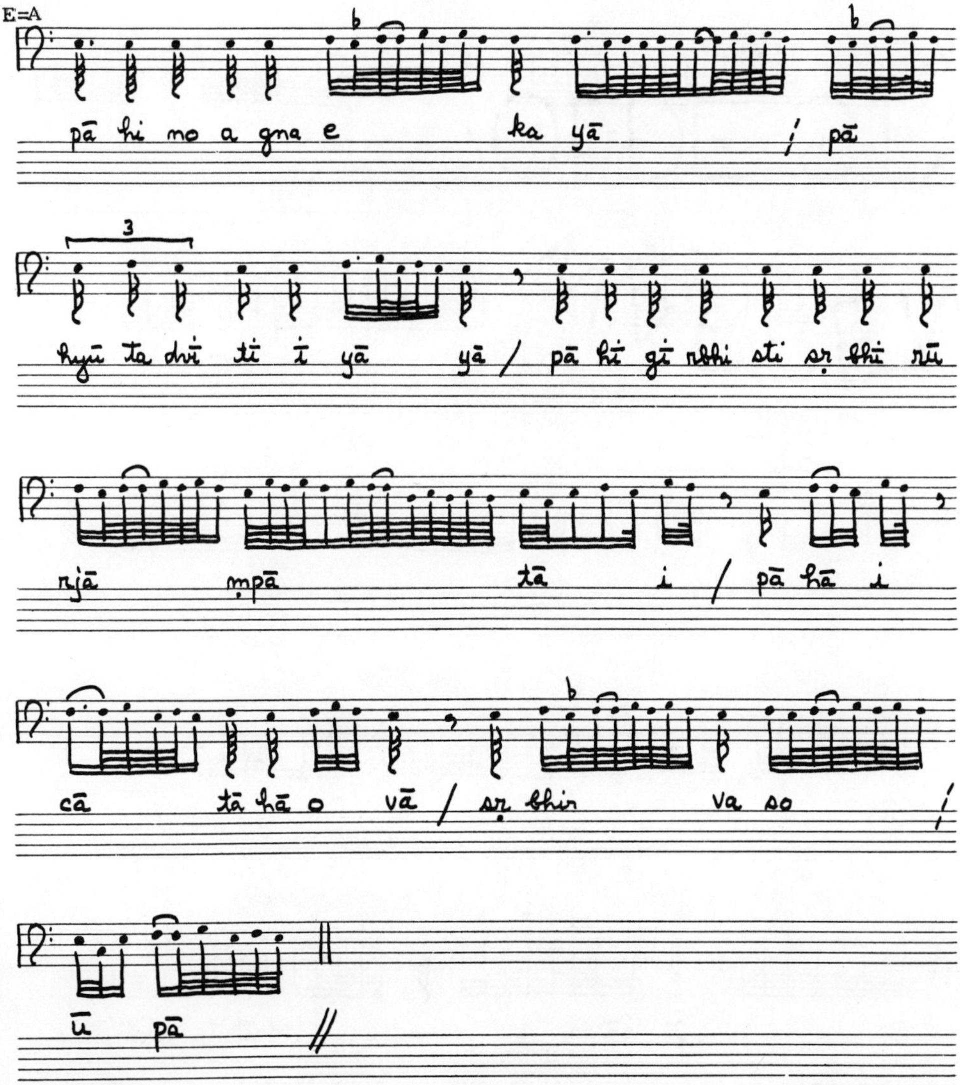

Tape IVb(7)
JGG from JS 1.2.2.1.1

♪ = 96

T. Rajagopala Aiyangar

E=A

JGG from JS 1.2.2.1.1 (cont.) T. Rajagopala Aiyangar

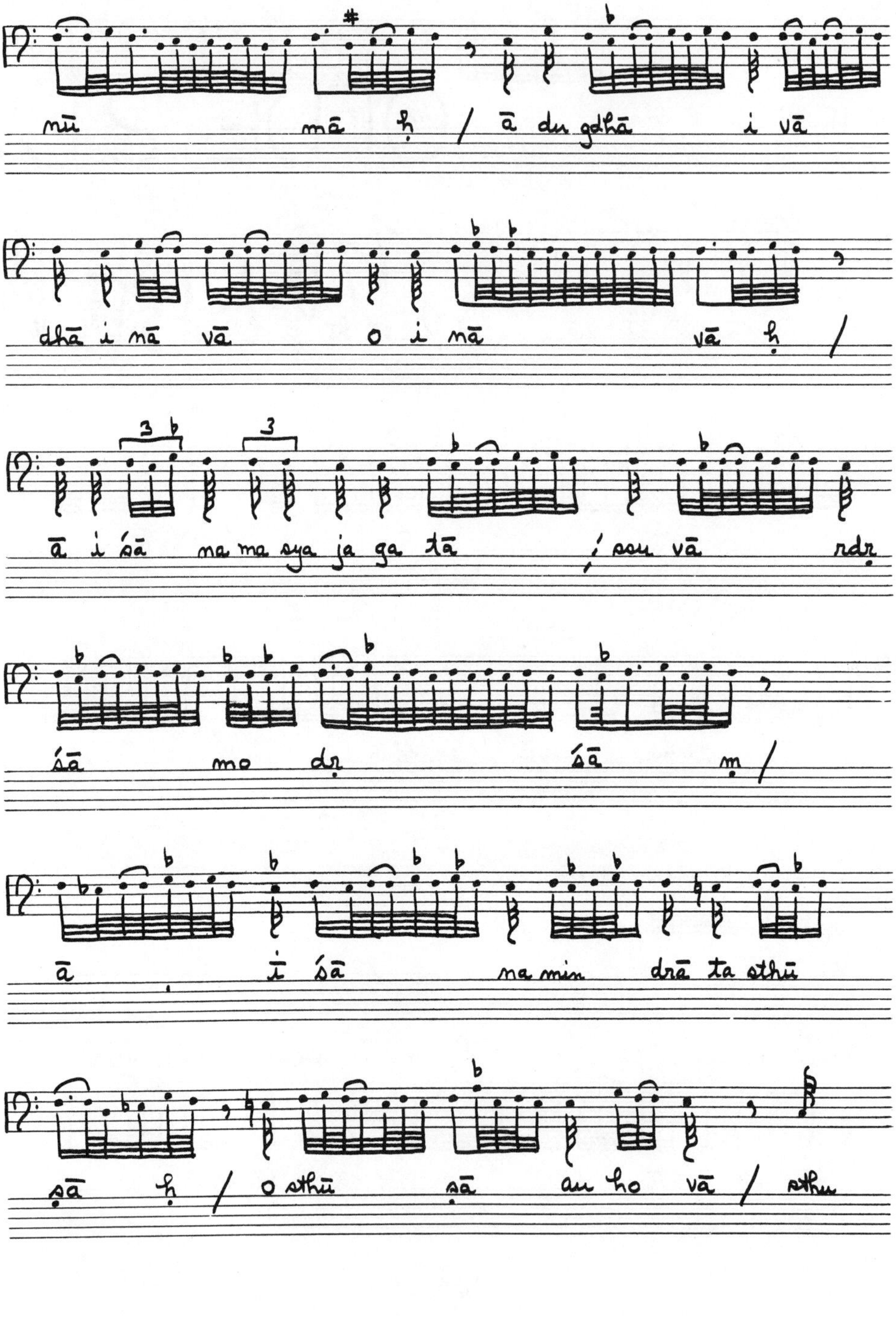

JGG from JS 1.2.2.1.1 (cont.) T. Rajagopala Aiyangar

Tape IVb(7) ♪= 96 T. Rajagopala Aiyangar
JGG from JS 1.2.2.1.1
E=A

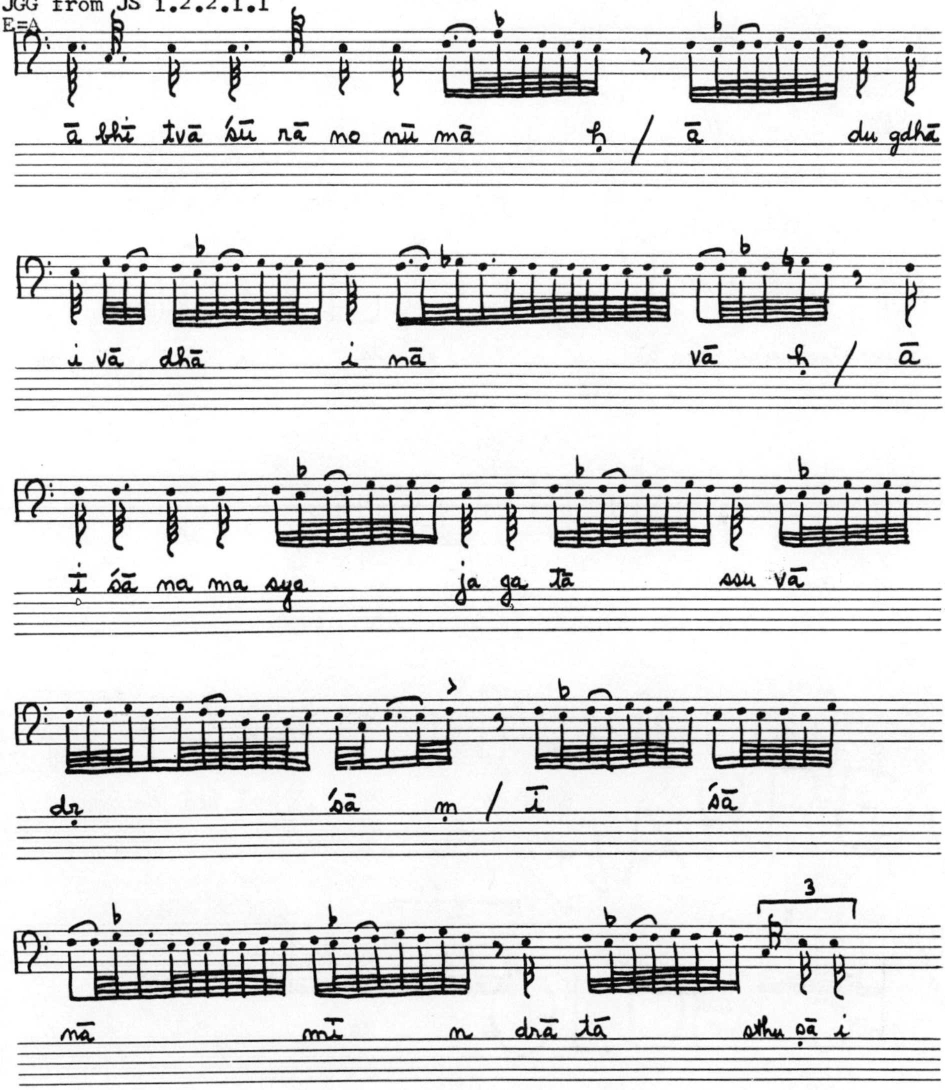

JGG from JS 1.2.2.1.1 (cont.) T. Rajagopala Aiyangar

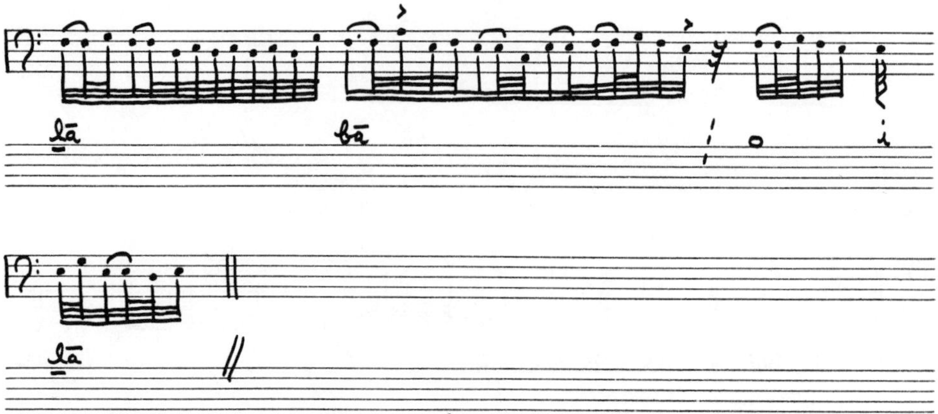

Tape IVb(8) T. Rajagopala Aiyangar
JGG from JS 1.2.3.5.1
E=A

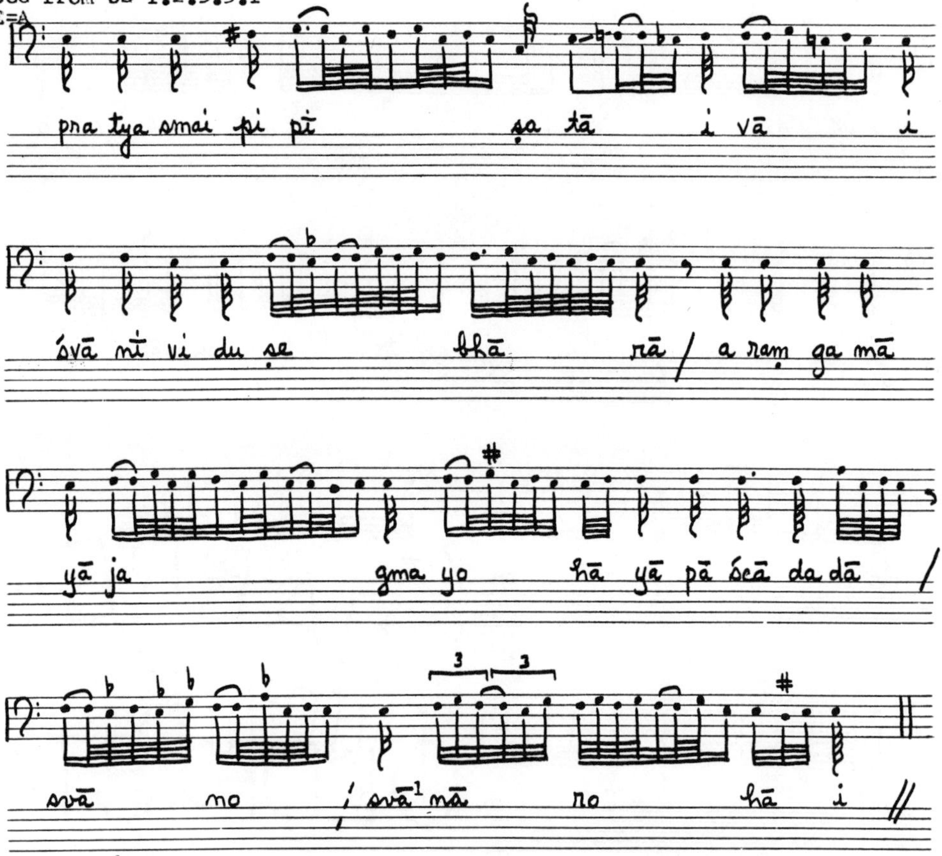

[1]Manuscript: bā.

Tape IVb(9)
JGG from JS 1.2.4.10.5 ♪ = 96 T. Rajagopala Aiyangar
E=A

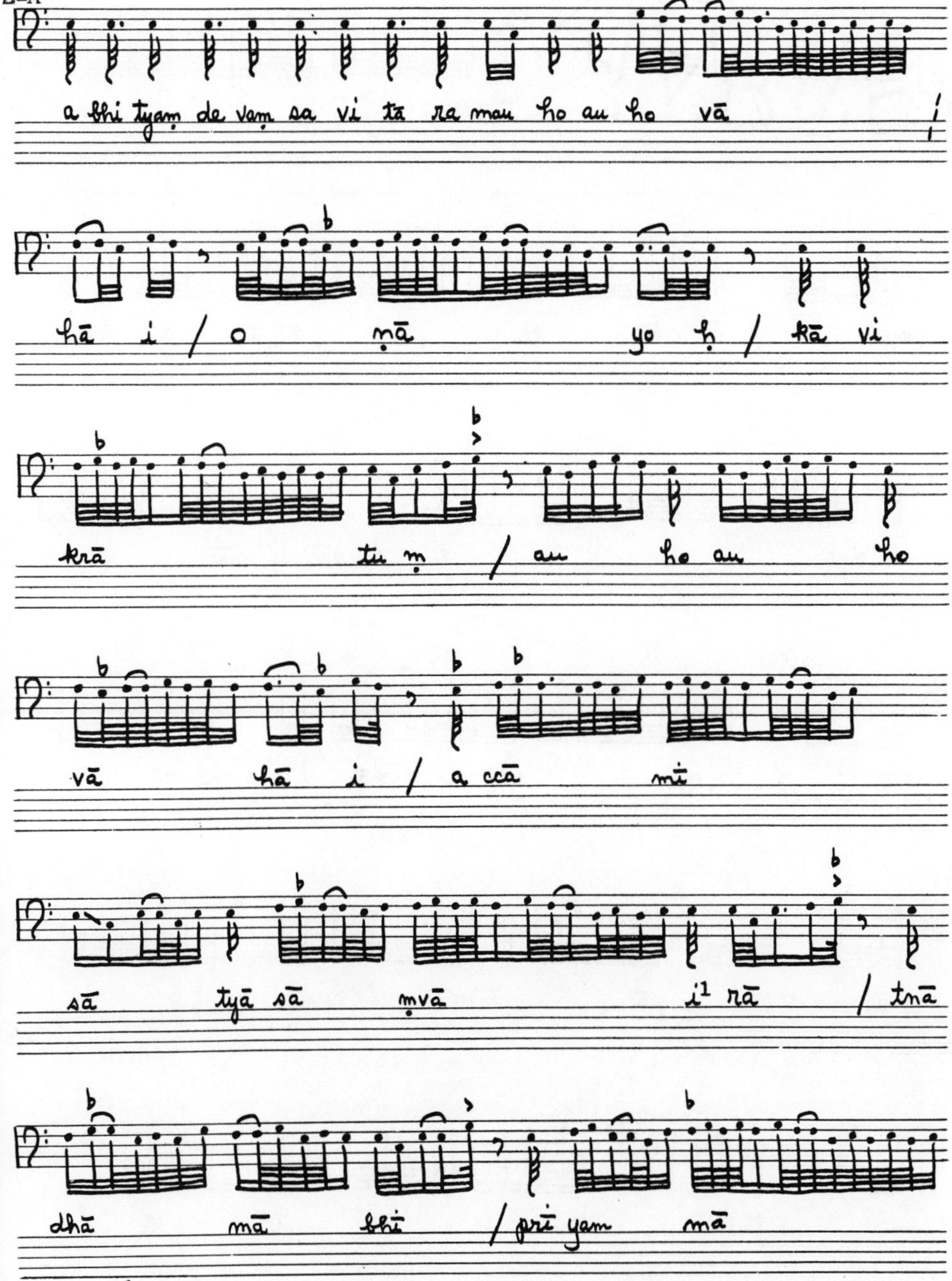

[1]Absent in the chanter's manuscript.

JGG from JS 1.2.4.10.5 (cont.) T. Rajagopala Aiyangar

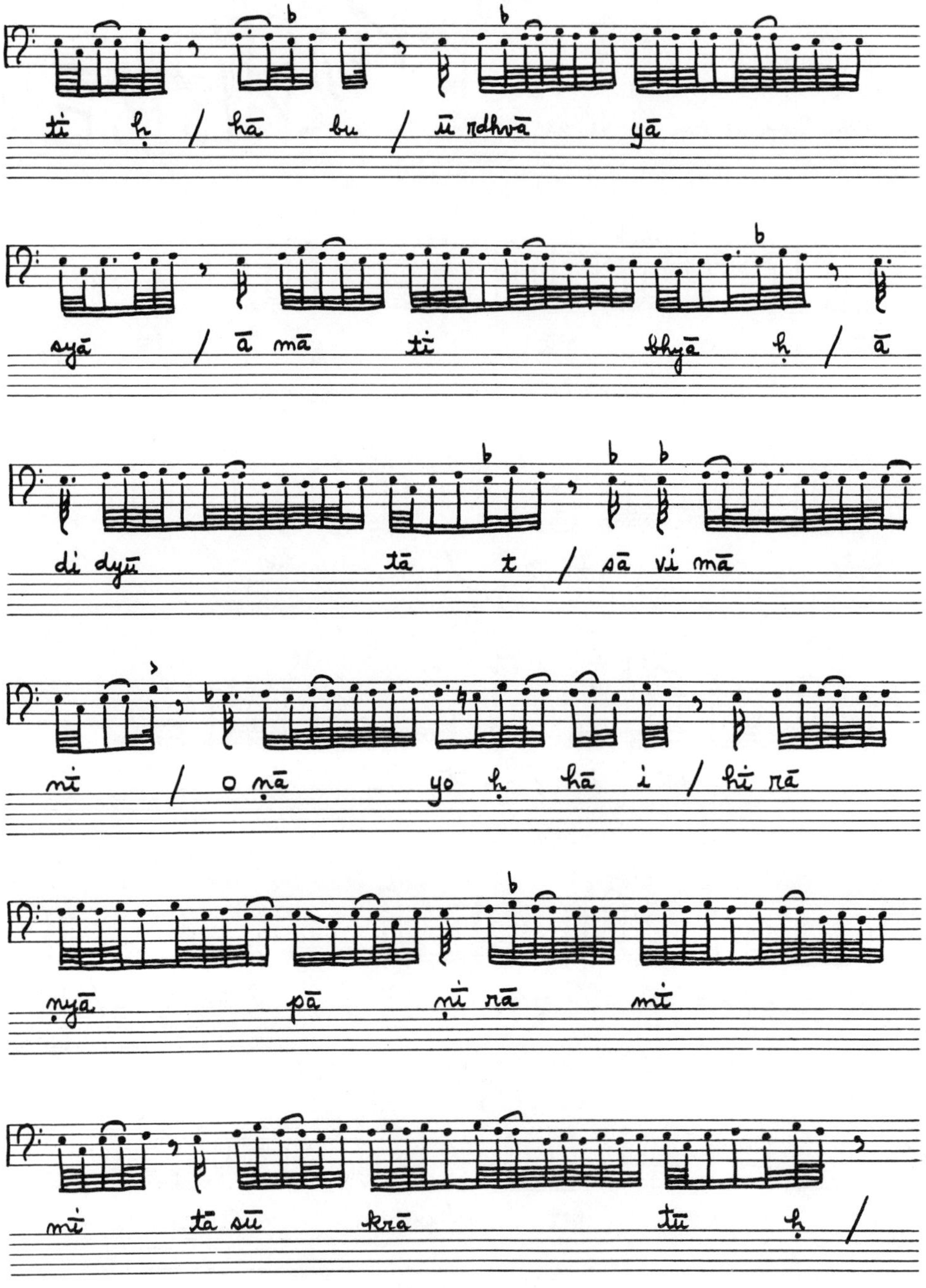

JGG from JS 1.2.4.10.5 (cont.) T. Rajagopala Aiyangar

hā u vā
e
kṛ pā
svā
ḥ

Tape IVb(10) T. Rajagopala Aiyangar
JGG from JS 1.3.1.1 ♪. = 96
D=G

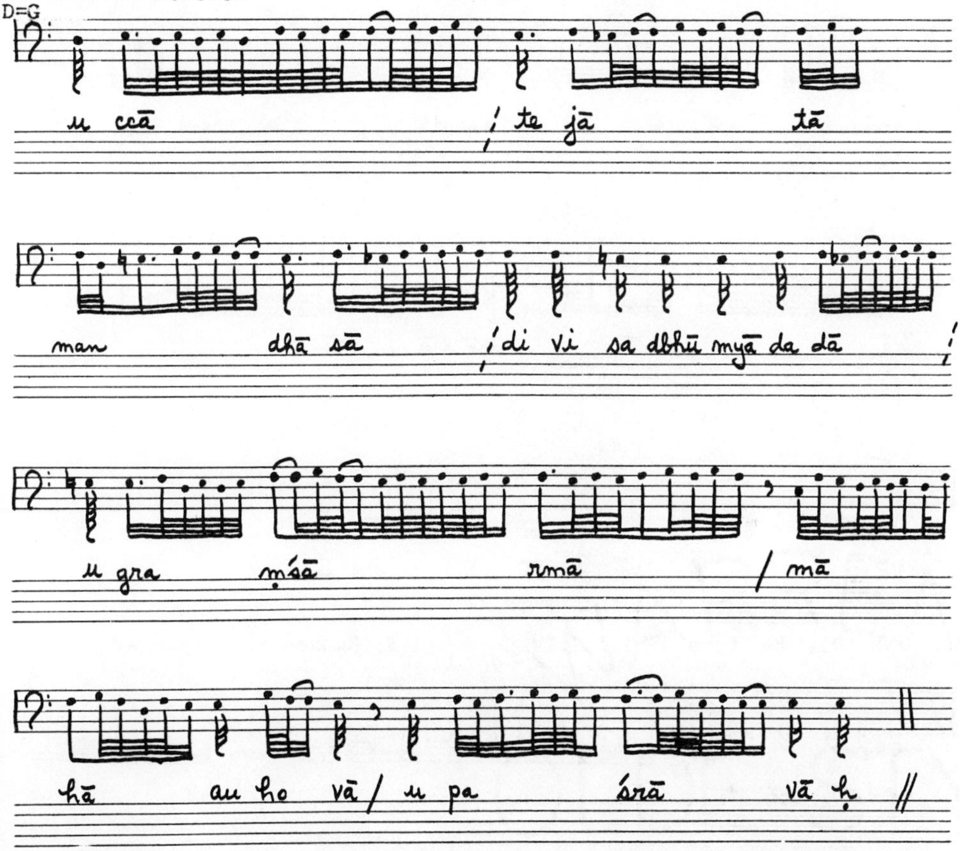
u ccā
te jā
tā
man
dhā sā
di vi sa dbhū myā da dā
u gra
ṃśā
rmā
mā
hā
au ho vā
u pa
śrā
vā ḥ

Tape IVb(10) T. Rajagopala Aiyangar
JGG from JS 1.3.1.1 ♪. = 96
E=A

u ccā te
jā
tā ma

JGG from JS 1.3.1.1 (cont.) T. Rajagopala Aiyangar

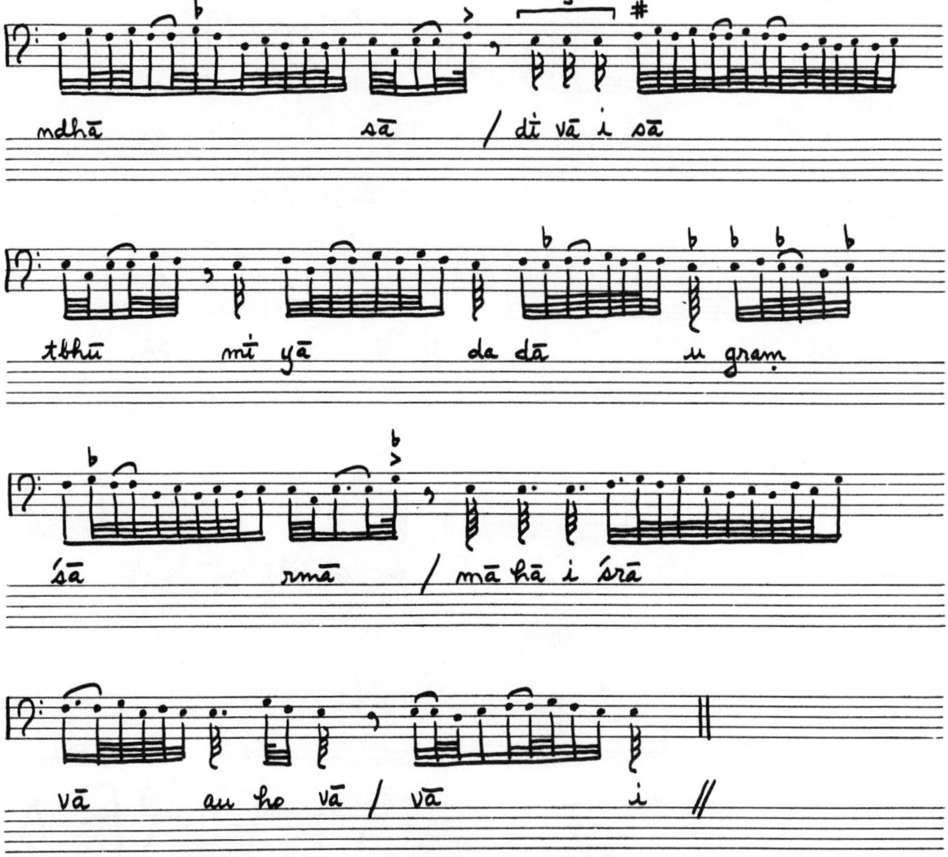
mdhā sā / di vā i sā
tbhū mi yā da dā u gram
śā rmā / mā hā i śrā
vā au ho vā / vā i //

Tape IVb(10); JGG from JS 1.3.1.1 ♪ = 96 T. Rajagopala Aiyangar
E=B♭

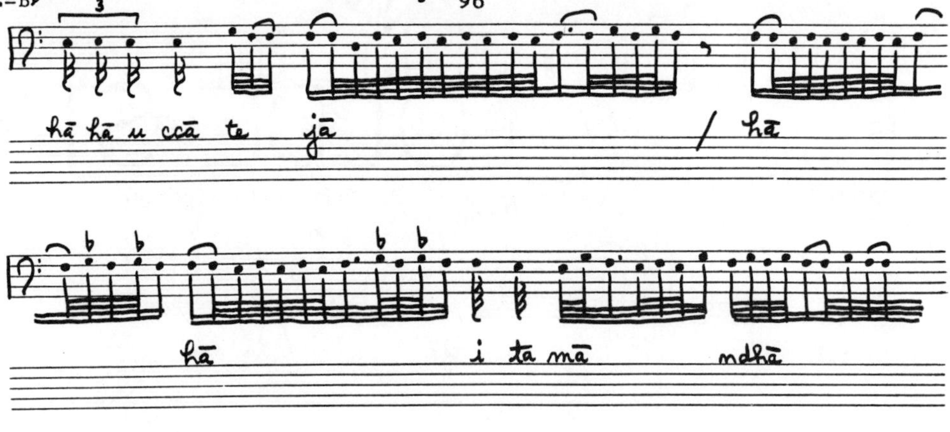
hā hā u ccā te jā / hā
hā i ta mā mdhā

JGG from JS 1.3.1.1 (cont.) T. Rajagopala Aiyangar

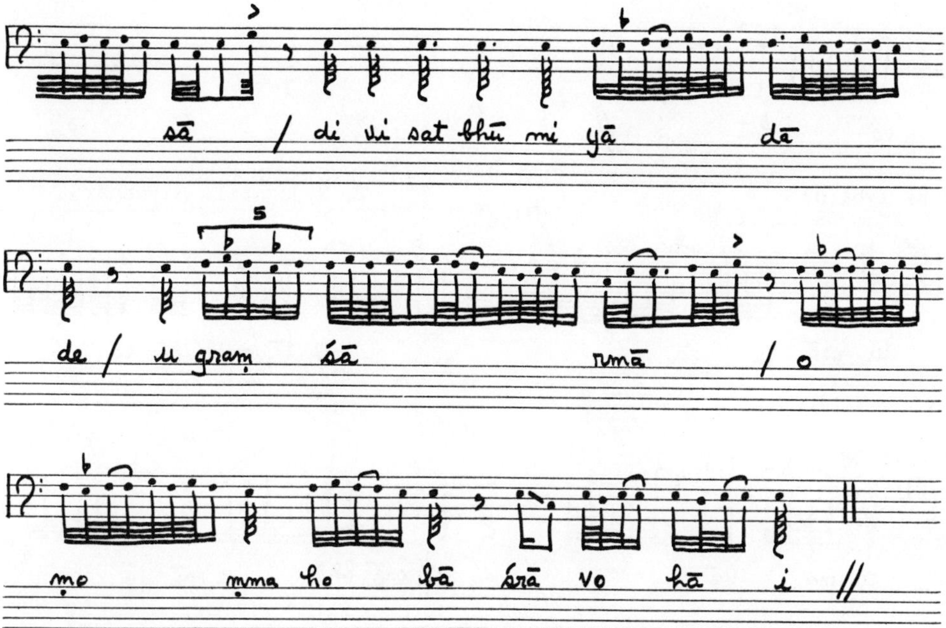

Tape IVb(10) ♪=96 T. Rajagopala Aiyangar
JGG from JS 1.3.1.1
F=B

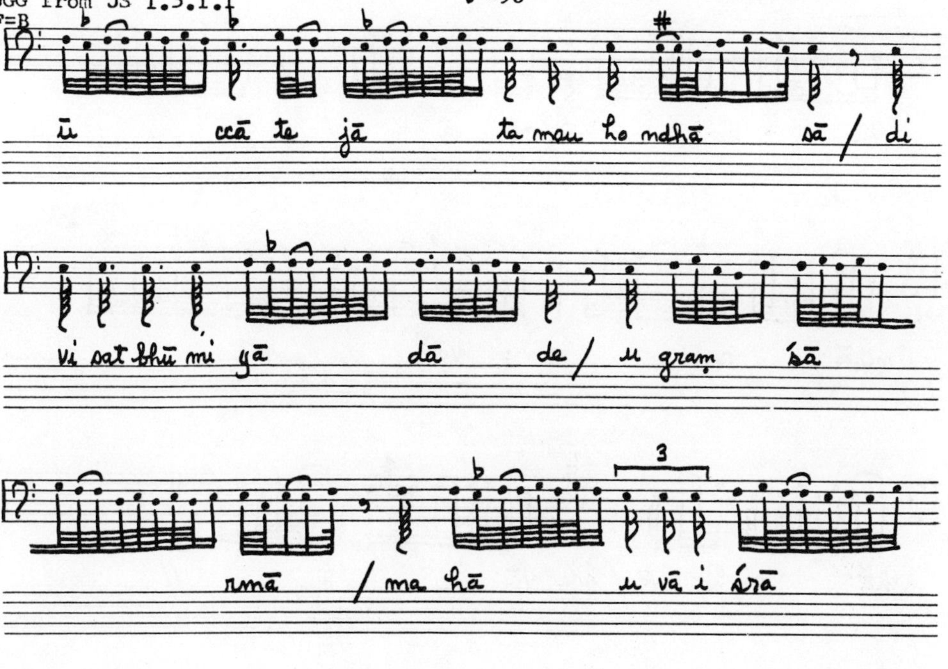

JGG from JS 1.3.1.1 (cont.) T. Rajagopala Aiyangar

Tape IVb(10) T. Rajagopala Aiyangar
JGG from JS 1.3.1.1
C=F#

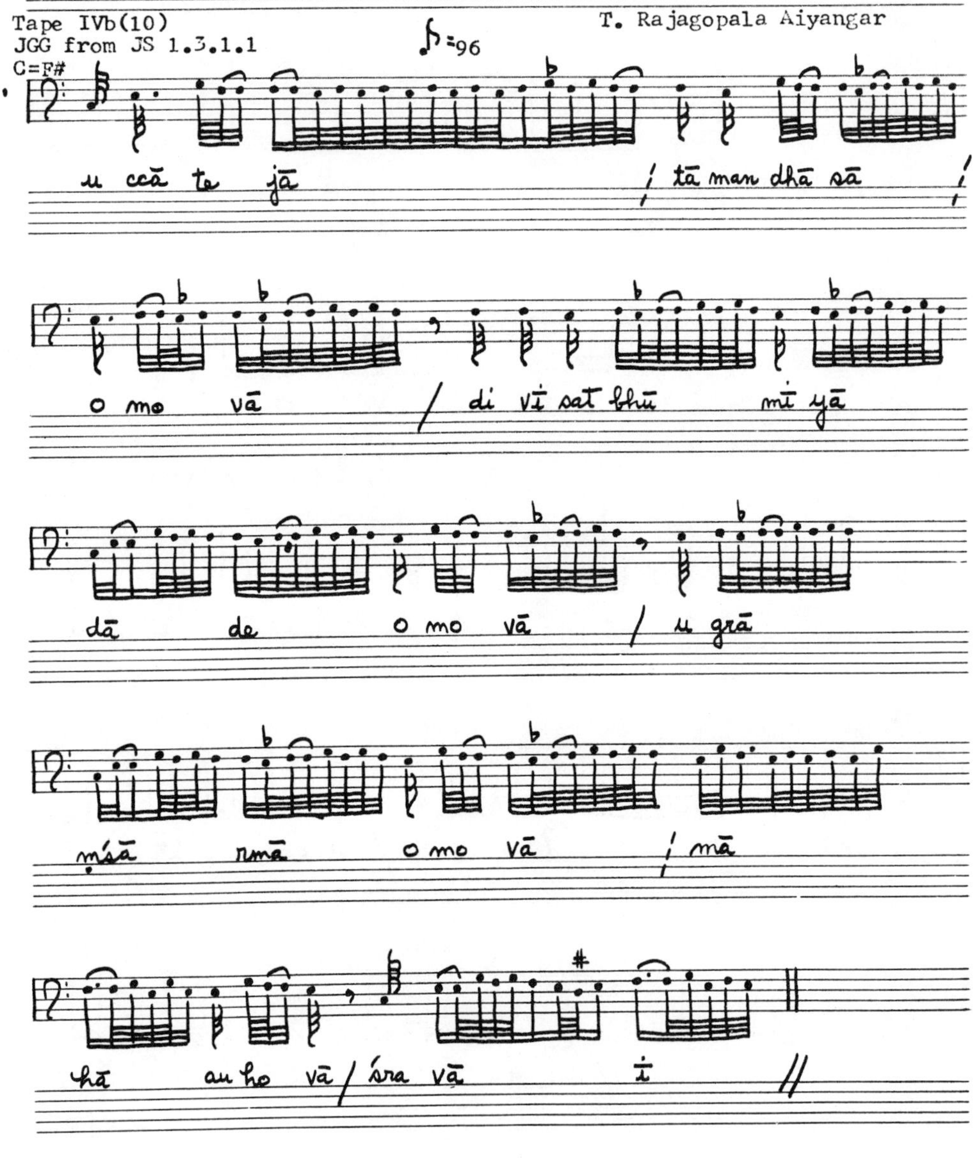

Tape IVb(10)
JGG from JS 1.3.1.1
E=B♭

♪ = 96

T. Rajagopala Aiyangar

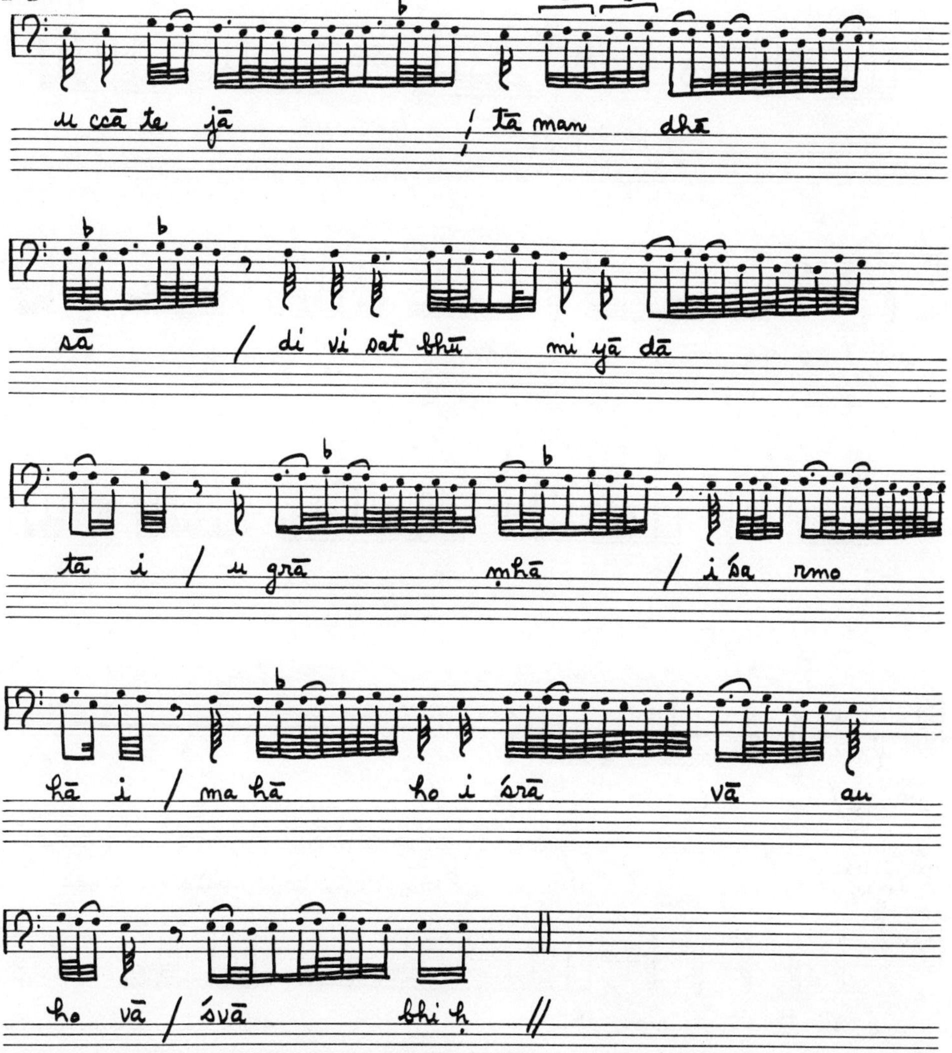

Tape IVb(10)
JGG from JS 1.3.1.1
E=B♭

♪ = 96

T. Rajagopala Aiyangar

JGG from JS 1.3.1.1 (cont.) T. Rajagopala Aiyangar

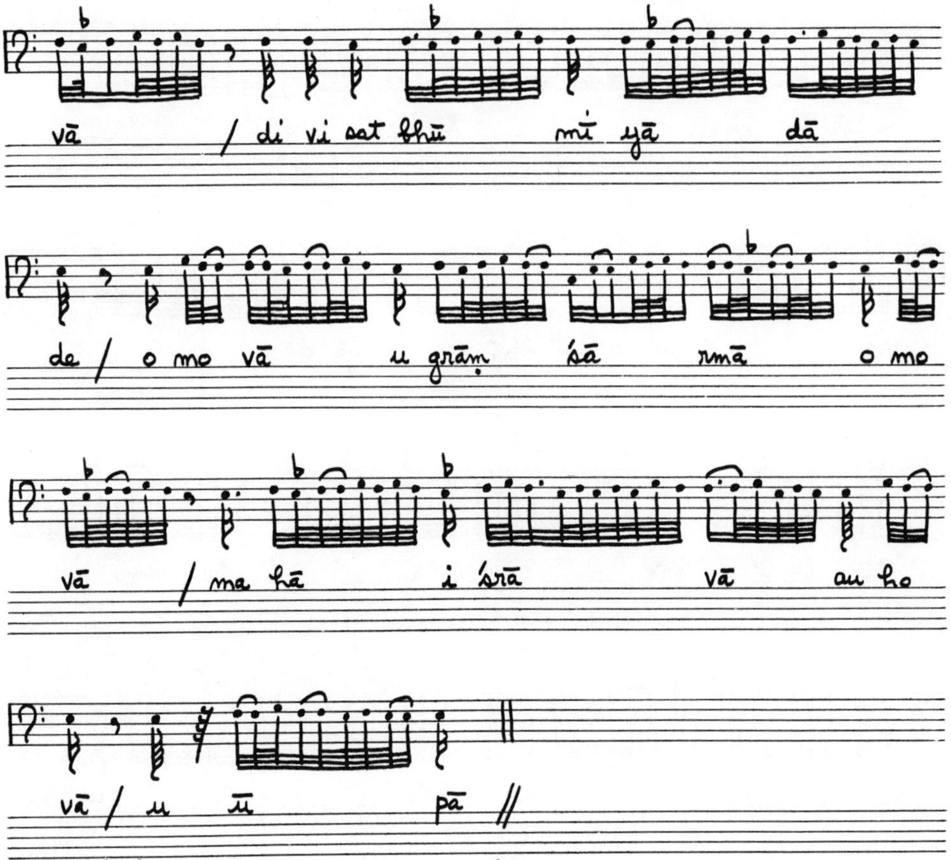
vā / di vi sat bhū mī yā dā
de / o mo vā u grām śā rmā o mo
vā / ma hā i śrā vā au ho
vā / u ū pā //

Tape IVb(10)
JGG from JS 1.3.1.1 ♪= 96 T. Rajagopala Aiyangar
C=F

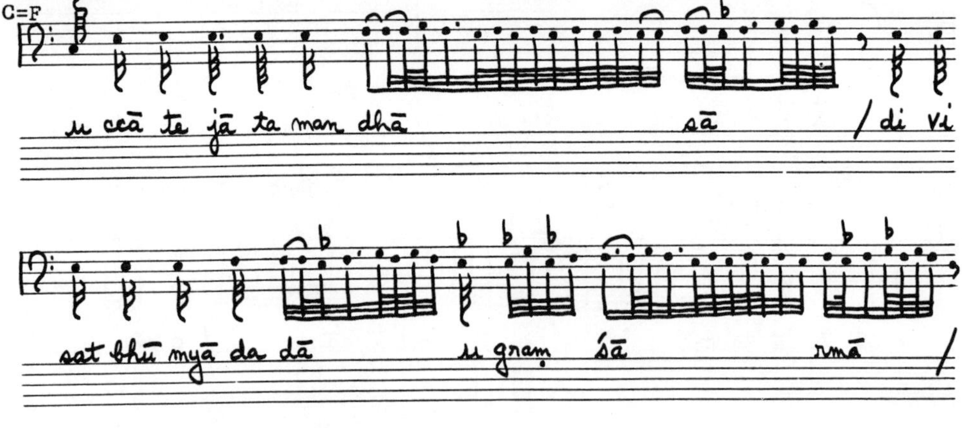
u ccā te jā ta man dhā sā / di vi
sat bhū myā da dā u gram śā rmā /

JGG from JS 1.3.1.1 (cont.) T. Rajagopala Aiyangar

Tape IVb(10)
JGG from JS 1.3.1.1 ♪=96 T. Rajagopala Aiyangar
E=B♭

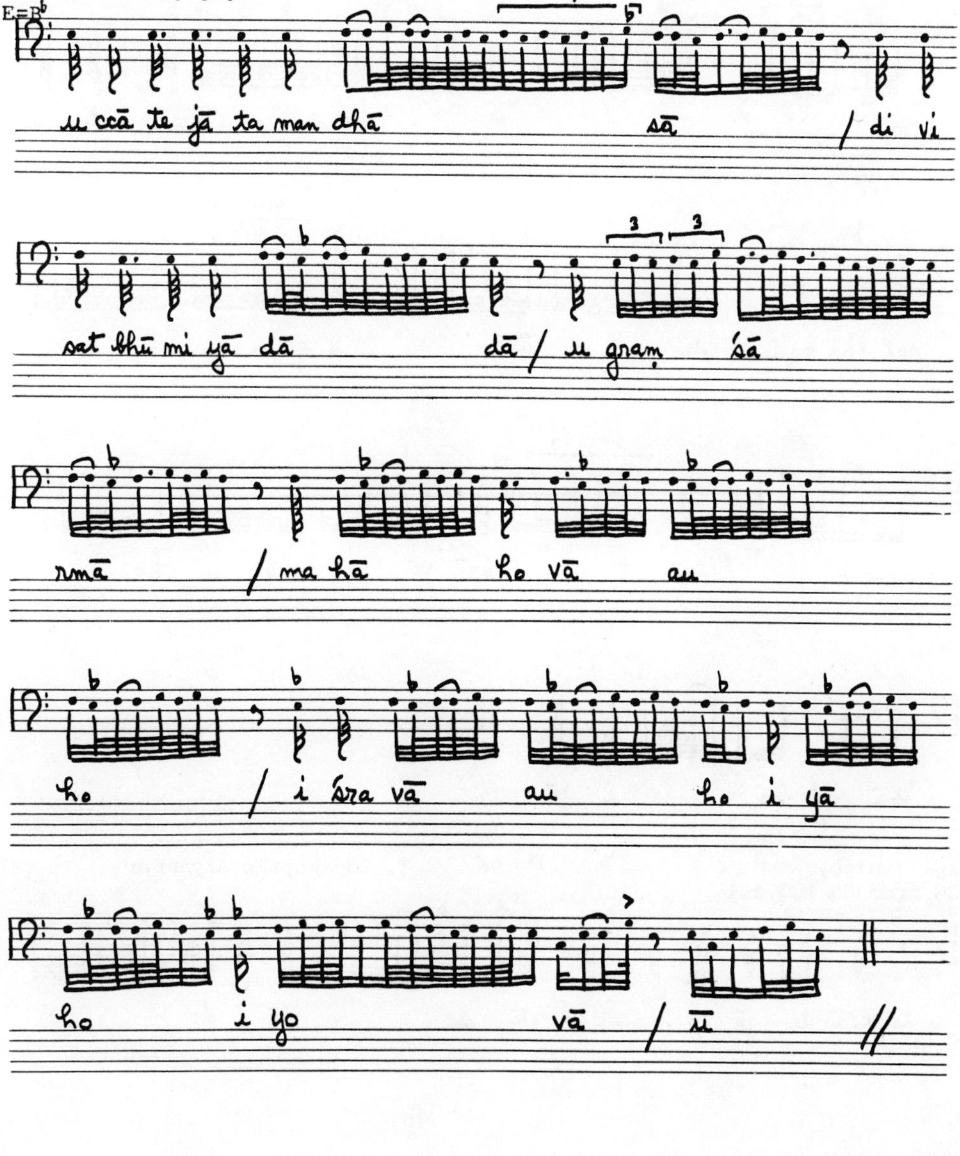

Tape IVb(10)
JGG from JS 1.3.1.1
C=F#

♪ = 96

T. Rajagopala Aiyangar

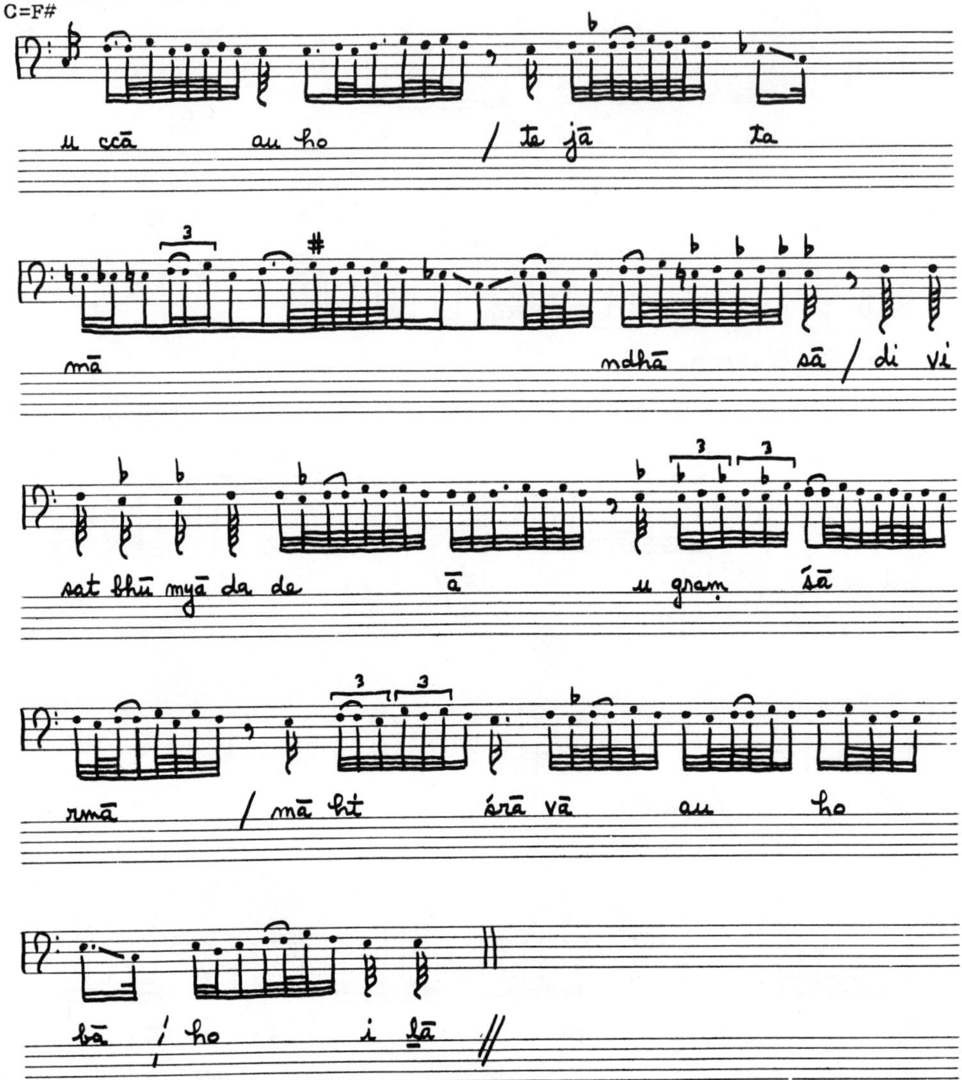

u ccā au ho / te jā ta
mā ndhā sā / di vi
sat bhū myā da de ā u gram śā
rmā / mā ht śrā vā au ho
bā / ho i lā //

Tape IVb(10)
JGG from JS 1.3.1.1
C=F

♪ = 96

T. Rajagopala Aiyangar

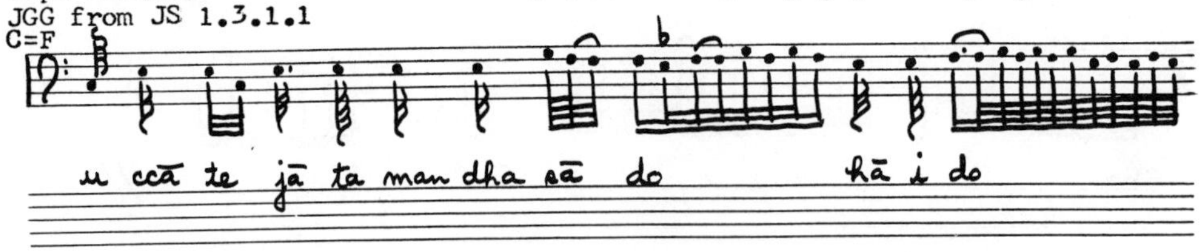

u ccā te jā ta man dha sā do hā i do

JGG from JS 1.3.1.1 (cont.)   T. Rajagopala Aiyangar

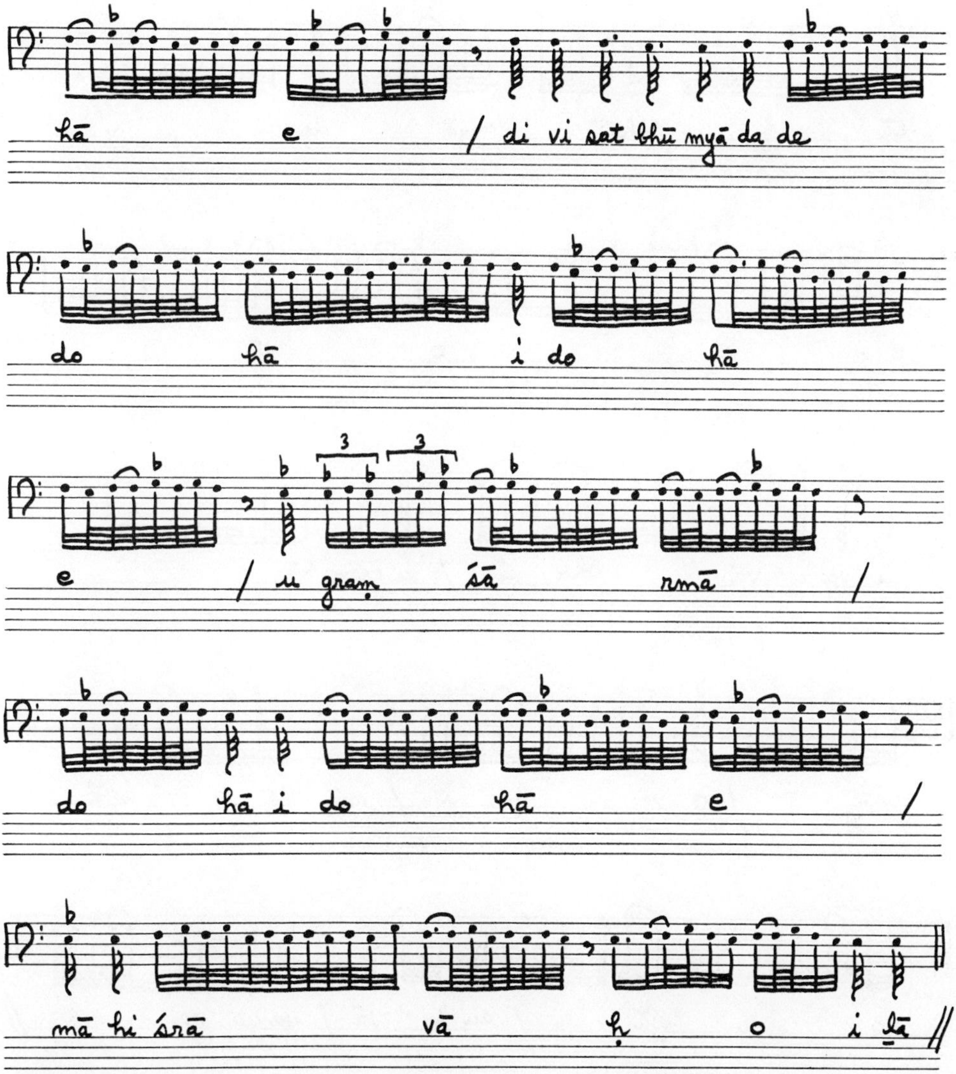

Tape IVb(10)
JGG from JS 1.3.1.1
E=B♭

♪ = 96   T. Rajagopala Aiyangar

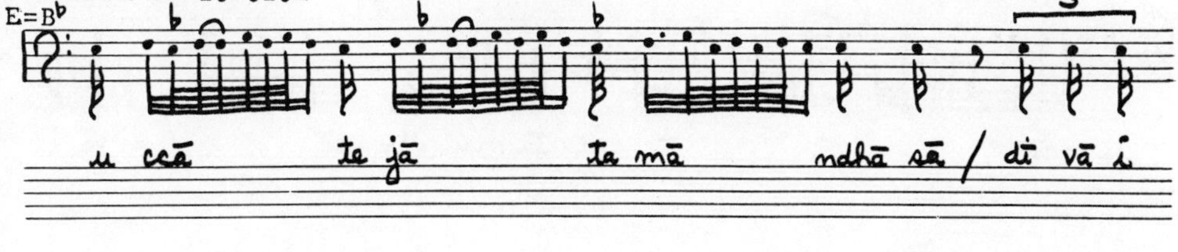

JGG from JS 1.3.1.1 (cont.) T. Rajagopala Aiyangar

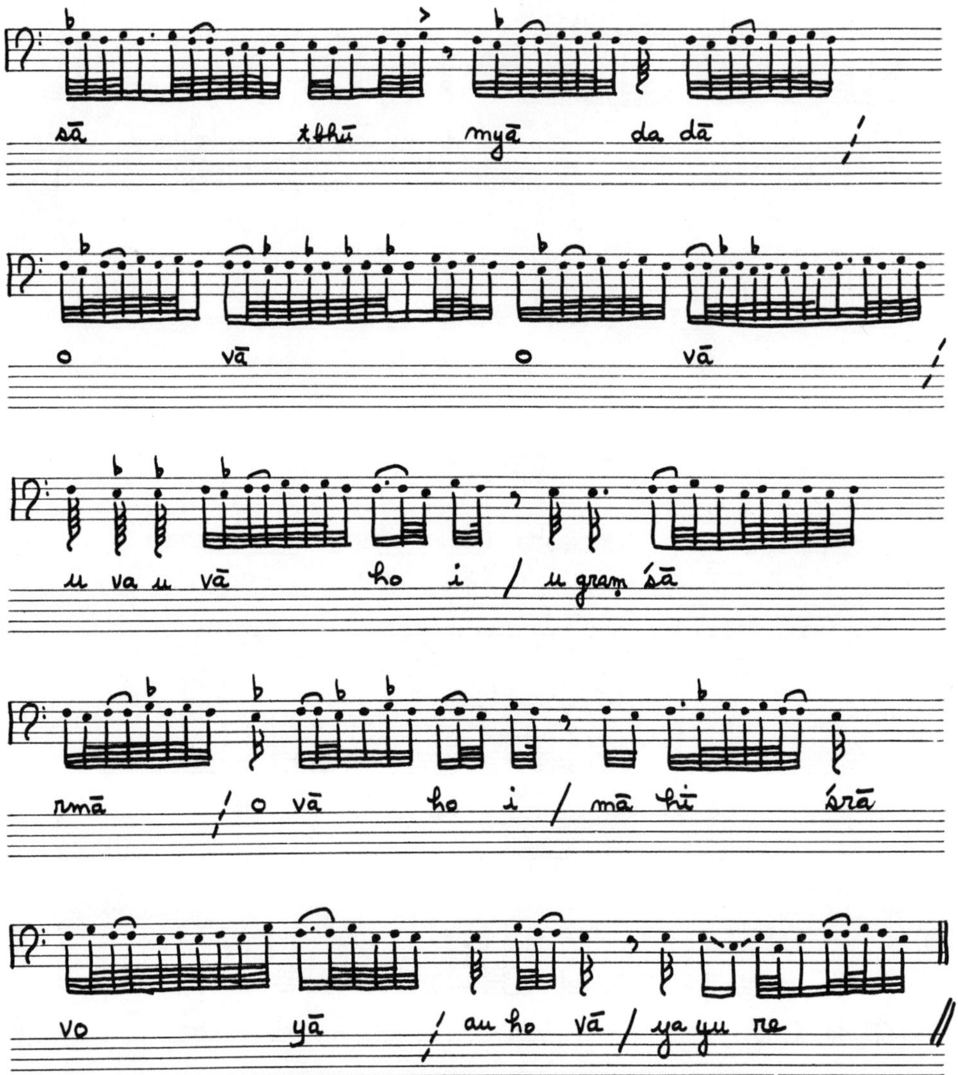

Tape IVb(10) T. Rajagopala Aiyangar
JGG from JS 1.3.1.1
C=F#

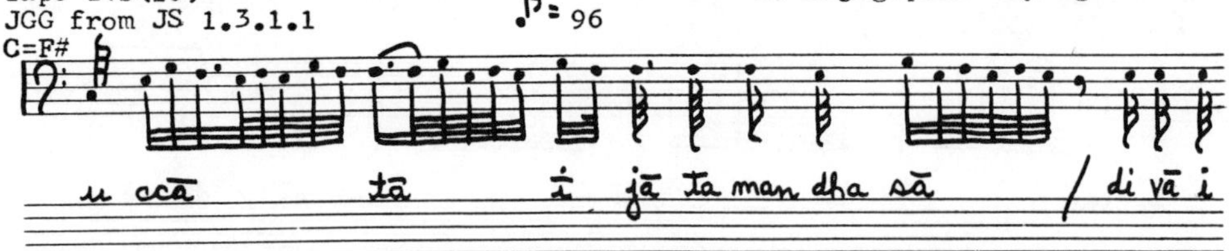

JGG from JS 1.3.1.1 (cont.) T. Rajagopala Aiyangar

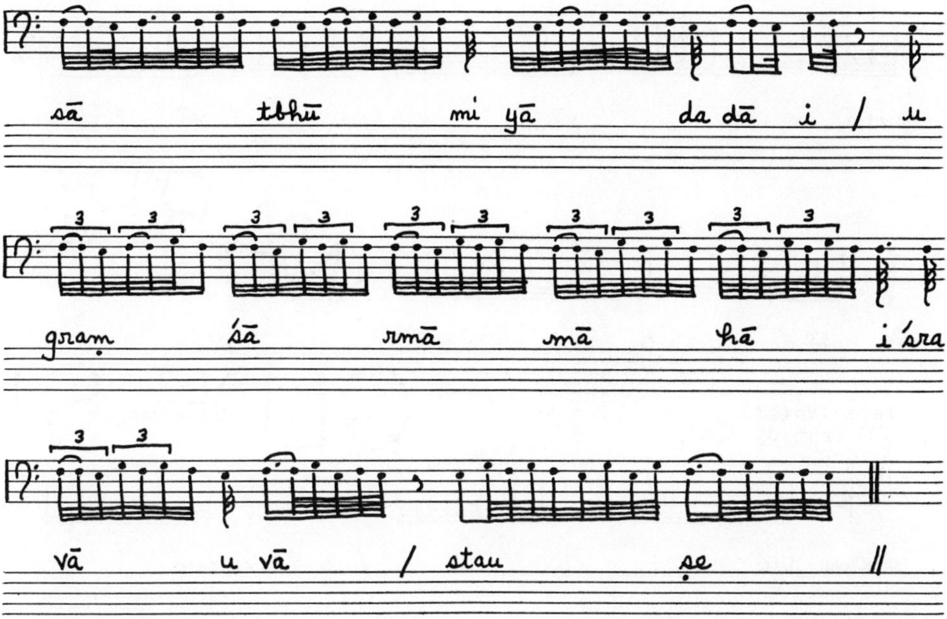

Tape IVb(12)A
Jaiminīya Gāyatram ♪ = 84 T. Rajagopala Aiyangar
D=G

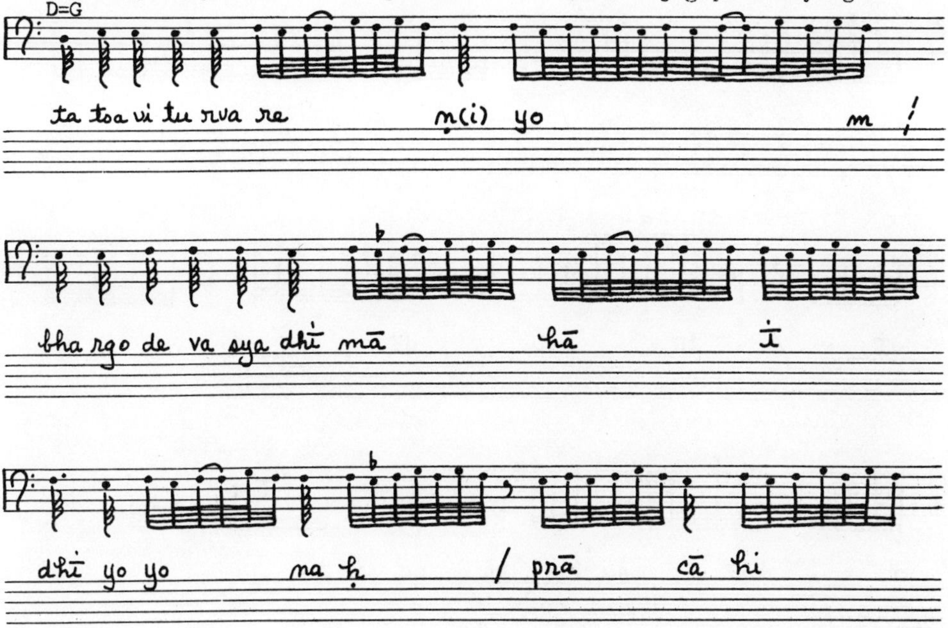

Jaiminīya Gāyatram (cont.)

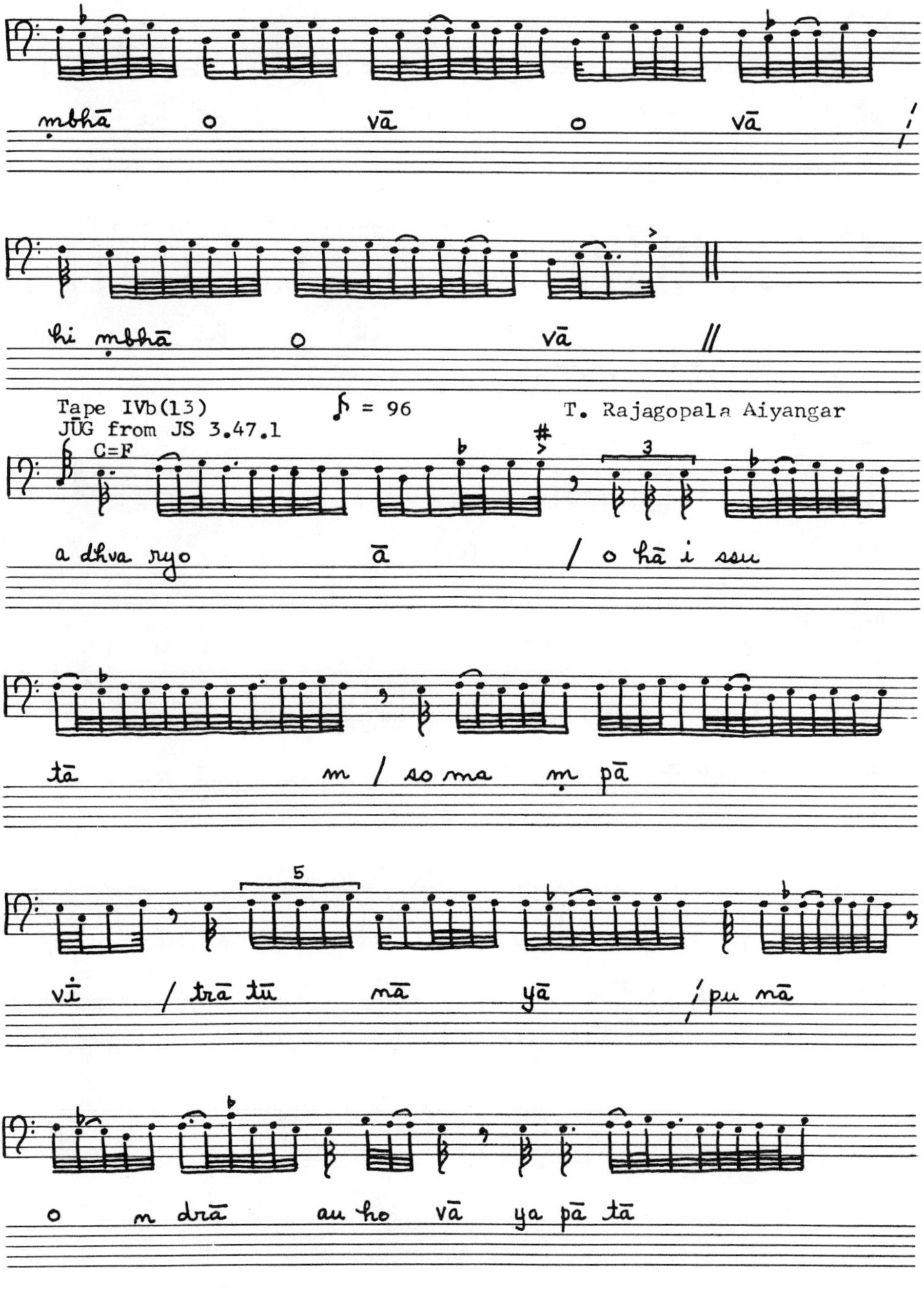
mbhā o vā o vā
hi mbhā o vā
Tape IVb(13)
JŪG from JS 3.47.1
= 96
T. Rajagopala Aiyangar
C=F
a dhva ryo ā / o hā i ssu
tā m / so ma m pā
vī / trā tū mā yā pu mā
o m drā au ho vā ya pā tā

JŪG from JS 3.47.1 (cont.) T. Rajagopala Aiyangar

Tape IVb(12)A ♪ = 96 T. Rajagopala Aiyangar
JRG on "utso devo hiranyayah . . ."

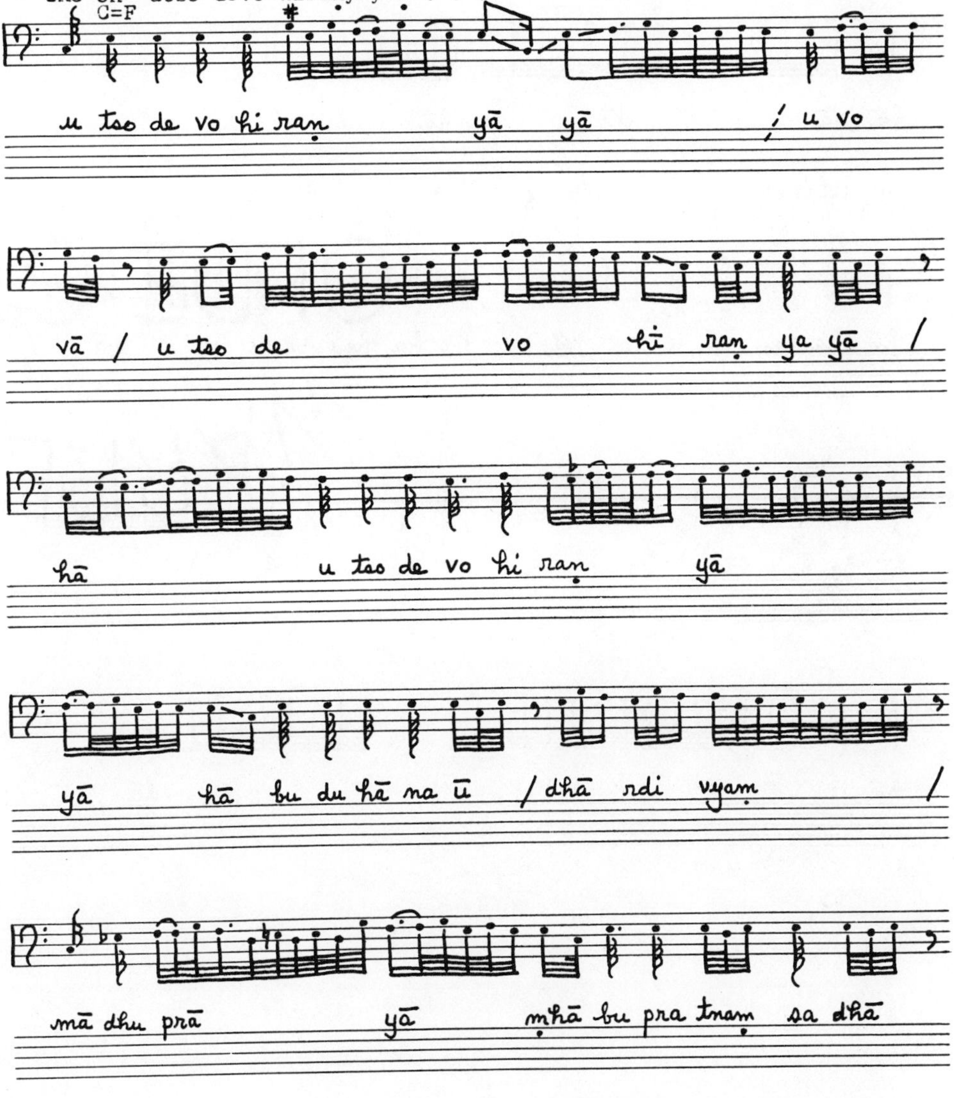

JRG on "utso devo hiranyayaḥ . . ." (cont.) T. Rajagopala Aiyangar

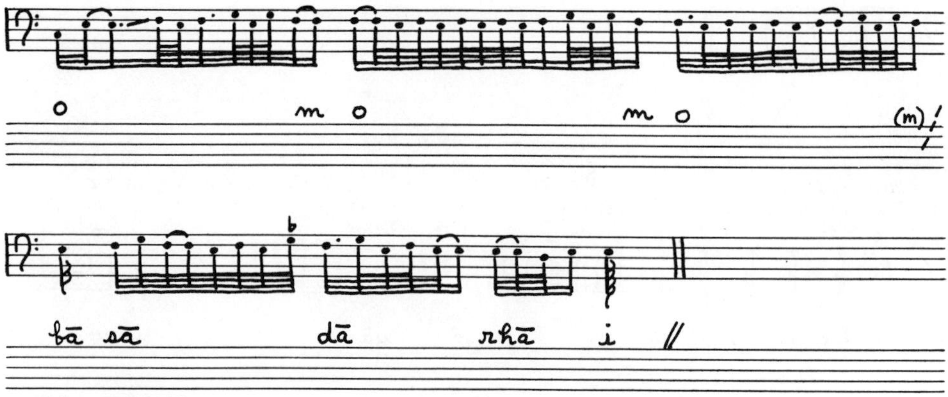

Tape IVb(14)
JRG from JS 3.30.10 ♪ = 96 T. Rajagopala Aiyangar
E=A

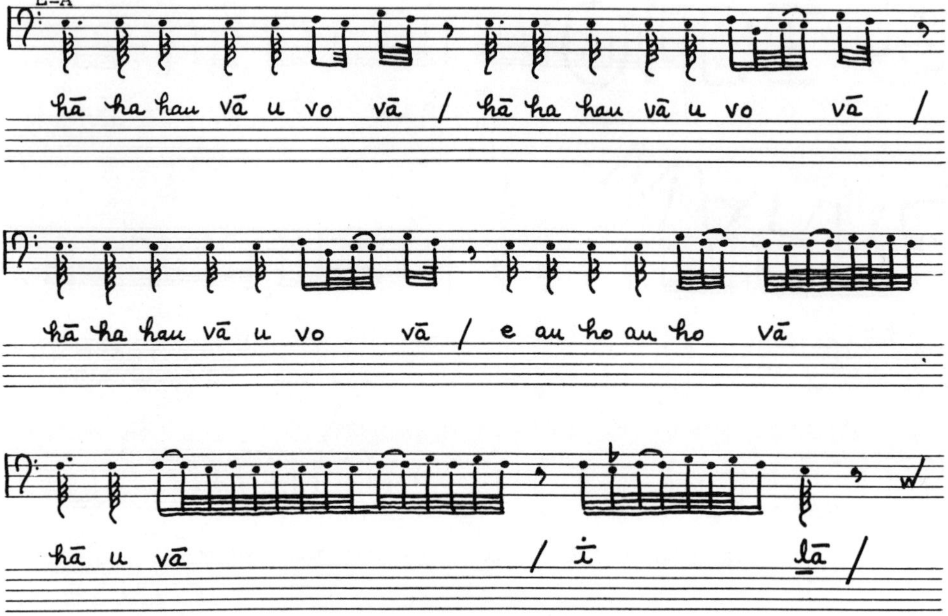

Tape VIIa(4)
JGG 1.1

♪ = 96

R. Narasimhan Aiyangar (Jaiminīya school), Srirangam. Originally from Vasishthapuram, S. Arcot District

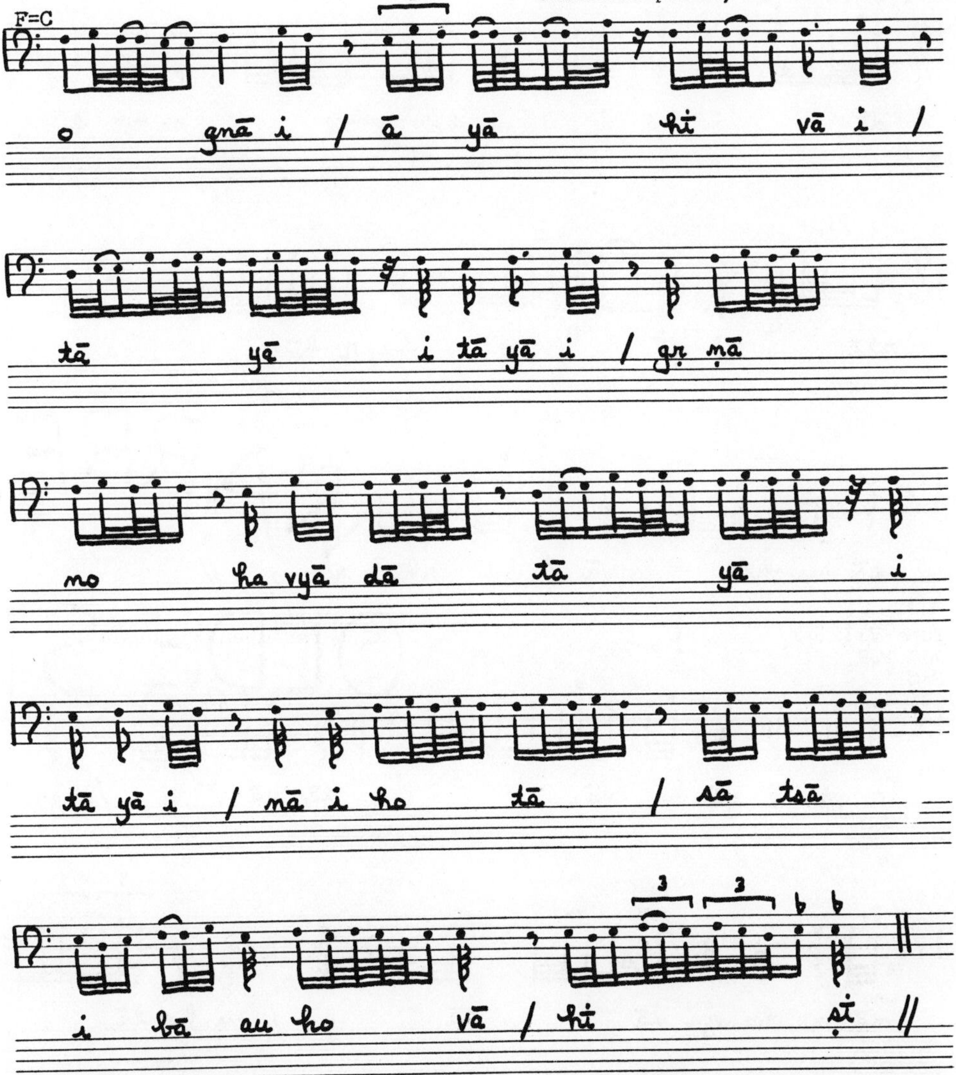

Tape VIIa(4), JGG 1.2

R. Narasimhan Aiyangar

JGG 1.2 (cont.) R. Narasimhan Aiyangar

dā tā yā i ni ho tā sa tsī ba
rhā i ṣī / ba r hā i
ṣā au ho vā / ba rhī ṣī //

Tape VIIa(4)
JGG 1.3
F=C

♪ = 96

R. Narasimhan Aiyangar

a gna ā yā hi vā i tā yā i / gṛ
ṇā no ha vya dā tā ye / ni ho tā
sā t / sā i bā / r hā ā i

JGG 1.3 (cont.) R. Narasimhan Aiyangar

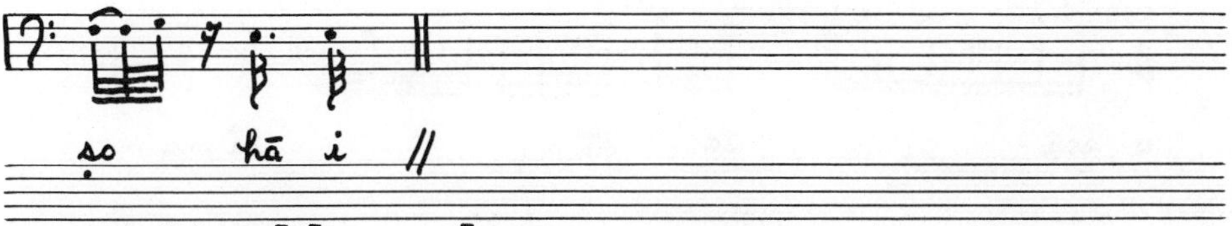
so hā i //

Tape VIIa(2): Prājāpatyaṃ Gāyatram ♪ = 96 R. Narasimhan Aiyangar

E=B

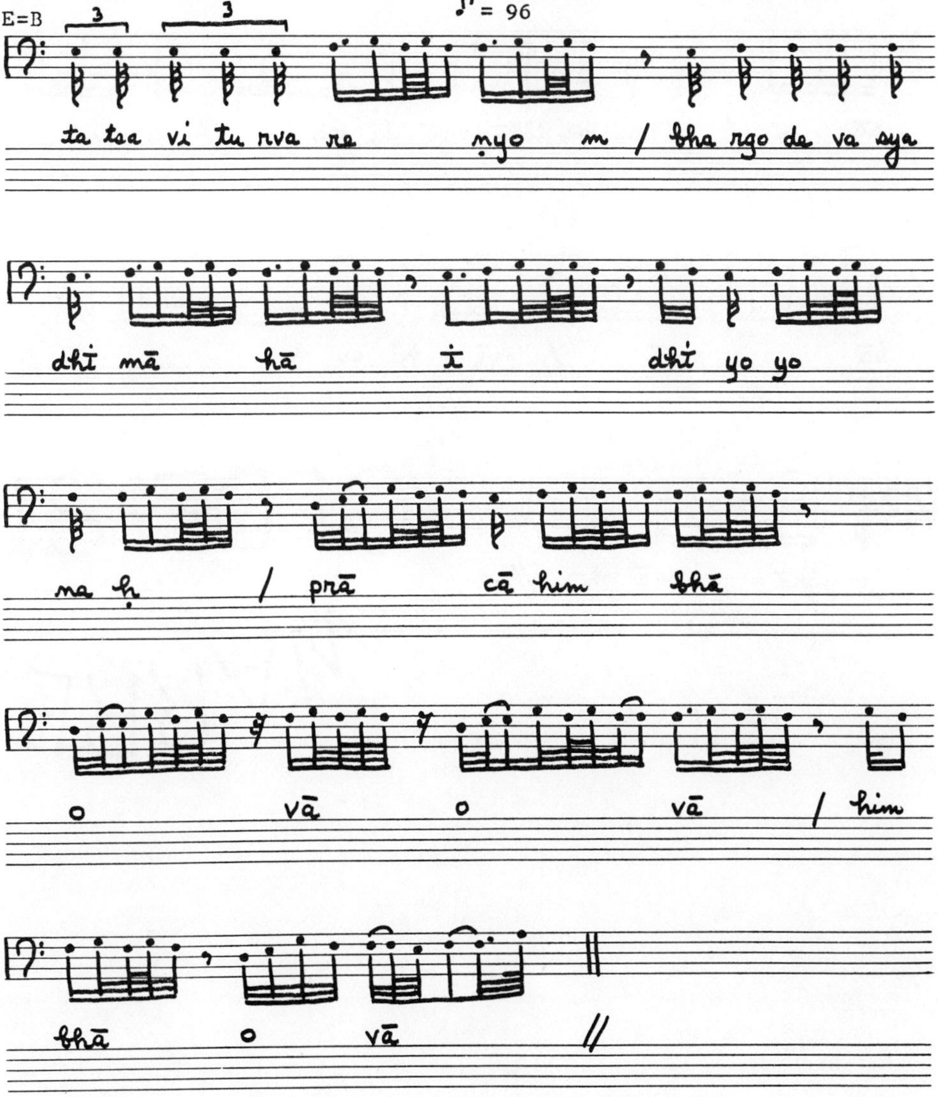
ta tsa vi tu rva re ṇyo ṃ / bha rgo de va sya
dhī mā hā ī dhī yo yo
na ḥ / prā cā him bhā
o vā o vā / him
bhā o vā //

Tape VIIa(8)
JGG from JS 1.3.1.1 (cf. GG 467.1)

R. Narasimhan Aiyangar

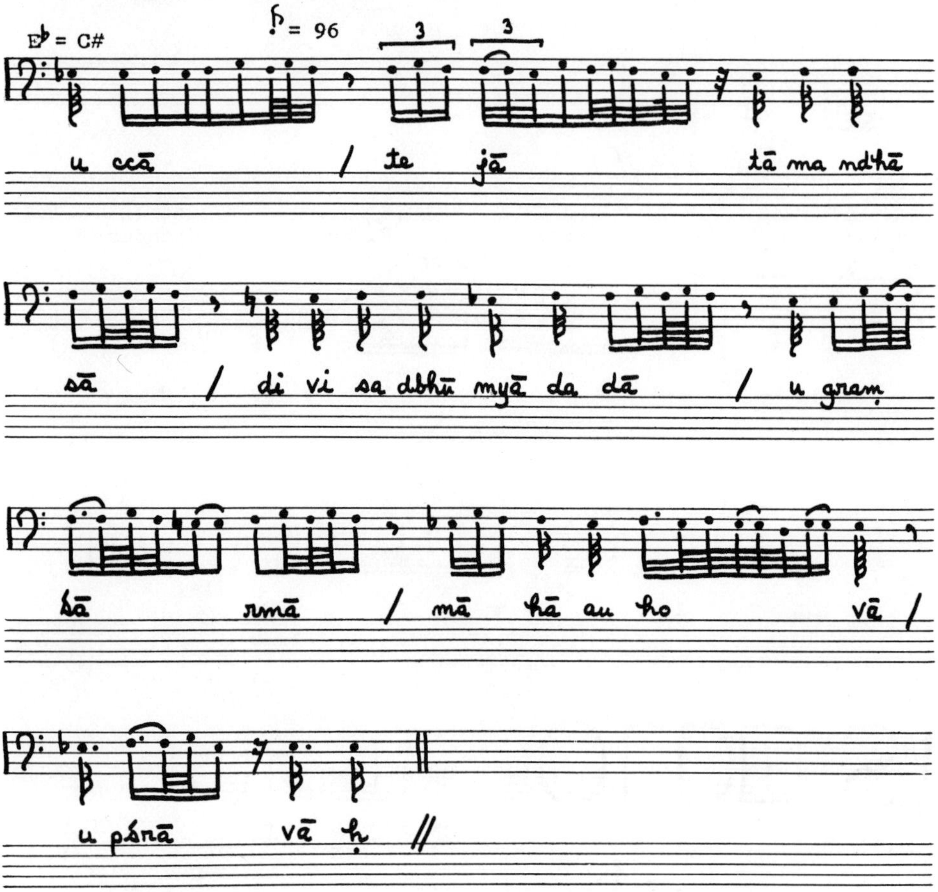
E♭ = C#
= 96
3
3
u ccā / te jā tā ma ndhā
sā / di vi sa dbhū myā da dā / u gram
śā rmā / mā hā au ho vā /
u pśnā vā ḥ //

Tape Xb(4)
JGG 1.1

Tiruvenkatanatha Sarma (Jaiminīya school)
Kotuntirappulli village, near Palghat

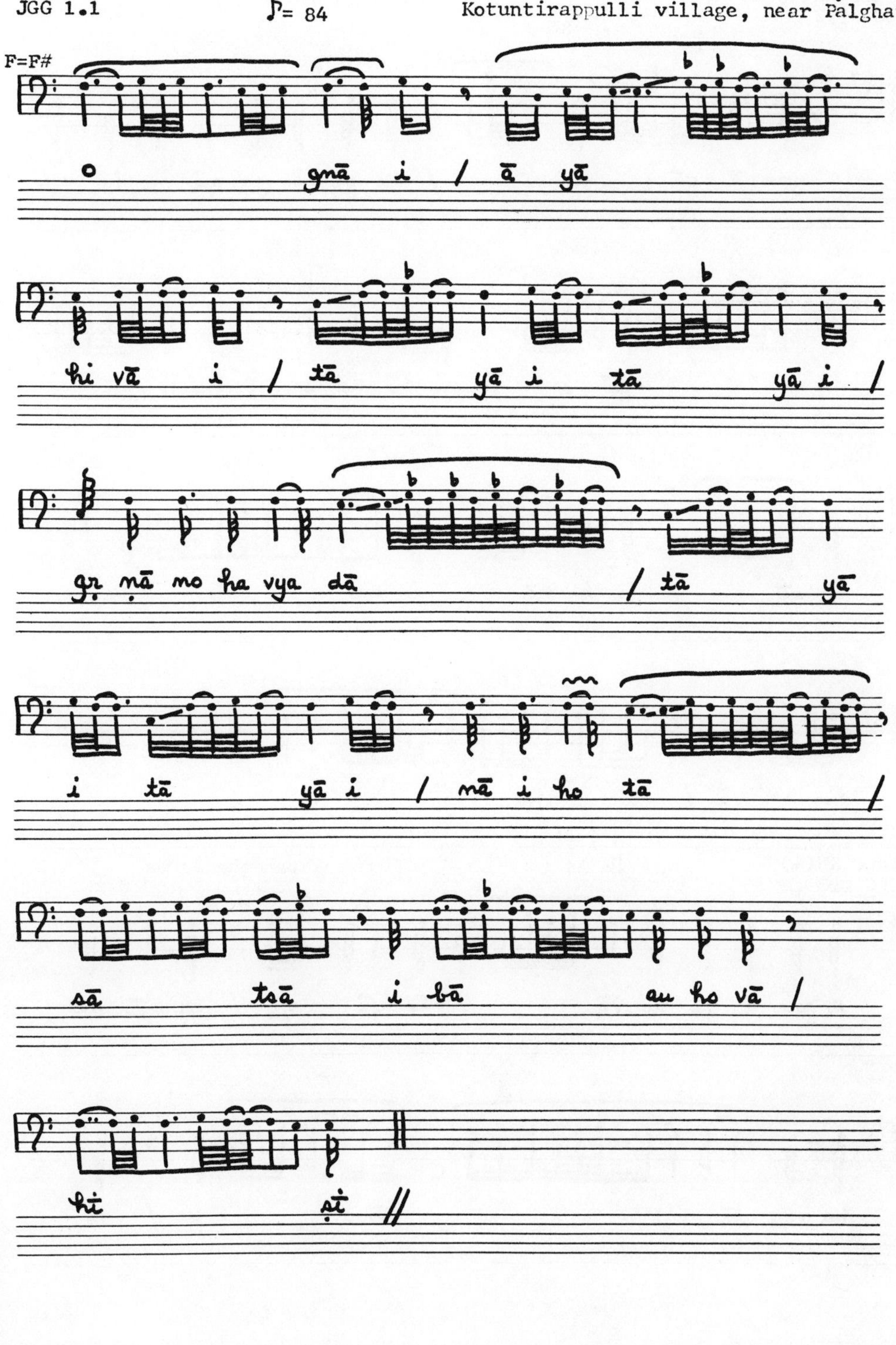
= 84
F=F#
o gnā i / ā yā
hi vā i / tā yā i tā yā i /
gṛ ṇā no ha vya dā / tā yā
i tā yā i / nā i ho tā /
sā tsā i bā au ho vā /
hi ṣi //

Tape Xb(4)
JGG 1.2

♪= 84

Tiruvenkatanatha Sarma

C=C#

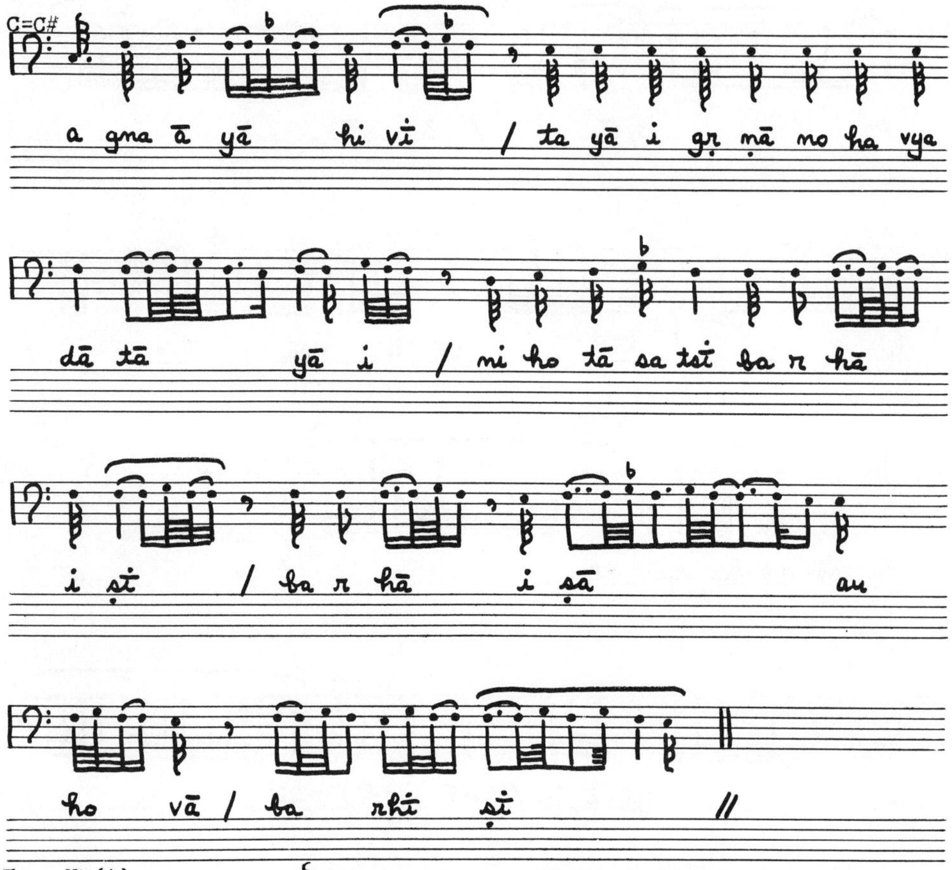

Tape Xb(4)
JGG 1.3

♪= 84

Tiruvenkatanatha Sarma

E=F

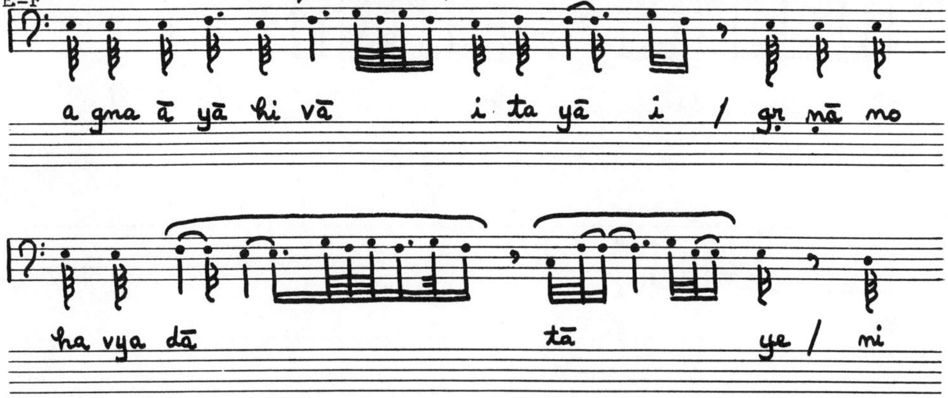

JGG 1.3 (cont.) Tiruvenkatanatha Sarma

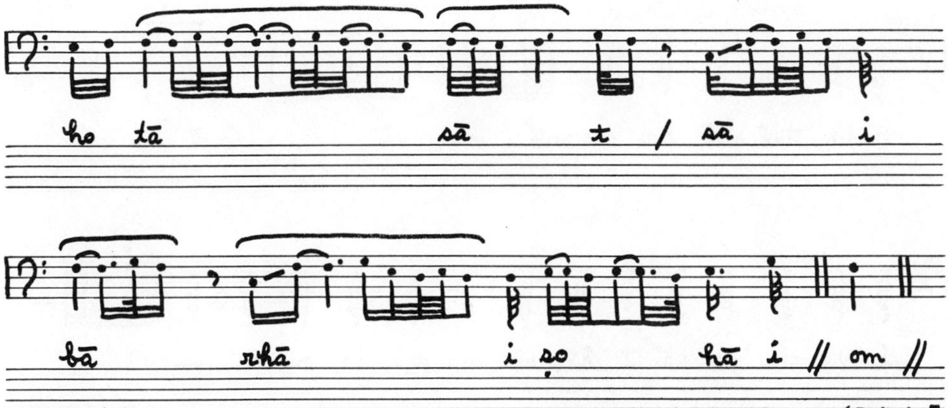
ho tā sā t / sā i
bā rhā i ṣo hā i // om //

Tape Xb(6)
Prajāpatyaṃ Gāyatram ♪ = 84

K. R. Venkatarama Sarma (Jaiminīya school) Kotuntirappulli, near Palghat

C=E

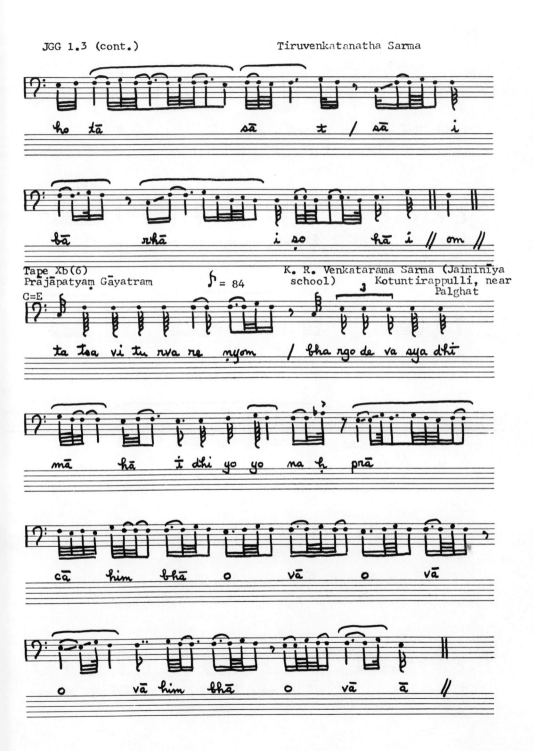

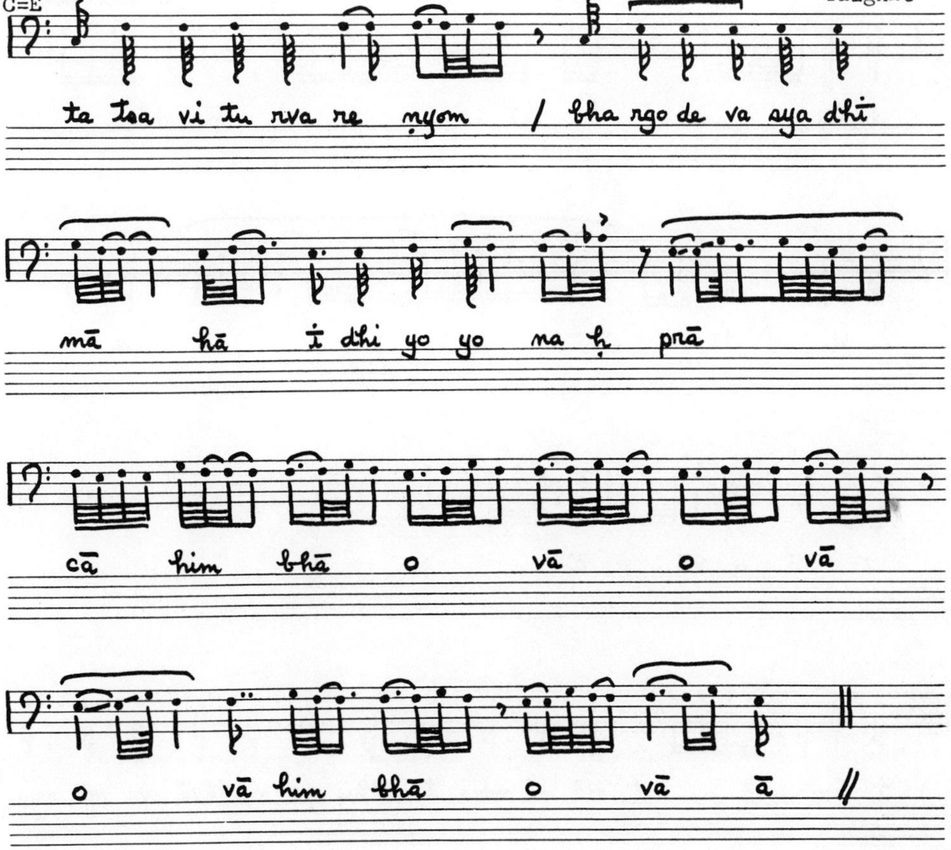
ta tsa vi tu rva re ṇyom / bha rgo de va sya dhī
mā hā ī dhi yo yo na ḥ prā
cā him bhā o vā o vā
o vā him bhā o vā ā //

Tape Xb(5)A
JRG from JS 3.4.1-2 (cf. RG 1.1.1)

K. R. Venkatarama Sarma

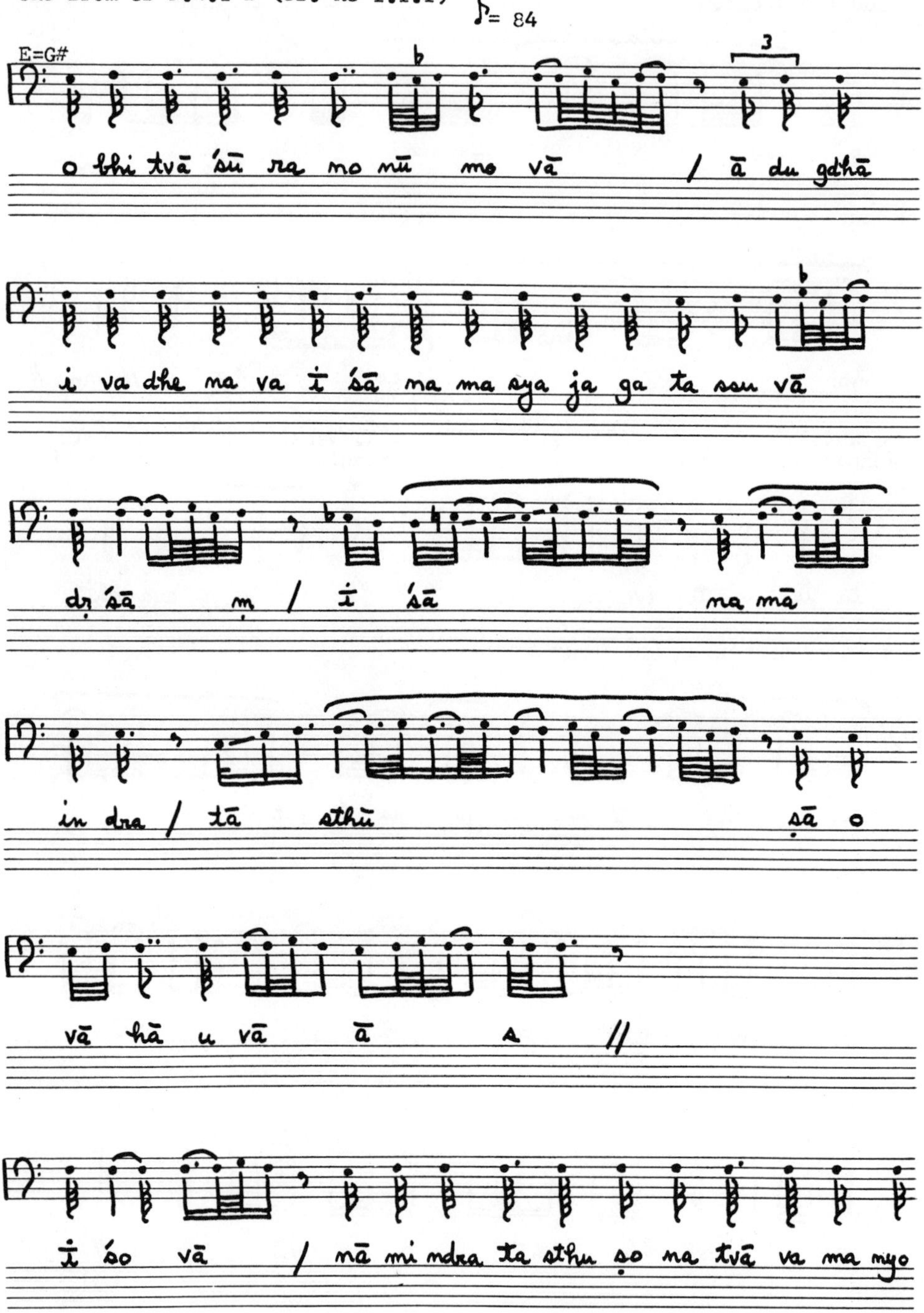

JRG from JS 3.4.1-2 (cont.) K. R. Venkatarama Sarma

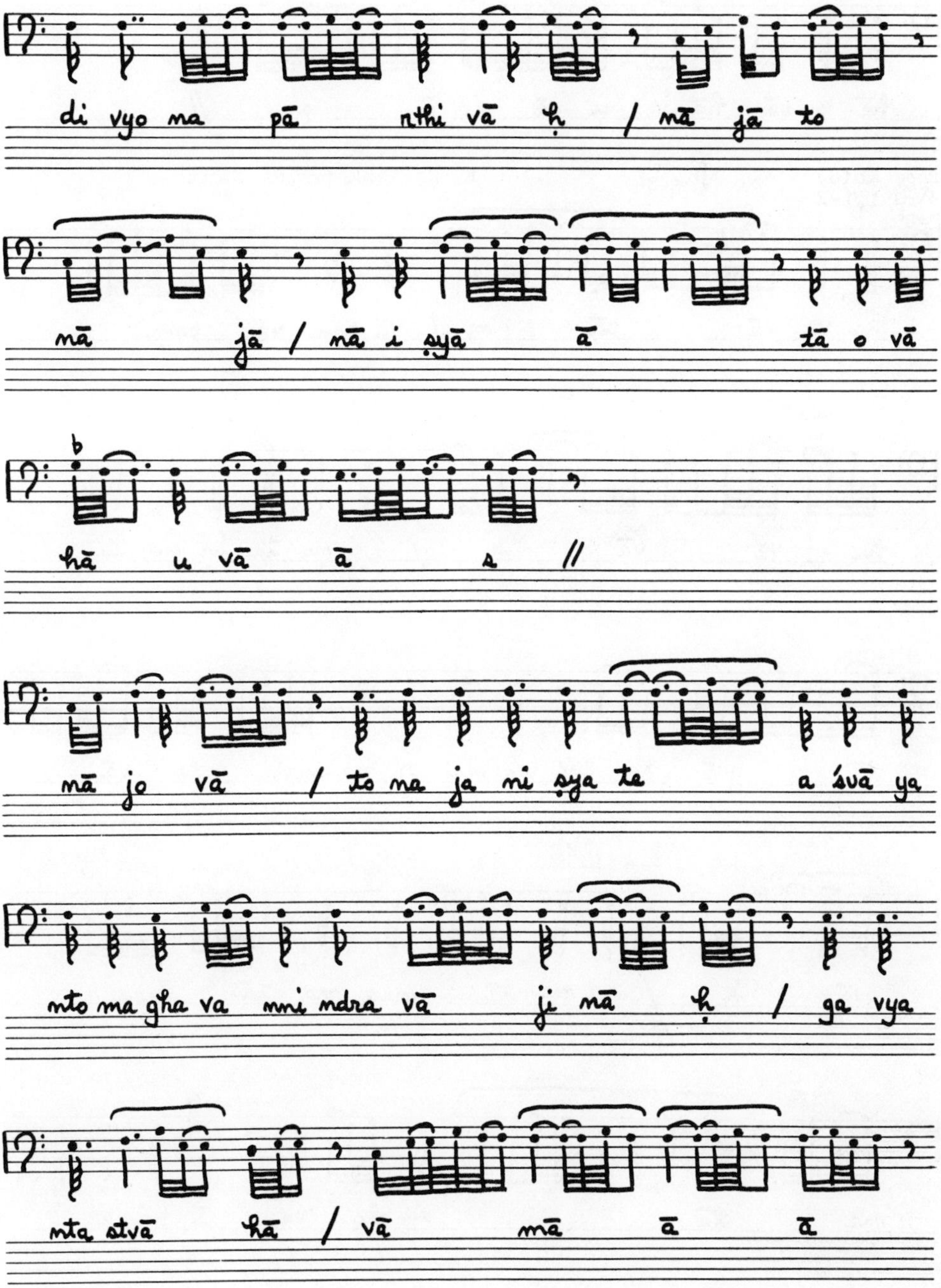

JRG from JS 3.4.1-2 (cont.) K. R. Venkatarama Sarma

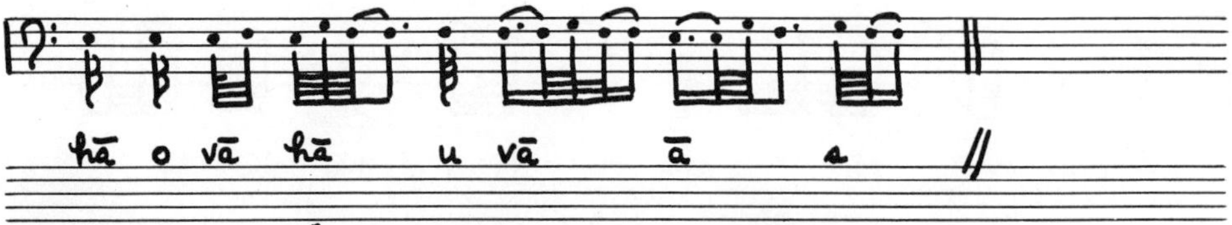
hā o vā hā u vā ā a //

Tape Xb(8) ♪ = 84 K. R. Venkatarama Sarma
JĀrG 1.1-2
F=B♭

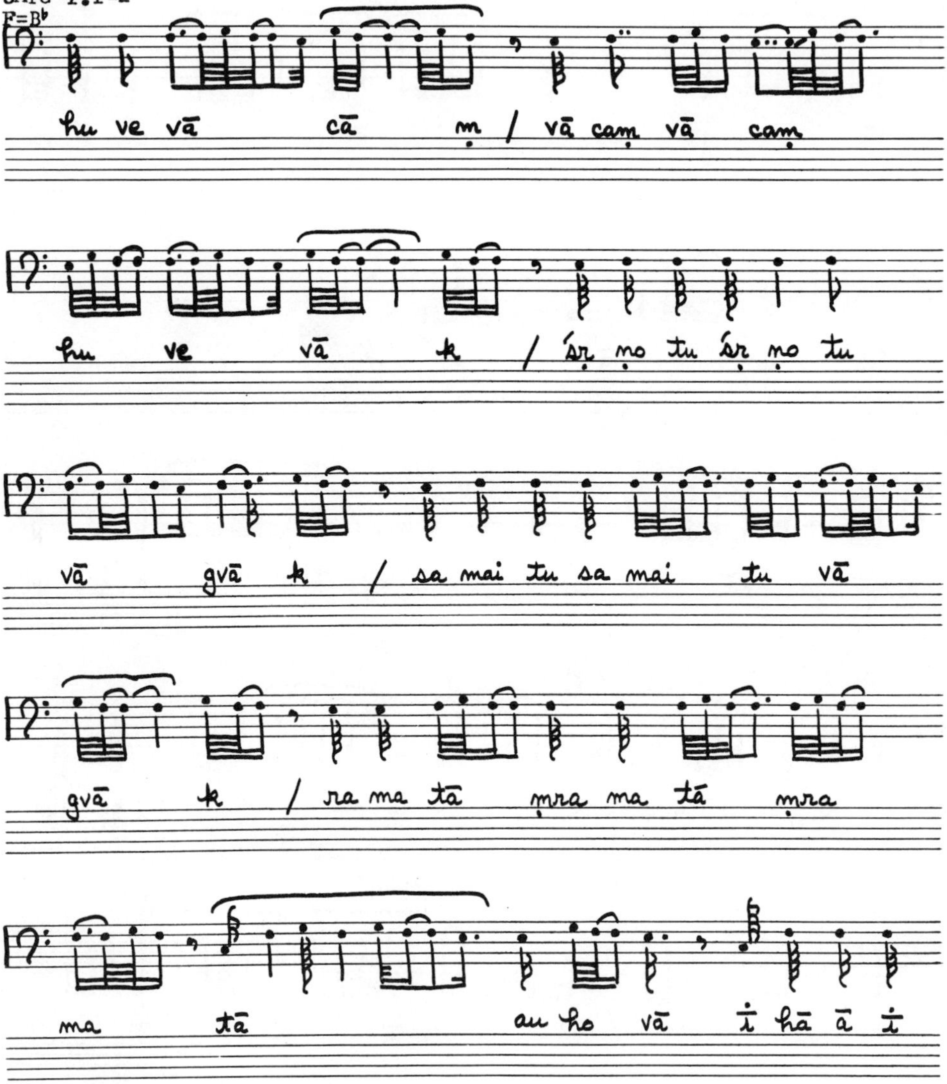
hu ve vā cā m / vā cam vā cam
hu ve vā k / śr no tu śr no tu
vā gvā k / sa mai tu sa mai tu vā
gvā k / ra ma tā mra ma tā mra
ma tā au ho vā ī hā ā ī

JĀrG 1.1 (cont.) K. R. Venkatarama Sarma

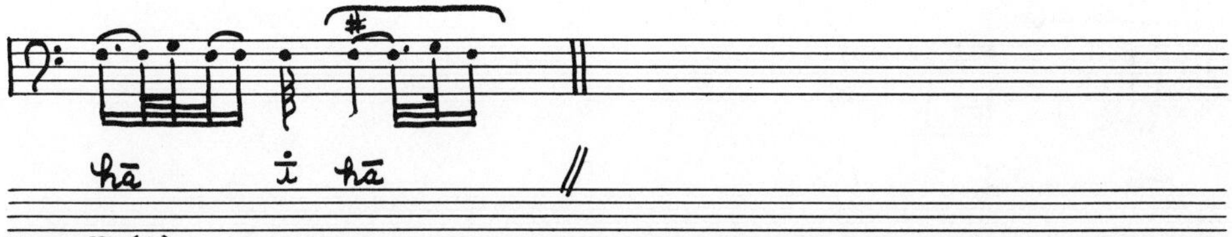

Tape Xb(8)
JĀrG 1.2 ♪ = 84 K. R. Venkatarama Sarma

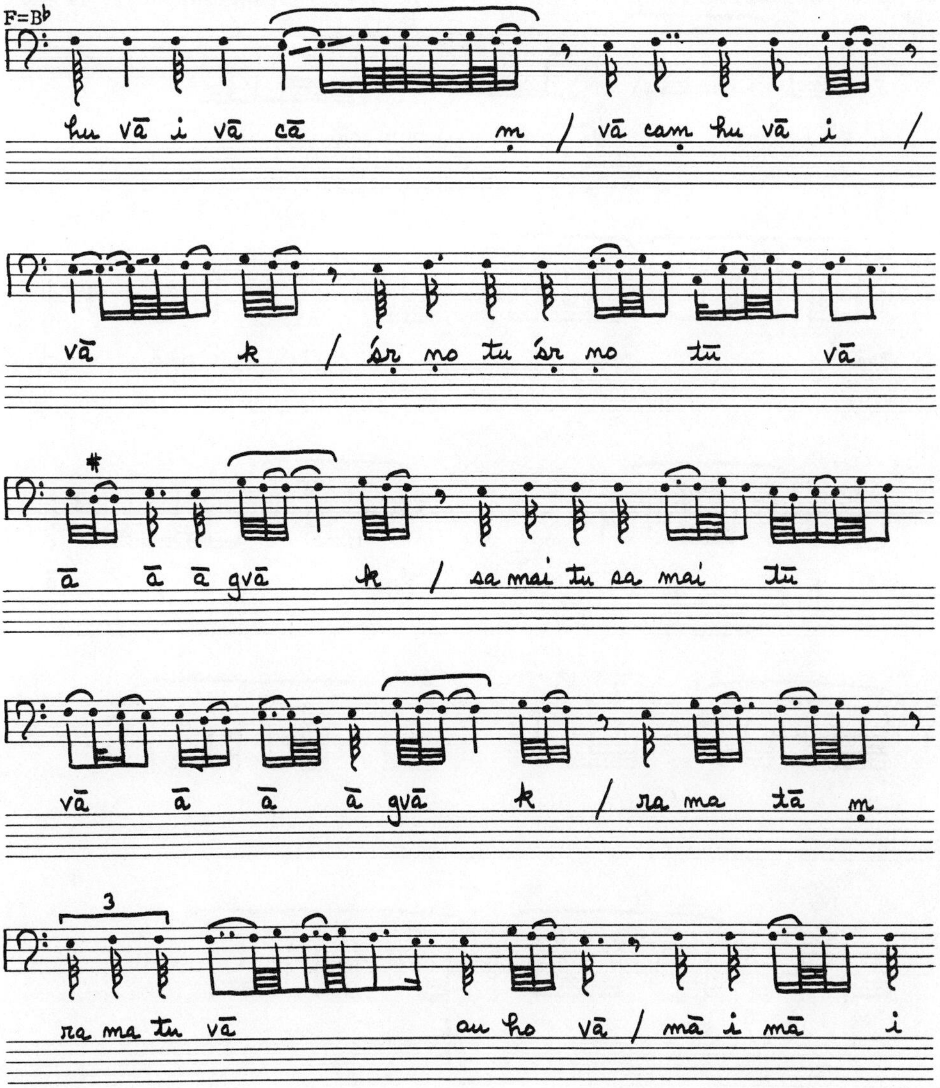

JĀrG 1.2 (cont.) K. R. Venkatarama Sarma

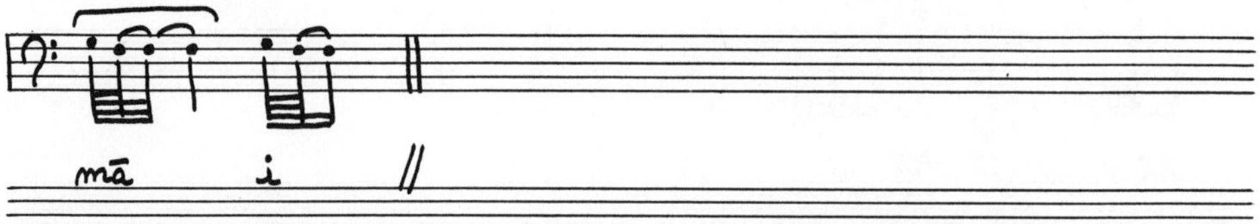

Tape Xb(14)A
JGG from JS 1.2.1.11.9
F=B♭

♪ = 84

K. N. Sahasranama Aiyar (Jaiminīya school), Kotuntirappulli, near Palghat

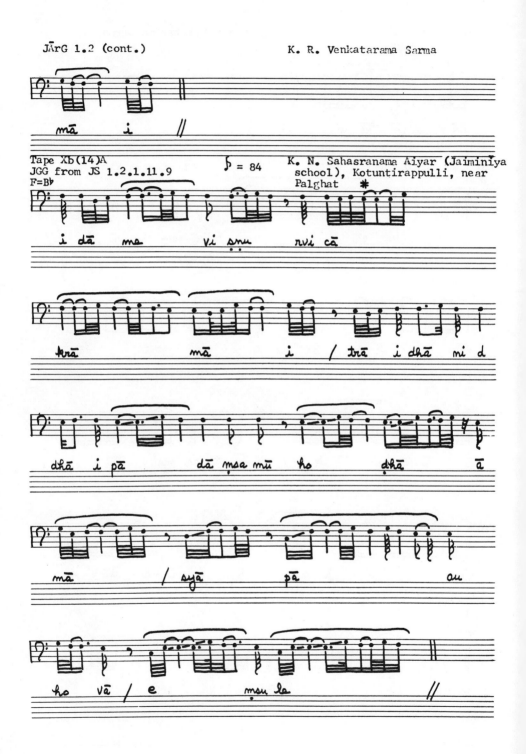

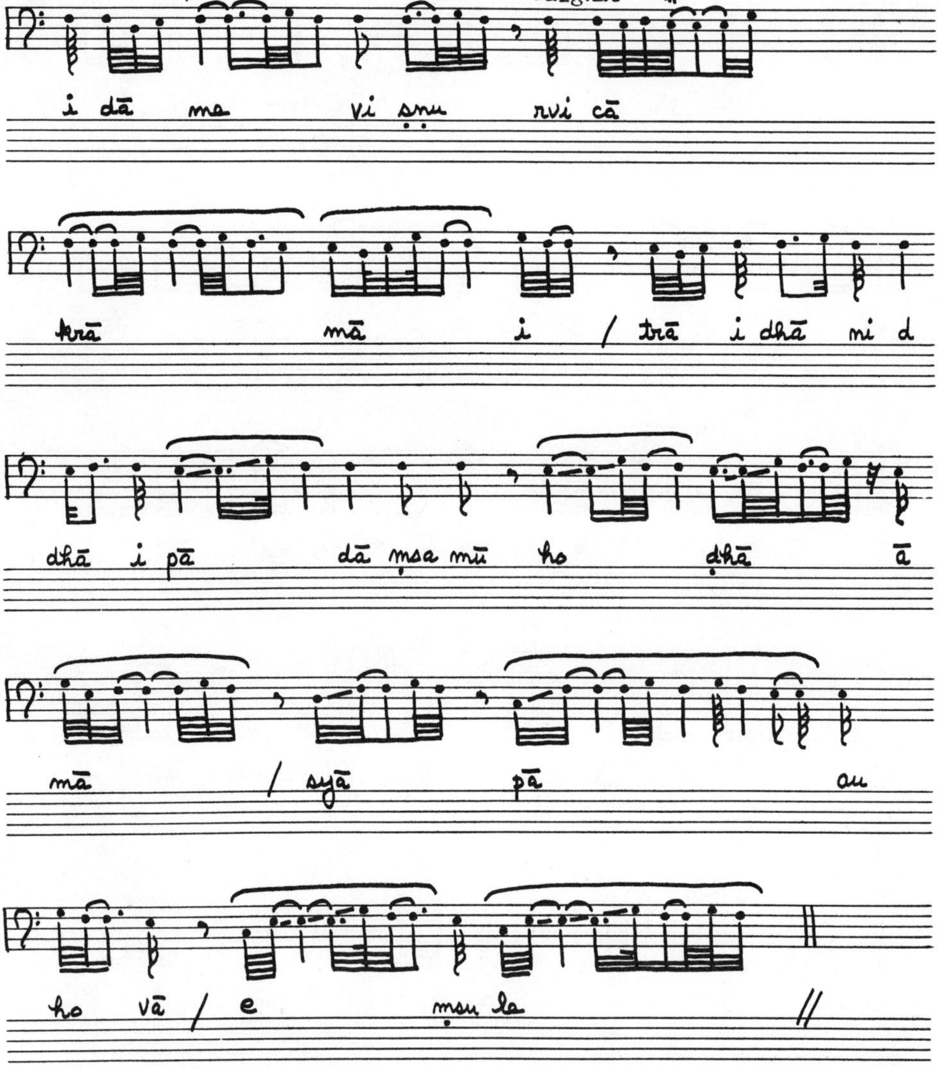

Tape Xb(14)B
JGG from JS 1.3.10.3 ♪ = 84 K. N. Sahasranama Aiyar

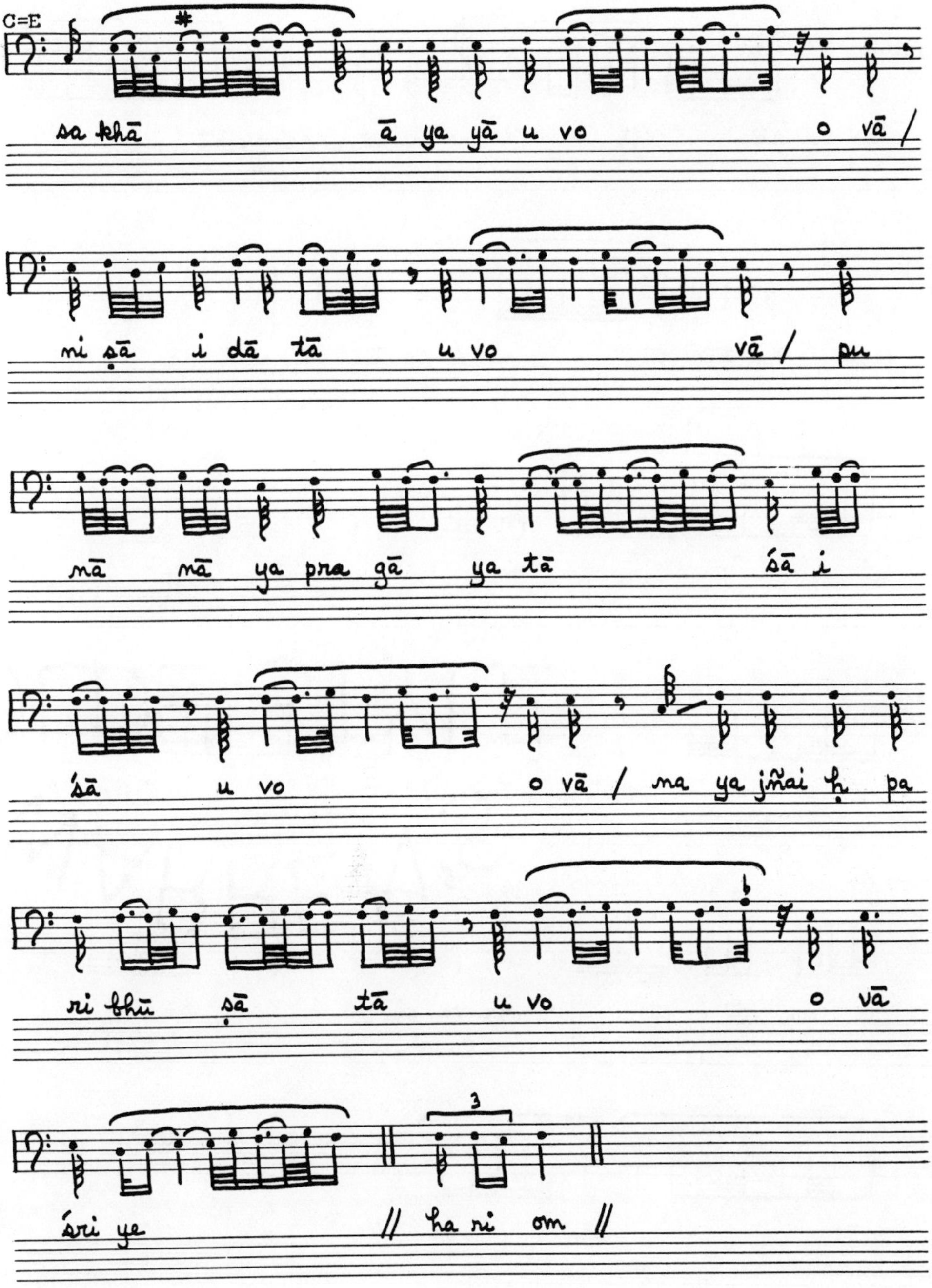
C=E
sa khā ā ya yā u vo o vā /
ni ṣā i dā tā u vo vā / pu
mā mā ya pra gā ya tā śā i
śā u vo o vā / ma ya jñai ḥ pa
ri bhū ṣā tā u vo o vā
śri ye // ha ri om //

Tape Xb(5)B
JGG from JS 1.1.7.7

♪ = 84

K. R. Venkatarama Sarma

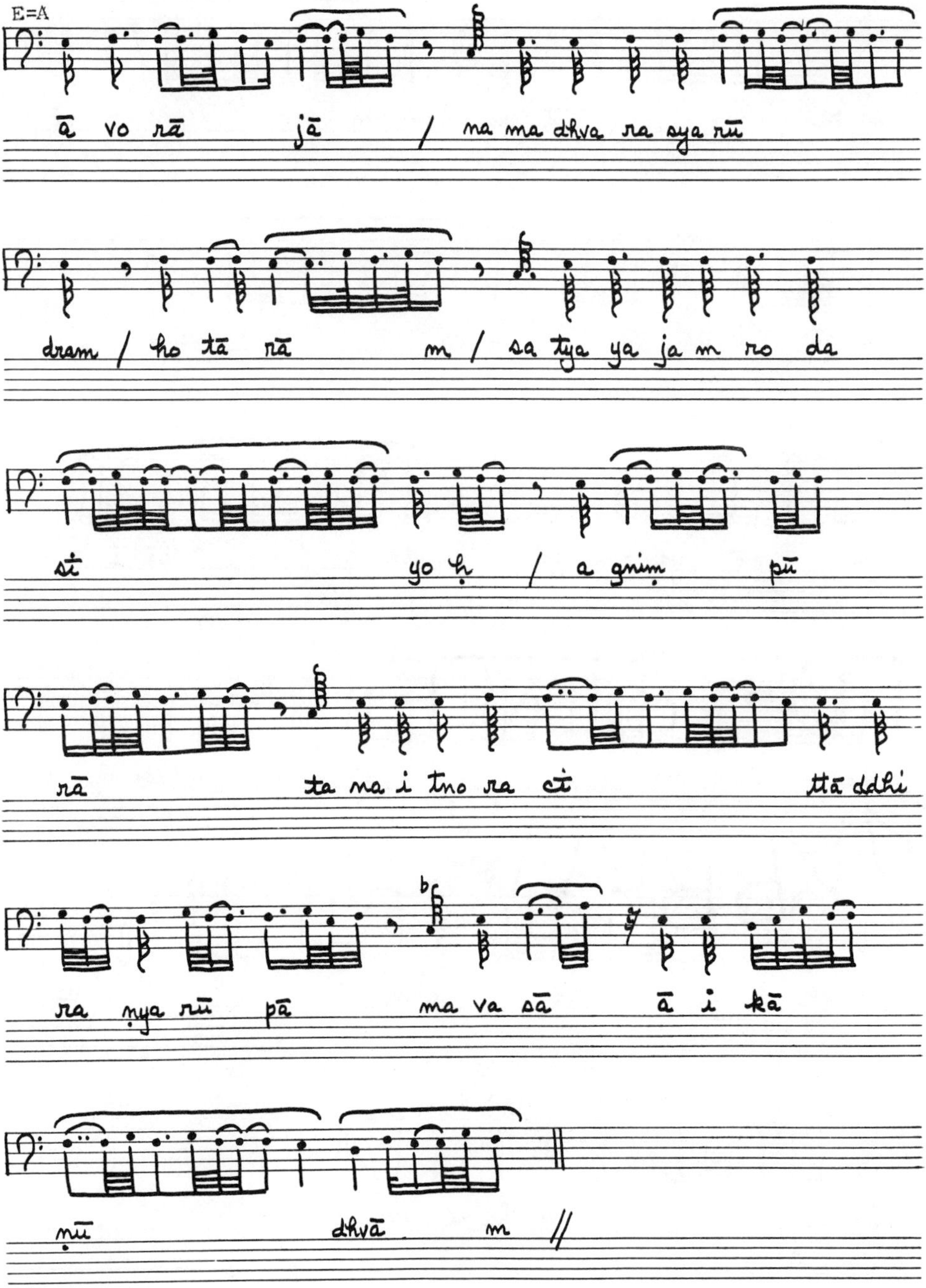

Tape VIIIb(1) ♪ = 84 Venkatacala Upadhyaya (Jaiminīya school), Tentirupperai village, Tirunělveli District
JGG 1.1

F=F

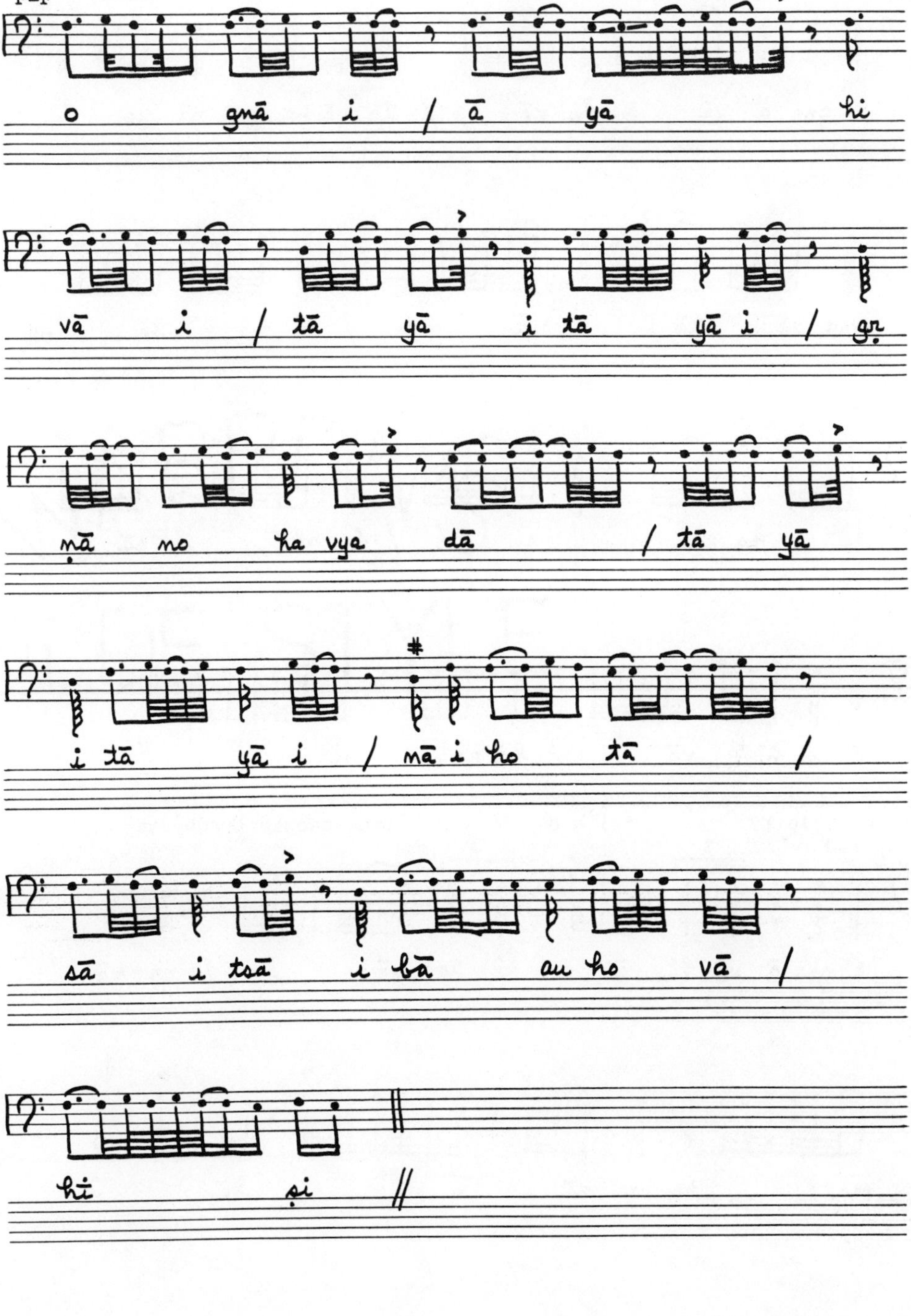
o gnā i / ā yā hi
vā i / tā yā i tā yā i / gṛ
ṇā no ha vya dā / tā yā
i tā yā i / mā i ho tā /
sā i tsā i bā au ho vā /
hī ṣi //

Tape VIIIb(1) ♪ = 84 Venkatacala Upadhyaya
JGG 1.2

D=D

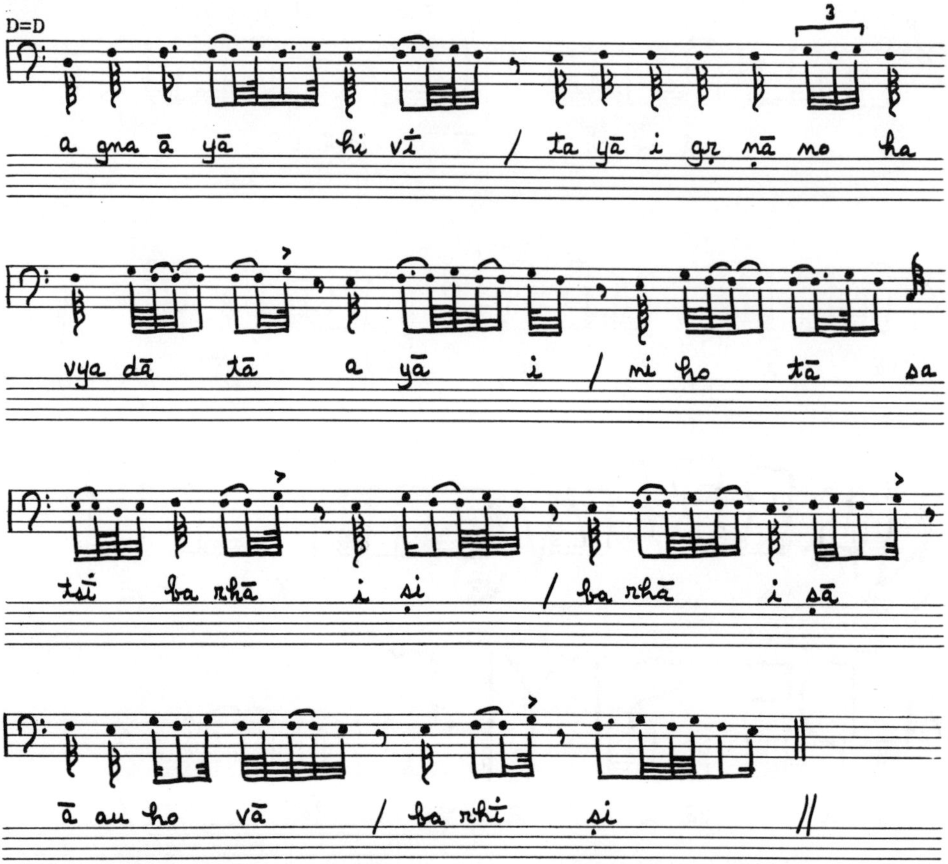

Tape VIIIb(1) ♪ = 84 Venkatacala Upadhyaya
JGG 1.3
D=D

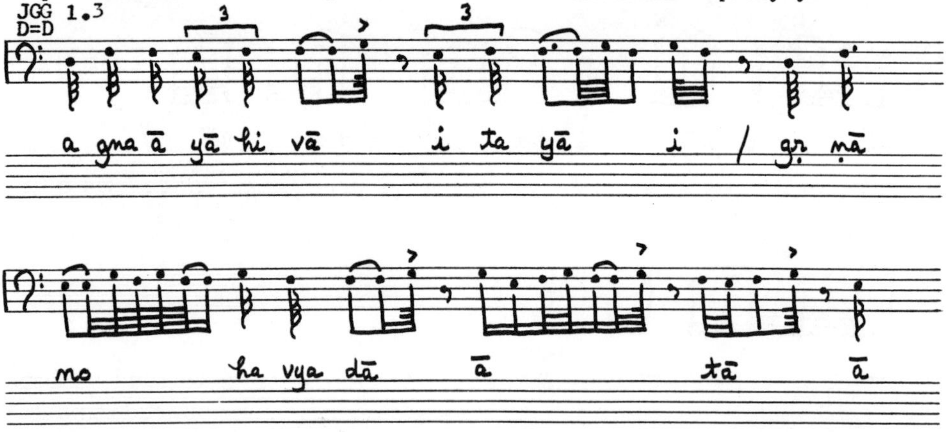

JGG 1.3 (cont.) Venkatacala Upadhyaya

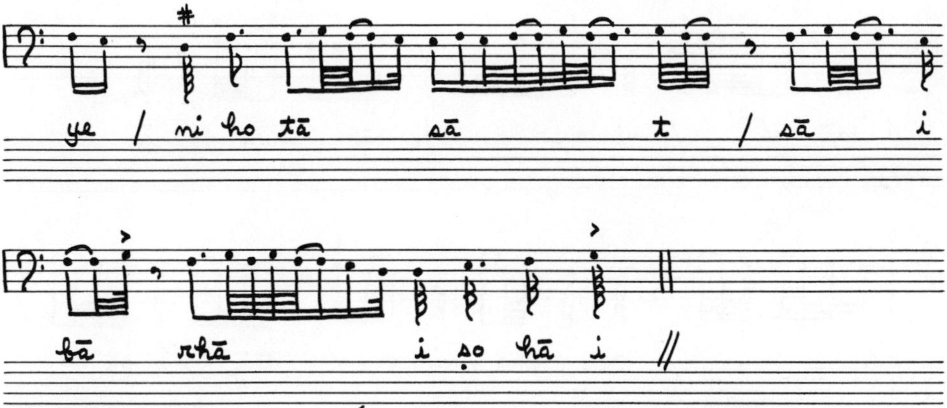

Tape VIIIb(17) = 84 Venkatacala Upadhyaya
Prajāpatyaṃ Gayatram
C=C

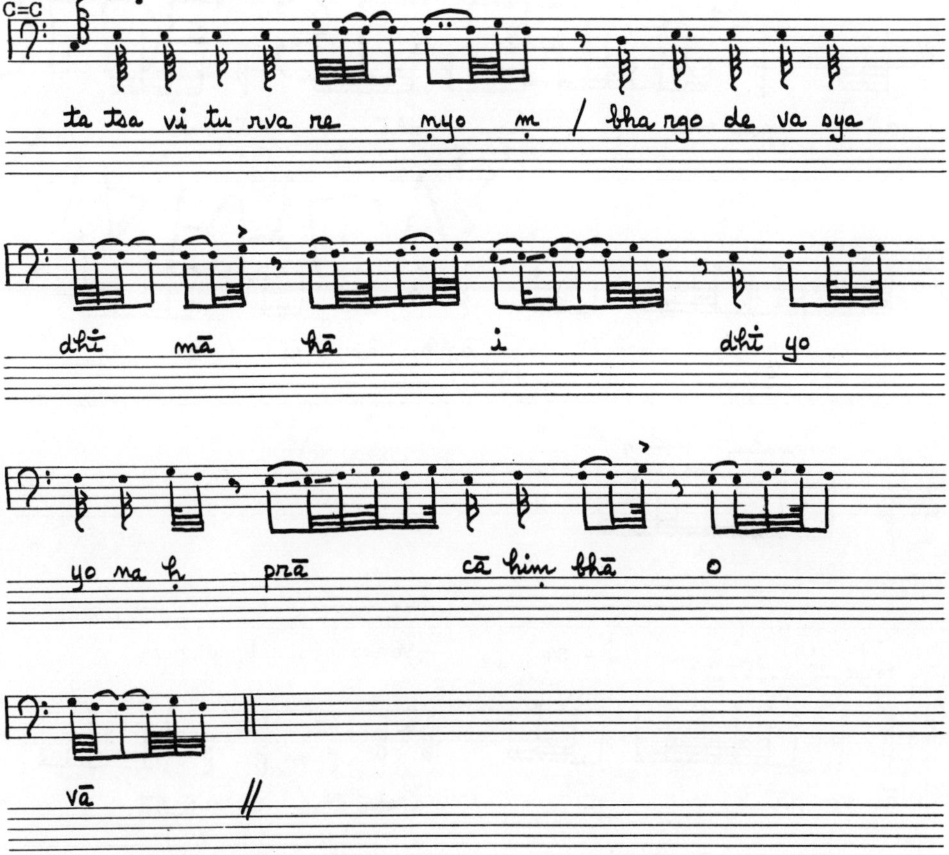

Tape VIIIb(4)
JGG from JS 1.2.1.11.9 ♪= 84 Venkatacala Upadhyaya

C=C

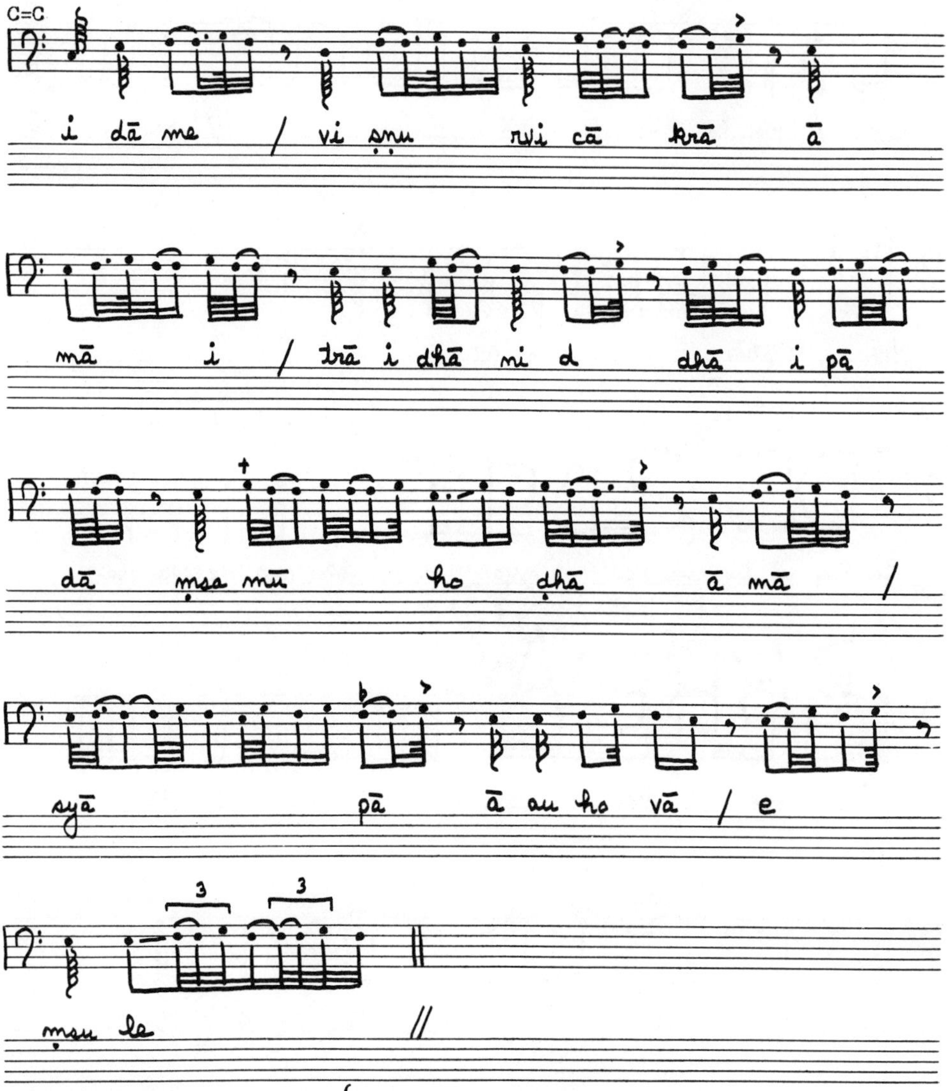

Tape VIIIb(6) ♪= 84 Venkatacala Upadhyaya
JGG from JS 1.1.7.7
E=E

JGG from JS 1.1.7.7 (cont.)   Venkatacala Upadhyaya

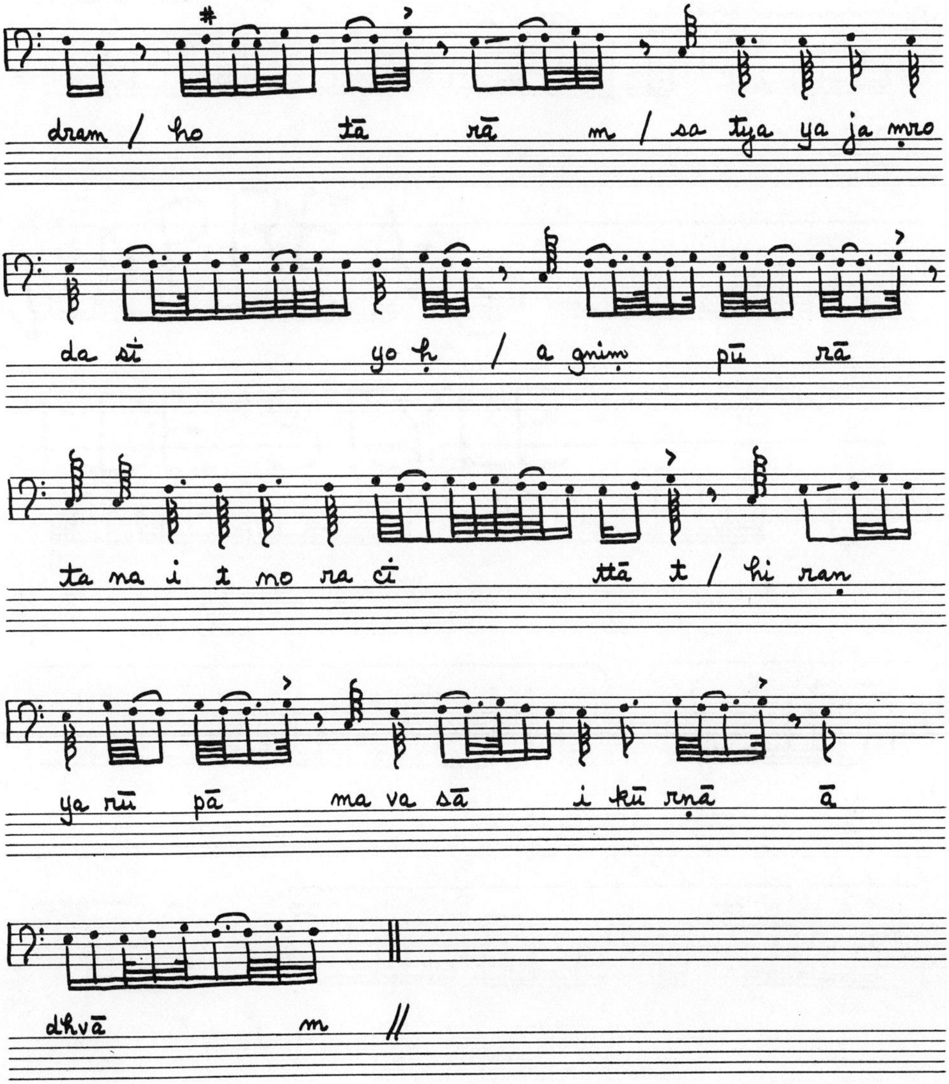

Tape IXa(13)
JGG 1.1

♪ = 116

Muttatukkattu Itti Ravi Nambudiri
Jaiminīya school, Panjal village,
Trichur District, Kerala

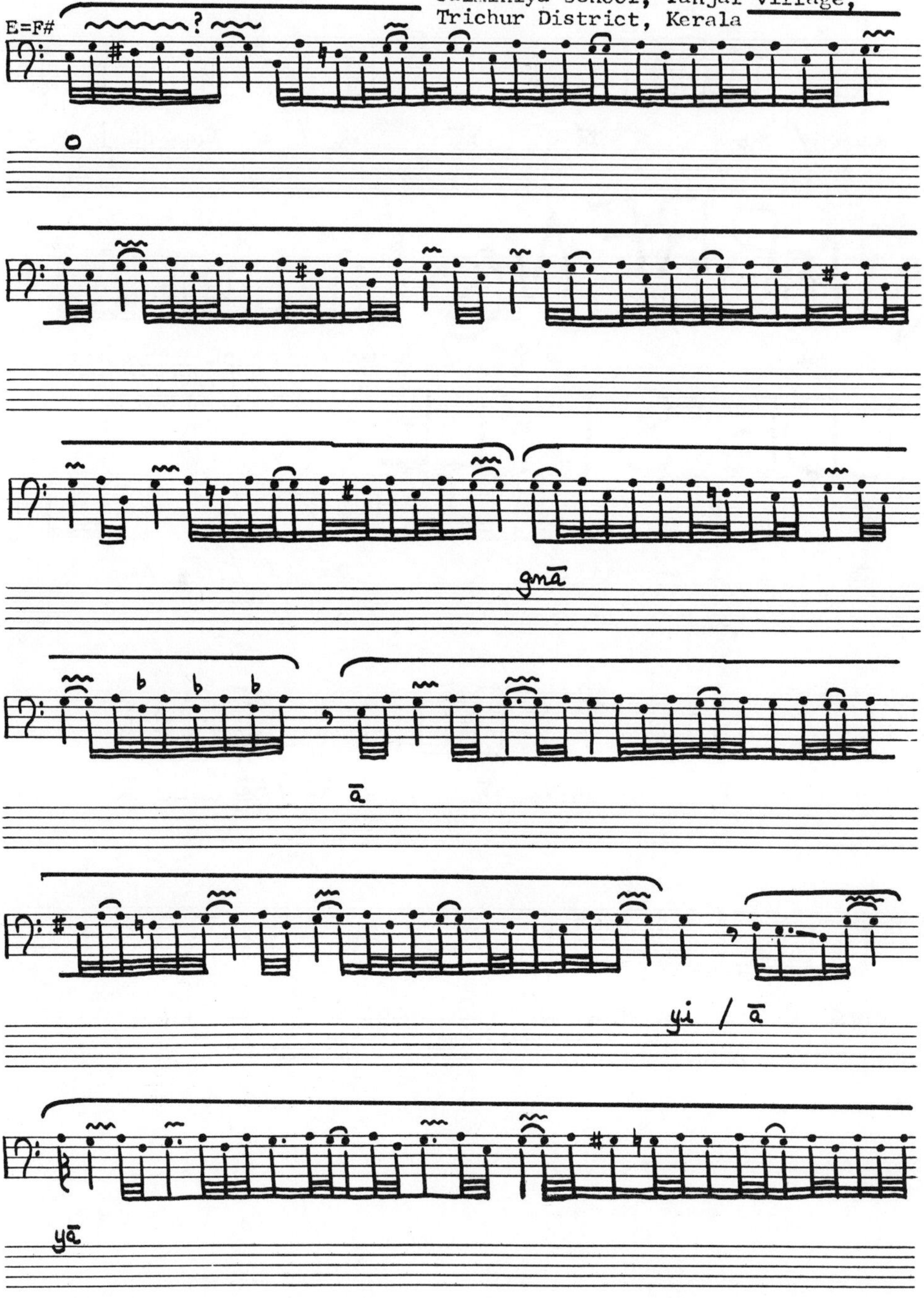

JGG 1.1 (cont.) M. Itti Ravi Nambudiri

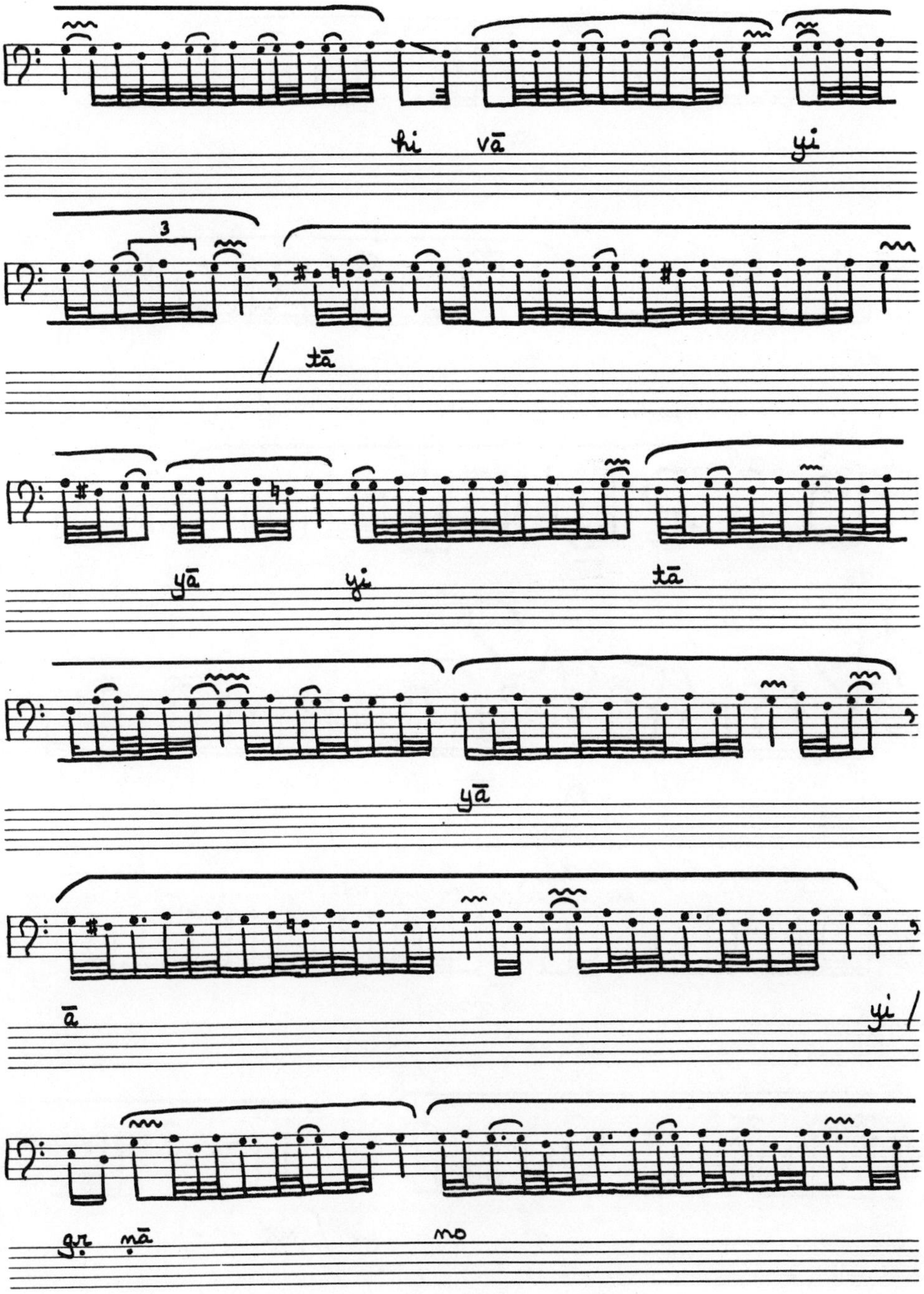

JGG 1.1 (cont.) M. Itti Ravi Nambudiri

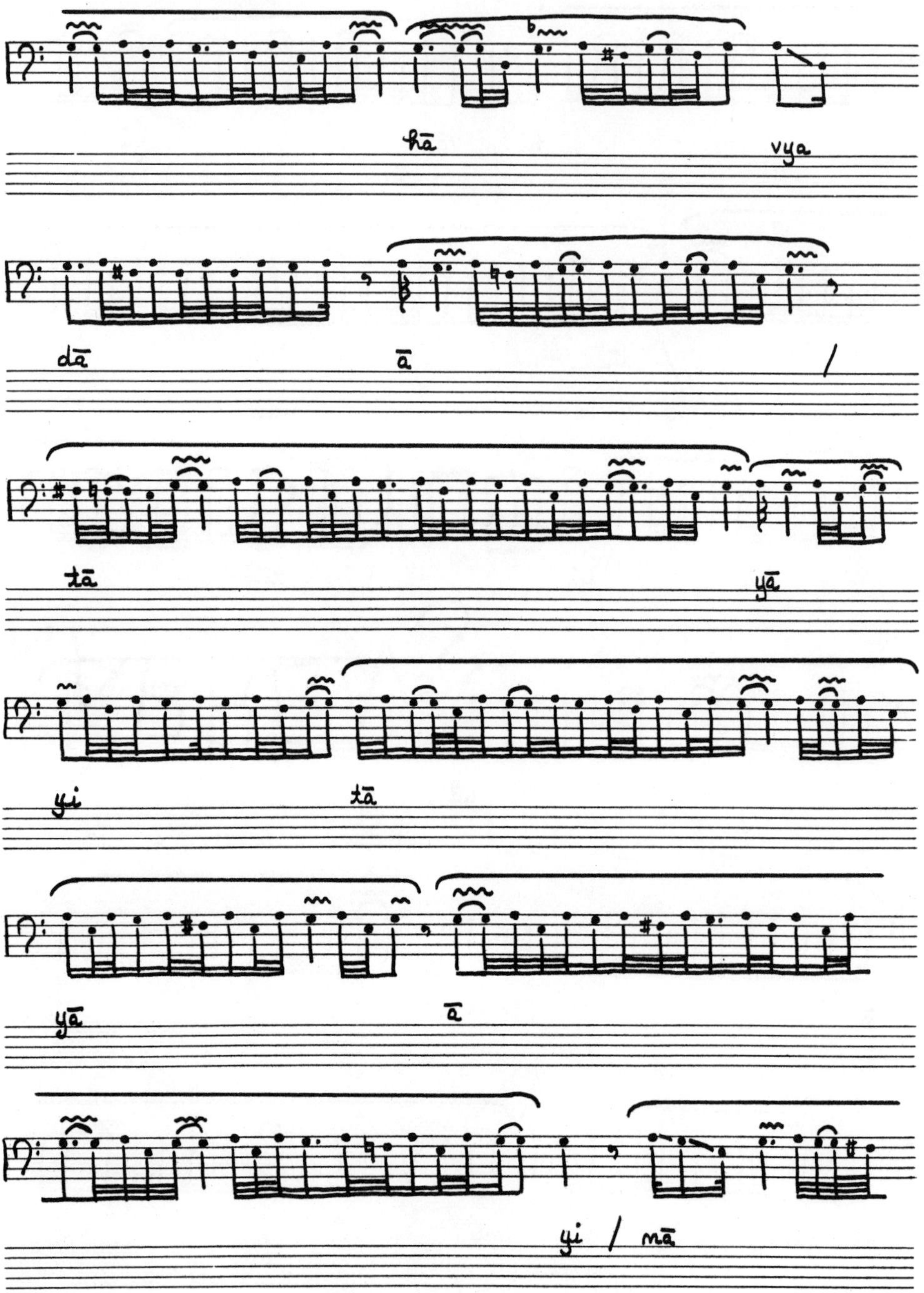

JGG 1.1 (cont.) M. Itti Ravi Nambudiri

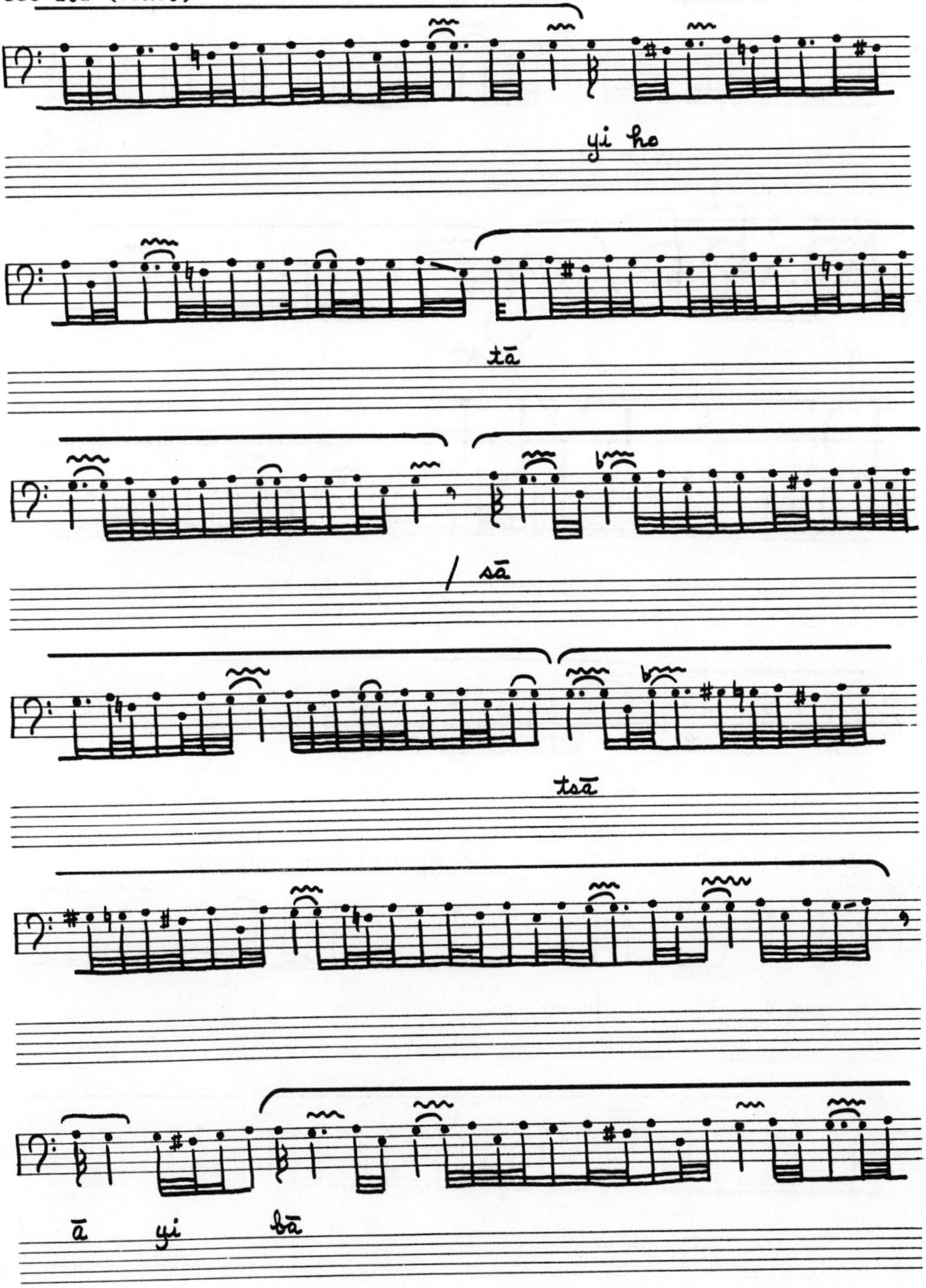
yi ho
tā
/ sā
tsā
ā yi bā

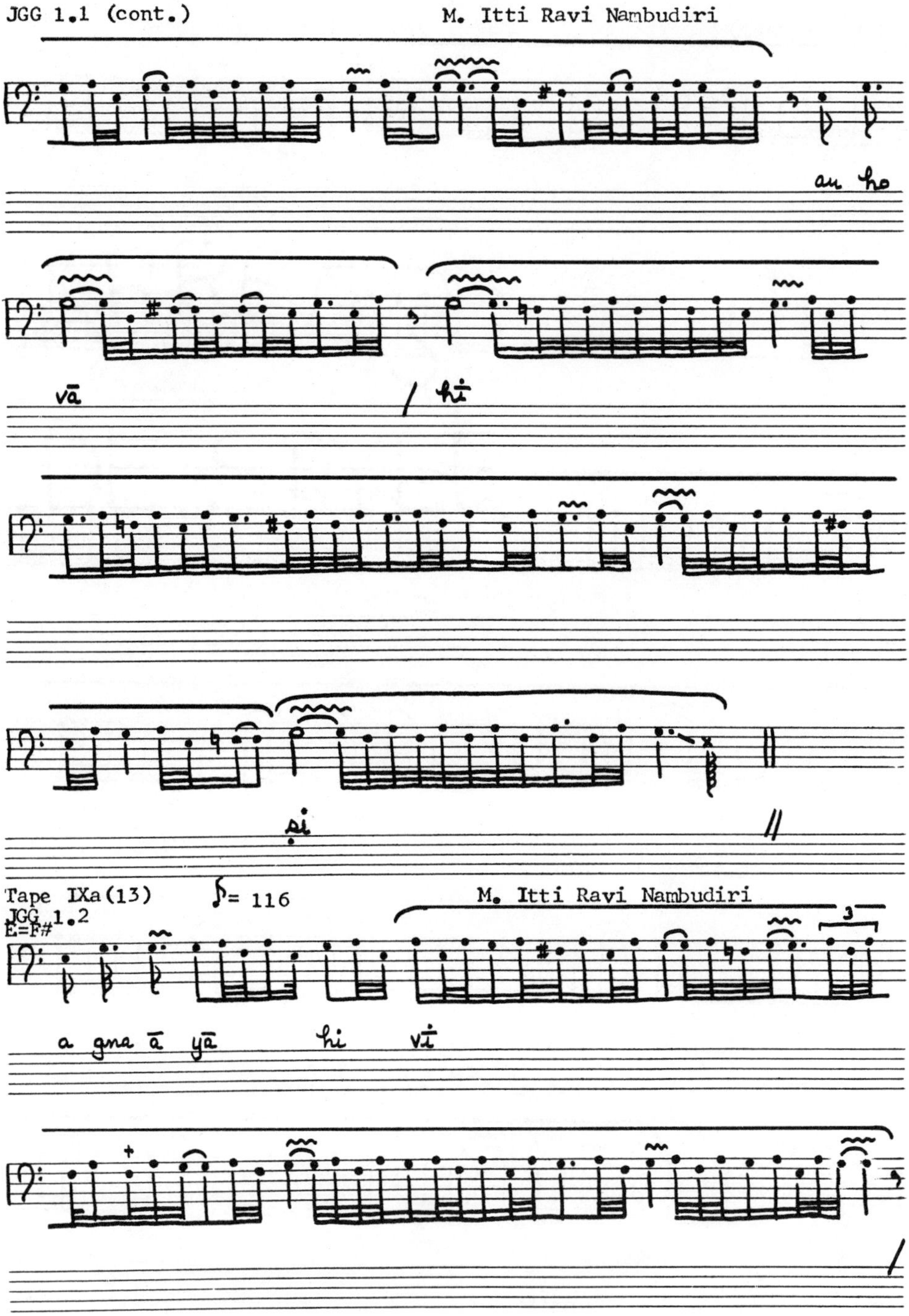
JGG 1.1 (cont.)
M. Itti Ravi Nambudiri
au ho
vā
hi
si
Tape IXa(13)
= 116
M. Itti Ravi Nambudiri
JGG 1.2
E=F#
3
a gna ā yā hi vi

JGG 1.2 (cont.) M. Itti Ravi Nambudiri

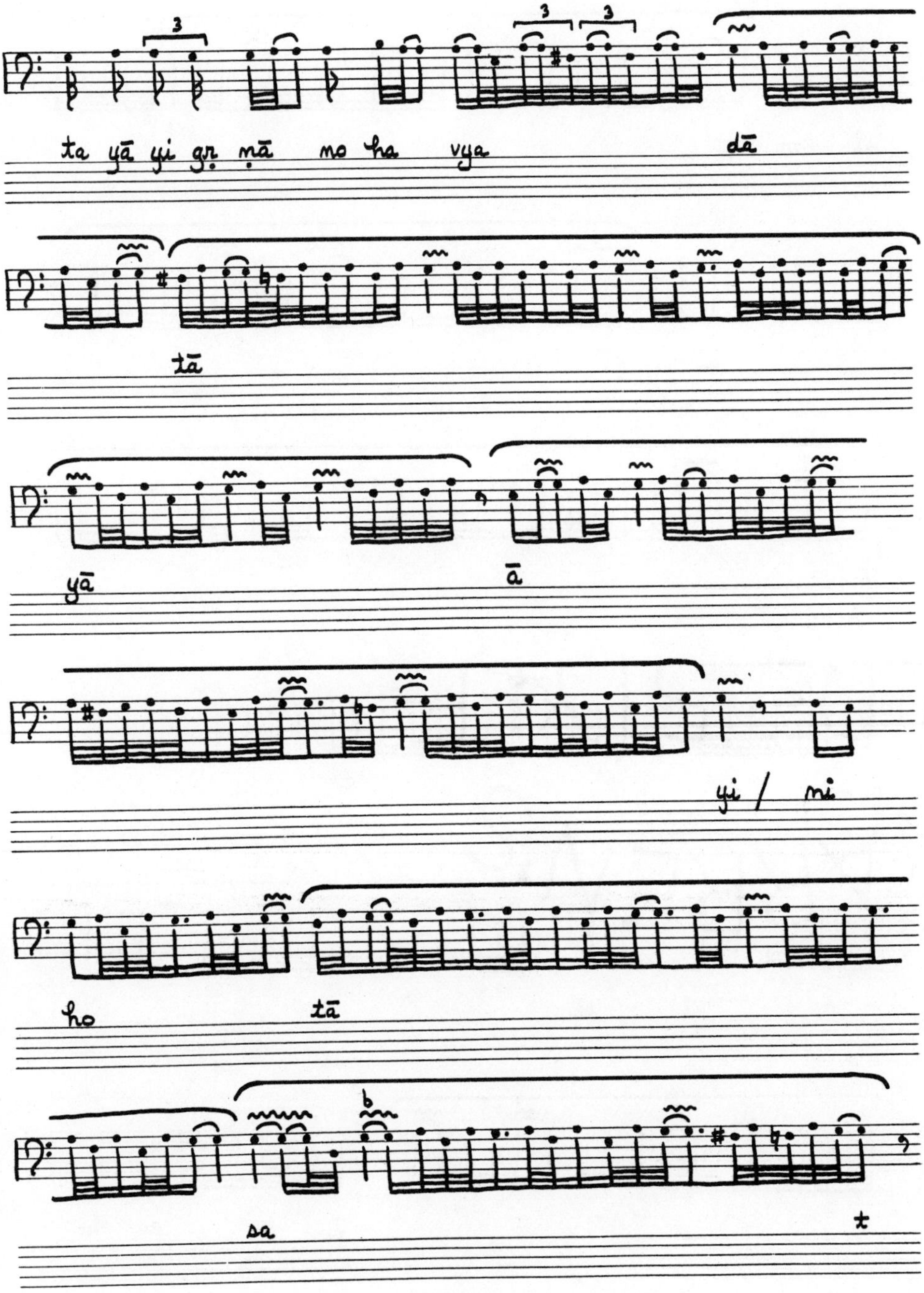

JGG 1.2 (cont.)

M. Itti Ravi Nambudiri

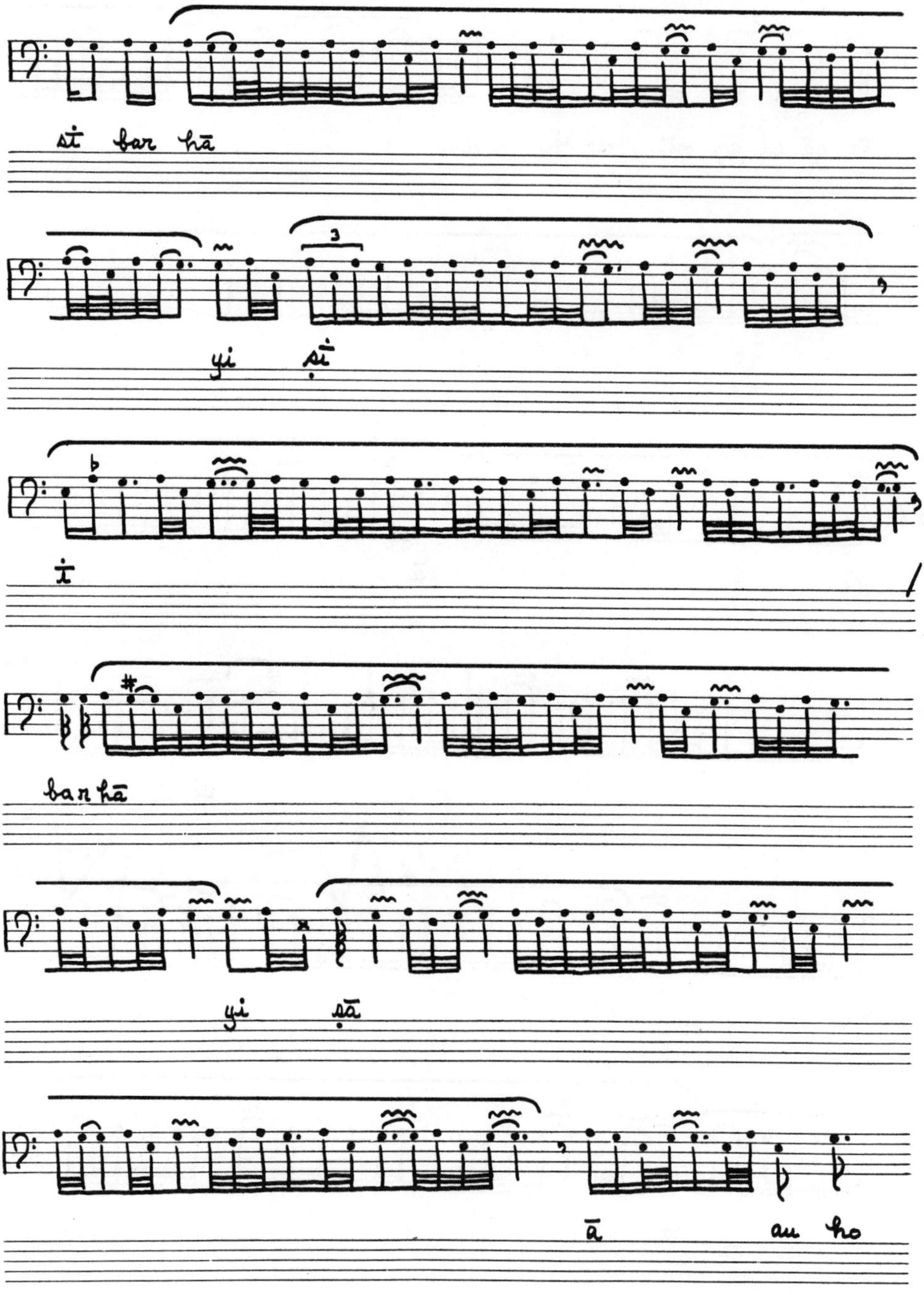

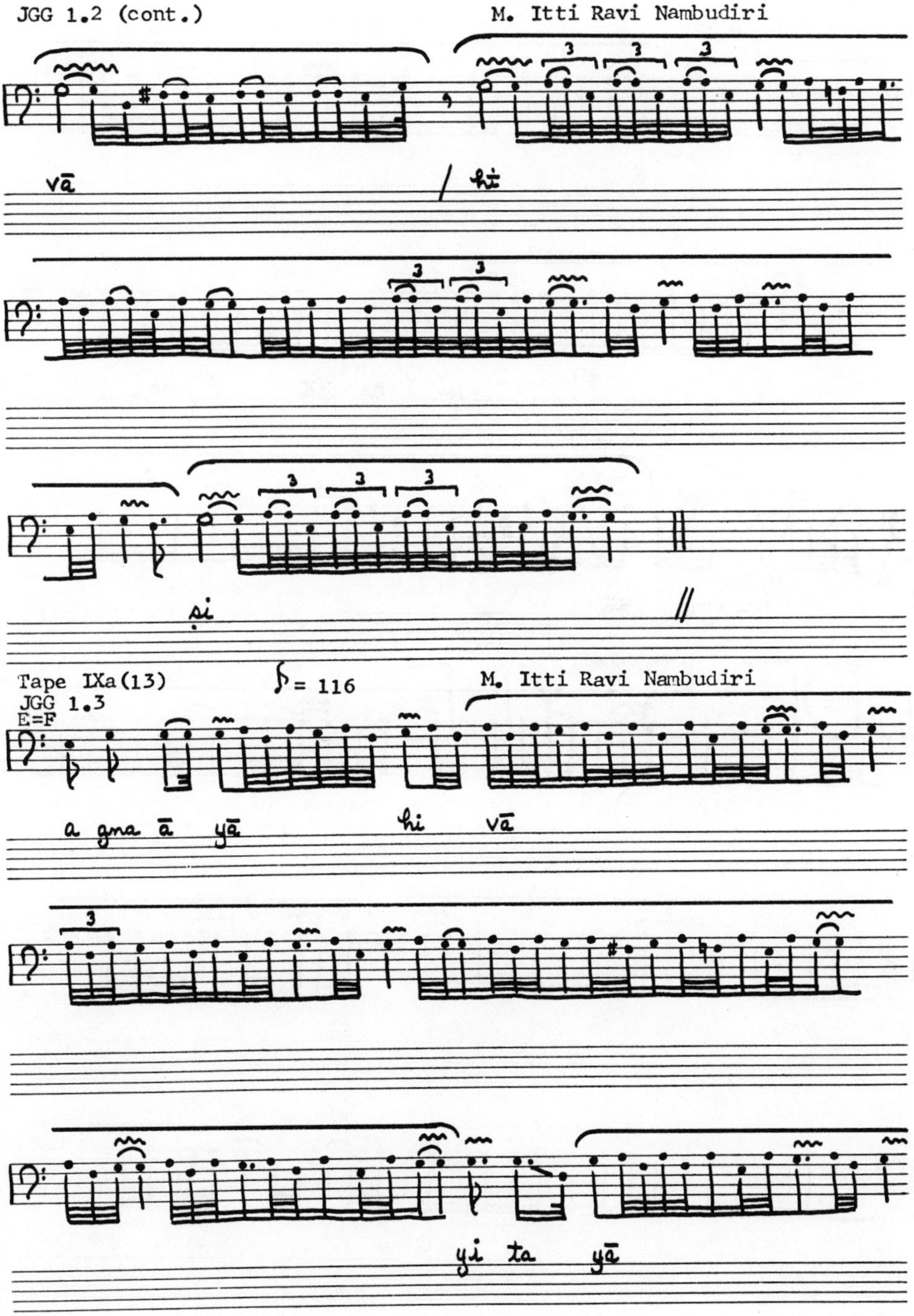
JGG 1.2 (cont.)
M. Itti Ravi Nambudiri
vā
hi
si
Tape IXa(13)
= 116
JGG 1.3
E=F
M. Itti Ravi Nambudiri
a gna ā yā
hi vā
yi ta yā

JGG 1.3 (cont.) M. Itti Ravi Nambudiri

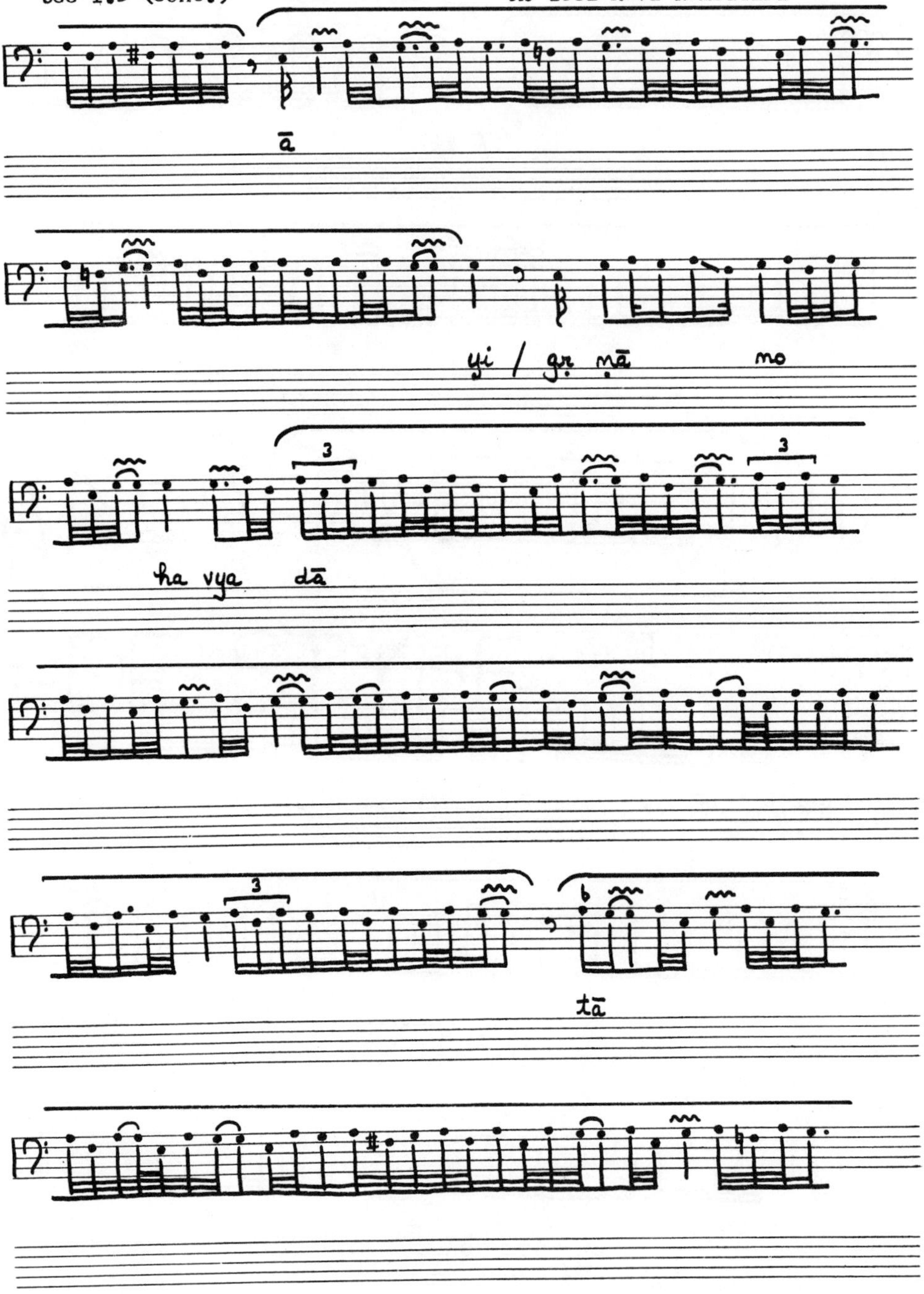
ā
yi / gṛ ṇā
mo
ha vya dā
tā

JGG 1.3 (cont.) M. Itti Ravi Nambudiri

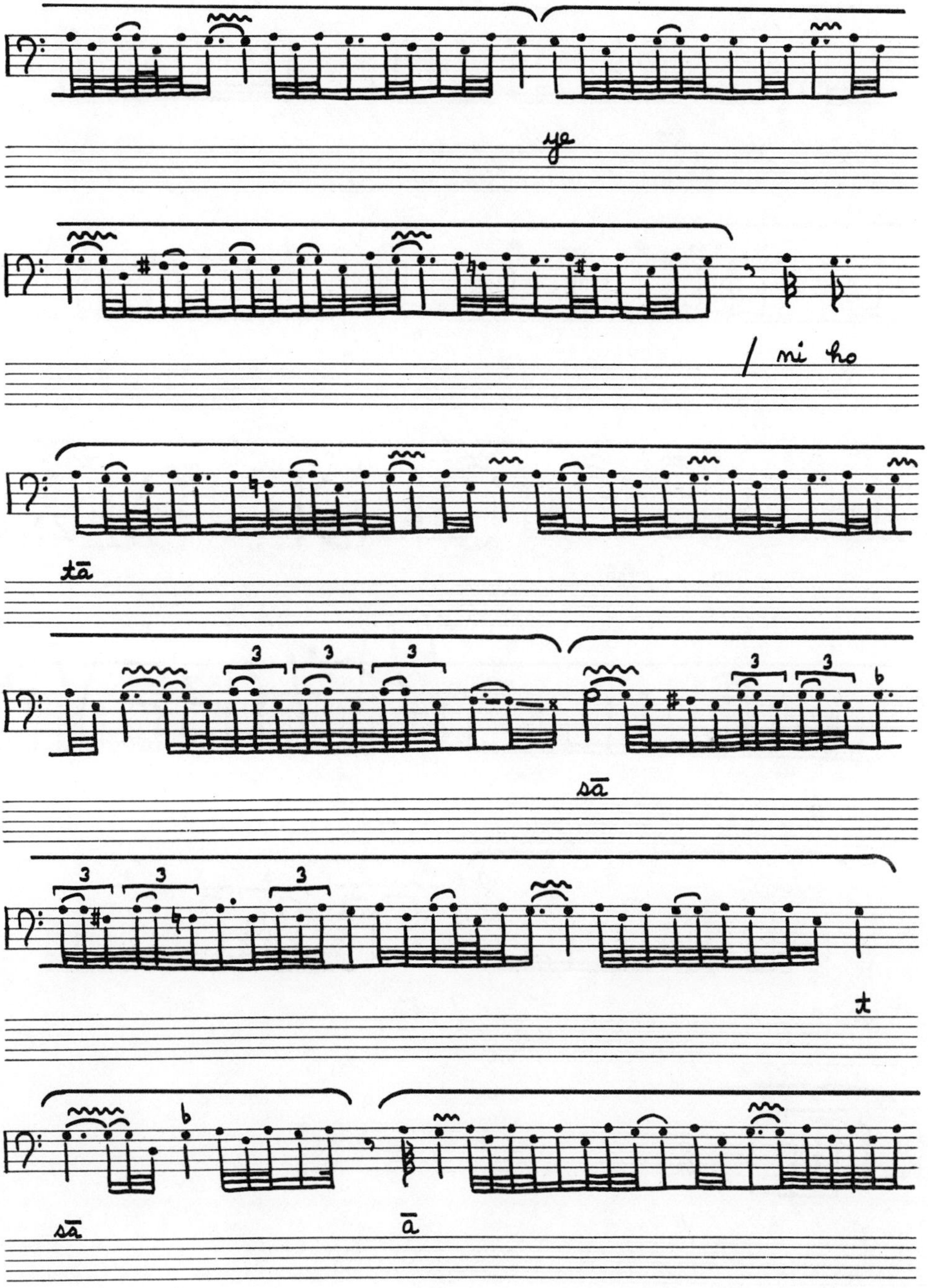
ye
/ ni ho
tā
sā
t
sā
ā

JGG 1.3 (cont.) M. Itti Ravi Nambudiri

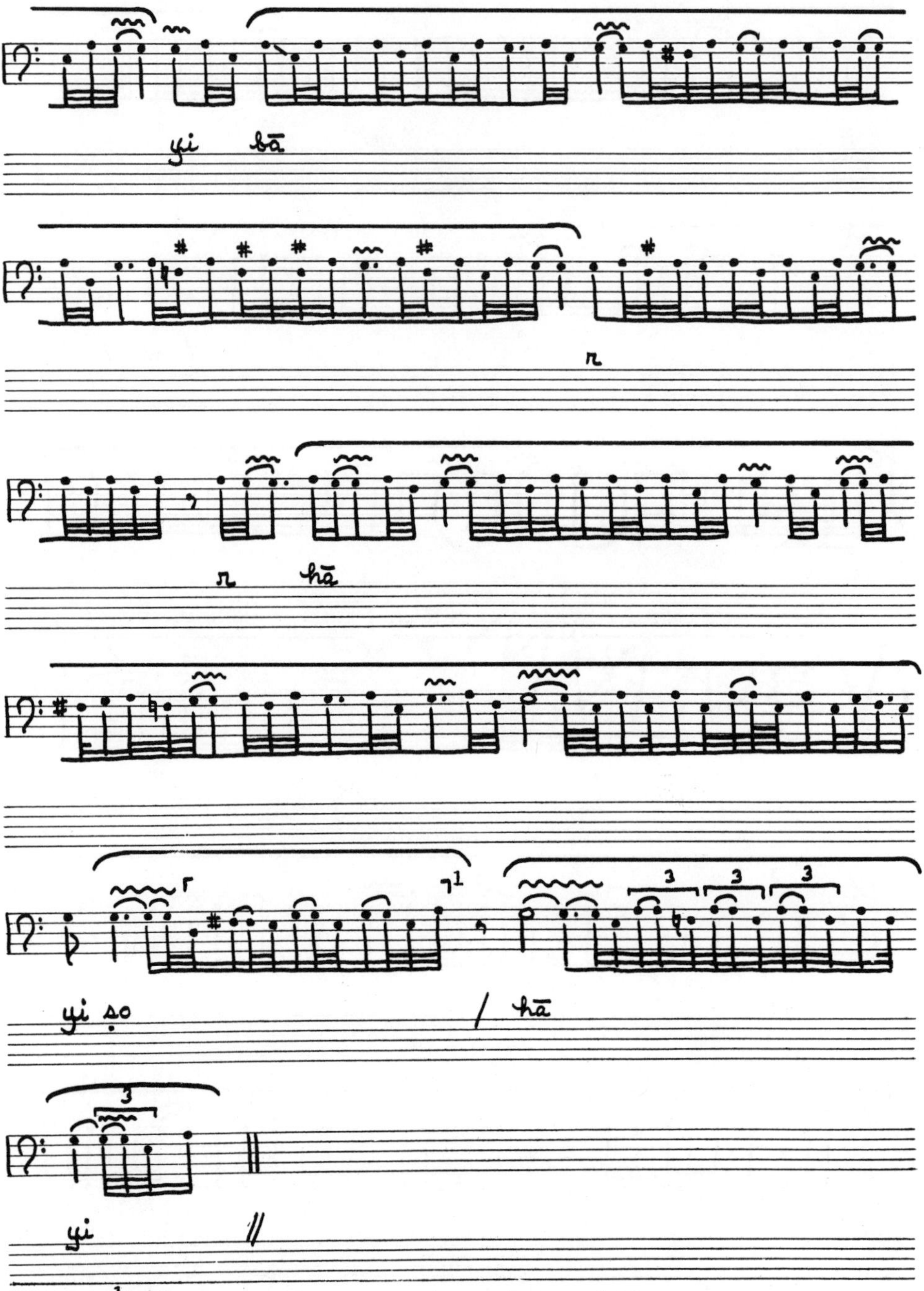

[1]Unclear on tape: approximate transcription.

Tape IXa(14)
JGG 1.1: abbreviated version ♪ = 116

M. Itti Ravi Nambudiri

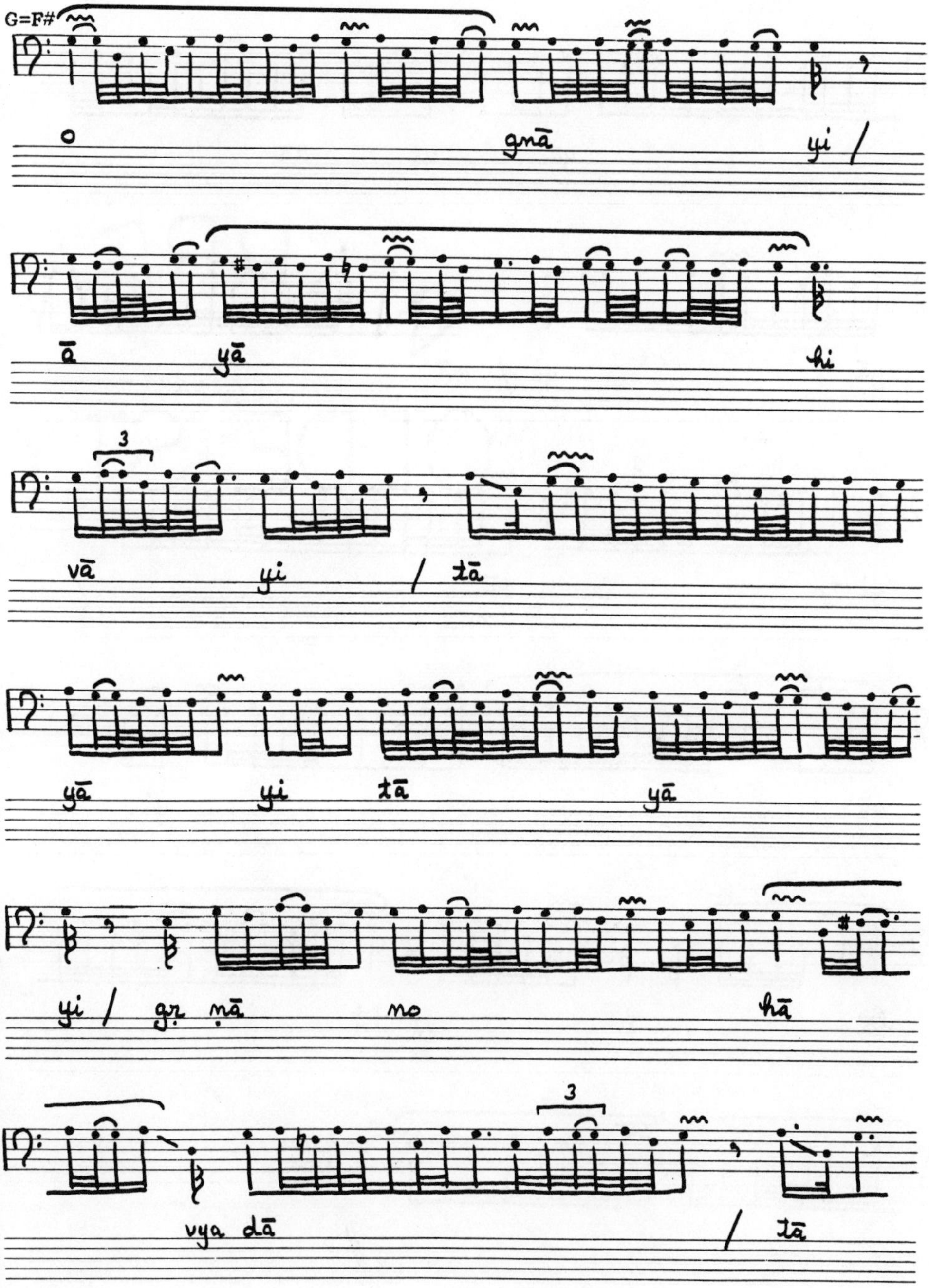

JGG 1.1: abbreviated version (cont.)   M. Itti Ravi Nambudiri

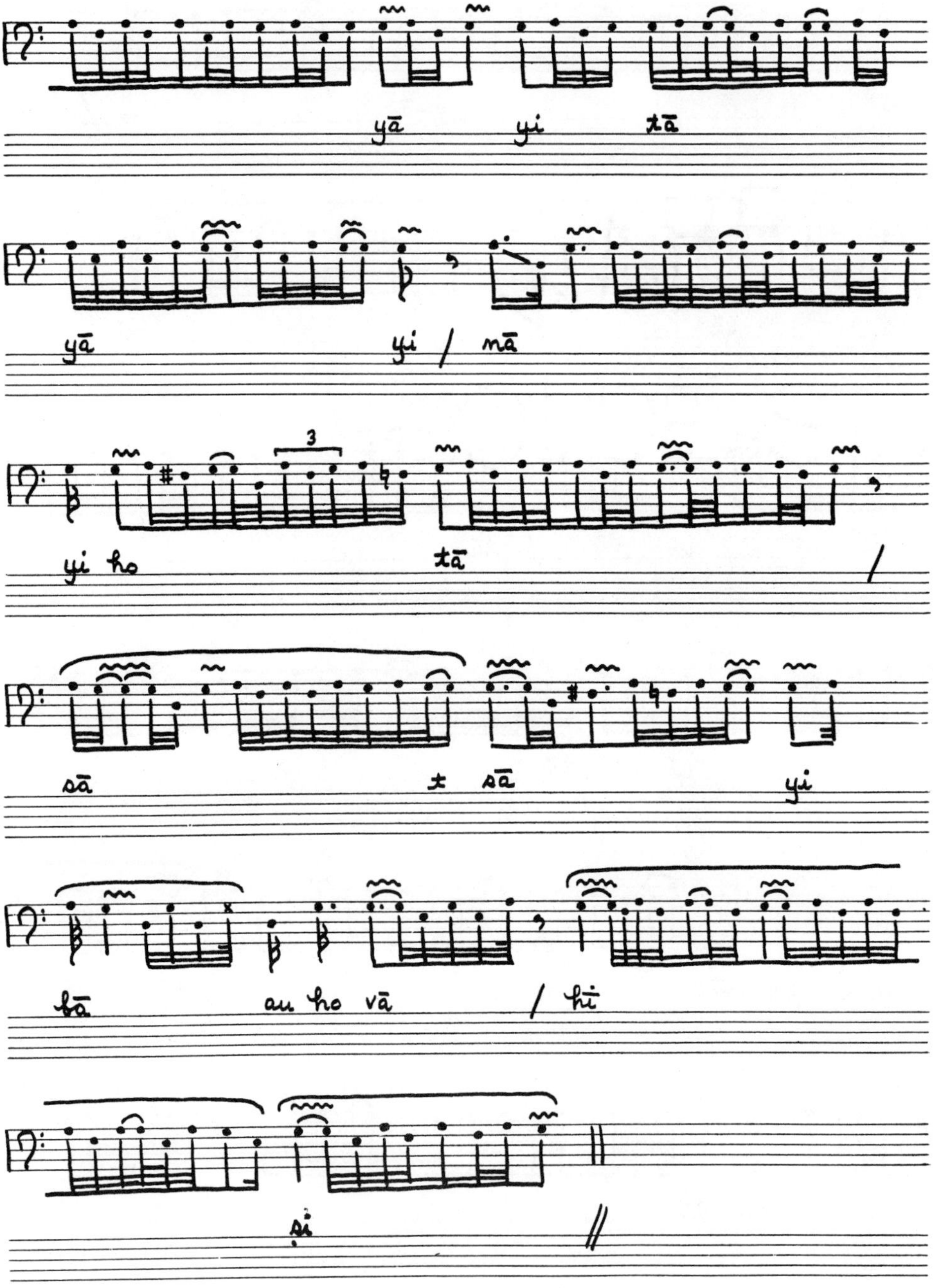
yā yi tā
yā yi / mā
yi ho tā /
sā t sā yi
bā au ho vā / hī
//

Tape IXa(14)
JGG 1.2: abbreviated version

♪ = 116

M. Itti Ravi Nambudiri

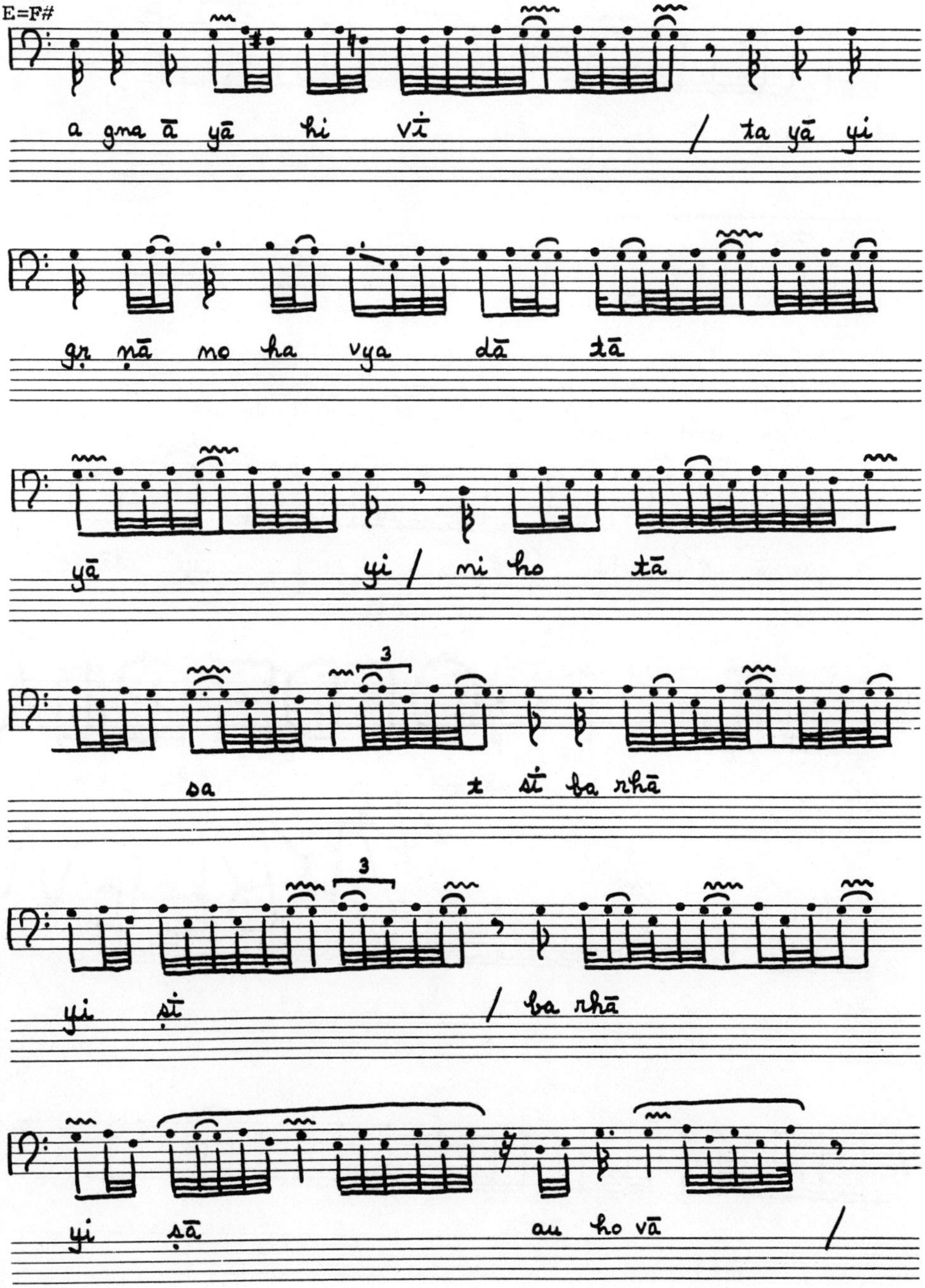
E=F#
a gna ā yā hi vi̇ / ta yā yi
gṛ ṇā mo ha vya dā tā
yā yi / mi ho tā
3
sa t sti̇ ba rhā
3
yi ṣi̇ / ba rhā
yi ṣā au ho vā /

JGG 1.2: abbreviated version (cont.) M. Itti Ravi Nambudiri

Tape IXa(14) ♪= 116 M. Itti Ravi Nambudiri
JGG 1.3: abbreviated version
E=E♭

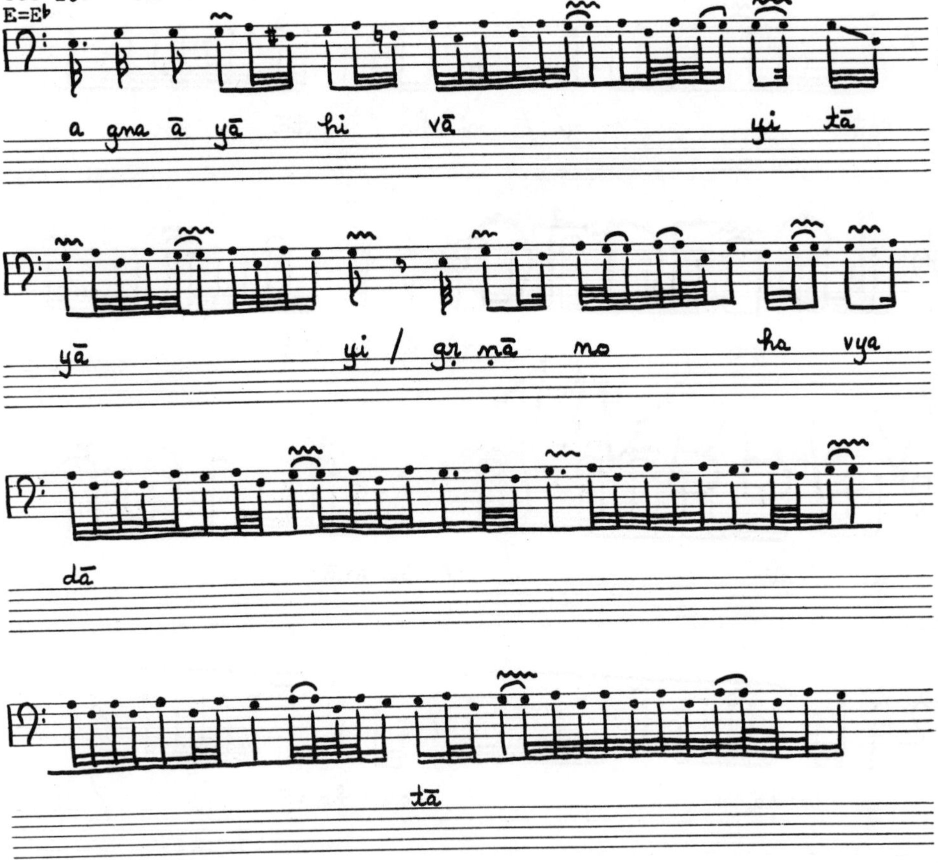

JGG 1.3: abbreviated version (cont.) M. Itti Ravi Nambudiri

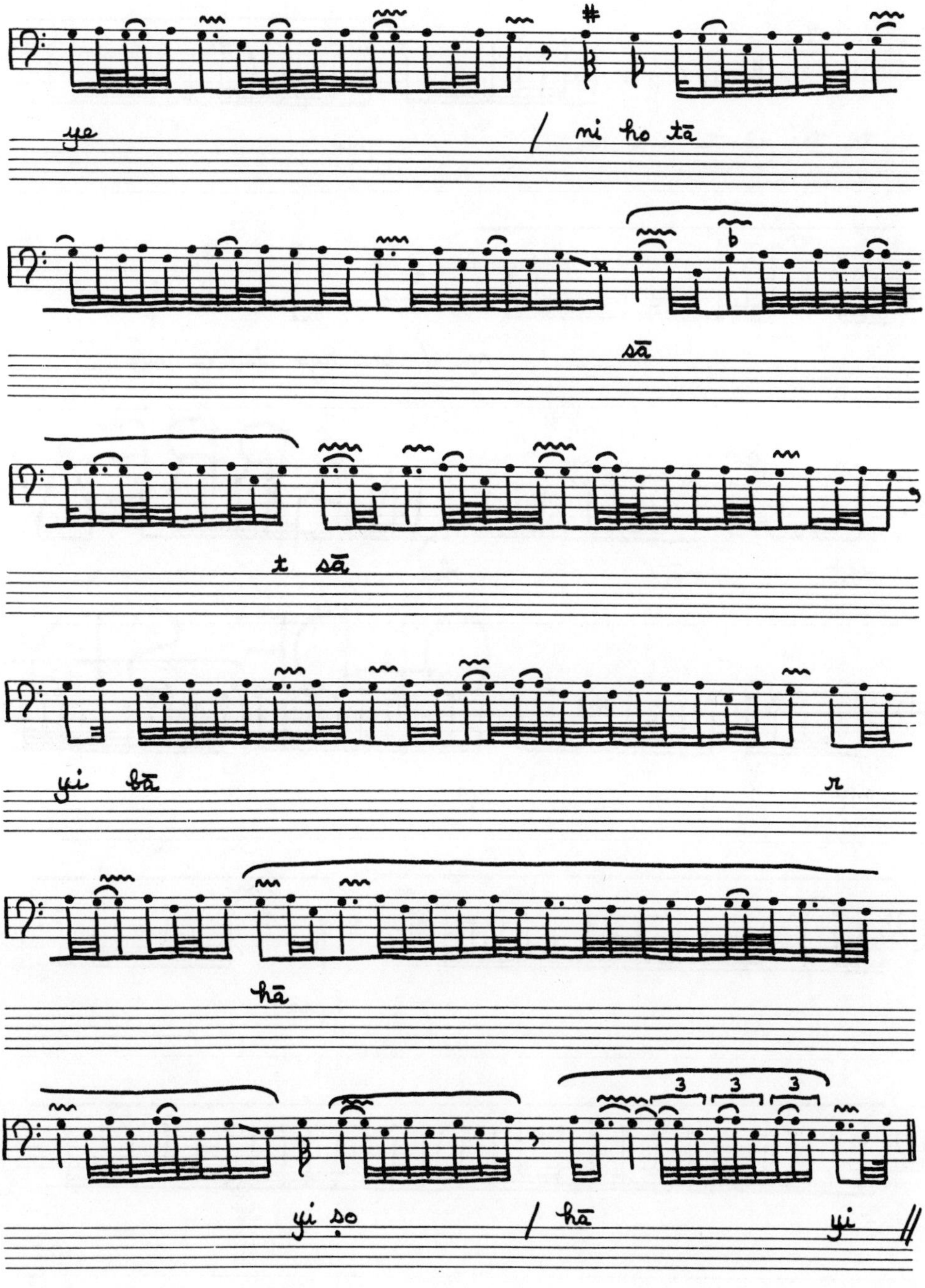

Tape IXb(2)
Jaiminīya Gāyatram

♪ = 116

M. Itti Ravi Nambudiri

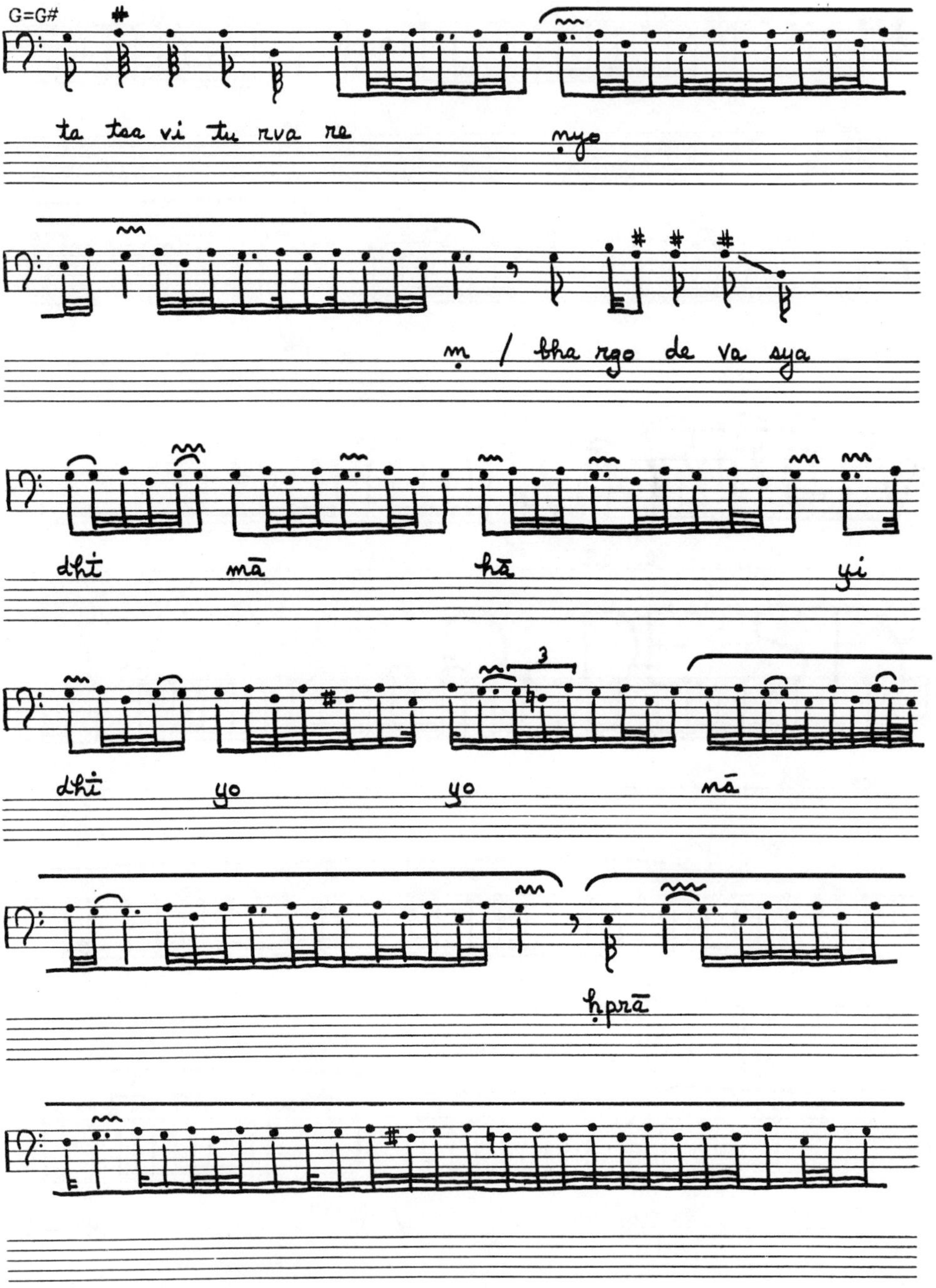
G=G#
ta tsa vi tu rva re
ṇyo
ṃ / bha rgo de va sya
dhī
mā
hā
yi
dhī
yo
yo
nā
ḥprā

Jaiminīya Gāyatram (cont.) M. Itti Ravi Nambudiri

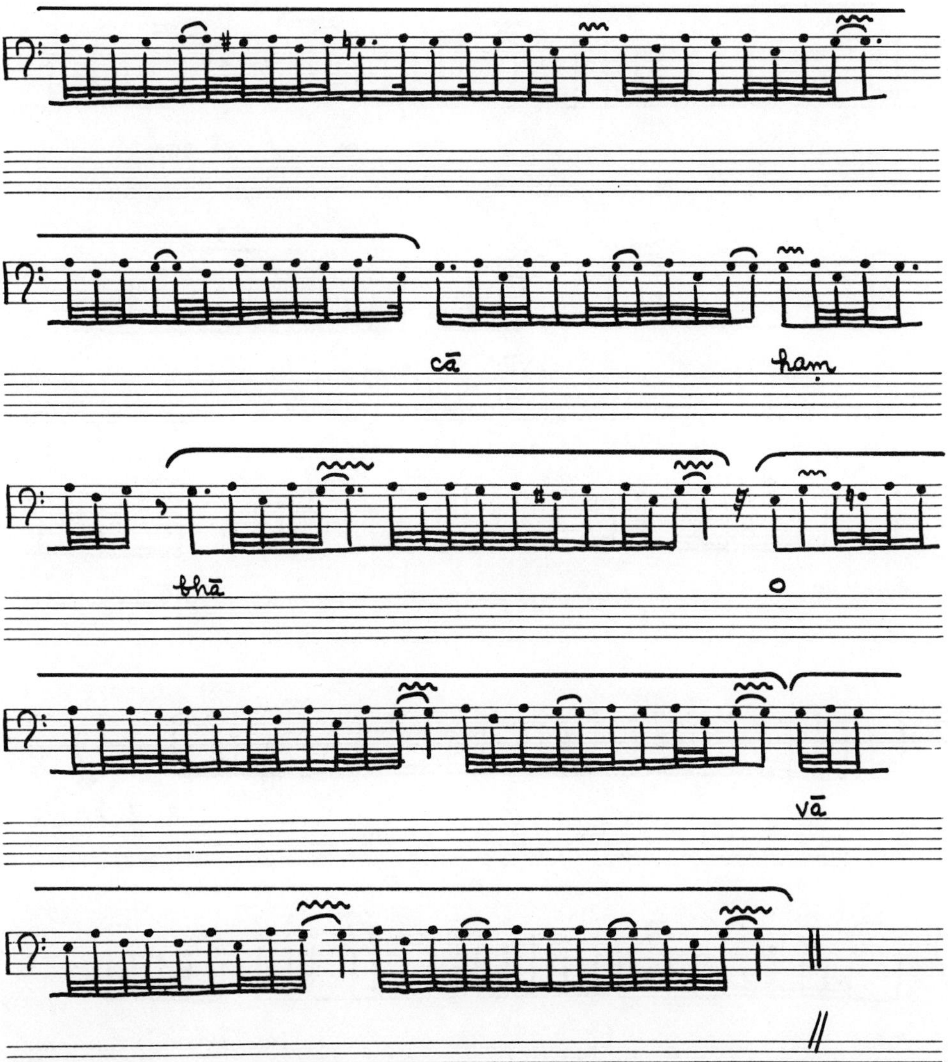

Tape IXb(7)B
JĀrG 1.1 ♪ = 116 T. Narayanan Nambudiri (Jaiminīya school)
Panjal village, Trichur District

D=C#

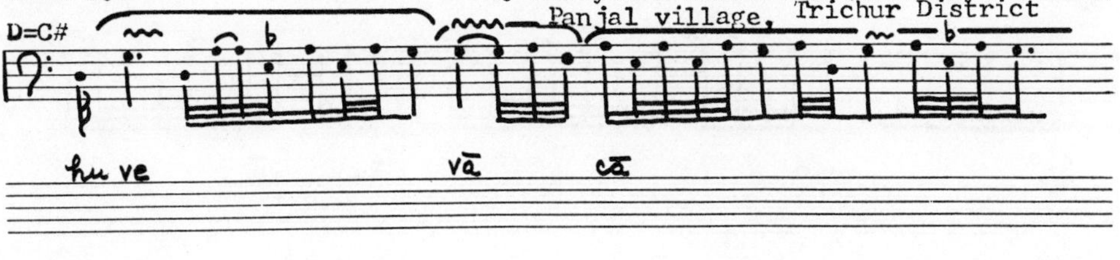

JĀrG 1.1 (cont.)   T. Narayanan Nambudiri

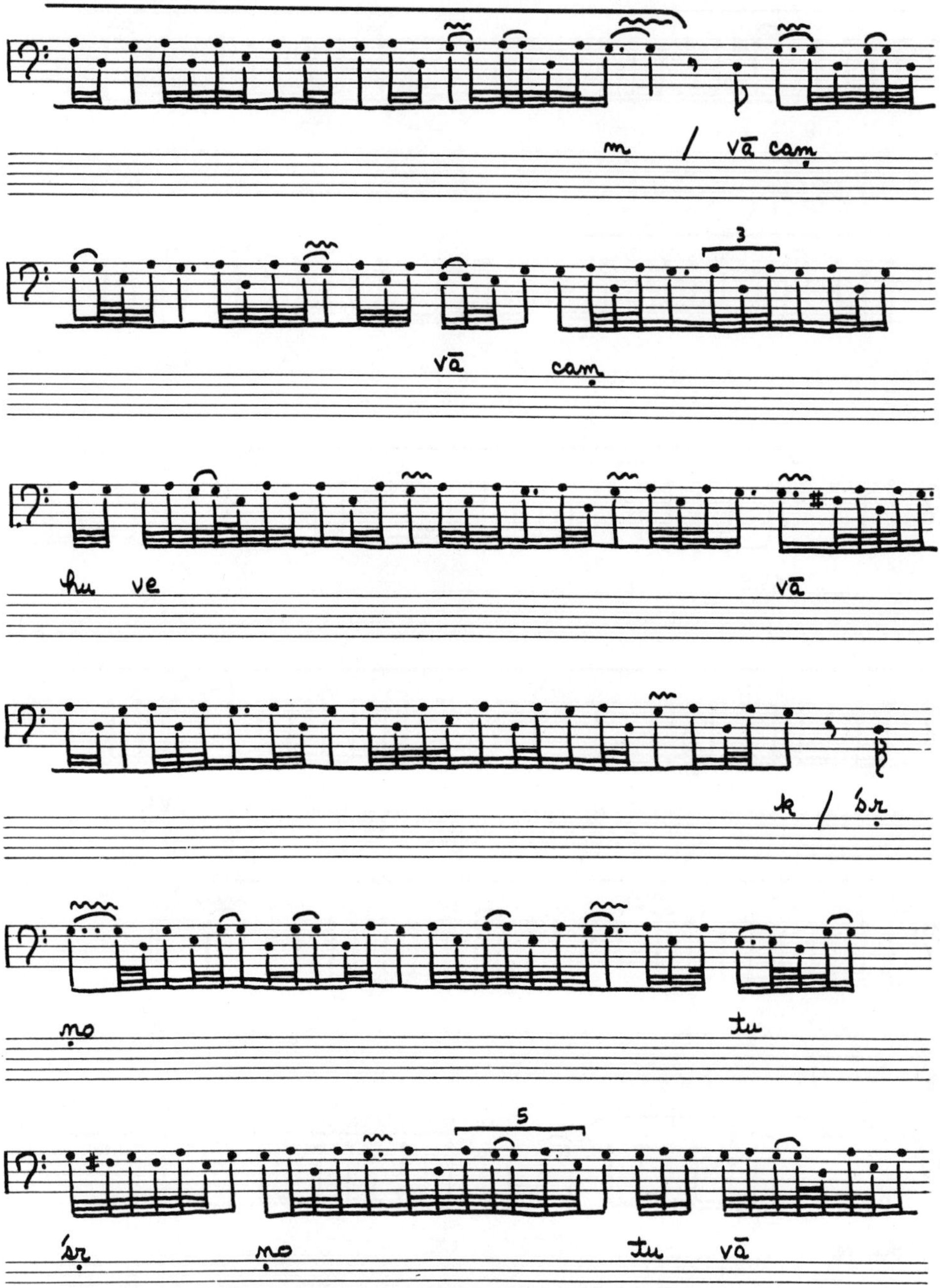

JĀrG 1.1 (cont.) T. Narayanan Nambudiri

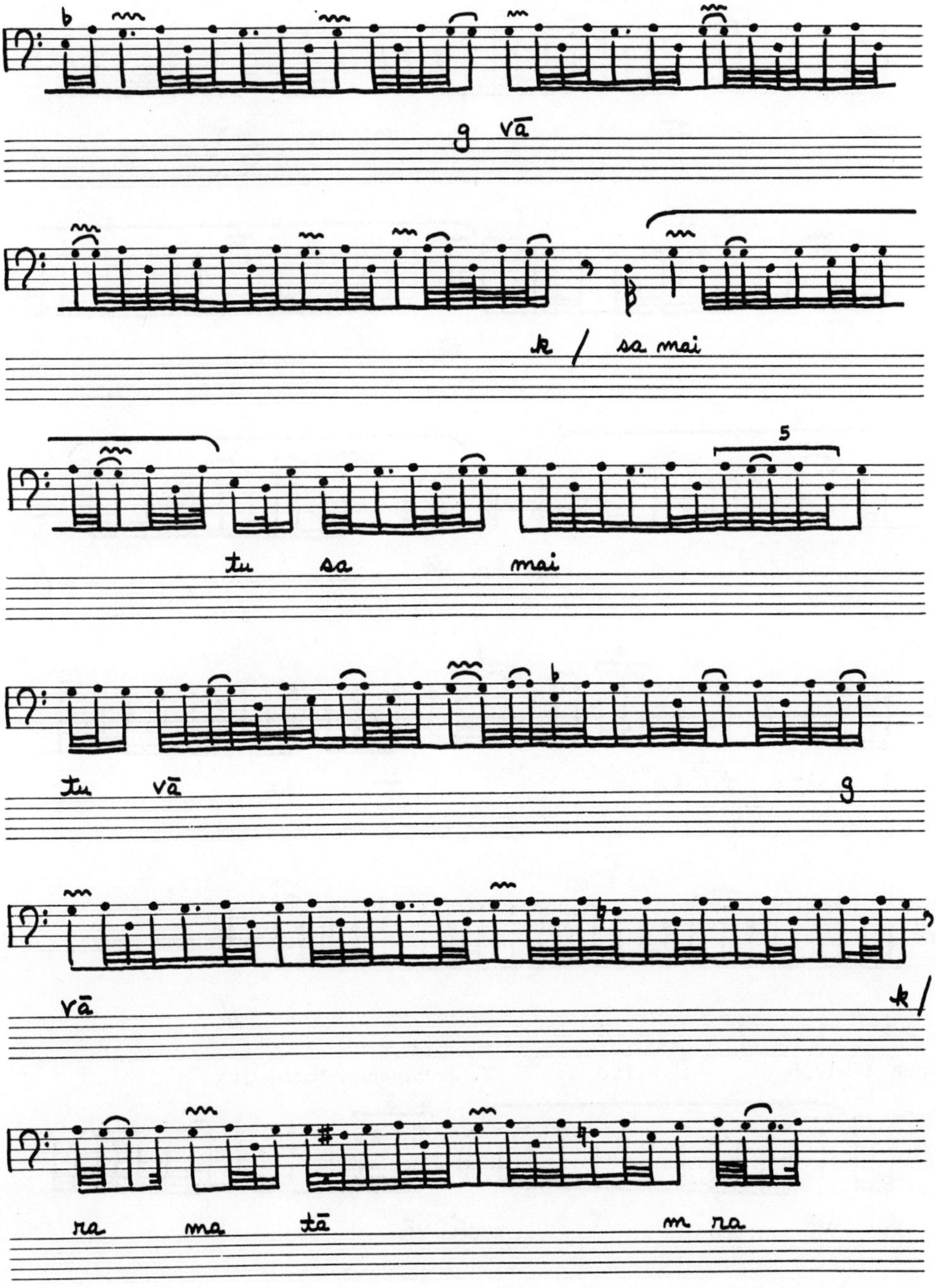

JĀrG 1.1 (cont.) T. Narayanan Nambudiri

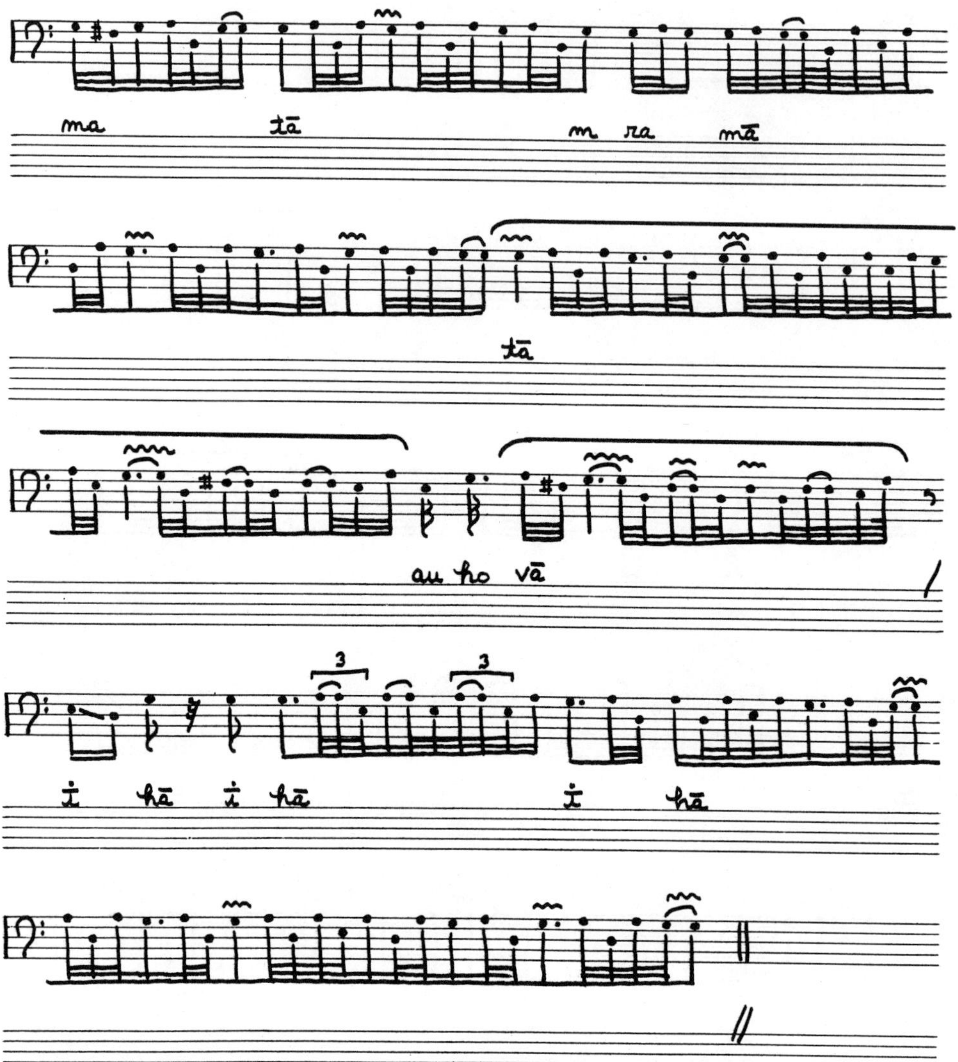

Tape IXb(7)B ♪ = 116 T. Narayanan Nambudiri
JĀrG 1.2
D=D

JĀrG 1.2 (cont.) T. Narayanan Nambudiri

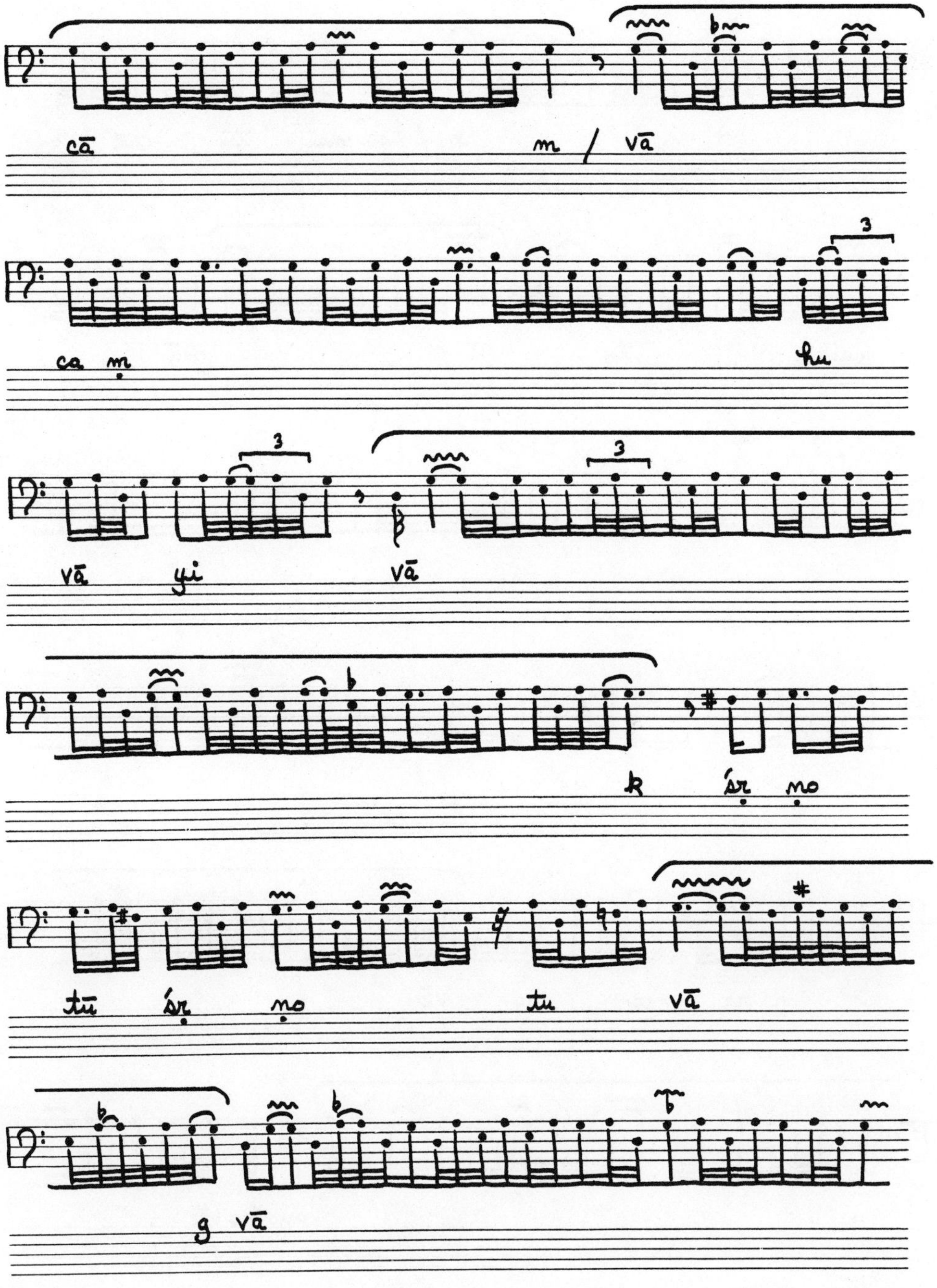

JĀrG 1.2 (cont.) T. Narayanan Nambudiri

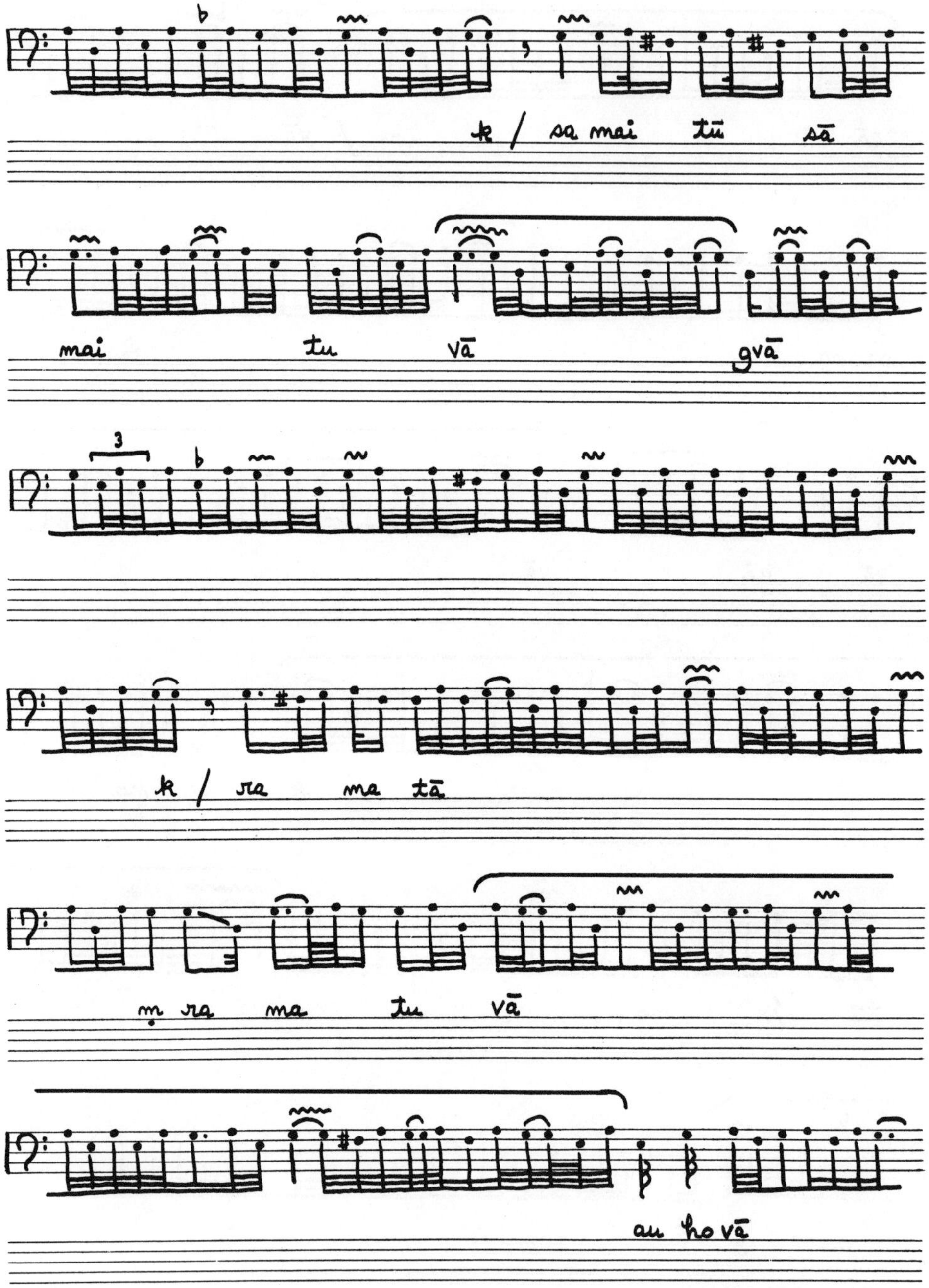

JĀrG 1.2 (cont.) T. Narayanan Nambudiri

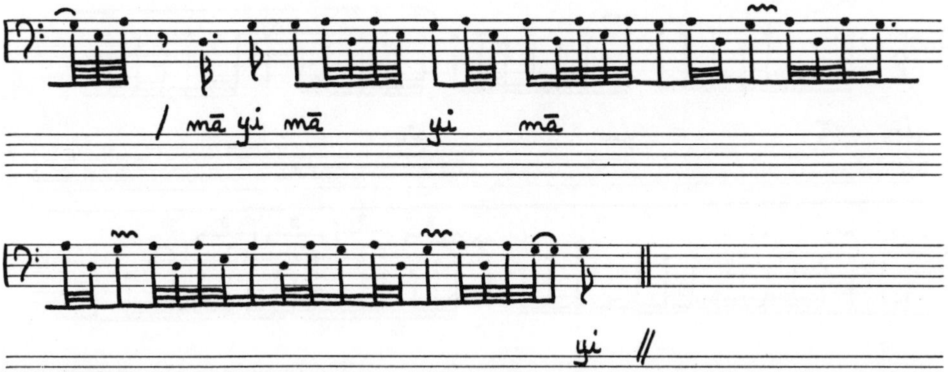

Tape Xb(2)
JUG from JS 3.6.9

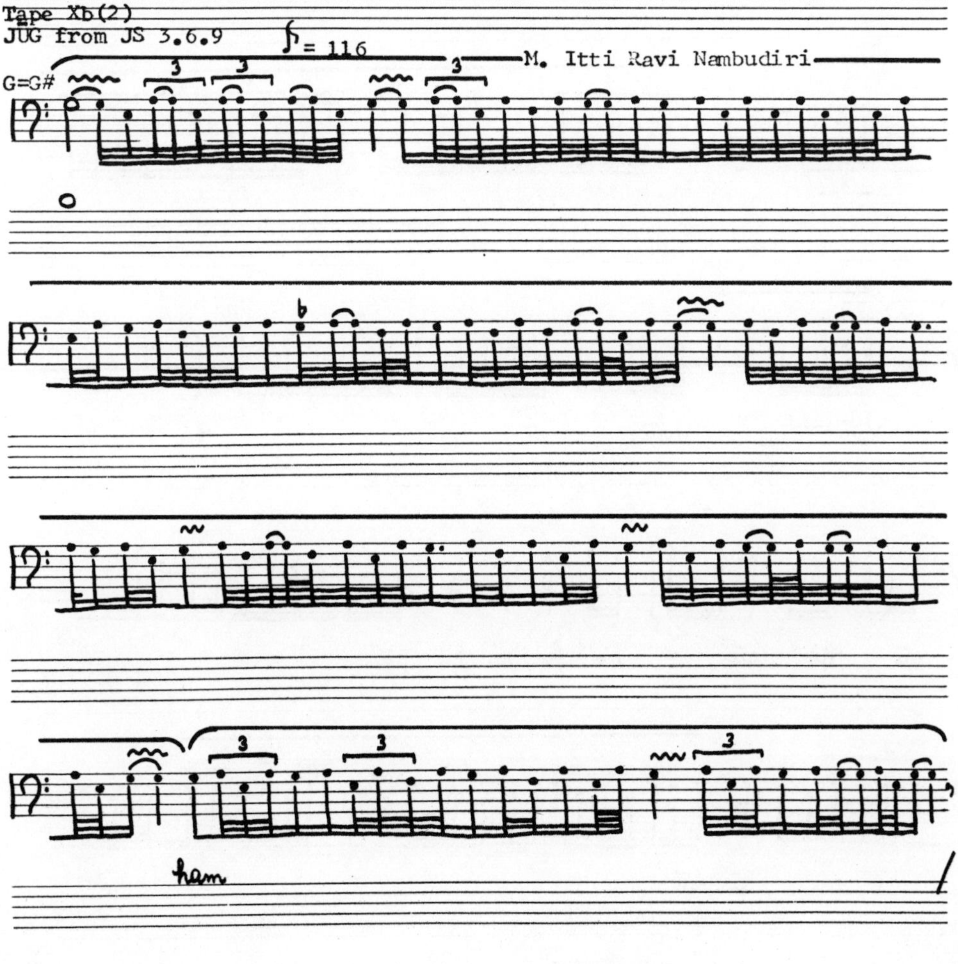

JŪG from JS 3.6.9 (cont.) M. Itti Ravi Nambudiri

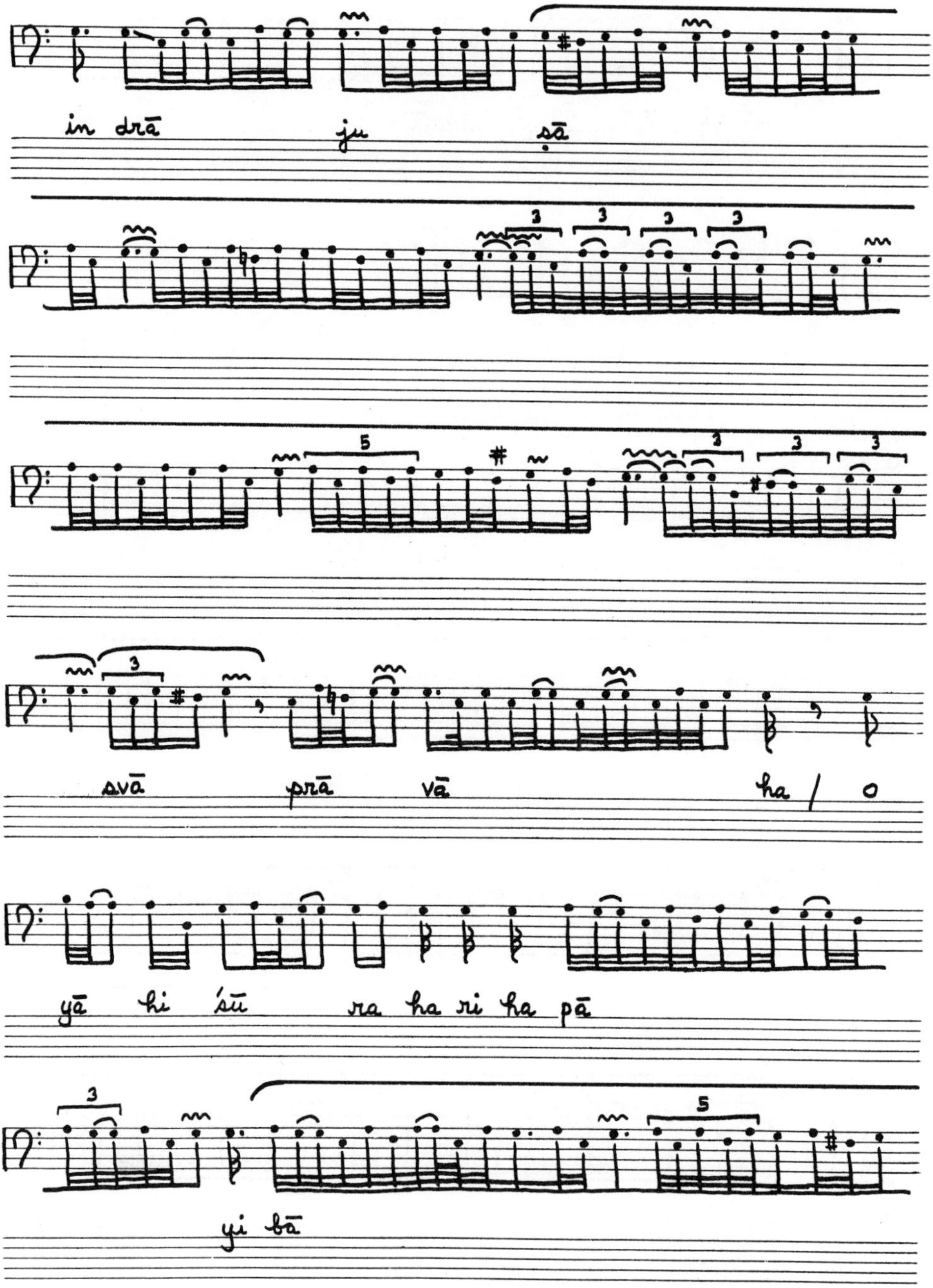

JŪG from JS 3.6.9 (cont.) M. Itti Ravi Nambudiri

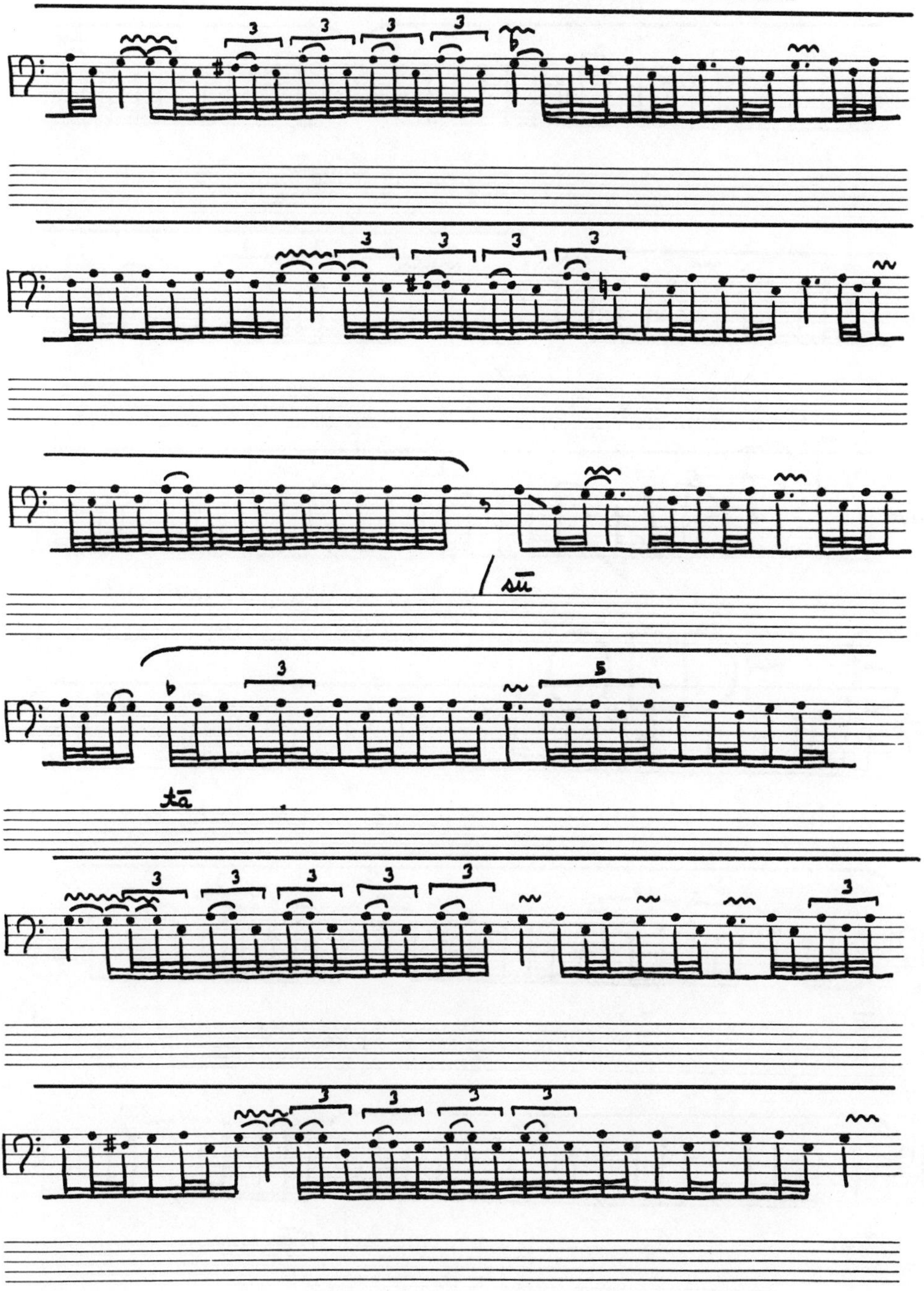

JŪG from JS 3.6.9 (cont.) M. Itti Ravi Nambudiri

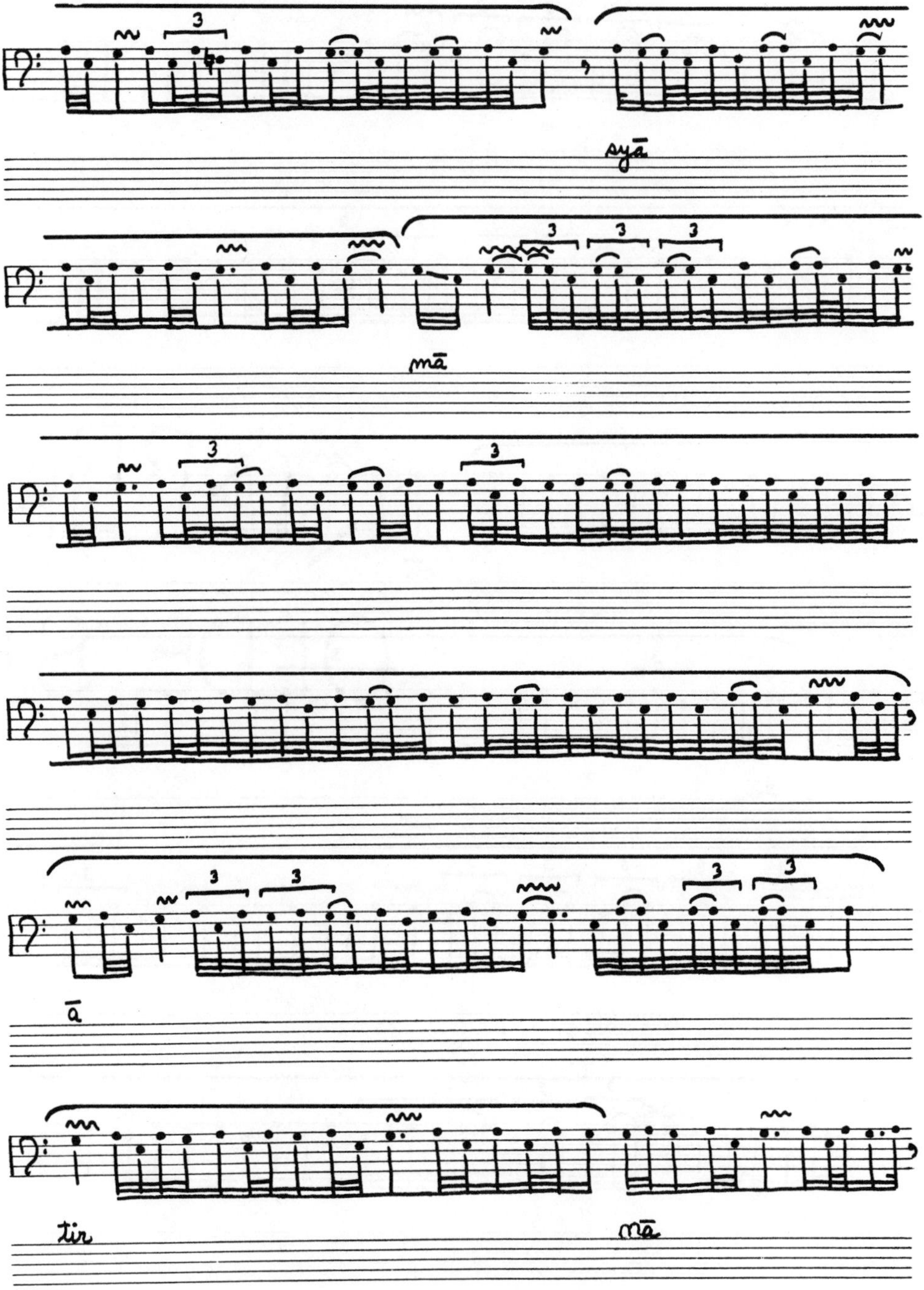

JŪG from JS 3.6.9 (cont.) M. Itti Ravi Nambudiri

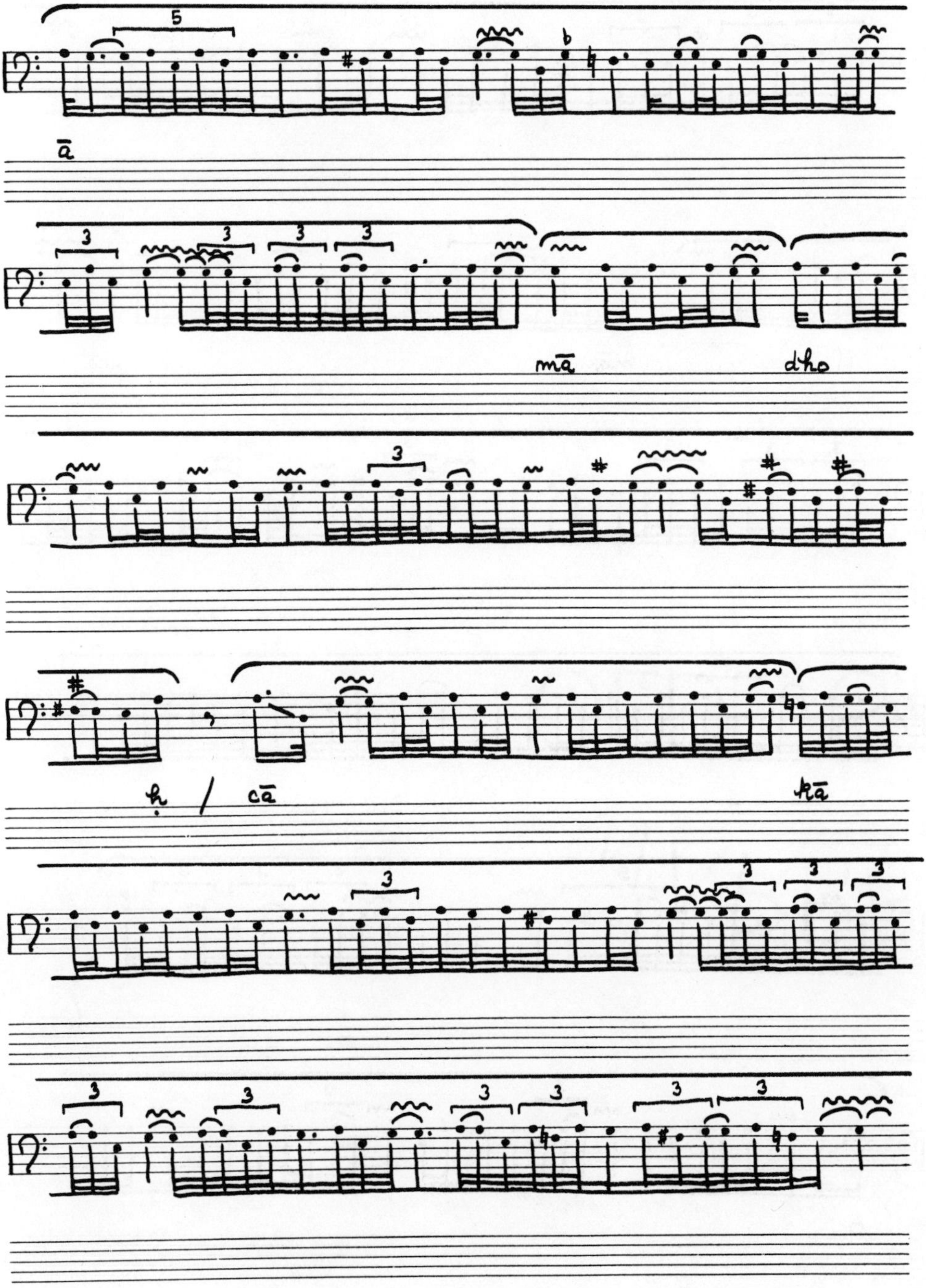

JŪG from JS 3.6.9 (cont.) M. Itti Ravi Nambudiri

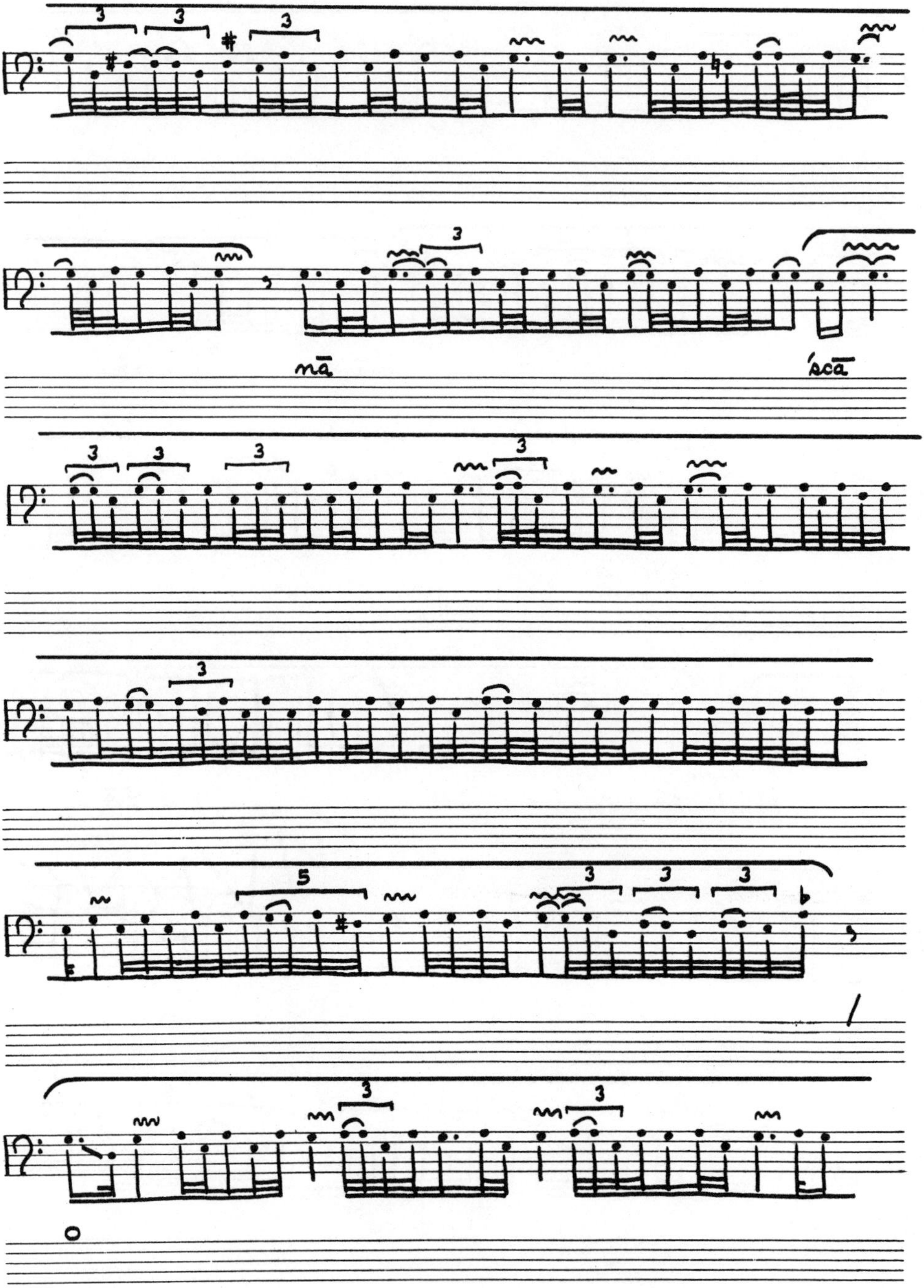

JŪG from JS 3.6.9 (cont.) M. Itti Ravi Nambudiri

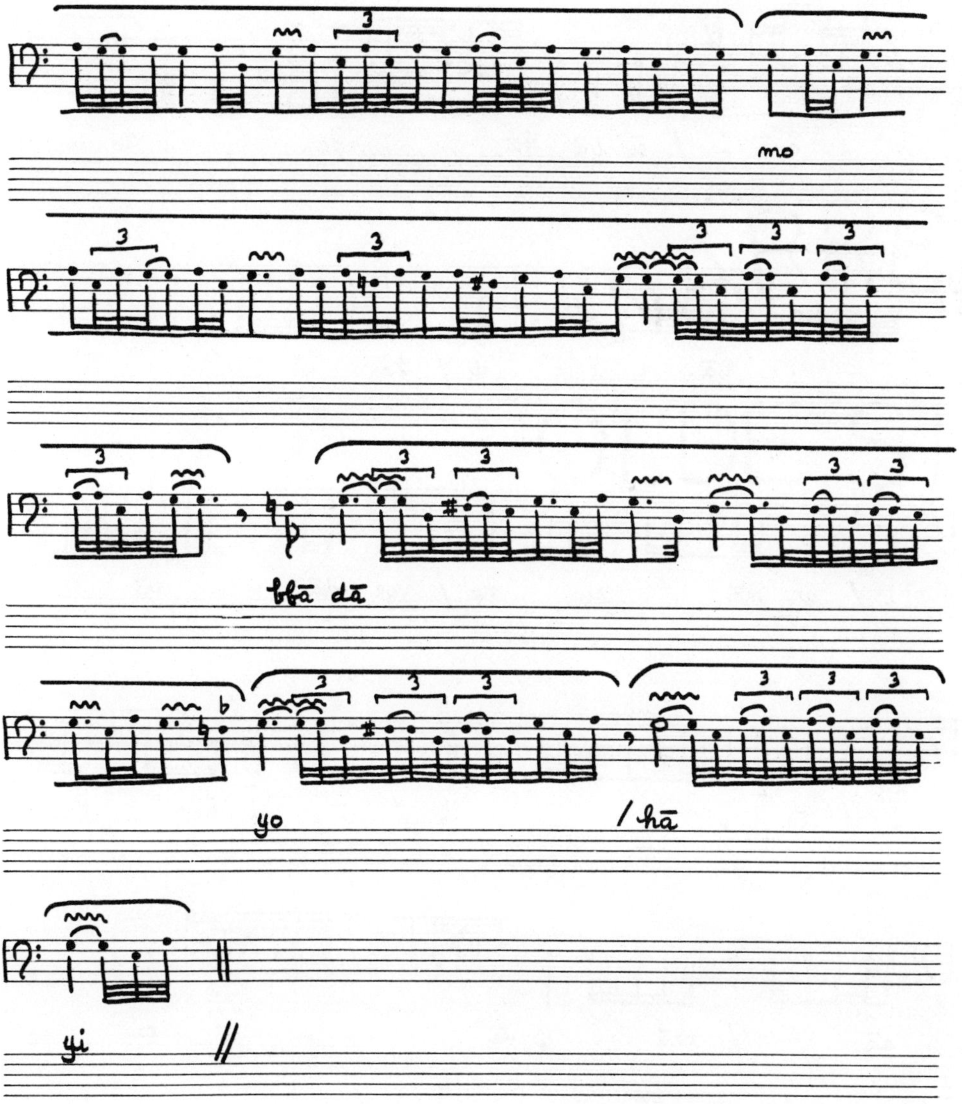

Tape XXVb(11)A · ♪ = 100
GG 1.1

M. Rajagopala Acarya (Jaiminiya[?] school), Matapadi, South Kannara District, Mysore

D=D

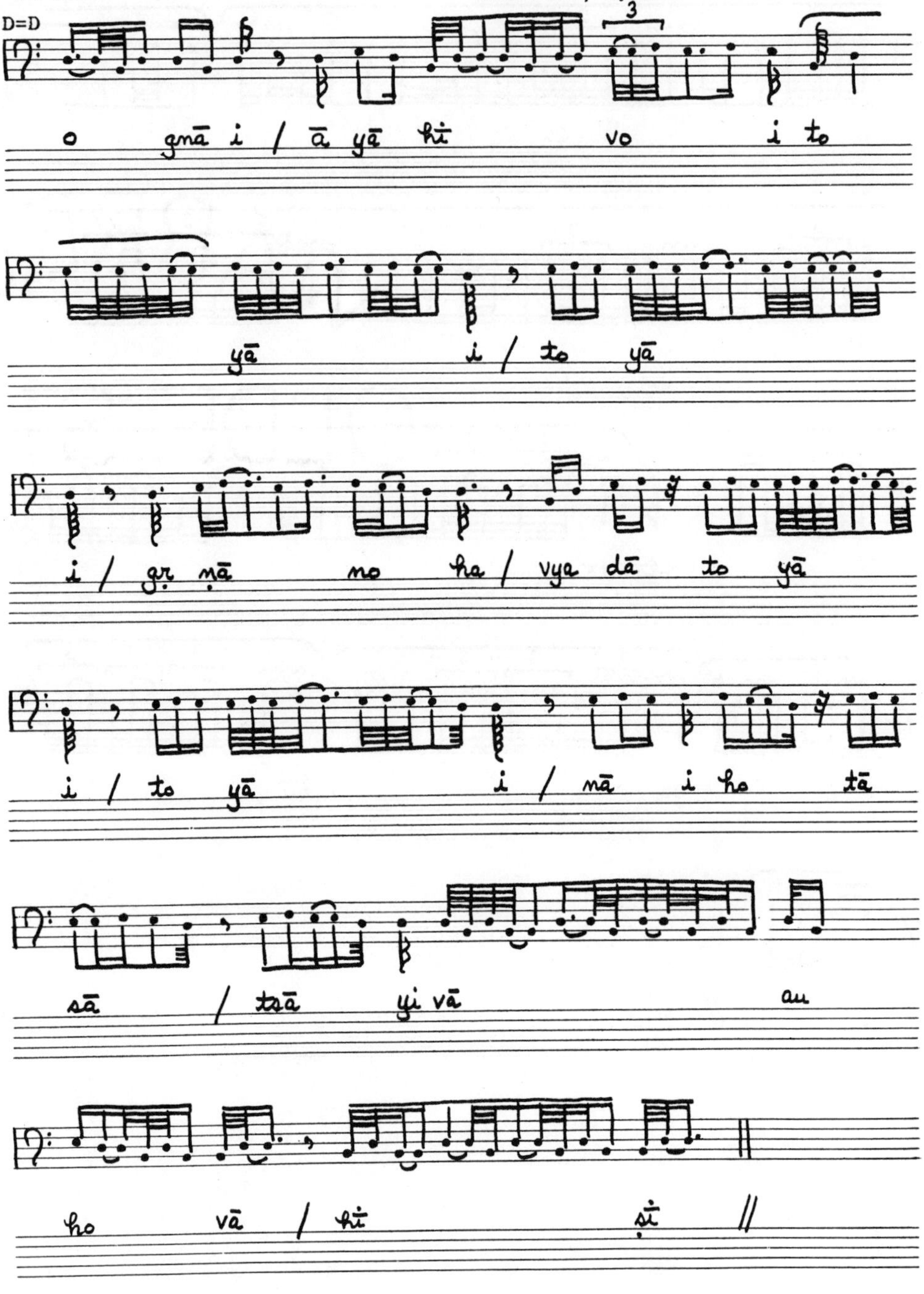
o gnā i / ā yā hi vo i to
yā i / to yā
i / gṛ ṇā no ha / vya dā to yā
i / to yā i / nā i ho tā
sā / tsā yi vā au
ho vā / hi ṣi //

Tape XXVb(16)A
Gāyatram

♪ = 100

M. Narasimha Acarya and his son
M. Ramamohana (Jaiminīya[?] school)
Matapadi, S. Kannara District, Mysore

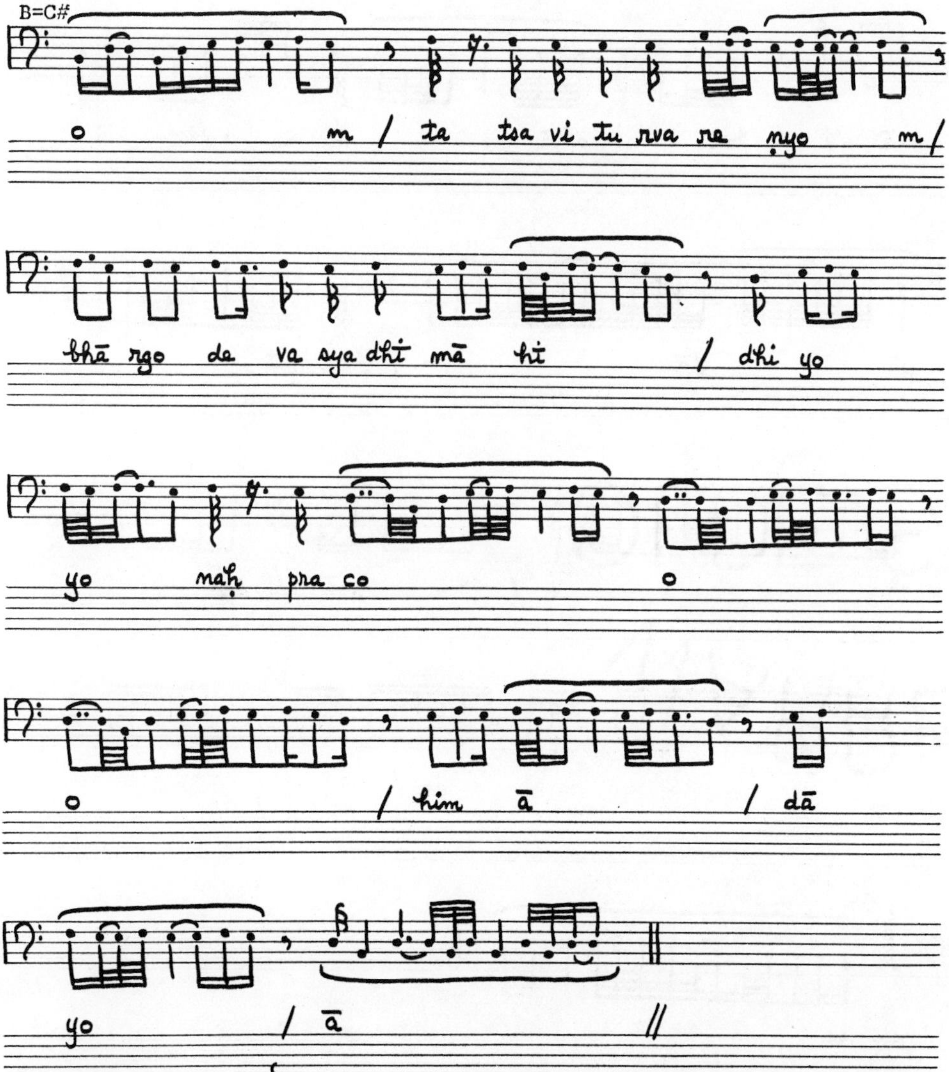

Tape XXVb(12)
GG 222.1

♪ = 100

M. Rajagopala Acarya

GG 222.1 (cont.) M. Rajagopala Acarya

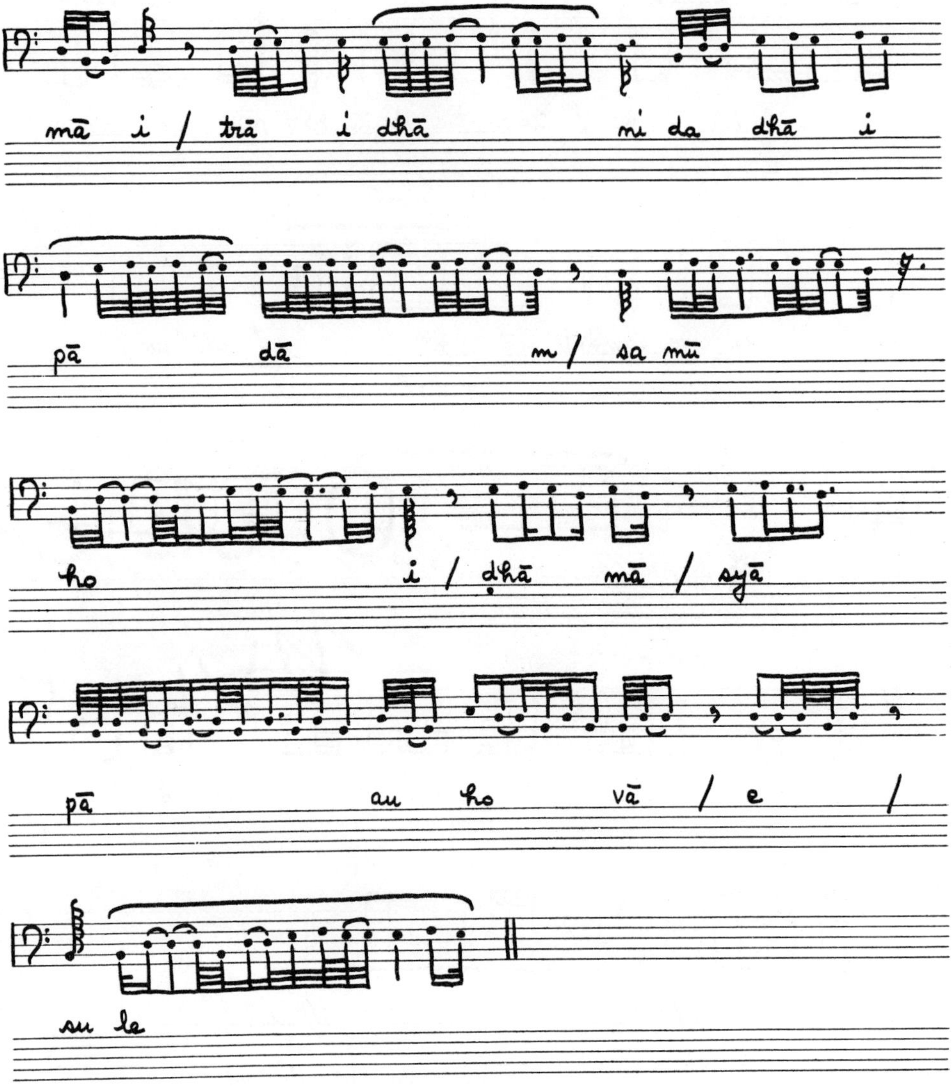
mā i / trā i dhā ni da dhā i
pā dā m / sa mū
ho i / ḍhā mā / syā
pā au ho vā / e /
su le

APPENDIX

CATALOGUE OF RECORDINGS MADE IN INDIA FROM DECEMBER 1970 TO DECEMBER 1971 (FULBRIGHT-HAYS GRANT)

Abbreviations

ṚGVEDA

AB	Aitareya Brāhmaṇa
ĀŚ	Āśvalāyana Śrauta Sūtra
ṚV	Ṛgveda Saṃhitā
ṚVKh	Khilas of the Ṛgveda
KB	Kauṣītaki Brāhmaṇa

KṚṢṆA YAJURVEDA

ĀpMB	Āpastamba Mantra Brāhmaṇa
TĀ	Taittirīya Āraṇyaka
TU	Taittirīya Upaniṣad
TB	Taittirīya Brāhmaṇa
TS	Taittirīya Saṃhitā
MahānU	Mahānārāyaṇa Upaniṣad
MG	Mānava Gṛhya Sūtra

ŚUKLA YAJURVEDA

ĪśāU	Īśāvāsya Upaniṣad
VS	Vājasaneyi Saṃhitā, Mādhyandina recension

VSK	Vājasaneyi Saṃhitā, Kāṇva recension
ŚB	Śatapatha Brāhmaṇa, Mādhyandina recension
ŚBK	Śatapatha Brāhmaṇa, Kāṇva recension

SĀMAVEDA

ĀrG	Āraṇyakagāna
ĀrS	Āraṇyaka Saṃhitā
ŪG	Ūhagāna
KenaU	Kena Upaniṣad
GG	Grāmageyagāna
ChU	Chāndogya Upaniṣad
JĀrG	Jaiminīya Āraṇyakagāna
JUB	Jaiminīya Upaniṣad Brāhmaṇa
JŪG	Jaiminīya Ūhagāna
JGG	Jaiminīya Grāmageyagāna
JRG	Jaiminīya Rahasyagāna (Ūhyagāna)
JS	Jaiminīya Saṃhitā
DB	Daivata Brāhmaṇa
PB	Pañcaviṃśa Brāhmaṇa
RG	Rahasyagāna (Ūhyagāna)
SUB	Saṃhitopaniṣad Brāhmaṇa
SV	Sāmaveda Saṃhitā

ATHARVAVEDA

AV	Atharvaveda Samhitā
GB	Gopatha Brāhmaṇa

NOTE: Names of North Indian _rāgas_ are followed by references to pages in Walter Kaufmann's _The Rāgas of North India_, Indiana University Press (Bloomington), 1968.

Recordings

TAPE Ia

(1) Yajurveda Gāyatrī (see VS 36.3): saṃhitā, pada, krama, jaṭā, puṣpamālā, kramamālā, viloma, śikhā, daṇḍa, dhvaja, ghana

By Virsen Vedasrami (Indore). Śākhā: Mādhyandina. Gotra: Kaśyapa.

Recorded at Nadiad (Gujarat) 5/II/71

(2) ṚV 1.2.1-9; 1.3.1-12

By Visvanatha Deva (Varanasi). Śākhā: Śākala. Gotra: Viṣṇuvṛddha. Sūtra: Āśvalāyana.

Recorded at Nadiad 7/II/71

(3) ĀrS 1.9; ĀrG 57.1

By Ganapati Sankar Kacarasankar (Ahmedabad). Śākhā: Kauthuma. Gotra: Kaśyapa. Sūtra: Gobhila.

Recorded at Nadiad 8/II/71

(4) SV 1.67; ĀrG 25.1

By Babubhai Maganlal Gor (Kaparavanj). Śākhā: Kauthuma. Gotra: Kauśika. Sūtra: Gobhila.

(5) AV 19.9.1; 1.21.1-4

By Lakshmisankar Gaurisankar Raval (Bhavnagar). Śākhā: Paippalāda, Śaunakapāṭha. Gotra: Bhāradvāja. Sūtra: Kauśika.

(6) SV 1.143; GG 143.2

By Naraharisankar Bhaisankar Ojha (Suklatirth). Śākhā: Kauthuma. Gotra: Kauśika. Sūtra: Gobhila.

TAPE Ia (continued)

(7) Īśā U (complete)

By Vishnudeva Sankalesvara Pandita (Ahmedabad).

Sakha: Mādhyandina. Gotra: Kāśyapa.

Recorded at Nadiad 10/II/71

(8) SV 1.1-3; GG 1.1-3

(9) Subrahmaṇyāhvāna

By Agnishvatt Sastri Agnihotri. Śākhā: Kauthuma.

Gotra: Vatsa. Sūtra: Gobhila.

Recorded at Varanasi 29/III/71

TAPE Ib

(1) ĀrG 57.1

(2) ĀrG 140.1

By Agnishvatt Sastri Agnihotri

Recorded at Varanasi 1/III/71

(3) GG 284.2

(4) ŪG 1.1.13.1; RG 1.1.1

(5) RG 1.1.5

(6) DB 4.1-5

(7) SUB 4.1-14

(8) PB 1.1.1-9

(9) ChU 8.6.1-6

By Krishnamurti Srauti(gal) (Maraiturai, Tanjore District). Śākhā: Kauthuma. Gotra: Vatsa. Sūtra: Drāhyāyaṇa.

Recorded at Varanasi 2/III/71

TAPE Ib (continued)

(10) ŪG 6.3.7; RG 1.1.1.1

(11) SV 2.812; Kauthuma Gāyatram; GG 1.1

(12) ĀrG 61.1

(13) GG 267.1

(14) ŪG 1.1.5

By Yajnarama Dikshita. Śākhā: Kauthuma. Gotra: Bhāradvāja. Sūtra: Drāhyāyaṇa.

Recorded at Pinnavasal (Tiruccirappalli District, near Lalgudi) 15/VI/71

(15) RG 1.1.1; ŪG 1.1.5

By P. T. Govinda Aiyangar (Terali, Madurai District). Śākhā: Chāndosāma (=Kauthuma). Gotra: Bhāradvāja. Sūtra: Drāhyāyaṇa.

(16) ŪG 5.3.2; RG 5.1.8

By P. K. Srinivasa Aiyangar (Terali, Madurai District). Śākhā: Chāndosāma. Gotra: Bhāradvāja. Sūtra: Drāhyāyaṇa.

(17) ĀrG, after 127.1:1-3; ĀrG 61.1

By P. T. Govinda Aiyangar and P. K. Srinivasa Aiyangar

Recorded at Srirangam 16/VI/71

TAPE IIa

(1) SV 1.1; GG 1.1-2

(2) SV 1.512; GG 512.1-3 (through "yo naryo 2 psuv antar ā")

(3) SV 1.512; GG 512.1-2, 5-6, 10-11

TAPE IIa (continued)

(4) bahiṣpavamānastotra: first stotriyā (see SV 2.1), in gāyatragāna, niruktagāna, and aniruktagāna

(5) Kauthuma Gāyatram

By Krishnamurti Srauti(gal). See above, Tape Ib(3-9).

Recorded at Varanasi 1/XII/70

(6) VS 3.60: saṃhitā, jaṭā

(7) VS 31.16: kramamālā

(8) VS 32.11: puṣpamālā

(9) VS 33.39: pañcasandhi

(10) VS 31.22: śikhā

(11) VS 17.36: rekha, dhvaja

(12) VS 23.20: daṇḍa

(13) VS 25.19: ratha (catuṣpāda)

(14) VS 1.29: ratha (dvipāda)

TAPE IIb

(1) VS 23.19: ghana

By Gajanan Sastri Musalgaonkar (originally from Gwalior). Śākhā: Mādhyandina. Gotra: Kauṇḍinya.

(2) TS 1.1.1-4: saṃhitā

(3) TS 1.1.1: pada, krama

(4) TS 6.6.10.9: jaṭā, ghana

(5) TA 10.10.1-3 (=MahānU 8.3-10.8)

(6) TA 10.11.1-2 (=MahānU 11.1-13)

(7) TU 3.1-10

TAPE IIb (continued)

(8) Lecture in Sanskrit

By S. Srinivasa Dikshita (Tiruvisainallur, Tanjore District). Śākhā: Taittirīya. Gotra: Śrīvatsa. Sūtra: Āpastamba.

Recorded at Varanasi 20/III/71

TAPE IIIa

(1) GG 11.1, 511.15-16; ĀrG 58.1-2, 14.1, 49.1

(2) SV 1.1; GG 1.1-3

(3) ĀrS 1.3; ĀrG 141.1

(4) ĀrS 1.1; ĀrG 12.1

(5) SV 1.512; GG 512.1-2

(6) SV 1.278; GG 278.1; ĀrG 1.1

By Jugal Kisor Sastri and Kisor Sastri (Yajurvedins). Śākhā: Mādhyandina. Gotra: Śāṇḍilya.

Recorded at Varanasi 28/I/71

(7) VS 31.1-22

(8) VS 10.1-18

By Kapiladeva Prasad Misra. Śākhā: Mādhyandina. Gotra: Vatsa.

Recorded at Varanasi 25/III/71

(9) AV 19.9.1-14

(10) AV 19.7.1-5; 19.8.1-7

(11) GB

By Narayan Sastri Ratate (Ṛgvedin). Śākhā: Śākala. Gotra: Kapi. Sūtra: Āśvalāyana.

Recorded at Varanasi 18/IV/71

TAPE IIIb

(1) ŚB

(2) ŚB

(3) VS 3.24: pañcasandhi

By Rajaram Bhatt Nirmale. Śākhā: Mādhyandina.
Gotra: Kṛṣṇātri.
Recorded at Varanasi 19/IV/71

(4) VSK 3.3.1-4; 4.5.1-2

(5) VSK 3.5.1-4: krama

(6) VSK 3.6.1-3; 3.7.3-4: pada

(7) ŚBK

By Lakshmikanta Sastri Khananga. Śākhā: Kāṇva.
Gotra: Gautama.
Recorded at Varanasi 20/IV/71

(8) Kauthuma Gāyatram; GG 1.1-3; ĀrG 57.1

By Srinivasa Mahadesikan. Śākhā: Kauthuma.
Gotra: Bhāradvāja. Sūtra: Drāhyāyaṇa.

(9) RG 1.1.5; 1.1.1-4

(10) ŪG 1.1.3; 1.1.5

By T. K. Devanathan (Śākhā: Gautama. Gotra:
Viśvāmitra. Sūtra: Drāhyāyaṇa) and
S. Srinivasan (Śākhā: Kauthuma. Gotra:
Bhāradvāja. Sūtra: Drāhyāyaṇa)
Recorded at Srirangam 27/V/71

TAPE IVa

(1) ṚV 1.1.1-9; 1.2.1-9

TAPE IVa (continued)

(2) ṚV 6.16.1-15

Recorded at Varanasi 6/IV/71

(3) ṚV 2.42.1-3; 2.43.1-3

(4) ṚV 10.90.1-16: pada

(5) ṚV 1.96.6-8: krama

(6) ṚV 1.22.17: jaṭā

(7) ṚV 1.43.1: ghana

(8) AB 3.2.24 (from "gṛhā vai pratiṣṭhā sūktaṃ")

Recorded at Varanasi 8/IV/71

By Anant Ram Punatambekar. Śākhā: Śākala.
Gotra: Bhāradvāja. Sūtra: Āśvalāyana.

(9) SV 1.1; GG 1.1-3

(10) ĀrG 57.1

(11) SV 2.812; Gautama Gāyatram

By K. Raman Aiyangar. Śākhā: Gautama. Gotra:
Bhāradvāja. Sūtra: Drāhyāyaṇa.

(12) GG 222.1; ĀrG 112.1; GG 524.4

(13) SV 1.189; GG 189.1

By two pupils of K. Raman Aiyangar

Recorded at Madras 21/V/71

(14) JĀrG from JS 2.3.6-9. See ĀrG 132.1--135.1

(15) A. Jaiminīya Gāyatram (Prājāpatyaṃ Gāyatram)
from JS 4.3.8

B. Jaiminīya Gāyatram (prayoga form) from JS 4.3.8

C. JĀrG from JS 2.5.1. See ĀrG 23.1

D. JGG from JS 1.1.12.10

TAPE IVa (continued)

(16) A. JGG from JS 1.2.1.11.9. See GG 222.1.

B. JGG from JS 1.2.1.9.2. See GG 195.1

By U. V. Narayanan Upadhyaya (Neduvenkurici, Tirunelveli District). Śākhā: Jaiminīya. Gotra: Viśvāmitra.

Recorded at Palayamkottai 6/XI/71

TAPE IVb

(1) GG 1.1-3

(2) GG 73.1; 192.1-2; 193.1; 318.1; 332.1-2; 333.1; 572.6; 582.1; ĀrG 74.1; 23.1; 57.1; SV 1.11-20

By Narayan Sankar and Hari Sankar Trivedi. Śākhā: Kauthuma. Gotra: Bhāradvāja. Sūtra: Gobhila/Lāṭyāyana.

Recorded at Varanasi 7/IV/71

(3) JGG from JS 1.1.1.1. See GG 1.1-3

(4) JGG from JS 1.1.2.7. See GG 17.3

(5) JGG from JS 1.1.4.1. See GG 35.3-4

(6) JGG from JS 1.1.4.2. See GG 36.2-3

(7) JGG from JS 1.2.2.1.1. See GG 233.1-2

(8) JGG from JS 1.2.3.5.1. See GG 352.3

(9) JGG from JS 1.2.4.10.5. See GG 464.1

(10) JGG from JS 1.3.1.1. See GG 467.1-13

(11) Subrahmaṇyāhvāna

(12) A. Jaiminīya Gāyatram from JS 4.3.8. See the Kauthuma Gāyatram

B. JRG on "utso devo hiraṇyayaḥ . . . ." See RG 5.1.6

TAPE IVb (continued)

(13) JŪG from JS 3.47.1. See ŪG 1.7.20.1

(14) JRG from JS 3.30.10

By T. Rajagopala Aiyangar (originally from Togur, Tanjore District). Śākhā: Jaiminīya. Gotra: Bhārgava.

(15) JGG from JS 1.2.4.10.10. See GG 465.3

By N. Makarabhushanam (Neduvenkurici, Tirunelveli District; Gotra: Viśvāmitra) and two other pupils of T. Rajagopala Aiyangar.

(16) ĀrG, after 177.1; ChU 8.15.1-2

By Srinivasa Mahadesikan. See above, Tape IIIb(8). Recorded at Srirangam 27/V/71

TAPE Va

Specimens of Tibetan Buddhist recitations, along with demonstrations of instrumental forms and the Tibetan alphabet. Copy of a recording by Mr. Ricardo Canzio. Recorded at Dharmsala, near Dalhousie (Himachal Pradesh, Chamba District) during September 1969.

TAPE Vb

(1) AV 7.26.4-5 (=ṚV 1.22.17-18): saṃhita (from "ni dadhe padā"), pada, krama, jaṭā, ghana (beginning only)

(2) AV 19.8.1-7

By a Maharashtrian Atnarvavedin (Ṛgvedin?)

(3) RV 1.164.50: saṃhitā, pada, krama, jaṭā, ghana

(4) ĀŚ

By a Maharashtrian Ṛgvedin. Śākhā: Śākala. Sūtra: Āśvalāyana.

TAPE Vb (continued)

(5) ĀrG 54.1 (Rāṇāyanīya), through the final "da 3 dhe" parvan of the udgitha

By Ramachandra Sastri Ratate (Ṛgvedin, originally from Maharashtra--now deceased). Śākhā: Śākala. Gotra: Kapi. Sūtra: Āśvalāyana.

Recorded at Varanasi 1961 (?). Copy of a tape belonging to Narayan Sastri Ratate (see above, Tape IIIa(9-11)).

(6) JGG from JS 1.2.1.11.9. See GG 222.1

(7) JRG on "utso devo hiraṇyayaḥ . . . ." See RG 5.1.6

(8) JĀrG from JS 2.4.5. See ĀrG 140.1

(9) sadas saṃbhāvanā: a chant "in the style of sāman" sung while dakṣiṇā is being distributed to participants in the soma sacrifice.

By K. Ramasvami Aiyangar (originally from Togur, Tanjore District). Śākhā: Jaiminīya. Gotra: Vasiṣṭha.

Recorded at Srirangam 29/V/71

(10) A. SV 2.812; Kauthuma Gāyatram

B. SV 1.1; GG 1.1-3

C. ĀrG 1.1

D. ŪG 1.1.1

E. bhakāra rathaṃtara (see RG 1.1.1.1-2)

(11) Subrahmaṇyāhvāna; UG 1.1.5

By Balasubrahmanya Srautigal. Śākhā: Kauthuma. Gotra: Bhāradvāja.

TAPE Vb (continued)

(12) TS 1.8.1.1-13

(13) TS 2.1.1.1-11

(14) ṚV 9.1.1-10; 9.2.1-10

(15) ṚV 1.1.1-9; 1.2.1-9

By V. R. Lakshmikanta Sarma (Yajurvedin). Śākhā: Taittirīya. Gotra: Kauṇḍinya. Sūtra: Āpastamba.

Recorded at Kumbakonam 30/V/71

TAPE VIa

(1) GG 1.1-3; 69.1 (first 7 parvans); 115.1; ĀrG 25.1-3; GG 383.1; 343.6; 484.1-2; ĀrG 1.4; after 127.1:1-3; 140.1; 57.1; 74.1; 23.1; ŪG 1.1.1-3; ĀrG 14.1; ŪG 1.1.5; RG 1.1.1.1; 4.1.7; Kauthuma Gāyatram; ChU 8.15

By P. A. Narayanan Aiyangar and (from ŪG 1.1.1) P. A. Tirumalai Aiyangar. Śākhā: Chāndosāma. Gotra: Bhāradvāja. Sūtra: Drāhyāyaṇa.

Recorded at Srirangam 14/VI/71

(2) TA 3.12.1-7; 3.13.1-2; 10.11.1-2; 10.12.1; 10.1.6a; TS 1.2.13.9-15; TB 2.4.6.2; 2.4.3.4b; 2.8.3.2c; 2.4.3.5c; ṚV 1.22.16-21

(3) TU 1.1.1--1.11.3

By K. K. A. P. Srinivasacariar. Śākhā: Taittirīya. Gotra: Śrīvatsa. Sūtra: Āpastamba.

Recorded at Srirangam 17/VI/71

TAPE VIb

(1) TS 1.5.6: saṃhitā

TAPE VIb (continued)

(2) TS 1.6.1: pada

(3) TS 1.6.9: krama

(4) TS 7.3.11.4-7: jaṭā (through "ā vṛñje suvaḥ")

(5) TS 6.1.2.12 (from "pra sāma"); 4.6.2.12; Sahasranāmastotra (final śloka): ghana

(6) A. TS 4.6.6.1 (first padam: "jīmūtasya"): varṇakrama

B. TA 1.1.1-3; 1.32.1-3

C. from the kāṭhakapraśna: TB 3.10.1.1-4

(7) from the mantrapraśna: ApMB 1.4.1-12

By Sauriraja Aiyangar. Sakha: Taittirīya. Gotra: Harita. Sūtra: Āpastamba.

Recorded at Srirangam 18/VI/71

(8) JĀrG from JS 1.2.2.5.8. See ĀrG 1.1

(9) JS 1.1.1.1; JGG 1.1 (through "gṛṇāno havyadā . . .")

By Thottam Sivakaran Nambudiri. Śākhā: Jaiminīya. Gotra: Vāsiṣṭha.

Recorded at Panjal (Trichur District, near Cheruthuruthy) 7/VII/71

TAPE VIIa

(1) JS ṛks (corresponding Kauthuma SV or ṚV mantras are given in parentheses)

JS 4.3.8 (SV 2.812); 1.1.10.1 (SV 1.91); 1.1.1.1 (SV 1.1); 1.2.1.1 (SV 1.115); 1.3.1.1 (SV 1.467); 2.5.1 (SV 1.589 = ĀrS 1.4); 1.2.3.1.9 (SV 1.321); 1.2.1.10.7 (SV 1.210);

TAPE VIIa (continued)

1.2.3.5.7 (SV 1.358); 1.2.3.6.10 (SV 1.369); 1.2.1.6.7 (SV 1.171); 3.28.6 (SV 2.334); 1.2.2.5.2 (SV 1.274); 1.2.3.1.3 (SV 1.320); 2.1.2 (SV 1.603); 1.2.1.11.9 (SV 1.222); 2.3.6 (SV 1.617 = ĀrS 4.3); 2.3.7 (SV 1.618 = ĀrS 4.4); 2.3.8 (SV 1.619 = ĀrS 4.5); 2.3.9 (SV 1.620 = ĀrS 4.6); 2.3.10 (SV 1.621 = ĀrS 4.7); 2.4.1 (ṚV 10.90.6); 2.4.2 (ṚV 10.90.15); 2.7.1 (SV 1.641-43 = ĀrS 6.1-3); 2.7.2 (SV 1.644-46 = ĀrS 6.4-6); 2.7.3 (SV 1.647-49 = ĀrS 6.7-9); 2.7.4 (SV 1.650 = ĀrS 6.10).

(2)-(45): Jaiminīya sāmans

(2) JS 4.3.8; Jaiminīya Gāyatram (chanted twice) from JS 4.3.8. See the Kauthuma Gāyatram.

(3) JS 1.1.10.1; JGG from JS 1.1.10.1. See GG 91.1

(4) JS 1.1.1.1; JGG from JS 1.1.1.1 (JGG 1.1 chanted twice). See GG 1.1-3

(5) JRG from JS 3.15.7-8. See RG 1.1.5

(6) JRG from JS 3.4.1-2. See RG 1.1.1

(7) JGG from JS 1.2.1.1. See GG 115.1-4

(8) JGG from JS 1.3.1.1. See GG 467.1

(9) JGG from JS 1.2.1.6.7. See GG 171.1

(10) JGG from JS 1.2.1.11.9. See GG 222.1

(11) JGG from JS 1.1.2.1. See GG 11.1

(12) JRG on "utso devo hiraṇyayaḥ . . . ." See RG 5.1.6

(13) JĀrG from JS 2.5.1. See ĀrG 23.1

TAPE VIIa (continued)

(14) JŪG from JS 3.3.1-3

(15) JRG from JS 4.16.7

(16) JGG from JS 1.2.1.9.2. See GG 195.1

(17) JGG from JS 1.1.8.7. See GG 79.1

(18) JŪG (?) from JS 3.21.13

(19) JĀrG from JS 2.4.3. See ĀrG 139.1

(20) JĀrG from JS 2.4.5. See ĀrG 140.1-4, 6, 5, 7-8

(21) JĀrG from JS 1.1.3.5. See ĀrG 70.1

(22) JĀrG (stobhas). See ĀrG, after 127.1:1-3

(23) JGG from JS 1.3.10.3. See GG 568.4-5

(24) JGG from JS 1.2.1.1.8. See GG 122.1-2

(25) JŪG from JS 3.4.3-5. See ŪG 1.1.5

(26) JGG from JS 1.2.3.4.9. See GG 350.1-2

(27) JĀrG from JS 1.2.2.1.1. See ĀrG 49.1

(28) JGG from JS 1.1.5.10. See GG 54.1-2

(29) JGG from JS 1.1.8.8. See GG 80.1

(30) JGG from JS 1.1.10.6. See GG 95.1

(31) JGG from JS 1.1.11.7. See GG 103.1

(32) JGG from JS 1.1.11.10. See GG 106.1

(33) JGG from JS 1.1.12.8. See GG 114.1

(34) JGG from JS 1.2.4.5.7. See GG 387.1

(35) JGG from JS 1.2.4.10.10. See GG 465.3-4

(36) JGG from JS 1.1.8.1. See GG 73.1

(37) JGG from JS 1.2.1.8.8. See GG 192.1-2

(38) JGG from JS 1.2.1.8.9. See GG 193.1

(39) JGG from JS 1.2.3.1.6. See GG 318.1

TAPE VIIa (continued)

(40) JGG from JS 1.2.3.3.2. See GG 333.1

(41) JGG from JS 1.3.10.7. See GG 572.6

(42) JGG from JS 1.3.11.5. See GG 582.1

(43) JGG from JS 1.2.4.8.1. See GG 437.1-2

(44) JGG from JS 1.2.1.6.5. See GG 169.1-2

(45) JRG from JS 4.11.4

TAPE VIIb

(1)-(31): Jaiminīya sāmans (continued)

(1) JĀrG from JS 2.3.6. See ĀrG 132.1

(2) JĀrG from JS 2.3.7. See ĀrG 133.1

(3) JĀrG from JS 2.3.8. See ĀrG 134.1

(4) JĀrG from JS 2.3.9. See ĀrG 135.1

(5) JĀrG from JS 2.3.10. See ĀrG 136.1

(6) JĀrG from JS 2.4.1

(7) JĀrG from JS 2.4.2

(8) JĀrG from JS 1.2.3.1.6. See ĀrG 58.1-2

(9) JĀrG 1.1-2 (stobhas). See ĀrG, before 94.1:1-2

(10) JĀrG from JS 2.2.7. See ĀrG 147.1

(11) JĀrG from JS 2.4.6. See ĀrG 161-162.1

(12) JĀrG on "bhūr bhuvaḥ svaḥ satyam . . . ." See RG 4.1.7

(13) JGG from JS 1.3.6.5. See GG 529.1

(14) JGG from JS 1.3.6.6. See GG 530.1-2

(15) JGG from JS 1.3.6.7. See GG 531.1

(16) JGG from JS 1.3.6.8. See GG 532.1

(17) JGG from JS 1.3.6.9. See GG 527.1-4

(18) JGG from JS 1.1.12.8. See GG 114.1

TAPE VIIb (continued)

(19) JGG from JS 1.1.8.8. See GG 80.1

(20) JGG from JS 1.2.4.2.7. See GG 415.1

(21) JRG from JS 3.15.7d-8. See RG 1.1.5.2-3

(22) JGG from JS 1.2.2.1.3. See GG 235.3

(23) JĀrG from JS 1.2.3.1.6. See ĀrG 123.2

(24) JĀrG from JS 2.6.2. See ĀrG 152.1

(25) JĀrG from JS 1.1.3.7. See ĀrG 153.1

(26) JĀrG from JS 2.3.2. See ĀrG 154.1

(27) JĀrG from JS 2.2.3. See ĀrG 155.1

(28) JĀrG from JS 2.3.2. See ĀrG 156.1-10

(29) JĀrG (stobha). See ĀrG, after 156.10

(30) JĀrG from JS 2.4.6. See ĀrG 157-159.1

(31) JĀrG from JS 1.2.2.4.8. See ĀrG 61.1

(32) JUB 4.27.1-18

By R. Narasimhan Aiyangar (Vasishthapuram, South Arcot District, near Tittaggudi). Śākhā: Jaiminīya. Gotra: Kāśyapa.

Recorded at Srirangam 17/VI/71

(33) JS 4.3.8; Jaiminīya Gāyatram. See the Kauthuma Gāyatram

(34) JS 1.1.10.1; JGG from JS 1.1.10.1. See GG 91.1

(35) JS 1.1.1.1; JGG from JS 1.1.1.1. See GG 1.1

(36) JS 1.2.1.1; JGG from JS 1.2.1.1. See GG 115.1

(37) JS 1.3.1.1; JGG from JS 1.3.1.1. See GG 467.1 (?)

(38) JS 2.3.6; JĀrG from JS 2.3.6. See ĀrG 132.1

(39) JGG from JS 1.1.1.1. See GG 1.1 (portion omitted)

TAPE VIIb (continued)

(40) JGG from JS 1.3.11.7. See GG 584-585.2

(41) JĀrG 1.1. See ĀrG, before 94.1:1

(42) JĀrG from JS 2.2.7. See ĀrG 147.1 (not completed)

By Muthuvenkata Acarya. Śākhā: Jaiminīya.
Gotra: Kauṇḍinya.

Recorded at Vasishthapuram 21/VI/71

TAPE VIIIa

(1) SV 1.1; GG 1.1-3; ŪG 3.1.6

(2) ŪG 1.1.13-14

(3) RG 2.2.9-10; 2.3.1-3

(4) RG 3.5

(5) RG 4.1.1-3

(6) RG 5.1.1; 1.2.10.1

(7) RG 1.2.10.2-3; 7.5.6

(8) Kauthuma Gāyatram

By P. T. Govinda Aiyangar. See above, Tape Ib(15, 17)

Recorded at Srirangam 23/VI/71

TAPE VIIIb

(1) JS 1.1.1.1; JGG from JS 1.1.1.1. See GG 1.1-3

(2) JS 1.2.1.1; JGG from JS 1.2.1.1. See GG 115.1

(3) JS 1.1.10.1; JGG from JS 1.1.10.1. See GG 91.1

(4) JS 1.2.1.11.9; JGG from JS 1.2.1.11.9. See GG 222.1

(5) JGG from JS 1.2.1.9.2. See GG 195.1

(6) JGG from JS 1.1.7.7. See GG 69.1

TAPE VIIIb (continued)

(7) JĀrG from JS 2.5.1. See ĀrG 23.1

(8) JGG from JS 1.3.7.8. See GG 539.1

(9) JĀrG from JS 1.2.2.4.8. See ĀrG 61.1

(10) JĀrG from JS 1.1.12.10

(11) JĀrG from JS 2.3.6. See ĀrG 132.1

(12) JĀrG from JS 2.3.7. See ĀrG 133.1

(13) JĀrG from JS 2.3.8. See ĀrG 134.1

(14) JĀrG from JS 2.3.9. See ĀrG 135.1

(15) JĀrG from JS 2.3.10. See ĀrG 136.1

(16) JGG from JS 1.3.10.3. See GG 568.1, 4

(17) JS 4.3.8 (repeated twice); Jaiminīya Gāyatram (Prājāpatyaṃ Gāyatram) from JS 4.3.8. See the Kauthuma Gāyatram

(18) Jaiminīya Gāyatram (prayoga form) from JS 4.3.8

(19) JĀrG on "bhūr bhuvaḥ svaḥ satyam . . . ." See RG 4.1.7

(20) Repetition of the two Gāyatram sāmans

By Venkatacala Upadhyaya. Śākhā: Jaiminīya. Gotra: Kāśyapa.

Recorded at Tentirupperai (Tirunelveli District, near Alvartirunagari) 26/VI/71

(21) JGG from JS 1.2.3.3.1. See GG 332.1-2

(22) JGG from JS 1.2.3.3.2. See GG 333.1

(23) JGG from JS 1.3.10.7. See GG 572.1

(24) JGG from JS 1.3.11.5. See GG 582.1

(25) JGG from JS 1.2.4.8.1. See GG 437.1

TAPE VIIIb (continued)

(26) JGG from JS 1.2.1.6.5. See GG 169.1-2

(27) JŪG from JS 3.4.3-5. See ŪG 1.1.5

(28) JĀrG (stobha). See ĀrG, after 127.1:1

By Kesava Upadhyaya. Śākhā: Jaiminīya. Gotra: Kāśyapa.

Recorded at Tentirupperai 26/VI/71

(29) RG 1.1.1-4

(30) bhakāra rathaṃtara (see RG 1.1.1)

(31) ŪG 1.1.5

(32) GG 222.1

(33) GG 222.1: sacrificial form

(34) ŪG 1.1.1

By Agnishvatt Sastri Agnihotri. See above, Tapes Ia(8-9), Ib(1-2)

Recorded at Varanasi 7/IX/71

TAPE IXa

(1) Ṛ̣V 1.1.1-9; 1.2.1-9: saṃhitā

(2) ṚV 1.1.1: saṃhitā (jaṭamātrā)

(3) ṚV 1.20.1: pada

(4) ṚV 1.1.1-9: pada

(5) ṚV 1.20.1: pada (jaṭamātrā)

(6) ṚV 1.1.1: krama (jaṭamātrā)

(7) ṚV 1.1.1: krama

(8) ṚV 1.20.1: jaṭā (from "janmane stomaḥ . . .")

(9) ṚV 1.20.1: ratha

By T. N. Paramesvaran Nambudiri and (in jaṭā and

TAPE IXa (continued)

ratha) his brother Sankaranarayanan. Gotra: Kāśyapa. Sūtra: Kauṣītaka

(10) A. Ṛv 1.22.6: ratha

By E. K. Madhavan Nambudiri (Gotra: Āṅgirasa. Sūtra Āśvalāyana) and E. K. Paramesvaran Nambudiri (Gotra: Viśvāmitra. Sūtra: Kauṣītaka)

B. Ṛv 1.20.1

Taught by E. K. Madhavan Nambudiri to eleven young Nambudiri Ṛgvedins

(11) Three kinds of kampa:

A. Ṛv 1.23.19 (through "bheṣajaṃ")

B. Ṛv 1.4.10 (through "mahān")

C. Ṛv 10.78.4 (through "sanābhayaḥ")

By T. N. Paramesvaran Nambudiri. See (1)-(9) above.

Recorded at Trichur 4/VII/71

(12) JS 1.1.1.1. See SV 1.1:

A. As it is taught

B. As it is performed

(13) JGG from JS 1.1.1.1. See GG 1.1-3

(14) JGG from JS 1.1.1.1, abbreviated version. See GG 1.1-3

(15) JRG from JS 3.4.1-2 (bhakāra rathaṃtara). See RG 1.1.1

(16) JŪG from JS 3.5.12. See ŪG 1.1.14.1

(17) JŪG from JS 3.5.12: First repetition of first stotriyā in first paryāya, with bhakāra substitutions.

(18) JŪG from JS 3.5.12-13. See ŪG 1.1.14.2-3

TAPE IXb

(1) Subrahmaṇyāhvāna

(2) JS 4.3.8; Jaiminīya Gāyatram from JS 4.3.8. See the Kauthuma Gāyatram

(3) JRG from JS 3.4.1-2. See RG 1.1.1

By Muttathukattu Itti Ravi Nambudiri. Śākhā: Jaiminīya. Gotra: Bhāradvāja.

Recorded at Panjal 6/VII/71

(4) A. JŪG from JS 3.24.9-11. See ŪG 1.4.19

B. JŪG from JS 3.23.6-8. See ŪG 1.4.12

C. JŪG from JS 3.23.12-14. See ŪG 1.4.13

D. JŪG from JS 3.23.15-16. See ŪG 1.4.14.1-2 (through "hovā hāi")

By Nilakantan Akkitiripad. Śākhā: Jaiminīya. Gotra: Bhāradvāja.

Recorded at Panjal II/71 by M. Itti Ravi Nambudiri

(5) KenaU (complete)

(6) TS 1.1.1-2

By Muttathukattu Itti Ravi Nambudiri. See above, Tapes IXa(12-16), IXb(1-3)

(7) A. JŪG from JS 3.3.1 (aniruktagāna: stotriyās 4-6 of the mādhyandinapavamānastotra)

B. JĀrG 1.1-2 (stobhas). See ĀrG, before 94.1:1-2

By Thottam Narayanan Nambudiri. Śākhā: Jaiminīya. Gotra: Vasiṣṭha.

Recorded at Panjal 6/VII/71

TAPE Xa

(1) Ślokas from Bhāgavatam (11.6.21--11.9.33, etc.), with commentary in Malayalam
By M. Sankaran Nambudiri (Manjur, Kottayam District)

(2) Bhajana in Rāga Śuruti, ādi tālam
By V. Doramani (Trichur)

(3) Lecture in Malayalam
By Madhavan Nambudiri (Guruvayur)

(4) JS 1.1.1.1; JGG from JS 1.1.1.1. See GG 1.1
By Krishna Nambudiri (Panjal). Śākhā: Jaiminīya. Gotra: Bhāradvāja.
Recorded at Guruvayur 8/VII/71

TAPE Xb

(1) JGG from JS 1.3.6.3. See GG 525.1-3

(2) JŪG from JS 3.6.9-11 (sixteenth stuti of the Nambudiri atirātra)
By M. Itti Ravi Nambudiri. See above, Tapes IXa(12-16), IXb(1-3, 5-6)
Recorded at Panjal 9/VII/71

(3) A. "abhivādaye nārāyaṇa śarmā nāma, aham asmi bhoḥ"
B. "suśarmāsi supratiṣṭhāno bṛhad ukṣe nama eṣa te yonir viśvebhyas tvā devebhyaḥ" (TS 1.4.26)
C. TS 1.1.1.1: sādhāraṇā mātrā, śālā mātrā, cantādikkal
By Madampu Narayanan Nambudiri. Śākhā: Taittirīya. Gotra: Viśvāmitra. Sūtra: Baudhāyana.
Recorded at Vadakkancheri 11/VII/71

TAPE Xb (continued)

(4) JS 1.1.1.1; JGG from JS 1.1.1.1. See GG 1.1-3

(5) A. JRG from JS 3.4.1-2. See RG 1.1.1

B. JGG from JS 1.1.7.7. See GG 69.1

(6) Jaiminīya Gāyatram from JS 4.3.8 (Prājāpatyaṃ Gāyatram). See the Kauthuma Gāyatram

(7) JŪG from JS 4.8.10. See ŪG 4.1.7.1

(8) JĀrG 1.1-2 (stobhas). See ĀrG, before 94.1:1-2

(9) A. JS 1.2.3.1.5; JGG from JS 1.2.3.1.5. See GG 317.5

B. JŪG from JS 3.24.9-10. See ŪG 1.4.19.1-2

(10) JS 1.2.3.1.9; JĀrG from JS 1.2.3.1.9

(11) JS 3.15.7; JRG from JS 3.15.7-9. See RG 1.1.5

(12) JGG from JS 1.2.2.1.2. See GG 234.1-2

By Tiruvenkatanatha Sarma (in 4, 7, and 9) and K. R. Venkatarama Sarma (in 5, 6, 8, 10, 11, and 12). Gotras: Viśvāmitra and Vasiṣṭha.

(13) JĀrG from JS 1.2.4.6.8. See ĀrG 54.1

(14) A. JGG from JS 1.2.1.11.9. See GG 222.1

B. JGG from JS 1.3.10.3. See GG 568.5

By K. N. Sahasranama Aiyar. Śākhā: Jaiminīya. Gotra: Bhārgava.

Recorded at Kotuntirappulli (near Palghat) 13/VII/71

TAPE XIa

(1) A. first ājyaśastram of the agniṣṭoma (see CH, pp. 230-34)

TAPE XIa (continued)

1. tūṣṇīṃjapaḥ
2. tūṣṇīṃśaṃsaḥ
3. puroruk
4. sūktam (Ṛ̣V 3.13.1-7)
5. ukthavīryam
6. yajyā

B. KB ("Prajāpatir vai saṃvatsaraḥ . . . ." See NVR, p. 53)

C. Yajurveda "vedīkaraṇam" ("ayaṃ vedaḥ pṛthivīm anvavindat . . . ." See CH, pp. 74-76)

D. Yajurveda "praiṣam"

1. "mamāgne varco . . . pavatāṃ kāme asmin" (TS 4.7.14.1-2)
2. "yajñasya ghoṣad asi . . . vahanti kavayaḥ purastād" (TS 1.1.2.1-3)

By Vaikkakkara Raman Nambudiri (Ṛgvedin; Gotra: Āṅgirasa. Sūtra: Kauṣītaka) and (in C and D) M. Itti Ravi Nambudiri (Sāmavedin; see above, Tapes IXa(12-16), IXb(1-3, 5-6), Xb(1-2))

Recorded at Panjal 9/VII/71

(2) Kṛti in (Hindusthānī) Rāga Śrī, ādi tālam (4+2+2); Venkataramanujam

(3) Kṛti in Rāga Garuḍadhvani, rūpakam tālam (2+4); Venkataramanujam

(4) Kṛti in (Hindusthānī) Rāga Pat-Dīp, ādi tālam; Venkataramanujam

TAPE XIa (continued)

By V. K. Venkataramanujam (violin), K. V. Krishnan (mṛdaṅgam), Balaji (violin), N. Ramanathan and Miss Rangamani (vocal)

Recorded at Banaras Hindu University 21/VIII/71

TAPE XIb

(1) Khyāl in Rāga Pūrya-Kalyān (Kaufmann 318-20, 62-63), ektāl (slow), tīntāl (fast)

(2) Ṭhumarī in Rāga Deś (Kaufmann 211-12), dīpchandi tāl

By Miss Ratnasri Mukharjee (vocal), Narayan Misra (sāraṅgī), Badri Maharaj (tabla)

Recorded at Banaras Hindu University 19/VIII/71

TAPE XIIa

(1) Khyāl in Rāga Yaman-Kalyān (Kaufmann 63-65), rūdra tāl (slow), tīntāl (fast)

By Rajabhan Singh (sitār), Badri Maharaj (tabla)

Recorded at Banaras Hindu University 19/VIII/71

TAPE XIIb

(1) Khyāl in Rāga Deś (Kaufmann 211-12), tīntāl

By Dr. K. C. Gangarade (sitār), Sankar Misra (tabla)

Recorded at Banaras Hindu University 20/VIII/71

TAPE XIIIa

(1) Varṇa in Rāga Kalyānī, ādi tālam ("vañjākṣiro . . .") composer unknown

TAPE XIIIa (continued)

(2) Kṛti in Rāga Baṅgālā, ādi tālam ("girirajasuta . . ."; Tyagaraja)

(3) Kṛti in Rāga Gaurīmanoharī, kaṇḍa cāpu tālam ("guruleka . . ."; Tyagaraja)

(4) Kṛti in Rāga Nāgasvarati, rūpakam tālam (Tyagaraja)

(5) Kṛti in Rāga Ritigaula, miśra cāpu tālam ("janani ninu vina . . ."; Subbaraya Sastri)

(6) Kṛti in Rāga Rāmapriya, rūpakam tālam (Patnam Subrahmanya Aiyar); ālāpana only (concluded Tape XVb(2))

By S. R. Kannan (vocal), T. S. Raghavan (mṛdaṅgam), N. Ramanathan (violin)

Recorded at Banaras Hindu University 20/VIII/71

TAPE XIIIb

(1) Khyāl in Rāga Rāgeśrī (Kaufmann 216-18), ektāl

(2) Ṭhumarī in Rāga Bahāri, tīntāl

By C. L. Srivastava (bāṃsurī), Sankar Misra (tabla)

Recorded at Durgā Mandir, Varanasi 20/VIII/71

(3) Khyāl in Rāga Mālkauṇs (Kaufmann 535-38), beginning

TAPE XIVa

(1) Rāga Mālkauṇs (conclusion)

By Madhu Misra (sāraṅgī), Chotelal Misra (tabla)

(2) Khyāl in Rāga Lalita (Kaufmann 323-27), vilambit ektāl

By Channulal Misra (vocal), Madhu Misra (sāraṅgī), Chotelal Misra (tabla)

Recorded at Varanasi 5/IX/71

TAPE XIVb

(1) Rāga Darbārī (Kaufmann 499-503), ālāp only

By Ravi Sankar (sitār)

Recorded at Varanasi, 1963 (?) Copy of a tape belonging to the Music College, Banaras Hindu University

TAPE XVa

(1) Khyāl in Rāga Gauḍa-Sāraṅga (Kaufmann 112-13), vilambit ektāl, tīntāl

(2) Khyāl in Rāga Sāraṅga (Kaufmann 449-51), ādachautāl. See also Rāga Mega-Mallāra (Kaufmann 395-401)

(3) Ṭhumarī in Rāga Bhairavī (Kaufmann 533-35), kaharwatāl

By Balavanta Ray Bhatt (vocal), Narayan Misra (sāraṅgī), Isvar Lal Misra (tabla)

Recorded at Banaras Hindu University 22/VIII/71

TAPE XVb

(1) Khyāl in Rāga Rāgeśrī (Kaufmann 216-18), rūpak tāl, then tīntāl

By C. L. Srivastava (bāṃsurī), Sivasankar Misra (tabla). See above, Tape XIIIb(1-2)

Recorded at Banaras Hindu University 22/VIII/71

(2) Kṛti in Rāga Rāmapriya (concluded from Tape XIIIa(6))

By S. R. Kannan (vocal), N. Ramanathan (violin), T. S. Raghavan (mṛdaṅgam). See above, Tape XIIIa(1-6).

Recorded at Banaras Hindu University 20/VIII/71

TAPE XVIa

(1) Bhajan in Rāga Bhairavī (Kaufmann 533-35): "Śrī Rāmacandra . . ."

By S. R. Kannan (vocal), Isvar Lal Misra (tabla). See above, Tapes XIIIa(1-6), XVb(2).

Recorded at Banaras Hindu University 22/VIII/71

(2) Ṭhumarī in Rāga Bhairavī (Kaufmann 533-35), sitārkhāni tāl

By Channulal Misra (vocal), Madhu Misra (sāraṅgī), Chotelal Misra (tabla). See above, Tape XIVa(2).

Recorded at Varanasi 5/IX/71

TAPE XVIb

(1) Mṛdaṅgam solo: ādi tālam (4+2+2)

(2) Mṛdaṅgam solo: kaṇḍa cāpu tālam (2+3)

By T. S. Raghavan

Recorded at Banaras Hindu University 19/VIII/71

(3) Khyāl in Rāga Mīyam Mallār (Kaufmann 402-4), ektāl, then tīntāl

By K. S. Avadhani (vocal), Narayan Misra (sāraṅgī), Sankar Misra (tabla)

Recorded at Banaras Hindu University 19/VIII/71

TAPE XVIIa

(1) Khyāl in Rāga Khambāvati (Kaufmann 219-22), vilambit ektāl, then tīntāl

(2) Ṭhumarī in Rāga Bahār (Kaufmann 385-89), tīntāl

TAPE XVIIa (continued)

(3) Ṭhumarī in Rāga Miśra Māṇḍ (Kaufmann 147-49), tīntāl

By M. V. Thakar (vocal), Narayan Misra (sāraṅgī), Babulal Pakhavji (tabla)

Recorded at Banaras Hindu University 22/VIII/71

TAPE XVIIb

Recital of aṣṭāpadis from Jayadeva's Gītagovinda by T. R. Sankaran Nambudiri, chief priest of the Śiva temple at Vaikom, Kerala. Accompanists are N. Ramanathan (violin) and K. V. Krishnan (mṛdaṅgam).

(1) Introduction; 1.1.1-2: Rāga Ārabhī, ādi tālam

(2) 1.1.3-4: Rāga Rītigauḷa, ādi tālam

(3) 1.1.5-6: Rāga Mukhāri, ādi tālam

(4) 1.1.7-8: Rāga Bauḷi, adi talam

(5) 1.1.9-11: Rāga Karṇāṭaka Devagānathāri, ādi tālam

(6) 1.1.12; 1.2.1-2: Rāga Śuruti, ādi tālam

(7) 1.2.3-4: Rāga Śivarañjani, ādi tālam

(8) 1.2.5-6: Rāga Dhanyāsi, ādi tālam

(9) 1.2.7,9: Rāga Nādanāmakriya, ādi tālam

(10) 11.1.1-3: Rāga Bhairavī, ādi tālam

(11) 11.1.4-5: Rāga Ānandabhairavī, ādi tālam

(12) 11.1.6-7: Rāga Hindolam, ādi tālam

(13) 11.1.8-9: Rāga Haṃsānandi, ādi tālam

TAPE XVIIIa

(1) 10.1.1-3: Rāga Mukhāri, kaṇḍa cāpu tālam

(2) 10.1.4-5: Rāga Śaṇmukhapriya, kaṇḍa cāpu tālam

TAPE XVIIIa (continued)

(3) 10.1.6-7: Rāga Ānandabhairavī, kaṇḍa cāpu tālam

(4) 10.1.8: Rāga Madhyamāvati, kaṇḍa cāpu tālam

Recorded at Varanasi 29/VIII/71

(5) Pañcaratna Kṛti in Rāga Śrī, ādi tālam (Telugu: "endaro mahānubhavulu . . ."; Tyagaraja)

(6) Kṛti in Rāga Haṃsadhvani, ādi tālam (Sanskrit: "vātapi gaṇapatim . . ."; Muthusvami Dikshitar)

(7) Kṛti in Rāga Deś, rūpakam tālam (Sanskrit: "śyāma sundarā . . ."; Venkataramanujam)

(8) Kṛti in Rāga Candrakauṇs, ādi tālam (Telugu: "samayamido . . ."; Venkataramanujam)

(9) Tillāna in Rāga Bhīmpalās, rūpakam tālam (Telugu: "tom tom tom . . ."; Venkataramanujam)

(10) Maṅgalam (Tyagaraja)

By V. K. Venkataramanujam (vocal), N. Ramanathan (violin), K. V. Krishnan (mṛdaṅgam). See above, Tape XIa(2-4).

Recorded at the home of Sri Venkataramanujam, Hanuman Ghat, Varanasi 8/IX/71. Recital continued, Tape XIXa.

TAPE XVIIIb

(1) A. Ṛ V 1.43.1-9: saṃhitā

B. ṚV 1.43.1-4: krama

C. ṚV 1.43.6: ghana

By D. V. Venkatakrishna Bhatta (Śākhā: Śākala. Gotra: Bhārgava. Sūtra: Āśvalāyana) and

TAPE XVIIIb (continued)

H. A. Krishnamurti Bhatta (Śākhā: Śākala. Gotra: Bhāradvāja. Sūtra: Āśvalāyana)

(2) A. TS 3.2.11.1-4; 1.7.1.1-3 (through "yajate"): saṃhitā

B. TS 2.2.11.6 ("etayā saṃjñānyā" through "samajānata"): krama

C. TS 2.5.4.9-11 (from "evainaṃ"): ghana

D. TB 2.7.14.2 (from "sa viṣṇu")

By A. Narayana Avadhani and N. Venkatasubha Avadhani. Śākhā: Taittirīya. Gotra: Bhāradvāja. Sūtra: Āpastamba.

(3) A. VSK

B. VSK

C. VSK

D. ŚBK

By G. Narayana Bhatta. Śākhā: Kāṇva. Gotra: Bhāradvāja. Sūtra: Kātyāyana.

(4) A. SV 1.1-10

B. GG 1.1-3

C. GG 91.1

D. GG 189.1

E. GG 222.1

F. RG 1.1.1

G. RG 1.1.5

H. ĀrG, after 177.1

I. ChU 2.23.1-3; 8.15.2

TAPE XVIIIb (continued)

By N. Lakshminarayana Srauti and S. Satyanarayana.

Śākhā: Kauthuma. Gotra: Bhāradvāja.

Sūtra: Drāhyāyaṇa.

Recorded at the Maharaja's Sanskrit College, Mysore 15/XI/71

TAPE XIXa

(1) Kṛti in Rāga Kauśikānaṛa, ādi tālam (Sanskrit: "himācala sute pāhimam . . ."; Venkataramanujam)

(2) Kṛti in Rāga Valaji, ādi tālam (Telugu: "nī pāda paṅkaja . . ."; Venkataramanujam)

(3) Kṛti in Rāga Durgā, ādi tālam (Sanskrit: "Śrī Durge sukhe . . ."; Venkataramanujam)

(4) Rāgam--Tānam--Pallavi in Rāga Kalyāni, caturaśrajāti jhampa tālam (4+1+2), Venkataramanujam

By V. K. Venkataramanujam (vocal), N. Ramanathan (violin), K. V. Krishnan (mṛdaṅgam). See above, Tapes XIa(2-4), XVIIIa(5-10).

Recorded at the home of Sri Venkataramanujam, Hanuman Ghat, Varanasi 8/IX/71

TAPE XIXb

Tabla recital by Suresh Chandra Srivastava

(1) Tīntāl (4+4+4+4)

(2) Rūpak tāl (3+2+2)

Recorded at the home of Sri Srivastava, Varanasi 12/IX/71

TAPES XXa-XXIVa(3)

Ottūṭṭu: the Vedic feast of the Nambudiri Taittirīyakas, recorded at the mana of Sri Desamangalam Sankaran Nambudiripad (Kadalasseri, Trichur District). The modus operandi is as follows:

In saṃhitā (cantādikkal), pada, and mantra, each paññāti (group of 50 words) is stated 6 times, once by a solo reciter "with svara" and 5 times by the full assembly "without svara" (i.e., "spoken"). Occasionally the group, for obvious structural reasons, recites with svara, and these exceptions are noted below by asterisks. Saṃhitā in valiyā mātrā, vallī, the prelude to kŏṭṭu, and ghoṣam are all recited with svara. Kŏṭṭu proper is performed in a quasi-responsorial manner, in which only the soloist uses musical pitches. TS numberings denote, respectively, kāṇḍa, prapāṭhaka, anuvāka, and paññāti. Recorded at Kadalasseri 26/IX/71

1. Saṃhitā in cantādikkal

TAPE XXa

*(1) TS 6.4.6.1

(2)-(11) TS 6.4.6.2--6.4.8.4

TAPE XXb

(1)-(12) TS 6.4.8.4--6.4.10.6

TAPE XXIa

(1)-(14) TS 6.4.11.1--6.5.3.2

TAPE XXIb

(1)-(3) TS 6.5.3.2-4

TAPE XXIb (continued).

2. Pada

*(4)-(8) TS 5.6.8.1-5

*(9) TS 5.6.8.6-7

TAPE XXIIa

3. Saṃhitā in cantādikkal

*(1) TS 6.5.4.1

(2)-(6) TS 6.5.4.2--6.5.5.4

4. Pada

(7)-(9) TS 5.6.9.1-4

5. Mantra

(10) TA 4.1

TAPE XXIIb

6. Vallī

(1) TU 2-3

7. Saṃhitā in valiyā mātrā

(2)-(3) TS 6.5.6.1-2

TAPE XXIIIa

(1)-(4) TS 6.5.6.3-6

8. Kŏṭṭu

(5) TS 1.4.36

(6) TS 5.7.25-26

TAPE XXIIIb

(1) TS 6.1.1-3

TAPE XXIVa

(1) TS 6.1.4

TAPE XXIVa (continued)

9. Ghoṣam

(2) TS 6.1.5.1-3

10. Kŏṭṭu

(3) TS 6.1.5.4-5 (in unison from "karoty asminn eva")

Participants:

Airil Saktidharan Bhattatiripad (Trippunithura, Ernakalam District)
Airil Narayanan Bhattatiripad (Urakam, Trichur District)
Ambalapilli Chittran Bhattatiripad (Thuravu, Trichur District)
Alakadu Nilakantan Nambudiri (Puthanchira, Trichur District)
Madampu Padmanabhan Nambudiri (Kiralur, Trichur District)
Kaplingat Vasudevan Nambudiri (Netumpura, Trichur District): ghoṣi
Kaplingat Vaidikan Anujan Nambudiri (Cerpu, Trichur District)
Kaplingat Vaidikan Divakaran Nambudiri (Perumpilisseri, Trichur District)
Kannamangalam Brahmadathan Nambudiri (Perumpilisseri, Trichur District)
Kannamangalam Vasudevan Nambudiri (Pallisseri, Trichur District)
Karolil Kunjunni Nambudiri (Urakam, Trichur District)
Karolil Kunju Nambudiri (Kadalasseri, Trichur District)
Vataketath Narayana Nambudiri (Perumpatappum, Trichur District)
Alakattur Narayana Nambudiri (Cherusseri, Trichur District)

TAPE XXIVa (continued)

(4) TS 4.5.1.1 (first padam: "namaste"): varṇakrama

By H. N. Narasimhamurti (Principal, Maharaja's Sanskrit College, Mysore). Śākhā: Taittirīya. Gotra: Bhāradvāja. Sūtra: Āpastamba.

Recorded at Mysore 15/XI/71

(5) GG 1.1-3

By Subbaraya Paramesvara Bhatta. Śākhā: Rāṇāyanīya. Gotra: Viśvāmitra. Sūtra: Drāhyāyaṇa.

Recorded at Hadinbal (North Kannara District, near Honnavar) 18/XI/71

TAPE XXIVb

(1) ṚV 1.189.1-8

(2) ṚV 2.21.6: saṃhitā, pada, krama, jaṭā, ghana

By Vignesvara Damodara Dikshita. Śākhā: Śākala. Gotra: Āṅgirasa. Sūtra: Āśvalāyana.

(3) A. ṚV 1.18.1-9: saṃhitā

B. ṚV 1.18.6-9: pada, krama

By Ganapati Harihara Maiyar (Gotra: Vasiṣṭha. Sūtra: Āśvalāyana) and Krishna Mannesvara Jogabhatta (Gotra: Kāśyapa. Sūtra: Āśvalāyana)

(4) TS 1.1.14.10-14

(5) TS 4.2.6.20: saṃhitā, pada, krama, jaṭā, ghana

By Gajanan Subrahmanya Bhatta (Gotra: Viśvāmitra. Sūtra: Baudhāyana) and Narasimha Vignesvara Bhatta (Gotra: Vasiṣṭha. Sūtra: Baudhāyana)

TAPE XXIVb (continued)

(6) Ṛgveda-Yajurveda "agnīṣomīya"

By Vignesvara Damodara Dikshita (maitrāvaruṇa) and Gajanan Subrahmanya Bhatta (adhvaryu)

Recorded at Gokarna 16/XI/71

(7) TS 7.5.24.2-4: saṃhitā, pada, krama, jaṭā, ghana

By Ramachandra Sastri Suri. Gotra: Vasiṣṭha. Sūtra: Baudhāyana.

Recorded at Kavalakki (North Kannara District) 17/XI/71

(8) ĀrG, before 94.1:1-2

By Subbaraya Ramachandra Bhatta. Śākhā: Rāṇāyanīya. Gotra: Viśvāmitra. Sūtra: Drāhyāyaṇa.

Recorded at Karki (North Kannara District) 17/XI/71

(9) TS 1.4.44.1: saṃhitā, pada, krama, jaṭā, ghana

(10) TB 2.7.7.1-7; TA 1.1.1; TB 2.8.8.4-6 ("devīṃ vācam" through "manuṣyā vadanti")

(11) TB 2.1.8.3; TS 7.5.24.2-4

By Vishnu Narasimha Bhatta (Bettageri, North Kannara District). Śākhā: Taittirīya. Gotra: Kāśyapa. Sūtra: Baudhāyana.

Recorded at Karki 17-18/XI/71

(12) ĀrG 58.1-2

By Subbaraya Ramachandra Bhatta. See (8) above.

Recorded at Karki 18/XI/71

TAPE XXIVb (continued)

(13) abhigīta, vinata, karṣaṇa, namata, preṅkha: speciminae (See, respectively, GG 9.1, 4.1, 1.1, 92.1, and 1.1)

By Subbaraya Paramesvaran Bhatta. Śākhā: Rāṇāyanīya. Gotra: Viśvāmitra. Sūtra: Drāhyāyaṇa.

(14) ĀrG 89.1

By Subbaraya Ramachandra Bhatta. See (8), (12) above.

(15) TB 3.5.10.4-5 (from "āśaste-yaṃ")

(16) TS 3.5.11.21: saṃhitā, daṇḍa

(17) TA 10.10.3

Recorded at Hadinbal 18/XI/71

(18) Ten "śānti" mantras: See TU 1.1.1; 2.1.1; 1.4.1; 1.10.1; MG 1.4.4; ṚV 10.20.1; TA 1.1.1. Three not identified.

(19) TA 10.1.16--10.2.1

(20) RVKh 5.87.1-15 (See ed. Scheftelowitz, pp. 72-73)

(21) TS 3.3.1.7-9: saṃhitā, jaṭā

(22) TS 4.6.6.18-20; 4.7.15.22

(23) TS 4.2.3.13, etc.

(24) TB 1.3.7.7, etc.

By Vishnu Narasimha Bhatta. See (9)-(11) above.

Recorded at Udipi 21/XI/71

TAPE XXVa

(1) GG 115.1-4

TAPE XXVa (continued)

(2) GG 372.1-3

(3) ĀrG 57.1

(4) ŪG 1.1.1

(5) GG 1.1-3

(6) GG 11.1

(7) ĀrG 141.1

(8) GG 222.1

(9) ŪG 1.1.5

(10) Rāṇāyanīya Gāyatram

(11) ĀrG 49.1

By Subbaraya Ramachandra Bhatta (in 1-7, 9, 11; see above, Tape XXIVb(8, 12, 14)) and his brother Siva Ramachandra (in 8 and 10).

Recorded at Arolli (near Honnavar) 17/XI/71

(12) The 301 typical parvans of the Hāvik Rāṇāyanīyas. See NVL, pp. 326-44.

A. ka-varga (92 examples)

By Subbaraya Ramachandra Bhatta. See above, Tapes XXIVb(8, 12, 14) and XXVa(1-7, 9, 11).

Recorded at Karki 17/XI/71

B. ca-varga (120 examples)

C. ṭa-varga (46 examples)

D. ta-varga (23 examples)

E. pa-varga (20 examples)

(13) ĀrG 102.1

By Subbaraya Paramesvaran Bhatta. See Tape XXIVb(13).

Recorded at Hadinbal 18/XI/71

TAPE XXVb

(1) A. SV 2.37-38.
    B. ŪG 1.1.7

(2) bahiṣpavamānastotra: first stotriyā (see SV 2.1), in aniruktagāna

(3) bhakāra rathaṃtara (see RG 1.1.1)

(4) GG 445.1

By Visvesvara Bhatta. Śākhā: Rāṇāyanīya. Gotra: Viśvāmitra. Sūtra: Drāhyāyaṇa.

Recorded at the Karikan Paramesvari Temple 19/XI/71

(5) SV 1.1-21

(6) ĀrG 51.1-3

(7) GG 92.1

(8) GG 255.1-3

(9) ĀrG, after 177.1

(10) ChU 8.15.2

By Subbaraya Ramachandra Bhatta. See above, Tapes XXIVb(8, 12, 14), XXVa(1-7, 9, 11-12A).

Recorded at Honnavar 19/XI/71

(11) GG 1.1; 175.1

(12) GG 222.1

(13) ĀrG 140.1 (without beginning and concluding stobhas)

By M. Rajagopala Acarya. Śākhā: Jaiminīya (?) Gotra: Viśvāmitra. Sūtra: Jaiminīya (?)

Recorded at Udipi 20/XI/71

(14) GG 92.1

By M. Ramamohana Acarya. Śākhā: Jaiminīya (?) Gotra: Viśvāmitra.

TAPE XXVb (continued)

(15) GG 233.1

By M. Narasimha Acarya. Śākhā: Jaiminīya (?)
Gotra: Viśvāmitra.

(16) A. Gāyatram

B. first ājyastotra: first stotriyā (see SV 2.10), in gāyatragāna

By M. Ramamohana Acarya (see 14 above) and M. Narasimha Acarya (see 15 above)

(17) A. Violin rendition of GG 1.1

B. The seven svaras of Samaveda: ārohaṇam, avarohaṇam

By M. Rajagopala Acarya (violin). See above, (11)-(13).

(18) Subrahmaṇyāhvāna

(19) ĀrG, after 166.1

(20) ĀrG 70.1

(21) ChU 2.24.3-6 (see CH, p. 129)

(22) bahiṣpavamānastotra: second stotriyā (see SV 2.2), in aniruktagāna

(23) ŪG 1.1.5

By M. Narasimha Acarya. See (15)-(16) above.

Recorded at Matapadi (South Kannara District) 21/XI/71

(24) ṚV 10.106.1-11: saṃhitā

(25) ṚV 9.1.1-10: pada

(26) ṚV 9.1.1-10: drutapada

TAPE XXVb (continued)

(27) Ṛ V 9.44.1-6; 9.45.1-6: krama

(28) Ṛ V 1.113.1-5: jaṭā

(29) Ṛ V 2.12.1-5: ghana

By Visvanatha Deva. See above, Tape Ia(2).

Recorded at Varanasi 6/XII/71

TAPE XXVIa

(1) ĀrG 57.1

(2) RG 1.1.1

(3) ŪG 1.1.5

(4) ĀrG, before 94.1:1-2

(5) GG 11.1

(6) ŪG 1.1.1

(7) RG 4.1.7

(8) GG 284.2

By Seshadri Sastrigal (Tiruvidaimarudur, Tanjore District). Śākhā: Kauthuma. Gotra: Gautama. Sūtra: Drāhyāyaṇa.

Recorded at Madras 27/XI/71

TAPE XXVIIa

(1) A. SV 1.1-20

B. SV 2.812; Rāṇāyanīya Gāyatram

C. GG 1.1-3; 2.1; 3.1

By Vedulu Gopala Avadhani and Srigovinda Sarma (Vijayanagaram, Andhra Pradesh). Śākhā: Rāṇāyanīya ("Gurjarapāṭha").

Recorded at Vijayawada

TAPE XXVIIa (continued)

(2) A. SV 2.812; SV 1.1-10

B. Rāṇāyanīya Gāyatram

C. GG 1.1-3; 2.1; 3.1

By Ramagopala Sastri and Narayana Sastri (Sitanagaram, Andhra Pradesh). Śākhā: Rāṇāyanīya.

Recorded at Vijayawada

(3) A. SV 2.812; Kauthuma Gāyatram

B. GG 1.1-3; 2.1; 3.1

By four Kauthuma Sāmavedins

(4) A. JGG from JS 1.1.1.1-3. See GG 1.1-3; 2.1; 3.1.

B. JĀrG 1.1-2 (stobhas). See ĀrG, before 94.1:1-2

C. JS 1.1.1.1-10

By M. Itti Ravi Nambudiri (see above, Tapes IXa(12-16), IXb(1-3, 5-6), Xb(1-2), XIa(1)) and T. Narayanan Nambudiri (in A and C; see above, Tape IXb(7))

TAPE XXVIIb

(1) third ājyastotra: complete in three paryāyas (JŪG from JS 3.2.7-9), in aniruktagāna

By Nilakantan Akkitiripad (Udgātar; see Tape IXb(4) above) and M. Itti Ravi Nambudiri (Prastotar and Pratihartar)

Recorded at an actual agniṣṭoma sacrifice

(2) JŪG from JS 3.3.1 (aniruktagāna: stotriyās 4-6 of the mādhyandinapavamānastotra)

TAPE XXVIIb (continued)

By M. Itti Ravi Nambudiri

NOTE: The items on Tape XXVII are copies of tapes belonging to Dr. E. R. Sreekrishna Sarma, Tirupati, Andhra Pradesh.

TAPE XXVIIIa

(1) GG 1.1

(2) bhakāra rathaṃtara (see RG 1.1.1)

(3) RG 1.1.1

(4) Kauthuma Gāyatram

(5) RG 1.1.5

By Mullantiram Ramanatha Dikshitar (Mullantiram, North Arcot District). Śākhā: Kauthuma.

Recorded by T. K. Rajagopala Aiyar (deceased)

(6) GG 1.1

(7) ŪG 1.1.5

(8) ĀrG 54.1

By Revasankar Becarbhai Trivedi (Paddhari, Gujarat). Śākhā: Kauthuma.

Recorded by T. K. Rajagopala Aiyar (deceased)

NOTE: The items on Tape XXVIIIa are copies of tapes belonging to Prof. J. F. Staal (Berkeley)

GLOSSARY[1]

A

ABHIGĪTA: In the *Kauthuma notation, a numerical sequence symbolized by the numeral 7 (North India) or the vowel a (South India). These signs signify that a *dvitīya (the number 2) of ½ *mātrā is followed by a *prathama (the number 1) of 1½ mātrās. Abhigīta is found almost always on short vowels.

ABHIGĪTA-KṚṢṬA: A lengthening of an *abhigīta syllable by the addition of a secondary (*vikṛti) numeral.

ĀBHOGI: In South Indian music, a *janya (derived) *rāga belonging to the twenty-second *meḷa, *Kharaharapriya. The rāga contains five tones in ascent and descent and is identified by some as resembling the gamut employed by adherents of the *Kauthuma school in South India.

ABHYĀSA: "Repetition." One of the ways in which the syllables of a source verse were altered so that they could fit a pre-existing melody.

ADHYARDHA: One and one-half.

ADHAḤ: "Low." One of the vertical levels at which

[1]Asterisks indicate separate entries.

*Nambūdiri *Sāmavedins hold the right hand while chanting a *sāman.

ĀDISVARA: "Beginning *svara." A term applied by *Nambūdiri *Sāmavedins to the first four svaras of the first chant of the *Jaiminīya *Grāmageyagāna (and perhaps to other chants as well). The four svaras correspond to four hand positions. In this instance, the right hand is first held in the high (*upari) position with palm facing the chanter and fingers straight upwards (see *malartti). Then *kaṇakku ("counting") takes place, in which three consecutive fingers are bent forward, beginning with the little finger.

ĀGAMA: "Augmentation." One of the ways in which the syllables of a source verse were altered so as to fit a pre-existing melody. The term implies the addition of extra letters or syllables to a radical word.

AGNI: The god of fire, especially of sacrificial flames. The first *parva (āgneyaṃ parva) of the *Grāmageyagāna of the Sāmaveda consists of chants addressed to this deity.

AGNICAYANA: A rite independent of, but sometimes proceeding simultaneously with, the *soma sacrifices. It involves "the piling [of bricks for an altar] of fire." The completed altar is in the shape of an eagle with wings outspread (see fig. 2 above, p. 26). Solo chants (*parisāman) are sung at designated spots around the altar as these parts are worshipped.

AGNIṢṬOMA: The first of seven varieties (*saṃsthās) of the

*jyotiṣṭoma, the prototype of all *soma sacrifices. The agniṣṭoma is made up of twelve lauds (*stotras) and draws its name from the twelfth and last of these, the agniṣṭomastotra or *yajñāyajñīyastotra.

AHĪNA: A *soma sacrifice comprising from two to twelve pressing days.

AIYAṄGĀR: The second most prominent sub-caste among *Tamil-speaking *Brāhmaṇs of South India. The Aiyaṅgārs are *vaiṣṇavas, who identify the god Viṣṇu as the supreme Being and worship Him above all other deities of the Hindu pantheon. The sect has split into northern (Vaḍagalai) and southern (Teṅgalai) branches.

AIYAR: The principal sub-caste among *Tamil-speaking *Brāhmaṇs of South India. They are known as smārta Brāhmaṇs in that they are said to be adherents to the precepts and laws of the *smṛti tradition. The heads of the community are the Śaṅkarācāryas of the pīṭhas at Śṛṅgeri and Kāñcīpuram (the latter known as the Kāmakoṭipītha). Probably as a response to the Tamil *vaiṣṇava movements, the Aiyars have developed *śaiva characteristics.

ĀJYA: Name given to four *stotras (chant complexes) sung at the morning service of a *soma sacrifice.

AKARṢAṆA: Absence of *karṣaṇa. A *sāman syllable which is not followed by a secondary numeral.

AKṢARA: A letter or syllable.

ĀḺVĀRTIRUNĀGARI: A place of *vaiṣṇava pilgrimage east of *Tirunělveli (Tinnevelly) in southern *Tamilnāṭu. An important village of *Jaiminīya *Sāmavedins, *Tĕntirupperai, is located a few miles east of Āḻvārtirunāgari.

ĀMAHĪYAVA: The melody comprising *_stotriyās_ 4-6 of the midday *_pavamāna_ laud (*_mādhyaṃdinapavamānastotra_) of a *_soma_ sacrifice.

ANĀMIKĀVAROHA: "_Anāmikā_" = "ring finger"; "_avaroha_" = "descent." Name given to the hand movement (*_kai-lakṣaṇa_) and sound (*_svara_) associated with the conjunct _pl_ of the *Jaiminīya syllable notation. The *Brāhmaṇs of *Kŏṭuntiṟappulli village in *Keraḷa refer to it alternately as _pla-svara_.

ANĀMIKODGAMA: "_Anāmikā_" = "ring finger"; "_udgama_" = "ascent." Name given to the hand movement (*_kai-lakṣaṇa_) and sound (*_svara_) associated with the nasal _ṇ_ of the *Jaiminīya syllable notation. The *Brāhmaṇs of *Kŏṭuntiṟappuḷḷi village in *Keraḷa refer to it alternately as _ṇa-svara_.

ĀNDHĪGAVA: The melody comprising *_stotriyās_ 12-14 of the *_ārbhavapavamānastotra_, the evening *_pavamāna_ laud of a *_soma_ sacrifice.

ĀNDHRA PRADESH: State in Southeast India lying north of *Tamiḻnāṭu and east of *Mysore. The principal language of Āndhra country is Telugu, a member of the Dravidian language family.

ANIRUKTAGĀNA: A method of sacrificial chanting in which the syllables of the *_udgītha_ and *_upadrava_ sections of the *_gāyatra_ melody are each replaced by the vowel _o_ (the original syllables are chanted mentally). Such "unuttered singing" is applied also to the first *pṛṣṭha-stotra (the *rathaṃtara), but here consonants rather than vowels are affected--certain vowels are preceded by bh and the original consonants are dropped.

ANTYA: "Last." The notational numeral of the *Kauthuma notation which is always listed in last place--the *atisvārya (the number 6).

ANUDĀTTA: See *udātta.

AṆUMĀTRĀ: One-fourth *mātrā--that is, one-fourth the duration of a short (*hrasva) vowel.

ANUNĀSIKA: The pure nasal, formed independently of any consonant by passing breath through the nose. It is indicated by the mark ँ.

ANUPADASTUBDHA: In *Rāṇāyanīya manuscripts, the designation (abbreviated an) for certain appearances of the notational pattern 2_3. It is not certain how anupadastubdha differs from the sequence *praṇata.

ANUSVĀRA: (1) In Sanskrit, the nasal sound indicated (in the *devanāgarī script) by a dot above the line.

(2) Another name for the *atisvārya.

ANVAṄGULYA (ANVAṄGULIMARDANAM, ANVAṄGULĪYAM): Name given to the hand movement (*kai-lakṣaṇa) and sound (*svara) associated with the consonant kh of the *Jaiminīya syllable notation.

APTORYĀMA: The seventh *saṃsthā of the *jyotiṣṭoma, the prototype of all *soma sacrifices. The aptoryāma is comprised of thirty-three lauds (*stotras).

APŪRVA: An independent rite, such as the *pravargya ceremony which precedes the *soma sacrifice.

ĀRAṆYAKA: A body of philosophical writings composed or studied in the forest. The Āraṇyaka of the Sāmaveda is appended to the *pūrvārcika of the *Saṃhitā.

ĀRAṆYAKAGĀNA (ĀRAṆYAGEYAGĀNA): The "Forest Songbook," containing melodies set to verses from the *pūrvārcika and the *Āraṇyaka Saṃhitā. All verses of the latter, taken in order but not necessarily consecutively, are set to at least one melody. Only selected pūrvārcika verses are melodized, and these do not appear in the original order.

ĀRAṆYAKA SAṂHITĀ: The *Āraṇyaka of the Sāmaveda, which is appended to the *pūrvārcika of the *Saṃhitā.

ĀRBHAVAPAVAMĀNA: A laud (*stotra) sung at the evening service of a *soma sacrifice.

ĀRCIKA: "Connected with a verse (*ṛc)." The verses of both Sāmaveda *saṃhitās (*Kauthuma-*Rāṇāyanīya and *Jaiminīya) are divided into two ārcikas, the *pūrvārcika ("first ārcika") and the *uttarārcika ("last ārcika").

ARDHACATASRA: "Containing a half for its fourth"--that is, $3\frac{1}{2}$.

ARDHATISRA: "Containing a half for its third"--that is, $2\frac{1}{2}$.

ARDHAMĀTRĀ: One-half *mātrā--that is, one-half the duration of a short (*hrasva) vowel.

ARKA: One of the divisions of the *Āraṇyakagāna. The

*Kauthumas and *Rāṇāyanīyas have it in first position; the *Jaiminīyas place it second.

ASSAM: State in extreme Northeast India. Assam is almost completely separated from India by Bangladesh. Shillong is the capital city.

ATHARVAN: The magical formulas and spells which comprise the greater part of the fourth Veda, the *Atharvaveda.

ATHARVAVEDA: Name of the fourth Veda (see *atharvan).

ATIKRAMA: In the *Kauthuma numeral notation, the omission of one or more numerals in ascent or descent. Eight cases are possible: 11 to 2, 1 to 3, 3 to 5, 1 to 5, 5 to 3, 5 to 2, 3 to 1, and 5 to 1.

ATIRĀTRA: The "over-night" rite, which is the sixth *saṃsthā of the *jyotiṣṭoma. An atirātra is comprised of twenty-nine lauds (*stotras).

ATISVĀRA: See *atisvārya.

ATISVĀRYA: In *Kauthuma and some *Rāṇāyanīya *gāna manuscripts, the notational numeral 6 (and thus the sound [*svara] indicated by the numeral). It is alternately called atisvāra, anusvāra, antya, or ṣaṣṭha.

ATYAGNIṢṬOMA: The second *saṃsthā of the *jyotiṣṭoma, the prototype of all *soma sacrifices. The atyagniṣṭoma consists of thirteen lauds (*stotras).

AUḌAVA: A *rāga which consists only of five tones.

AUŚANA: A melody in the *Ūhagana which comprises *stotriyās 13-15 of the midday *pavamāna laud (*mādhyaṃdinapavamāna-stotra).

AVAGRAHA: In Sanskrit, the mark ऽ, indicating grammatical separation. The *Kauthuma notation uses the symbol for designating *_atikrama_, *_vinata_, and *_namana_. Occasionally it is placed before the first secondary numeral following a primary numeral.

AVANARDANA: A trill. Because of its alternation of two numerals, the sequence 2_{1212} of the *_gāyatra_-melody is often quoted as an example.

AVAROHA (AVAROHAṆA): "Descent." Name given to the hand movement (*_kai_-_lakṣaṇa_) and sound (*_svara_) associated with the consonant _k_ of the *Jaiminīya syllable notation.

AVAROHAKṢEPAṆA: Name given to the hand movement (*_kai_-_lakṣaṇa_) and sound (*_svara_) associated with the consonant _g_ of the *Jaiminīya syllable notation. This consonant designates a compound: _k_ (*_avaroha_) + _p_ (*_kṣepaṇa_).

AVAROHAMARŚANA: Name given to the hand movement (*_kai_-_lakṣaṇa_) and sound (*_svara_) associated with the consonant _j_ of the *Jaiminīya syllable notation. This consonant designates a compound: _k_ (*_avaroha_) + _y_ (*_marśana_).

AVAROHĀVARTA: Name given to the hand movement (*_kai_-_lakṣaṇa_) and sound (*_svara_) associated with the semivowel _v_ of the *Jaiminīya syllable notation. This semivowel designates a compound: _k_ (*_avaroha_) + _t_ (*_āvarta_).

AVAROHAYĀNA: Name given to the hand movement (*_kai_-_lakṣaṇa_) and sound (*_svara_) associated with the semivowel _l_ of the *Jaiminīya syllable notation. This semivowel designates a compound: _k_ (*_avaroha_) + _ṭ_ (*_yāna_).

AVAROHOTTĀNA: Name given to the hand movement (*kai-lakṣaṇa) and sound (*svara) associated with the consonant ṭh of the *Jaiminīya syllable notation. This consonant designates a compound: k (*avaroha) + tha (*uttāna). An alternate name is nīcair upakramya uttānam.

ĀVARTA: "Turning, revolving." Name given to the hand movement (*kai-lakṣaṇa) and sound (*svara) associated with the consonant t of the *Jaiminīya syllable notation.

ĀVARTAKṢEPAṆA: Name given to the hand movement (*kai-lakṣaṇa) and sound (*svara) associated with the consonant jh of the *Jaiminīya syllable notation. This consonant designates a compound: t (*āvarta) + p (*kṣepaṇa).

ĀVARTAMARŚANA: Name given to the hand movement (*kai-lakṣaṇa) and sound (*svara) associated with the consonant ḍh of the *Jaiminīya syllable notation. This consonant designates a compound: t (*āvarta) + y (*marśana).

B

BAHIṢPAVAMĀNASTOTRA: The "out-of-doors *pavamāna laud," sung during the morning service of a *soma sacrifice. The text comprises three *tṛcas, each verse of which is sung to the *gāyatra melody.

BANĀRAS: See *Vārāṇasī.

BENGAL: State in Northeast India. The principal tongue is Bengali, which belongs to the Indo-European language family. Calcutta is the capital and largest city.

BHAKĀRA: The consonant bh, which, in the first *pṛṣṭhastotra (the *rathaṃtara) of the *soma sacrifice, precedes the vowels of the *udgītha, thus replacing the original consonants. There is some dispute among the authorities as to whether the original vowels should be retained or else replaced by the a-vowel. Some texts permit the chanting of the final four syllables in their unaltered form, with both original consonants and vowels.

BHAKĀRA-RATHAṂTARA: A sacrificial form of the *rathaṃtara-*sāman. See *bhakāra.

BHAKTI: A division of a Sāmavedic chant. The five standard bhaktis--*prastāva, *udgītha, *pratihāra, *upadrava, and *nidhana--may be increased to seven by adding the *praṇava (the syllable om, inserted after the prastāva) and the *hiṃkāra (the syllable hum, placed before the prastāva).

BIHĀR: State in Northeast India bordered on the north by Nepal, on the east by Bengal, on the south by Orissa, on the southwest by Madhya Pradesh, and on the west by Uttar Pradesh. Patna (Pāṭaliputra) is the capital city. See also *Darbhaṅga.

BINDU: The zero (o), found in South Indian *Kauthuma *gāna manuscripts in place of the *repha (the semivowel r, which designates a syllable worth two *mātrās). When found within rather than above the line of text (in the *grantha script), the bindu represents *anusvāra or *anunāsika.

BRĀHMAṆ: See *Brāhmaṇa.

BRĀHMAṆA: (1) The highest of the four Hindu castes, the other three comprising the Kṣatriyas (warriors, rulers), Vaiśyas (merchants, farmers), and Śūdras (servants of the three higher castes). A Brāhmaṇa (usually abbreviated Brāhmaṇ) is a priest; his principal duty is the study and recitation of the Veda to which he belongs by birth. In modern India, however, only an extremely small percentage of Brāhmaṇ society honors its traditional obligations; most members of the caste function simply as laymen. (2) A text which explains the functions of a particular Veda in the sacrifices. The principal Sāmavedic Brāhmaṇas are the Pañcaviṃśa, Ṣaḍviṃśa (these first two of the *Kauthuma and *Rāṇāyanīya schools), and Jaiminīya (of the *Jaiminīya school).

BṚHASPATI: A priestly deity who serves as an intermediary between the gods and mankind.

C

CANDRASĀMAN: *Nambūdiri term for a chant of the Āraṇyakagāna.

CATURTHA: "Fourth." The notational numeral 4 of the *Kauthuma notation; also the sound (**svara*) indicated by that numeral.

CATURTHADHĀRI: In *Rāṇāyanīya manuscripts, the designation (abbreviated *rtha*) for a particular numerical succession, perhaps 3 4 3.

CATURVEDIN: One who has knowledge of four Vedas.

CAUBE: Same as **caturvedin*.

CĔRICCU: One of the hand positions which *Nambūdiri *Sāmavedins employ while chanting. According to the leading Nambūdiri chanter, the term refers to "the palm turned sideways to the left."

CHANDAS: Meter, and the class of works which represent it as one of the six *_vedāṅgas_ ("limbs of the Veda").

CHANDOGAPARIŚIṢṬA: See *Mātrālakṣaṇa.

D

DAṆḌA: In Sāmavedic *_gāna_ manuscripts, the vertical line which separates one *_parvan_ from another. It thus marks the spot where a pause (*_virāma_) occurs and consequently where breath is taken.

DAKṢIṆA: "Right." One of three horizontal hand positions employed by *Nambūdiri Sāmavedins while chanting.

DARBHAṄGA: A center of Sāmavedic chanting in *Bihār State, where the mahārājā has sponsored the teaching of the southern *Kauthuma style of *Tanjore. The city, sixty miles northeast of Patna, is in the Darbhaṅga District.

DARŚAPŪRṆAMĀSA: Sacrifices of the new and full moon. These ceremonies consist of offerings of butter and cakes but not of *_soma_; hence Sāmavedic priests do not take part.

DEVANĀGARĪ: "Divine city writing." The script in which Sanskrit is usually written in North India.

DHĀRAṆALAKṢAṆA: A treatise by Sabhāpati which lists and explains the symbols associated with the Jaiminīya syllable notation.

DHARMAŚĀSTRA: A book of law.

DĪRGHA: "Long; a long vowel." The *Mātrālakṣaṇa specifies that long vowels of (*Kauthuma) chants are worth two *_mātrās_.

DĪRGHA-KARṢAṆA: See *_karṣaṇa_.

DRUTA: "Fast." One of three tempi (*_vṛttis_) admitted by the *Mātrālakṣaṇa for Sāmavedic chanting.

DUBE (DŪBE): A *Brāhmaṇ sub-caste. Same as *Dvivedī.

DVANDVA: One of the divisions of the *Āraṇyakagāna. The *Kauthumas and *Rāṇāyanīyas have it in second place; the *Jaiminīyas place it third.

DVITĪYA: "Second." The notational numeral 2 of the *Kauthuma notation; also the sound (*_svara_) indicated by that numeral.

DVIVEDĪ: Having knowledge of two Vedas. A *Brāhmaṇ sub-caste.

E

EKĀHA: A sacrifice comprising only one day on which stalks of *_soma_ are pressed.

G

GĀNA: "Songbook." See *Grāmageyagāna, *Āraṇyakagāna, *Ūhagāna, *Ūhyagāna.

GARBHINĪ: One of the patterns (*_viṣṭutis_) according to which the verses of a three-verse group (*_tṛca_) or two-verse group (*_pragātha_) in the *_uttarārcika_ are sung in order to form a laud (*_stotra_). All _viṣṭutis_ are comprised of three rounds (*_paryāyas_), and each round must contain at least one setting of each of the three verses (_pragāthas_ are changed into _tṛcas_ by a process of overlapping). The *_hiṃkāra_ (the syllable _hum_) precedes each round. If the verses are numbered 1-2-3, then the _garbhinī viṣṭuti_ may be represented as follows:

hum,1,1,1,2,3; *hum*,1,2,2,2,3; *hum*,1,2,2,2,3,3,3. The four **pṛṣṭha*-**stotras* of the **agniṣṭoma* are each sung to this pattern.

GATI: An addition of a palatal or labial vowel to a guttural vowel. Thus *ā* may become *ā*-*i* (or *ā*-*yi*) or *ā*-*u*.

GĀYATRA: The most sacred chant of the Sāmavedic repertoire. Its text is based upon the famous Sāvitrī verse (in the Gāyatrī meter and addressed to the sun god Savitṛ), which is repeated by every *Brāhmaṇ at his morning and evening devotions:

tat savitur vareṇyam bhargo devasya dhīmahi /
dhiyo yo naḥ pracodayāt // (SV 2.812)
May we attain that excellent glory of Savitar the God:
So may he stimulate our prayers! (translation of Ralph T. H. Griffith)

The *Kauthuma-*Rāṇāyanīya version of the Gāyatra-**sāman* (also called Gāyatram) is as follows:

```
2      1            r         1 r  r
o 3 m / tat savitur vareṇiyom / bhārgo devasya

  r          2 1r  r        2        1
dhīmāhī 2̄ / dhiyo  yo naḥ praco 1 2 1 2 / hum ā 2̄ /

 1    2 1 1 1
dāyo / ā 3 4 5 //
```

A *Jaiminīya version (from a *Kōṭuntir̲appuḷḷi manuscript) reads:

```
ca                 ṡū                          _ṭe   ca ka
tat savitur vareṇyom / bhargo devasya dhīmahā / ī dhiyo

   ṭi  saṭ ca ṡa kac   ṭāc  ṭāc sa ṭac    kāc ca ṡa
yo naḥ prāco huṃ bhā o vā o vā  o  vā huṃ bhā o vā //
```

Verses from the *uttarārcika which are not set to melodies notated in the *Uttaragāna are to be sung to the Gāyatra melody, which, either because it is so well-known or because it is so venerated, is not notated in the *gānas. During sacrificial rites, the syllables of the *udgītha and *upadrava sections of the melody are replaced by the vowel o, and the resulting chant is known as *aniruktagāna.

GOKARṆA: A Hindu pilgrimage city in the North Kannara District of *Mysore State, on the coast of the Arabian Sea. It is an important Vedic center, with large numbers of Ṛgvedins and *Kṛṣṇa Yajurvedins. However, no Sāmavedins reside there.

GOTRA: "Family." The *Brāhmaṇ caste is said to be composed of forty-nine gotras, who bear the names of revered *ṛṣis such as Gautama, Bharadvāja, and so on.

GRĀMA: "Village." See *Grāmageyagāna.

GRĀMAGEYAGĀNA: "Village Songbook." The Sāmavedic songbook containing melodies (*sāmans) to be studies or chanted within the village (grāma). The hymns are arranged according to divinity (*Agni, *Indra, *Soma) and meter. Each verse of the *pūrvārcika, taken in order, is set to one or more melodies.

GRANTHA: The script in which most South Indian Vedic manuscripts are written.

GṚHYA: "Domestic." That which relates to marriage, birth, death, and so on.

GṚHYASŪTRA: A manual which gives clues to the proper function of a certain Veda in domestic ceremonies and rituals.

GUJARĀT: State in West India bounded by *Mahārāṣṭra to the south, *Rājāsthān to the north, *Madhya Pradesh to the east, and the Arabian Sea to the west. Its capital is Ahmedabad, and the principal language is Gujarāti, a member of the Indo-European group.

H

HĀVIK: A *_śaiva_ *Brāhmaṇ sect of North Kannara in *Mysore State. Hāviks are not priests exclusively but engage also in other occupations. The *Rāṇāyanīya Sāmavedins around the town *Honnāvār are Hāviks.

HIMĀCĀL PRADESH: State in northern India bordered on the north by *Jammu and Kashmir, on the east by China and *Uttar Pradesh, and on the west and southwest by *Panjāb and Haryana.

HIṂKĀRA: The syllable _hum_, sung at the beginning of each round (*_paryāya_) and between *_udgītha_ and *_pratihāra_ of Sāmavedic ritual chants (*_stotras_).

HONNĀVĀR: Town in the North Kannara District of *Mysore. Several *Rāṇāyanīya villages are nearby.

HRASVA: A short vowel, whose length is the basic temporal unit (*_mātrā_) of *Kauthuma chant.

HRASVA-KARṢAṆA: See *_karṣaṇa_.

HUM: See *_hiṃkāra_.

I

IḶAKKAM: "Shaking." The term *Nambūdiri Sāmavedins use in describing the tonal movement of their chants.

INDRA: The chief god of atmosphere and sky, who subordinated the forces of evil by hurling his thunderbolt (*vajra*). The second **parva* (*aindraṃ parva*) of the *Grāmageyagāna of the Sāmaveda consists of chants addressed to Indra.

ITIHĀSA: History, particularly heroic history as narrated in the Hindu epics Mahābhārata and Rāmāyana.

J

JAIMINĪYA: One of three extant schools of Sāmavedic chant. Jaiminīyas can be found only at a very few villages and towns in South India.

JAMMU and KASHMIR: India's northernmost states, bounded on the north by China, on the west by Afghanistan, and on the east by Tibet.

JANYA: A South Indian **rāga* derived from one of forty-four parent *rāgas* (**meḷas*).

JYOTIṢA: A type of **vedāṅga* text dealing with the science of the movements of heavenly bodies and the divisions of time which depend on such movements.

JYOTIṢṬOMA: The prototype for all **soma* sacrifices. Seven varieties (**saṃsthās*) of the *jyotiṣṭoma* are distinguishable. From shortest to longest in duration, they are: **agniṣṭoma*, **atyagniṣṭoma*, **ukthya*, **ṣoḍaśin*, **vājapeya*, **atirātra*, and **aptoryāma*.

K

KAI-KĀṬṬUKA: "Hand showing." The term used by the *Nambūdiri Sāmavedins of *Keraḷa for the hand movements employed while chanting a *sāman.

KAI-LAKṢAṆA: "Hand indication." A term used by the Sāmavedins of *Kŏṭuntiṟappuḷḷi village in *Keraḷa when referring to the hand movements employed during Sāmavedic chanting.

KALĀ: A fixed temporal unit in *Kauthuma time measurement. A *mātrā (the length of a short syllable) may consist of three, four, or five kalās, depending upon the tempo (*vṛtti) chosen by the chanter.

KĀLEYA: The melody of the fourth *pṛṣṭhastotra of a *soma sacrifice.

KALPA: The sixth *vedāṅga ("limb of the Veda"), which deals with sacrificial procedures.

KAMIḺTTI: From kamiḺttuka: "to upset, to be turned upside down." One of four ways in which the *Nambūdiri Sāmagas of *Keraḷa hold the hand while chanting. In this case, the back of the hand faces the chanter when the hand is held in the high position; when it is held in the low position, the back faces the onlooker.

KAMPA: "Trembling, shaking." Trilling, which is employed frequently during the chanting of Sāmavedic hymns. Kampa is not indicated by any of the notational systems but nevertheless is present to some extent in the recitals of almost all Sāmavedins.

KAṆAKKU: "Counting." A procedure observed by *Nambūdiri Sāmavedins while they chant certain *sāmans. Counting is carried out by bending forward each finger of the right hand in turn, beginning with the little finger, when the hand is motionless. It is done mostly in the *upari ("high") position but may be performed in other positions as well.

KANIṢṬHIKĀBHIMARŚANA: Name given to the hand movement (*kai-lakṣaṇa) and sound (*svara) associated with the conjunct tr of the *Jaiminīya syllable notation. It is known also as tra-svara.

KANIṢṬHIKODGAMA: Name given to the hand movement (*kai-lakṣaṇa) and sound (*svara) associated with the nasal ṅ of the *Jaiminīya syllable notation. It is known also as ṅa-svara.

KAṆṬHYA: A guttural sound.

KARMAKĀṆḌA: The elements of Vedic revelation which relate to sacrificial observances.

KARṢAṆA: "Extending, drawing out, prolonging." A musical extension of certain syllables of a Sāmavedic chant. Karṣaṇa is indicated in the *Kauthuma notation by the placement, after the syllables in question, of numerals within the line of text. Five types of karṣaṇa (all on *vṛddha or augmented syllables) are listed by the *Mātrā-lakṣaṇa: 1_2, 1_{23}, 1_{234}, 1_{2345}, and 5_6. In each case the *svara ("sound") indicated by the first numeral is worth two *mātrās, and each subsequent numeral designates a _svara_ worth one _mātrā_. _Karṣaṇa_ on long (*_dīrgha_) and short (*_hrasva_) syllables are viewed as special cases; each _svara_ of the former is worth two _mātrās_, and each of the latter is worth one _mātrā_. The sequences *_pratyutkrama_, *_atikrama_, and *_svāra_ are to be considered forms of _karṣaṇa_.

KAUTHUMA: One of the three extant schools of Sāmavedic chant. Sāmavedins calling themselves Kauthumas are found in both the North and the South, but it is possible that true Kauthumas are found only in the North, particularly in *Uttar Pradesh and *Gujarāt. The Kauthumas are the only school which notate their chants numerically. Otherwise, however, their texts are almost identical to those of the *Rāṇāyanīyas.

KĀVA: The melody comprising *_stotriyās_ 15-17 of the evening *_pavamāna_ laud (*_ārbhavapavamānastotra_) of a *_soma_ sacrifice.

KERAḶA: State in Southwest India bordered on the east by a mountain range called the Western Ghāṭs and on the west by the Arabian Sea. The indigenous *Brāhmaṇs of Keraḷa are the *Nambūdiris, who employ distinctive styles of reciting and chanting the Vedas. The native language is *Malayāḷam.

KEVALOTTĀNA: See *_uttāna_.

KHARAHARAPRIYA: The twenty-second *_meḷa_ (parent *_rāga_) of South Indian classical music.

KŌṬUNTIṞAPPUḶḶI: A village, best known as a community of *Aiyar *Jaiminīya Sāmavedins, located a few miles west of

*Pālghāt (Pālakkāṭu) in *Keraḷa State. The *Brāhmaṇs here speak *Tamil̠ but write in the *Malayāḷam script.

KṚṢṆA YAJURVEDA: See *Yajurveda.

KRUṢṬA: (1) One of the seven *svaras enumerated by the *Nārada Śikṣā and other treatises on the *Kauthuma-*Rāṇāyanīya Sāmaveda. Kruṣṭa is indicated in the song-books either by 1 or 11. The former, however, usually designates another svara, the *prathama; where it designates the kruṣṭa can be known only through oral tradition. Among the svaras, kruṣṭa is usually listed in first place, a circumstance which has prompted numerous scholars to consider it the "highest" of seven "tones" making up the Kauthuma gamut. In India there is a saying that the kruṣṭa is heard only by the gods. One Sāmavedin told me in fact that he intones this svara only for "a split second." In practice, however, the seven numerals of the Kauthuma notation do not represent seven individual tones, and nothing extraordinary occurs in Sāmavedic recitals at the spots where kruṣṭa appears in the notation. (2) Name given to the hand movement (*kai-lakṣaṇa) and sound (*svara) associated with the syllable kru of the *Jaiminīya syllable notation. The syllable is said to be notated in only one *sāman of the Jaiminīya *Prakṛtigāna.

KUMBAKOṆAM: An important center of Vedic activity in the *Tanjore District of *Tamil̠nāṭu.

KUŚĀ: A small piece of wood used to mark the occurrence of each *stotriyā during the chanting of a laud (*stotra) at a *soma sacrifice. The kuśā sticks are placed in certain designs according to patterns (*viṣṭutis) prescribed for chanting the stotras.

KṢATRIYA: See *Brāhmaṇa.

KṢEPAṆA: Name given to the hand movement (*kai-lakṣaṇa) and sound (*svara)associated with the consonant p of the *Jaiminīya syllable notation.

KṢEPAṆAMARŚANA: Name given to the hand movement (*kai-lakṣaṇa) and sound (*svara) associated with the consonant dh of the *Jaiminīya syllable notation. This consonant designates a compound: p (*kṣepaṇa) + y (*marśana).

L

LOPA: "Disappearance." One of the ways in which the syllables of a source verse were altered so as to fit a pre-existing melody.

LUCKNOW: The capital of *Uttar Pradesh. Near here are said to be villages where *Kauthuma chanting is kept alive.

M

MADHYAMA: "Middle." (1) See *tṛtīya. (2) One of the vertical levels at which *Nambūdiri Sāmagas hold the right hand while chanting. (3) One of three *vṛttis (tempi) admitted by the *Mātrālakṣaṇa for Sāmavedic chanting. The term madhyama in this case implies chanting at a moderate tempo, in which the *mātrā (temporal unit) is said to consist of four *kalās (temporal subdivisions).

MADHYAMĀṄGULYA: Name given to the hand movement (*_kai-lakṣaṇa_) and sound (*_svara_) associated with the consonant _ph_ of the *Jaiminīya syllable notation. The Sāmavedins of *Kŏṭuntiṟappuḷḷi village in *Keraḷa refer to it as _pha_-_svara_.

MĀDHYAṂDINA: A recension (*_śākhā_) of the *Śukla ("White") Yajurveda.

MĀDHYAṂDINAPAVAMĀNASTOTRA: "Midday *_pavamāna_ laud." The first *_stotra_ (chant complex) of the midday service of the *_soma_ sacrifice. It is based upon a *_tṛca_ followed by a *_pragātha_ and a second _tṛca_. The initial _tṛca_ is sung first to the *Gāyatra melody, then to the *_āmahīyava_. The _prāgatha_ (transformed by overlapping into a _tṛca_) is sung first to the _raurava_, then to the *_yaudhājaya_. The concluding _tṛca_ is sung once to the *_auśana_ melody.

MADHYA PRADESH: State in Central India whose capital is Bhopal. The principal language is Hindi, a member of the Indo-European family.

MADRAS: Capital and largest city of *Tamiḻnāṭu.

MAHĀRĀṢṬRA: State in West Central India, whose principal language is Marāthī, an Indo-European tongue. Bombay is the capital and largest city.

MAHĀVEDI: The "great altar," where the principal events of the *_soma_ sacrifice take place (see fig. 1 above, p. 15).

MALARTTI: From _malarttuka_: "to place on the back, to lay open, to turn face upward." One of the ways in which *Nambūdiri Sāmagas hold the right hand while chanting a *sāman. The palm of the hand faces the chanter when the hand is held in the high (*upari) position; when it is held in the low (*adhaḥ) position, the palm faces the onlooker.

MALAYĀḶAM: A member of the Dravidian family of languages. It is the principal tongue of *Keraḷa State in Southwest India.

MANDRA: See *pañcama.

MARAITURAI: A Vedic center in the *Tanjore District of *Tamiḻnāṭu. Also known as Vedaprī.

MARDANA: "Crushing." Name given to the hand movement (*kai-lakṣaṇa) and sound (*svara) associated with the consonant bh of the *Jaiminīya syllable notation.

MARŚANA: Name given to the hand movement (*kai-lakṣaṇa) and sound (*svara) associated with the semivowel y of the *Jaiminīya syllable notation.

MAṬAKI-PIṬIKKA: From maṭakku ("to bend as the arms or knees, draw in, fold") and piṭi ("to catch, seize, clutch, cling to"). One of the ways in which *Nambūdiri Sāmavedins hold the right hand while chanting. The position is that of the hand held as a fist.

MĀTRĀ: The basic temporal unit of Sāmavedic chant. The *Mātrālakṣaṇa defines it as equivalent to the length of a short (*hrasva) vowel. See also *kalā.

MEḶA: In South Indian art music, one of seventy-two primary scales, from which are derived numerous subordinate patterns (*janya *rāgas).

MUDRĀ: "Seal, sign." Any one of a number of finger positions employed by a Sāmavedin as he chants a *sāman.

MUḶḶANṬIRAM: A village in the North Arcot District of *Tamilnāḍu where the old (*prācīna) style of *Kauthuma (= *Rāṇāyanīya?) chanting was handed down.

MYSORE: State in South India whose principal tongue is Kannaḍa, a member of the Dravidian language family. The capital city is Bangalore. Important centers of *Rāṇāyanīya Sāmaveda are located in the North Kannara District.

N

NAMANA (NAMATA): "Bowing down, sinking." A sequence of the *Kauthuma numeral notation which begins with the *prathama and ends with the *tṛtīya. Ordinarily it is designated by either the *avagraha (followed by the numeral 3 in the line of text) or (in South Indian manuscripts) the syllable na. Namana is found on augmented vowels and is worth a total of three *mātrās.

NAMBŪDIRI (NAṂPŪTIRI): Caste name of the *Malayāḷam-speaking *Brāhmaṇs of *Keraḷa. They are the only Brāhmaṇ community in this state whose origin cannot be traced elsewhere. Nambūdiri Sāmavedins belong to the *Jaiminīya school, and their style of singing is markedly different from Sāmavedic chanting elsewhere in India.

NĀRADA ŚIKṢĀ (NĀRADĪYĀ ŚIKṢĀ): "Textbook of [the sage] Nārada." A treatise which, among other things, relates the *Kauthuma notational numerals to the tones of the secular scale and to the cries of animals. It also describes the hand positions (**mudrās*) corresponding to **kruṣṭa*, **prathama*, and so on. The exact age of the treatise is not known, and its value for Sāmavedic research is questionable.

ṄA-SVARA: See **kaniṣṭhikodgama*.

ṆA-SVARA: See **anāmikodgama*.

NAUDHASA: The melody of the third **pṛṣṭhastotra* of the *Kauthuma-*Rāṇāyanīya **agniṣṭoma*.

NIDHANA: The fifth and final section (**bhakti*) of a Sāmavedic chant. It is sung by *Prastotar, *Udgātar, and *Pratihartar together.

NIGADA: (1) In the *Kauthuma notation, the numeral succession 3^{111}_{2345}, which is one of three types of **svāra*. The five numbers signify **svara*s ("sounds") worth $3 + 2 + 1 + 1 + 1 = 8$ **mātrā*s. (2) The invocation which forms the greater part of the **subrahmaṇyā* litany.

NIRUKTA: Explanation by Yaska of difficult Vedic words found in the lists called Nighaṇṭus. The work is one of the six **vedāṅga*s ("limbs of the Veda").

NĪTIŚĀSTRA: A work on political ethics or morals.

O

OKĀRA: The vowel *o*, which replaces the textual syllables of the **udgītha* and the **upadrava* during **aniruktagāna*, a sacrificial version of the *Gāyatra melody. Sāmavedins of the *Nambūdiri sect in *Keraḷa open their ritual chants (which they call **stuti*s rather than *stotra*s) with an *okāra* followed by a **hiṃkāra* (the syllable *hum*).

OṂKĀRA: The mystic syllable *om*, which is inserted into sacrificial chants between **prastāva* and **udgītha* as an additional **bhakti*, the **praṇava*. It is chanted by the *Udgātar.

ORISSA: State in East India south of *Bihār.

OṢṬHYA: A labial sound.

P

PĀDA: Quarter-verse. More specifically, that part of a verse which is treated as a euphonic unit.

PADĀNUSVĀRA: The number sequence 5_{656} (also called *pari-svāra*) of the *Kauthuma notation. The sequence appears invariably on augmented (**vṛddha*) vowels. The term *padānusvāra* by definition calls for nasalization; this is observed in the chants of the *Hāvik *Rāṇāyanīyas of *Mysore and the "Old School" Kauthumas of North Arcot. The sequence ordinarily occurs on the final syllable of certain chants.

PĀLGHĀT (PĀLAKKĀṬU): A district and its capital city in *Keraḷa State, Southwest India. Near Pālghāt City is the village *Kŏṭuntiṟappuḷḷi, an important center for *Jaiminīya Sāmaveda. The tradition here is kept alive by *Tamiḻ-speaking *Aiyar *Brāhmaṇs. Exponents of the *Kauthuma school also are to be found in the district.

PAÑCAMA: "Fifth." The notational numeral 5 of the *Kauthuma notation; also the sound (**svara*) indicated by that numeral.

PAÑCAPAÑCINĪ: "Five-fold." A pattern (*viṣṭuti) according to which the required number (*stoma) of verses (*stotriyās) of certain lauds (*stotras) are sung. A viṣṭuti is made up of three rounds (*paryāyas), each preceded by the *hiṃkāra (the syllable hum) and consisting of at least one appearance of each verse. If the three verses are numbered 1, 2, 3, then the pañcapañcinī scheme can be represented as follows: hum,1,1,1,2,3; hum,1,2,2,2,3; hum,1,2,3,3,3. Therefore fifteen stotriyās are derived.

PANJĀB: State in Northwest India.

PÃÑÑĀL: A village in the *Trichur District of *Kerala State. Located a few miles southeast of Cer̲utūrutti, Pāññāl is one of the few places where *Nambūdiri Sāmaveda is kept alive.

PARISĀMAN: A solo chant. Several are sung at independent ceremonies such as the *agnicayana and *pravargya, which are only peripherally connected with the *soma rite.

PARIŚIṢṬAM: A supplement or appendix, such as that to the *Āraṇyakagāna.

PARISVĀRA: See *padānusvāra.

PARVAN: "Division, section." Every Sāmavedic chant is composed of a number of parvans, which vary in length. In the *gāna manuscripts, parvans are separated from one another by vertical lines (*daṇḍas), which mark the spots where breath is to be taken. Certain *Rāṇāyanīya manuscripts present around three hundred parvans extracted from various chants of the repertoire. These "typical parvans" represent by and large all of the musical material of that school. Every Rāṇāyanīya chant was "composed" by selecting certain parvans from that basic repository of three hundred. Chants of the other two schools also are constructed according to this "cento-nization" principle.

PARYĀYA: One of three "rounds" of a *viṣṭuti (chant pattern). A paryāya contains at least one appearance of each *stotriyā of a laud (*stotra). The syllable huṃ (the *hiṃkāra) precedes each round.

PĀṬHAŚĀLĀ: A school. A vedapāṭhaśālā is a school where the Vedas are taught.

PAUṢKALA: The melody comprising stotriyā 8 of the *ārbhava-pavamāna laud, which is sung during the evening service of a *soma sacrifice.

PAVAMĀNA: The strained--and hence "purified" or "clear"-- *soma liquid.

PHA-SVARA: See *madhyamāṅgulya.

PLA-SVARA: See *anāmikāvaroha.

PLUTA: "Protracted, lengthened." A three-*mātrā vowel formed by the addition of two mātrās to a short (*hrasva) vowel.

PRACAYA: See *udātta.

PRĀCĪNA: "Ancient, old." A term applied to a style of *sāman-singing prevalent among *Kauthumas of the North Arcot District of *Tamiḻnāṭu.

PRAGĀTHA: A mixed strophic meter, common among groups of two verses in the *uttarārcika of the Sāmaveda. Of the two types of pragāthas, the kākubha pragātha appears less often. It consists of a kakubh combined with a sato-bṛhatī verse according to the following arrangement of syllables:

(8 + 12) + 8

(12 + 8) + (12 + 8)

The bārhata pragātha occurs more frequently. It is a combination of bṛhatī and satobṛhatī verses in the following pattern:

(8 + 8) + (12 + 8)

(12 + 8) + (12 + 8)

PRAKṚTI: The "original or primary form."

PRAKṚTIGĀNA: Same as *Pūrvagāna.

PRAṆATA: "Bowed, inclined, bent." In the *Kauthuma notation, the numeral 2 in the primary position (that is, above the line of text) followed immediately by the numeral 3 in the secondary position (that is, within the line of text). The circumflex, notated above 3, is an optional sign which more often than not is omitted. The two numerals of praṇata have the following respective *mātrā distribution:

augmented (*vṛddha) vowels: $1\frac{1}{2} + \frac{1}{2}$

long (*dīrgha) vowels: $\frac{1}{2} + \frac{1}{2}$

short (*hrasva) vowels: $\frac{1}{2} + \frac{1}{2}$

PRAṆAVA: The syllable om, which may be inserted into a ritual chant as an additional *bhakti. It is chanted by the *Udgātar immediately prior to the *udgītha section.

PRASTĀVA: The first section (*_bhakti_) of a Sāmavedic chant, sung by a priest called the *Prastotar.

PRASTOTAR: One of a trio of Sāmavedic priests whose duty is the chanting of lauds (*_stotra_s) at the *_soma_ sacrifices. The *_prastāva_ or opening section (*_bhakti_) of a melody is sung by the Prastotar alone. He joins the other priests in chanting the closing section (*_nidhana_).

PRATHAMA: "First." The notational numeral 1 of the *Kauthuma notation; also the sound (*_svara_) indicated by that numeral. The figure designates optionally another _svara_, the *_kruṣṭa_.

PRATIHĀRA: The third of five principal sections (*_bhakti_s) of a Sāmavedic chant. It is sung by a priest known as the *Pratihartar.

PRATIHARTAR: One of a trio of Sāmavedic priests whose duty is the chanting of lauds (*_stotra_s) at the *_soma_ sacrifices. The *_pratihāra_ or third principal section (*_bhakti_) of a melody is sung by the Pratihartar alone. He joins the other priests in chanting the closing section (*_nidhana_).

PRĀTIŚĀKHYA: One of a group of treatises, each belonging to a particular Vedic school, which deals with euphonic combination (*_saṃdhi_) and related subjects (tone, length of tone, syllabication, and so on).

PRATYAVAROHA: "Descent." A number sequence of the *Kauthuma notation. The *Puṣpasūtra gives 1_{234} as an example.

PRATYUTKRAMA: In the *Kauthuma notation, a number followed

by a "higher" number. Eight varieties are listed by the *Mātrālakṣaṇa: 6 to 5, 5 to 4, 4 to 3, 3 to 2, 2 to 1, 5 to 3, 5 to 2, and 3 to 1. Wherever the first numeral of any type falls in the primary (*_prakṛti_) position (that is, above the line of text) and the second numeral appears in the secondary (*_vikṛti_) position (that is, within the line of text), the respective *_mātrā_ distribution is 2_{+1} or 3 _mātrās_ total for the sequence.

PRAVARGYA: A ceremony preliminary to the *_soma_ sacrifice. It is an independent (*_apūrva_) ritual featuring an offering of fresh milk heated in a special vessel called _gharma_ or _mahāvīra_. During this rite, solo chants (*_parisāman_) are sung by a priest called the *Prastotar.

PRAYOGA: "Application, employment, use." Chanting for "use" in the *_soma_ sacrifices, in contradistinction to *_svādhyāya_, or chanting to oneself.

PREṄKHA: In the *Kauthuma songbooks, the numerical sequence 1_2, indicated in South Indian manuscripts by the syllable _pre_. From an example offered by the *Mātrālakṣaṇa, _preṅkha_ is seen as a form of *_karṣaṇa_ having a total duration of three *_mātrās_ (time units), distributed 2_{+1}. Occasionally a chant from the *Uttaragāna has _preṅkha_ in the spot where *_vinata_ occurs in the identical *Pūrvagāna chant.

PṚṢṬHA: Name given to four lauds (*_stotras_) sung at the midday service of a *_soma_ sacrifice.

PṚṢṬHASTOTRA: See *_pṛṣṭha_.

PŪJĀ: Worship, homage.

PURĀṆA: "Ancient, old." One of a group of sacred tales and legends about the gods--Viṣṇu, Śiva, and so on.

PŪRVAGĀNA: "First Songbook," as opposed to the *Uttaragāna ("Last Songbook"). The Pūrvagāna comprises both *Grāmageyagāna ("Village Songbook") and *Āraṇyakagāna ("Forest Songbook"). Many of the chants of the Uttaragāna (*Ūhagāna + *Rahasyagāna) are taken, often in modified form, from the Pūrvagāna. Also called Prakṛtigāna.

PŪRVĀRCIKA: The "first *_ārcika_" of the Sāmaveda *Saṃhitā. It consists of verses arranged according to divinity (*Agni, *Indra, *Soma) and meter. Attached to it is the *Āraṇyaka Saṃhitā.

PUṢPASŪTRA: A *_prātiśākhya_ of the Sāmaveda. It deals mainly with the adaptation of *Pūrvagāna melodies to different texts (as found in the *_uttarārcika_). The treatise is attributed to Vararuci and is known in South India as the Phullasūtra.

R

RĀGA: "Color, atmosphere." One of many tonal schemes upon which the art music of both North and South India is based. These "melody patterns" have certain tones that are more outstanding than others. Moreover, the ascending tonal material may be different from that used in descent, and these ascending and descending "scales" may proceed in zigzag fashion. A large number of _rāgas_ are associated with certain typical phrases.

RAHASYAGĀNA: Known also as *Ūhyagāna. It is the fourth songbook (*gāna) of the Sāmaveda, containing (1) chants from the *Āraṇyakagāna which are changed or modified (ūhya) for sacrificial purposes, and (2) chants found only in the Rahasyagāna. Most of the melodies (*sāmans) are notated three times consecutively to different texts, which are drawn mainly from the *uttarārcika of the *Saṃhitā.

RĀJĀSTHĀN: State in Northwest India bordered on the west by Pakistan, on the east by *Madhya Pradesh, on the south by *Gujarāt, on the north by *Panjāb and Haryana, and on the northeast by *Uttar Pradesh. Jaipur is the state capital.

RĀṆĀYANĪYA: One of three extant schools of Sāmavedic chanting. Rāṇāyanīyas may be found in *Gujarāt, *Andhra Pradesh, and among the *Hāvik *Brāhmaṇs of North Kannara, *Mysore. The Sāmavedins in South India who call themselves *Kauthumas may in fact be Rāṇāyanīyas. The latter use a syllable notation which was at one time known to the former.

RATHAṂTARA: The first *pṛṣṭha-*stotra of the *soma sacrifice. See also *bhakāra.

RAURAVA: The melody forming *stotriyās 7-9 of the *mādhyaṃdinapavamānastotra, the midday *pavamāna laud of the *soma sacrifice.

ṚC (ṚK): "Verse," particularly a recited verse in praise of a deity. It is to be distinguished from chanted melodies (*sāmans), sacrificial formulae (*yajus), and magical spells (*atharvan). See also *Ṛgveda.

REPHA: The letter *r*, which, when placed above a syllable of a *Kauthuma chant, denotes a time value of two **mātrās* (temporal units). The South Indian equivalent is the **bindu*.

ṚGVEDA: The "Veda of Verses," which is the most ancient of the Vedic collections.

ṚṢI: One of the seers to whom the Vedic hymns were revealed.

RUDRA: In Vedic times, an atmospheric god of storms and tempests. Rudra later is identified as Śiva, one of the three principal deities of the Hindu pantheon.

RŪPĀNTARA: The form of Sāmavedic chants notated in the *Pūrvagāna, as opposed to the **svarūpa* or sacrificial form of *Uttaragāna chants.

S

ŚAIVA: Connected with the god Śiva.

ŚĀKHĀ: A school of Vedic recitation or chant. *Brāhmaṇs of the same *śākhā* (a *Vaidika belongs by birth to only one school) generally follow the same text, but their interpretations may not necessarily coincide stylistically.

SĀMAGA (SĀMAGĀ): A Sāmavedic chanter. Same as Sāmavedin.

SĀMAN: A Sāmavedic chant.

SĀMAVEDA: The Veda consisting of a collection of verses, each of which is set to one or more melodies (**sāmans*). These chants are brought together in four songbooks (**gānas*): *Grāmageyagāna, *Āraṇyakagāna, *Ūhagāna, and *Rahasyagāna (Ūhyagāna). Ūhagāna and Rahasyagāna present the hymns in the order in which they are sung at the **soma* rituals, where each laud (*_stotra_) is sung by a trio of Sāmavedic priests: *Prastotar, *Udgātar, and *Pratihartar.

SĀMAVEDIN: Same as *Sāmaga.

SAṂDHI: Euphonic combination.

SAṂHITA: The melody comprising *_stotriyās_ 4-6 of the evening *_pavamāna_ laud (*_ārbhavapavamāna_-*_stotra_) of the *_soma_ sacrifice.

SAṂHITĀ: (1) One of several "collections" of hymns, verses, or sacrificial formulas which form the essential and primary part of Vedic literature. Each Veda has one or more Saṃhitās, which are to be distinguished from the auxiliary *Brāhmaṇas, *Āraṇyakas, and *Upaniṣads. (2) The continuous text of the Vedas (as found in the Saṃhitās), in contradistinction to the division into isolated words (*_padas_). See *_saṃhitāpāṭha_.

SAṂHITĀPĀṬHA: Recitation carried out by observing the laws of euphonic combination (*_saṃdhi_) of final and initial sounds of individual words (*_padas_).

SAṂPRASĀRAṆA: See *_svāra_.

SAṂSTHĀ: One of seven varieties of the *_jyotiṣṭoma_, the basic form of all *_somayāgas_. The seven, in order of duration, are: *_agniṣṭoma_, *_atyagniṣṭoma_, *_ukthya_, *_ṣoḍaśin_, *_vājapeya_, *_atirātra_, and *_aptoryāma_. Each _saṃsthā_ is divided into morning, afternoon, and evening services. The length of the evening service distinguishes one type from another.

SAPHA: The melody comprising the seventh *_stotriyā_ of the

evening *_pavamāna_ laud (*_ārbhavapavamāna_-*_stotra_) of the *_soma_ sacrifice.

SAPTASAPTINĪ: "Seven-fold." A pattern (*_viṣṭuti_) according to which the required number (*_stoma_) of verses (*_stotriyās_) of a particular laud (*_stotra_) are sung. A _viṣṭuti_ is made up of three rounds (*_paryāyas_), each preceded by the *_hiṃkāra_ (the syllable _hum_) and consisting of at least one appearance of each verse. As each _stotriyā_ is sung, a *_kuśā_ stick is placed on the ground; a particular pattern of sticks emerges for each _paryāya_ as the singing of the laud proceeds. If the three source verses are numbered 1-2-3, the _saptasaptinī_ scheme may be represented as: _hum_,1,1,1,2,3; _hum_,1,2,2,2,3,3,3; _hum_,1,1,1,2,2,2,3,3,3. Therefore twenty-one _stotriyās_ are derived in this fashion. The final _stotra_ of the *_agniṣṭoma_ is sung according to this _viṣṭuti_.

ṢAṢṬHA: "Sixth." See *_atisvārya_.

SATTRA: "Session." A *_soma_ sacrifice consisting of twelve or more pressing days. At *_ekāha_ and *_ahīna_ rites, the sacrificer (*_yajamāna_) may belong to either of the higher three castes (*Brāhmaṇa, Kṣatriya, or Vaiśya). At a _sattra_ ceremony, however, each of the priests is himself the _yajamāna_ (all, of course, are Brāhmaṇs), who reaps the benefits of the observance.

SĀVITRĪ: See *Gāyatra.

ŚIKṢĀ: "Instruction, precept." The *_vedāñga_ ("limb of the Veda") which teaches the correct utterance of the Vedic texts. See *Nārada Śikṣā.

ŚIVALLI: Tulu-speaking Mādhva (and hence *vaiṣṇava) *Brāhmaṇs of South Kannara, *Mysore.

SMĀRTA: See *Aiyar.

SMṚTI: That which is remembered, in contradistinction to that which was revealed to the *ṛṣis through a "hearing" (*śruti). Within the sphere of smṛti are comprehended the six *vedāṅgas ("limbs of the Veda": *śikṣā, *chandas, *vyākaraṇa, *nirukta, *jyotiṣa, *kalpa), the *śrauta- and *gṛhya-*sūtras, the *dharmaśāstras, the *itihāsas, the *purāṇas, and the *nītiśāstras.

ṢOḌAŚIN: "Having sixteen parts." One of the seven *saṃsthās of the *jyotiṣṭoma, the prototype for all *soma sacrifices. The ṣoḍaśin is the fourth of the seven and consists of sixteen lauds (*stotras), the last of which is known among *Nambūdiri *Sāmagas as the ṣoḍaśi-*sāman.

SOMA: The intoxicating juice of the soma plant. Sāmavedic chanting takes place during *somayāgas--sacrifices at which libations of the liquid are offered to the gods.

SOMAYĀGA: "Soma sacrifice." A sacrifice at which the most important libation is that of the *soma liquid. Somayāgas are the only rites at which Sāmavedic chanting can be heard in its ritualistic form, as performed by a trio of Sāmavedic priests.

ŚRAUTA: That which relates to the *śruti tradition (that is, the Vedas), especially as it is applied at the sacrifices.

ŚRAUTASŪTRA: A text which provides clues to the proper

function of a Veda at particular sacrifices.

ŚRAUTIN: Same as *_śrotriya_.

ŚRĪRAṄGAM: A temple town and *_vaiṣṇava_ pilgrimage place a few miles north of *Tiruccirāppaḷḷi in *Tamiḻnāṭu. The imposing Śrī Raṅganātha temple here is famous throughout India. The streets surrounding the edifice are inhabited principally by *Aiyaṅgār *Brāhmaṇs, among them Sāmavedins of the *Kauthuma (= *Rāṇāyanīya?) and *Jaiminīya schools. A Jaiminīya *_pāṭhaśālā_ has been established here under the tutelage of T. Rājagopāla Aiyaṅgār, the principal *Tamiḻ exponent of this *_śākhā_.

ŚROTRIYA: A *Brāhmaṇ who has knowledge of the Veda, especially of its sacrificial functions.

ŚRUTI: (1) A "hearing." The sacred, revealed knowledge ("Veda") which is transmitted orally by the *Brāhmaṇs from father to son, teacher to pupil, generation after generation. (2) A microtone of Indian classical music.

STHIRAMĀTRĀ: "Fixed (or motionless?) *_mātrā_." A term whose abbreviations, _sthi_ and _sthira_, appear as notational symbols in some *Rāṇāyanīya chants. The precise meaning of the word is not known.

STOBHA: A non-textual insertion in a Sāmavedic chant. One of the most common interjections is comprised of the "nonsense" syllables _au_-_ho_-_vā_, although some _stobhas_ are in fact legitimate words or phrases. All of these insertions are considered to have magical or mystical properties. They were perhaps added when the original texts required extra syllables in order to more closely fit pre-existing melodies or melody fragments. Some chants are made up entirely of stobhas.

STOMA: The necessary number of verses (*stotriyās) for any given ritual chant (*stotra).

STOTRA: Name given to the ritual chants sung at the *soma sacrifices. Stotras are chanted by three Sāmavedic priests--Prastotar, Udgātar, Pratihartar--and are thus distinguished from the *parisāmans or solo chants. The verses (*stotriyās) of certain stotras are required to be sung according to prescribed repetition schemes called *viṣṭutis.

STOTRIYĀ: A *stotra verse.

STUTI: The *Nambūdiri term for *stotra.

SUBRAHMAṆYA: See *subrahmaṇyā.

SUBRAHMAṆYĀ: A formula whose calling (āhvāna) is entrusted to a fourth (after *Prastotar, *Udgātar, and *Pratihartar) Sāmaveda priest, the Subrahmaṇya. It is intoned on the day of *soma pressing (the sutyā), as well as on each of the preliminary festival (upasad) days. The formula proper is addressed to the god *Indra (there is also a subrahmaṇyā litany to *Agni), who is invited, along with gods and *Brāhmaṇs, to be present at the sacrifice. The litany consists of the word subrahmaṇyā combined with the sacred syllable om (thus: subrahmaṇyom) stated three times, followed by a prayer (*nigada). The *Kauthuma-*Rāṇāyanīya version, in eleven sections (*vacanas), reads as follows (text and translation after Parpola in L/DSS I:1, pp. 114-15; I:2, pp. 47-51--syllables bearing the *udātta* accent are marked with a *u*):

u u u
I. subrahmaṇyom subrahmaṇyom subrahmaṇyom

[Subrahmaṇyā, Om! Subrahmaṇyā, Om! Subrahmaṇyā, Om!]

u u u
II. indrāgaccha

O Indra, Come!

u u u u
III. hariva āgaccha

O Thou with the bay steeds, Come!

u u
IV. medhātither meṣa

O ram of Medhātithi!

u u
V. vṛṣaṇaśvasya mene

O Menā of Vṛṣaṇaśva!

u u
VI. gaurāvaskandinn

O buffalo leaping down!

u u
VII. ahalyāyāi jāra

O lover of Ahalyā!

u u
VIII. kauśika brāhmaṇa!

O brāhmaṇa of the clan of Kuśika!

u u
IX. gautama bruvāṇa

O Thou that callest thyself Gautama!

u u u
X. adya sutyām āgaccha maghavan

[O munificent one, come today to the *soma* pressing!]

u u u u u u u u

XI. devā brahmāṇa āgacchata āgacchata āgacchata

u u u u u u

[or: āgacchatāgacchatāgacchata]

O Gods! O Brāhmaṇs! Come ye! Come ye!

Come ye!

The god Indra "has committed many a naughty trick on earth: when the priest Medhātithi had bought soma-grass in view of an approaching sacrificial festival, Indra assuming in hasty gluttony the appearance of a ram ate all the stalks in which the juice was contained; and when the brahmin Gautama for a short while was away from home, Indra in Gautama's shape enjoyed the loveliness of Ahalyā; nay even, in order to make acquaintance with the pleasures of love on the female side, he became the wife of Vṛṣaṇaśva, a man so strong that he put bulls instead of horses before his cart." (SSV, p. 23)

Certain callings of the subrahmaṇyā should include the nāmagrāha, in which the name of the sacrificer and his ancestors and descendants are mentioned.

ŚŪDRA: See *Brāhmaṇa.

ŚUKLA YAJURVEDA: See *Yajurveda.

ŚUKRIYA: One of the divisions of the *Āraṇyakagāna. It is found in fourth place in both the *Kauthuma/*Rāṇāyanīya and *Jaiminīya recensions.

SŪRYA: A Vedic solar deity (different from Savitṛ) who is pulled through the sky in a chariot by seven horses or mares.

SŪTRA: "Thread, string." A short aphorism or collection of aphorisms which prescribe the proper function of a Veda during the sacrificial (*śrauta) rites or domestic (*gṛhya) ceremonies. To each of the three Sāmavedic śākhās belong one śrauta- and one gṛhya-sūtra. The Lāṭyāyana-śrauta-sūtra, Drāhyāyaṇa-śrauta-sūtra, and Jaiminīya-śrauta-sūtra belong to the *Kauthuma, *Rāṇāyanīya, and *Jaiminīya schools respectively. Likewise, to the three schools (taken in the same order) belong the Gobhila-gṛhya-sūtra, Khādira (or Drāhyāyaṇa)-gṛhya-sūtra, and Jaiminīya-gṛhya-sūtra.

SVĀDHYĀYA: Reciting or chanting the Veda alone to oneself rather than at the sacrifices.

SVARA: "Sound." The relation of this term to Vedic music has been the subject of much debate. The post-Vedic *Nārada Śikṣā formulates a descending scale by listing seven svaras (corresponding, doubtlessly, to the numerals 11, 1, 2, 3, 4, 5, and 6 of the *Kauthuma notation) and equating them with the tones of secular music. Such an analogy, however, does not withstand comparison with the oral traditions. It is apparent from them that the *parvan--that portion of a chant sung in one breath--is the musical unit and that parvans with the same numerical sequence (Kauthuma manuscripts), the same notational syllable (*Rāṇāyanīya manuscripts), or the same sequence of notational syllables (*Jaiminīya manuscripts) have basically the same musical content. Since the number of differently notated parvans is limited to about three hundred, adherents to a particular style of chant can claim for their repertoire the same number of motives or typical phrases, which are combined in various ways to form individual chants. Thus the Sāmavedic concept of *svara* is much broader than previously imagined and is oriented towards tone patterns rather than single pitches.

SVĀRA (SVĀRYA, SAṂPRASĀRAṆA): Term for three related sequences (numeral successions) of the *Kauthuma notation (**mātrā* values are in parentheses):

1. $1_{2345}^{\;\;111}$ (3+3+1+1+1)
2. 2_{345}^{111} (3+1+1+1)
3. $3_{2345}^{\;\;111}$ (3+2+1+1+1)

The numeral 1 above the final three numbers of each type is an indication that the **svaras* ("sounds") corresponding to these numbers are worth one *mātrā* apiece. *Svāra* occurs only on augmented (**vṛddha*) vowels and is found most often on final syllables of **nidhanas*, the concluding sections of Sāmavedic chants.

SVARABHAKTI: A vowel sound separating *r* or *l* from a following consonant.

SVARABHEDA: One of thirty-three **svaras* listed, along with corresponding notational signs, by Sabhāpati in his *Dhāraṇalakṣaṇa. The treatise belongs to the *Jaiminīya school of Sāmaveda.

SVARITA: See **udātta*.

SVARŪPA: The "natural form" of Sāmavedic chant as revealed

at the *soma sacrifices and notated in the *Ūha- and *Rahasyagānas.

SVĀRYA: See *svāra.

ŚYĀVĀŚVA: The melody comprising *stotriyās 9-11 of the *ārbhavapavamāna-stotra (evening *pavamāna laud) of the *soma sacrifice.

T

TAITTIRĪYA: A recension of the Kṛṣṇa ("Black") *Yajurveda.

TĀLAVYA: A palatal sound.

TAMIḺ: The principal language of *Tamiḻnāṭu. It is the least Sanskritized of the Dravidian tongues.

TAMIḺNĀṬU: "Tamiḻ Country." State in Southeast India (formerly known as Madras State) whose chief language is Tamiḻ, a member of the Dravidian group of languages. Madras is the state capital.

TANJORE (TAÑJĀVŪR): A district (and its capital city) in *Tamiḻnāṭu. The Tanjore District is widely known for its large numbers of Vedic reciters and chanters. Most of the Sāmavedins here call themselves *Kauthumas; a much smaller number belong to the *Jaiminīya school. Ṛgveda and both Kṛṣṇa and Śukla *Yajurveda are still transmitted in the district.

TARJANĪ MARŚANA: "Touching of the index finger." Name given to the hand movement (*kai-lakṣaṇa) and sound (*svara) associated with the sibilant ṣ of the *Jaiminīya syllable notation.

TĔNTIRUPPERAI: A village of *Jaiminīya Sāmavedins in the *Tirunĕlveli District of *Tamiḻnāṭu, near *Āḻvārtirunāgari. The *Brāhmaṇs here are *Aiyaṅgārs of the Teṅgalai sect.

TIRUCCIRĀPPAḶḶI (TRICHINOPOLY): A district (and its capital city) in *Tamiḻnāṭu. The *_vaiṣṇava_ temple town *Śrīraṅgam is near Tiruccirāppaḷḷi City.

TIRUNĔLVELI (TINNEVELLY): A district (and its capital city) in southern *Tamiḻnāṭu. *Jaiminīya Sāmaveda is extant at the village *Tĕntirupperai, near *Āḻvārtirunāgari.

TIRUPATI: A city in the Chittur District of Andhra Pradesh. The famous Śrī Veṅkateśvara Temple, reputedly the wealthiest in India, is situated at nearby Tirumalai. The shrine is visited by thousands of Hindu pilgrims daily. Most of the *Vaidikas resident at Tirupati and environs belong to the *Taittirīya school of Kṛṣṇa *Yajurveda. No Sāmavedins are to be found in the area.

TIVĀRI: A caste name among North Indian *Brāhmaṇs.

TOGŪR: A *Jaiminīya village in the *Tanjore District of *Tamiḻnāṭu, near Grand Amicut.

TRA-SVARA: See *_kaniṣṭhikābhimarśana_.

TṚCA: In the *_uttarārcika_ of the Sāmaveda *Saṃhitā, a strophe comprised of three verses. The first verse ordinarily is found also in the *_pūrvārcika_.

TRICHUR (TṚŚŚIVAPERŪR): A district (and its capital city) in *Keraḷa State. Here are to be found important centers of *Nambūdiri Ṛg-, Yajur-, and Sāmaveda.

TRIṢṬUBH: A Vedic meter consisting of four verses, each with eleven syllables, arranged in two hemistichs.

TRIVEDĪ: Having knowledge of three Vedas. It is a common title among *Brāhmaṇs.

TṚTĪYA: "Third." The notational numeral 3 of the *Kauthuma notation; also the sound (*svara) indicated by that numeral. Alternately it is called madhyama ("middle").

TṚTĪYADHARI: In *Rāṇāyanīya manuscripts, the designation (abbreviated tra) for a particular number sequence, perhaps the pattern 4-3-4.

U

UDĀTTA: In Vedic literature, the principal or "raised" accent, which normally is preceded by the anudātta ("not raised") and followed by the svarita ("sounded"). The svarita is a falling or transitional accent, and the accentless syllables which sometimes follow it are termed pracaya ("multitude"). It is not uncommon for two or more udāttas to appear consecutively in a Vedic sentence; moreover, an udātta is followed by an anudātta--not by a svarita--if the latter is itself followed by an udātta. The udātta is a fixed accent and can not be shifted or changed, but it can be lost entirely, in which case we find a svarita (now "independent" of the udātta, which has disappeared) preceded by an anudātta.

The *Ṛgveda *Saṃhitā does not mark udātta and pracaya. The anudātta is indicated by a horizontal stroke beneath a syllable, the *svarita* by a vertical stroke above. An independent *svarita* not followed by an *anudātta* is marked either by the figure 1 (in the case of a short vowel) or by the figure 3 (in the case of a long vowel). In both instances the *svarita* and *anudātta* strokes appear, respectively, above and below the numeral.

The Sāmaveda *Saṃhitā (*Kauthuma-*Rāṇāyanīya) uses the figures 1-2-3 to mark the accents. The 1 and the 3 always represent *udātta* and *anudātta*, respectively. The 2 usually stands for the *svarita*, but it is the symbol for the *udātta* when a *svarita* does not follow. When two *udāttas* occur in succession, the second is left undesignated while 2r is placed above the following *svarita*. If in such a case a *svarita* does not follow, 2u is placed above the first *udātta*. The independent *svarita* has the symbol 2r, and the *anudātta* which precedes it is marked by the sign 3k. *Pracaya* syllables are left unmarked.

The methods of the Ṛgveda and Sāmaveda can be illustrated by Ṛgveda Saṃhitā 6.16.10 (= Sāmaveda Saṃhitā 1.1). These are followed by an interpretation of N. Lakṣmīnārāyaṇa Śrautigal, a Kauthuma chanter from Mysore City.

Ṛgveda: agna ā yāhi vītaye gṛṇāno havyadātaye /

ni hotā satsi barhiṣi //

```
            2  3 1  2    3 1 2    3 2  3  1 2
Sāmaveda:  agna ā yāhi vītaye gṛṇāno havyadātaye /
            1   2r        3  1 2
           ni hotā satsi barhiṣi //
```

"Come, Agni, praised with song, to feast and sacrificial offering: sit
As Hotar on the holy grass!" (trans. Ralph T. H. Griffith)

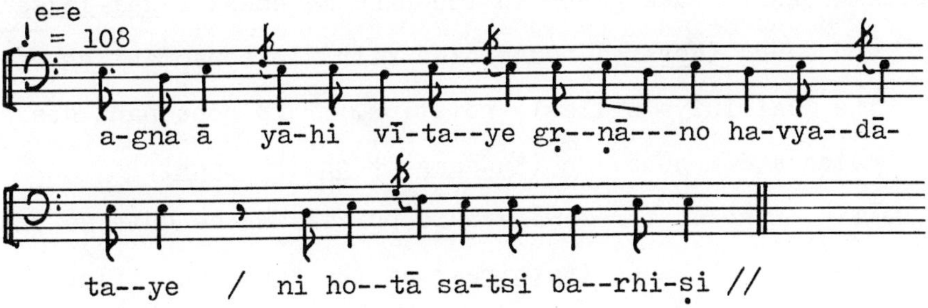
e=e
♪ = 108
a-gna ā yā-hi vī-ta--ye gṛ--ṇā---no ha-vya--dā-
ta--ye / ni ho--tā sa-tsi ba--rhi-ṣi //

UDGAMA: "Ascent." Name given to the hand movement (*kai-lakṣaṇa) and sound (*svara) associated with the consonant c of the *Jaiminīya syllable notation.

UDGAMAKṢEPAṆA: Name given to the hand movement (*kai-lakṣaṇa) and sound (*svara) associated with the consonant ḍ of the *Jaiminīya syllable notation. This consonant designates a compound: c (*udgama) + p (*kṣepaṇa).

UDGAMĀVARTA: Name given to the hand movement (*kai-lakṣaṇa) and sound (*svara) associated with the semivowel ḷ of the *Jaiminīya syllable notation. This semivowel designates a compound: c (*udgama) + t (*āvarta).

UDGAMAMARŚANA: Name given to the hand movement (*kai-lakṣaṇa) and sound (*svara) associated with the consonant d of the *Jaiminīya syllable notation. This consonant designates a compound: c (*udgama) + y (*marśana).

UDGAMAYĀNA: Name given to the hand movement (*kai-lakṣaṇa) and sound (*svara) associated with the aspiration h of the *Jaiminīya syllable notation. This aspiration designates a compound: c (*udgama) + ṭ (*yāna).

UDGAMOTTĀNA: Name given to the hand movement (*kai-lakṣaṇa) and sound (*svara) associated with the consonant ch of the *Jaiminīya syllable notation. This consonant designates a compound: c (*udgama) + th (*uttāna).

UDGĀTAR: One of three Sāmavedic priests whose duty is the chanting of lauds (*stotras) at the *soma sacrifices. Two sections (*bhaktis) of a melody, *udgītha and *upadrava, are sung by the Udgātar alone. He also chants the *praṇava (the syllable om) when it is inserted between *prastāva and udgītha. The closing section (*nidhana) is sung by the three priests together.

UDGĪTHA: The second and principal section (*bhakti) of a Sāmavedic chant, sung by the *Udgātar.

UDŪHA: In the *Kauthuma numeral notation, a number which is equal to another number minus three. Thus *prathama, *dvitīya, and *tṛtīya (1, 2, and 3) are the respective udūhas of *caturtha, *mandra, and *atisvārya (4, 5, and 6). Barend Faddegon views the udūhas as "harmonic derivatives," for which the other *svaras could be considered substitutes.

ŪHA: "Modification." A chant of the *Ūhagāna or *Rahasyagāna which is derived from a source chant (*yoni) of the *Grāmageyagāna or *Āraṇyakagāna.

ŪHAGĀNA: Name of the third songbook (*gāna) of the Sāmaveda. It presents chants arranged for use in the *soma sacrifices. Contained in the songbook are both chants from the *Grāmageyagāna which undergo modification (*ūha) for sacrificial purposes and chants peculiar only to the Ūhagāna. Most of the melodies of the Ūha- and *Rahasyagānas are notated three times consecutively to different texts, which are drawn mainly from the *uttarārcika of the *Saṃhitā.

ŪHYAGĀNA: Same as *Rahasyagāna.

UKTHYA: The third of seven varieties (*saṃsthās) of the *jyotiṣṭoma. Ukthya rites are comprised of fifteen lauds (*stotras).

UPADRAVA: The fourth *bhakti of a Sāmavedic chant. It is sung by a priest called the *Udgātar.

UPANIṢAD: A class of mystical writings which seek to expound the hidden meaning of the Veda. They form the basis of the Vedānta and Sāṃkhya philosophies. Two Upaniṣads properly belong to the Sāmaveda, the Chāndogyopaniṣad of the *Kauthumas and *Rāṇāyanīyas and the Kenopaniṣad of the *Jaiminīyas.

UPARI: "High." One of the vertical levels at which *Nambūdiri *Sāmagas hold the right hand while chanting.

UPARIṢṬHA-PIṬIKKA: One of the hand positions used by *Nambūdiri *Sāmavedins while chanting. The right hand is turned sideways so that the edge of the little finger faces the onlooker. The position is known also as *c̆ericcu, which is the palm turned sideways to the left.

UPĀYA: In the *Kauthuma numeral notation, a *svāra numeral succession on the *stobha syllable vā.

ŪṢĀNI: A term for the chants of the *Rahasyagāna.

UTSVARITA: The sequence 4_5 of the *Kauthuma numeral notation. According to the *Mātrālakṣaṇa, the *caturtha (4) is worth ½ *mātrā and the *mandra (5) 1½ mātrās. These values hold true regardless of syllable length.

UTTĀNA: "Stretched out, spread out, lying on the back." Name given to the hand movement (*kai-lakṣaṇa) and sound (*svara) associated with the consonant th of the *Jaiminīya syllable notation. Known also as kevalottāna.

UTTARAGĀNA: The *Ūhagāna and *Rahasyagāna, which are based largely upon the verses of the *uttarārcika of the Sāmaveda *Saṃhitā.

UTTARĀRCIKA: "Last ārcika." One of the two large divisions (*ārcikas) of the Sāmaveda *Saṃhitā. In the uttarārcika verses are arranged--usually in groups of two or three--in an order suited to sacrificial requirements. The first verse of each group may ordinarily be found in the *pūrvārcika ("first ārcika") also.

UTTAR PRADESH: "Northern Province." State in northern India whose capital is *Lucknow. The Hindu pilgrimage city *Vārāṇasī (Banāras), one of the leading Vedic centers in North India, is situated on the Ganges River in this state. The principal language is Hindi, a member of the Indo-European language family.

VACANA: A section of the **subrahmaṇyā* litany. *Nambūdiri chanters use the term for that part of a chant sung in one breath. See **parvan*.

VAIDIKA: A *Brāhmaṇ who knows the Veda.

VAIRĀJANIDHANA: In the *Kauthuma notation, a **nidhana* (the concluding section of a chant) which consists of the sequence 3_{2345}^{111} sung on the long *ī*-vowel. The **mātrās* corresponding to the individual numerals are $3_{+2+1+1+1}$. See **svāra*.

VAIṢṆAVA: Connected with the god Viṣṇu.

VAIŚYA: See *Brāhmaṇa.

VĀJAPEYA: The fifth of seven varieties (**saṃsthās*) of the **jyotiṣṭoma*, the prototype of all **soma* sacrifices. The *vājapeya* consists of seventeen lauds (**stotras*).

VĀJASANEYI SAṂHITĀ: The continuous text of the Śukla *Yajurveda, which appears in two recensions: Mādhyaṃdina and Kāṇva.

VAKRA: "Curved, bent." A characteristic of certain **rāgas*, whereby the tones--either in ascent or descent--proceed in oblique or zigzag fashion.

VĀMA: "Left." One of three horizontal positions at which *Nambūdiri Sāmavedins hold the right hand while chanting.

VĀMADEVYA: The melody of the second **pṛṣṭha*-**stotra* of the **soma* sacrifice.

VĀRĀṆASĪ (BANĀRAS, KĀŚĪ): The famous Hindu pilgrimage city located on a bank of the Ganges River in *Uttar Pradesh. *Kauthuma chanting in both its northern and southern styles is carried on within the city limits.

VARGA: A class of consonants. Five such categories are taken by the *Rāṇāyanīyas as the basis for their syllable notation. They are: ka-varga (gutturals), ca-varga (palatals), ṭa-varga (linguals), ta-varga (dentals), and pa-varga (labials). The consonants of each class may combine with ten vowels (a, ā, i, ī, u, ū, e, ai, o, au), *anusvāra, and *visarga (these last two preceded by the short a-vowel). Each resulting syllable is assigned to a certain *parvan in the songbooks. The syllables of the five vargas correspond to parvans beginning with the notational numerals 1, 2, 3, 4, and 5, respectively, though no two parvans are notated exactly alike. Taken together, however, they constitute all of the musical material of the school.

VĀYU: The Vedic wind deity.

VEDĀṄGA: "Limb of the Veda." A group of writings, arranged in six classes, which expound the proper usage, reading, and understanding of the Vedas. See *śikṣā, *chandas, *vyākaraṇa, *nirukta, *jyotiṣa, and *kalpa.

VIKĀRA: "Modification." One of the methods by which a source verse was altered in order to fit a pre-existing melody. A common transformation was the replacement of original vowels by new vowels.

VIKARṢAṆA: "Suspension." One of the methods by which a source verse was altered in order to fit a pre-existing melody. A syllable was broken up into two parts with intervening secondary (*vikṛti) numerals: ye, for example, becomes yā 2 3 yi.

VIKṚTI: "Derived or modified form." In the *Kauthuma notation, a numeral notated within the line of text. Also the sound (*svara) indicated by that numeral. See also *prakṛti.

VILAṄṄATTIL: "In transverse." An arm movement employed by *Nambūdiri Sāmavedins as they intone a vibrato. The thumb is placed upon the index finger as the right arm is moved horizontally to and fro.

VINATA: "Bent, curved, sunk down." In the *Kauthuma notation, the numeral 1 in the primary (*prakṛti) position followed immediately by the numeral 2 in the secondary (*vikṛti) position. The sequence is indicated by either the superscribed *avagraha (in northern manuscripts) or the syllable vi (in southern manuscripts). The two numbers have the following respective *mātrā values:

augmented (*vṛddha) vowels: $1\frac{1}{2} + \frac{1}{2}$

long (*dīrgha) vowels: $\frac{1}{2} + \frac{1}{2}$

short (*hrasva) vowels: $\frac{1}{2} + \frac{1}{2}$

A chant which appears both in the Pūrvagāna and the Uttaragāna may have the sequence *preṅkha in the latter at the spot where vinata appears in the former.

VIRĀMA: "Pause, cessation, stop." (1) In Sāmavedic chants, the pause--indicated in the notation by a vertical stroke (*daṇḍa)--which occurs between two *parvans. (2) One of the methods by which a source verse was altered in order to fit a pre-existing melody. In this case, the syllables of a word are divided between two parvans.

VISARGA (VISARJANĪYA): A grammatical sign indicating an aspiration. It is marked by two dots (:) and is usually transliterated ḥ.

VIŚLEṢAṆA: "Dissolution." One of the methods by which a source verse was altered in order to fit a pre-existing melody. An example is the word vītaye, transformed in the songbooks into voyitoyā 2 yi.

VIṢṬUTI: A pattern according to which the melodizations of the three verses of a *tṛca are sung. All viṣṭutis consist of three rounds (*paryāyas). Each paryāya goes through, at least once, a setting of each of the three verses. The three rounds are each preceded by the *hiṃkāra (the syllable hum).

VRATA: One of the divisions of the *Āraṇyakagāna. The *Kauthumas and *Rāṇāyanīyas have it in third place; the *Jaiminīyas place it first.

VṚDDHA: "Augmented." In the songbooks of the *Kauthumas and *Rāṇāyanīyas, vṛddha vowels are long vowels which lack the superscribed repha (the semivowel r) or (in South India) bindu (the sign o). If no numerals follow within the line of text, vṛddha vowels are worth three *mātrās (temporal units).

VṚDHEŚVARA: In the *Kauthuma notation, the sequence 32_1.

VṚTTI: Tempo. Three tempi are prescribed by the *Mātrālakṣaṇa: slow (*vilambita), moderate (*madhyama), and fast (*druta).

VYĀKARAṆA: A work dealing with grammatical analysis, the most notable example of which is Pāṇini's Aṣṭādhyāyī. The category comprises one of the six *vedāṅgas.

Y

YAJAMĀNA: "Sacrificer." The patron or sponsor of a sacrifice. He must belong to one of the three upper castes (*Brāhmaṇa, Kṣatriya, Vaiśya).

YAJÑĀYAJÑĪYA: The twelfth and final laud (*stotra) of the *agniṣṭoma sacrifice.

YAJURVEDA: The Veda of verses and prose formulas for utterance at the sacrifices. It has been passed down in two forms. The Kṛṣṇa ("Black") Yajurveda contains explanatory matter mixed in with the verses and formulas. The Śukla ("White") Yajurveda is without such interpolations.

YAJUS: A prose formula uttered by a *Yajurveda priest at a sacrifice.

YĀNA: Name given to the hand movement (*kai-lakṣaṇa) and sound (*svara) associated with the consonant ṭ of the *Jaiminīya syllable notation.

YĀNAKṢEPAṆA: Name given to the hand movement (*kai-lakṣaṇa) and sound (*svara) associated with the consonant b of the *Jaiminīya syllable notation. This consonant designates a compound: ṭ (*yāna) + p (*kṣepaṇa).

YĀNAMARŚANA: Name given to the hand movement (*kai-lakṣaṇa)

and sound (*svara) associated with the consonant gh of the *Jaiminīya syllable notation. This consonant designates a compound: ṭ (*yāna) + y (*marśana).

YĀNĀNVAṄGULYA: Name given to the hand movement (*kai-lakṣaṇa) and sound (*svara) associated with the consonant n of the *Jaiminīya syllable notation. This consonant designates a compound: ṭ (*yāna) + kh (*anvaṅgulya).

YAUDHĀJAYA: A melody which comprises *stotriyās 10-12 of the *mādhyaṃdinapavamānastotra ("midday *pavamāna laud").

YONI: "Source, origin." (1) The verse on which a chant is based. (2) A chant of the *Prakṛtigāna.

Select Bibliography

Apel, Willi. *Gregorian Chant*. Bloomington: Indiana University Press, 1958.

Apte, V. M. "Sound-Records of Sāmagānas: A Prospect and Retrospect." *Bulletin of the Deccan College Postgraduate and Research Institute* 4 (1942-43): 296-314.

________. "The 'Spoken Word' in Sanskrit Literature." *Bulletin of the Deccan College Postgraduate and Research Institute* 4 (1942-43): 277.

Bake, Arnold A. "The Practice of Sāmaveda." *Proceedings and Transactions of the Seventh All-India Oriental Conference*. Baroda: Oriental Institute (1935), pp. 143-55.

Bhaṭṭa Drāviḍa, Lakṣmaṇa Śaṅkara. "The Mode of Singing Sāma Gāna." *The Poona Orientalist* 4 (April-July 1939): 1-21.

Burnell, A. C. *Catalogue of a Selection of Sanskrit Manuscripts*. Pt. 1: *Vedic Manuscripts*. London: Trübner & Co., 1869.

________, ed. *The Ārsheyabrāhmaṇa (Being the Fourth Brāhmaṇa) of the Sāmaveda*. Mangalore: Basel Mission Press, 1876.

________, ed. *The Jaiminīya Text of the Ārsheyabrāhmaṇa of the Sāmaveda*. Mangalore: Basel Mission Press, 1878.

________, ed. *Saṃhitopanishadbrāhmaṇa*. Mangalore: Basel Mission Press, 1877.

Burrow, T., and Emeneau, M. B. *A Dravidian Etymological Dictionary*. Oxford: Clarendon Press, 1961.

Caland, Willem. *Die Jaiminīya-Saṃhitā, mit einer Einleitung über die Sāmavedaliteratur*. Vol. 2 of *Indische Forschungen*. Edited by Alfred Hillebrandt. Breslau: M. & H. Marcus, 1907.

________. *Pañcaviṃśa-Brāhmaṇa: The Brāhmaṇa of Twenty Five Chapters*. Work 255 of *Bibliotheca Indica*. Calcutta: Asiatic Society of Bengal, 1931.

Caland, Willem, and Henry, Victor. *L'Agniṣṭoma, description complète de la forme normale du sacrifice de soma dans le culte védique*. 2 vols. Paris: Ernest Leroux, 1906-7.

Dīkṣita, A. M. Rāmanātha, ed. *Ūhagānam--Ūhyagānam*. Vedic Research Series, Banāras Hindu University, vol. 3. Varanasi: Banaras Hindu University Press, 1967.

Faddegon, Barend. *Studies on the Sāmaveda, Part I*. Vol. 57:1 of *Verhandelingen der koninklijke nederlandse Akademie van Wetenschappen, afd. Letterkunde*. Amsterdam: North-Holland Publishing Co., 1951.

Felber, Erwin, and Geiger, Bernhard. Die indische Musik der vedischen und der klassischen Zeit. Vol. 170:7 of Sitzungsberichte der philosophisch-historischen Klasse der kaiserlichen Akademie der Wissenschaften. Vienna: Alfred Hölder, 1912.

Fox Strangways, A. H. The Music of Hindostan. Oxford: Clarendon Press, 1914.

Hillebrandt, Alfred. Ritual-Litteratur: Vedische Opfer und Zauber. Vol. 3:2 of Grundriss der Indo-Arischen Philologie und Altertumskunde. Edited by G. Bühler. Strassburg: Verlag von Karl J. Trübner, 1897.

Hoogt, J. M. van der. The Vedic Chant Studied in Its Textual and Melodic Form. Wageningen: H. Veenman & Sons' Press, 1929.

Kaufmann, Walter. The Rāgas of North India. Bloomington: Indiana University Press, 1968.

________. "Some Reflections on the Notations of Vedic Chant." Essays in Musicology: A Birthday Offering for Willi Apel. Edited by Hans Tischler. Bloomington Indiana University School of Music, 1968.

Keith, A. B. Catalogue of the Sanskrit Manuscripts in the Library of the India Office. London: Secretary of State for India in Council, 1887-1935.

Nāradīya Śikṣā. Edited by Śrī Pītambara Pīṭha Saṃskṛta Pariṣad. Jhansi: Śrī Rām Press, 1964.

Nārāyaṇasvāmi, R., ed. Grāmageyagānam--Āraṇyageyagānam. Pardi: Svādhyāyamaṇḍala, 1958.

Parpola, Asko. The Śrautasūtras of Lāṭyāyana and Drāhyāyaṇa and Their Commentaries: An English Translation and Study. Vol. 42:2 of Commentationes Humanarum Litterarum. Helsinki: Societas Scientiarum Fennica, 1968-69.

_______. "The Literature and Study of the Jaiminīya Sāmaveda." Studia Orientalia 43:6 (1973): 1-33.

Renou, Louis. Classical India. Vol. 3: Vedic India. Translated by Philip Spratt. Delhi: Indological Book House, 1971.

_______. Les écoles védiques et la formation du Veda. Vol. 9 of Cahiers de la Société Asiatique. Paris: Imprimerie Nationale, 1947.

_______. Vocabulaire du rituel védique. Paris: Librairie C. Klincksieck, 1954.

Raghavan, V. "Present Position of Vedic Chanting and Its Future." Bulletin of the Institute of Traditional Cultures 1 (1957): 48-69.

Śāstrī, M. Śeṣagiri, and Raṅgācārya, M. A Descriptive Catalogue of the Sanskrit Manuscripts in the Government Oriental Manuscripts Library, Madras. Vol. 1: Vedic Literature. Madras: Government Press, 1901-5.

Sātvalekar, Dāmodar, ed. Sāmaveda [Saṃhitā]. Pardi: Svādhyāyamaṇḍala, 1956.

Sharma, B. R., ed. Devatādhyāya--Saṃhitopaniṣad--Vaṃśa--Brāhmaṇas. Tirupati: Kendriya Sanskrit Vidyapeetha, 1965.

________, ed. Jaiminīyārṣeya--Jaiminīyopaniṣad--Brāhmaṇas. Tirupati: Kendriya Sanskrit Vidyapeetha, 1967.

________, ed. Pañcavidha-Sūtra and Mātrālakṣaṇa, with Commentaries. Tirupati: Kendriya Sanskrit Vidyapeetha, 1970.

________, ed. Sāmavidhāna Brāhmaṇa. Tirupati: Kendriya Sanskrit Vidyapeetha, 1964.

Simon, Richard. "Die Notationen der vedischen Liederbücher." Wiener Zeitschrift für die Kunde des Morgenlandes 28 (1913): 305-46.

________. Das Pañcavidhasūtra. Vol. 5 of Indische Forschungen. Edited by Alfred Hillebrandt. Breslau: M. & H. Marcus, 1913.

________. Das Puṣpasūtra mit Einleitung und Übersetzung. Vol. 23:3 of Abhandlungen der philosophisch-philologischen Klasse der königlichen Bayerischen Akademie der Wissenschaften. Munich: n.p., 1908.

Staal, J. F. Nambudiri Veda Recitation. Vol. 5 of Disputationes Rheno-Trajectinae. Edited by Jan Gonda. The Hague: Mouton, 1961.

________. "Notes on Some Brahmin Communities of South India." Arts and Letters: Journal of the Royal India Pakistan and Ceylon Society 32 (1958): 1-7.

________. "Some Vedic Survivals: Report on Research Done in India, Dec. 1970--March 1971, A.I.I.S. Grant." Varanasi, 20 March 1971.

________. "The Twelve Ritual Chants of the Nambudiri Agniṣṭoma." Pratidānam: Indian, Iranian and Indo-European Studies Presented to Franciscus Bernardus Jacobus Kuiper on his Sixtieth Birthday. Edited by J. C. Heesterman, G. H. Schokker, and V. I. Subramoniam. The Hague: Mouton, 1968.

Tripāṭhī, Rishisaṅkar, ed. Sāmavedīyarudrajapavidhiḥ. Compiled by Yamunā Prasād Tripāṭhī. Varanasi: Chowkhamba, 1963.

Index